SOURCES
of the
WESTERN
TRADITION

SOURCES of the WESTERN TRADITION

NINTH EDITION

VOLUME I: FROM ANCIENT TIMES TO THE ENLIGHTENMENT

Marvin Perry

Baruch College, City University of New York

George W. Bock, Editorial Associate

WADSWORTH
CENGAGE Learning·

Australia • Brazil • Japan • Korea • Mexico • Singapore • Spain • United Kingdom • United States

WADSWORTH
CENGAGE Learning

Sources of the Western Tradition:
Volume I: From Ancient Times
to the Enlightenment, **Ninth Edition**
Marvin Perry

Senior Publisher: Suzanne Jeans

Acquiring Sponsoring Editor: Brooke Barbier

Development Editor: Lauren Floyd

Assistant Editor: Jamie Bushell

Editorial Assistant: Katie Coaster

Managing Media Editor: Lisa Ciccolo

Executive Brand Manager: Melissa Larmon

Senior Content Project Manager: Jane Lee

Senior Art Director: Cate Rickard Barr

Manufacturing Planner: Sandee Milewski

Senior Rights Acquisition Specialist:
Jennifer Meyer Dare

Production Service: PreMediaGlobal

Cover Designer: Lori Leahy, Mighty Quinn
Graphic Design

Cover Image: Marinari, Onorio (1627–1715)
(attributed to). *Saint Catherine of Alexandria*,
ca. 1670. Oil on canvas, 75.2 × 106.4 cm.
Credit: By kind permission of the Trustees of the
Wallace Collection, London/Art Resource, NY.

Compositor: PreMediaGlobal

For product information and technology assistance, contact us at
Cengage Learning Customer & Sales Support, 1-800-354-9706

For permission to use material from this text or product,
submit all requests online at **www.cengage.com/permissions.**
Further permissions questions can be emailed to
permissionrequest@cengage.com.

Library of Congress Control Number: 2012949049

ISBN-13: 978-1-133-93525-4

ISBN-10: 1-133-93525-7

Wadsworth
20 Channel Center Street
Boston, MA 02210
USA

Cengage Learning is a leading provider of customized learning solutions with office locations around the globe, including Singapore, the United Kingdom, Australia, Mexico, Brazil, and Japan. Locate your local office at:
international.cengage.com/region

Cengage Learning products are represented in Canada by
Nelson Education, Ltd.

For your course and learning solutions, visit **www.cengage.com.**

Purchase any of our products at your local college store or at our preferred online store **www.cengagebrain.com.**

Instructors: Please visit **login.cengage.com** and log in to access instructor-specific resources.

Printed in the United States of America
1 2 3 4 5 6 7 16 15 14 13 12

Contents

Preface

Teachers of the Western Civilization survey have long recognized the pedagogical value of primary sources, which are the raw materials of history. The ninth edition of *Sources of the Western Tradition* contains a wide assortment of documents—over 200 in each volume, principally primary sources—that have been carefully selected and edited to fit the needs of the survey and to supplement standard texts.

I have based my choice of documents for the two volumes on several criteria. To introduce students to those ideas and values that characterize the Western tradition, *Sources of the Western Tradition* emphasizes the works of the great thinkers. While focusing on the great ideas that have shaped the Western heritage, however, the volumes also provide a balanced treatment of political, economic, and social history. I have tried to select documents that capture the characteristic outlook of an age and provide a sense of the movement and development of Western history. The readings are of sufficient length to convey their essential meaning, and I have carefully extracted those passages that focus on the documents' main ideas.

An important feature of the compilation is the grouping of several documents that illuminate a single theme; such a constellation of related readings reinforces understanding of important themes and invites comparison, analysis, and interpretation. For example, in volume I, the section "The Humanists' Fascination with Antiquity" (see chapter 9), concerning the Renaissance, contains four interrelated readings: in the first, Petrarch shows his commitment to classical culture; in the second, Leonardo Bruni discusses the value of studying Greek literature and proposes a humanist educational program; in the third, Petrus Paulus Vergerius also discusses the importance of liberal studies; and in the fourth, Lorenzo de' Medici expresses a quest for fame and glory in the manner of the ancients. In volume II, the section "Resistance" (see chapter 13), which concerns World War II, contains four readings: in the first, Albert Camus explains why he joined the French Resistance; the second reproduces the leaflets distributed during the war by Hans and Sophie Scholl denouncing the Nazis; the third selection is by Marek Edelman, one of the surviving commanders of the memorable Warsaw Ghetto uprising; and the final selection by Tadeusz Bor-Komorowski, commander of the Polish Home Army, recounts the Poles' valiant effort to drive the Germans from Warsaw.

An overriding concern of mine in preparing this compilation was to make the documents accessible—to enable students to comprehend and to interpret historical documents on their own. I have provided several pedagogical features to facilitate this aim. Introductions of three types explain the historical setting, the authors' intent, and the meaning and significance of the readings. First, introductions to each chapter—thirteen in volume I and fifteen in volume II—provide comprehensive overviews of periods. Second, introductions to each numbered section or grouping treat the historical background for the reading(s) that follow(s). Third, each reading has a brief headnote that provides specific details about that reading.

Within some readings, interlinear notes, clearly set off from the text of the document, serve as transitions and suggest the main themes of the passages that follow. Used primarily in longer extracts of the great thinkers, these interlinear notes help to guide students through the readings.

To aid students' comprehension, brief editorial definitions or notes that explain unfamiliar or foreign terms are inserted into the running text. When terms or concepts in the documents require fuller explanations, these appear at the bottom of pages as footnotes. Where helpful, I have retained the footnotes of authors, translators, or editors from whose works the documents were acquired. (Within the running text, original author or editor notes appear in parentheses, while my insertions appear in brackets. Within footnotes, my explanatory notes are distinguished by "—Eds." at the end of each one.) The review questions that appear at the ends of sections enable students to check their understanding of the documents; sometimes the questions ask for comparisons with other readings, linking or contrasting key concepts.

For ancient sources, I have generally selected recent translations that are both faithful to the text and readable. For some seventeenth- and eighteenth-century English documents, the archaic spelling has been retained, when this does not preclude comprehension, in order to show students how the English language has evolved over time.

For the ninth edition I have reworked most chapters, dropping some documents and adding new ones. All new documents have been carefully edited: extraneous passages deleted, notes inserted to explain historical events, names identified, and technical terms defined. Throughout the book, I have extended the constellation format that groups related documents into one section.

In the ninth edition, volume I contains seventeen new documents. Among the chapters concerning the ancient world, chapter 1 now includes a selection depicting terrible punishments, including a flood, inflicted by Mesopotamian gods who, it was believed, controlled human destiny. In chapter 2, the section on Hebrew law has been expanded. The section, "Hellenistic Culture: Rationalism, Universalism, and Individualism" in chapter 3 has been restructured. In chapter 4, I have added a speech by Cicero denouncing exploitation of the provincials. The section "Roman Stoicism" in chapter 5 has been enhanced with the addition of Musonius Rufus' enlightened lectures on women. Chapter 6 includes two new selections: Josephus' treatment of the essential outlook of the Essenes, and Justin Martyr's account of Christianity's high moral standards.

Turning to the Middle Ages, chapter 7 now includes excerpts from a work written by Dhouda, a Frankish noblewoman, in the Carolingian era. In this work, Dhouda instructs her eldest son on the proper behavior toward the king, high nobles, his father, and God. Enriching the section "Medieval Learning: Synthesis of Reason and Christian Faith" in chapter 8 is an excerpt from Abelard's *Sic et Non.* Also new to chapter 8 is a sermon by a Dominican preacher denouncing the rich and powerful, which further depicts the fourteenth century as an age of adversity.

Among the chapters concerning Early Modern Europe, in chapter 9, I have improved the constellation "The Humanists' Fascination with Antiquity" with a letter written by Lorenzo de' Medici in which he unabashedly expresses a quest for fame and glory in the manner of the ancients. Also added to chapter 9 is a passage from Montaigne's *Essays,* which aptly illustrates the efforts of Renaissance writers to explore their own lives, thoughts, and feelings; and an excerpt from Leonardo da Vinci's writings on the art and science of painting, which further illustrates his genius. The fourth new selection in chapter 9 is comprised of excerpts from *The Worth of Women,* written by Moderata Fonte, a wealthy Venetian lady. The subtitle of the book—*Wherein Is Clearly Revealed Their Nobility and Their Superiority to Men*—shows the author's intent. In chapter 11, an account of the Spanish Inquisition by a sixteenth-century priest and chronicler reveals the attitude of the clergy toward Jews and Judaism, and the cruelty this attitude engendered. Also in chapter 11, the selection by John Newton, a slave trader who came to support abolitionism, enhances the constellation "The Atlantic Slave Trade." In chapter 12, a passage from Blaise Pascal's *Pensées* depicts another side of the Scientific Revolution—the fear that the new science could stir doubt, uncertainty, and anxiety, and threaten Christian beliefs. Chapter 13 now contains a selection from the brilliant Madame du Châtelet in which she makes a fervent appeal for educating women.

Volume II contains twenty-seven new selections. Chapter 1, "The Rise of Modernity," now contains a section dealing with several aspects of the Atlantic slave trade, including the buying and transporting of Africans and the views of both critics and defenders of slavery. The new selections for chapter 2, "The Scientific Revolution," and Chapter 3, "The Enlightenment," which are reproduced from volume I, are described on the previous page.

In the chapters concerning Modern Europe, chapter 4 has gained three new selections: Arthur Young's account of the plight of French peasants prior to the revolutionary era, an edict by a French district calling for de-Christianization, and Madame de Staël's scathing criticism of Napoleon.

Chapter 6 now includes a selection featuring two excerpts that deal with the spread of liberal ideals from revolutionary France to tsarist Russia. In chapter 7, the section "Realism in Literature" has been enriched with the inclusion of an excerpt from Émile Zola's *The Experimental Novel*. Added to the section "The Lower Classes" in chapter 8 is a passage from Jeanne Bouvier's memoirs describing the pains of poverty in late nineteenth-century France. In chapter 9, the section "European Rule in Africa" has been broadened by a selection from Ndabaningi Sithole, an anti-imperialist African who notes imperialism's positive achievements for Africans. In chapter 10, the section "The Political Potential of the Irrational" has been enhanced by the inclusion of a passage from the works of Vilfredo Pareto, a prominent sociologist.

All chapters in the third part of volume II, "Western Civilization in Crisis," have been expanded. Complementing the section "Pan-Serbism: Nationalism and Terrorism" in chapter 11 is the inclusion of a memorandum from the Austrian ambassador to Serbia after the assassination of Archduke Francis Ferdinand calling for crushing the Serbs.

In chapter 12, the section "Soviet Indoctrination" now includes a clever and humorous attack on censorship published in Moscow the year Stalin died. A new section, "The Fledgling Weimar Republic," has also been added to chapter 12 and contains two new readings; one illustrates the pervasive antidemocratic thought of the time, the other depicts the trauma caused by inflation—which fittingly complements the selection on the Depression that is retained from the previous edition. Also in chapter 12, added to the section "The Nazification of Culture and Society," is an eye-witness description of the monster rallies staged at Nuremberg. In chapter 13, a thoughtful passage by a German veteran of the Stalingrad campaign has been added to the section "Stalingrad: A Turning Point."

In the final part, concerning the contemporary world, chapter 15 has been considerably revised. Added to the section "Globalization: Patterns and Problems" is a selection by Thomas L. Friedman, who argues that a country's economic success depends more on the quality of its education than the abundance of its natural resources. Also added to this section is an excerpt from Daron Acemoglu and James A. Robinson, *Why Nations Fail*, in which the authors link economic failure to political systems that concentrate power in the hands of a narrow elite. The new selection in the brand-new section "War in the Twenty-first Century" maintains that, contrary to the prevailing view, violent conflicts are now in decline. Also added to chapter 15 is a new section dealing with ethnic cleansing and genocide in Rwanda. Enhancing the section "Female Oppression" is a new account of sex trafficking, a horrific and expanding abuse that is becoming increasingly more profitable for organized criminal elements.

I wish to thank the following instructors for their critical reading of the manuscript: LeNie Adolphson, Sauk Valley Community College; Julian Bourg, Boston College; Richard Brabander, Bridgewater State College; Carol Carbine, Loyola University; Janusz Duzinkiewicz, Purdue University; Erin Jordan,

Old Dominion University; Philip Napoli, Brooklyn College; Elena Osokina, University of South Carolina; and George W. Whitton, SUNYIT Utica/Rome.

I am grateful to the staff of Wadsworth/ Cengage Learning who lent their talents to the project. Nancy Blaine, who served as senior sponsoring editor for several editions, is no longer with the company but her contribution is still felt. Brooke Barbier, the new acquiring sponsoring editor, has made several significant recommendations. A special thanks to Lauren H. Floyd, development editor, who conscientiously and efficiently prepared the revision for production, as she has done for my other books. I thank also Jane Lee, senior content project manager, who, with the very capable assistance of project manager Valarmathy Munuswamy, skillfully guided the book through production. Also deserving of my gratitude are Will Moore, who served as both copy-editor and proofreader and who read the manuscript with a trained eye; Jennifer Wagner, senior permissions project manager, who, assisted by Sarah Carey, managed the difficult task of obtaining text permissions smoothly; Catherine Schnurr, senior image research and permissions project manager, who oversaw the selection and research of the chapter-opening photos; and Cate Rickard Barr, senior art director, who managed the design of the cover. And I thank my friend and colleague Howard E. Negrin who checked the accuracy of the citations for several documents.

I thank my wife, Phyllis Perry, for her encouragement and computer expertise, which saved me time and aggravation. Unfortunately, Angela Von Laue, who had assisted me since the death of her husband Theo in 2000, has taken a too-early retirement from the book. I continue to miss her research. I am saddened that my friend George Bock, who insightfully evaluated proposed selections and introductions, and diligently proofread, passed away. He will be missed.

M.P.

Prologue
Examining Primary Sources

When historians try to reconstruct and apprehend past events, they rely on primary or original sources—official documents prepared by institutions and eyewitness reports. Similarly, when they attempt to describe the essential outlook or worldview of a given era, people, or movement, historians examine other types of primary sources—the literature, art, philosophy, and religious expressions of the time. These original sources differ from secondary or derivative sources—accounts of events and times written at a later date by people who may or may not have had access to primary sources. *Sources of the Western Tradition* consists principally of primary sources, which are the raw materials of history; they provide historians with the basic facts, details, and thinking needed for an accurate reconstruction of the past.

Historians have to examine a document with a critical spirit. The first question asked is: Is the document authentic and reliable? An early illustration of critical historical awareness was demonstrated by the Renaissance thinker Lorenzo Valla (c. 1407–1457) in *Declamation Concerning the False Decretals of Constantine*. The so-called Donation of Constantine, which was used by popes to support their claim to temporal authority, stated that the fourth-century Roman emperor Constantine had given the papacy dominion over the western Empire. By showing that some of the words in the document were unknown in Constantine's time and therefore could not have been used by the emperor, Valla proved that the document was forged by church officials several hundred years after Constantine's death. A more recent example of the need for caution is shown by the discovery of the "Hitler Diaries" in the mid-1980s. Several prominent historians "authenticated" the manuscript before it was exposed as a forgery—the paper dated from the 1950s and

Hitler died in 1945. Nor can all eyewitness accounts be trusted, something Thucydides, the great Greek historian, noted 2,400 years ago.

[E]ither I was present myself at the events which I have described or else I heard of them from eye-witnesses whose reports I have checked with as much thoroughness as possible. Not that even so the truth was easy to discover: different eye-witnesses give different accounts of the same events, speaking out of partiality for one side or the other or else from imperfect memories.

An eyewitness's personal bias can render a document worthless. For example, in *The Auschwitz Lie* (1973), Thies Christophersen, a former SS guard at Auschwitz-Birkenau, denied the existence of gas chambers and mass killings in the notorious Nazi death camp, which he described as a sort of resort where prisoners, after work, could swim, listen to music in their rooms, or visit a brothel. Years later he was captured on videotape—he mistakenly thought the interviewers were fellow neo-Nazis—confessing that he had lied about the gas chambers because of loyalty to the SS and his desire to protect Germany's honor.

After examining the relevant primary sources and deciding on their usefulness, historians have to construct a consistent narrative and provide a plausible interpretation. Ideally, this requires that they examine documentary evidence in a wholly neutral, detached, and objective way. But is it possible to write history without being influenced by one's own particular viewpoint and personal biases?

No doubt several historians examining the same material might draw differing conclusions, and each could argue his or her position persuasively. This is not surprising, for history is not an exact science, and historians, like all individuals, are influenced by their upbringing and education, by their thoughts and feelings. Conflicting interpretations of historical events and periods are expected and acceptable features of historiography. But what is not acceptable is the deliberate distortion and suppression of evidence in order to substantiate one's own prejudices.

A flagrant example of writers of history misusing sources and distorting evidence in order to fortify their own prejudices is the recent case of British historian David Irving, author of numerous books on World War II, several of them well reviewed. Increasingly Irving revealed an undisguised admiration for Hitler and an antipathy toward Jews, which led him to minimize and disguise atrocities committed by the Third Reich. Addressing neo-Nazi audiences in several lands, he asserted that the Holocaust is "a major fraud. . . . There were no gas chambers. They were fakes and frauds." In *Lying About Hitler: History, Holocaust and the David Irving Trial* (2001), Richard J. Evans, a specialist in modern German history with a broad background in archival research, exposed instance after instance of how Irving, in his attempt to whitewash Hitler, misquoted sources, "misrepresented data, . . . skewed documents [and] ignored or deliberately suppressed material when it ran counter to his arguments. . . . [When I] followed Irving's claims and statements back to the original documents on which they purported to rest . . . Irving's work in this respect was revealed as a house of cards, a vast apparatus of deception and deceit."

The sources in this anthology can be read on several levels. First, they enhance understanding of the historical period in which they were written, shedding light on how people lived and thought and the chief concerns of the time. Several of the sources, written by some of humanity's greatest minds, have broader implications. They are founts of wisdom, providing insights of enduring value into human nature and the human condition. The documents also reveal the evolution of those core ideas and values—reason, freedom, and respect for human dignity—that constitute the Western heritage. Equally important, several documents reveal the precariousness of these values and the threats to them. It is the hope of the editors that an understanding of the evolution of the Western tradition will foster a renewed commitment to its essential ideals.

The documents in these volumes often represent human beings struggling with the vital questions of their day. As such they invite the reader to react actively and imaginatively to the times in which they were produced and to the individuals who produced them. The documents should also be approached with a critical eye. The reader has always to raise several pointed questions regarding the author's motivation, objectivity, logic, and accuracy. In addition, depending on the content of a particular document, the reader should consider the following questions: What does the document reveal about the times in which it was written? About the author? About the nature, evolution, and meaning of the Western tradition? About human nature and human relations? About good and evil? About progress? About war and peace? About gender relations? About life and death? Doubtless other questions will come to mind. In many instances, no doubt, the documents will impel readers to reflect on current issues and their own lives.

CHAPTER 1

The Near East

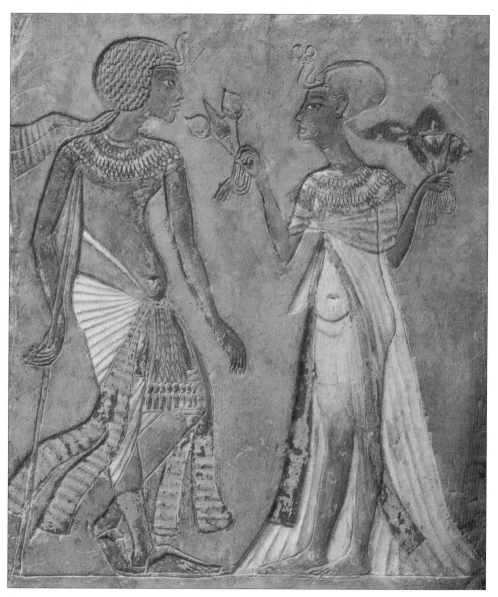

TUTANKHAMUN AND HIS WIFE ANKHESENAMUN, painted limestone, Eighteenth Dynasty, c. 1350 B.C. This relief shows the pharaoh and his wife taking a stroll in the garden. *(bpk, Berlin/Aegyptisches Museum/Margarete Buesing/Art Resource, NY)*

The world's first civilizations arose some five thousand years ago in the river valleys of Mesopotamia (later Iraq) and Egypt. In these Near Eastern lands people built cities, organized states with definite boundaries, invented writing, engaged in large-scale trade, practiced specialization of labor, and erected huge monuments: all activities that historians associate with civilization. Scholars emphasize the fact that civilizations emerged in the river valleys—the Tigris and Euphrates in Mesopotamia and the Nile in Egypt. When they overflowed their banks, these rivers deposited fertile soil, which could provide a food surplus required to sustain life in cities. The early inhabitants of these valleys drained swamps and built irrigation works, enabling them to harness the rivers for human advantage. In the process they also strengthened the bonds of cooperation, a necessary ingredient of civilization.

Religion and myth were the central forces in these early civilizations. They pervaded all phases of life, providing people with satisfying explanations for the operations of nature and the mystery of death and justifying traditional rules of morality. Natural objects—the sun, the river, the mountain—were seen as either gods or as the abodes of gods. The political life of the Near East was theocratic; that is, people regarded their rulers either as divine or as representatives of the gods and believed that law originated with the gods. Near Eastern art and literature were dominated by religious themes.

The Sumerians, founders of urban life in Mesopotamia, developed twelve city-states in the region of the lower Euphrates near the Persian Gulf. Each city-state included a city and the farmland around it; each had its own government and was independent of the other city-states. In time the Sumerians were conquered, and their cities were incorporated into kingdoms and empires. However, as Akkadians, Elamites, Babylonians, and other peoples of the region adopted and built upon Sumerian religion, art, and literary forms, the Sumerian achievement became the basis of a coherent Mesopotamian civilization that lasted some three thousand years.

Early in its history Egypt became a centralized state under the rule of a pharaoh, who was viewed as both a man and a god. The pharaoh's authority was all-embracing, and all Egyptians were subservient to him. Early in their history, the Egyptians developed cultural patterns that were to endure for three thousand years; the ancient Egyptians looked to the past, seeking to maintain the ways of their ancestors.

Although the cultural patterns of both civilizations were similar—in both, religion and theocratic kingship played a dominant role—there were significant differences between the two. First, whereas in Egypt the pharaoh was considered divine, rulers in Mesopotamia were regarded as exceptional human beings whom the gods had selected to act as their agents. Second, the natural environment of the Egyptians fostered a sense of security and an optimistic outlook toward life.

Natural barriers—deserts, the Mediterranean Sea, and cataracts in the Nile—protected Egypt from invasion, and the overflowing of the Nile was regular and predictable, ensuring a good harvest. In contrast, Mesopotamia, without natural barriers, suffered from frequent invasions, and the Tigris and Euphrates rivers were unpredictable. Sometimes there was insufficient overflow, and the land was afflicted with drought; at other times, rampaging floods devastated the fields. These conditions promoted a pessimistic outlook, which pervaded Mesopotamian civilization.

After 1500 B.C., the Near East entered a period of empire building. In the late sixth century B.C., the Persians, the greatest of the empire builders, conquered all the lands from the Nile River to the Indus River in India. Persia united Egypt, Mesopotamia, and other Near Eastern lands into a world-state and brought together the region's various cultural traditions. In the first half of the fifth century B.C., the Persians tried to add the city-states of Greece to their empire; the ensuing conflict was of critical importance for the history of Western civilization.

Egyptians, Mesopotamians, and other Near Eastern peoples developed a rich urban culture and made important contributions to later civilizations. They established bureaucracies, demonstrated creativity in art and literature, fashioned effective systems of mathematics, and advanced the knowledge of architecture, metallurgy, and engineering. The wheel, the plow, the phonetic alphabet, and the calendar derive from the Near East. Both the Hebrews and the Greeks, the principal sources of Western civilization, had contact with these older civilizations and adopted many of their cultural forms. But, as we shall see, even more important for the shaping of Western civilization was how the Hebrews and the Greeks broke with the essential style of Near Eastern society and conceived new outlooks, new points of departure for the human mind.

1 Mesopotamian Protest against Death

The *Epic of Gilgamesh*, the greatest work of Mesopotamian literature, was written about 2000 B.C. It utilized legends about Gilgamesh, probably a historical figure who ruled the city of Uruk about 2600 B.C. The story deals with a profound theme—the human protest against death. In the end, Gilgamesh learns to accept reality: there is no escape from death. While the *Epic of Gilgamesh* is an expression of the pessimism that pervaded Mesopotamian life, it also reveals the Mesopotamians' struggle to come to terms with reality.

EPIC OF GILGAMESH[1]

The *Epic of Gilgamesh* involves the gods in human activities. Because King Gilgamesh, son of a human father and the goddess Ninsun, drives his subjects too hard, they appeal to the gods for help. The gods decide that a man of Gilgamesh's immense vigor and strength requires a rival with similar attributes with whom he can contend. The creation goddess, Aruru, is instructed to create a man worthy of Gilgamesh. From clay she fashions Enkidu in the image of Anu, the god of the heavens and father of all the gods. Enkidu is a powerful man who roams with the animals and destroys traps set by hunters, one of whom appeals to King Gilgamesh. The two of them, accompanied by a harlot, find Enkidu at a watering place frequented by animals. The harlot removes her clothes and seduces Enkidu, who spends a week with her, oblivious to everything else. After this encounter, the bond between Enkidu and the animals is broken. He now enters civilization and is befriended by Gilgamesh, with whom he slays the terrible monster Humbaba.

Returning to Uruk after the encounter with Humbaba, Gilgamesh washes away the grime of battle and dons his royal clothes; thus arrayed he attracts the goddess of love, Ishtar, patroness of Uruk, who proposes marriage, but because of Ishtar's previous marriages and infidelities, Gilgamesh refuses. Ishtar falls into a bitter rage and appeals to her father, the god Anu, to unleash the fearful Bull of Heaven on Gilgamesh. However, Gilgamesh and Enkidu together slay the beast. To avenge the deaths of Humbaba and the Bull of Heaven, the gods decide that Enkidu shall die. In the following passage, Enkidu dreams of his impending death and the House of Darkness, from which no one returns.

When the daylight came Enkidu got up and cried to Gilgamesh, "O my brother, such a dream I had last night. Anu, Enlil, Ea and heavenly Shamash took counsel together, and Anu said to Enlil, 'Because they have killed the Bull of Heaven, and because they have killed Humbaba who guarded the Cedar Mountain one of the two must die.'. . ."

So Enkidu lay stretched out before Gilgamesh: his tears ran down in streams and he said to Gilgamesh, "O my brother, so dear as you are to me, brother, yet they will take me from you." Again he said, "I must sit down on the threshold of the dead and never again will I see my dear brother with my eyes."

. . . In bitterness of spirit he poured out his heart to his friend. "It was I who cut down the cedar, I who levelled the forest, I who slew Humbaba and now see what has become of me. Listen, my friend, this is the dream I dreamed last night. The heavens roared, and earth rumbled back an answer; between them stood I before an awful being, the sombre-faced man-bird; he had directed on me his purpose. His was a vampire face, his foot was a lion's foot, his hand was an eagle's talon. He fell on me and his claws were in my hair, he held me fast and I smothered; then he transformed me so that my arms became wings covered with feathers. He turned his stare towards me, and he led me away to the palace of Irkalla, the Queen of Darkness, to the house from which none who enters ever returns, down the road from which there is no coming back.

"There is the house whose people sit in darkness; dust is their food and clay their meat.

The Epic of Gilgamesh, pp. 89, 91–97, 101, translated by N.K. Sandars (Penguin Classics, 1960, Third edition 1972). Copyright © N.K. Sandars, 1950, 1964, 1972. Reproduced by permission of Penguin Books Ltd.

[1]Throughout this volume, titles original to the source appear in italics. Titles added by the editors are not italicized. —Eds.

They are clothed like birds with wings for covering, they see no light, they sit in darkness. I entered the house of dust and I saw the kings of the earth, their crowns put away forever; rulers and princes, all those who once wore kingly crowns and ruled the world in the days of old. They who had stood in the place of the gods like Anu and Enlil, stood now like servants to fetch baked meats in the house of dust, to carry cooked meat and cold water from the waterskin. In the house of dust which I entered were high priests and acolytes, priests of the incantation and of ecstasy; there were servers of the temple, and there was Etana, that king of Kish whom the eagle carried to heaven in the days of old. I saw also Samuqan, god of cattle, and there was Ereshkigal the Queen of the Underworld; and Belit-Sheri squatted in front of her, she who is recorder of the gods and keeps the book of death. She held a tablet from which she read. She raised her head, she saw me and spoke: 'Who has brought this one here?' Then I awoke like a man drained of blood who wanders alone in a waste of rushes; like one whom the bailiff has seized and his heart pounds with terror."

Gilgamesh had peeled off his clothes, he listened to his words and wept quick tears, Gilgamesh listened and his tears flowed. . . .

This day on which Enkidu dreamed came to an end and he lay stricken with sickness. One whole day he lay on his bed and his suffering increased. He said to Gilgamesh, the friend on whose account he had left the wilderness, "Once I ran for you, for the water of life, and I now have nothing." A second day he lay on his bed and Gilgamesh watched over him but the sickness increased. A third day he lay on his bed, he called out to Gilgamesh, rousing him up. Now he was weak and his eyes were blind with weeping. Ten days he lay and his suffering increased, eleven and twelve days he lay on his bed of pain. Then he called to Gilgamesh, "My friend, the great goddess cursed me and I must die in shame. I shall not die like a man fallen in battle; I feared to fall, but happy is the man who falls in the battle, for I must die in shame." And Gilgamesh wept over Enkidu. With the first light of dawn he raised his voice and said to the counsellors of Uruk:

"Hear me, great ones of Uruk,
I weep for Enkidu, my friend,
Bitterly moaning like a woman mourning
I weep for my brother.
O Enkidu, my brother,
You were the axe at my side,
My hand's strength, the sword in my belt,
The shield before me,
A glorious robe, my fairest ornament;
An evil Fate has robbed me.

.   .   .

All the people of Eridu
Weep for you Enkidu.

.   .   .

What is this sleep which holds you now?
You are lost in the dark and cannot hear me."

He touched his heart but it did not beat, nor did he lift his eyes again. When Gilgamesh touched his heart it did not beat. So Gilgamesh laid a veil, as one veils the bride, over his friend. He began to rage like a lion, like a lioness robbed of her whelps. This way and that he paced round the bed, he tore out his hair and strewed it around. He dragged off his splendid robes and flung them down as though they were abominations.

In the first light of dawn Gilgamesh cried out, "I made you rest on a royal bed, you reclined on a couch at my left hand, the princes of the earth kissed your feet. I will cause all the people of Uruk to weep over you and raise the dirge of the dead. The joyful people will stoop with sorrow; and when you have gone to the earth I will let my hair grow long for your sake, I will wander through the wilderness in the skin of a lion." The next day also, in the first light, Gilgamesh lamented; seven days and seven nights he wept for Enkidu, until the worm fastened on him. Only then he gave him up to the earth, for the Anunnaki, the judges [of the dead],[2] had seized him. . . .

---

[2]Throughout the volume, words in brackets have been added as notes by the editors of this text. Notes originating with the source appear in parentheses to distinguish them. —Eds.

In his despair, Gilgamesh is confronted with the reality of his own death. Yearning for eternal life, he seeks Utnapishtim, legendary king of the city of Shurrupak, a man to whom the gods had granted everlasting life.

Bitterly Gilgamesh wept for his friend Enkidu; he wandered over the wilderness as a hunter, he roamed over the plains; in his bitterness he cried, "How can I rest, how can I be at peace? Despair is in my heart. What my brother is now, that shall I be when I am dead. Because I am afraid of death I will go as best I can to find Utnapishtim whom they call the Faraway, for he has entered the assembly of the gods." So Gilgamesh travelled over the wilderness, he wandered over the grasslands, a long journey, in search of Utnapishtim, whom the gods took after the deluge; and they set him to live in the land of Dilmun, in the garden of the sun; and to him alone of men they gave everlasting life. . . .

In the garden of the gods, Gilgamesh speaks with Siduri, the divine winemaker, who tells him that his search for eternal life is hopeless.

". . . My friend who was very dear to me and who endured dangers beside me, Enkidu my brother, whom I loved, the end of mortality has overtaken him. I wept for him seven days and nights till the worm fastened on him. Because of my brother I am afraid of death, because of my brother I stray through the wilderness and cannot rest. But now, young woman, maker of wine, since I have seen your face do not let me see the face of death which I dread so much."

She answered, "Gilgamesh, where are you hurrying to? You will never find that life for which you are looking. When the gods created man they allotted to him death, but life they retained in their own keeping. As for you, Gilgamesh, fill your belly with good things; day and night, night and day, dance and be merry, feast and rejoice. Let your clothes be fresh, bathe yourself in water, cherish the little child that holds your hand, and make your wife happy in your embrace; for this too is the lot of man."

But Gilgamesh said to Siduri, the young woman, "How can I be silent, how can I rest, when Enkidu whom I love is dust, and I too shall die and be laid in the earth. You live by the seashore and look into the heart of it; young woman, tell me now, which is the way to Utnapishtim, the son of Ubara-Tutu? What directions are there for the passage; give me, oh, give me directions, I will cross the Ocean if it is possible; if it is not I will wander still farther in the wilderness.". . .

Siduri instructs Gilgamesh how to reach Utnapishtim. Ferried across the "waters of death" by a boatman, Gilgamesh meets Utnapishtim. But he, too, cannot give Gilgamesh the eternal life for which he yearns.

. . . "Oh father Utnapishtim, you who have entered the assembly of the gods, I wish to question you concerning the living and the dead, how shall I find the life for which I am searching?"

Utnapishtim said, "There is no permanence. Do we build a house to stand for ever, do we seal a contract to hold for all time? Do brothers divide an inheritance to keep for ever, does the flood-time of rivers endure? It is only the nymph of the dragon-fly who sheds her larva and sees the sun in his glory. From the days of old there is no permanence. The sleeping and the dead, how alike they are, they are like a painted death. What is there between the master and the servant when both have fulfilled their doom? When the Anunnaki, the judges, come together, and Mammetun the mother of destinies, together they decree the fates of men. Life and death they allot but the day of death they do not disclose."

The tale concludes with one of several Near Eastern flood stories that preceded the account of Noah in Genesis.

REVIEW QUESTIONS

1. Describe the condition of the dead as envisioned in Enkidu's dream.
2. Describe the stages of Gilgamesh's reaction to Enkidu's death. Do these seem plausible psychologically? Explain.
3. What philosophic consolation did the goddess Siduri and Utnapishtim offer Gilgamesh?
4. Historians often comment on the pessimism or sense of the tragic that is reflected in Mesopotamian literature. To what extent is this true in the story of Gilgamesh?

---

2 Mesopotamian Concepts of Justice

A significant source of information about the life of the ancient peoples of Mesopotamia is a code of laws issued about 1750 B.C. by the Babylonian king Hammurabi (ruled 1792–1750 B.C.). Discovered by archaeologists in 1901, the code was inscribed on a stone that shows the king accepting the laws from the sun god, Shamash, who was also the Babylonian god of justice.

These laws offer striking insights into the moral values, class structure, gender relationships, and roles of kingship and religion in Babylonian society. The 282 laws cover a range of public and private matters: marriage and family relations, negligence, fraud, commercial contracts, duties of public officials, property and inheritance, crimes and punishments, and techniques of legal procedure. The prologue to the code reveals the Mesopotamian concept of the priest-king— a ruler chosen by a god to administer his will on earth. In it, Hammurabi asserted that he had a divine duty to uphold justice in the land, to punish the wicked, and to further the welfare of the people.

CODE OF HAMMURABI

Two distinct approaches to choice of punishment for crime are found in Hammurabi's code with its numerous laws. In some instances, the guilty party is required to pay a monetary compensation to the victim, a tradition traceable to the earliest known Sumerian laws. Another approach, also found in the later Hebrew codes of law, is the principle of exact retaliation: "an eye for an eye, a tooth for a tooth."

Another feature of Hammurabi's code is that the penalties vary according to the social status of the victim. Three classes are represented: free men and women (called *patricians* in the following excerpt); commoners (or *plebeians*), not wholly free, but dependents of the state or perhaps serfs on landed estates; and slaves. The patricians are protected by the law of retaliation. People of the lower classes receive only monetary compensation if they are victims of a crime.

196. If a man has knocked out the eye of a patrician, his eye shall be knocked out.

197. If he has broken the limb of a patrician, his limb shall be broken.

198. If he has knocked out the eye of a plebeian or has broken the limb of a plebeian, he shall pay one mina[1] of silver.

199. If he has knocked out the eye of a patrician's servant, or broken the limb of a patrician's servant, he shall pay half his value.

200. If a patrician has knocked out the tooth of a man that is his equal, his tooth shall be knocked out.

201. If he has knocked out the tooth of a plebeian, he shall pay one-third of a mina of silver. . . .

209. If a man has struck a free woman with child, and has caused her to miscarry, he shall pay ten shekels[2] for her miscarriage.

210. If that woman die, his daughter shall be killed.

211. If it be the daughter of a plebeian, that has miscarried through his blows, he shall pay five shekels of silver.

212. If that woman die, he shall pay half a mina of silver.

213. If he has struck a man's maid and caused her to miscarry, he shall pay two shekels of silver.

214. If that woman die, he shall pay one-third of a mina of silver.

Many laws relating to business transactions show the importance of trade in Mesopotamian society and the willingness of the government to intervene in order to regulate the practices of the marketplace.

---

218. If a surgeon has operated with the bronze lancet on a patrician for a serious injury, and has caused his death, or has removed a cataract for a patrician, with the bronze lancet,

and has made him lose his eye, his hands shall be cut off.

219. If the surgeon has treated a serious injury of a plebeian's slave, with the bronze lancet, and has caused his death, he shall render slave for slave.

220. If he has removed a cataract with the bronze lancet, and made the slave lose his eye, he shall pay half his value.

221. If a surgeon has cured the limb of a patrician, or has doctored a diseased bowel, the patient shall pay five shekels of silver to the surgeon.

222. If he be a plebeian, he shall pay three shekels of silver.

223. If he be a man's slave, the owner of the slave shall give two shekels of silver to the doctor. . . .

228. If a builder has built a house for a man, and finished it, he shall pay him a fee of two shekels of silver, for each *Sar*[3] built on.

229. If a builder has built a house for a man, and has not made his work sound, and the house he built has fallen, and caused the death of its owner, that builder shall be put to death.

230. If it is the owner's son that is killed, the builder's son shall be put to death.

231. If it is the slave of the owner that is killed, the builder shall give slave for slave to the owner of the house.

232. If he has caused the loss of goods, he shall render back whatever he has destroyed. Moreover, because he did not make sound the house he built, and it fell, at his own cost he shall rebuild the house that fell. . . .

271. If a man has hired oxen, a wagon, and its driver, he shall pay one hundred and sixty *Ka*[4] of corn daily. . . .

275. If a man has hired a boat, its hire is three *Še*[5] of silver daily.

Babylonian and Assyrian Contracts and Letters, ed. C. M. W. Johns (New York: Charles Scribner's Sons, 1904), pp. 44–67 passim.

---

[1]The mina was a weight of silver used to express monetary value. —Eds.

[2]The shekel, also a weight of monetary value, was worth far less than the mina. —Eds.

[3]*Sar* was a measure of land. —Eds.

[4]*Ka* stood for a bulk measure. —Eds.

[5]*Še* was another monetary weight of silver. —Eds.

The outcome of some procedures depended on the will of the gods: for example, an accused woman could place her fate in the hands of a god by plunging into a river, canal, or reservoir; if she did not drown, she was declared innocent. In other cases, legal culpability could be removed by invoking a god to bear witness to the truth of one's testimony. The law was particularly harsh on perjurers and those who made grave charges that they could not prove in court.

property. The buyer shall recoup himself from the seller's estate.

The laws concerned with family relationships placed great power in the hands of husbands and fathers, yet the code tried to protect women and children from neglect and mistreatment. Divorce initiated by either husband or wife was permitted under specific circumstances.

1. If a man has accused another of laying a *nêrtu* (death spell?) upon him, but has not proved it, he shall be put to death.

2. If a man has accused another of laying a *kišpu* (spell) upon him, but has not proved it, the accused shall go to the sacred river, he shall plunge into the sacred river, and if the sacred river shall conquer him, he that accused him shall take possession of his house. If the sacred river shall show his innocence and he is saved, his accuser shall be put to death. He that plunged into the sacred river shall appropriate the house of him that accused him.

3. If a man has borne false witness in a trial, or has not established the statement that he has made, if that case be a capital trial, that man shall be put to death.

4. If he has borne false witness in a civil law case, he shall pay the damages in that suit. . . .

9. If a man has lost property and some of it be detected in the possession of another, and the holder has said, "A man sold it to me, I bought it in the presence of witnesses"; and if the claimant has said, "I can bring witnesses who know it to be property lost by me"; then the alleged buyer on his part shall produce the man who sold it to him and the witnesses before whom he bought it; the claimant shall on his part produce the witnesses who know it to be his lost property. The judge shall examine their pleas. The witnesses to the sale and the witnesses who identify the lost property shall state on oath what they know. Such a seller is the thief and shall be put to death. The owner of the lost property shall recover his lost

141. If a man's wife, living in her husband's house, has persisted in going out, has acted the fool, has wasted her house, has belittled her husband, he shall prosecute her. If her husband has said, "I divorce her," she shall go her way; he shall give her nothing as her price of divorce. If her husband has said, "I will not divorce her," he may take another woman to wife; the wife shall live as a slave in her husband's house.

142. If a woman has hated her husband and has said, "You shall not possess me," her past shall be inquired into, as to what she lacks. If she has been discreet, and has no vice, and her husband has gone out, and has greatly belittled her, that woman has no blame, she shall take her marriage-portion and go off to her father's house.

143. If she has not been discreet, has gone out, ruined her house, belittled her husband, she shall be drowned. . . .

148. If a man has married a wife and a disease has seized her, if he is determined to marry a second wife, he shall marry her. He shall not divorce the wife whom the disease has seized. In the home they made together she shall dwell, and he shall maintain her as long as she lives. . . .

168. If a man has determined to disinherit his son and has declared before the judge, "I cut off my son," the judge shall inquire into the son's past, and, if the son has not committed a grave misdemeanor such as should cut him off from sonship, the father shall (not) disinherit his son.

169. If he has committed a grave crime against his father, which cuts him off from sonship, for

the first offence he shall pardon him. If he has committed a grave crime a second time, the father shall cut off his son from sonship. . . .

195. If a son has struck his father, his hands shall be cut off.

One of the most unusual features of the law dealt with the failure of the government officials of a city or a district to prevent banditry. The code held the governor responsible for the breach of the peace and required him to compensate the bandit's victim. Government officials found guilty of extortion, bribery, or use of public employees for private purposes were severely punished.

---

23. If the highwayman has not been caught, the man that has been robbed shall state on oath what he has lost and the city or district governor in whose territory or district the robbery took place shall restore to him what he has lost.

24. If a life (has been lost), the city or district governor shall pay one mina of silver to the deceased's relatives. . . .

34. If either a governor, or a prefect, has appropriated the property of a levymaster,[6] has hired him out, has robbed him by high-handedness at a trial, has taken the salary which the king gave to him, that governor, or prefect, shall be put to death. . . .

---

[6]A levymaster was a military official. —Eds.

REVIEW QUESTIONS

1. What does Hammurabi's code reveal about the social structure of Babylonian society?
2. Explain the role of religion in the administration of law in Babylonia.
3. How did Hammurabi seek to regulate business practices among the Babylonian people?
4. What do the laws indicate about the status of women in Babylonian society?
5. How did Hammurabi try to control corrupt practices among the government officials of Babylonia?

---

3   Divine Kingship in Egypt

Theocratic monarchy, in which the ruler was considered either a god or a representative of the gods, was the basic political institution of ancient Near Eastern civilization. Kings were believed to rule in accordance with divine commands, and law was viewed as god-given. Theocracy as a form of government that subordinates the individual to the gods and their earthly representatives is compatible with mythical thought that sees nature and human destiny controlled by divine beings.

The theocratic mind of the Near East did not conceive the idea of political freedom. Mesopotamians and Egyptians were not free citizens but subjects who obeyed unquestioningly the edicts of their god-kings or priest-kings. Nor did Near Easterners arrive at a rational way of analyzing the nature and purpose of government and the merits or demerits of political institutions. To them the power of their gods and rulers was absolute and not an issue for discussion or reflection.

Divine kingship was the basic political institution of ancient Egyptian civilization. The Egyptians believed their king, or pharaoh, to be both a god and a man, the earthly embodiment of the god Horus. He was regarded as a benevolent protector who controlled the flood waters of the Nile, kept the irrigation system in working order, maintained justice in the land, and expressed the will of the gods by his words. It was expected that when the pharaoh died and joined his fellow gods, he would still help his living subjects. The Egyptians rejoiced in the rule of their all-powerful god-king.

HYMNS TO THE PHARAOHS

The first reading is a hymn to the new god-king Ramesses IV (c. 1166 B.C.). The second reading is a hymn to a deceased pharaoh, perhaps Unnos (c. 2600 B.C.).

TO RAMESSES IV

What a happy day! Heaven and earth rejoice, (for) thou art the great lord of Egypt.

They that had fled have come again to their towns, and they that were hidden have again come forth.

They that hungered are satisfied and happy, and they that thirsted are drunken.

They that were naked are clad in fine linen, and they that were dirty have white garments.

They that were in prison are set free, and he that was in bonds is full of joy.

They that were at strife in this land are reconciled. High Niles [beneficial floods] have come from their sources, that they may refresh the hearts of others.

Widows, their houses stand open, and they suffer travellers to enter.

Maidens rejoice and repeat their songs of gladness (?). They are arrayed in ornaments and say (?): "——— he createth generation on generation. Thou ruler, thou wilt endure for ever."

The ships rejoice on the deep ———.
They come to land with wind or oars,
They are satisfied . . . when it is said:
"King Hekmaatrē-Beloved-of-Amūn[1] again
   weareth the crown.

The son of [the sun-god] Rē, Ramesses, hath
   received the office of his father."
All lands say unto him:
"Beautiful is Horus on the throne of Amūn
   who sendeth him forth,
(Amūn) the protector of the Prince, who
   bringeth every land."

TO A DECEASED PHARAOH

The King has not died the death: he has become one who rises (like the morning sun) from the horizon. He rests from life (like the setting sun) in the West, but he dawns anew in the East. O King, you have not departed dead: you have departed living! Have you said that he would die?—nay, he dies not: this king lives for ever. He has escaped his day of death. O lofty one among the imperishable stars!—you shall not ever perish. Loose the embalming bandages!—they are not bandages (at all): they are the tresses of the goddess Nephthys (as she leans down over you). Men fall, and their name ceases to be: therefore God takes hold of this king by his arm, and leads him to the sky, that he may not die upon earth amongst men. This king flies away from you, you mortals. He is not of the earth, he is of the sky. He flies as a cloud to the sky, he who was like a bird

Adolph Erman, *The Ancient Egyptians: A Sourcebook of Their Writings*, trans. Aylward M. Blackman (New York: Harper Torchbooks, 1966), pp. 279–280. Reproduced by permission of Taylor & Francis Books UK.

Arthur Weigall, *A History of the Pharaohs,* vol. 1 (London: T. Butterworth, 1925), p. 215.

[1]Hekmaatrē was another name of this pharaoh. —Eds.

at the masthead. He goes up to heaven like the hawks, and his feathers are like those of the wild geese; he rushes at heaven like a crane, he kisses heaven like the falcon, he leaps to heaven like the locust. He ascends to the sky! He ascends to the sky on the wind, on the wind! The stairs of the sky are let down for him that he may ascend thereon to heaven. O gods, put your arms under the king: raise him, lift him to the sky. To the sky! To the sky! To the great throne amongst the gods!

GUIDELINES FOR THE RULER

Generally, pharaohs were mindful of their responsibilities. To prepare his son to rule, a pharaoh or his vizier (a high executive officer) might compile a list of instructions, like the ones that follow.

If thou art a leader and givest command to the multitude, strive after every excellence, until there be no fault in thy nature. Truth is good and its worth is lasting, and it hath not been disturbed since the day of its creator,[1] whereas he that transgresseth its ordinances is punished. It lieth as a (right) path in front of him that knoweth nothing. Wrong-doing (?) hath never yet brought its venture to port. Evil indeed winneth wealth, but the strength of truth is that it endureth, and the (upright) man saith: "It is the property of my father."...[2]

The following excerpts come from the instructions of Amenemhet I (ruled 1991–1962 B.C.), who prepared them for his son.

I gave to the poor and nourished the orphan, I caused him that was nothing to reach the goal, even as him that was of account....

None hungered in my years, none thirsted in them. Men dwelt in (peace) through that which I wrought; ... all that I commanded was as it should be....

These instructions were prepared for pharaoh Merikare (c. 2050 B.C.) by his father.

Be not evil, it is good to be kindly. Cause thy monument[3] to endure through the love of thee.... Then men thank God on thine account, men praise thy goodness and pray for thine health.... But keep thine eyes open, one that is trusting will become one that is afflicted....

Do right so long as thou abidest on the earth. Calm the weeper, oppress no widow, expel no man from the possessions of his father.... Take heed lest thou punish wrongfully.

Exalt not the son of one of high degree more than him that is of lowly birth, but take to thyself a man because of his actions.

Adolph Erman, *The Ancient Egyptians: A Sourcebook of Their Writings*, trans. Aylward M. Blackman (New York: Harper Torchbooks, 1966), pp. 57, 72, 74, 76–78. Reproduced by permission of Taylor & Francis Books UK.

[1] Rē [the sun god], who brought truth into the world.
[2] That my father brought me up in the ways of truth is the best thing that he has bequeathed me.
[3] The remembrance of thee.

REVIEW QUESTIONS

1. What were the duties expected of an Egyptian pharaoh?
2. Discuss the role of religion in sustaining the authority of rulers over their subjects.

4 Religious Inspiration of Akhenaten

Pharaoh Amenhotep IV (ruled 1369–1353 B.C.) was a religious mystic who conceived of divinity in a manner approaching monotheism. He suppressed the worship of the many gods of Egypt and insisted that only Aton—the sun god—and himself, the king and son of Aton, be worshiped by the Egyptians. Aton was viewed as the creator of the world, a god of love, peace, and justice. To promote the exclusive worship of Aton and himself, Amenhotep changed his name to Akhenaten ("It is well with Aton"), and near modern Tell El-Amarna he built a new capital city, Akhetaten, which became the center of the new religious cult. The new religion perished quickly after Akhenaten's death. There is no evidence that this step toward a monotheistic conception of the divine had any later influence on the Hebrews.

The masses of Egypt were not influenced by Akhenaten's religious inspiration, and he was resisted by the priests, who clung to traditional beliefs. His immediate successors abandoned the new capital and had the monuments to Aton destroyed.

HYMN TO ATON

Akhenaten's religious outlook inspired remarkable works of art and literature. In the following hymn, Akhenaten glorifies Aton in words that are reminiscent of Psalm 104.

Thou appearest beautifully on the horizon of
   heaven,
Thou living Aton, the beginning of life!
When thou art risen on the eastern horizon,
Thou hast filled every land with thy beauty.
Thou art gracious, great, glistening, and high
   over every land;
Thy rays encompass the lands to the limit of all
   that thou hast made. . . .
At daybreak, when thou arisest on the horizon,
When thou shinest as the Aton by day,
Thou drivest away the darkness and givest thy rays.
The Two Lands[1] are in festivity *every day*,
Awake and standing upon (their) feet,
For thou hast raised them up.
Washing their bodies, taking (their) clothing,

Their arms are (raised) in praise at thy appearance.
All the world, they do their work.

All beasts are content with their pasturage;
Trees and plants are flourishing.
The birds which fly from their nests,
Their wings are (stretched out) in praise to thy *ka*.[2]
All beasts spring upon (their) feet.
Whatever flies and alights,
They live when thou hast risen (for) them.
The ships are sailing north and south as well,
For every way is open at thy appearance.
The fish in the river dart before thy face;
Thy rays are in the midst of the great green sea.

Creator of seed in women,
Thou who makest fluid into man,

James B. Pritchard, ed., *Ancient Near Eastern Texts Relating to the Old Testament*, 3rd ed., with supplement, pp. 100–101. Copyright © 1950, 1955, 1969, renewed 1978 by Princeton University Press. Reprinted by permission of Princeton University Press.

[1]The Two Lands were the two political divisions of Egypt—Upper and Lower Egypt. They were usually governed by the same king. —Eds.
[2]The *ka* was a protective and guiding spirit, which each person was thought to have. —Eds.

Who maintainest the son in the womb of his
    mother,
Who soothest him with that which stills his
    weeping,
Thou nurse (even) in the womb,
Who givest breath to sustain all that he had made!
When he descends from the womb to *breathe*
On the day when he is born,
Thou openest his mouth completely,
Thou suppliest his necessities.
When the chick in the egg speaks within the shell,
Thou givest him breath within it to maintain him.
When thou hast made him his fulfillment
    within the egg, to break it,
He comes forth from the egg to speak at his
    completed (time);
He walks upon his legs when he comes forth
    from it.

How manifold it is, what thou hast made!
They are hidden from the face (of man).
O sole god, like whom there is no other!
Thou didst create the world according to thy
    desire,
Whilst thou wert alone:
All men, cattle, and wild beasts,
Whatever is on earth, going upon (its) feet,

And what is on high, flying with its wings.
The countries of Syria and Nubia,[3] the *land* of
    Egypt,
Thou settest every man in his place,
Thou suppliest their necessities:
Everyone has his food, and his time of life is
    reckoned.
Their tongues are separate in speech,
And their natures as well;
Their skins are distinguished,
As thou distinguishest the foreign peoples.
Thou makest a Nile in the underworld,[4]
Thou bringest it forth as thou desirest
To maintain the people (of Egypt)
According as thou madest them for thyself,
The lord of all of them, wearying (himself)
    with them,
The lord of every land, rising for them,
The Aton of the day, great of majesty.

————

[3]Syria was an ancient country, larger than modern Syria,
north of modern Israel and Jordan; Nubia was a kingdom
located south of the first cataract of the Nile. It is now in
Sudan. —Eds.
[4]The Egyptians believed that the source of their Nile was
in a huge body of water, which they called Nun, under the
earth. —Eds.

REVIEW QUESTIONS

1. Why was the sun a likely choice for a god conceived as one and universal?
2. What were some of the gifts of Aton to humanity?
3. What does the poem reveal about Akhenaten's view of the world and its peoples?

---

5 Love, Passion, and Misogyny in Ancient Egypt

As in most ancient societies, Egyptian women were concerned principally with
marriage, children, and household. But in comparison to other societies, Egyptian women suffered fewer disabilities. They had legal rights, could enter the
priesthood, a truly prestigious position, and, like men, were thought to have access to the other world after death.

Both men and women came under love's power, and the Egyptians wrote numerous poems that expressed both the joy and pain of love.

LOVE POETRY

In the first selection, a young man admires his loved one's beauty. In this instance, the word *sister*[1] is probably not to be taken literally; it is intended as an expression of endearment.

The *One*, the sister without peer,
The handsomest of all!
She looks like the rising morning star
At the start of a happy year.
Shining bright, fair of skin,
Lovely the look of her eyes,
Sweet the speech of her lips,
She has not a word too much.
Upright neck, shining breast,
Hair true lapis lazuli;
Arms surpassing gold,
Fingers like lotus buds.
Heavy thighs, narrow waist,
Her legs parade her beauty;
With graceful step she treads the ground,
Captures my heart by her movements.
She causes all men's necks
To turn about to see her;
Joy has he whom she embraces,
He is like the first of men!

Without his love the young man suffers.

Seven days since I saw my sister,
And sickness invaded me;
I am heavy in all my limbs,
My body has forsaken me.
When the physicians come to me,
My heart rejects their remedies;
The magicians are quite helpless,
My sickness is not discerned.
To tell me "She is here" would revive me!

Her name would make me rise;
Her messenger's coming and going,
That would revive my heart!
My sister is better than all prescriptions,
She does more for me than all medicines;
Her coming to me is my amulet,
The sight of her makes me well!
When she opens her eyes my body is young,
Her speaking makes me strong;
Embracing her expels my malady—
Seven days since she went from me!

Egyptian women also experience love and vent their feelings.

My heart *flutters* hastily,
When I think of my love of you;
It lets me not act sensibly,
It leaps (from) its place.
It lets me not put on a dress,
Nor wrap my scarf around me;
I put no paint upon my eyes,
I'm even not anointed.

"Don't wait, go there," says it to me,
As often as I think of him;
My heart, don't act so stupidly,
Why do you play the fool?
Sit still, the brother comes to you,
And many eyes as well!
Let not the people say of me:
"A woman fallen through love!"
Be steady when you think of him,
My heart, do not *flutter*!

Miriam Lichtheim, *Ancient Egyptian Literature: A Book of Readings,* vol. 2, 1976, pp. 182, 185, 183–184, 166–180. © 1976 University of California Press. Reprinted by permission of the University of California Press.

[1]Since Egyptians were interested in maintaining pure bloodlines, incestuous relationships, including brother and sister, were not uncommon. Therefore, the word *sister,* when used by a lover, may be taken figuratively or literally, depending on the circumstances. —Eds.

THE INSTRUCTION OF ANKHSHESHONQ

Some Egyptian men held unflattering views of women. In his advice to his son, the priest Ankhsheshonq, who lived sometime between 300 B.C. and 50 B.C., expresses such misogynistic views.

Do not take to yourself a woman whose husband is alive, lest he become your enemy. . . .

Let your wife see your wealth; do not trust her with it. . . .

Do not open your heart to your wife or to your servant.

Open it to your mother; she is a woman of discretion. . . .

Instructing a woman is like having a sack of sand whose side is split open.

Her savings are stolen goods.

What she does with her husband today she does with another man tomorrow. . . .

Do not rejoice in your wife's beauty; her heart is set on her lover. . . .

A woman lets herself be loved according to the character of her husband. . . .

He who violates a married woman on the bed will have his wife violated on the ground. . . .

He who makes love to a woman of the street will have his purse cut open on its side. . . .

He who makes love to a married woman is killed on her doorstep. . . .

Do not marry an impious woman, lest she give your children an impious upbringing.

If a woman is at peace with her husband they will never fare badly.

If a woman whispers about her husband [they will never] fare well.

If a woman does not desire the property of her husband she has another man [in her] heart. . . .

If a wife is of nobler birth than her husband he should give way to her.

Miriam Lichtheim, *Ancient Egyptian Literature: A Book of Readings*, vol. 2, 1976, pp. 182, 185, 183–184, 166–180. © 1976 University of California Press. Reprinted by permission of the University of California Press.

REVIEW QUESTIONS

1. On the basis of these poems, what similarities do you discern between our standards of beauty and an ancient Egyptian's?
2. Which piece of the priest's advice would a misogynist today consider the wisest?

6 Empire Builders: The Assyrians and Persians

After 1500 B.C. Near Eastern history was marked by empire building, which led to the intermingling of peoples and cultural traditions and to the extension of civilization well beyond the river valleys. Two of the leading empire builders were the Assyrians and the Persians.

INSCRIPTION OF TIGLATH-PILESER I

The Assyrians, a Semitic people from the region of what is now northern Iraq, went through several stages of empire building. At its height in the seventh century B.C., the Assyrian Empire stretched from Egypt to Persia (modern Iran). The king, representative of the god Ashur, governed absolutely, and nobles, appointed by the crown, kept order in the provinces. Traveling inspectors checked on the performance of these officials. A network of roads and an effective messenger service enabled Assyrian rulers to keep informed about potential unrest and to crush rebellions. Conquered peoples were permitted a substantial amount of independence so long as they paid tribute to their Assyrian overlords, but uprisings were ruthlessly suppressed.

In the following reading, Tiglath-pileser I (1115–1077 B.C.) describes his conquests and the subjugation of rebellious subjects.

Tiglath-pileser, the powerful king, king of hosts, who has no rival, king of the four quarters (of the world), king of all rulers, lord of lords, king of kings; the lofty prince . . . who rules over the nations, . . . the legitimate shepherd whose name is exalted above all rulers; the lofty judge, whose weapons Ashur[1] has sharpened, and whose name, as ruler over the four quarters (of the world), he has proclaimed forever; the conqueror of distant lands, which form the boundaries on north and south; the brilliant day, whose splendour overthrows the world's regions; the terrible, destroying flame, which like the rush of the storm sweeps over the enemy's country; who . . . has no adversary, and overthrows the foes of Ashur.

Ashur and the great gods who have enlarged my kingdom, who have given me strength and power as my portion, commanded me to extend the territory of their (the gods') country, putting into my hand their powerful weapons, the cyclone of battle. I subjugated lands and mountains, cities and their rulers, enemies of Ashur, and conquered their territories. With sixty kings I fought, spreading terror (among them), and achieved a glorious victory over them. A rival in combat, or an adversary in battle, I did not have. To Assyria I added more land, to its people I added more people, enlarging the boundaries of my land and conquering all (neighbouring?) territories.

In the beginning of my government, five kings . . . with an army of twenty thousand men . . .—and whose power no king had ever broken and overcome in battle—trusting to their strength rushed down and conquered the land of Qummuh (Commagene).[2] With the help of Ashur, my lord, I gathered my war chariots and assembled my warriors; I made no delay, but traversed Kashiari,[3] an almost impassable region. I waged battle in Qummuh with these five kings and their twenty thousand soldiers and accomplished their defeat. Like the Thunderer (the storm god Adad) I crushed the corpses of their warriors in the battle that caused their overthrow. I made their blood to flow over all the ravines and high places of mountains. I cut off their heads and piled them up at the walls of their cities like heaps of grain. I carried off their booty, their goods, and their property beyond reckoning. Six thousand, the rest of their

---

R. F. Harper, *Assyrian and Babylonian Literature* (New York: D. Appleton, 1904), pp. 12–14.

---

[1] Ashur was the patron god of the Assyrians. He is identified with the earlier Babylonian god Marduk. —Eds.
[2] Commagene was a region along the upper Euphrates River in northern Syria. —Eds.
[3] Kashiari was a mountainous area in Mesopotamia. —Eds.

troops, who had fled before my weapons and had thrown themselves at my feet, I took away as prisoners and added to the people of my country.

At that time I marched also against the people of Qummuh, who had become unsubmissive, withholding the tax and tribute due to Ashur, my lord. I conquered Qummuh to its whole extent, and carried off their booty, their goods, and their property; I burned their cities with fire, destroyed, and devastated.

INSCRIPTIONS OF CYRUS AND DARIUS I

Under Cyrus the Great and his son and successor, Cambyses, the Persians conquered all lands between the Nile in Egypt and the Indus River in India. This conquest took twenty-five years, from 550 to 525 B.C. The Near Eastern conception of absolute monarchy justified by religion reached its culminating expression in the person of the Persian king who, it was believed, ruled this vast empire with divine approval. The Persian kings developed an effective system of administration—based in part on an Assyrian model—which gave stability and a degree of unity to their extensive territories.

In the following inscription, Cyrus the Great describes his accomplishments.

I am Cyrus, king of the world, great king, legitimate king, king of Babylon, king of Sumer and Akkad, king of the four rims (of the earth), son of Cambyses, great king, king of Anshan, grandson of Cyrus, great king, king of Anshan, descendant of Teispes, great king, king of Anshan, of a family (which) always (exercised) kingship; whose rule Bel and Nebo love, whom they want as king to please their hearts.

When I entered Babylon as a friend and (when) I established the seat of the government in the palace of the ruler under jubilation and rejoicing, Marduk, the great lord, (induced) the magnanimous inhabitants of Babylon (to love me), and I was daily endeavouring to worship him. My numerous troops walked around in Babylon in peace, I did not allow anybody to terrorize (any place) of the (country of Sumer) and Akkad. I strove for peace in Babylon and in all his (other) sacred cities. As to the inhabitants of Babylon, (I abolished) the *corvée*[1] (lit.: yoke) which was against their (social) standing. I brought relief to their dilapidated housing, putting (thus) an end to their (main) complaints. Marduk, the great lord, was well pleased with my deeds and sent friendly blessings to myself, Cyrus, the king who worships him, to Cambyses, my son, the offspring of (my) loins, as well as to all my troops, and we all (praised) his great (godhead) joyously, standing before him in peace.

All the kings of the entire world from the Upper to the Lower Sea, those who are seated in throne rooms, (those who) live in other (types of buildings as well as) all the kings of the West land living in tents,[2] brought their heavy tributes and kissed my feet in Babylon. (As to the region) from . . . as far as Ashur and Susa, Agade, Eshnunna, the towns Zamban, Me-Turnu, Der as well as the region of the Gutians, I returned to (these) sacred cities on the other side of the Tigris, the sanctuaries of which have been ruins for a long time, the images which

---

James B. Pritchard, ed., *Ancient Near Eastern Texts Relating to the Old Testament,* 2nd ed., p. 316. Copyright © 1950, 1955, 1969, renewed 1978 by Princeton University Press. Reprinted by permission of Princeton University Press.

[1]The *corvée* was labor that local authorities required of ordinary citizens, often on public works such as the maintenance of roads. —Eds.

[2]This phrase refers either to the way of life of a nomadic or a primitive society in contradistinction to that of an urban.

(used) to live therein and established for them permanent sanctuaries. I (also) gathered all their (former) inhabitants and returned (to them) their habitations. Furthermore, I resettled upon the command of Marduk, the great lord, all the gods of Sumer and Akkad whom Nabonidus has brought into Babylon to the anger of the lord of the gods, unharmed, in their (former) chapels, the places which make them happy.

May all the gods whom I have resettled in their sacred cities ask daily Bel and Nebo for a long life for me and may they recommend me (to him); to Marduk, my lord, they may say this: "Cyrus, the king who worships you, and Cambyses, his son, . . ." . . . all of them I settled in a peaceful place . . . ducks and doves, . . . I endeavoured to fortify/repair their dwelling places. . . . (six lines destroyed)

Besides providing impressive political and administrative unity, the Persian Empire fused and perpetuated the various cultural traditions of the Near East. This cultural fusion is reflected in the following inscription, which describes the construction of the palace at Susa by King Darius I (ruled 522–486 B.C.).

A great god is Ahuramazda, who created this earth, who created yonder firmament, who created man, who created welfare for man, who made Darius king, one king of many, one lord of many.—I am Darius, great king, king of kings, king of countries, king of this earth, son of Hystaspes, the Achaemenian.—Says Darius the king: Ahuramazda the greatest of gods, he created me; he made me king; he to me this kingdom granted, the great (kingdom), with good horses, with good men. By the grace of Ahuramazda my father Hystaspes and Arsames my grandfather

then both were living when Ahuramazda made me king of this earth. Ahuramazda created for me the horse on the whole earth, and man; he made me king. Ahuramazda granted me aid, Ahuramazda I reverenced, Ahuramazda the greatest of gods—what he told me to do, all that by my hand was done, all that Ahuramazda did.—By the grace of Ahuramazda this palace I made which at Susa was made. From afar to here its ornamentation was brought.

The earth was dug until I came to rock-bottom. When the excavation was made, then rubble was filled in, one part 40 feet in depth, the other 20 feet in depth. On this rubble the palace was constructed.— And that the earth was dug down, and that rubble was filled in and that brick was moulded, the Babylonian folk, it did (that). The timber cedar, this—a mountain named Lebanon—from there was brought; the Assyrian folk, it brought it to Babylon; from Babylon the Karkians and Ionians brought it to Susa. The oak from Gandara was brought and from Carmania. The gold from Sardis and from Bactria was brought, which was wrought here. The stone—lapis lazuli and serpentine— which was wrought here, this from Sogdiana was brought. The stone hematite, this from Chorasmia was brought, which was wrought here. The silver and the copper from Egypt were brought. The ornamentation with which the wall was adorned, that from Ionia was brought. The ivory, which was brought here, from Ethiopia and from India and from Arachosia was brought. The stone pillars which here were wrought—a place named Abirāduš in Uja—from there were brought; the stone-masons who there worked, those were Ionians and Sardians.—The artisans who the structure wrought, those were Medes and Egyptians;

those who worked on the fine stones, those
were Sardians and Egyptians. The men who
worked on the brick (work), those were Babylonians and Ionians; those who (worked) at the
wall, those were
Medes and Egyptians.—Says Darius the king:
   by the grace

of Ahuramazda (this) fine well-laid well-walled
   (palace)
I made. Me may Ahuramazda protect, and what
   by me was
done, and what my father (has done), and my
   country.

REVIEW QUESTIONS

1. What role do the inscriptions suggest the gods played in establishing and extending
   the rule of the Assyrian and Persian kings?
2. What appear to have been the character and purposes of warfare in the Assyrian and
   Persian empires?
3. In what ways did the great royal palace at Susa symbolize both the culture and
   extent of the Persian Empire?

---

7   The Myth-Making Outlook of the Ancient Near East

The civilizations of the ancient Near East were based on a way of thinking that
is fundamentally different from the modern scientific outlook. The peoples of
Mesopotamia and Egypt interpreted nature and human experience through
myths, which narrated the deeds of gods who in some distant past had brought
forth the world and human beings. These myths made the universe and life
intelligible for Near Eastern people.

The difference between scientific thinking and mythical thinking is
profound. The scientific mind views physical nature as an *it*—inanimate,
impersonal, and governed by universal law. The myth-making (mythopoeic)
mind sees nature as personified—alive, with individual wills, gods, and demons who manipulate things according to their desires. The scientific mind
holds that natural objects obey universal rules; hence the location of planets, the speed of objects, and the onset of a hurricane can be predicted. The
myth-making mind has no awareness of repetitive laws inherent in nature;
rather it attributes all occurrences to the actions of gods, whose behavior is
often unpredictable. The scientific mind appeals to reason—it analyzes nature
logically and systematically and searches for general principles that govern the
phenomena. The myth-making mind explains nature and human experience
by narrating stories about the gods and their deeds. Myth is an expression of
the poetic imagination; it proclaims a truth that is emotionally satisfying, not
one produced by intellectual analysis and synthesis. It gives order to human
experiences and justifies traditional rules of morality. Mythical explanations of
nature and human experience, appealing essentially to the imagination, enrich
perception and feeling; they make life seem less overwhelming and death less
frightening.

PERSONIFICATION OF NATURAL OBJECTS

The myth-making mind accounts for causation by personifying inanimate substances. To explain through personification is to seek the *who* behind events, to attribute these events to the will of a god (or to an object suffused with divine presence). Thus if a river did not rise, it was because it refused to do so; either the river or the gods were angry at the people.

The following excerpts from Mesopotamian literature are examples of personification. While we regard table salt as an ordinary mineral, to the Mesopotamians it was alive, a fellow being. In one passage, a person appeals to salt to end his bewitchment. In another, an afflicted person who believes himself bewitched calls on fire to destroy his enemies.

O SALT

O Salt, created in a clean place,
For food of gods did *Enlil* [father of the
    Sumerian gods] destine thee.
Without thee no meal is set out in *Ekur*,
Without thee god, king, lord, and prince do
    not smell incense.
I am so-and-so, the son of so-and-so,
Held captive by enchantment,
Held in fever by bewitchment.
O Salt, break my enchantment! Loose my spell!

———

From *The Intellectual Adventure of Ancient Man: An Essay on Speculative Thought in the Ancient Near East*, by Henri Frankfort, H.A. Frankfort, John A. Wilson, Thorkid Jacobsen, and William A. Irwin, eds. © 1977 University of Chicago Press. Reprinted with permission of University of Chicago Press.

Take from me the bewitchment!—And as My
    Creator
I shall extol thee.

SCORCHING FIRE

Scorching Fire, warlike son of Heaven,
Thou, the fiercest of thy brethren,
Who like Moon and Sun decidest lawsuits—
Judge thou my case, hand down the verdict.
Burn the man and woman who bewitched me;
Burn, O Fire, the man and woman who
    bewitched me;
Scorch, O Fire, the man and woman who
    bewitched me;
Burn them, O Fire;
Scorch them, O Fire;
Take hold of them, O Fire;
Consume them, O Fire;
Destroy them, O Fire.

ATRAHASIS DIVINE PUNISHMENT

The tale of the great flood appeared in many ancient cultures, including a Mesopotamian version, *Atrahasis,* which recounts the deeds of the wise Atrahasis, who built an ark to escape the flood sent by the gods in order to reduce an expanding population. The Mesopotamian account, which is replete with disasters inflicted on the people by the gods, illustrates the Mesopotamian belief that the gods controlled human destiny. The following excerpts describe the terrible punishments inflicted by the gods prior to unleashing the great flood.

Ellil organized his assembly,
Addressed the gods his sons. . . .
 "I have become restless at their noise,
 Sleep cannot overtake me because of their racket!
 Cut off food from the people,
 Let vegetation be too scant for their stomachs!
 Let Adad on high make his rain scarce,
 Let him block below, and not raise flood-
  water from the springs!
 Let the field decrease its yield,
 Let Nissaba turn away her breast,
 Let the dark fields become white,
 Let the broad countryside breed alkali,
 Let earth clamp down her teats
 So that no vegetation sprouts, no grain grows.
 Let *ašakku*[1] be inflicted on the people,
 Let the womb be too tight to let a baby out!"
They cut off food for the people,
Vegetation . . . became too scant for their stomachs.
Adad on high made his rain scarce,
Blocked below, and did not raise flood-water
  from the springs.
The field decreased its yield,
Nissaba turned away her breast,
The dark fields became white,
The broad countryside bred alkali.
Earth clamped down her teats:
No vegetation sprouted, no grain grew.
Ašakku was inflicted on the people.
The womb was too tight to let a baby out.
Ea kept guard over the bolt that bars the sea,
Together with his *lahmu*-heroes.
Above, Adad made his rain scarce,
Blocked below, and did not raise flood-water
  from the springs.

The field decreased its yield. . . .
The dark fields became white,
The broad countryside bred alkali.
Earth clamped down her teats:
No vegetation sprouted, no grain grew.
Ašakku was inflicted on the people.
The womb was too tight to let a baby out.
When the second year arrived
They had depleted the storehouse.
When the third year arrived
(The people's looks) were changed (by
  starvation).
When the fourth year arrived
Their upstanding bearing bowed,
Their well-set shoulders slouched,
People went out in public hunched over.
When the fifth year arrived,
A daughter would eye her mother coming in;
A mother would not even open her door to her
  daughter.
A daughter would watch the scales (at the sale
  of her) mother,
A mother would watch the scales (at the sale of
  her) daughter.
When the sixth year arrived
They served up a daughter for a meal,
Served up a son for food.

The people are also afflicted with the flood,
which "roared like a bull. Like a wild ass
screaming, the winds [howled]. The darkness was total, there was no sun." Atrahasis,
who built a boat that he stocked with animals, survived with his family.

Stephanie Dalley, ed. and trans., *Myths from Mesopotamia:
Creation, the Flood, Gilgamesh, and Others* (New York:
Oxford University Press, 2008), pp. 24–26.

[1] Illness and misfortune personified as demons. —Eds.

REVIEW QUESTIONS

1. What is myth? How does mythopoeic thinking differ from scientific thinking?
2. It has been said that humans are myth-making animals and that all human societies
   sustain themselves by creating myths. Discuss.
3. On what occasions might the ancient Mesopotamians have turned to the gods for help?
4. How did the ancient Mesopotamians explain natural disasters?

CHAPTER 2

The Hebrews

JEWISH CAPTIVES, relief from the triumphal Arch of Titus, c. A.D. 90. The captives are bearing the menorah and vessels from the Temple of Jerusalem, burned by the Romans following Jewish revolt in A.D. 70. *(Alinari/Art Resource, NY)*

Two ancient peoples, the Hebrews (Jews) and the Greeks, are the principal founders of Western civilization. From the Hebrews derives the concept of *ethical monotheism*—the belief in one God who demands righteous behavior from his human creations—which is an essential element of the Western tradition.

According to biblical tradition, the Hebrews originated in Mesopotamia and migrated to Canaan (Palestine). Some Hebrews who journeyed to Egypt to become farmers and herdsmen were forced to labor for the Egyptian state. In the thirteenth century B.C., Moses, who believed that he was doing God's bidding, led the Hebrews from Egypt—the biblical Exodus. While wandering in the Sinai Desert, the Hebrews were uplifted and united by a belief in Yahweh, the One God. In the eleventh century B.C., some two hundred years after they had begun the conquest of Canaan, the Hebrews were unified under the leadership of Saul, the first king of Israel. Under Solomon (d. 922 B.C.) the kingdom of Israel reached the height of its power and splendor.

The Hebrews borrowed elements from the older civilizations of the Near East. Thus there are parallels between Babylonian literature and biblical accounts of the Creation, the Flood, and the Tower of Babel. Nevertheless, Israelite religion marks a profound break with the outlook of the surrounding civilizations of the Near East.

There are two fundamental characteristics of ancient Near Eastern religion. First, the Near Eastern mind saw gods everywhere in nature: the moon and stars, rivers and mountains, thunder and wind storms were either gods or the dwelling places of gods. The Near Eastern mind invented myths—stories about the gods' birth, deeds, death, and resurrection. Second, Near Eastern gods were not fully sovereign. They were not eternal but were born or created; their very existence and power depended on some prior realm. They grew old, became ill, required food, and even died—all limitations on their power. The gods were subject to magic and destiny—forces that preceded them in time and surpassed them in power—and if the gods did wrong, destiny, or fate, punished them.

Hebrew religious thought evolved through the history and experience of the Jewish people. Over the centuries the Hebrew view of God came to differ markedly from Near Eastern ideas about the gods and the world. For the Hebrews, God was not only one, he was also *transcendent*—above nature. This means that natural objects were not divine, holy, or alive, but were merely God's creations. In contrast to the Near Eastern gods, Yahweh was fully *sovereign*, absolutely free; there were no limitations whatsoever on his power. He was eternal and the source of all in the universe; he did not answer to fate but himself determined the consequences of wrongdoing; he was not subject to any primordial power or to anything outside or above him.

The Hebrew conception of God led to a revolutionary view of the human being. The Hebrews believed that God had given the individual moral autonomy—the capacity to choose between good and evil. Therefore, men and women had to measure their actions by God's laws and were responsible for their own behavior. Such an outlook led people to become aware of themselves—their moral potential and personal worth. From the Hebrews came a fundamental value of the Western tradition—the inviolable worth and dignity of the individual.

1 Hebrew Cosmogony and Anthropology

The Hebrew scriptures, which form the Old Testament of the Christian Bible, are a collection of thirty-nine books written over several centuries by multiple authors. It is a record of more than a thousand years of ancient Jewish history and religious development. Among the topics treated in Genesis, the first book of the Bible, are God's creation of the universe and human beings, the original human condition in the Garden of Eden, and the origin of evil with Adam and Eve's disobedience of God and their resultant expulsion from Eden.

GENESIS

Portions of the first two chapters from the book of Genesis follow. The first chapter presents the *cosmogony* and *anthropology* of the Jews. Hebrew cosmogony—that is, their view of the generation of the universe and all that is in it—exemplifies God's majesty and power. Although Genesis is similar to other Near Eastern creation myths, it also sharply breaks with the essential outlook of the time. In Genesis, nature is no longer inhabited by mythical gods, and inanimate objects are not suffused with life. The Hebrews did not worship the moon and stars and mountains and rivers, but they regarded nature as the orderly creation of one supreme and eternal being.

How the Hebrews conceived of the creation of men and women and their position in the universe—the anthropology of the Jews—is dealt with in verses 26–31. The Hebrews' conception of the individual created in God's image and subordinate to nothing except God is as revolutionary as their idea of God, for this conception confers great value and dignity upon human beings.

1 In the beginning God created the heavens and the earth. [2]The earth was without form and void, and darkness was upon the face of the deep; and the Spirit of God was moving over the face of the waters.

3 And God said, "Let there be light"; and there was light. [4]And God saw that the light was good; and God separated the light from the darkness. [5]God called the light Day, and the darkness he called Night. And there was evening and there was morning, one day.

6 And God said, "Let there be a firmament in the midst of the waters, and let it separate the waters from the waters." [7]And God made the firmament and separated the waters which

were under the firmament from the waters which were above the firmament. And it was so. [8]And God called the firmament Heaven. And there was evening and there was morning, a second day.

9 And God said, "Let the waters under the heavens be gathered together into one place, and let the dry land appear." And it was so. [10]God called the dry land Earth, and the waters that were gathered together he called Seas. And God saw that it was good. [11]And God said, "Let the earth put forth vegetation, plants yielding seed, and fruit trees bearing fruit in which is their seed, each according to its kind, upon the earth." And it was so. [12]The earth brought forth vegetation, plants yielding seed according to their own kinds, and trees bearing fruit in which is their seed, each according to its kind. And God saw that it was good. [13]And there was evening and there was morning, a third day.

14 And God said, "Let there be lights in the firmament of the heavens to separate the day from the night; and let them be for signs and for seasons and for days and years, [15]and let them be lights in the firmament of the heavens to give light upon the earth." And it was so. [16]And God made the two great lights, the greater light to rule the day, and the lesser light to rule the night; he made the stars also. [17]And God set them in the firmament of the heavens to give light upon the earth, [18]to rule over the day and over the night, and to separate the light from the darkness. And God saw that it was good. [19]And there was evening and there was morning, a fourth day.

20 And God said, "Let the waters bring forth swarms of living creatures, and let birds fly above the earth across the firmament of the heavens." [21]So God created the great sea monsters and every living creature that moves, with which the waters swarm, according to their kinds, and every winged bird according to its kind. And God saw that it was good. [22]And God blessed them, saying, "Be fruitful and multiply and fill the waters in the seas,

and let birds multiply on the earth." [23]And there was evening and there was morning, a fifth day.

24 And God said, "Let the earth bring forth living creatures according to their kinds: cattle and creeping things and beasts of the earth according to their kinds." And it was so. [25]And God made the beasts of the earth according to their kinds and the cattle according to their kinds, and everything that creeps upon the ground according to its kind. And God saw that it was good.

26 Then God said, "Let us make man in our image, after our likeness; and let them have dominion over the fish of the sea, and over the birds of the air, and over the cattle, and over all the earth, and over every creeping thing that creeps upon the earth." [27]So God created man in his own image, in the image of God he created him; male and female he created them. [28]And God blessed them, and God said to them, "Be fruitful and multiply, and fill the earth and subdue it; and have dominion over the fish of the sea and over the birds of the air and over every living thing that moves upon the earth." [29]And God said, "Behold, I have given you every plant yielding seed which is upon the face of all the earth, and every tree with seed in its fruit; you shall have them for food. [30]And to every beast of the earth, and to every bird of the air, and to everything that creeps on the earth, everything that has the breath of life, I have given every green plant for food." And it was so. [31]And God saw everything that he had made, and behold, it was very good. And there was evening and there was morning, a sixth day. [Genesis 1]

The second chapter of Genesis contains a more detailed description of God's creation of woman.

---

18 Then the LORD God said, "It is not good that the man should be alone; I will make him a helper fit for him." [19]So out of the ground

the LORD God formed every beast of the field and every bird of the air, and brought them to the man to see what he would call them; and whatever the man called every living creature, that was its name. ²⁰The man gave names to all cattle, and to the birds of the air, and to every beast of the field; but for the man there was not found a helper fit for him. ²¹So the LORD God caused a deep sleep to fall upon the man, and while he slept took one of his ribs and closed up its place with flesh; ²²and the rib which the LORD God had taken from the

man he made into a woman and brought her to the man.
23 Then the man said,
"This at last is bone of my bones
　and flesh of my flesh;
she shall be called Woman,
　because she was taken out of Man."
24 Therefore a man leaves his father and his mother and cleaves to his wife, and they become one flesh. ²⁵And the man and his wife were both naked, and were not ashamed. [Genesis 2]

REVIEW QUESTIONS

1. What conception of God emerges from these two chapters in Genesis?
2. What does the book of Genesis reveal about Hebrew conceptions of male and female relationships?
3. What relationship does the book of Genesis suggest between humans and other creations of God such as the earth, plants, and animals?

2 Human Sinfulness

The Hebrews defined sin as a violation of God's laws and a breach of his Covenant — their agreement to be faithful to God. This offense against God corrupts his created order, which was intended to be beneficial to human beings, and brings suffering into the world. Biblical writers regarded sin as a universal phenomenon, an ever-present menace to both individual and group life, deserving of God's punishment. Yet even when God inflicts terrible pain on the Hebrews for violating his law, he still remains compassionate and merciful, an inducement to sinners to renew their commitment to God's teachings.

GENESIS
THE ORIGINS OF SIN

The third chapter of Genesis deals with the origin of sin. When the first man and woman, Adam and Eve, disobeyed God by eating from the tree of knowledge, they were driven from the Garden of Eden. For the Hebrews the expulsion from paradise marks the beginning of human history, suffering, and death. This passage provides one of the fundamental explanations of evil in the Western tradition, the Judaic conception, later to be refashioned by Saint Paul into the Christian notion of original sin. The language of the biblical narrative is seemingly naive and framed in mythic imagery, but the ideas that it presents are profound and timeless.

1 Now the serpent was more subtle than any other wild creature that the LORD God had made. He said to the woman, "Did God say, 'You shall not eat of any tree of the garden'?" [2]And the woman said to the serpent, "We may eat of the fruit of the trees of the garden; [3]but God said, 'You shall not eat of the fruit of the tree which is in the midst of the garden, neither shall you touch it, lest you die.'" [4]But the serpent said to the woman, "You will not die. [5]For God knows that when you eat of it your eyes will be opened, and you will be like God, knowing good and evil." [6]So when the woman saw that the tree was good for food, and that it was a delight to the eyes, and that the tree was to be desired to make one wise, she took of its fruit and ate; and she also gave some to her husband, and he ate. [7]Then the eyes of both were opened, and they knew that they were naked; and they sewed fig leaves together and made themselves aprons.

8 And they heard the sound of the LORD God walking in the garden in the cool of the day, and the man and his wife hid themselves from the presence of the LORD God among the trees of the garden. [9]But the LORD God called to the man, and said to him, "Where are you?" [10]And he said, "I heard the sound of thee in the garden, and I was afraid, because I was naked; and I hid myself." [11]He said, "Who told you that you were naked? Have you eaten of the tree of which I commanded you not to eat?" [12]The man said, "The woman whom thou gavest to be with me, she gave me fruit of the tree, and I ate." [13]Then the LORD God said to the woman, "What is this that you have done?" The woman said, "The serpent beguiled me, and I ate."

14 The LORD God said to the serpent,
"Because you have done this,
    cursed are you above all cattle,
    and above all wild animals;
upon your belly you shall go,
    and dust you shall eat
    all the days of your life.

[15]I will put enmity between you and the
        woman,
    and between your seed and her seed;
he shall bruise your head,
    and you shall bruise his heel."
[16]To the woman he said,
"I will greatly multiply your pain in
        childbearing;
    in pain you shall bring forth children,
yet your desire shall be for your husband,
    and he shall rule over you."
17 And to Adam he said,
"Because you have listened to the voice of
        your wife,
    and have eaten of the tree
of which I commanded you,
    'You shall not eat of it,'
cursed is the ground because of you;
    in toil you shall eat of it all the days of
        your life;
[18]thorns and thistles it shall bring forth to you;
    and you shall eat the plants of the field.
[19]In the sweat of your face
    you shall eat bread
till you return to the ground,
    for out of it you were taken;
you are dust,
    and to dust you shall return."

20 The man called his wife's name Eve, because she was the mother of all living. [21]And the LORD God made for Adam and for his wife garments of skins, and clothed them.

22 Then the LORD God said, "Behold, the man has become like one of us, knowing good and evil; and now, lest he put forth his hand and take also of the tree of life, and eat, and live for ever"—[23]therefore the LORD God sent him forth from the garden of Eden, to till the ground from which he was taken. [24]He drove out the man; and at the east of the garden of Eden he placed the cherubim [winged angels], and a flaming sword which turned every way, to guard the way to the tree of life. [Genesis 3]

REVIEW QUESTION

What does the story of Adam and Eve reveal about Hebrew conceptions of good and evil?

3 The Covenant and the Ten Commandments

Central to Hebrew religious thought was the Covenant that the Hebrews believed had been made between God and themselves. The Hebrews believed that God had chosen them to be the first recipients of his law. They did not hold that this honor was bestowed on them because they were better than other nations or that they had done something special to earn it. Rather they viewed the Covenant as an awesome responsibility; God had chosen them to set an example of righteous behavior to the other nations.

EXODUS
THE COVENANT

As described in the book of Exodus, the Israelite leader Moses received the Covenant on Mount Sinai at the time of the Hebrews' flight from Egypt and wanderings in the wilderness of the Sinai Desert.

3 And Moses went up to God, and the LORD called to him out of the mountain, saying, "Thus you shall say to the house of Jacob, and tell the people of Israel: ^{4}You have seen what I did to the Egyptians, and how I bore you on eagles' wings and brought you to myself. ^{5}Now therefore, if you will obey my voice and keep my covenant, you shall be my own possession among all peoples; for all the earth is mine, ^{6}and you shall be to me a kingdom of priests and a holy nation. These are the words which you shall speak to the children of Israel."

7 So Moses came and called the elders of the people, and set before them all these words which the LORD had commanded him. ^{8}And all the people answered together and said, "All that the LORD has spoken we will do." And Moses reported the words of the people to the LORD. ^{9}And the LORD said to Moses, "Lo, I am coming to you in a thick cloud, that the people may hear when I speak with you, and may also believe you for ever." [Exodus 19]

EXODUS
THE TEN COMMANDMENTS

Together with the Covenant, Moses received the Ten Commandments, which specified God's moral laws.

17 Then Moses brought the people out of the camp to meet God; and they took their stand at the foot of the mountain. ^{18}And Mount

Sinai was wrapped in smoke, because the LORD descended upon it in fire; and the smoke of it went up like the smoke of a kiln, and the whole mountain quaked greatly. [19]And as the sound of the trumpet grew louder and louder, Moses spoke, and God answered him in thunder. [20]And the LORD came down upon Mount Sinai, to the top of the mountain; and the LORD called Moses to the top of the mountain, and Moses went up. [Exodus 19]

— — —

1 And God spoke all these words, saying,

2 "I am the LORD your God, who brought you out of the land of Egypt, out of the house of bondage.

3 "You shall have no other gods before me.

4 "You shall not make yourself a graven image, or any likeness of anything that is in heaven above, or that is in the earth beneath, or that is in the water under the earth; [5]you shall not bow down to them or serve them; for I the LORD your God am a jealous God, visiting the iniquity of the fathers upon the children to the third and the fourth generation of those who hate me, [6]but showing steadfast love to thousands of those who love me and keep my commandments.

7 "You shall not take the name of the LORD your God in vain; for the LORD will not hold him guiltless who takes his name in vain.

8 "Remember the sabbath day, to keep it holy. [9]Six days you shall labor, and do all your work; [10]but the seventh day is a sabbath to the LORD your God; in it you shall not do any work, you, or your son, or your daughter, your manservant, or your maidservant, or your cattle, or the sojourner who is within your gates; [11]for in six days the LORD made heaven and earth, the sea, and all that is in them, and rested the seventh day; therefore the LORD blessed the sabbath day and hallowed it.

12 "Honor your father and your mother, that your days may be long in the land which the LORD your God gives you.

13 "You shall not kill.

14 "You shall not commit adultery.

15 "You shall not steal.

16 "You shall not bear false witness against your neighbor.

17 "You shall not covet your neighbor's house; you shall not covet your neighbor's wife, or his manservant, or his maidservant, or his ox, or his ass, or anything that is your neighbor's."

18 Now when all the people perceived the thunderings and the lightnings and the sound of the trumpet and the mountain smoking, the people were afraid and trembled; and they stood afar off, [19]and said to Moses, "You speak to us, and we will hear; but let not God speak to us, lest we die." [20]And Moses said to the people, "Do not fear; for God has come to prove you, and that the fear of him may be before your eyes, that you may not sin."

21 And the people stood afar off, while Moses drew near to the thick cloud where God was. [Exodus 20]

REVIEW QUESTIONS

1. What were the terms of the Covenant between God and the Hebrews?
2. The belief that some laws were divine in origin was shared by many Near Eastern peoples, including the Hebrews. How has this belief shaped subsequent Western civilization?

4 Humaneness of Hebrew Law

The new awareness of the individual that was produced by the Hebrew concept of God found expression in Hebrew law, which was recorded in the Torah, the first five books of the scriptures. For the Hebrews, the source of law was, of course, God, and because God is good, his law must be concerned with human welfare. Thus Hebrew law showed a respect for life: it protected the stranger, widows, orphans, and the destitute and slaves from cruel masters. Elders and judges who implemented the law were expected to be guided by God's command to pursue righteousness as the prophet Micah enjoined: "And what does the Lord require of you but to do justice and to love kindness and to walk humbly with your God?"

Israelite law incorporated elements of the customary law and legal codes of the older civilizations of the Near East. For example, in Deuteronomy the law prescribes the treatment of a murder committed in areas where there are no witnesses and no indication of who committed the crime. The elders in the nearest village are required to declare that the inhabitants of their village did not commit the murder and to assume responsibility for bringing the unknown assailant to justice. These requirements bear striking similarity to several Near Eastern texts. Another example involves the theft of a herd or flock animal. The penalties in both Exodus and Babylonian documents are similar: the guilty party has to return more animals than were stolen. And both Babylonian and Hebrew law endorse the principle of "an eye for an eye." However, it seems that for the Hebrews, this law of retaliation was eventually replaced by the formula of proportionate compensation for the damage inflicted. The person responsible for the loss of another's eye or tooth could compensate the injured party in other ways.

There are also fundamental differences between biblical law and the other law codes of the Near East. Hebrew laws were more concerned with people than with property. For example, whereas Babylonian law prescribed death for house invasion and theft, the Bible does not permit taking a life for a crime against property. Hebrew law rejected the idea, so clearly demonstrated in the Code of Hammurabi, of one law for nobles and another for commoners. Nor did Hebrew law permit substitutionary punishment common to Near Eastern law codes. For example, if due to faulty construction a house collapsed killing the homeowner's son, Babylonian law required that the builder's son be put to death. No such provision is found in biblical law. Hebrew law was more considerate of the slave than the law codes of other Near Eastern peoples: "When you buy a Hebrew slave, he shall serve six years, and in the seventh he shall go out free, for nothing." Also in contrast to Near Eastern law, a Hebrew father had no legal sanction to kill his daughter for having premarital sex.

While biblical law valued human life and was concerned with human welfare, it also contained provisions that shock us as cruel, for example: ordering the slaughter of the enemies in war, the stoning to death of one's family members who chose to serve other gods, and the execution of homosexuals. Over the centuries, however, there arose an oral and interpretive tradition that made the written law less rigid and led the Hebrews to adapt to changing cultural conditions.

EXODUS
CRIME AND PUNISHMENT

For the Hebrews the most serious crimes were grave sins against God, including idolatry, blasphemy, apostasy, profaning the sabbath, and adultery,[1] which were all punishable by death. They viewed such rebellion as a threat to the entire community, for it might cause God to annul the Covenant, the special relationship he had with the Hebrews that was the foundation of their existence as a nation. Believing that God would blame them if they failed to take action, the entire community felt a responsibility to punish by death these dangerous offenders in their midst.

Hebrew law dealt with a multiplicity of crimes, including assaults and murder. Because each human being was a bearer of God's image, murder was viewed as an attack on God. In Near Eastern legal codes, if a noble killed a commoner, his punishment might be financial compensation to the family. Such class differences did not enter into Israelite law, which required the murderer to pay with his own life; there was no death penalty in cases of involuntary homicide, and the law provided places of refuge where the person who killed by accident would be protected from people seeking vengeance. Hebrew law also prescribed the death penalty for children who physically or verbally abused their parents. However, because the parents' approval was necessary for the court to implement the law, it is highly likely that only rarely was it put into effect. Kidnapping with the object of selling the victim to caravan traders for transportation to foreign slave markets was another capital crime.

The following passages from Exodus illustrate Hebrew views of crime and punishment.

12 "Whoever strikes a man so that he dies shall be put to death. [13]But if he did not lie in wait for him, but God let him fall into his hand, then I will appoint for you a place to which he may flee. [14]But if a man wilfully attacks another to kill him treacherously, you shall take him from my altar, that he may die.

15 "Whoever strikes his father or his mother shall be put to death.

16 "Whoever steals a man, whether he sells him or is found in possession of him, shall be put to death.

17 "Whoever curses his father or his mother shall be put to death.

18 "When men quarrel and one strikes the other with a stone or with his fist and the man does not die but keeps his bed, [19]then if the man rises again and walks abroad with his staff, he that struck him shall be clear; only he shall pay for the loss of his time, and shall have him thoroughly healed.

20 "When a man strikes his slave, male or female, with a rod and the slave dies under his hand, he shall be punished. [21]But if the slave survives a day or two, he is not to be punished; for the slave is his money.

22 "When men strive together, and hurt a woman with child, so that there is a miscarriage, and yet no harm follows, the one who hurt her shall be fined, according as the woman's husband

---

[1]Although the scriptures exhort husbands to be faithful, the death penalty only applied if his infidelity were conducted with another man's wife. No exception was made for an adulteress wife.

shall lay upon him; and he shall pay as the judges determine. ^{23}If any harm follows, then you shall give life for life, ^{24}eye for eye, tooth for tooth, hand for hand, foot for foot, ^{25}burn for burn, wound for wound, stripe for stripe.

26 "When a man strikes the eye of his slave, male or female, and destroys it, he shall let the slave go free for the eye's sake. ^{27}If he knocks out the tooth of his slave, male or female, he shall let the slave go free for the tooth's sake. [Exodus 21]

— — —

16 "If a man seduces a virgin who is not betrothed, and lies with her, he shall give the marriage present for her, and make her his wife. ^{17}If her father utterly refuses to give her to him, he shall pay money equivalent to the marriage present for virgins.

18 "You shall not permit a sorceress to live.

19 "Whoever lies with a beast shall be put to death.

20 "Whoever sacrifices to any god, save to the LORD only, shall be utterly destroyed.

21 "You shall not wrong a stranger or oppress him, for you were strangers in the land of Egypt. ^{22}You shall not afflict any widow or orphan. ^{23}If you do afflict them, and they cry out to me, I will surely hear their cry; ^{24}and my wrath will burn, and I will kill you with the sword, and your wives shall become widows and your children fatherless.

25 "If you lend money to any of my people with you who is poor, you shall not be to him as a creditor, and you shall not exact interest from him. ^{26}If ever you take your neighbor's garment in pledge, you shall restore it to him before the sun goes down; ^{27}for that is his only covering, it is his mantle for his body; in what else shall he sleep? And if he cries to me, I will hear, for I am compassionate.

28 "You shall not revile God, nor curse a ruler of your people. [Exodus 22]

LEVITICUS
NEIGHBOR AND COMMUNITY

To the Hebrews, laws governing economic, social, and political relationships gave practical expression to God's universal standards of morality. Leviticus, the third book in the scriptures, contains laws governing actions dealing with neighbors and the community.

9 "When you reap the harvest of your land, you shall not reap your field to its very border, neither shall you gather the gleanings after your harvest. ^{10}And you shall not strip your vineyard bare, neither shall you gather the fallen grapes of your vineyard; you shall leave them for the poor and for the sojourner: I am the LORD your God.

11 "You shall not steal, nor deal falsely, nor lie to one another. ^{12}And you shall not swear by my name falsely, and so profane the name of your God: I am the LORD.

13 "You shall not oppress your neighbor or rob him. The wages of a hired servant shall not remain with you all night until the morning. ^{14}You shall not curse the deaf or put a stumbling block before the blind, but you shall fear your God: I am the LORD.

15 "You shall do no injustice in judgment; you shall not be partial to the poor or defer to

the great, but in righteousness shall you judge your neighbor. ^{16}You shall not go up and down as a slanderer among your people, and you shall not stand forth against the life of your neighbor: I am the LORD.

17 "You shall not hate your brother in your heart, but you shall reason with your neighbor, lest you bear sin because of him. ^{18}You shall not take vengeance or bear any grudge against the sons of your own people, but you shall love your neighbor as yourself: I am the LORD. . . .

33 "When a stranger sojourns with you in your land, you shall not do him wrong. ^{34}The stranger who sojourns with you shall be to you as the native among you, and you shall love him as yourself. . . ." [Leviticus 19]

DEUTERONOMY
JUDGES, WITNESSES, AND JUSTICE

The book of Deuteronomy was composed in the seventh century B.C., some six centuries after the Exodus from Egypt. Written as though it were a last speech of Moses advising the people how to govern themselves as they entered the land of Canaan, Deuteronomy reflects the new problems faced by the Hebrews who had already established a kingdom and lived in a settled urban society. In presenting their reform program, the authors of Deuteronomy linked their message to the authority of Moses. The central theme of these verses is the attainment of justice.

18 "You shall appoint judges and officers in all your towns which the LORD your God gives you, according to your tribes; and they shall judge the people with righteous judgment. ^{19}You shall not pervert justice; you shall not show partiality; and you shall not take a bribe, for a bribe blinds the eyes of the wise and subverts the cause of the righteous. ^{20}Justice, and only justice, you shall follow, that you may live and inherit the land which the LORD your God gives you." [Deuteronomy 16]

— — —

15 "A single witness shall not prevail against a man for any crime or for any wrong in connection with any offence that he has committed; only on the evidence of two witnesses, or of three witnesses, shall a charge be sustained. ^{16}If a malicious witness rises against any man to accuse him of wrongdoing, ^{17}then both parties to the dispute shall appear before the LORD, before the priests and the judges who are in office in those days; ^{18}the judges shall inquire diligently, and if the witness is a false witness and has accused his brother falsely, ^{19}then you shall do to him as he had meant to do to his brother; so you shall purge the evil from the midst of you." [Deuteronomy 19]

— — —

15 "You shall not give up to his master a slave who has escaped from his master to you; ^{16}he shall dwell with you, in your midst, in the place which he shall choose within one of your towns, where it pleases him best; you shall not oppress him." [Deuteronomy 23]

— — —

14 "You shall not oppress a hired servant who is poor and needy, whether he is one of your brethren or one of the sojourners who are in your land within your towns; ^{15}you shall give him his hire on the day he earns it, before the sun goes down (for he is poor, and sets his heart upon it); lest he cry against you to the LORD, and it be sin in you.

16 "The fathers shall not be put to death for the children, nor shall the children be put to death for the fathers; every man shall be put to death for his own sin.

17 "You shall not pervert the justice due to the sojourner or to the fatherless, or take a widow's garment in pledge; [18]but you shall remember that you were a slave in Egypt and the LORD your God redeemed you from there; therefore I command you to do this.

19 "When you reap your harvest in your field, and have forgotten a sheaf in the field, you shall not go back to get it; it shall be for the sojourner, the fatherless, and the widow; that the LORD your God may bless you in all the work of your hands. [20]When you beat your olive trees, you shall not go over the boughs again; it shall be for the sojourner, the fatherless, and the widow. [21]When you gather the grapes of your vineyard, you shall not glean it afterward; it shall be for the sojourner, the fatherless, and the widow. [22]You shall remember that you were a slave in the land of Egypt; therefore I command you to do this." [Deuteronomy 24]

There are passages in the biblical law that we would regard as cruel, for example the following excerpt from Deuteronomy that calls for stoning to death Israelites who urge serving other gods.

---

6 "If your brother, the son of your mother, or your son, or your daughter, or the wife of your bosom, or your friend who is as your own soul, entiles you secretly, saying, 'Let us go and serve other gods,' which neither you nor your fathers have known, [7]some of the gods of the peoples that are round about you, whether near you or far off from you, firm the one end of the earth to the other, [8]you shall not yield to him, not shall your eye pity him, nor shall you spare him, nor shall you conceal him; [9]but you shall kill him; your hand shall be first against him to put him to death, and afterwards the hand of all the people. [10]You shall stone him to death with stones because he sought to draw you away from the LORD your God, who brought you out of the land of Egypt, out of the house of bondage. And all Israel shall hear, and fear, and never again do any such wickedness as this among you." [Deuteronomy 13]

REVIEW QUESTIONS

1. Show how an awareness of social justice pervaded Hebrew law.
2. How did the legal procedures of Hebrew law try to ensure fair treatment of all ranks of society?
3. What facets of Hebrew law do you consider especially humane? Excessively severe?

---

5 God's Greatness and Human Dignity

The Hebrew view of God produced a remarkable new concept of human dignity. In God's plan for the universe, the Hebrews believed, human beings are the highest creation, subordinate only to God. Of all God's creatures, only they have been given the freedom to choose between good and evil. To human beings God granted dominion over the earth and the seas.

The Psalms in the Hebrew scriptures contain 150 hymns extolling Yahweh, some of them written by King David, who ruled c. 1000–961 B.C. In addition to his great success as a warrior and administrator, David was renowned as a harpist and composer.

PSALM 8

In the following song, the psalmist rejoices in the greatness of God. He marvels in the Lord's love for human beings, expressed in their having been given dominion over the earth and its creatures.

O LORD, our Lord,
how majestic is thy name in all the earth!

Thou whose glory above the heavens is
    chanted
    ²by the mouth of babes and infants,
thou hast founded a bulwark because of thy
    foes,
    to still the enemy and the avenger.

³When I look at thy heavens, the work of thy
    fingers,
    the moon and the stars which thou hast
    established;
⁴what is man that thou art mindful of him,

and the son of man that thou dost care for
    him?
⁵Yet thou hast made him little less than God,
    and dost crown him with glory and honor.
⁶Thou hast given him dominion over the works
    of thy hands;
    thou hast put all things under his feet,
⁷all sheep and oxen,
    and also the beasts of the field,
⁸the birds of the air, and the fish of the sea,
    whatever passes along the paths of the sea.

⁹O LORD, our Lord,
    how majestic is thy name in all the earth!

PSALM 104

Psalm 104 praises God's majesty and lauds him for the wonders of his creation—
the earth and all its creatures.

Bless, the LORD, O my soul!
O LORD my God, thou art very great!
Thou art clothed with honor and majesty,
²who coverest thyself with light as with a garment,
who hast stretched out the heavens like a tent,
³who hast laid the beams of thy chambers
    on the waters,
who makest the clouds thy chariot,
    who ridest on the wings of the wind,
⁴who makest the winds thy messengers,
    fire and flame thy ministers.
⁵Thou didst set the earth on its foundations, so
    that it should never be shaken.
⁶Thou didst cover it with the deep as with a
    garment;
    the waters stood above the mountains. . . .

¹⁴Thou dost cause the grass to grow for the
    cattle,
    and plants for man to cultivate,
that he may bring forth food from the earth,
¹⁵and wine to gladden the heart of man,
oil to make his face shine,
    and bread to strengthen man's heart.
¹⁶The trees of the LORD are watered abundantly,
    the cedars of Lebanon   which he planted.
¹⁷In them the birds build their nests;
    the stork has her home in the fir trees.
¹⁸The high mountains are for the wild goats;
    the rocks are a refuge for the badgers.
¹⁹Thou hast made the moon to mark the
    seasons;
    the sun knows its time for setting. . . .

²⁴O LORD, how manifold are thy works!
  In wisdom hast thou made them all;
  the earth is full of thy creatures.
²⁵Yonder is the sea, great and wide,
  which teems with things innumerable,

living things both small and great....
³¹May the glory of the LORD endure for ever,
  may the LORD rejoice in his works....

REVIEW QUESTIONS

1. What do the Psalms reveal about the Hebrew view of God? Of human beings? Of nature?
2. Compare Psalm 104 with Akhenaten's *Hymn to Aton* (chapter 1, pages 13–14).

---

6 The Age of Classical Prophecy

Ancient Jewish history was marked by the rise of prophets—spiritually inspired persons who believed that God had chosen them to remind the Jews of their duties to God and his law. These prophets carried God's message to the leaders and the people and warned of divine punishments for disobedience to God's commandments.

The prophetic movement—the age of classical prophecy—which emerged in the eighth century B.C., creatively expanded Hebrew religious thought. Prophets denounced exploitation of the poor, the greed of the wealthy, and the oppressive behavior of the powerful as a betrayal of God, a violation of his moral laws. They insisted that the core of Hebrew faith was not ritual but morality. Their concern for the poor and their attack on injustice received reemphasis in the Christian faith and thus became incorporated into the Western ideal of social justice.

AMOS AND *ISAIAH*
SOCIAL JUSTICE

By the eighth century B.C., even as Jewish religious institutions flourished, a significant disparity existed between the wealthy and the poor. Small farmers in debt to moneylenders faced the loss of their land or even bondage. Amos and Isaiah of Jerusalem, mid-eighth-century prophets, spoke out in the name of God against these injustices and insisted that the essence of God's law was not rituals, but rather righteous living. Scholars agree that Isaiah of Jerusalem did not write all sixty-six chapters that make up the book of Isaiah. Some material appears to have been written by his disciples and interpreters, and Chapters 40–55, composed some two centuries later, are attributed to a person given the name Second Isaiah.

²¹"I hate, I despise your feasts,
      and I take no delight in your solemn
          assemblies.
²²Even though you offer me your burnt
          offerings and cereal offerings,
   I will not accept them,
and the peace offerings of your fatted beasts
   I will not look upon.
²³Take away from me the noise of your songs;
      to the melody of your harps I will not listen.
²⁴But let justice roll down like waters,
      and righteousness like an everflowing stream."
          [Amos 5]

¹¹What to me is the multitude of your
          sacrifices?
      says the LORD;
I have had enough of burnt offerings of rams
      and the fat of fed beasts;
I do not delight in the blood of bulls, or of
      lambs, or of he-goats. . . .
¹³Bring no more vain offerings;
      incense is an abomination to me.
   New moon and sabbath and the calling of
          assemblies—
   I cannot endure iniquity and solemn
          assembly.

¹⁴Your new moons and your appointed feasts
      my soul hates;
they have become a burden to me,
   I am weary of bearing them.
¹⁵When you spread forth your hands,
      I will hide my eyes from you;
even though you make many prayers,
      I will not listen;
   your hands are full of blood.
¹⁶Wash yourselves; make yourselves clean;
      remove the evil of your doings
      from before my eyes;
cease to do evil,
¹⁷ learn to do good;
seek justice,
      correct oppression;
defend the fatherless,
      plead for the widow.
      [Isaiah 1]

¹³The LORD has taken his place to contend,
      he stands to judge his people.
¹⁴The LORD enters into judgment
      with the elders and princes of his people:
"It is you who have devoured the vineyard,
      the spoil of the poor is in your houses.
¹⁵What do you mean by crushing my people,
      by grinding the face of the poor?"
          says the Lord GOD of hosts.
          [Isaiah 3]

ISAIAH
PEACE AND HUMANITY

Isaiah of Jerusalem envisioned the unity of all people under God. This universalism drew out the full implications of Hebrew monotheism. In Isaiah's vision all peoples would live together in peace and harmony. Some of these lines are inscribed on the building that houses the United Nations in New York City.

²It shall come to pass in the latter days
   that the mountain of the house of the LORD
shall be established as the highest of the
     mountains,
   and shall be raised above the hills;
and all the nations shall flow to it,
³and many peoples shall come, and say:
"Come, let us go up to the mountain of the
    LORD,
   to the house of the God of Jacob;
that he may teach us his ways
   and that we may walk in his paths."

For out of Zion shall go forth the law,
   and the word of the LORD from Jerusalem.
⁴He shall judge between the nations,
   and shall decide for many peoples;
and they shall beat their swords into
    plowshares,
   and their spears into pruning hooks;
nation shall not lift up sword against nation,
   neither shall they learn war any more.
   [Isaiah 2]

REVIEW QUESTIONS

1. What were some of the ritual acts and ceremonies practiced by the Hebrews?
2. What was the prophets' attitude toward rituals?
3. What social reforms did the prophets seek?
4. What does the concept *humanity* mean? The Hebrew prophets are one source of the idea of humanity. Discuss this statement.

CHAPTER 3

The Greeks

THE ACROPOLIS, the sacred hill of ancient Athens, largely constructed in the fifth century B.C. Many of Athens' most important temples, including the Parthenon, were located on the Acropolis. *(© Georgescu Gabriel/Shutterstock.Com)*

Hebrew ethical monotheism, which gave value to the individual, is one source of Western civilization. Another source derives from the ancient Greeks, who originated scientific and philosophic thought, created democracy, and developed a humanistic outlook. From about 750 B.C. to 338 B.C. the Greek world consisted of small, independent, and self-governing city-states. Within this political-social context, the Greeks made their outstanding contributions to civilization.

In contrast to the Egyptians and Mesopotamians, the Greeks developed rational-scientific, rather than mythical, interpretations of nature and the human community. In trying to understand nature, Greek philosophers proposed physical explanations; that is, they gradually omitted the gods from their accounts of how nature came to be the way it is. Greek intellectuals also analyzed government, law, and ethics in logical and systematic ways. It was the great achievement of Greek thinkers to rise above magic, miracles, mystery, and custom and to assert that reason was the avenue to knowledge. The emergence of rational attitudes did not, of course, end traditional religion, particularly for the peasants, who remained devoted to their ancient cults, gods, and shrines. But what distinguishes the Greeks is that alongside an older religious-mythical tradition arose a philosophic-scientific view of the natural world and human culture.

The Greeks, who defined human beings by their capacity to use reason, also defined the principle of political liberty. Egyptians and Mesopotamians were subject to the authority of god-kings and priest-kings; the common people did not participate in political life, and there was no awareness of individual liberty. In contrast, many Greek city-states, particularly Athens, developed democratic institutions and attitudes. In the middle of the fifth century B.C., when Athenian democracy was at its height, adult male citizens were eligible to hold public office and were equal before the law; in the Assembly, which met some forty times a year, they debated and voted on the key issues of state. Whereas Mesopotamians and Egyptians believed that law had been given to them by the gods, the Greeks came to understand that law was a human creation, a product of human reason. The Athenians abhorred rule by absolute rulers and held that men can govern themselves. While expressing admiration for the Greek political achievement, modern critics also point out several limitations of Greek democracy, notably slavery and the inability of women to participate in political life.

The Greeks originated the Western humanist tradition. They valued the human personality and sought the full cultivation of human talent. In the Greek view, a man of worth pursued excellence; that is, he sought to mold himself in accordance with the highest standards and ideals. Greek art, for example, made the human form the focal point of attention and exalted the nobility, dignity, self-assurance, and beauty of the human being.

Greek culture has a distinctive style that enables us to see it as an organic whole. To the English classicist H. D. F. Kitto, the common thread that runs through Greek philosophy, literature, and art is "a sense of the wholeness of things"—the conviction that the universe contains an inherent order, that law governs both nature and human affairs, and that this orderliness can be comprehended by human reason.

Although the Greek city-states shared a common culture, they frequently warred with each other. Particularly ruinous was the Peloponnesian War (431–404 B.C.) between Athens and Sparta and their allies. The drawn-out conflict, marked by massacres and civil wars within city-states, shattered the Greek world spiritually. Increasingly, a narrow individualism and worsening factional disputes weakened the bonds of community within the various city-states. Moreover, learning little from the Peloponnesian War, the Greeks continued their internecine conflicts. Finally, by 338 B.C., the weakened city-states were conquered by Philip II of Macedonia, a kingdom to the north of Greece.

Philip's famous son, Alexander the Great, a romantic adventurer and brilliant commander, inherited the Macedonian kingdom and conquered the vast Persian Empire. After Alexander died in 323 B.C. at the age of thirty-two, his generals could not hold together the empire, which extended from Egypt to the frontiers of India. By 275 B.C. it was broken into three parts, each named for a dynasty: the Ptolemies in Egypt, the Seleucids in Asia, and the Antigonids in Macedonia and Greece. The rulers of these kingdoms were Macedonians, and their generals and high officials were Greek; the style of government, not in the democratic tradition of the Greek city-states, was modeled after the absolute rule by priest-kings and god-kings typical of the Near East.

Alexander's conquest of the Near East marks a second stage in the evolution of Greek civilization (Hellenism). The first stage, the *Hellenic Age*, began about 800 B.C. with the earliest city-states and lasted until Alexander's death. Subsequently Greek civilization entered the *Hellenistic Age*, which lasted until 30 B.C., when Egypt, the last Hellenistic kingdom, lost its independence to Rome.

The Hellenistic Age inherited many cultural achievements of the earlier Hellenic Age, but two crucial differences exist between the two eras. First, the self-sufficient and independent *polis* (city-state), the center of life in the Hellenic Age, was diminished in power and importance by larger political units, kingdoms headed by absolute monarchs. Although Greek cities continued to exercise considerable control over domestic affairs, they had lost to powerful monarchs their freedom of action in foreign affairs.

A second characteristic of the Hellenistic Age was cosmopolitanism, an intermingling of peoples and cultural traditions. In the Hellenic Age, the Greeks had drawn a sharp distinction between Greek and non-Greek. In the wake of Alexander's conquests, however, thousands of Greek soldiers, merchants, and administrators settled in Near Eastern lands, bringing with them Greek language, customs, and culture. Many upper-class citizens of Near Eastern cities, regardless of their ethnic backgrounds, came under the influence of Greek civilization. At the same time, Mesopotamian, Egyptian, and Persian ways, particularly religious practices and beliefs, spread westward into regions under the sway of Greek civilization.

---

1 Homer: The Educator of Greece

The poet Homer, who probably lived during the eighth century B.C., helped shape the Greek outlook. His great epics, *The Iliad* and *The Odyssey*, contain the embryo of the Greek humanist tradition: the concern with man and his achievements. "To strive always for excellence and to surpass all others"—in these words lies the essence of the Homeric hero's outlook. In the warrior-aristocratic world of Homer, excellence is primarily interpreted as bravery and skill in battle. The Homeric hero is driven to demonstrate his prowess, to assert himself, to win honor, and to earn a reputation.

The Iliad deals in poetic form with the Trojan War, which probably was waged in the thirteenth century B.C., between the Mycenaean Greeks and the Trojans of Asia Minor. At the outset Homer states his theme: the wrath of Achilles that brought so much suffering to the Greeks. Agamemnon, their king, has deprived the great warrior Achilles of his rightful prize, the captive girl Briseis. Achilles will not submit to this grave insult to his honor and refuses to join the Greeks in combat against the Trojans. In this way he intends to make Agamemnon pay for his arrogance, for without the Greeks' greatest warrior, Agamemnon will have no easy victories. With Achilles on the sidelines, the Greeks suffer severe losses.

Destiny is at work: the "wicked arrogance" of Agamemnon and the "ruinous wrath" of Achilles have caused suffering and death among the Greek forces. For Homer, human existence has a pattern—a universal plan governs human affairs. People, even the gods, operate within a certain unalterable framework; their deeds are subject to the demands of destiny or necessity. Later Greek thinkers would express this idea of a universal order in philosophic and scientific terms.

Homer
THE ILIAD

The following passages from *The Iliad* illustrate the Homeric ideal of excellence. In the first, Hector of Troy, son of King Priam, prepares for battle. Hector's wife Andromache pleads with him to stay within the city walls, but Hector, in the tradition of the Homeric hero, feels compelled to engage in combat to show his worth and gain honor.

Hector looked at his son and smiled, but said nothing. Andromache, bursting into tears, went up to him and put her hand in his. "Hector," she said, "you are possessed. This bravery of yours will be your end. You do not think of your little boy or your unhappy wife, whom you will make a widow soon. Some day the Achaeans [Greeks] are bound to kill you in a massed attack. And when I lose you I might as well be dead. There will be no comfort left, when you have met your doom—nothing but grief. I have no father, no mother, now. My father fell to the great Achilles when he sacked our lovely town, Cilician Thebe[1] of the High Gates. . . . I had seven brothers too at home. In one day all of them went down to Hades' House.[2] The great Achilles of the swift feet killed them all. . . .

"So you, Hector, are father and mother and brother to me, as well as my beloved husband. Have pity on me now; stay here on the tower; and do not make your boy an orphan and your wife a widow. . . ."

"All that, my dear," said the great Hector of the glittering helmet, "is surely my concern. But if I hid myself like a coward and refused to fight, I could never face the Trojans and the Trojan ladies in their trailing gowns. Besides, it would go against the grain, for I have trained myself always, like a good soldier, to take my place in the front line and win glory for my father and myself. . . ."

As he finished, glorious Hector held out his arms to take his boy. But the child shrank back with a cry to the bosom of his girdled nurse, alarmed by his father's appearance. He was frightened by the bronze of the helmet and the horsehair plume that he saw nodding grimly down at him. His father and his lady mother had to laugh. But noble Hector quickly took his helmet off and put the dazzling thing on the ground. Then he kissed his son, dandled him in his arms, and prayed to Zeus [the chief god] and the other gods: "Zeus, and you other gods, grant that this boy of mine may be, like me, pre-eminent in Troy; as strong and brave as I; a mighty king of Ilium [Troy]. May people say, when he comes back from battle, 'Here is a better man than his father.' Let him bring home the blood-stained armour of the enemy he has killed, and make his mother happy."

Hector handed the boy to his wife, who took him to her fragrant breast. She was smiling through her tears, and when her husband saw this he was moved. He stroked her with his hand and said: "My dear, I beg you not to be too much distressed. No one is going to send me down to Hades before my proper time. But Fate is a thing that no man born of woman, coward or hero, can escape. Go home now, and attend to your own work, the loom and the spindle, and see that the maidservants get on with theirs. War is men's business; and this war is the business of every man in Ilium, myself above all."

From *The Iliad* by Homer, translated by E. V. Rieu, pp. 128–130, 450–451. Copyright © the Estate of E. V. Rieu, 1946. Reprinted by permission of Penguin Books Ltd.

---

[1]In *The Iliad* the Cilices lived in southern Asia Minor. —Eds.
[2]Hades refers both to the god of the underworld and to the underworld itself. —Eds.

Many brave Greek warriors die in battle, including Achilles' best friend Patroclus, slain by the Trojan Hector. Achilles now sets aside his quarrel with Agamemnon (who has appealed to Achilles) and joins the battle. King Priam urges his son not to fight the mighty Achilles, but Hector, despite his fears, faces Achilles and meets his death. In this passage, the grief-stricken Priam goes to Achilles and requests Hector's body. Achilles responds with compassion. This scene shows that although Homer sees the essence of life as the pursuit of glory, he is also sensitive to life's brevity and to the suffering that pervades human existence.

. . . Big though Priam was, he came in unobserved, went up to Achilles, grasped his knees and kissed his hands, the terrible, man-killing hands that had slaughtered many of his sons. Achilles was astounded when he saw King Priam, and so were all his men. . . .

But Priam was already praying to Achilles. "Most worshipful Achilles," he said, "think of your own father, who is the same age as I, and so has nothing but miserable old age ahead of him. No doubt his neighbours are oppressing him and there is nobody to save him from their depredations. Yet he at least has one consolation. While he knows that you are still alive, he can look forward day by day to seeing his beloved son come back from Troy; whereas my fortunes are completely broken. I had the best sons in the whole of this broad realm, and now not one, not one I say, is left. There were fifty when the Achaean expedition came. Nineteen of them were borne by one mother and the rest by other ladies in my palace. Most of them have fallen in action, and Hector, the only one I still could count on, the bulwark of Troy and the Trojans, has now been killed by you, fighting for his native land. It is to get him back from you that I have come to the Achaean ships, bringing this princely ransom with me. Achilles, fear the gods, and be merciful to me, remembering your own father, though I am even more entitled to compassion, since I have brought myself to do a thing that no one else on earth has done—I have raised to my lips the hand of the man who killed my son."

Priam had set Achilles thinking of his own father and brought him to the verge of tears. Taking the old man's hand, he gently put him from him; and overcome by their memories they both broke down. Priam, crouching at Achilles' feet, wept bitterly for man-slaying Hector, and Achilles wept for his father, and then again for Patroclus. The house was filled with the sounds of their lamentation. But presently, when he had had enough of tears and recovered his composure, the excellent Achilles leapt from his chair, and in compassion for the old man's grey head and grey beard, took him by the arm and raised him. Then he spoke to him from his heart: "You are indeed a man of sorrows and have suffered much. How could you dare to come by yourself to the Achaean ships into the presence of a man who has killed so many of your gallant sons? You have a heart of iron. But pray be seated now, here on this chair, and let us leave our sorrows, bitter though they are, locked up in our own hearts, for weeping is cold comfort and does little good. We men are wretched things, and the gods, who have no cares themselves, have woven sorrow into the very pattern of our lives."

REVIEW QUESTIONS

1. What glimpses do we get from Homer's *Iliad* of the respective roles of men and women in Greek society?
2. Homer's epic poems were studied and even memorized by Greek schoolchildren. What values would the poems have taught these youngsters to emulate?
3. What lessons about the human condition did Achilles draw from the tragic events of the Trojan War?

2 Lyric Poetry

During the seventh century B.C., lyric poetry began to supplant epic poetry. Greek lyric poetry was intended to be sung to the musical accompaniment of a lyre, a stringed instrument. In fact the word *lyric* means "accompanied by the lyre." Lyric poetry was much more concerned with a poet's own opinions and inner emotions than with the great deeds of heroes as recounted in epic poetry.

Sappho
LOVE, PASSION, AND FRIENDSHIP

The greatest female lyric poet in antiquity was Sappho, who lived around 600 B.C. on the island of Lesbos. She was a member of the aristocracy and married a man named Cercylas, with whom she had one daughter, Cleïs. Unfortunately, just one complete poem, of twenty-eight lines, still remains; the rest of her poems exist only in fragments. Nonetheless, Sappho is credited with creating the metric stanza that bears her name—*Sapphic*. She established a "finishing" school to teach music and singing to well-to-do girls and to prepare them for marriage. With great tenderness, she wrote poems of friendship and love. Although some of her poems are about love between women and men, a number of verses are addressed to women, suggesting a homo-erotic interest. The sensual and erotic nature of these poems indicates that Sappho was bisexual. Such sexual behavior was, however, tolerated in ancient Greece, for it did not deprive a woman of her status as a virgin, since it was nonprocreative.

In this first fragment, Sappho likens her absent friend, Anactoria, to a defiant Helen of Troy, who (in spite of Homer's claims to the contrary) willingly left Sparta to sail away to Troy with her lover Paris, son of Priam, the Trojan king.

Some an army on horseback, some an army on
    foot
and some say a fleet of ships is the loveliest sight
on this dark earth; but I say it is whatever you
    desire:

and it is perfectly possible to make this clear
to all; for Helen, the woman who by far surpassed
all others in her beauty, left her husband—
the best of all men—

behind and sailed far away to Troy; she did not
    spare

a single thought for her child nor for her dear
    parents
but [the goddess of love] led her astray
[to desire. . . .]

                              [. . . which]
reminds me now of Anactoria
although far away,

whose long-desired footstep, whose radiant,
    sparkling face
I would rather see before me than the chariots
of Lydia[1] or the armour of men
who fight wars on foot. . . .

From *Sappho: Poems and Fragments*, translated by Josephine Balmer, Bloodaxe Books Ltd., 1992, pp. 39, 46, 49, 63, and 66. Reprinted with permission of Bloodaxe Books Ltd.

[1]Lydia was an ancient kingdom in the western part of Asia Minor. —Eds.

The following poetic fragments also deal with the power of love. In the first one, Sappho addresses passion between women.

. . . frankly I wish that I were dead:
she was weeping as she took her leave from me

and many times she told me this:
"Oh what sadness we have suffered,
Sappho, for I'm leaving you against my will."
So I gave this answer to her:
"Go, be happy but remember
me there, for you know how we have cherished
   you,

if not, then I would remind you
[of the joy we have known,] of all
the loveliness that we have shared together;

for many wreaths of violets,
of roses and of crocuses
. . . you wove around yourself by my side

. . . and many twisted garlands
which you had woven from the blooms
of flowers, you placed around your slender neck

. . . and you were anointed with
a perfume, scented with blossom,
. . . although it was fit for a queen

and on a bed, soft and tender
. . . you satisfied your desire. . . ."

In this fragment, Sappho admits that Aphrodite, the goddess of love, has left her powerless to resist desire.

Mother dear, I simply cannot weave my cloth;
                              I'm overpowered
by desire for a slender youth—and it's all
                              Aphrodite's fault

Sappho loved her daughter dearly and speaks of her love for Cleïs in the following fragment.

I have a child; so fair
As golden flowers is she,
My Cleïs, all my care.
I'd not give her away
For Lydia's wide sway
Nor lands men long to see.

A lost love is the subject of this fragment, as Aphrodite responds to Sappho's plea for assistance.

Immortal Aphrodite, on your patterned throne,
daughter of Zeus, guile-weaver,
I beg you, goddess, don't subjugate my heart
with anguish, with grief

but come here to me now, if ever in the past
you have heard my distant pleas
and listened; leaving your father's golden house
you came to me then

with your chariot yoked; beautiful swift sparrows
brought you around the dark earth
with a whirl of wings, beating fast, from heaven
down through the mid-air

to reach me quickly; then you, my sacred
   goddess,
your immortal face smiling,
asked me what had gone wrong this time and
   this time
why was I begging

and what in my demented heart, I wanted
   most:
"Who shall I persuade this time
to take you back, yet once again, to her love;
who wrongs you, Sappho?

For if she runs away, soon she shall run after,
if she shuns gifts, she shall give,
if she does not love you, soon she shall even
against her own will."

So come to me now, free me from this aching
   pain,
fulfil everything that

my heart desires to be fulfilled: you, yes you,
will be my ally.

Greek society mandated that women should
marry and bear children, thus surrendering
their symbol of female honor—virginity. In
this poem, Sappho recounts the trauma a
woman may experience when she loses her
virginity.

FIRST VOICE
Virginity O my virginity!
Where will you go when I lose you?

SECOND VOICE
I'm off to a place I shall never come back from
Dear Bride!
I shall never come back to you
Never!

REVIEW QUESTION

Which lines in Sappho's poems have the most appeal for you? Why?

---

3   The Emancipation of Thought from Myth

In the sixth century B.C., Greeks living in the city of Miletus in Ionia, the coast
of Asia Minor, conceived a nonmythical way of viewing nature, a feat that marks
the origins of philosophic and scientific thought. Traditionally, natural occurrences like earthquakes and lighting had been attributed to the gods. But early
Greek thinkers, called cosmologists because they were interested in the nature
and structure of the universe, were the first to see nature as a system governed
by laws that the intellect could ascertain. The cosmologists sought physical
rather than supernatural explanations for natural events. This new approach
made possible a self-conscious and systematic investigation of nature and a critical appraisal of proposed theories; in contrast, the mythical view that the gods
regulate nature did not invite discussion and questioning.

Thales of Miletus (c. 624–c. 548 B.C.) is considered the founder of Ionian philosophy. He wanted to know how nature came to be the way it is, and he did not
turn to traditional legends for an answer. Thales said that water was the basic element of nature and that through a natural process—similar to the formation of ice
or steam—water gave rise to everything else in the universe. Thales revolutionized thought because in searching for a first cause in nature he omitted the gods.

Anaximander (c. 611–547 B.C.), another Ionian, also held that a single element
was the wellspring of nature, but he rejected any specific substance such as water,
holding instead that something indefinite, which he called the Boundless or the
Infinite, was the source of all things. Anaximander attempted to explain how natural objects and living things had derived from this primary mass. Like Thales,
what is remarkable about Anaximander's cosmogony was the omission of the gods
or any supernatural agency in the origin of life and the formation of the world.

Pythagoras (c. 580–507 B.C.) was born on the island of Samos, a major Greek
cultural and commercial center in the eastern Aegean Sea; as a young man, he
migrated to southern Italy, where the Greeks had established colonies. A deep
religiosity pervaded the thought of Pythagoras and his followers, who sought

to purify the soul and to achieve salvation. Believing that the soul undergoes a reincarnation in animals, Pythagoreans would not eat meat. The Pythagoreans' great contribution to scientific thought was their conviction that nature contains an inherent mathematical order. Thus, continuity exists between the Pythagoreans and Isaac Newton and Albert Einstein, who expressed the laws underlying the cosmos in mathematical terms more than two thousand years later.

The method of inquiry initiated by the Ionian natural philosophers found expression in other areas of Greek culture. Thus, in the Greek medical school headed by Hippocrates (c. 460–377 B.C.) on the island of Cos, doctors consciously attacked magical practices and beliefs, seeing them as hindrances to understanding causes and cures of disease. The historian Thucydides (c. 460–400 B.C.) sought logical explanations for human events, and the Sophists (seventh to fifth centuries B.C.) applied reason to traditional religion, law, and morality.

Hippocrates
THE SACRED DISEASE:
THE SEPARATION OF MEDICINE FROM MYTH

In the following excerpt from *The Sacred Disease*, a Hippocratic doctor rejects the belief that epilepsy is a sacred disease. Instead he maintains that epilepsy, like all other diseases, has a natural explanation and denounces as "charlatans and quacks" those who claim that gods cause the disease.

I. I am about to discuss the disease called "sacred." It is not, in my opinion, any more divine or more sacred than other diseases, but has a natural cause, and its supposed divine origin is due to men's inexperience, and to their wonder at its peculiar character. Now while men continue to believe in its divine origin because they are at a loss to understand it, they really disprove its divinity by the facile method of healing which they adopt, consisting as it does of purifications and incantations. But if it is to be considered divine just because it is wonderful, there will be not one sacred disease but many, for I will show that other diseases are no less wonderful and portentous, and yet nobody considers them sacred. For instance, quotidian fevers, tertians and quartans seem to me to be no less sacred and god-sent than this disease,[1] but nobody wonders at them. . . .

II. My own view is that those who first attributed a sacred character to this malady were like the magicians, purifiers, charlatans and quacks of our own day, men who claim great piety and superior knowledge. Being at a loss, and having no treatment which would help, they concealed and sheltered themselves behind superstition, and called this illness sacred, in order that their utter ignorance might not be manifest. They added a plausible story, and established a method of treatment that secured their own position.

Reprinted by permission of the publishers and the Trustees of the Loeb Classical Library from Hippocrates, *Volume II: Prognostic,* Loeb Classical Library Volume 148, translated by W. H. S. Jones, Cambridge, Mass.: Harvard University Press, 1923, pp. 139–141, 145. The Loeb Classical Library® is a registered trademark of the President and Fellows of Harvard College.

[1]Because of the regularity of the attacks of fever, which occur every day (quotidians), every other day (tertians), or with intermission of two whole days (quartans).

They used purifications and incantations; they forbade the use of baths, and of many foods that are unsuitable for sick folk. . . .

But if to eat or apply these things engenders and increases the disease, while to refrain works a cure, then neither is godhead to blame nor are the purifications beneficial; it is the foods that cure or hurt, and the power of godhead disappears.

III. Accordingly I hold that those who attempt in this manner to cure these diseases cannot consider them either sacred or divine; for when they are removed by such purifications and by such treatment as this, there is nothing to prevent the production of attacks in men by devices that are similar. If so, something human is to blame, and not godhead. He who by purifications and magic can take away such an affliction can also by similar means bring it on, so that by this argument the action of godhead is disproved. By these sayings and devices they claim superior knowledge, and deceive men by prescribing for them purifications and cleansings, most of their talk turning on the intervention of gods and spirits.

In this passage, using a scientific approach, a Hippocratic physician observes a fever.

Erasinus lived by the gully of Bootes. Was seized with fever after supper; a troubled night.

First day. Quiet, but the night was painful.
Second day. General exacerbation; delirium at night.
Third day. Pain and much delirium.
Fourth day. Very uncomfortable; no sleep at night; dreams and wandering. Then worse symptoms, of a striking and significant character; fear and discomfort.
Fifth day. Early in the morning was composed, and in complete possession of his senses. But long before mid-day was madly delirious; could not restrain himself; extremities cold and rather livid; urine suppressed; died about sunset.

In this patient the fever was throughout accompanied by sweat; the hypochondria {upper parts of the abdomen} were swollen, distended and painful. Urine black, with round, suspended particles which did not settle. There were solid discharges from the bowels. Thirst throughout not very great. Many convulsions with sweating about the time of death.

Reprinted by permission of the publishers and the Trustees of the Loeb Classical Library from Hippocrates, *Volume I: Ancient Medicine*, Loeb Classical Library Volume 147, translated by W. H. S. Jones, Cambridge, Mass.: Harvard University Press, 1923, p. 145. The Loeb Classical Library® is a registered trademark of the President and Fellows of Harvard College.

Thucydides
METHOD OF HISTORICAL INQUIRY

Thucydides' historiography was another expression of the movement from myth to reason that pervaded every aspect of Greek culture. Mesopotamians and Egyptians kept annals purporting to narrate the deeds of gods and their human agents. The Greeks carefully investigated events—the first people to examine the past with a critical eye. Thucydides examined men's actions and their motives, explicitly rejected divine explanations for human occurrences, searched for natural causes, and based his conclusions on evidence. In this approach, he was influenced by the empiricism of the Hippocratic physicians. For Thucydides, a work of history, as distinguished from poetry, was a creation of the rational mind and not an expression of the poetic imagination. Thus, in Thucydides' *History of the Peloponnesian War* there was no place for legend, for myth, for the fabulous—all hindrances to historical truth. In the following passage, Thucydides describes his method of inquiry.

[I began my history at the very outbreak of the war,] in the belief that it was going to be a great war and more worth writing about than any of those which had taken place in the past. My belief was based on the fact that the two sides were at the very height of their power and preparedness, and I saw, too, that the rest of the Hellenic [Greek] world was committed to one side or the other; even those who were not immediately engaged were deliberating on the courses which they were to take later. This was the greatest disturbance in the history of the Hellenes, affecting also a large part of the non-Hellenic world, and indeed, I might almost say, the whole of mankind. For though I have found it impossible, because of its remoteness in time, to acquire a really precise knowledge of the distant past or even of the history preceding our own period, yet, after looking back into it as far as I can, all the evidence leads me to conclude that these periods were not great periods either in warfare or in anything else. . . .

In investigating past history, and in forming the conclusions which I have formed, it must be admitted that one cannot rely on every detail which has come down to us by way of tradition. People are inclined to accept all stories of ancient times in an uncritical way—even when these stories concern their own native countries. . . .

. . . Most people, in fact, will not take trouble in finding out the truth, but are much more inclined to accept the first story they hear.

However, I do not think that one will be far wrong in accepting the conclusions I have reached from the evidence which I have put forward. It is better evidence than that of the poets, who exaggerate the importance of their themes, or of the prose chroniclers, who are less interested in telling the truth than in catching the attention of their public, whose authorities cannot be checked, and whose subject-matter, owing to the passage of time, is mostly lost in the unreliable streams of mythology. We may claim instead to have used only the plainest evidence and to have reached conclusions which are reasonably accurate, considering that we have been dealing with ancient history. As for this present war, even though people are apt to think that the war in which they are fighting is the greatest of all wars and, when it is over, to relapse again into their admiration of the past, nevertheless, if one looks at the facts themselves, one will see that this was the greatest war of all.

In this history I have made use of set speeches some of which were delivered just before and others during the war. I have found it difficult to remember the precise words used in the speeches which I listened to myself and my various informants have experienced the same difficulty; so my method has been, while keeping as closely as possible to the general sense of the words that were actually used, to make the speakers say what, in my opinion, was called for by each situation.

And with regard to my factual reporting of the events of the war I have made it a principle not to write down the first story that came my way, and not even to be guided by my own general impressions; either I was present myself at the events which I have described or else I heard of them from eyewitnesses whose reports I have checked with as much thoroughness as possible. Not that even so the truth was easy to discover: different eyewitnesses give different accounts of the same events, speaking out of partiality for one side or the other or else from imperfect memories. And it may well be that my history will seem less easy to read because of the absence in it of a romantic element. It will be enough for me, however, if these words of mine are judged useful by those who want to understand clearly the events which happened in the past and which (human nature being what it is) will, at some time or other and in much the same ways, be repeated in the future. My work is not a piece of writing designed to meet the taste of an immediate public, but was done to last for ever.

From *History of the Peloponnesian War* by Thucydides, translated by Rex Warner, pp. 35, 46–48. © 1954. Reproduced by permission of Penguin Books Ltd.

Critias
RELIGION AS A HUMAN INVENTION

After the Greek philosophers of Asia Minor began to employ natural, rather than supernatural, explanations for nature, Greek thinkers on the mainland applied reason to human affairs. Exemplifying this trend were the Sophists, who wandered from city to city teaching rhetoric, grammar, poetry, mathematics, music, and gymnastics. The Sophists sought to develop their students' minds, and they created a secular curriculum—for these reasons they enriched the humanist tradition of the West.

The Sophist Critias (c. 480–403 B.C.) was a poet, philosopher, orator, and historian; also he was originally an eager follower of Socrates. Later, Critias became the most bloodthirsty of the so-called Thirty Tyrants, oligarchs who seized control of Athens in 404 B.C. and massacred their democratic opponents. The following passage, a surviving fragment of a play by Critias, demonstrates the Sophists' use of critical thought.

There was a time when the life of men was unordered, bestial and the slave of force, when there was no reward for the virtuous and no punishment for the wicked. Then, I think, men devised retributory laws, in order that Justice might be dictator and have arrogance as its slave, and if anyone sinned, he was punished. Then, when the laws forbade them to commit open crimes of violence, and they began to do them in secret, a wise and clever man invented fear (of the gods) for mortals, that there might be some means of frightening the wicked, even if they do anything or say or think it in secret. Hence he introduced the Divine (religion), saying that there is a God flourishing with immortal life, hearing and seeing with his mind, and thinking of everything and caring about these things, and having divine nature,

who will hear everything said among mortals, and will be able to see all that is done. And even if you plan anything evil in secret, you will not escape the gods in this; for they have surpassing intelligence. In saying these words, he introduced the pleasantest of teachings, covering up the truth with a false theory; and he said that the gods dwelt there where he could most frighten men by saying it, whence he knew that fears exist for mortals and rewards for the hard life: in the upper periphery, where they saw lightnings and heard the dread rumblings of thunder, and the starry-faced body of heaven, the beautiful embroidery of Time the skilled craftsman, whence come forth the bright mass of the sun, and the wet shower upon the earth. With such fears did he surround mankind, through which he well established the deity with his argument, and in a fitting place, and quenched lawlessness among men. . . . Thus, I think, for the first time did someone persuade mortals to believe in a race of deities.

Kathleen Freeman, *Ancilla to the Pre-Socratic Philosophers* (Cambridge: Harvard University Press, 1948), pp. 56–57.

REVIEW QUESTIONS

1. Hippocrates distinguishes between magic and medicine. Discuss this statement.
2. What were some of the methods that Thucydides promised to use to make his history more accurate and credible?
3. What was revolutionary about Critias' approach to religion?

4 Humanism

The Greeks conceived the humanist outlook, one of the pillars of Western civilization. They urged human beings to develop their physical, intellectual, and moral capacities to the fullest, to shape themselves according to the highest standards, and to make their lives as harmonious as a flawless work of art. Such an aspiration required intelligence and self-mastery.

Pindar
THE PURSUIT OF EXCELLENCE

The poet Pindar (c. 518–438 B.C.) expressed the Greek view of excellence in his praise for a victorious athlete. Life is essentially tragic—triumphs are short-lived, misfortunes are many, and ultimately death overtakes everyone; still, human beings must demonstrate their worth by striving for excellence.

He who wins of a sudden, some noble prize
In the rich years of youth
Is raised high with hope; his manhood takes
    wings;
He has in his heart what is better than wealth,

But brief is the season of man's delight.
Soon it falls to the ground;
Some dire decision uproots it.
—Thing of a day! such is man: a shadow in a
    dream.
Yet when god-given splendour visits him
A bright radiance plays over him, and how
    sweet is life!

From *The Greeks*, Revised Edition, poem translated by H.D.F. Kitto, pp. 174–175. © 1957. Reprinted by permission of Penguin Books Ltd.

Sophocles
LAUDING HUMAN TALENTS

In a famous passage from his play *Antigone*, Sophocles (c. 496–406 B.C.) lauded human talents.

Wonders are many, and none is more wonderful than man; the power that crosses the white sea, driven by the stormy south-wind, making a path under surges that threaten to engulf him; and Earth, the eldest of the gods, the immortal, the unwearied, doth he wear, turning the soil, with the offspring of horses, as the ploughs go to and fro year to year.

And the light-hearted race of birds, and the tribes of savage beasts, and the sea-brood of the deep, he snares in the meshes of his woven toils, he leads captive, man excellent in wit. And he masters by his arts the beast whose lair is in the wilds, who roams the hills; he tames the horse of shaggy mane, he puts the yoke upon its neck, he tames the tireless mountain bull.

Excerpted from *Three Theban Plays: Antigone, Oedipus The King, and Oedipus at Colonus* by Sophocles, edited by Theodore Howard Banks, pp. 13–17, 19–22. Copyright © 1956. By permission of Oxford University Press.

And speech, and wind-swift thought, and all the moods that mould a state, hath he taught himself; and how to flee the arrows of the frost, when 'tis hard lodging under the clear sky, and the arrows of the rushing rain; yea, he hath resource for all; without resources he meets nothing that must come: only against Death shall he call for aid in vain; but from baffling maladies he hath devised escapes.

Cunning beyond fancy's dream is the fertile skill which brings him, now to evil, now to good. When he honors the laws of the land, and that justice which he hath sworn by the gods to uphold, proudly stands his city: no city hath he who, for his rashness, dwells with sin. Never may he share my hearth, never think my thoughts, who doth these things!

REVIEW QUESTIONS

1. In what sense does Pindar consider life to be tragic?
2. What human virtues did the Greek poets extoll?

---

5 The Persian Wars

In 499 B.C., the Ionian Greeks in Asia Minor revolted against their Persian rulers; Athens sent twenty ships to aid the Ionians. To punish the Athenians, Darius I, king of Persia, sent a force to the peninsula of Attica, where Athens is located. In 490 B.C., on the plains of Marathon, an Athenian army of about ten thousand men defeated the Persians. Ten years later, Xerxes, Darius' son and heir, organized a huge invasion force aimed at making Greece a Persian province. Realizing that their independence and freedom were at stake, many Greek cities put aside their quarrels and united against the common enemy. In 480 B.C., on the Bay of Salamis near Athens, the Athenian navy defeated the Persian armada, and the next year the Spartan army crushed the Persians at Plataea.

Herodotus
THE HISTORIES

Herodotus (c. 484–c. 424 B.C.), often called "the father of history," wrote about the most important events of his lifetime, the Persian Wars. He took note of the strategy that lay behind the Greek victory in the battle of Salamis. He tells us that the Athenian general Themistocles (c. 527–460 B.C.) sent a slave to the Persian commander with the story that some of Athens' allies, fearing entrapment, were planning to sail out of the Bay of Salamis. As Themistocles hoped, the Persians, eager for a decisive victory, sailed into the narrow waters of the bay. Unable to deploy its more numerous ships in this cramped space, the Persian fleet was destroyed by the Greek ships.

Although the gods were present in Herodotus' narrative, they played a far less important role than they had in Greek mythology or in Near Eastern annals.

Herodotus visited Persian lands and found much to praise there. Nevertheless, he was struck by the contrast between Greek freedom and Persian absolutism, between the free Greek citizen and the Persian subject who knew only obedience to the king's commands.

A second theme prevalent in *The Histories* is punishment for *hubris*, or arrogance. Xerxes, in seeking to rule both Asia and Greece, was seen as exhibiting such arrogance. In the following excerpt, Herodotus discusses Xerxes' ambition.

In this book, the result of my inquiries into history, I hope to do two things: to preserve the memory of the past by putting on record the astonishing achievements both of our own and of the Asiatic peoples; secondly, and more particularly, to show how the two races came into conflict. . . .

———

Xerxes began his reign by building up an army for a campaign in Egypt. The invasion of Greece was at first by no means an object of his thoughts; but Mardonius—the son of Bogryas and Darius' sister and thus cousin to the king—who was present in court and had more influence with Xerxes than anyone else in the country, used constantly to talk to him on the subject. "Master," he would say, "the Athenians have done us great injury, and it is only right that they should be punished for their crimes. By all means finish the task you already have in hand; but when you have tamed the arrogance of Egypt, then lead an army against Athens. Do that, and your name will be held in honour all over the world, and people will think twice in future before they invade your country." And to the argument for revenge he would add that Europe was a very beautiful place; it produced every kind of garden tree; the land there was everything that land should be—it was, in short, too good for anyone in the world except the Persian king. Mardonius' motive for urging the campaign was love of mischief and adventure and the hope of becoming governor of Greece

himself; and after much persistence he persuaded Xerxes to make the attempt. . . .

After the conquest of Egypt, when he was on the point of taking in hand the expedition against Athens, Xerxes called a conference of the leading men in the country, to find out their attitude towards the war and explain to them his own wishes. When they met, he addressed them as follows: "Do not suppose, gentlemen, that I am departing from precedent in the course of action I intend to undertake. We Persians have a way of living, which I have inherited from my predecessors and propose to follow. . . . Of our past history you need no reminder; for you know well enough the famous deeds of Cyrus,[1] Cambyses,[2] and my father Darius, and their additions to our empire. Now I myself, ever since my accession, have been thinking how not to fall short of the kings who have sat upon this throne before me, and how to add as much power as they did to the Persian empire. And now at last I have found a way to win for Persia not glory only but a country as large and as rich as our own—indeed richer than our own—and at the same time to get satisfaction and revenge. That, then, is the object of this meeting—that I may disclose to you what it is that I intend to do. I will bridge the Hellespont[3] and march an army through Europe into Greece, and punish the Athenians

———

Herodotus, *The Histories*, pp. 13, 414–419, translated by Aubrey de Selincourt, revised by A. R. Burn, Penguin Classics, 1954. © The Estate of Aubrey de Selincourt, 1954, © A. R. Burn, 1972. Reproduced by permission of Penguin Books Ltd.

[1]Cyrus, the founder of the Persian Empire, ruled from 559 to 529 B.C. —Eds.
[2]Cambyses was king of Persia from 529 to 521 B.C. When he conquered Egypt, it temporarily became a Persian province. —Eds.
[3]The Hellespont is the narrow strait connecting the Aegean Sea with the Sea of Marmora. At one point it is less than a mile wide. —Eds.

for the outrage they committed upon my father and upon us. As you saw, Darius himself was making his preparations for war against these men; but death prevented him from carrying out his purpose. I therefore on his behalf, and for the benefit of all my subjects, will not rest until I have taken Athens and burnt it to the ground, in revenge for the injury which the Athenians without provocation once did to me and my father. These men, you remember, came to Sardis with Aristagoras[4] the Milesian— a mere slave of ours—and burnt the temples, and the trees that grew about them; and you know all too well how they served our troops under Datis and Artaphernes.[5] when they landed upon Greek soil. For these reasons I have now prepared to make war upon them, and, when I consider the matter, I find several advantages in the venture: if we crush the Athenians and their neighbours in the Peloponnese,[6] we shall so extend the empire of Persia that its boundaries will be God's own sky. With your help I shall pass through Europe from end to end and make it all one country, so that the sun will not look down upon any land beyond the boundaries of what is ours. For if what I am told is true, there is not a city or nation in the world which will be able to withstand us, once Athens and Sparta are out of the way. Thus the guilty and the innocent alike shall bear the yoke of servitude. . . ."

The first to speak after the king was Mardonius. "Of all Persians who have ever lived," he began, "and of all who are yet to be born, you, my lord, are the greatest. Every word you have spoken is true and excellent, and you will not allow the wretched Ionians in Europe to make fools of us. It would indeed be an odd thing if we who have defeated and enslaved the Sacae, Indians, Ethiopians, Assyrians,[7] and many other great nations for no fault of their own, but merely to extend the boundaries of our empire, should fail now to punish the Greeks who have been guilty of injuring us without provocation. . . . Well then, my lord, who is likely to resist you when you march against them with the millions of Asia at your back, and the whole Persian fleet? Believe me, it is not in the Greek character to take so desperate a risk. But should I be wrong—should the courage born of ignorance and folly drive them to do battle with us, then they will learn that we are the best soldiers in the world. Nevertheless, let us take this business seriously and spare no pains; success is never automatic in this world—nothing is achieved without trying."

Xerxes' proposals were made to sound plausible enough by these words of Mardonius, and when he stopped speaking there was a silence. For a while nobody dared to put forward the opposite view, until Artabanus, taking courage from the fact of his relationship to the king— he was a son of Hystaspes and therefore Xerxes' uncle—rose to speak. . . . "It is my duty to tell you what you have to fear from them: you have said you mean to bridge the Hellespont and march through Europe to Greece. Now suppose—and it is not impossible—that you were to suffer a reverse by sea or land, or even both. These Greeks are said to be great fighters—and indeed one might well guess as much from the fact that the Athenians alone destroyed the great army we sent to attack them under Datis and Artaphernes. Or, if you will, suppose they were to succeed upon one element only—suppose they fell upon our fleet and defeated it, and then sailed to the Hellespont and

---

[4]Aristagoras, the ruler of Miletus, encouraged the other cities of Ionia to revolt against the Persians. —Eds.

[5]Datis and Artaphernes were the commanders of the Persian forces defeated by the Athenians at Marathon. —Eds.

[6]The Peloponnese (Peloponnesus) is the largst peninsula of southern Greece. —Eds.

[7]The Sacae lived in Bactria, above the Iranian Plateau; the Indians just west of the Indus River. Ethiopia of that time means a land along the west side of the Red Sea. The Assyrians were a people inhabiting land between the Tigris and Euphrates rivers. —Eds.

destroyed the bridge: then, my lord, you would indeed be in peril. . . .

"I urge you, therefore, to abandon this plan; take my advice and do not run any such terrible risk when there is no necessity to do so. . . .

"You know, my lord, that amongst living creatures it is the great ones that God smites with his thunder, out of envy of their pride. The little ones do not vex him. It is always the great buildings and the tall trees which are struck by lightning. It is God's way to bring the lofty low. Often a great army is destroyed by a little one, when God in his envy puts fear into the men's hearts, or sends a thunderstorm, and they are cut to pieces in a way they do not deserve. For God tolerates pride in none but Himself."

REVIEW QUESTIONS

1. What were the motives of the Persians in planning Xerxes' invasion of Greece? What do these motives suggest about the nature of the Persian imperial system?
2. What factors did the Persians consider in choosing a strategy for the war?
3. Herodotus was not a witness to the debate between Mardonius and Artabanus. Which lines do you think represent his own view rather than that of the Persians?
4. What dangers did Artabanus foresee in the proposed invasion of Greece?

---

6 Greek Drama

Western drama is an art form that originated in Greece. It had its beginnings in the religious ceremonies of the Greeks and initially served a ritual function linking the Greeks with their gods. In the hands of the great Greek dramatists, drama gradually became less concerned with the activities of the gods, emphasizing instead human personality and universal human themes.

Sophocles
ANTIGONE

In *Antigone*, the dramatist Sophocles expresses the Greeks' high esteem for humanity and its potential. He also deals with a theme that recurs in Western thought over the centuries: the conflict between individual morality and the requirements of the state, between personal conscience and the state's laws. Creon, king of Thebes, forbids the burial of Polyneikes, Antigone's brother, because he rebelled against the state. The body, decrees Creon, shall remain unburied, food for dogs and vultures, despite the fact that Antigone is his niece and betrothed to his son, Haemon. Antigone believes that a higher law compels her to bury her brother, even though this means certain death for her and for her sister Ismene, if the latter helps Antigone.

SCENE II

CREON (*to* ANTIGONE)
You there. You, looking at the ground. Tell me.
Do you admit this or deny it? Which?

ANTIGONE
Yes, I admit it. I do not deny it.

CREON (*to* GUARD)
Go. You are free. The charge is dropped.
                              Exit GUARD
                              Now you,
Answer this question. Make your answer brief.
You knew there was a law forbidding this?

ANTIGONE
Of course I knew it. Why not? It was public,

CREON
And you have dared to disobey the law?

ANTIGONE
Yes, For this law was not proclaimed by Zeus,
Or by the gods who rule the world below.
I do not think your edicts have such power
That they can override the laws of heaven,
Unwritten and unfailing, laws whose life
Belongs not to today or yesterday
But to time everlasting; and no man
Knows the first moment that they had
    their being.
If I transgressed these laws because I feared
The arrogance of man, how to the gods
Could I make satisfaction? Well I know,
Being a mortal, that I have to die,
Even without your proclamations. Yet
If I must die before my time is come,
That is a blessing. Because to one who lives,
As I live, in the midst of sorrows, death
Is of necessity desirable.
For me, to face death is a trifling pain
That does not trouble me. But to have left
The body of my brother, my own brother,
Lying unburied would be bitter grief.

Excerpted from *Three Theban Plays: Antigone, Oedipus The King, and Oedipus at Colonus* by Sophocles, edited by Theodore Howard Banks, pp. 13–17, 19–22. Copyright © 1956. By permission of Oxford University Press.

And if these acts of mine seem foolish
    to you,
Perhaps a fool accuses me of folly.

CHORUS
The violent daughter of a violent father,
She cannot bend before a storm of evils.

CREON (*to* ANTIGONE)
Stubborn? Self-willed? People like that, I tell
    you,
Are the first to come to grief. The hardest
    iron,
Baked in the fire, most quickly flies to
    pieces.
An unruly horse is taught obedience
By a touch of the curb. How can you be so
    proud?
You, a mere slave? (*to* CHORUS) She was well
    schooled already
In insolence, when she defied the law.
And now look at her! Boasting, insolent,
Exulting in what she did. And if she triumphs
and goes unpunished, I am no man—she is.
If she were more than niece, if she were
    closer
Than anyone who worships at my altar,
She would not even then escape her doom,
A dreadful death. Nor would her sister. Yes,
Her sister had a share in burying him.
(*to* ATTENDANT) Go bring her here. I have just
    seen her, raving,
Beside herself. Even before they act,
Traitors who plot their treason in the dark
Betray themselves like that. Detestable!
(*to* ANTIGONE) But hateful also is an
    evil-doer
Who, caught red-handed, glorifies the
    crime.

ANTIGONE
Now you have caught me, will you do more
    than kill me?

CREON
No, only that. With that I am satisfied.

ANTIGONE
Then why do you delay? You have said nothing

I do not hate. I pray you never will.
And you hate what I say. Yet how could I
Have won more splendid honor than by giving
Due burial to my brother? All men here
Would grant me their approval, if their lips
Were not sealed up in fear. But you, a king,
Blessed by good fortune in much else besides,
Can speak and act with perfect liberty.

CREON
All of these Thebans disagree with you.

ANTIGONE
No. They agree, but they control their tongues.

CREON
You feel no shame in acting without their
help?

ANTIGONE
I feel no shame in honoring a brother.

CREON
Another brother died who fought against him.

ANTIGONE
Two brothers. The two sons of the same
parents.

CREON
Honor to one is outrage to the other.

ANTIGONE
Eteocles will not feel himself dishonored.

CREON
What! When his rites are offered to a traitor?

ANTIGONE
It was his brother, not his slave, who died.

CREON
One who attacked the land that he defended.

ANTIGONE
The gods still wish those rites to be performed.

CREON
Are they just pleased with the unjust as their
equals?

ANTIGONE
That may be virtuous in the world below.

CREON
No. Even there a foe is never a friend.

ANTIGONE
I am not made for hatred but for love.

CREON
Then go down to the dead. If you must love,
Love them. While I yet live, no woman
rules me.

CHORUS
Look there. Ismene, weeping as sisters weep,
The shadow of a cloud of grief lies deep.
On her face, darkly flushed; and in her pain
Her tears are falling like a flood of rain.
Enter ISMENE *and* ATTENDANTS

CREON
You viper! Lying hidden in my house,
Sucking my blood in secret, while I reared,
Unknowingly, two subverters of my throne.
Do you confess that you have taken part
In this man's burial, or deny it? Speak.

ISMENE
If she will recognize my right to say so,
I shared the action and I share the blame.

ANTIGONE
No. That would not be just. I never let you
Take any part in what you disapproved of.

ISMENE
In your calamity, I am not ashamed
To stand beside you, beaten by this tempest.

ANTIGONE
The dead are witnesses of what I did,
To love in words alone is not enough.

ISMENE
Do not reject me, Sister! Let me die
Beside you, and do honor to the dead.

ANTIGONE
No. You will neither share my death nor claim
What I have done. My death will be sufficient.

ISMENE
What happiness can I have when you are gone?

ANTIGONE
Ask Creon that. He is the one you value.

ISMENE
Do you gain anything by taunting me?

ANTIGONE
Ah, no! by taunting you, I hurt myself.

ISMENE
How can I help you? Tell me what I can do.

ANTIGONE
Protect yourself. I do not grudge your safety.

ISMENE
Antigone! Shall I not share your fate?

ANTIGONE
We both have made our choices, life and death.

ISMENE
At least I tried to stop you. I protested.

ANTIGONE
Some have approved your way; and others,
    mine.

ISMENE
Yet now I share your guilt. I too am ruined.

ANTIGONE
Take courage. Live your life. But I long since
Gave myself up to death to help the dead. . . .

Haemon, grief-stricken at the condemnation of his fiancée Antigone, approaches his
father, Creon, and tries to resolve the crisis.
Creon is suspicious about Haemon's loyalty.

CREON
We soon shall know better than seers could tell
    us.
My son, Antigone is condemned to death.
Nothing can change my sentence. Have you
    learned
Her fate and come here in a storm of anger,
Or do you love me and support my acts?

HAEMON
Father, I am your son. Your greater knowledge

Will trace the pathway that I mean to follow.
My marriage cannot be of more importance
Than to be guided always by your wisdom.

CREON
Yes, Haemon, this should be the law you
    live by!
In all things to obey your father's will.
Men pray for children round them in their
    homes
Only to see them dutiful and quick
With hatred [for their father's enemies] . . .
With honor to repay their father's friend.
But what is there to say of one whose children
Prove to be valueless? That he has fathered
Grief for himself and laughter for his foes.
Then, Haemon, do not, at the rule of pleasure,
Unseat your reason for a woman's sake.
This comfort soon grows cold in your embrace:
A wicked wife to share your bed and home.
Is there a deeper wound than to find worthless
The one you love? Turn from this girl with
    loathing,
As from an enemy, and let her go
To get a husband in the world below.
For I have found her openly rebellious,
Her only out of all the city. Therefore,
I will not break the oath that I have sworn.
I will have her killed. Vainly she will invoke
The bond of kindred blood the gods make
    sacred.
If I permit disloyalty to breed
In my own house, I nurture it in strangers.
He who is righteous with his kin is righteous
In the state also. Therefore, I cannot pardon
One who does violence to the laws or thinks
To dictate to his rulers; for whoever
May be the man appointed by the city,
That man must be obeyed in everything,
Little or great, just or unjust. And surely
He who was thus obedient would be found
As good a ruler as he was a subject;
And in a storm of spears he would stand fast
With loyal courage at his comrade's side.
But disobedience is the worst of evils.
For it is this that ruins cities; this
Makes our homes desolate; armies of allies

Through this break up in rout. But most men find
Their happiness and safety in obedience.
Therefore we must support the law, and never
Be beaten by a woman. It is better
To fall by a man's hand, if we must fall,
Than to be known as weaker than a girl.

CHORUS
We may in our old age have lost our judgment,
And yet to us you seem to have spoken wisely.

HAEMON
The gods have given men the gift of reason,
Greatest of all things that we call our own.
I have no skill, nor do I wish to have it,
To show where you have spoken wrongly. Yet
Some other's thought, beside your own, might prove
To be of value. Therefore it is my duty,
My natural duty as your son, to notice,
On your behalf, all that men say, or do,
Or find to blame. For your frown frightens them,
So that the citizen dares not say a word
That would offend you. I can hear, however,
Murmurs in darkness and laments for her.
They say: "No woman ever less deserved
Her doom, no woman ever was to die
So shamefully for deeds so glorious.
For when her brother fell in bloody battle,
She would not let his body lie unburied
To be devoured by carrion dogs or birds.
Does such a woman not deserve reward,
Rewards of golden honor?" This I hear,
A rumor spread in secrecy and darkness.
Father, I prize nothing in life so highly
As your well-being. How can children have
A nobler honor than their father's fame?
Or father than his son's? Then do not think
Your mood must never alter; do not feel
Your word, and yours alone, must be correct.
For if a man believes that he is right
And only he, that no one equals him
In what he says or thinks, he will be found
Empty when searched and rested. Because
    a man

Even if he wise, feels no disgrace
In learning many things, in taking care
Not to be over-rigid. You have seen
Trees on the margin of a stream in winter:
Those yielding to the flood save every twig,
And those resisting perish, root and branch.
So, too, the mariner who never slackens,
His taut sheet overturns his craft and spends
Keel uppermost the last part of his voyage.
Let your resentment die. Let yourself change.
For I believe—if I, a younger man,
May have a sound opinion—it is best
That men by nature should be wise in all
    things.
But most men find they cannot reach that goal;
And when this happens, it is also good
To learn to listen to wise counselors.

CHORUS
Sir, when his words are timely, you should heed
    them.
And Haemon, you should profit by his words.
Each one of you has spoken reasonably.

CREON
Are men as old as I am to be taught
How to behave by men as young as he?

HAEMON
Not to do wrong. If I am young, ignore
My youth. Consider only what I do.

CREON
Have you done well in honoring the rebellious?

HAEMON
Those who do wrong should not command
    respect.

CREON
Then that disease has not infected her?

HAEMON
All of our city with one voice denies it.

CREON
Does Thebes give orders for the way I rule?

HAEMON
How young you are! How young in saying
    that!

CREON	CREON
Am I to govern by another's judgment?	A city is the king's. That much is sure.
HAEMON	HAEMON
A city that is one man's is no city.	You would rule well in a deserted country.

REVIEW QUESTIONS

1. What was Antigone's justification for disobeying the command of the king? Provide examples of historical figures who have employed a similar justification for their actions.
2. Why did Creon react so violently to Antigone's action?
3. Which lines best reveal Antigone's position? Creon's position?

---

7 Athenian Greatness

The Persian Wars were decisive in the history of the West. Had the Greeks been defeated, it is very likely that their cultural and political vitality would have been aborted. The confidence and pride that came with victory, however, propelled Athens into a golden age.

Thucydides
THE FUNERAL ORATION OF PERICLES

The central figure in Athenian political life for much of the period after the Persian Wars was Pericles (c. 495–429 B.C.), a gifted statesman and military commander. In the opening stage of the Peloponnesian War between Athens and Sparta (431–404 B.C.), Pericles delivered an oration in honor of the Athenian war dead. In this speech, as reconstructed by the historian Thucydides, Pericles brilliantly described Athenian greatness.

Pericles contrasted Sparta's narrow conception of excellence with the Athenian ideal of the self-sufficiency of the human spirit. The Spartans subordinated all personal goals and interests to the demands of the Spartan state. As such, Sparta—a totally militarized society—was as close as the ancient Greeks came to a modern totalitarian society. The Athenians, said Pericles, did not require grinding military discipline in order to fight bravely for their city. Their cultivation of the mind and love of beauty did not make them less courageous.

To be sure, Pericles' "Funeral Oration," intended to bolster the morale of a people locked in a brutal war, idealized Athenian society. Athenians did not always behave in accordance with Pericles' high principles. Nevertheless, as both Pericles and Thucydides knew, Athenian democracy was an extraordinary achievement.

"Let me say that our system of government does not copy the institutions of our neighbours. It is more the case of our being a model to others, than of our imitating anyone else. Our constitution is called a democracy because power is in the hands not of a minority but of the whole people. When it is a question of settling private disputes, everyone is equal before the law; when it is a question of putting one person before another in positions of public responsibility, what counts is not membership of a particular class, but the actual ability which the man possesses. No one, so long as he has it in him to be of service to the state, is kept in political obscurity because of poverty. And, just as our political life is free and open, so is our day-to-day life in our relations with each other. We do not get into a state with our next-door neighbour if he enjoys himself in his own way, nor do we give him the kind of black looks which, though they do no real harm, still do hurt people's feelings. We are free and tolerant in our private lives; but in public affairs we keep to the law. This is because it commands our deep respect.

"We give our obedience to those whom we put in positions of authority, and we obey the laws themselves, especially those which are for the protection of the oppressed, and those unwritten laws which it is an acknowledged shame to break.

"And here is another point. When our work is over, we are in a position to enjoy all kinds of recreation for our spirits. There are various kinds of contests [in poetry, drama, music, and athletics] and sacrifices regularly throughout the year; in our own homes we find a beauty and a good taste which delight us every day and which drive away our cares. Then the greatness of our city brings it about that all the good things from all over the world flow in to us, so that to us it seems just as natural to enjoy foreign goods as our own local products.

"Then there is a great difference between us and our opponents, in our attitude towards

military security. Here are some examples: Our city is open to the world, and we have no periodical deportations in order to prevent people observing or finding out secrets which might be of military advantage to the enemy. This is because we rely, not on secret weapons, but on our own real courage and loyalty. There is a difference, too, in our educational systems. The Spartans, from their earliest boyhood, are submitted to the most laborious training in courage; we pass our lives without all these restrictions, and yet are just as ready to face the same dangers as they are. Here is a proof of this: When the Spartans invade our land, they do not come by themselves, but bring all their allies with them; whereas we, when we launch an attack abroad, do the job by ourselves, and, though fighting on foreign soil, do not often fail to defeat opponents who are fighting for their own hearths and homes. As a matter of fact none of our enemies has ever yet been confronted with our total strength, because we have to divide our attention between our navy and the many missions on which our troops are sent on land. Yet, if our enemies engage a detachment of our forces and defeat it, they give themselves credit for having thrown back our entire army; or, if they lose, they claim that they were beaten by us in full strength. There are certain advantages, I think, in our way of meeting danger voluntarily, with an easy mind, instead of with a laborious training, with natural rather than with state-induced courage. We do not have to spend our time practising to meet sufferings which are still in the future; and when they are actually upon us we show ourselves just as brave as these others who are always in strict training. This is one point in which, I think, our city deserves to be admired. There are also others:

"Our love of what is beautiful does not lead to extravagance; our love of the things of the mind does not make us soft. We regard wealth as something to be properly used, rather than as something to boast about. As for poverty, no one need be ashamed to admit it:

From *History of the Peloponnesian War*, by Thucydides, translated by Rex Warner, pp. 145–148. © 1954. Reproduced by permission of Penguin Books Ltd.

the real shame is in not taking practical measures to escape from it. Here each individual is interested not only in his own affairs but in the affairs of the state as well: even those who are mostly occupied with their own business are extremely well-informed on general politics—this is a peculiarity of ours: we do not say that a man who takes no interest in politics is a man who minds his own business; we say that he has no business here at all. We Athenians, in our own persons, take our decisions on policy or submit them to proper discussions: for we do not think that there is an incompatibility between words and deeds; the worst thing is to rush into action before the consequences have been properly debated. And this is another point where we differ from other people. We are capable at the same time of taking risks and of estimating them beforehand. Others are brave out of ignorance; and, when they stop to think, they begin to fear. But the man who can most truly be accounted brave is he who best knows the meaning of what is sweet in life and of what is terrible, and then goes out undeterred to meet what is to come.

"Again, in questions of general good feeling there is a great contrast between us and most other people. We make friends by doing good to others, not by receiving good from them. This makes our friendship all the more reliable, since we want to keep alive the gratitude of those who are in our debt by showing continued goodwill to them: whereas the feelings of one who owes us something lack the same enthusiasm, since he knows that, when he repays our kindness, it will be more like paying back a debt than giving something spontaneously. We are unique in this. When we do kindnesses to others, we do not do them out of any calculations of profit or loss: we do them without afterthought, relying on our free liberality. Taking everything together then, I declare that our city is an education to Greece, and I declare that in my opinion each single one of our citizens, in all the manifold aspects of life, is able to show himself the rightful lord and owner of his own person, and do this, moreover, with exceptional grace and exceptional versatility. And to show that this is no empty boasting for the present occasion, but real tangible fact, you have only to consider the power which our city possesses and which has been won by those very qualities which I have mentioned. Athens, alone of the states we know, comes to her testing time in a greatness that surpasses what was imagined of her. In her case, and in her case alone, no invading enemy is ashamed at being defeated, and no subject can complain of being governed by people unfit for their responsibilities. Mighty indeed are the marks and monuments of our empire which we have left. Future ages will wonder at us, as the present age wonders at us now."

REVIEW QUESTIONS

1. According to Pericles, what are the chief characteristics of a democratic society?
2. What were the attitudes of the Athenians to such things as wealth, learning, and public affairs?
3. How did the Athenians differ from the Spartans in their views on education and military training?

8 The Status of Women in Classical Greek Society

Women occupied a subordinate position in Greek society. A woman's chief functions were to bear male heirs for her husband and to manage his household. In Athens, respectable women were secluded in their homes; they did not go into the marketplace or eat at the same table as their husbands and guests. Nor did women have political rights; they could not vote or hold office. In order to exercise her property rights, a woman was represented by a male guardian—usually a father, husband, brother, or son.

Parents usually arranged the marriage of their daughters. A father who discovered that his daughter had been unchaste could sell her into slavery. Adultery was a crime. A husband was compelled by law to divorce his adulterous wife and could have her lover executed.

Euripides
MEDEA

The Greek dramatist Euripides (c. 485–406 B.C.) applied a keen critical spirit to the great question of individual life versus the demands of society. His play *Medea* focuses on a strong-willed woman whose despair at being cast off by her husband leads her to exact a terrible revenge. But in the following passage, Medea might speak for the deepest feelings of any Greek woman.

It was everything to me to think well of one man,
And he, my own husband, has turned out
    wholly vile.
Of all things which are living and can form a
    judgement
We women are the most unfortunate creatures.
Firstly, with an excess of wealth it is required
For us to buy a husband and take for our bodies
A master; for not to take one is even worse.
And now the question is serious whether we take
A good or bad one; for there is no easy escape
For a woman, nor can she say no to her marriage.
She arrives among new modes of behaviour
    and manners,
And needs prophetic power, unless she has
    learnt at home,

How best to manage him who shares the bed
    with her.
And if we work out all this well and carefully,
And the husband lives with us and lightly
    bears his yoke,
Then life is enviable. If not, I'd rather die.
A man, when he's tired of the company in his
    home,
Goes out of the house and puts an end to his
    boredom
And turns to a friend or companion of his own
    age.
But we are forced to keep our eyes on one
    alone.
What they say of us is that we have a peaceful
    time
Living at home, while they do the fighting in war.
How wrong they are! I would very much
    rather stand
Three times in the front of battle than bear one
    child.

From *Medea*, translated by Rex Warner, in *Euripedes* vol. 3 of Richard Lattimore *The Complete Greek Tragedies*, pp. 101, 96. © 1959 by The Bodley Head, published by Bodley Head. Reproduced with permission of Curtis Brown Group Ltd, London on behalf of the Estate of Rex Warner. © Rex Warner, 1944.

Aristophanes
LYSISTRATA

Aristophanes (c. 448–c. 380 B.C.), the greatest Athenian comic playwright, wrote *Lysistrata* in 412 B.C. to convey his revulsion for the Peloponnesian War that was destroying Greece. In the play, the women of Athens, led by Lysistrata, resolve to refrain from sexual relations with their husbands until the men make peace. When the women seize the Acropolis—the rocky hill in the center of Athens— the men resort to force but are doused with water. At this point a commissioner, accompanied by four constables, enters and complains about the disturbance; Koryphaios, one of the doused men, vents his anger. The ensuing dialogue between the commissioner and Lysistrata reflects some attitudes of Greek men and women toward each other.

COMMISSIONER . . . That's what women are good for: a complete disaster.

MAN I Save your breath for actual crimes, Commissioner. Look what's happened to us. Insolence, insults, insufferable effrontery, and apart from that, they've soaked us. It looks as though we pissed in our tunics.

COMMISSIONER By Poseidon, that liquid deity, you got what you deserved. It's all our own fault. We taught them all they know. We are the forgers of fornication. We sowed in them sexual license and now we reap rebellion . . . *(shrugs)* What do you expect? This is what happens. . . . *(indicates doors of Acropolis)* Take my own case.

I'm the Commissioner for Public Safety. I've got men to pay. I need the money and look what happens. The women have shut me out of the public treasury. *(taking command)* All right, men. On your feet. Take up that log over there. Form a line. Get a move on. You can get drunk later. I'll give you a hand. *(They ram the gates without success. After three tries, as they are stepping back, Lysistrata opens the door. Calonike and Myrrhine accompany her.)*

LYSISTRATA Put that thing down! I'm coming out of my own free will. What we want here is not bolts and bars and locks, but common sense.

COMMISSIONER Sense? Common sense? You . . . you . . . you . . . Where's a policeman? Arrest her! Tie her hands behind her back.

LYSISTRATA *(who is carrying wool on a spindle or a knitting needle)* By Artemis, goddess of the hunt, if he touches me, you'll be dropping one man from your payroll. *(Lysistrata jabs him)*

COMMISSIONER What's this? Retreat? Get back in there. Grab her, the two of you.

MYRRHINE *(holding a large chamber pot)* By Artemis, goddess of the dew, if you lay a hand on her, I'll kick the shit out of you.

COMMISSIONER Shit? Disgusting. Arrest her for using obscene language.

CALONIKE *(carrying a lamp)* By Artemis, goddess of light, if you lay a finger on her, you'll need a doctor.

COMMISSIONER Apprehend that woman. Get her, NOW!

BOEOTIAN *(from the roof, with a broom)* By Artemis, goddess of witchcraft, if you go near her, I'll break your head open.

COMMISSIONER Good God, what a mess. Athens' finest disgraced! Defeated by a gaggle of girls. Close ranks, men! On your marks, get set, CHARGE!

LYSISTRATA *(holds her hands up and they stop)* Hold it! We've got four battalions of fully equipped infantry women back there.

COMMISSIONER Go inside and disarm them.

LYSISTRATA *(gives a loud whistle and women crowd the bottlenecks and the doorway with brooms, pots and pans, etc.)* Attack! Destroy them, you sifters of flour and beaters of eggs, you pressers of garlic, you dough girls, you bar maids, you market militia. Scratch them and tear them, bite and kick. Fall back, don't strip the enemy—the day is ours. *(the policemen are overpowered)*

COMMISSIONER *(in tears)* Another glorious military victory for Athens!

LYSISTRATA What did you think we were? There's not an ounce of servility in us. A woman scorned is something to be reckoned with. You underestimated the capacity of freeborn women.

COMMISSIONER Capacity? I sure as hell did. You'd cause a drought in the saloons if they let you in.

MAN I Your honor, there's no use talking to animals. I know you're a civil servant, but don't overdo it.

MAN II Didn't we tell you? They gave us a public bath, fully dressed, without any soap.

WOMAN I What did you expect, sonny? You made the first move—we made the second. Try it again and you'll get another black eye. *(flute)* We are really sweet little stay-at-homes by nature, all sweetness and light, good little virgins, perfect dolls *(they all rock to and fro coyly)*. But if you stick your finger in a hornet's nest, you're going to get stung.

MEN ALL *(and drums—they beat their feet rhythmically on the ground)*
Oh Zeus, Oh Zeus.
Of all the beasts that thou has wrought,
What monster's worse than woman?
Who shall encompass with his thought
Their endless crimes? Let me tell you . . . no man!

They've seized the heights, the rock, the shrine.
But to what end I know not.
There must be *reasons* for the crime *(to audience)*
Do you know why? *(pause)* I thought not.

MAN I Scrutinize those women. Assess their rebuttals.

MAN II 'Twould be culpable negligence not to probe this affair to the bottom.

COMMISSIONER *(as if before a jury)* My first question is this, gentlemen of the . . . What possible motive could you have had in seizing the Treasury?

LYSISTRATA We wanted to keep the money. *No money, no war.*

COMMISSIONER You think that money is the cause of the war?

LYSISTRATA Money is the cause of all our problems. . . . They'll not get another penny.

COMMISSIONER Then what do you propose to do?

LYSISTRATA Control the Treasury.

COMMISSIONER Control the Treasury?

LYSISTRATA Control the Treasury. National economics and home economics—they're one and the same.

COMMISSIONER No, they're not.

LYSISTRATA Why do you say so?

COMMISSIONER The national economy is for the war effort.

LYSISTRATA Who needs the war effort?

COMMISSIONER How can we protect the city?

LYSISTRATA Leave that to us.

ALL MEN You?

ALL WOMEN Us.

COMMISSIONER God save us.

LYSISTRATA Leave that to us.

COMMISSIONER Subversive nonsense!

LYSISTRATA Why get so upset? There's no stopping us now.

COMMISSIONER It's a downright crime.

LYSISTRATA We *must* save you.

COMMISSIONER *(pouting)* What if I don't want to be saved?

LYSISTRATA All the more reason to.

COMMISSIONER Might I ask where you got these ideas of war and peace?

LYSISTRATA If you'll allow me, I'll tell you.

COMMISSIONER Out with it then, or I'll . . .

LYSISTRATA Relax and put your hands down.

COMMISSIONER I can't help myself. You make me so damned angry.

CALONIKE Watch it.

COMMISSIONER Watch it yourself, you old wind bag.

LYSISTRATA Because of our natural self-restraint, we women have tolerated you men ever since this war began. We tolerated you and kept our thoughts to ourselves. (You never let us utter a peep, anyway.) But that does not mean that we were happy with you. We knew you all too well. Very often, in the evening, at suppertime, we would listen to you talk of some enormously important decision you had made. Deep down inside all we felt was pain, but we would force a smile and ask, "How was the assembly today, dear? Did you get to talk about peace?" And my husband would answer, "None of your business. Shut up!" And I would shut up.

CALONIKE I wouldn't have.

COMMISSIONER I'd have shut your mouth for you.

LYSISTRATA But then we would find out that you had passed a more disgusting resolution, and I would ask you, "Darling, how did you manage to do something so absolutely stupid?" And my husband would glare at me and threaten to slap my face if I did not attend to the distaff side of things. And then he'd always quote Homer: "The men must see to the fighting."

COMMISSIONER Well done. Well done.

LYSISTRATA What do you mean? Not to let us advise against your idiocy was bad enough, but then again we'd actually hear you out in public saying things like, "Who can we draft? There's not a man left in the country." Someone else would say, "Quite right, not a man left. Pity." And so we women got together and decided to save Greece. There was no time to lose. Therefore, you keep quiet for a change and listen to us. For we have valuable advice to give this country. If you'll listen, we'll put you back on your feet again.

COMMISSIONER You'll do what? I'm not going to put up with this. I'm not going . . .

LYSISTRATA SILENCE!

COMMISSIONER I categorically decline to be silent for a woman. Women wear hats.

LYSISTRATA If that's what is bothering you, try one on and shut up! *(puts one on him)*

CALONIKE Here's a spindle.

MYRRHINE And a basket of wool.

CALONIKE Go on home. There's a sweetheart. Put on your girdle, wind your wool, and mind the beans don't boil over.

LYSISTRATA THE WOMEN MUST SEE TO THE FIGHTING.

COMMISSIONER Beside the point, beside the point. Things are in a tangle. How can you set them straight?

LYSISTRATA Simple.

COMMISSIONER Explain.

LYSISTRATA Do you know anything about weaving? Say the wool gets tangled. We lift it up, like this, and work out the knots by winding it this way and that, up and down, on the spindles. That's how we'll unravel the war. We'll send our envoys this way and that, up and down, all over Greece.

COMMISSIONER Wool? Spindles? Are you out of your mind? War is a serious business.

LYSISTRATA If you had any sense, you'd learn a lesson from women's work.

COMMISSIONER Prove it.

LYSISTRATA The first thing we have to do is give the wool a good wash, get the dirt out of the fleece. We beat out the musk and pick out the hickies. Do the same for the city. Lambast the loafers and discard the dodgers. Then our spoiled wool—that's like your job-hunting sycophants—sack the spongers, decapitate the dabblers. But toss together into the wool basket the good [resident] aliens, the allies, the strangers, and begin spinning them into a ball. The colonies are loose threads; pick up the ends and gather them in. Wind them all into one, make a great bobbin of yarn, and weave, without bias or seam, a garment of government fit for the people.

COMMISSIONER It's all very well this weaving and bobbing—when you have absolutely no earthly idea what a war means.

LYSISTRATA You disgusting excuse for a man! The pain of giving birth was only our first pain. You took our boys and sent *them to their deaths in Sicily.*

COMMISSIONER Quiet! I beg you, let that memory lie still.

LYSISTRATA And now, when youth and beauty are still with us and our blood is hot, you take our husbands away, and we sleep alone. That's bad enough for us married women. But I pity the virgins growing old, alone in their beds.

COMMISSIONER Well, men grow old too, you know.

LYSISTRATA But it's not the same. A soldier's discharged, bald as a coot he may be, and . . . zap! he marries a nymphette. But a woman only has one summer, and when that has slipped by, she can spend her days and her years consulting oracles and fortune tellers, but they'll never send her a husband.

———

MEN ALL There's something rotten in the state of Athens.

An ominous aroma of constitutional rot.
My nose can smell a radical dissenter,
An anarchist, tyrannous, feminist plot.

The Spartans are behind it.
They must have masterminded
This anarchist, tyrannous, feminist plot.

REVIEW QUESTIONS

1. List several reasons Medea gives to support her claim that "we women are the most unfortunate creatures."

2. What were the grievances of Greek women as listed by Aristophanes?
3. What attitudes of ancient Greek males toward females are reflected in the contemporary world?

---

9   The Peloponnesian War

After the defeat of the Persian invaders in 479 B.C., the Athenians organized a mutual defense pact, called the Delian League, among the smaller Greek states. With the largest population and greatest wealth and naval forces, Athens became the dominant power within the league. In the course of time, Athens converted the alliance from an organization of equal sovereign states to an empire under Athenian control. This outcome aroused suspicion among the other Greek states in the Peloponnese, particularly Sparta, that an imperialistic Athens was a threat to their own independence and freedom. That fear precipitated the Peloponnesian War (431–404 B.C.), which devastated the Greek world during the late fifth century B.C.

Elected general during the war, Thucydides was banished from Athens for failing to rescue Amphipolis, a town under attack by Sparta. During his twenty-year exile, Thucydides gathered information about the war, which he correctly viewed as an event of world-historical importance. He was also right to regard his account as a unique documentary achievement that would serve as a model for future historians.

Above all, Thucydides studied politics, the lifeblood of Athenian society. For him, history was essentially the study of political behavior. Consistent with the Greek character, Thucydides sought underlying patterns and general truths pertaining to statesmanship and political power. His chronicle contains rich insights into human nature, the techniques of demagogues, the ruinous consequences of mob behavior, and the spiritual deterioration of men under the stress of war.

Thucydides
THE MELIAN DIALOGUE AND
THE REVOLUTION AT CORCYRA

The Athenians, who saw no conflict between imperialism and democracy, considered it natural for strong states to dominate weaker ones. This view coincided with the position of those Sophists who argued that might makes right. The classic expression of this view is found in Thucydides' history.

During the war, Athens decided to invade the island of Melos, which resisted this unprovoked act of aggression. Thucydides reconstructed a dialogue based on a meeting between Athenian envoys and Melian officials, who tried unsuccessfully to persuade the Athenians not to launch an unjust war. Subsequently, Athens attacked. After capturing the town, the Athenians slaughtered the men, enslaved the women and children, and colonized the territory. The first selection is the famous Melian Dialogue. In the second selection, Thucydides describes the revolution of Corcyra, one of several conflicts that broke out within the city-states during the Peloponnesian War.

MELIANS No one can object to each of us putting forward our own views in a calm atmosphere. That is perfectly reasonable. What is scarcely consistent with such a proposal is the present threat, indeed the certainty, of your making war on us. We see that you have come prepared to judge the argument yourselves, and that the likely end of it all will be either war, if we prove that we are in the right, and so refuse to surrender, or else slavery.

ATHENIANS If you are going to spend the time in enumerating your suspicions about the future, or if you have met here for any other reason except to look the facts in the face and on the basis of these facts to consider how you can save your city from destruction, there is no point in our going on with this discussion. If, however, you will do as we suggest, then we will speak on.

MELIANS It is natural and understandable that people who are placed as we are should have recourse to all kinds of arguments and different points of view. However, you are right in saying that we are met together here to discuss the safety of our country and, if you will have it so, the discussion shall proceed on the lines that you have laid down.

ATHENIANS Then we on our side will use no fine phrases saying, for example, that we have a right to our empire because we defeated the Persians, or that we have come against you now because of the injuries you have done us—a great mass of words that nobody would believe. And we ask you on your side not to imagine that you will influence us by saying that you, though a colony of Sparta, have not joined Sparta in the war, or that you have never done us any harm. Instead we recommend that you

should try to get what it is possible for you to get, taking into consideration what we both really do think; since you know as well as we do that when these matters are discussed by practical people, the standard of justice depends on the equality of power to compel and that in fact the strong do what they have the power to do and the weak accept what they have to accept.

MELIANS Then in our view (since you force us to leave justice out of account and to confine ourselves to self-interest)—in our view it is at any rate useful that you should not destroy a principle that is to the general good of all men—namely, that in the case of all who fall into danger there should be such a thing as fair play and just dealing, and that such people should be allowed to use and to profit by arguments that fall short of a mathematical accuracy. And this is a principle which affects you as much as anybody, since your own fall would be visited by the most terrible vengeance and would be an example to the world. . . .

ATHENIANS . . . What we shall do now is to show you that it is for the good of our own empire that we are here and that it is for the preservation of your city that we shall say what we are going to say. We do not want any trouble in bringing you into our empire, and we want you to be spared for the good both of yourselves and of ourselves.

MELIANS And how could it be just as good for us to be the slaves as for you to be the masters?

ATHENIANS You, by giving in, would save yourselves from disaster; we, by not destroying you, would be able to profit from you.

MELIANS So you would not agree to our being neutral, friends instead of enemies, but allies of neither side?

ATHENIANS No, because it is not so much your hostility that injures us; it is rather the

---

From *History of the Peloponnesian War*, by Thucydides, translated by Rex Warner, pp. 401–407. © 1954. Reproduced by permission of Penguin Books Ltd.

case that, if we were on friendly terms with you, our subjects would regard that as a sign of weakness in us, whereas your hatred is evidence of our power. . . . [Our subjects think] that those who still preserve their independence do so because they are strong, and that if we fail to attack them it is because we are afraid. So that by conquering you we shall increase not only the size but the security of our empire. We rule the sea and you are islanders, and weaker islanders too than the others; it is therefore particularly important that you should not escape. . . .

MELIANS Then surely, if such hazards are taken by you to keep your empire . . . we who are still free would show ourselves great cowards and weaklings if we failed to face everything that comes rather than submit to slavery.

ATHENIANS No, not if you are sensible. This is no fair fight, with honour on one side and shame on the other. It is rather a question of saving your lives and not resisting those who are far too strong for you.

MELIANS Yet we know that in war fortune sometimes makes the odds more level than could be expected from the difference in numbers of the two sides. And if we surrender, then all our hope is lost at once, whereas, so long as we remain in action, there is still a hope that we may yet stand upright.

ATHENIANS Hope, that comforter in danger! If one already has solid advantages to fall back upon, one can indulge in hope. . . . [D]o not be like those people who, as so commonly happens, miss the chance of saving themselves in a human and practical way, and, when every clear and distinct hope has left them in their adversity, turn to what is blind and vague, to prophecies and oracles and such things which by encouraging hope lead men to ruin.

MELIANS It is difficult, and you may be sure that we know it, for us to oppose your power. . . . Nevertheless we trust that the gods will give us

fortune as good as yours, because we are standing for what is right against what is wrong; and as for what we lack in power, we trust that it will be made up for by our alliance with the Spartans, who are bound, if for no other reason, then for honour's sake, and because we are their kinsmen, to come to our help. Our confidence, therefore, is not so entirely irrational as you think. . . .

ATHENIANS . . . Our opinion of the gods and our knowledge of men lead us to conclude that it is a general and necessary law of nature to rule wherever one can. . . . [W]ith regard to your views about Sparta and your confidence that she, out of a sense of honour, will come to your aid, we must say that we congratulate you on your simplicity but do not envy you your folly. . . .

. . . You, if you take the right view . . . will see that there is nothing disgraceful in giving way to the greatest city in Hellas when she is offering you such reasonable terms—alliance on a tribute-paying basis and liberty to enjoy your own property. And, when you are allowed to choose between war and safety, you will not be so insensitively arrogant as to make the wrong choice. This is the safe rule—to stand up to one's equals, to behave with deference towards one's superiors, and to treat one's inferiors with moderation. Think it over again, then, when we have withdrawn from the meeting, and let this be a point that constantly recurs to your minds—that you are discussing the fate of your country, that you have only one country, and that its future for good or ill depends on this one single decision which you are going to make.

The Athenians then withdrew from the discussion. The Melians, left to themselves, reached a conclusion which was much the same as they had indicated in their previous replies. Their answer was as follows:

MELIANS Our decision, Athenians, is just the same as it was at first. We are not prepared to give up in a short moment the liberty which our city has enjoyed from its foundation for

700 years. We put our trust in the fortune that the gods will send and which has saved us up to now, and in the help of men—that is, of the Spartans; and so we shall try to save ourselves. But we invite you to allow us to be friends of yours and enemies to neither side, to make a treaty which shall be agreeable to both you and us, and so to leave our country.

During the war, revolutions broke out in several city-states as democrats, those who believed in decision making by citizen participation, and oligarchs, those who wanted the rule of a select few, competed for power. In these conflicts, traditional standards of morality were set aside and dangerous passions were unleashed. Thucydides' account of the revolution at Corcyra shows how the stresses of war precipitated a moral collapse and a deterioration in the quality of political life.

. . . The Corcyraeans continued to massacre those of their own citizens whom they considered to be their enemies. Their victims were accused of conspiring to overthrow the democracy, but in fact men were often killed on grounds of personal hatred or else by their debtors because of the money that they owed. There was death in every shape and form. And, as usually happens in such situations, people went to every extreme and beyond it. There were fathers who killed their sons; men were dragged from the temples or butchered on the very altars; some were actually walled up in the temple of Dionysus [a god of drunken revelry] and died there.

So savage was the progress of this revolution, and it seemed all the more so because it was one of the first which had broken out. Later, of course, practically the whole of the Hellenic world was convulsed, with rival parties in every state—democratic leaders trying to bring in

From *History of the Peloponnesian War*, by Thucydides, translated by Rex Warner, pp. 241–245. © 1954. Reproduced by permission of Penguin Books Ltd.

the Athenians, and oligarchs trying to bring in the Spartans. In peacetime there would have been no excuse and no desire for calling them in, but in time of war, when each party could always count upon an alliance which would do harm to its opponents and at the same time strengthen its own position, it became a natural thing for anyone who wanted a change of government to call in help from outside. In the various cities these revolutions were the cause of many calamities—as happens and always will happen while human nature is what it is, though there may be different degrees of savagery, and, as different circumstances arise, the general rules will admit of some variety. In times of peace and prosperity cities and individuals alike follow higher standards, because they are not forced into a situation where they have to do what they do not want to do. But war is a stern teacher; in depriving them of the power of easily satisfying their daily wants, it brings most people's minds down to the level of their actual circumstances.

So revolutions broke out in city after city, and in places where the revolutions occurred late the knowledge of what had happened previously in other places caused still new extravagances of revolutionary zeal, expressed by an elaboration in the methods of seizing power and by unheard-of atrocities in revenge. To fit in with the change of events, words, too, had to change their usual meanings. What used to be described as a thoughtless act of aggression was now regarded as the courage one would expect to find in a party member; to think of the future and wait was merely another way of saying one was a coward; any idea of moderation was just an attempt to disguise one's unmanly character; ability to understand a question from all sides meant that one was totally unfitted for action. Fanatical enthusiasm was the mark of a real man, and to plot against an enemy behind his back was perfectly legitimate self-defence. Anyone who held violent opinions could always be trusted, and anyone who objected to them became a suspect. To plot successfully was a sign of intelligence, but it was still cleverer to see that a plot was hatching. If one attempted to provide against having to do either, one was disrupting the unity of the party and acting out of fear of the opposition. In short, it was equally praiseworthy to get one's blow in first against someone who was going to do wrong, and to denounce someone who had no intention of doing any wrong at all. Family relations were a weaker tie than party membership, since party members were more ready to go to any extreme for any reason whatever. These parties were not formed to enjoy the benefits of the established laws, but to acquire power by overthrowing the existing regime, and the members of these parties felt confidence in each other not because of any fellowship in a religious communion, but because they were partners in crime. If an opponent made a reasonable speech, the party in power, so far from giving it a generous reception, took every precaution to see that it had no practical effect. . . .

Love of power, operating through greed and through personal ambition, was the cause of all these evils. To this must be added the violent fanaticism which came into play once the struggle had broken out. Leaders of parties in the cities had programmes which appeared admirable—on one side political equality for the masses, on the other the safe and sound government of the aristocracy—but in professing to serve the public interest they were seeking to win the prizes for themselves. In their struggles for ascendancy nothing was barred; terrible indeed were the actions to which they committed themselves, and in taking revenge they went farther still. Here they were deterred neither by the claims of justice nor by the interests of the state; their one standard was the pleasure of their own party at that particular moment, and so, either by means of condemning their enemies on an illegal vote or by violently usurping power over them, they were always ready to satisfy the hatreds of the hour. Thus neither side had any use for conscientious motives; more interest was shown in those who could produce attractive

arguments to justify some disgraceful action. As for the citizens who held moderate views, they were destroyed by both the extreme parties, either for not taking part in the struggle or in envy at the possibility that they might survive.

As the result of these revolutions, there was a general deterioration of character throughout the Greek world. The simple way of looking at things, which is so much the mark of a noble nature, was regarded as a ridiculous quality and soon ceased to exist. Society had become divided into two ideologically hostile camps, and each side viewed the other with suspicion. As for ending this state of affairs, no guarantee could be given that would be trusted, no oath sworn that people would fear to break; everyone had come to the conclusion that it was hopeless to expect a permanent settlement, and so, instead of being able to feel confident in others, they devoted their energies to providing against being injured themselves. As a rule those who were least remarkable for intelligence showed the greater powers of survival. Such people recognized their own deficiencies and the superior intelligence of their opponents; fearing that they might lose a debate or find themselves outmanoeuvred in intrigue by their quick-witted enemies, they boldly launched straight into action; while their opponents, over-confident in the belief that they would see what was happening in advance, and not thinking it necessary to seize by force what they could secure by policy, were the more easily destroyed because they were off their guard.

Certainly it was in Corcyra that there occurred the first examples of the breakdown of law and order. There was the revenge taken in their hour of triumph by those who had in the past been arrogantly oppressed instead of wisely governed; there were the wicked resolutions taken by those who, particularly under the pressure of misfortune, wished to escape from their usual poverty and coveted the property of their neighbours; there were the savage and pitiless actions into which men were carried not so much for the sake of gain as because they were swept away into an internecine struggle by their ungovernable passions. Then, with the ordinary conventions of civilized life thrown into confusion, human nature, always ready to offend even where laws exist, showed itself proudly in its true colours, as something incapable of controlling passion, insubordinate to the idea of justice, the enemy to anything superior to itself; for, if it had not been for the pernicious power of envy, men would not so have exalted vengeance above innocence and profit above justice. Indeed, it is true that in these acts of revenge on others men take it upon themselves to begin the process of repealing those general laws of humanity which are there to give a hope of salvation to all who are in distress, instead of leaving those laws in existence, remembering that there may come a time when they, too, will be in danger and will need their protection.

REVIEW QUESTIONS

1. In what way did the debate between the Athenians and Melians reflect the new rationalist spirit in Greek society?
2. Evaluate the performance of the Melian negotiators.
3. What types of political behavior did Thucydides hold in contempt?

10 Socrates: The Rational Individual

Socrates (469–399 B.C.) marked a decisive turning point in Greek philosophy and in the history of Western thought. The Socratic conception of the rational individual became an essential component of the tradition of classical humanism. Socrates agreed with the Sophists that the study of physical nature was less important than the study of man. But whereas the Sophists concentrated on teaching specific skills—how to excel in debates, for example—Socrates was concerned with comprehending and improving human character. Although ethical concerns lay at the center of Socrates' thought, he never provided a list of ethical commands; in Socratic philosophy, there is nothing comparable to the Ten Commandments. What he did provide was a method—the dialectic or dialogue—of arriving at knowledge, including moral values.

For Socrates, the dialogue (the asking and answering of questions between two or more individuals) was the sole avenue to moral insights and self-knowledge. The interchange implied that a human mind was not a passive vessel into which a teacher poured knowledge. Participants in a dialogue were obliged to play an active role and to think critically about human values. The use of the dialogue implied further that relations between people should involve rational discussion through which people learn from each other and improve themselves.

When Socrates was seventy, he was accused by his enemies of corrupting the youth of Athens and of not believing in the city's gods but in other, new divinities, and he went on trial for his life.

Plato
THE APOLOGY

Knowledge of Socrates' trial comes principally from *The Apology* written by Plato, Socrates' most illustrious student. (The original meaning of *apology* was a defense or explanation.) In the first passage from *The Apology*, presented below, Socrates tells the court that the Delphic Oracle, the prophetess of Apollo at Delphi, had said that there was no one wiser than Socrates. Not considering himself wise, Socrates resolved to discover what the oracle meant, by conversing with people reputed to be wise.

I went to a man who seemed wise: thinking that there, if anywhere, I should prove the answer wrong, and be able to say to the oracle, "You said that I am the wisest of men; but this man is wiser than I am." So I examined him—I need not tell you his name, he was a public man, but this was the result, Athenians. When I conversed with him, I came to see that, though many persons, and chiefly he himself, thought that he was wise, yet he was not wise. And then I tried to show him that he was not wise, though he fancied that he was; and by that I gained his hatred, and the hatred of many of the bystanders. So when I went away, I thought to myself, "I am wiser than this man: neither of us probably knows anything that is really good, but he thinks that he has knowledge, when he has it not, while I, seeing that I have no knowledge, do not think that I have." In this point, at least, I seem to be a little wiser than he is; I do not think that I know what I do not know. Next I went to another man, who seemed to be still wiser, with just the same result. And there again I gained his hatred. . . . After the public men I went to the poets, tragic, dithyrambic [frenzied], and others, thinking there to find myself manifestly more ignorant than they. So I took up the poems on which I thought that they had spent most pains, and asked them what they meant, wishing also for instruction. I am ashamed to tell you the truth, my friends, but I must say it. In short, almost any of the bystanders would have spoken better about the works of these poets than the poets themselves. So I soon found that it is not by wisdom that the poets create their works, but by a certain natural power, and by inspiration, like soothsayers and prophets: for though such persons say many fine things, they know nothing of what they say. And the poets seemed to me to be in a like case. And at the same time I perceived that, because of their poetry, they thought that they were the wisest of men in other matters too, which they were not. So I went away again, thinking that I had the same advantage over them as over the public men.

Finally I went to the artisans: for I was conscious, in a word, that I had no knowledge at all, and I was sure that I should find that they knew many fine things. And in that I was not mistaken. They knew what I did not know, and so far they were wiser than I. But, Athenians, it seemed to me that the skilled craftsmen made the same mistake as the poets. Each of them claimed to have great wisdom in the highest matters because he was skilful in his own art; and this fault of theirs threw their real wisdom into the shade. So I asked myself on behalf of the oracle whether I would choose to remain as I was, neither wise in their wisdom nor ignorant in their ignorance, or to have both, as they had them. And I made answer to myself and to the oracle that it were better for me to remain as I was.

This search, Athenians, has gained me much hatred of a very fierce and bitter kind, which has caused many false accusations against me; and

The Trial and Death of Socrates, trans. F. J. Church (London: Macmillan, 1880), pp. 37–41, 50–53, 56–57.

I am called by the name of wise. For the by-standers always think that I am wise myself in any matter wherein I convict another man of ignorance. But in truth, my friends, perhaps it is God who is wise: and by this oracle he may have meant that man's wisdom is worth little or nothing. He did not mean, I think, that Socrates is wise: he only took me as an example, and made use of my name, as though he would say to men: "He among you is wisest, who, like Socrates, is convinced that for wisdom he is verily worthless." And therefore I still go about searching and testing every man whom I think wise, whether he be a citizen or a stranger, according to the word of the God [Apollo]; and whenever I find that he is not wise, I point that out to him in the service of the God. And I am so busy in this pursuit that I have never had leisure to take any part worth mentioning in public matters, or to look after my private affairs. I am in very great poverty by my service to the God.

And besides this, the young men who follow me about, who are the sons of wealthy persons and with much leisure, by nature delight in hearing men cross-questioned: and they often imitate me among themselves: then they try their hand at cross-questioning other people. And, I imagine, they find a great abundance of men who think that they know a great deal, when in truth they know little or nothing. And then the persons who are cross-questioned are angry with me instead of with themselves: and say that Socrates is an abominable fellow who corrupts the young. And when they are asked, Why, what does he do? what does he teach? they have nothing to say; but, not to seem at a loss, they repeat the stock charges against all philosophers, and say that he investigates things in the air and under the earth, and that he teaches people to disbelieve in the gods, and "to make the worst appear the better reason." For I fancy they would not like to confess the truth, that they are shown up as mere ignorant pretenders to knowledge. And so they have filled your ears with their fierce slanders for a long time, for they are zealous and fierce and numerous: they are well-disciplined too, and plausible in speech. . . .

Had Socrates been willing to compromise and to stop teaching his philosophy, it is likely that he would not have received the death penalty. However, for Socrates the pursuit of truth was the highest human activity; it involved the person's whole being. It transformed the individual, enabling him to live in accordance with moral values that had been arrived at through thought and that could be defended rationally.

. . . But I know well that it is evil and base to do wrong and to disobey my better, whether he be man or god. And I will never choose what I know to be evil, and fear and fly from what may possibly be a good. And so, even if you acquit me now, and do not listen to Anytus' [his prosecutor's] argument that I ought never to have been brought to trial if I was to be acquitted, and that, as it is, you are bound to put me to death, because if I were to escape, all your children would forthwith be utterly corrupted by practising what Socrates teaches: if you were therefore to say to me, "Socrates, this time we will not listen to Anytus: we will let you go: but on this condition, that you cease from carrying on this search, and from philosophy: if you are found doing that again, you shall die": I say, if you offered to let me go on these terms, I should reply:—"Athenians, I hold you in the highest regard and love; but I will obey the God rather than you: and as long as I have breath and power I will not cease from philosophy, and from exhorting you and setting forth the truth to any of you whom I meet, saying as I am wont, 'My excellent friend, you are a citizen of Athens, a city very great and very famous for wisdom and power of mind: are you not ashamed of caring so much for the making of money, and for reputation and honour? Will you not spend thought or care on wisdom and truth and the perfecting of your soul?' " And if he dispute my words, and say that he does care for these things, I shall not forthwith release him and go away: I shall question him and cross-examine him: and if I think that he has not virtue, though he says that he has, I shall reproach him for setting the least value on the most important things; and the greater value on the more worthless. This shall I do to every one whom I meet, old or young, citizen or stranger; but especially to the citizens, for they are more nearly akin to me. For know well, the God commands me so to do. And I think that nothing better has ever happened to you in your city than my service to the God. For I spend my whole life in going about persuading you all, both young and old, to give your first and chiefest care to the perfection of your souls: and not till you have done that to care for your bodies or your wealth. I tell you, that virtue does not come from wealth, but that wealth and every other good, whether public or private, which men have, come from virtue. If then I corrupt the youth by this teaching, the mischief is great; but if any man says that I teach anything else, he speaks falsely. And therefore, Athenians, I say, either listen to Anytus, or do not listen to him: either acquit me, or do not acquit me: but be sure that I shall not alter my life; no, not if I have to die for it many times.

Do not interrupt me, Athenians. Remember the request which I made to you, and listen to my words. I think that it will do you good to hear them. I have something more to say to you, at which perhaps you will cry out: but do not do that. Be sure that if you kill me, a man such as I say I am, you will harm yourselves more than you will harm me. Meletus [another prosecutor] and Anytus can do me no harm; that is impossible, for I do not think that God will allow a good man to be harmed by a bad one. They may indeed kill me, or drive me into exile, or deprive me of my civil rights; and perhaps Meletus and others think these things great evils. But I do not think so: I think that to do as he is doing, and to try to kill a man unjustly, is a much greater evil. And now, Athenians, I am not going to argue for my own sake at all, as you might think, but for yours, that you may not sin against the God and reject his gift to you, by condemning me. If you put me to death, you will hardly find another man to fill my place. The God has

sent me to attack the city, if I may use a ludicrous simile, just as if it were a great and noble horse, which was rather sluggish from its size and needed a gadfly to rouse it: and I think that I am the gadfly that the God has set upon the city: for I never cease settling on you as it were at every point, and rousing, and exhorting, and reproaching each man of you all day long. You will hardly find anyone else, my friends, to fill my place: and, if you take my advice, you will spare my life. You are indignant, as drowsy persons are when they are awakened, and, of course, if you are persuaded by Anytus, you could easily kill me with a single blow, and then sleep on undisturbed for the rest of your lives. . . .

Perhaps someone will say, "Why cannot you withdraw from Athens, Socrates, and hold your peace?" It is the most difficult thing in the world to make you understand why I cannot do that. If I say that I cannot hold my peace because that would be to disobey the God, you will think that I am not in earnest and will not believe me. And if I tell you that no greater good can happen to a man than to discuss human excellence every day and the other matters about which you have heard me arguing and examining myself and others, and that an unexamined life is not worth living, then you will believe me still less. But that is so, my friends, though it is not easy to persuade you. . . .

Socrates is convicted and sentenced to death.

. . . Perhaps, my friends, you think that I have been convicted because I was wanting in the arguments by which I could have persuaded you to acquit me, if I had thought it right to do or to say anything to escape punishment. It is not so. I have been convicted because I was wanting, not in arguments, but in impudence and shamelessness—because I would not plead before you as you would have liked to hear me plead, or appeal to you with weeping and wailing, or say and do many other things which I maintain are unworthy of me, but which you have been accustomed to from other men. But when I was defending myself, I thought that I ought not to do anything unworthy of a free man because of the danger which I ran, and I have not changed my mind now. I would very much rather defend myself as I did, and die, than as you would have had me do, and live. . . .

And now I wish to prophesy to you, Athenians, who have condemned me. For I am going to die, and that is the time when men have most prophetic power. And I prophesy to you who have sentenced me to death that a far more severe punishment than you have inflicted on me will surely overtake you as soon as I am dead. You have done this thing, thinking that you will be relieved from having to give an account of your lives. But I say that the result will be very different. There will be more men who will call you to account, whom I have held back, though you did not recognize it. And they will be harsher toward you than I have been, for they will be younger, and you will be more indignant with them. For if you think that you will restrain men from reproaching you for not living as you should, by putting them to death, you are very much mistaken. That way of escape is neither possible nor honorable. It is much more honorable and much easier not to suppress others, but to make yourselves as good as you can. This is my parting prophecy to you who have condemned me.

REVIEW QUESTIONS

1. What is the nature of Socrates' wisdom?
2. Was Socrates a subversive force in Athenian society? Explain your answer.
3. According to Socrates, what is the true vocation of a philosopher? What price may the philosopher pay for his effort?
4. Compare and contrast the vocation of Socrates as a philosopher to that of the Hebrew prophets.
5. Why did some Athenians believe that Socrates corrupted the young?
6. What did Socrates say would be his reaction if he were offered an acquittal on the condition that he give up teaching his philosophy? What were his reasons?

11 Plato: The Philosopher-King

Plato (c. 429–347 B.C.), an Athenian aristocrat and disciple of Socrates, based his philosophy on Socrates' teachings. Plato was greatly affected by the deterioration of Athenian politics during and immediately after the Peloponnesian War. The rise of demagogues, the violent conflicts between oligarchs and democrats, and the execution of Socrates convinced Plato that Athenian democracy was a failure. His hostility toward democracy also stemmed from his upper-class background and temperament.

Socratic philosophy held promise of reforming the individual through the critical use of reason. Plato felt that the individual could not undergo a moral transformation while living in a wicked and corrupt society. For the individual to be able to achieve virtue, the state must be reformed.

Plato
THE REPUBLIC

In *The Republic*, Plato proposed organizing government in harmony with the needs of human nature. Those people who are driven by a desire for food, possessions, and sexual gratification, Plato said, should be farmers, tradesmen, or artisans. Those who are naturally courageous and assertive should be soldiers. And the few who have the capacity for wisdom—the philosophers—should be entrusted with political power.

In the ideal state, Plato asserted, the many would be ruled by the few who have a natural endowment for leadership. These philosopher-kings, the finest product of the state's carefully designed educational program, would wield absolute power: the people would lose their right to participate in political affairs, and the state would manufacture propaganda and strictly control education in order to keep the masses obedient. In exchange, the citizens would gain leaders distinguished by their rationality, wisdom, and virtue. In the form of a dialogue between Socrates and a man called Glaucon, Plato in the following reading presents his views on the character of the philosopher.

[SOCRATES] Unless either philosophers become kings in their countries or those who are now called kings and rulers come to be sufficiently inspired with a genuine desire for wisdom; unless that is to say, political power and philosophy meet together . . . there can be no rest from troubles, my dear Glaucon, for states, nor yet, as I believe, for all mankind. . . . There is no other way of happiness either for the state or for the individual. . . .

Now . . . we must, I think, define . . . whom we mean by these lovers of wisdom who, we have dared to assert, ought to be our rulers. Once we have a clear view of their character, we shall be able to defend our position by pointing to some who are naturally fitted to combine philosophic study with political leadership, while the rest of the world should accept their guidance and let philosophy alone.

[GLAUCON] Yes, this is the moment for a definition. . . .

[S] . . . One trait of the philosophic nature we may take as already granted: a constant passion for

any knowledge that will reveal to them something of that reality which endures for ever and is not always passing into and out of existence. And, we may add, their desire is to know the whole of that reality; they will not willingly renounce any part of it as relatively small and insignificant, as we said before when we compared them to the lover and to the man who covets honour.

[G] True.

[S] Is there not another trait which the nature we are seeking cannot fail to possess—truthfulness, a love of truth and a hatred for falsehood that will not tolerate untruth in any form?

[G] Yes, it is natural to expect that.

[S] It is not merely natural, but entirely necessary that an instinctive passion for any object should extend to all that is closely akin to it; and there is nothing more closely akin to wisdom than truth. So the same nature cannot love wisdom and falsehood; the genuine lover of knowledge cannot fail, from his youth up, to strive after the whole of truth.

[G] I perfectly agree.

[S] Now we surely know that when a man's desires set strongly in one direction, in every other channel they flow more feebly, like a stream

Republic of Plato translated by F. M. Cornford (1941), from pp. 178–179, 181, 190–192, 228–231, 282–283, 286, 288–289. By permission of Oxford University Press.

diverted into another bed. So when the current has set towards knowledge and all that goes with it, desire will abandon those pleasures of which the body is the instrument and be concerned only with the pleasure which the soul enjoys independently—if, that is to say, the love of wisdom is more than a mere pretence. Accordingly, such a one will be temperate and no lover of money; for he will be the last person to care about the things for the sake of which money is eagerly sought and lavishly spent.

[G] That is true.

[S] Again, in seeking to distinguish the philosophic nature, you must not overlook the least touch of meanness. Nothing could be more contrary than pettiness to a mind constantly bent on grasping the whole of things, both divine and human.

[G] Quite true.

[S] And do you suppose that one who is so high-minded and whose thought can contemplate all time and all existence will count this life of man a matter of much concern?

[G] No, he could not.

[S] So for such a man death will have no terrors.

[G] None.

[S] A mean and cowardly nature, then, can have no part in the genuine pursuit of wisdom.

[G] I think not.

[S] And if a man is temperate and free from the love of money, meanness, pretentiousness, and cowardice, he will not be hard to deal with or dishonest. So, as another indication of the philosophic temper, you will observe whether, from youth up, he is fair-minded, gentle, and sociable.

[G] Certainly.

[S] Also you will not fail to notice whether he is quick or slow to learn. No one can be expected to take a reasonable delight in a task in which much painful effort makes little headway. And if he cannot retain what he learns, his forgetfulness will leave no room in his head for knowledge; and so, having all his toil for

nothing, he can only end by hating himself as well as his fruitless occupation. We must not, then, count a forgetful mind as competent to pursue wisdom; we must require a good memory.

[G] By all means.

[S] Further, there is in some natures a crudity and awkwardness that can only tend to a lack of measure and proportion; and there is a close affinity between proportion and truth. Hence, besides our other requirements, we shall look for a mind endowed with measure and grace, which will be instinctively drawn to see every reality in its true light.

[G] Yes.

[S] Well then, now that we have enumerated the qualities of a mind destined to take its full part in the apprehension of reality, have you any doubt about their being indispensable and all necessarily going together?

[G] None whatever.

[S] Then have you any fault to find with a pursuit which none can worthily follow who is not by nature quick to learn and to remember, magnanimous and gracious, the friend and kinsman of truth, justice, courage, temperance?

Plato said that genuine philosophers are "those whose passion it is to see the truth." For Plato, unlike the Sophists, standards of beauty, justice, and goodness exist that are universally valid—that apply to all peoples at all times. Plato held that these standards are in a higher world, the realm of Forms or Ideas. This world of Forms is known only through the mind, not the senses. For example, a sculptor observes many bodies, but they all possess flaws; in his mind's eye he perceives the world of Ideas and tries to reproduce with his art the perfect human form. Plato says that the ordinary person, basing opinion on everyday experience, has an imperfect understanding of beauty, goodness, and justice, whereas the philosopher, through reason, reaches beyond sense perception to the realm of Forms and discovers truth. Such people are the natural rulers of the state; only they are capable of a correct understanding of justice; only they have the wisdom to reform the state in the best interests of all its citizens.

The distinction between a higher world of truth and a lower world of imperfection, deception, and illusion is illustrated in Plato's famous Allegory of the Cave. Plato, through the dialogue of Socrates and Glaucon, compares those persons without a knowledge of the Forms to prisoners in a dark cave.

[S] Next, said I, here is a parable to illustrate the degrees in which our nature may be enlightened or unenlightened. Imagine the condition of men living in a sort of cavernous chamber underground, with an entrance open to the light and a long passage all down the cave. Here they have been from childhood, chained by the leg and also by the neck, so that they cannot move and can see only what is in front of them, because the chains will not let them turn their heads. At some distance higher up is the light of a fire burning behind them; and between the prisoners and the fire is a track with a parapet built along it, like the screen at a puppet-show, which hides the performers while they show their puppets over the top.

[G] I see, said he.

[S] Now behind this parapet imagine persons carrying along various artificial objects, including figures of men and animals in wood or stone or other materials, which project above the parapet. Naturally, some of these persons will be talking, others silent.

[G] It is a strange picture, he said, and a strange sort of prisoners.

[S] Like ourselves, I replied; for in the first place prisoners so confined would have seen nothing of themselves or of one another, except the shadows thrown by the fire-light on the wall of the Cave facing them, would they?

[G] Not if all their lives they had been prevented from moving their heads.

[S] And they would have seen as little of the objects carried past.

[G] Of course.

[S] Now, if they could talk to one another, would they not suppose that their words referred only to those passing shadows which they saw?

[G] Necessarily.

[S] And suppose their prison had an echo from the wall facing them? When one of the people crossing behind them spoke, they could only suppose that the sound came from the shadow passing before their eyes.

[G] No doubt.

[S] In every way, then, such prisoners would recognize as reality nothing but the shadows of those artificial objects.

[G] Inevitably. . . .

To the prisoners chained in the cave, the shadows of the artificial objects constitute reality. When a freed prisoner ascends from the cave to the sunlight, he sees a totally different world. Returning to the cave, he tries to tell the prisoners that the shadows are only poor imitations of reality, but they laugh at him, for their opinions have been shaped by the only world they know. The meaning of the parable is clear: the philosophers who ascend to the higher world of Forms possess true knowledge; everyone else possesses mere opinions, deceptive beliefs, and illusions. The philosophers have a duty to guide the ignorant.

[S] Now consider what would happen if their release from the chains and the healing of their unwisdom should come about in this way. Suppose one of them were set free and forced suddenly to stand up, turn his head, and walk with eyes lifted to the light; all these movements would be painful, and he would be too dazzled to make out the objects whose shadows he had been used to see. What do you think he would say, if someone told him that what he had formerly seen was meaningless illusion, but now, being somewhat nearer to reality and turned towards more real objects, he was getting a truer view? Suppose further that he were shown the various objects being carried by and were made to say, in reply to questions, what each of them was.

Would he not be perplexed and believe the objects now shown him to be not so real as what he formerly saw?

[G] Yes, not nearly so real.

[S] And if he were forced to look at the fire-light itself, would not his eyes ache, so that he would try to escape and turn back to the things which he could see distinctly, convinced that they really were clearer than these other objects now being shown to him?

[G] Yes.

[S] And suppose someone were to drag him away forcibly up the steep and rugged ascent and not let him go until he had hauled him out into the sunlight, would he not suffer pain and vexation at such treatment, and, when he had come out into the light, find his eyes so full of its radiance that he could not see a single one of the things that he was now told were real?

[G] Certainly he would not see them all at once.

[S] He would need, then, to grow accustomed before he could see things in that upper world. At first it would be easiest to make out shadows, and then the images of men and things reflected in water, and later on the things themselves. After that, it would be easier to watch the heavenly bodies and the sky itself by night, looking at the light of the moon and stars rather than the Sun and the Sun's light in the day-time.

[G] Yes, surely.

[S] Last of all, he would be able to look at the Sun and contemplate its nature, not as it appears when reflected in water or any alien medium, but as it is in itself in its own domain.

[G] No doubt.

[S] And now he would begin to draw the conclusion that it is the Sun that produces the seasons and the course of the year and controls everything in the visible world, and moreover is in a way the cause of all that he and his companions used to see.

[G] Clearly he would come at last to that conclusion.

[S] Then if he called to mind his fellow prisoners and what passed for wisdom in his former dwelling place, he would surely think himself happy in the change and be sorry for them. They may have had a practice of honouring and commending one another, with prizes for the man who had the keenest eye for the passing shadows and the best memory for the order in which they followed or accompanied one another, so that he could make a good guess as to which was going to come next. Would our released prisoner be likely to covet those prizes or to envy the men exalted to honour and power in the Cave? Would he not feel like Homer's Achilles, that he would far sooner "be on earth as a hired servant in the house of a landless man" or endure anything rather than go back to his old beliefs and live in the old way?

[G] Yes, he would prefer any fate to such a life.

[S] Now imagine what would happen if he went down again to take his former seat in the Cave. Coming suddenly out of the sunlight, his eyes would be filled with darkness. He might be required once more to deliver his opinion on those shadows, in competition with the prisoners who had never been released, while his eyesight was still dim and unsteady; and it might take some time to become used to the darkness. They would laugh at him and say that he had gone up only to come back with his sight ruined; it was worth no one's while even to attempt the ascent. If they could lay hands on the man who was trying to set them free and lead them up, they would kill him.

[G] Yes, they would.

[S] Every feature in this parable, my dear Glaucon, is meant to fit our earlier analysis. The prison dwelling corresponds to the region revealed to us through the sense of sight, and the firelight within it to the power of the Sun. The ascent to see the things in the upper world you may take as standing for the upward journey of the soul into the region of the intelligible; then you will be in possession of what I surmise, since that is what you wish to be told.

Heaven knows whether it is true; but this, at any rate, is how it appears to me. In the world of knowledge, the last thing to be perceived and only with great difficulty is the essential Form of Goodness. Once it is perceived, the conclusion must follow that, for all things, this is the cause of whatever is right and good; in the visible world it gives birth to light and to the lord of light, while it is itself sovereign in the intelligible world and the parent of intelligence and truth. Without having had a vision of this Form no one can act with wisdom, either in his own life or in matters of state. . . .

For Plato, the perfect state, like the well-formed soul, is one governed by reason. By contrast, in the imperfect state, as in the imperfect soul, greed, selfishness, desire, and disorder predominate. Democracy is flawed, said Plato, because most people lack the ability to deal intelligently with matters of state. In the end, said Plato, the democratic state degenerates into anarchy, and the way is prepared for a tyrant. Plato viewed the tyrant as the most despicable of persons. A slave to his own passions, said Plato, the tyrant is like a lunatic who "dreams that he can lord it over all mankind and heaven besides." The character of the philosopher is the very opposite of the sick soul of the tyrant. In the following passage, Plato discusses what he regards as democracy's weaknesses.

[S] And when the poor win, the result is a democracy. They kill some of the opposite party, banish others, and grant the rest an equal share in civil rights and government, officials being usually appointed by lot.

[G] Yes, that is how a democracy comes to be established, whether by force of arms or because the other party is terrorized into giving way.

[S] Now what is the character of this new régime? Obviously the way they govern themselves will throw light on the democratic type of man.

[G] No doubt.

[S] First of all, they are free. Liberty and free speech are rife everywhere; anyone is allowed to do what he likes.

[G] Yes, so we are told.

[S] That being so, every man will arrange his own manner of life to suit his pleasure. The result will be a greater variety of individuals than under any other constitution. So it may be the finest of all, with its variegated pattern of all sorts of characters. Many people may think it the best, just as women and children might admire a mixture of colours of every shade in the pattern of a dress. At any rate if we are in search of a constitution, here is a good place to look for one. A democracy is so free that it contains a sample of every kind; and perhaps anyone who intends to found a state, as we have been doing, ought first to visit this emporium of constitutions and choose the model he likes best.

[G] He will find plenty to choose from.

[S] Here, too, you are not obliged to be in authority, however competent you may be, or to submit to authority, if you do not like it; you need not fight when your fellow citizens are at war, nor remain at peace when they do, unless you want peace; and though you may have no legal right to hold office or sit on juries, you will do so all the same if the fancy takes you. . . .

. . . When he [the democrat] is told that some pleasures should be sought and valued as arising from desires of a higher order, others chastised and enslaved because the desires are base, he will shut the gates of the citadel against the messengers of truth, shaking his head and declaring that one appetite is as good as another and all must have their equal rights. So he spends his days indulging the pleasure of the moment, now intoxicated with wine and music, and then taking to a spare diet and drinking nothing but water; one day in hard training, the next doing nothing at all, the third apparently immersed in study. Every now and then he takes a part in politics, leaping to his feet to say or do whatever comes into his head. . . . His life is subject to no order or restraint, and he has no wish to change an existence which he calls pleasant, free, and happy.

That well describes the life of one whose motto is liberty and equality. . . .

In a democratic country you will be told that liberty is its noblest possession, which makes it the only fit place for a free spirit to live in.

[G] True; that is often said.

[S] Well then, as I was saying, perhaps the insatiable desire for this good to the neglect of everything else may transform a democracy and lead to a demand for despotism. A democratic state may fall under the influence of unprincipled leaders, ready to minister to its thirst for liberty with too deep draughts of this heady wine; and then, if its rulers are not complaisant enough to give it unstinted freedom, they will be arraigned as accursed oligarchs and punished. Law-abiding citizens will be insulted as nonentities who hug their chains; and all praise and honour will be bestowed, both publicly and in private, on rulers who behave like subjects and subjects who behave like rulers. In such a state the spirit of liberty is bound to go to all lengths. . . .

. . . The parent falls into the habit of behaving like the child, and the child like the parent: the father is afraid of his sons, and they show no fear or respect for their parents, in order to assert their freedom. . . . To descend to smaller matters, the schoolmaster timidly flatters his pupils, and the pupils make light of their masters as well as of their attendants. Generally speaking, the young copy their elders, argue with them, and will not do as they are told; while the old, anxious not to be thought disagreeable tyrants, imitate the young and condescend to enter into their jokes and amusements. . . .

Putting all these items together, you can see the result: the citizens become so sensitive that they resent the slightest application of control as intolerable tyranny, and in their resolve to have no master they end by disregarding even the law, written or unwritten.

[G] Yes, I know that only too well.

[S] Such then, I should say, is the seed, so full of fair promise, from which springs despotism.

REVIEW QUESTIONS

1. According to Plato, what were the character traits a philosopher should possess? What traits should he avoid?
2. In terms of the Allegory of the Cave, what is real and what is illusion?
3. Why did Plato believe that philosophers would make the best rulers?
4. In Plato's view, what were the principal arguments against democracy? What is your assessment of his critique?

12 Aristotle: Science, Politics, and Ethics

Aristotle (384–322 B.C.) was born at Stagira, a Greek city-state on the Macedonian coast. About 367 B.C., he came to Athens to study with Plato, and he remained a member of Plato's Academy for twenty years. In 342 B.C., Philip II, king of Macedonia, invited Aristotle to tutor his son Alexander, who was then fourteen years old. When Alexander succeeded Philip and set out to conquer the Persian Empire, Aristotle left Macedonia for Athens, where he opened a school of philosophy called the Lyceum, named for a nearby temple to Apollo Lyceus. Aristotle synthesized the thought of earlier philosophers, including his teacher Plato, and was the leading authority of his day in virtually every field of knowledge.

Aristotle
HISTORY OF ANIMALS, POLITICS, AND NICOMACHEAN ETHICS

Scientific thinking encompasses both rationalism and empiricism. Rationalism—pursuit of truth through thought alone, independent of experience with the natural world—was advocated by Plato. This approach points in the direction of theoretical mathematics. Like Plato, Aristotle valued reason, but unlike his teacher he also had great respect for the concrete details of nature obtained through sense experience. In *History of Animals*, Aristotle demonstrated his empirical approach: observing nature and collecting, classifying, and analyzing data. Aristotle's empiricism is the foundation of such sciences as geology, botany, and biology. The first excerpt, a careful observation of the development of a chick embryo, illustrates Aristotle's empiricism.

When he turned to the study of politics, Aristotle also followed an empirical methodology. He undertook a series of historical studies of the constitutions of 158 Greek states. The most significant and complete study that has survived describes the constitution of Athens. On the basis of these extensive surveys, Aristotle proceeded to write *Politics*, his masterwork of political philosophy, excerpted in the second reading.

Like Socrates and Plato, Aristotle based his ethics on reason. People could achieve moral well-being, said Aristotle, when they avoided extremes of behavior and rationally chose the way of moderation. In his *Nicomachean Ethics*, dedicated to his son Nicomachus, Aristotle described the "proud man." This passage, excerpted in the third reading, sketches characteristics that make up the Greek ideal of excellence.

HISTORY OF ANIMALS

. . . With the common hen after three days and three nights there is the first indication of the embryo; with larger birds the interval being longer, with smaller birds shorter. Meanwhile the yolk comes into being, rising towards the sharp end, where the primal element of the egg is situated, and where the egg gets hatched; and the heart appears, like a speck of blood, in the white of the egg. This point beats and moves as though endowed with life, . . . and a membrane carrying bloody fibres now envelops the yolk. . . . A little afterwards the body is differentiated, at

From *The Oxford Translation of Aristotle: History of the Animals, Politics & Ethics* edited by W. D. Ross. (1925) By permission of Oxford University.

first very small and white. The head is clearly distinguished, and in it the eyes, swollen out to a great extent. This condition of the eyes lasts on for a good while, as it is only by degrees that they diminish in size and collapse. At the outset the under portion of the body appears insignificant in comparison with the upper portion. . . . The life-element of the chick is in the white of the egg, and the nutriment comes through the navel-string out of the yolk.

When the egg is now ten days old the chick and all its parts are distinctly visible. The head is still larger than the rest of its body, and the eyes larger than the head, but still devoid of vision. The eyes, if removed about this time, are found to be larger than beans, and black; if the cuticle be peeled off them there is a white and cold liquid inside, quite glittering in the sunlight, but there is no hard substance whatsoever. Such is the condition of the head and eyes. At this time also the larger internal organs are visible. . . .

About the twentieth day, if you open the egg and touch the chick, it moves inside and chirps; and it is already coming to be covered with down, when, after the twentieth day is past, the chick begins to break the shell. The head is situated over the right leg close to the flank, and the wing is placed over the head. . . .

POLITICS

In the following selection from *Politics*, Aristotle begins by defining the nature of a state and its purpose.

It is clear therefore that the state cannot be defined merely as a community dwelling in the same place and preventing its members from wrong-doing and promoting the exchange of goods and services. Certainly all these must be present if there is to be a state, but even the presence of every one of them does not *ipso facto* [by that fact] make a state. The state is intended to enable all, in their households and their kinships, to live *well*, meaning by that a full and satisfying life. . . .

. . . "Where ought the sovereign power of the state to reside?" With the people? With the propertied classes? With the good? With one man, the best of all the good? With one man, the tyrant? There are objections to all these. Thus suppose we say the people is the supreme authority, then if they use their numerical superiority to make a distribution of the property of the rich, is not that unjust? It has been done by a valid decision of the sovereign power, yet what can we call it save the very height of injustice? Again, if the majority, having laid their hands on everything, distribute the possessions of the few, they are obviously destroying the state. But that cannot be goodness which destroys its possessor and justice cannot be destructive of the

state. So it is clear that this process, though it may be the law, cannot be just. Or, if that is just, the actions taken by a tyrant must be just; his superior power enables him to use force, just as the masses force their will on the rich. Thirdly, if it is just for the few and wealthy to rule, and if they too rob and plunder and help themselves to the goods of the many, is that just? If it is, then it is just in the former case also. The answer clearly is that all these three are bad and unjust. The fourth alternative, that the good should rule and have the supreme authority, is also not free from objection; it means that all the rest must be without official standing, debarred from holding office under the constitution. The fifth alternative, that one man, the best, should rule, is no better; by making the number of rulers fewer we leave still larger numbers without official standing. It might be objected too that it is a bad thing for any human being, subject to all possible disorders and affections of the human mind, to be the sovereign authority, which ought to be reserved for the law itself. . . .

. . . [A]t the moment it would seem that the most defensible, perhaps even the truest, answer to the question would be to say that the majority ought to be sovereign. . . . For where there are many people, each has some share of goodness and intelligence, and when these are brought together, they become as it were one multiple man with many pairs of feet and hands and many minds. So too in regard to character and powers of perception. That is why the general public is a better judge of works of music and poetry; some judge some parts, some others, but their joint pronouncement is a verdict upon the whole. . . .

Aristotle seeks to determine what is the best constitution. His conclusion reflects the premise developed in his *Ethics* that moderation, or the middle way, is the path to virtue in all things. So, Aristotle says that in forming a constitution for the state, power should reside in the hands of the middle class rather than the aristocracy or the poor.

If we were right when in our *Ethics* we stated that Virtue is a Mean and that the happy life is life free and unhindered and according to virtue, then the best life must be the middle way, [or the mean] . . . between two extremes which it is open to those at either end to attain. And the same principle must be applicable to the goodness or badness of cities and states. For the constitution of a city is really the way it lives.

In all states there are three sections of the community—the very well-off, the very badly off, and those in between. Seeing therefore that it is agreed that moderation and a middle position are best, it is clear that in the matter of possessions to own a middling amount is best of all. This condition is most obedient to reason, and following reason is just what is difficult both for the exceedingly rich, handsome, strong, and well-born, and for the opposite, the extremely poor, the weak, and the downtrodden. The former commit deeds of violence on a large scale, the latter are delinquent and wicked in petty ways. The misdeeds of the one class are due to *hubris* [overweening pride, arrogance], the misdeeds of the other to rascality. . . . There are other drawbacks about the two extremes. Those who have a super-abundance of all that makes for success, strength, riches, friends, and so forth, neither wish to hold office nor understand the work; and this is ingrained in them from childhood on; even at school they are so full of their superiority that they have never learned to do what they are told. Those on the other hand who are greatly deficient in these qualities are too subservient. So they cannot command and can only obey in a servile régime, while the others cannot obey in any régime and can command only in a master-slave relationship. The result is a state not of free men but of slaves and masters, the one full of envy, the other of contempt. Nothing could be farther removed from friendship or from the whole idea of a shared partnership in a state. . . . The state aims to consist as far as possible of those who are like and equal, a condition found chiefly among the middle section. . . . The middle class is also the steadiest element, the least eager for change. They neither covet, like the poor, the possessions of others, nor do others covet theirs, as the poor covet those of the rich. . . .

It is clear then both that the political partnership which operates through the middle class is best, and also that those cities have every chance of being well-governed in which the middle class is large, stronger if possible than the other two together, or at any rate stronger than one of them. . . . For this reason it is a happy state of affairs when those who take part in the life of the state have a moderate but adequate amount of property. . . . Tyranny often emerges from an over-enthusiastic democracy or from an oligarchy, but much more rarely from middle-class constitutions or from those very near to them.

The superiority of the middle type of constitution is clear also from the fact that it alone is free from fighting among factions. Where the middle element is large, there least of all arise faction and counter-faction among citizens. . . .

NICOMACHEAN ETHICS

The following selection from *Ethics* shows how Aristotle's ethical theory rests on the principles of moderation and balance. Aristotle notes that some people become "angry at the wrong things, more than is right, and longer, and cannot be appeased until they inflict vengeance or punishment." On the other extreme, foolish and slavish people endure every insult without defending themselves. Between these extremes is the proud man, "who is angry at the right thing and with the right people, and, as he ought, when he ought, and as long as he ought." Even-tempered and moderate in all things, such a man "tends to be unperturbed and not to be led by passion."

. . . In the first place, then, as has been said, the proud man is concerned with honours; yet he will also bear himself with moderation towards wealth and power and all good or evil fortune, whatever may befall him, and will be neither over-joyed by good fortune nor over-pained by evil. For not even towards honour does he bear himself as if it were a very great thing. . . .

He does not run into trifling dangers, nor is he fond of danger, because he honours few things; but he will face great dangers, and when he is in danger he is unsparing of his life, knowing that there are conditions on which life is not worth having. And he is the sort of man to confer benefits, but he is ashamed of receiving them; for the one is the mark of a superior, the other of an inferior. And he is apt to confer greater benefits in return; for thus the original benefactor besides being paid will incur a debt to him, and will be the gainer by the transaction. They seem also to remember any service they have done, but not those they have received (for he who receives a service is inferior to him who has done it, but the proud man wishes to be superior), and to hear of the former with pleasure, of the latter with displeasure. . . . It is a mark of the proud man also to ask for nothing or scarcely anything, but to give help readily, and to be dignified towards people who enjoy high position and good fortune, but unassuming towards those of the middle class; for it is a difficult and lofty thing to be superior to the former, but easy to be so to the latter, and a lofty bearing over the former is no mark of ill-breeding, but among humble people it is as vulgar as a display of strength against the weak. Again, it is characteristic of the proud man not to aim at the things commonly held in honour, or the things in which others excel; to be sluggish and to hold back except where great honour or a great work is at stake, and to be a man of few deeds, but of great and notable ones. He must also be open in his hate and in his love (for to conceal one's feelings, i.e., to care less for truth than for what people will think, is a coward's part), and must speak and act openly; for he is free of speech because he is contemptuous, and he is given to telling the truth, except when he speaks in irony to the vulgar. He must be unable to make his life revolve round another, unless it be a friend; for this is slavish, and for this reason all flatterers are servile, and people lacking in self-respect are flatterers. Nor is he given to admiration; for nothing to him is great. Nor is he mindful of wrongs; for it is not the part of a proud man to have a long memory, especially for wrongs, but rather to overlook them. Nor is he a gossip; for he will speak neither about himself nor about another, since he cares not to be praised nor for others to be blamed; nor again is he given to praise; and for the same reason he is not an evil-speaker, even about his enemies, except from haughtiness. With regard to necessary or small matters he is least of all men given to lamentation or the asking of favours; for it is the part of one who takes such matters seriously to behave so with respect to them. He is one who will possess beautiful and profitless things rather than profitable and useful ones; for this is more proper to a character that suffices to itself.

Further, a slow step is thought proper to the proud man, a deep voice, and a level utterance; for the man who takes few things seriously is not likely to be hurried, nor the man who thinks nothing great to be excited, while a shrill voice and a rapid gait are the results of hurry and excitement.

Such, then, is the proud man; the man who falls short of him is unduly humble, and the man who goes beyond him is vain.

REVIEW QUESTIONS

1. What evidence in Aristotle's description of a chick's embryo development illustrates his use of empirical methods of scientific inquiry?
2. Why did Aristotle believe that state power was best left in the hands of the middle classes? Why did he fear government by the poor, the tyrant, the few, the good, or the rich?
3. According to Aristotle, how did the "proud man," a man of excellence, relate to others? To worldly success and riches?
4. What kind of moral values did the proud man cultivate?
5. Aristotle urged both self-sufficiency and moderation as guiding principles in human life. In what specific ways would the proud man demonstrate these virtues?

13 Hellenistic Culture:
Rationalism, Universalism, and Individualism

During the Hellenistic Age, Greek civilization spread to the Near East in the wake of Alexander's conquests, and Mesopotamian, Egyptian, Persian, and Jewish traditions—particularly religious beliefs—moved westward. Thousands of Greeks settled in newly established cities throughout the ancient Near East, carrying with them Greek urban institutions and culture—laws, cults, educational methods, artistic and architectural styles, customs, and dress. The new Hellenistic cities were dominated by a Greek upper class, which recruited native non-Greeks to its ranks to the degree that they became *Hellenized*—that is, they adopted the Greek language and lifestyle. Through intermarriage, education in Greek schools, and the prospect of political and economic advantage, non-Greeks came to participate in and contribute to a common Greek civilization that spread from the western Mediterranean to the Indus River.

Cultural exchange permeated all phases of cultural life. Sculpture showed the influence of many lands. Historians wrote world histories, not just local ones. Greek astronomers worked with data collected over the centuries by the Babylonians. Greeks increasingly demonstrated a fascination with Near Eastern religious cults. Philosophers helped to break down the barriers between peoples by asserting that all inhabit a single fatherland. As the philosopher Crates said, "My fatherland has no single tower, no single roof. The whole earth is my citadel, a home ready for us all to live in."

Plutarch
CULTURAL FUSION

The Greek biographer Plutarch (c. A.D. 46–120) provides a glowing account of Alexander the Great in the following passage. Plutarch saw Alexander as a philosopher in action and an apostle of universalism and human brotherhood. Many modern historians reject this assessment of Alexander's intentions, but the scope of his conquests and their significance in reducing the distinctions between Near Easterners and Greeks remain impressive.

[W]hen Alexander was civilizing Asia, Homer was commonly read, and the children of the Persians, of the Susianians, and of the Gedrosians[1] learned to chant the tragedies of Sophocles and Euripides. . . . yet through Alexander Bactria[2] and the Caucasus learned to revere

[1]The Susianians lived in and near the city of Susa, the capital of the Persian Empire; the Gedrosians lived just north of the Arabian Sea, in what is now southeastern Iran and western Pakistan. —Eds

[2]Bactria, a northeastern province of the ancient Persian Empire, was located in the area of modern Afghanistan and Central Asia. —Eds

the gods of the Greeks. Plato wrote a book on the One Ideal Constitution, but because of its forbidding character he could not persuade anyone to adopt it; but Alexander established more than seventy cities among savage tribes, and sowed all Asia[3] with Grecian magistracies, and thus overcame its uncivilized and brutish manner of living. Although few of us read Plato's *Laws*, yet hundreds of thousands have made use of Alexander's laws, and continue to use them. Those who were vanquished by Alexander are happier than those who escaped his hand; for these had no one to put an end to the wretchedness of their existence, while the victor compelled those others to lead a happy life. . . . Thus Alexander's new subjects would not have been civilized, had they not been vanquished; Egypt would not have its Alexandria, nor Mesopotamia its Seleuceia, nor Sogdiana its Prophthasia, nor India its Bucephalia,[4] nor the Caucasus a Greek city hard by; for by the founding of cities in these places savagery was extinguished and the worse element, gaining familiarity with the better, changed under its influence. If, then, philosophers take the greatest pride in civilizing and rendering adaptable the intractable and untutored elements in human character, and if Alexander has been shown to have changed the savage natures of countless tribes, it is with good reason that he should be regarded as a very great philosopher.

Moreover, the much-admired *Republic* of Zeno, the founder of the Stoic sect, may be summed up in this one main principle: that all the inhabitants of this world of ours should not live differentiated by their respective rules of justice into separate cities and communities, but that we should consider men to be of one community and one polity, and that we should have a common life and an order common to us all, even as a herd that feeds together and shares the pasturage of a common field. This Zeno wrote, giving shape to a dream or, as it were, shadowy picture of a well-ordered and philosophic commonwealth; but it was Alexander who gave effect to the idea. For Alexander did not follow Aristotle's advice to treat the Greeks as if he were their leader, and other peoples as if he were their master; to have regard for the Greeks as for friends and kindred, but to conduct himself toward other peoples as though they were plants or animals; for to do so would have been to cumber his leadership with numerous battles and banishments and festering seditions. But, as he believed that he came as a heaven-sent governor to all, and as a mediator for the whole world, those whom he could not persuade to unite with him, he conquered by force of arms, and he brought together into one body all men everywhere, uniting and mixing in one great loving-cup, as it were, men's lives, their characters, their marriages, their very habits of life. He bade them all consider as their fatherland the whole inhabited earth, as their stronghold and protection his camp, as akin to them all good men, and as foreigners only the wicked; they should not distinguish between Grecian and foreigner by Grecian cloak and targe [shield], or scimitar [curved sword] and jacket; but the distinguishing mark of the Grecian should be seen in virtue, and that of the foreigner in iniquity; clothing and food, marriage and manner of life they should regard as common to all, being blended into one by ties of blood and children. . . .

[3]"All Asia" referred to western Asia Minor at first, then, as Alexander's conquests spread further, the term was broadened to include the other territory to the east, extending to what is now India and Central Asia. —Eds

[4]Seleuceia (named for one of Alexander's generals) was near modern Baghdad. Prophthasia, a city founded by Alexander, was in Sogdiana, north of modern Afghanistan. Bucephalia, on a northern branch of the Indus River, was named for Alexander's horse Bucephalus. —Eds

. . . For he did not overrun Asia like a robber nor was he minded to tear and rend it, as if it were booty and plunder bestowed by unexpected good fortune, after the manner in which Hannibal later descended upon Italy. . . . But Alexander desired to render all upon earth subject to one law of reason and one form of government and to reveal all men as one people, and to this purpose he made himself conform. But if the deity that sent down Alexander's soul into this world of ours had not recalled him quickly, one law would govern all mankind, and they all would look toward one rule of justice as though toward a common source of light. But as it is, that part of the world which has not looked upon Alexander has remained without sunlight.

Philo of Alexandria
JEWISH APPRECIATION OF GREEK CULTURE AND SYNTHESIS OF REASON AND REVELATION

Like other Near Eastern people, the Jews—both in Judea and the Diaspora (Jews who lived outside Palestine)—came under the influence of Hellenism. As Greek settlements sprang up in Judea, Jews had increasing contact with Greek soldiers, artisans, and merchants. Some Jewish scholars came to admire the rich Greek philosophical tradition. The Hebrew scriptures were translated into Greek for use by Greek-speaking Jews, Greek words entered the Hebrew language, and newly constructed synagogues employed Hellenistic architectural styles. Radical Hellenizers, mainly prosperous aristocrats, adopted Greek games, dress, entertainment, and eating habits; these efforts to assimilate pagan ways were resisted by simple folk and the devout who clung tenaciously to Mosaic law. Thus Greek influences both enriched Hebrew culture and threatened its integrity.

Living in the cosmopolitan world of Alexandria dominated by Greek thought and culture, Alexandrian Jews felt compelled to demonstrate that their faith was not incompatible with reason, that there was no insurmountable gulf separating Mosaic religion from Greek philosophy. The leading figure in this effort to explain and justify the Hebrew scriptures in terms of Greek philosophy—to prove that Mosaic law, revealed by God, was compatible with truth discovered by natural reason—was Philo of Alexandria (c. 20 B.C.–A.D. 50). Scion of a wealthy, aristocratic Jewish family, Philo was intimately familiar with the Greek cultural tradition and greatly admired Plato. He believed that Plato's view of God, as presented in the *Timaeus*, was compatible with Hebrew scripture. In that work Plato had posited an eternal God who had existed prior to his creation of the world and continued to exist as an incorporeal and transcendent being.

On several points Philo disagreed with Greek philosophy. For example, holding that only God was eternal, he could not accept the Platonic view of the eternity of Ideas or Forms. Nor could he accept the position of Greek philosophy that the laws of nature were inexorable, for this precluded divine miracles. In these and other instances, Philo skillfully used the tools of Greek logic to harmonize differing viewpoints. His blending of Platonism with scripture would be continued by Christian thinkers who also admired Philo's achievement.

In the following selections from *Preliminary Studies in Philosophy*, Philo expresses his admiration for Greek culture.

There was a time when I had leisure for philosophy and for the contemplation of the universe and its contents, when I made its spirit my own in all its beauty and loveliness and true blessedness, when my constant companions were divine themes and verities, wherein I rejoiced with a joy that never cloyed or sated. I had no base or abject thoughts nor grovelled in search of reputation or of wealth or bodily comforts, but seemed always to be borne aloft into the heights with a soul possessed by some God-sent inspiration, a fellow-traveller with the sun and moon and the whole heaven and universe. Ah then I gazed down from the upper air, and straining the mind's eye beheld, as from some commanding peak, the multitudinous world-wide spectacles of earthly things, and blessed my lot in that I had escaped by main force from the plagues of mortal life. But, as it proved, my steps were dogged by the deadliest of mischiefs, the hater of the good, envy, which suddenly set upon me and ceased not to pull me down with violence till it had plunged me in the ocean of civil cares, in which I am swept away, unable even to raise my head above the water. Yet amid my groans I hold my own, for, planted in my soul from my earliest days I keep the yearning for culture which ever has pity and compassion for me, lifts me up and relieves my pain. To this I owe it that sometimes I raise my head and with the soul's

eyes—dimly indeed because the mist of extraneous affairs has clouded their clear vision—I yet make shift to look around me in my desire to inhale a breath of life pure and unmixed with evil. And if unexpectedly I obtain a spell of fine weather and a calm from civil turmoils, I get me wings and ride the waves and almost tread the lower air, wafted by the breezes of knowledge which often urges me to come to spend my days with her [philosophy], a truant as it were from merciless masters in the shape not only of men but of affairs, which pour in upon me like a torrent from different sides. Yet it is well for me to give thanks to God even for this, that though submerged I am not sucked down into the depths, but can also open the soul's eyes, which in my despair of comforting hope I thought had now lost their sight, and am irradiated by the light of wisdom, and am not given over to lifelong darkness. So behold me daring, not only to read the sacred messages of Moses, but also in my love of knowledge to peer into each of them and unfold and reveal what is not known to the multitude.

———

. . . For instance when first I was incited by the goads of philosophy to desire her I consorted in early youth with one of her handmaids, Grammar, and all that I begat by her, writing, reading and study of the writings of the poets, I dedicated to her mistress. And again I kept company with another, namely Geometry, and was charmed with her beauty, for she shewed symmetry and proportion in every part. Yet I took none of her children for my private use, but brought them as a gift to the lawful wife. Again my ardour moved me to keep company with a third; rich in rhythm, harmony and melody was she, and her name was Music, and from her I begat diatonics, chromatics and enharmonics, conjunct and disjunct melodies, conforming with the consonance of the fourth, fifth or octave intervals. And again of none of these did I make a secret hoard, wishing to see the lawful wife a lady of wealth with a host of servants ministering to her.

Philo sought to demonstrate the truth of Judaism to a non-Jewish culture. In the selection below, he employs the categories of Greek philosophy to provide proof for God's existence and his creation of the universe.

Doubtless hard to unriddle and hard to apprehend is the Father and Ruler of all, but that is no reason why we should shrink from searching for Him. But in such searching two principal questions arise which demand the consideration of the genuine philosopher. One is whether the Deity exists, a question necessitated by those who practise atheism, the worst form of wickedness, the other is what the Deity is in essence. Now to answer the first question does not need much labour, but the second is not only difficult but perhaps impossible to solve. Still, both must be examined.

We see then that any piece of work always involves the knowledge of a workman. Who can look upon statues or painting without thinking at once of a sculptor or painter? Who can see clothes or ships or houses without getting the idea of a weaver and a shipwright and a housebuilder? And when one enters a well-ordered city in which the arrangements for civil life are very admirably managed, what else will he suppose but that this city is directed by good rulers? So then he who comes to the truly Great City, this world, and beholds hills and plains teeming with animals and plants, the rivers, spring-fed or winter torrents, streaming along, the seas with their expanses, the air with its happily tempered phases, the yearly seasons passing into each other, and then the sun and moon ruling the day and night, and the other heavenly bodies fixed or planetary and the whole firmament revolving in rhythmic order, must he not naturally or rather necessarily gain the conception of the Maker and Father and Ruler also? For none of the works of human art is self-made, and the highest art and knowledge is shewn in this universe, so that surely it has been wrought by one of excellent knowledge and absolute perfection. In this way we have gained the conception of the existence of God.

Epicurus
SELF-SUFFICIENCY

Hellenistic philosophy marks a second stage in the evolution of Greek thought. In the Hellenic Age, philosophers dealt primarily with the individual's relationship to the city-state. In the Hellenistic Age, philosophers were concerned with defining the individual's relationship to a wider, often competitive and hostile community that consisted of a variety of peoples and cultures. In particular, the later philosophers sought to help people become ethically self-sufficient so that they could attain peace of mind in such an environment. Among the most significant schools of philosophy that emerged during the Hellenistic Age were Stoicism (see pages 107, 136) and Epicureanism.

Epicureanism was named for its founder, Epicurus (341–270 B.C.), who established a school at Athens in 307 or 306 B.C. To achieve peace of mind, taught

Epicurus, one should refrain from worrying about death or pleasing the gods, avoid intense involvements in public affairs, cultivate friendships, and pursue pleasure prudently. The following excerpts from Epicurus' works reveal his prescription for achieving emotional well-being. The passages have been grouped according to particular subjects.

THE GODS

. . . We must grasp this point, that the principal disturbance in the minds of men arises because they think that these celestial bodies are blessed and immortal, and yet have wills and actions and motives inconsistent with these attributes; and because they are always expecting or imagining some everlasting misery [inflicted on them by the gods], such as is depicted in legends, or even fear the loss of feeling in death . . . and, again, because they are brought to this pass not by reasoned opinion, but rather by some irrational presentiment . . . and, by learning the true causes of celestial phenomena and all other occurrences that come to pass from time to time, we shall free ourselves from all which produces the utmost fear in other men.

———

It is vain to ask of the gods what a man is capable of supplying for himself.

DEATH

. . . So death, the most terrifying of ills, is nothing to us, since so long as we exist, death is not with us; but when death comes, then we do not exist. It does not then concern either the living or the dead, since for the former it is not, and the latter are no more.

But the many at one moment shun death as the greatest of evils, at another yearn for it as a respite from the evils in life. But the wise man neither seeks to escape life nor fears the cessation of life, for neither does life offend him nor does the absence of life seem to be any evil. And

———

Epicurius, *The Extant Remains*, translated by Cyril Bailey (1926) from pp. 53, 83, 89, 97, 101, 115, 117, 119. By permission of Oxford University Press.

just as with food he does not seek simply the larger share and nothing else, but rather the most pleasant, so he seeks to enjoy not the longest period of time, but the most pleasant.

REASON AND PHILOSOPHY

Let no one when young delay to study philosophy, nor when he is old grow weary of his study. For no one can come too early or too late to secure the health of his soul. And the man who says that the age for philosophy has either not yet come or has gone by is like the man who says that the age for happiness is not yet come to him, or has passed away. Wherefore both when young and old a man must study philosophy, that as he grows old he may be young in blessings through the grateful recollection of what has been and that in youth he may be old as well, since he will know no fear of what is to come. We must then meditate on the things that make our happiness, seeing that when that is with us we have all, but when it is absent we do all to win it.

———

A man cannot dispel his fear about the most important matters if he does not know what is the nature of the universe but suspects the truth of some mythical story. So that without natural science it is not possible to attain our pleasures unalloyed.

———

We must not pretend to study philosophy, but study it in reality: for it is not the appearance of health that we need, but real health.

LIVING WELL

When, therefore, we maintain that pleasure is the end, we do not mean the pleasures of profligates and those that consist in sensuality, as is supposed by some who are either ignorant or disagree with us or do not understand, but freedom from pain in the body and from trouble in the mind. For it is not continuous drinkings and revellings, nor the satisfaction of lusts, nor the enjoyment of fish and other luxuries of the wealthy table, which produce a pleasant life, but sober reasoning, searching out the motives for all choice and avoidance, and banishing mere opinions, to which are due the greatest disturbance of the spirit.

Of all this the beginning and the greatest good is prudence. Wherefore prudence is a more precious thing even than philosophy; for from prudence are sprung all the other virtues, and it teaches us that it is not possible to live pleasantly without living prudently and honourably and justly. . . .

———

Of all the things which wisdom acquires to produce the blessedness of the complete life, far the greatest is the possession of friendship.

———

We must release ourselves from the prison of affairs and politics.

———

A free life cannot acquire many possessions, because this is not easy to do without servility to mobs or monarchs. . . .

———

The noble soul occupies itself with wisdom and friendship. . . .

———

The first measure of security is to watch over one's youth and to guard against what makes havoc of all by means of pestering desires.

REVIEW QUESTIONS

1. According to Plutarch, what benefits did Alexander confer on the peoples he conquered?
2. In Plutarch's view, how did Alexander's policies reflect Stoic philosophic ideals?
3. What Hellenistic elements are revealed in the writings of Philo of Alexandria?
4. Why were some Jews attracted to Greek philosophy? Why were others repelled?
5. What did Epicurus believe were the chief causes of emotional distress among human beings?
6. What advice did he offer for achieving inner peace and happiness?
7. How did Epicurean teachings both continue and break with traditional Greek values?

CHAPTER 4

The Roman Republic

A ROMAN WARSHIP WITH LEGIONNAIRES, on a relief from the Temple of Fortuna Primigenia, first century B.C. Roman soldiers fought on sea as well as on land, conquering nations throughout the Mediterranean area during the eras of the Republic and the Empire. *(Scala / Art Resource, NY)*

The city-state was the foundation of Greek society in the Hellenic Age; in the Hellenistic Age, Greek cities became subordinate to kingdoms, larger political units ruled by autocratic monarchs. Hellenistic philosophers conceived of a still broader political arrangement: a world-state in which people of different nationalities were bound together by the ties of common citizenship and law that applied to all. It was Rome's great achievement to construct such a world-state.

Roman history falls into two broad periods—the Republic and Empire. The Roman Republic began in 509 B.C. with the overthrow of the Etruscan monarchy and lasted until 27 B.C., when Augustus (formerly Octavian) became in effect the first Roman emperor, ending almost five hundred years of republican self-government. For the next five hundred years, Rome would be governed by emperors.

In 264 B.C., when the Roman Republic had established dominion over the Italian peninsula, there were four other great powers in the Mediterranean world: Carthage controlled North Africa, Corsica, Sardinia, and parts of Spain and Sicily. The other powers—Macedonia, Egypt, and Syria—were the three Hellenistic kingdoms carved out of the empire of Alexander the Great. By 146 B.C., Rome had emerged victorious over the other powers, and by 30 B.C. these Mediterranean lands were all Roman provinces.

The Roman Republic, which had conquered a vast empire, was destroyed not by foreign armies but by internal weaknesses. In the century after Tiberius Gracchus' assassination in 133 B.C. (see pages 120–121), the Senate, which had governed Rome well during its march to empire, degenerated into a self-seeking oligarchy; it failed to resolve critical domestic problems and fought to preserve its own power and prestige. When Rome had been threatened by foreign enemies, all classes united in a spirit of patriotism. This social harmony broke down when the threat from outside diminished, and the Republic was torn by internal dissension and civil war.

1 Rome's March to World Empire

By 146 B.C., Rome had become the dominant state in the Mediterranean world. Roman expansion had occurred in three main stages: the uniting of the Italian peninsula, which gave Rome the manpower that transformed it from a city-state into a great power; the collision with Carthage, from which Rome emerged as ruler of the western Mediterranean; and the subjugation of the Hellenistic states, which brought Romans in close contact with Greek civilization. As Rome expanded territorially, its leaders enlarged their vision. Instead of restricting citizenship to people having ethnic kinship, Rome assimilated other peoples into its political community. Just as law had grown to cope with the earlier grievances of the plebeians, so it adjusted to the new situations resulting from the creation of a multinational empire. The city of Rome was evolving into the city of humanity—the cosmopolis envisioned by the Stoics.

Polybius
THE ROMAN ARMY

The discipline and dedication of the citizen-soldiers help explain Rome's success in conquering a world empire. In the following account, Polybius (c. 200–c. 118 B.C.) tells how the commanders enforced obedience and fostered heroism.

A court-martial composed of the tribunes immediately sits to try him [a soldier], and if he is found guilty, he is punished by beating (*fustuarium*). This is carried out as follows. The tribune takes a cudgel and lightly touches the condemned man with it, whereupon all the soldiers fall upon him with clubs and stones, and usually kill him in the camp itself. But even those who contrive to escape are no better off. How indeed could they be? They are not allowed to return to their homes, and none of their family would dare to receive such a man into the house. Those who have once fallen into this misfortune are completely and finally ruined. The *optio* [lieutenant] and the *decurio* [sergeant] of the squadron are liable to the same punishment if they fail to pass on the proper orders at the proper moment to the patrols and the *decurio* of the next squadron. The consequence of the extreme severity of this penalty and of the absolute impossibility of avoiding it is that the night watches of the Roman army are faultlessly kept.

The ordinary soldiers are answerable to the tribunes [elected military administrators] and the tribunes to the consuls [commanders]. A tribune, and in the case of the allies a prefect [commander of a large unit], has power to inflict fines, distrain on [confiscate] goods, and

to order a flogging. The punishment of beating to death is also inflicted upon those who steal from the camp, those who give false evidence, those who in full manhood commit homosexual offences, and finally upon anyone who has been punished three times for the same offence. The above are the offences which are punished as crimes. The following actions are regarded as unmanly and dishonourable in a soldier: to make a false report to the tribune of your courage in the field in order to earn distinction; to leave the post to which you have been assigned in a covering force because of fear; and similarly to throw away out of fear any of your weapons on the field of battle. For this reason the men who have been posted to a covering force are often doomed to certain death. This is because they will remain at their posts even when they are overwhelmingly outnumbered on account of their dread of the punishment that awaits them. Again, those who have lost a shield or a sword or any other weapon on the battlefield often hurl themselves upon the enemy hoping that they will either recover the weapon they have lost, or else escape by death from the inevitable disgrace and the humiliations they would suffer at home.

If it ever happens that a large body of men break and run in this way and whole maniples [units of 120 to 300 men] desert their posts under extreme pressure, the officers reject the idea of beating to death or executing all who are guilty, but the solution they adopt is as

Polybius The Rise of the Roman Empire, translated by Ian Scott-Kilvert, selected with an introduction by F. W. Walbank, pp. 332–335. (Penguin Classics, 1979) Copyright © Ian Scott-Kilvert, 1979. Reproduced by permission of Penguin Books Ltd.

effective as it is terrifying. The tribune calls the legion [large military unit] on parade and brings to the front those who are guilty of having left the ranks. He then reprimands them sharply, and finally chooses by lot some five or eight or twenty of the offenders, the number being calculated so that it represents about a tenth[1] of those who have shown themselves guilty of cowardice. Those on whom the lot has fallen are mercilessly clubbed to death in the manner I have already described. The rest are put on rations of barley instead of wheat, and are ordered to quarter themselves outside the camp in a place which has no defences. The danger and the fear of drawing the fatal lot threatens every man equally, and since there is no certainty on whom it may fall, and the public disgrace of receiving rations of barley is shared by all alike, the Romans have adopted the best possible practice both to inspire terror and to repair the harm done by any weakening of their warlike spirit.

The Romans also have an excellent method of encouraging young soldiers to face danger. Whenever any have especially distinguished themselves in a battle, the general assembles the troops and calls forward those he considers to have shown exceptional courage. He praises them first for their gallantry in action and for anything in their previous conduct which is particularly worthy of mention, and then he distributes gifts such as the following: to a man who has wounded one of the enemy, a spear; to one who has killed and stripped an enemy, a cup if he is in the infantry, or horse-trappings if in the cavalry—originally the gift was simply a lance. These presentations are not made to men who have wounded or stripped an enemy in the course of a pitched battle, or at the storming of a city, but to those who during a skirmish or some similar situation in which there is no necessity to engage in single combat, have voluntarily and deliberately exposed themselves to danger.

At the storming of a city the first man to scale the wall is awarded a crown of gold. In the same way those who have shielded and saved one of their fellow-citizens or of the allies are honoured with gifts from the consul, and the men whose lives they have preserved present them of their own free will with a crown; if not, they are compelled to do so by the tribunes who judge the case. Moreover, a man who has been saved in this way reveres his rescuer as a father for the rest of his life and must treat him as if he were a parent. And so by means of such incentives even those who stay at home feel the impulse to emulate such achievements in the field no less than those who are present and see and hear what takes place. For the men who receive these trophies not only enjoy great prestige in the army and soon afterwards in their homes, but they are also singled out for precedence in religious processions when they return. On these occasions nobody is allowed to wear decorations save those who have been honoured for their bravery by the consuls, and it is the custom to hang up the trophies they have won in the most conspicuous places in their houses, and to regard them as proofs and visible symbols of their valour. So when we consider this people's almost obsessive concern with military rewards and punishments, and the immense importance which they attach to both, it is not surprising that they emerge with brilliant success from every war in which they engage.

---

[1]This custom is the origin of the word *decimate*, from the Latin *decem*, "ten."—Eds.

REVIEW QUESTIONS

1. How did the Romans ensure good discipline among their soldiers?
2. What factors mentioned by Polybius help explain Rome's emergence as a great power?

2 The Punic Wars

In 264 B.C., Rome, which had just completed its conquest of Italy, went to war with Carthage, the dominant power in the western Mediterranean. A threat to the north Sicilian city of Messana (now Messina) was the immediate cause of the war. Rome feared that Carthage might use Messana as a springboard from which to attack the cities of southern Italy, which were allied to Rome, or to interfere with their trade. The First Punic War (264–241 B.C.) was a grueling conflict; drawing manpower from its loyal allies, Rome finally prevailed. Carthage surrendered Sicily to Rome, and three years later Rome seized the large islands of Corsica and Sardinia, west of Italy, from a weakened Carthage.

Livy
THE SECOND PUNIC WAR: THE THREAT FROM HANNIBAL

Carthaginian expansion in Spain led to the Second Punic War (218–201 B.C.). The Carthaginian army was led by Hannibal (247–183 B.C.), whose military genius impressed and frightened Rome. Hannibal brought the battle to Rome by leading his seasoned army, including war elephants, across the Alps into Italy.

Hannibal demonstrated his superb generalship at the battle of Cannae in 216 B.C., where the Carthaginians destroyed a Roman army of sixty thousand. Hannibal removed some of his soldiers in the center and commanded the thin line to retreat as the Romans charged. Believing that the enemy was on the run, the Romans continued their headlong thrust into the Carthaginian center. Then, according to plan, Carthaginian troops stationed on the wings attacked the Roman flanks and the cavalry closed in on the Roman rear, completely encircling the Roman troops. News of the disaster, one of the worst in the Republic's history, brought anguish to Romans, who feared that Hannibal would march on the capital itself. Adding to Rome's distress was the desertion of some of its Italian allies to Hannibal. In the following passage, the Roman historian Livy (59 B.C.–A.D. 17) describes the mood in Rome after Cannae.

. . . Never, without an enemy actually within the gates, had there been such terror and confusion in the city [Rome]. To write of it is beyond my strength, so I shall not attempt to describe what any words of mine would only make less than the truth. In the previous year a consul and his army had been lost at Trasimene [location of an overwhelming defeat for Rome], and now there was news not merely of another similar blow, but of a multiple calamity—two consular armies annihilated, both consuls[1] dead, Rome left without a force in the field, without a

Livy, *The War with Hannibal*, translated by Aubrey de Selincourt, pp. 154–156, 165. Copyright © 1965 The Estate of Aubrey de Selincourt. Reprinted by permission of Penguin Books Ltd.

[1]The consuls served dual offices as elected magistrates of Rome in peacetime and commanders-in-chief of the Roman army. —Eds.

commander, without a single soldier, Apulia and Samnium [two provinces in southern Italy] in Hannibal's hands, and now nearly the whole of Italy overrun. No other nation in the world could have suffered so tremendous a series of disasters, and not been overwhelmed. It was unparalleled in history: the naval defeat off the Aegates islands,[2] a defeat which forced the Carthaginians to abandon Sicily and Sardinia and suffer themselves to pay taxes and tribute to Rome; the final defeat in Africa to which Hannibal himself afterwards succumbed—neither the one nor the other was in any way comparable to what Rome had now to face, except in the fact that they were not borne with so high a courage.

The praetors[3] Philus and Pomponius summoned the Senate[4] to meet . . . to consider the defence of the City, as nobody doubted that Hannibal, now that the armies were destroyed, would attack Rome—the final operation to crown his victory. It was not easy to work out a plan: their troubles, already great enough, were made worse by the lack of firm news; the streets were loud with the wailing and weeping of women, and nothing yet being clearly known, living and dead alike were being mourned in nearly every house in the city. In these circumstances, Quintus Fabius Maximus[5] put forward some proposals: riders, he suggested, lightly equipped, should be sent out along the Appian and Latin Ways[6] to question any survivors they might meet roaming the countryside, and report any tidings they could get from them of what had happened to the consuls and the armies. If the gods, in pity for the empire, had suffered any of the Roman name to survive, they should inquire where they were, where Hannibal went after the battle, what his plans were, what he was doing, and what he was likely to do next. The task of collecting this information should be entrusted to vigorous and active men. There was also a task, Fabius suggested, for the Senate itself to perform, as there was a lack of public officers: this was, to get rid of the general confusion in the city and restore some sort of order. Women must be forbidden to appear out of doors, and compelled to stay in their homes; family mourning should be checked, and silence imposed everywhere; anyone with news to report should be taken to the praetors, and all individuals should await in their homes the news which personally concerned them. Furthermore, guards should be posted at the gates to prevent anyone from leaving the city, and every man and woman should be made to believe that there was no hope of safety except within the walls of Rome. Once, he ended, the present noise and disorder were under control, then would be the proper time to recall the Senate and debate measures for defence.

The proposals of Fabius won unanimous support. The city magistrates cleared the crowds out of the forum and the senators went off to restore some sort of order in the streets. . . .

How much more serious was the defeat at Cannae than those which had preceded it can be seen by the behaviour of Rome's allies: before that fatal day their loyalty had remained unshaken; now it began to waver, for the simple reason that they despaired of the survival of Roman power. The following peoples went over to the Carthaginian cause: the Atellani, Calatini, Hirpini, some of the Apulians, all the Samnites except the Pentri, the Bruttii, the Lucanians, the Uzentini, and nearly all the Greek settlements on the coast, namely Tarentum, Metapontum, Croton, and Locri, and all the Gauls on the Italian side of the Alps.

But neither the defeats they had suffered nor the subsequent defection of all these allied peoples moved the Romans ever to breathe a word about peace.

---

[2]The end of the First Punic War in 241 B.C.

[3]Praetors were magistrates who governed the city of Rome when the consuls were absent. —Eds.

[4]The Senate, originally drawn from the patrician caste, was the true ruler of Rome. It advised the magistrates on all matters of public policy. —Eds.

[5]Fabius (Quintus Fabius Maximus Verrucosus, nicknamed "the Delayer," d. 203 B.C.) was elected consul several times, but his tactics in trying to avoid pitched battles displeased the Romans. However, Fabius' successors were totally defeated at Cannae, and Fabius, elected consul for the fifth time, recaptured Tarentum in 209. —Eds.

[6]The Appian Way, parts of which exist today, was the main highway from Rome southward to Campania. The Latin Way (*Via Latina*), a parallel route, passed through hill towns before rejoining the Appian Way. —Eds.

Appian of Alexandria
THE THIRD PUNIC WAR:
THE DESTRUCTION OF CARTHAGE

Despite his brilliant victory at Cannae, Hannibal lacked the manpower to deal Rome a knockout blow, and the Romans, respecting Hannibal's generalship, refused to engage his army in another major encounter. Finally, when Rome invaded North Africa and threatened Carthage, Hannibal quit Italy to defend his homeland and was defeated at the battle of Zama in 202 B.C.

Although Carthage, now a second-rate power, no longer posed a threat, Rome started the Third Punic War in 149 B.C. Driven by old hatreds and the traumatic memory of Hannibal's near conquest of Italy, Rome resolved to destroy Carthage. After Carthage fell in 146 B.C., Rome sold the survivors into slavery, obliterated the city, and turned the land into a province, which was named Africa. The savage and irrational behavior of Rome toward a helpless Carthage showed an early deterioration in senatorial leadership. In the following passage, Appian of Alexandria (A.D. 95–c. 165) describes the destruction of Carthage by the Romans under Scipio Aemilianus (185–129 B.C.).

Now Scipio hastened to the attack of Byrsa, the strongest part of the city [of Carthage], where the greater part of the inhabitants had taken refuge. There were three streets ascending from the forum to this fortress, along which, on either side, were houses built closely together and six stories high, from which the Romans were assailed with missiles. They were compelled, therefore, to possess themselves of the first ones and use those as a means of expelling the occupants of the next. When they had mastered the first, they threw timbers from one to another over the narrow passageways, and crossed as on bridges. While war was raging in this way on the roofs, another fight was going on among those who met each other in the streets below. All places were filled with groans, shrieks, shouts, and every kind of agony. Some were stabbed, others were hurled alive from the roofs to the pavement, some of them alighting on the heads of spears or other pointed weapons, or swords. No one dared to set fire to

the houses on account of those who were still on the roofs, until Scipio reached Byrsa. Then he set fire to the three streets all together, and gave orders to keep the passageways clear of burning material so that the army might move back and forth freely.

Then came new scenes of horror. As the fire spread and carried everything down, the soldiers did not wait to destroy the buildings little by little, but all in a heap. So the crashing grew louder, and many corpses fell with the stones into the midst. Others were seen still living, especially old men, women, and young children who had hidden in the inmost nooks of the houses, some of them wounded, some more or less burned, and uttering piteous cries. Still others, thrust out and falling from such a height with the stones, timbers, and fire, were torn asunder in all shapes of horror, crushed and mangled. Nor was this the end of their miseries, for the street cleaners, who were removing the rubbish with axes, mattocks, and forks, and making the roads passable, tossed with these instruments the dead and the living together into holes in the ground, dragging them along like sticks and stones and

The Roman History of Appian of Alexandria, trans. Horace White (London: Macmillan, 1899), vol. 1, pp. 229–232.

turning them over with their iron tools. Trenches were filled with men. Some who were thrown in head foremost, with their legs sticking out of the ground, writhed a long time. Others fell with their feet downward and their heads above ground. Horses ran over them, crushing their faces and skulls, not purposely on the part of the riders, but in their headlong haste. Nor did the street cleaners do these things on purpose; but the tug of war, the glory of approaching victory, the rush of the soldiery, the orders of the officers, the blast of the trumpets, tribunes and centurions[1] marching their cohorts hither and thither—all together made everybody frantic and heedless of the spectacles under their eyes.

Six days and nights were consumed in this kind of fighting, the soldiers being changed so that they might not be worn out with toil, slaughter, want of sleep, and those horrid sights. . . .

Scipio, beholding this city, which had flourished 700 years from its foundation and had ruled over so many lands, islands, and seas, rich with arms and fleets, elephants and money, equal to the mightiest monarchies but far surpassing them in bravery and high spirit (since without ships or arms, and in the face of famine, it had sustained continuous war for three years), now come to its end in total destruction— Scipio, beholding this spectacle, is said to have shed tears and publicly lamented the fortune of the enemy. After meditating by himself a long time and reflecting on the rise and fall of cities, nations, and empires, as well as of individuals, upon the fate of Troy, that once proud city, upon that of the Assyrians, the Medes, and the Persians, greatest of all, and later the splendid Macedonian empire, either voluntarily or otherwise the words of the poet escaped his lips:—

"The day shall come in which our
    sacred Troy
And Priam,[2] and the people over whom
Spear-bearing Priam rules, shall perish all."

Being asked by Polybius in familiar conversation (for Polybius had been his tutor) what he meant by using these words, he said that he did not hesitate frankly to name his own country, for whose fate he feared when he considered the mutability of human affairs. And Polybius wrote this down just as he heard it came to Rome and increased Roman knowledge of Hellenic culture.

---

[1]Centurions were noncommissioned officers, each commanding a hundred men; attached to each legion were six military tribunes, who had been voted in by the citizens of Rome in the general elections. —Eds.

[2]Priam, in Homer's epic poem *The Iliad*, was the king of Troy at the time of the Trojan War. —Eds.

REVIEW QUESTIONS

1. Describe the mood in Rome after the battle of Cannae.
2. After the Roman disaster at Cannae, what actions did Quintus Fabius Maximus propose?
3. What do you think prompted Scipio Aemilianus to quote the lines from Homer's *Iliad*?

---

3 The Spread of Greek Philosophy to Rome

One of the chief consequences of Roman expansion was growing contact with Greek culture. During the third century B.C., Greek civilization started to exercise an increasing and fruitful influence on the Roman mind. Greek teachers, both slave and free, came to Rome and increased Roman knowledge of Hellenic culture.

As they conquered the eastern Mediterranean, Roman generals began to ship libraries and works of art from Greek cities to Rome. Roman sculpture and painting imitated Greek prototypes. In time, Romans acquired from Greece knowledge of scientific thought, medicine, and geography. Roman writers and orators used Greek history, poetry, and oratory as models. Roman philosophers borrowed the ideas of Greek philosophical schools and adapted them to Roman culture.

Lucretius
DENUNCIATION OF RELIGION

The writings of the Greek philosopher Epicurus soon won admirers in Rome. Lucretius (c. 96–c. 55 B.C.), the leading Roman Epicurean philosopher, lived in a time of civil war, which was fostered by two generals, Marius and Sulla. Distraught by the seemingly endless strife, Lucretius yearned for philosophical tranquillity. Like Epicurus, he believed that religion prompted people to perform evil deeds and caused them to experience terrible anxiety about death and eternal punishment. Like his mentor, Lucretius advanced a materialistic conception of nature, one that left no room for the activity of gods—mechanical laws, not the gods, governed all physical happenings. To dispel the fear of punishment after death, Lucretius marshaled arguments to prove that the soul perishes with the body. He proposed that the simple life, devoid of political involvement and excessive passion, was the highest good. Epicurus' disparagement of politics and public service and rejection of the goals of power and glory ran counter to the accepted Roman ideal of virtue. On the other hand, his praise of the quiet life amid a community of friends and his advice on how to deal with life's misfortunes with serenity had great appeal to first-century Romans who were disgusted with civil strife.

The following selection from *On the Nature of Things* shows Lucretius' hostility to religion. In the first excerpt, Lucretius admires Epicurus, "the first to stand firm in defiance" of the fables about the gods.

When before our eyes man's life lay groveling,
    prostrate,
Crushed to the dust under the burden of Religion
(Which thrust its head from heaven, its
    horrible face
Glowering over mankind born to die),
One man, a Greek [Epicurus], was the first
    mortal who dared
Oppose his eyes, the first to stand firm in
    defiance.

Not the fables of gods, nor lightning, nor the
    menacing
Rumble of heaven could daunt him, but all
    the more
They whetted his keen mind with longing to be
First to smash open the tight-barred gates of
    Nature.
His vigor of mind prevailed. . . .
Religion now lies trampled beneath our feet,
And we are made gods by the victory.

Lucretius, *On the Nature of Things: De rerum natura,* trans. Anthony M. Esolen, pp. 26–27, 191–193. © 1995 The Johns Hopkins University Press. Reprinted with permission of The Johns Hopkins University Press.

Lucretius attempts to explain why people came to believe in powerful gods.

How the idea of gods spread to all nations,
Stocking their cities with altars and making
    men tremble
To undertake the solemn rites, which flourish
With all our luxury and magnificence
(Even now sowing in us the seeds of horror,
Urging us on to rear across the world
New shrines to the gods to crowd on festival days),
Is not hard to explain in a few words.
In those days mortal men saw while awake
The excellent countenances of the gods,
Or rather in dreams they gasped at their vast
    size.
Men lent sensation to these giant forms
For they moved their limbs, it seemed, and
    spoke proud words
As arrogant as their beauty and great strength.
Eternal life they gave them, for their faces
And their physiques persisted ever-present,
And they thought that beings endowed with
    such great power
Could never be put to rout by any force.
They thought the gods preeminently blest,
For the fear of death could hardly trouble them;
Also because in dreams they saw them do
Miraculous things, and many, without an effort.
Then too they saw the systems of the sky
Turn in sure order, and the changing seasons,
But could not understand why this occurred.
Their refuge, then: assign to the gods all things,
Have them steer all things with a single nod.
In the heavens they placed the holy haunts of
    the gods. . . .

Unhappy human race—to grant such feats
To gods, and then to add vindictiveness!
What wailing did they bring forth for
    themselves,
What wounds for us, what tears for our
    descendants!
It's no piety to be seen at every altar,
To cover your head and turn to the stone idol,
Or to flatten yourself on the ground and lift
    your palms
To the shrines, or to spray altars with the blood
Of cattle—so much!—or to string vow on vow.
To observe all things with a mind at peace

Is piety. For when we look up to the heavenly
Shrines of this great world, the stars that
    glitter, the sky
Studded, when we think of the journeying sun
    and moon,
Then in hearts heavy-laden with other cares
Trouble is roused to boot, and rears its
    head—
That the limitless power of gods, the power
    that wheels
The stars and planets, may be aimed at us.
Then ignorance assails the mind in doubt
About the universe's origin,
About the end, how long the walls of the world
Can suffer the straining of such stir and motion,
Or whether, granted everlasting health
By the gods, they can in endless course disdain
The turning age and the vast strength of time.
And worse, whose soul does not contract in fear
Of the gods, whose limbs don't crawl with
    terror when
The scorched earth under the terrible
    lightning bolt
Quakes, and a grumbling rolls through the
    great sky?
Don't people and nations tremble, and
    arrogant kings
Cringe, stricken into shock by fear of the gods,
Lest for some foul deed done or proud word said
The heavy time has come to pay the price?
When a high hard gale across the plains of the sea
Rakes a commander and his fleet along
With all his mighty elephants and legions,
Won't he beseech the "Peace of the Gods" in
    terror
And pray for peaceful breezes and fair winds?
In vain, for the whirlpool's got him anyway
And borne him down unto the shoals of
    Death.
So thoroughly is human grandeur crushed
By a hidden force; the glorious rods and axes,
Those splendid mockeries, are trampled under.
Well, when the whole earth staggers underfoot
And cities are battered and fall, or threaten to fall,
What wonder if self-loathing seizes men
And they grant wondrous power over all affairs
To gods, to steer and rule the universe?

Cicero
ADVOCATE OF STOICISM

Marcus Tullius Cicero (106–43 B.C.), a leading Roman statesman, was also a distinguished orator, an unsurpassed Latin stylist, and a student of Greek philosophy. His letters, more than eight hundred of which have survived, provide modern historians with valuable insights into late-republican politics. His orations before the Senate and law courts have been models of eloquence and rhetorical technique for students of Latin and later European languages.

Like many other Romans, Cicero was influenced by the Greek philosophy of Stoicism. Cicero adopted the Stoic belief that natural law governs the universe and applies to all and that all belong to a common humanity. The gift of reason, which is common to all people, enables us to comprehend this natural law and to order our lives in accordance with its principles, which are unchangeable and eternal. Natural law as understood by right reason commands people to do what is right and deters them from doing what is wrong. Thus there is a unity of knowledge and virtue. For Cicero, the laws of the state should accord with the natural law underlying the universe. Adherence to such rationally formulated laws creates a moral bond among citizens and the peoples of all nations and states. In the following passage from his philosophic treatise *The Laws*, Cicero explores the implications of the Stoic concept of natural law.

. . . Now let us investigate the origins of Justice.

Well then, the most learned men have determined to begin with Law, and it would seem that they are right, if, according to their definition, Law is the highest reason, implanted in Nature, which commands what ought to be done and forbids the opposite. This reason, when firmly fixed and fully developed in the human mind, is Law. And so they believe that Law is intelligence whose natural function it is to command right conduct and forbid wrongdoing. . . . [T]he origin of Justice is to be found in Law, for

Reprinted by permission of the publishers and the Trustees of the Loeb Classical Library from *Cicero: Volume XVI, De Republica, De Legibus*, Loeb Classical Library Volume 213, translated by Clinton W. Keyes, Cambridge, Mass.: Harvard University Press, 1936, pp. 317, 319, 321, 323, 325, 329, 331, 333. Copyright © 1936 by the President and Fellows of Harvard College. The Loeb Classical Library® is a registered trademark of the President and Fellows of Harvard College.

Law is a natural force; it is the mind and reason of the intelligent man, the standard by which Justice and Injustice are measured. But since our whole discussion has to do with the reasoning of the populace, it will sometimes be necessary to speak in the popular manner, and give the name of law to that which in written form decrees whatever it wishes, either by command or prohibition. For such is the crowd's definition of law. But in determining what Justice is, let us begin with that supreme Law which had its origin ages before any written law existed or any State had been established.

. . . I shall seek the root of Justice in Nature, under whose guidance our whole discussion must be conducted.

. . . [T]hat animal which we call man, endowed with foresight and quick intelligence, complex, keen, possessing memory, full of reason and prudence, has been given a certain distinguished status by the supreme God who created him; for he is the only one among so many different kinds and varieties of living beings who has a share in reason and thought, while all the rest are deprived of it. But what is more divine, I will not say in man only, but in all heaven and earth, than reason? And reason, when it is full grown and perfected, is rightly called wisdom. Therefore, since there is nothing better than reason, and since it exists both in man and God, the first common possession of man and God is reason. But those who have reason in common must also have right reason in common. And since right reason is Law, we must believe that men have Law also in common with the gods. Further, those who share Law must also share Justice; and those who share these are to be regarded as members of the same commonwealth. If indeed they obey the same authorities and powers, this is true in a far greater degree; but as a matter of fact they do obey this celestial system, the divine mind, and the God of transcendent power. Hence we must now conceive of this whole universe as one commonwealth of which both gods and men are members.

Moreover, virtue exists in man and God alike, but in no other creature besides; virtue, however, is nothing else than Nature perfected and developed to its highest point; therefore there is a likeness between man and God. As this is true, what relationship could be closer or clearer than this one? For this reason, Nature has lavishly yielded such a wealth of things adapted to man's convenience and use that what she produces seems intended as a gift to us, and not brought forth by chance; and this is true, not only of what the fertile earth bountifully bestows in the form of grain and fruit, but also of the animals; for it is clear that some of them have been created to be man's slaves, some to supply him with their products, and others to serve as his food. Moreover innumerable arts have been discovered through the teachings of Nature; for it is by a skilful imitation of her that reason has acquired the necessities of life. . . .

. . . [O]ut of all the material of the philosophers' discussions, surely there comes nothing more valuable than the full realization that we are born for Justice, and that right is based, not upon men's opinions, but upon Nature. This fact will immediately be plain if you once get a clear conception of man's fellowship and union with his fellow-men. For no single thing is so like another, so exactly its counterpart, as all of us are to one another. Nay, if bad habits and false beliefs did not twist the weaker minds and turn them in whatever direction they are inclined, no one would be so like his own self as all men would be like all others. And so, however we may define man, a single definition will apply to all. This is a sufficient proof that there is no difference in kind between man and man; for if there were, one definition could not be applicable to all men; and indeed reason, which alone raises us above the level of the beasts and enables us to draw inferences, to prove and disprove, to discuss and solve problems, and to come to conclusions, is certainly common to us all, and, though varying in what it learns, at least in the capacity to learn it is invariable. For the same things are invariably perceived by the senses, and those things which stimulate the senses, stimulate them in the same way in all men; and those rudimentary beginnings of intelligence to which I have referred, which are imprinted on our minds, are imprinted on all minds alike; and speech, the mind's interpreter, though differing in the choice of words, agrees in the sentiments expressed. In fact, there is no human being of any race who, if he finds a guide, cannot attain to virtue.

Cato the Elder
HOSTILITY TO GREEK PHILOSOPHY

Some conservative Romans were hostile to the Greek influence, which threatened, they felt, traditional Roman values. Cato the Elder (also "the Censor"; 234–149 B.C.) denounced Socrates for undermining respect for Athenian law and warned that Greek philosophy might lure Roman youth into similar subversive behavior. The following passage is by Plutarch, the second-century A.D. Greek biographer; it shows Cato's hostility to Greek philosophy.

He was now grown old, when Carneades the Academic, and Diogenes the Stoic, came as deputies from Athens to Rome, praying for release from a penalty of five hundred talents laid on the Athenians, in a suit, to which they did not appear, in which the Oropians were plaintiffs and Sicyonians[1] judges. All the most studious youth immediately waited on these philosophers, and frequently, with admiration, heard them speak. But the gracefulness of Carneades's oratory, whose ability was really greatest, and his reputation equal to it, gathered large and favourable audiences, and ere long filled, like a wind, all the city with the sound of it. So that it soon began to be told that a Greek, famous even to admiration, winning and carrying all before him, had impressed so strange a love upon the young men, that quitting all their pleasures and pastimes, they ran mad, as it were, after philosophy; which indeed much pleased the Romans in general; nor could they but with much pleasure see the youth receive so welcomely the Greek literature, and frequent the company of learned men. But Cato, on the other side, seeing the passion for words flowing into the city, from the beginning took it ill, fearing lest the youth should be diverted that way, and so should prefer the glory of speaking well before that of arms and doing

well. And when the fame of the philosophers increased in the city, and Caius Acilius, a person of distinction, at his own request, became their interpreter to the senate at their first audience, Cato resolved, under some specious pretence, to have all philosophers cleared out of the city; and, coming into the senate, blamed the magistrates for letting these deputies stay so long a time without being despatched, though they were persons that could easily persuade the people to what they pleased; that therefore in all haste something should be determined about their petition, that so they might go home again to their own schools, and declaim to the Greek children, and leave the Roman youth to be obedient, as hitherto, to their own laws and governors.

Yet he did this not out of any anger, as some think, to Carneades; but because he wholly despised philosophy, and out of a kind of pride scoffed at the Greek studies and literature; as, for example, he would say, that Socrates was a prating, seditious fellow, who did his best to tyrannise over his country, to undermine the ancient customs, and to entice and withdraw the citizens to opinions contrary to the laws. Ridiculing the school of Isocrates,[2] he would add,

---

"Life of Cato the Elder," from Plutarch, *Plutarch's Lives: The Translation Called Dryden's*, corrected from the Greek and revised by A. H. Clough (Boston: Little Brown & Co., 1875), vol. 2, pp. 345–347.

[1]The Oropians came from the town of Oropus in east-central Greece. Sicyonians came from the city of Sicyon in southern Greece. —Eds
[2]Isocrates (436–338 B.C.) was an Athenian orator whose students distinguished themselves as orators, historians, and statesmen. —Eds

that his scholars grew old men before they had done learning with him, as if they were to use their art and plead causes in the court of Minos in the next world. And to frighten his son from anything that was Greek, in a more vehement tone than became one of his age, he pronounced, as it were, with the voice of an oracle, that the Romans would certainly be destroyed when they began once to be infected with Greek literature; though time indeed has shown the vanity of this his prophecy; as, in truth, the city of Rome has risen to its highest fortune while entertaining Grecian learning. Nor had he an aversion only against the Greek philosophers, but the physicians also; for having, it seems, heard how Hippocrates, when the king of Persia sent for him, with offers of a fee of several talents, said, that he would never assist barbarians who were enemies of the Greeks; he affirmed, that this was now become a common oath taken by all physicians, and enjoined his son to have a care and avoid them.

REVIEW QUESTIONS

1. Why was Lucretius critical of religion?
2. According to Lucretius, why did people first begin to believe in gods? Compare his view to that of Critias (p. 52).
3. What is Cicero's view on the nature of law? What conclusions does he derive from it?
4. Why does Cicero conclude that the sense of justice is common to all humans? What implication does he draw from this conclusion?
5. Why did Cato fear Carneades in particular and Greek thought in general?

4   Exploitation of the Provinces

The Greeks expressed their genius in philosophy and the arts, the Romans in government and law. Rome generally allowed its subjects a large measure of self-government, respected local religions and customs, and reduced the constant warfare that had plagued the Mediterranean world. But there was also a negative side to Roman rule. The conquest of a great number of lands and peoples gave the Roman ruling class innumerable opportunities to enhance their wealth by exploiting the empire's subjects. Senators appointed to govern provinces frequently amassed large fortunes through bribery, extortion, the confiscation of properties, and the enslavement and sale of the captured populace.

Efforts by provincial victims to seek justice by prosecuting the malefactors before the extortion court in Rome were often thwarted by collusion between the senators accused and the senators who served as judges and jurors. One such case was the trial of Gaius Verres, ex-governor of Sicily, who was prosecuted for his crimes by Cicero. Expecting the worst, Verres fled Rome before a verdict was reached. Found guilty, he was fined *in absentia*.

Cicero
ORATION AGAINST VERRES

Cicero, acting on behalf of the Sicilians, portrays Verres' crimes while the defendant was governor of Sicily. He links them to the greater problem of the disastrous decline in the moral reputation and authority of the whole senatorial order.

. . . Nothing, he declares, is too sacred to be corrupted by money; nothing too strong to resist its attack. If the secrecy with which his projects are put into effect were comparable to the criminality which inspires their design, he might, to some extent or at some stage, have kept them from my notice. But so far, conveniently enough, his unbelievable unscrupulousness has been matched by a peculiar degree of folly. He has grabbed his wealth without any attempt at concealment; and he has let everyone see the schemes and intrigues by which he hopes to corrupt his judges. . . .

But the most conspicuous and numerous instances and demonstrations of his criminality come from his governorship in Sicily. For three long years he so thoroughly despoiled and pillaged the province that its restoration to its previous state is out of the question. A succession of honest governors, over a period of many years, could scarcely achieve even a partial rehabilitation. While Verres was governor the Sicilians enjoyed the benefit neither of their own laws, nor of the Roman Senate's decrees, nor even of the rights to which everyone in the world is entitled. All the property that anyone in Sicily still has for his own today is merely what happened to escape the attention of this avaricious lecher, or survived his glutted appetites.

In Sicily, during those three years, not a single lawsuit was decided without his connivance. Inheritances from a father or grandfather, however authentic, were cancelled — if Verres said the word. Under a new and immoral ruling, the properties of farmers were robbed of countless sums. Allies of unassailable loyalty were treated as enemies; Roman citizens were tortured and put to death like slaves. Criminals of the deepest dye would bribe their way to acquittal, while men of impeccable honesty were prosecuted in their absence, and convicted and banished unheard. Powerfully fortified harbours, great and well-protected cities, were left open for pirates and robbers to attack. Sicilian soldiers and sailors, allies and friends of ours, were starved to death. Splendid, beautifully equipped fleets were squandered and thrown away. It was an appalling disgrace for our country.

Then again, ancient monuments given by wealthy monarchs to adorn the cities of Sicily, or presented or restored to them by victorious Roman generals, were ravaged and stripped bare, one and all, by this same governor. Nor was it only statues and public monuments that he treated in this manner. Among the most sacred and revered Sicilian sanctuaries, there was not a single one which he failed to plunder; not one single god, if only Verres detected a good work of art or a valuable antique, did he leave in the possession of the Sicilians.

When I turn to his adulteries and similar outrages, considerations of decency deter me from giving details of these loathsome manifestations of his lusts. Besides, 1 do not want, by describing them, to worsen the calamities of the people who have not been permitted to save their children and their wives from Verres' sexual passions. It is, however, incontestable that he himself did not take the slightest precaution to prevent these abominations from becoming universally known. On the contrary, 1 believe that every man alive who has heard the name of Verres would be able to recount the atrocities which he has committed. . . .

Cicero Selected Works, translated by Michael Grant (Baltimore: Penguin Books, 1960), pp. 38–39, 41–42, 52–53. Reprinted by permission of Penguin Books Ltd.

. . . When Gaius Verres was in Sicily, a number of people heard him saying this sort of thing on various occasions: "I have a powerful friend! Whatever I steal from the province, I am sure he will protect me. My intention is not just to make money for myself: I have mapped out the three years of my Sicilian governorship like this. I shall consider myself to be doing nicely if I can earmark one year's profits for my own use, the second year's for my protectors and counsel, and the whole of the third year's — the richest and most lucrative — for the judges who try me!" . . .

In God's name, gentlemen, I pray you to devote all your care and all your foresight to facing this situation. It is evident to me, and I give you solemn warning, that heaven itself has vouchsafed you this opportunity of rescuing our entire Order from its present unpopularity, disgrace, ill-fame, and scandal.

REVIEW QUESTIONS

1. What crimes did Cicero attribute to Verres?
2. What danger did he see in such behavior by Roman officials?

---

5 Roman Slavery

Slavery was practiced in ancient times, in many lands, and among most peoples. Although conditions might vary in detail from place to place, essentially a slave was considered legally to be a piece of property, not a person with normal citizen rights. Age, sex, skills, ethnic origin, demeanor, appearance, and personal character determined a slave's value in the marketplace. The status of slave was usually hereditary, but a person might be enslaved for debt or as a penalty for crime. Pirates would kidnap and sell their captives as slaves. But the most common source of slaves was defeated people captured during wars. They were assigned to all kinds of work, and their labors were vital in sustaining the luxury and leisure of the Roman upper classes. Even families of modest fortunes could usually afford a slave to do domestic chores, to help farm, or to assist in the family's business or craft.

Diodorus Siculus
SLAVES: TORMENT AND REVOLT

The Roman war machine created hundreds of thousands of slaves during the last centuries of the Republic and the early centuries of the imperial age. Under the Republic, the Romans were notably harsh toward slaves; until the full influence of Greek Stoic philosophy penetrated the governing class, little was done to protect them from the absolute power of their Roman masters. Diodorus Siculus, a Greek historian, describes the condition of Roman slaves toiling in silver and gold mines in Iberia (present-day Spain) and then tells of an uprising of slaves that lasted from 135 to 132 B.C.

THE ORDEAL OF SLAVES IN THE MINES

. . . After the Romans had made themselves masters of Iberia, a multitude of Italians have swarmed to the mines and taken great wealth away with them, such was their greed. For they purchase a multitude of slaves whom they turn over to the overseers of the working of the mines; and these men, opening shafts in a number of places and digging deep into the ground, seek out the seams of earth which are rich in silver and gold; and not only do they go into the ground a great distance, but they also push their diggings many stades [measure equalling about 607 feet] in depth and run galleries off at every angle, turning this way and that, in this manner bringing up from the depths the ore which gives them the profit they are seeking. . . .

But to continue with the mines, the slaves who are engaged in the working of them produce for their masters revenues in sums defying belief, but they themselves wear out their bodies both by day and by night in the diggings under the earth, dying in large numbers because of the exceptional hardships they endure. For no respite or pause is granted them in their labours, but compelled beneath blows of the overseers to endure the severity of their plight, they throw away their lives in this wretched manner, although certain of them who can endure it, by virtue of their bodily strength and their persevering souls, suffer such hardships over a long period; indeed death in their eyes is more to be desired than life, because of the magnitude of the hardships they must bear.

A SLAVE REVOLT IN SICILY

There was never a sedition of slaves so great as that which occurred in Sicily, whereby many cities met with grave calamities, innumerable men and women, together with their children, experienced the greatest misfortunes, and all the island was in danger of falling into the power of fugitive slaves. . . .

. . . The Servile [slave] War broke out for the following reason. The Sicilians, having shot up in prosperity and acquired great wealth, began to purchase a vast number of slaves, to whose bodies, as they were brought in droves from the slave markets, they at once applied marks and brands. The young men they used as cowherds, the others in such ways as they happened to be useful. But they treated them with a heavy hand in their service, and granted them the most meagre care, the bare minimum for food and clothing. . . .

The slaves, distressed by their hardships, and frequently outraged and beaten beyond all reason, could not endure their treatment. Getting together as opportunity offered, they discussed the possibility of revolt, until at last they put their plans into action. . . . The beginning of the whole revolt took place as follows.

There was a certain Damophilus of Enna [a city in central Sicily], a man of great wealth but insolent of manner; he had abused his slaves to excess, and his wife Megallis vied even with her husband in punishing the slaves and in her general inhumanity towards them. The slaves, reduced by this degrading treatment to the level of brutes, conspired to revolt and to murder their masters. Going to Eunus [a Syrian slave believed to be a seer and magician] they asked him whether their resolve had the favour of the gods. He, resorting to his usual mummery, promised them the favour of the gods, and soon persuaded them to act at once. Immediately, therefore, they brought together four hundred of their fellow slaves and, having armed themselves in such ways as opportunity permitted, they fell upon the city of Enna, with Eunus at their head and working his miracle of the flames of fire for their benefit. When they found their way into the houses they shed much blood, sparing not even suckling babes. Rather they tore them from the breast and dashed them to the ground, while as for the women—and under their husbands' very eyes—but words cannot tell the extent of their outrages and acts of lewdness! By now a great multitude of slaves from the city had joined them, who, after first demonstrating against their own masters their utter ruthlessness, then turned to the slaughter of others. When Eunus and his men learned that Damophilus and his wife were in the garden that lay near the city, they sent some of their band and dragged them off, both the man and his wife, fettered and with hands bound behind their backs, subjecting them to many outrages along the way. Only in the case of the couple's daughter were the slaves seen to show consideration throughout, and this was because of her kindly nature, in that to the extent of her power she was always compassionate and ready to succour the slaves. Thereby it was demonstrated that the others were treated as they were, not because of some "natural savagery of slaves," but rather in revenge for wrongs previously received. The men appointed to the task, having dragged Damophilus and Megallis into the city, as we said, brought them to the theatre, where the crowd of rebels had assembled. But when Damophilus attempted to devise a plea to get them off safe and was winning over many of the crowd with his words, Hermeias and Zeuxis, men bitterly disposed towards him, denounced him as a cheat, and without waiting for a formal trial by the assembly the one ran him through the chest with a sword, the other chopped off his head with an axe. Thereupon Eunus was chosen king, not for his manly courage or his ability as a military leader, but solely for his marvels and his setting of the revolt in motion. . . .

Established as the rebels' supreme commander, he called an assembly and put to death all the citizenry of Enna except for those who were skilled in the manufacture of arms: these he put in chains and assigned them to this task. He gave Megallis to the maidservants to deal with as they might wish; they subjected her to torture and threw her over a precipice. He himself murdered his own masters, Antigenes and Pytho. Having set

a diadem upon his head, and arrayed himself in full royal style, he proclaimed his wife queen (she was a fellow Syrian and of the same city), and appointed to the royal council such men as seemed to be gifted with superior intelligence. . . .

. . . In three days Eunus had armed, as best he could, more than six thousand men, besides others in his train who had only axes and hatchets, or slings, or sickles, or fire-hardened stakes, or even kitchen spits; and he went about ravaging the countryside. Then, since he kept recruiting untold numbers of slaves, he ventured even to do battle with Roman generals, and on joining combat repeatedly overcame them with his superior numbers, for he now had more than ten thousand soldiers.

Soon after, engaging in battle with a general arrived from Rome, Lucius Hypsaeus [the Roman governor], who had eight thousand Sicilian troops, the rebels were victorious, since they now numbered twenty thousand. Before long their band reached a total of two hundred thousand,[1] and in numerous battles with the Romans they acquitted themselves well, and failed but seldom. As word of this was bruited about, a revolt of one hundred and fifty slaves, banded together, flared up in Rome, of more than a thousand in Attica, and of yet others in Delos [an island off the southeastern Greek coast] and many other places. But thanks to the speed with which forces were brought up and to the severity of their punitive measures, the magistrates of these communities at once disposed of the rebels and brought to their senses any who were wavering on the verge of revolt. In Sicily, however, the trouble grew. Cities were captured with all their inhabitants, and many armies were cut to pieces by the rebels, until Rupilius, the Roman commander, recovered Tauromenium [Taormina] for the Romans by placing it under strict siege and confining the rebels under conditions of unspeakable duress and famine: conditions such that, beginning by eating the children, they progressed to the women, and did not altogether abstain even from eating one another. . . .

---

[1]The ancients often exaggerated numbers; the slaves probably raised an army of some 70,000.—Eds.

Finally, after Sarapion, a Syrian, had betrayed the citadel, the general laid hands on all the runaway slaves in the city, whom, after torture, he threw over a cliff. From there he advanced to Enna, which he put under siege in much the same manner, bringing the rebels into extreme straits and frustrating their hopes. . . . Rupilius captured this city also by betrayal, since its strength was impregnable to force of arms. Eunus, taking with him his bodyguards, a thousand strong, fled in unmanly fashion. . . .

. . . He met such an end as befitted his knavery, and died at Morgantina [in central Sicily]. Thereupon Rupilius, traversing the whole of Sicily with a few picked troops, sooner than had been expected rid it of every nest of robbers.

Appian of Alexandria
THE REVOLT OF SPARTACUS

In 73 B.C., gladiators led by Spartacus broke out of their barracks and were joined by tens of thousands of runaways. Spartacus aimed to escape from Italy to Gaul and Thrace (northeast of Greece), the homelands—Spartacus was a Thracian—of many slaves. The slave army, which grew to perhaps as many as 120,000, defeated Roman armies and devastated southern Italy before the superior might of Rome prevailed. Some six thousand of the defeated slaves were tortured and crucified on the road from Capua to Rome. The following account of the rebellion was written by Appian of Alexandria in the second century A.D.

In Italy, at this same time, Spartacus, a Thracian who had once fought against the Romans and after being taken prisoner and sold had become a gladiator in a troop which was kept to provide entertainments at Capua, persuaded about seventy of his fellows to risk their lives for freedom rather than for exhibition as a spectacle. With them, he overpowered their guards and escaped. Then he equipped himself and his companions with staves and daggers seized from travellers and took refuge on Mount Vesuvius, where he allowed many runaway domestic slaves and some free farm hands to join him. With the gladiators Oenomaus and Crixus as his subordinates he plundered the nearby areas, and because he divided the spoils in equal shares his numbers quickly swelled. The first commander sent against him was Varinius Glaber, and the second Publius Valerius; instead of legionary forces they had anyone they

could quickly conscript on the way, because the Romans did not yet class the affair as a war, but as a kind of raid akin to piracy, and they were defeated when they attacked him. Spartacus himself actually captured Varinius' horse from under him; so nearly was a Roman general taken prisoner by a gladiator. After this, people flocked in still greater numbers to join Spartacus: his army now numbered 70,000 and he began to manufacture weapons and gather stores.

The government in Rome now despatched the consuls with two legions. Crixus, at the head of 3,000 men, was defeated and killed by one of them at Mount Garganus, with the loss of two-thirds of his force. Spartacus, who was eager to go through the Apennines to the Alpine regions, and then to Celtic lands from the Alps, was intercepted and prevented from escaping by the other consul, while his colleague conducted the pursuit. But Spartacus turned on each of them and defeated them separately. In the aftermath they retreated in confusion, while Spartacus, first sacrificing 300 Roman prisoners to Crixus, made

From Appian, *The Civil Wars*, translated by John Carter, Bk. 1, secs. 116–120, pp. 65–67. Copyright © 1996. Reproduced by permission of Penguin Books Ltd.

for Rome with 120,000 foot soldiers after burning the useless equipment and putting all the prisoners to death and slaughtering the draught animals to free himself of all encumbrances; and although a large number of deserters approached him he refused to accept any of them. When the consuls made another stand in Picenum, there was a further great struggle and on that occasion also a great Roman defeat. Spartacus, however, changed his mind about marching on Rome because he was not yet a match for the defenders and his troops did not all have soldier's arms and equipment (no town had joined their cause, and they were all slaves, deserters and human flotsam). He seized the mountains around Thurii, together with the town itself, and then prevented traders bringing in gold and silver, barred his own men from acquiring any, and bought exclusively iron and bronze at good prices without harming those who brought them. As a result they had plenty of raw material and were well equipped and made frequent raiding expeditions. They again confronted the Romans in battle, defeated them, and on that occasion too returned to camp laden with booty.

The war had now lasted three years and was causing the Romans great concern, although at the beginning it had been laughed at and regarded as trivial because it was against gladiators. When the appointment of other generals was proposed there was universal reluctance to stand, and no one put himself forward until Licinius Crassus, distinguished both for his family and his wealth, undertook to assume the post, and led six legions against Spartacus; to these he added the two consular legions when he reached the front. He immediately punished the latter for their repeated defeats, making them draw lots for every tenth man to be put to death. According to some, this was not what happened; instead, when he himself had suffered defeat after engaging the enemy with his whole force he had them all draw lots for the tenth place and put to death up to 4,000 men without being in the least deterred by their numbers. Whatever the truth, he established himself in the eyes of his men as more to be feared than a defeat at the hands

of the enemy, and forthwith won a victory over 10,000 of Spartacus' men who were encamped separately somewhere. He killed two-thirds of them and marched confidently against Spartacus himself. After winning a brilliant victory, he pursued Spartacus as he fled towards the sea with the intention of sailing across to Sicily, overtook him, and walled him in with ditches, earthworks, and palisades. Spartacus then tried to force his way out and reach the Samnite country, but Crassus killed almost 6,000 of his opponents at the beginning of the day and nearly as many more at evening, at the cost of three dead and seven wounded from the Roman army; so effective had their punishment been in altering their will to win. Spartacus, who was waiting for some cavalry that were on their way to him, no longer went into battle with his full force, but conducted many separate harassing operations against his besiegers; he made sudden and repeated sorties against them, set fire to bundles of wood which he had thrown into the ditches, and made their work difficult. He crucified a Roman prisoner in no-man's land to demonstrate to his own troops the fate awaiting them if they were defeated. When the government at Rome heard of the siege and contemplated the dishonour they would incur from a protracted war with gladiators, they appointed Pompeius, who had recently arrived from Spain, to an additional command in the field, in the belief that the task of dealing with Spartacus was now substantial and difficult. As a result of this appointment Crassus pressed on urgently with every means of attacking Spartacus, to stop Pompeius stealing his glory, while Spartacus, thinking to forestall Pompeius, invited Crassus to negotiate. When Crassus spurned the offer, Spartacus decided to make a desperate attempt, and with the cavalry which had by now arrived forced a way through the encircling fortifications with his whole army and retired towards Brundisium, with Crassus in pursuit. But when he discovered that Lucullus, who was on his way back from his victory over Mithridates, was there, he despaired of everything and, at the head of a still large force, joined battle with Crassus. The fight was long, and bitterly contested, since so many tens of thousands of men had no other hope. Spartacus himself was wounded by a spear-thrust in the thigh, but went down on one knee, held his shield in front of him, and fought off his attackers until he and a great number of his followers were encircled and fell. The rest of his army was already in disorder and was cut down in huge numbers; consequently their losses were not easy to estimate (though the Romans lost about 1,000 men), and Spartacus' body was never found. Since there was still a very large number of fugitives from the battle in the mountains, Crassus proceeded against them. They formed themselves into four groups and kept up their resistance until there were only 6,000 survivors, who were taken prisoner and crucified all the way along the road from Rome to Capua.

REVIEW QUESTIONS

1. What was the character of slavery under the early Romans?
2. According to Diodorus Siculus, what was the impact of slavery on the moral character of both masters and slaves? Compare with that of Seneca (see chapter 5, page 138).
3. Judging from Appian's account, how would you describe Spartacus' character?

6 Women in Republican Society

The status of women in late-republican Roman society was considerably better than that of Greek women during the classical age. Like Greek law, Roman law had originally placed each female under the jurisdiction of a male, the *paterfamilias* (literally, "family father"), but Roman women obtained some freedom from male control during the times of the late Republic and the early Empire. Although women never achieved full civil equality and they could not formally participate in the political institutions of Rome, they did eventually exercise much practical control over their own property and indirectly exercised political influence through their husbands, sons, and fathers.

Quintus Lucretius Vespillo
A FUNERAL EULOGY FOR A ROMAN WIFE

Documenting intimate relationships between Roman men and women is difficult because ordinary people were unlikely to write about such things. Although personal records are scant or now lost, glimpses have survived in the writings of historians and poets or as inscriptions on tombstones.

In the late Republic, it became more common for distinguished men to pronounce funeral eulogies for distinguished female as well as male members of their families. One such eulogy was composed by the ex-Consul Quintus Lucretius Vespillo for his wife, Turia, who died about 8 B.C. Though marriages among persons of the higher social ranks were usually undertaken for political and economic considerations, clearly this couple had gone beyond such a formal alliance to achieve a most touching love.

Before the day fixed for our marriage, you were suddenly left an orphan, by the murder of your parents in the solitude of the country. . . .

Through your efforts chiefly, their death did not remain unavenged. . . .

In our day, marriages of such long duration, not dissolved by divorce, but terminated by death alone, are indeed rare. For our union was prolonged in unclouded happiness for forty-one years. Would that it had been my lot to put an end to this our good fortune and that I as the older—which was more just—had yielded to fate.

Why recall your inestimable qualities, your modesty, deference, affability, your amiable disposition, your faithful attendance to the household duties, your enlightened religion, your unassuming elegance, the modest simplicity and refinement of your manners? Need I speak of your attachment to your kindred, your affection for your family—when you respected my mother as you did your own parents and cared for her tomb as you did for that of your own mother and father,—you who share countless other virtues with Roman ladies most jealous of their fair name? These qualities which I claim for you are your own, equalled or excelled by but few; for the experience of men teaches us how rare they are.

With common prudence we have preserved all the patrimony which you received from your parents. Intrusting it all to me, you were not troubled with the care of increasing it; thus did we share the task of administering it, that I undertook to protect your fortune, and you to guard mine. . . .

You gave proof of your generosity not only towards several of your kin, but especially in your filial devotion. . . . You brought up in your own home, in the enjoyment of mutual benefits, some young girls of your kinship. And that these might attain to a station in life worthy of our family, you provided them with dowries. . . .

I owe you no less a debt than Cæsar Augustus [27 B.C.–A.D. 14, emperor of Rome] himself, for this my return from exile to my native land. For unless you had prepared the way for my safety, even Cæsar's promises of assistance had been of no avail. So I owe no less a debt to your loyal devotion than to the clemency of Cæsar.

Why shall I now conjure up the memory of our domestic counsels and plans stored away in the hidden recesses of the heart?—That, aroused by the sudden arrival of messages from you to a realization of the present and imminent perils, I was saved by your counsel? That you suffered me not to be recklessly carried away by a foolish rashness, or that, when bent on more temperate plans, you provided for me a safe retreat, having as sharers in your plans for my safety, when an exile,—fraught with danger as they were for you all,—your sister and her husband. . . .

Vespillo then relates what happened to his wife when she begged his enemy M. Lepidus to honor her husband's writ of pardon from Caesar Augustus.

. . . Then prostrating yourself at his feet, he not only did not raise you up,—but, dragged along and abused as though a common slave, your body all covered with bruises, yet with unflinching steadfastness of purpose, you recalled to him Cæsar's edict (of pardon) and the letter of felicitation on my return, that accompanied it. Braving his taunts and suffering the most brutal treatment, you denounced these cruelties publicly so that he (Lepidus) was branded as the author of all my perils and misfortunes. And his punishment was not long delayed.

Could such courage remain without effect? Your unexampled patience furnished the occasion for Cæsar's clemency, and, by guarding my life, he branded the infamous and savage cruelty (of the tyrant Lepidus). . . .

A Source Book of Roman History, ed. Dana C. Munro (Boston: D. C. Heath, 1904), pp. 201–204.

When all the world was again at peace and the Republic reestablished, peaceful and happy days followed. We longed for children, which an envious fate denied us. Had Fortune smiled on us in this, what had been lacking to complete our happiness? But an adverse destiny put an end to our hopes. . . . Disconsolate to see me without children . . . you wished to put an end to my chagrin by proposing to me a divorce, offering to yield the place to another spouse more fertile, with the only intention of searching for and providing for me a spouse worthy of our mutual affection, whose children you assured me you would have treated as your own. . . .

I will admit that I was so irritated and shocked by such a proposition that I had difficulty in restraining my anger and remaining master of myself. You spoke of divorce before the decree of fate [death] had forced us to separate, and I could not comprehend how you could conceive of any reason why you, still living, should not be my wife, you who during my exile had always remained most faithful and loyal. . . .

Would that our time of life had permitted our union to have endured until I, the older, had passed away—which was more just—and that you might perform for me the last sad rites and that I might have departed, leaving you behind, with a daughter to replace me at your side.

By fate's decree your course was run before mine. You left me the grief, the heart-ache, the longing for you, the sad fate to live alone. . . .

The conclusion of this discourse will be that you have deserved all, and that I remain with the chagrin of not being able to give you all. Your wishes have always been my supreme law; and whatever it will be permitted me to accord them still, in this I shall not fail.

May the gods, the Manes [spirits of dead ancestors, considered godlike], assure and protect your repose!

REVIEW QUESTIONS

1. What does Vespillo's eulogy reveal about the virtues a Roman husband might expect in his wife? What duties were expected of a wife?
2. In your opinion, what was Turia's most commendable quality?

---

7   The Decline of the Republic

In 133 B.C. the Romans effectively controlled all the lands bordering the Mediterranean Sea. The old enemies of Rome, Carthage and Macedonia, had become Roman provinces; the Hellenistic kingdoms of Syria and Egypt were clients of Rome without effective power to challenge Roman hegemony. The Mediterranean Sea had become a "Roman lake."

Yet, at the very moment of its imperial supremacy, the internal order and institutions of the Roman Republic began to break down. The senatorial leaders, who had served Rome responsibly in its march to empire, no longer governed effectively. The ruling class engaged in shameless corruption in administering the provinces, resorted to bribery and force to maintain control over public offices, and failed to solve the deeply rooted problems that afflicted the state.

Triggering the Republic's downhill slide was an agricultural crisis that destroyed the small independent peasant.

Plutarch
TIBERIUS GRACCHUS

The wars of expansion had a disastrous effect on Roman agriculture. Hannibal's ravaging of Italian farmlands and the obligatory military service that kept peasants away from their fields for long periods left many small farms in near ruins. The importation of thousands of prisoners of war to toil as slaves on large plantations deprived small farmers of this work. Sinking ever deeper into debt and poverty, many lost their lands and went to Rome, where lack of jobs condemned them to permanent poverty. The once sturdy and independent Roman farmer, who had done all that his country had asked of him, became part of a vast urban underclass—poor, embittered, and alienated.

Tiberius Gracchus (163–133 B.C.), a scion of one of Rome's most honored families, was distressed by this injustice. Moreover, he realized that small landowners were the backbone of the Roman army. Elected tribune (an office created in 493 B.C. to protect plebeian rights), Tiberius Gracchus in 133 B.C. proposed land reforms that the senatorial nobility regarded as a potential menace to their property. They also viewed Tiberius Gracchus as a threat to their political authority. The Roman nobility feared that this popular reformer was building a following among the commoners in order to undermine senatorial rule and that his real ambition was to subvert republican institutions and to become a tyrant, a one-man ruler. This fear was strengthened when Tiberius, in violation of constitutional custom, announced that he would seek reelection as tribune. Senatorial extremists killed Tiberius Gracchus and some three hundred of his followers. The Republic had entered an age of political violence that would eventually destroy it. (Tiberius' younger brother, Gaius, became tribune in 123 B.C. and suffered a fate similar to his brother's.) The following account of Tiberius Gracchus is by Plutarch, the second-century A.D. Greek biographer.

Of the territory which the Romans won in war from their neighbours, a part they sold, and a part they made common land, and assigned it for occupation to the poor and indigent among the citizens, on payment of a small rent into the public treasury. And when the rich began to offer larger rents and drove out the poor, a law was enacted forbidding the holding by one person of more than five hundred acres of land. For a short time this enactment gave a check to the rapacity of the rich, and was of assistance to the poor, who remained in their places on the land which they had rented and occupied the allotment which each had held from the outset.

But later on the neighbouring rich men, by means of fictitious personages, transferred these rentals to themselves, and finally held most of the land openly in their own names. Then the poor, who had been ejected from their land, no longer showed themselves eager for military service, and neglected the bringing up of children, so that soon all Italy was conscious of a dearth of freemen, and was filled with gangs of foreign slaves, by whose aid the rich cultivated their estates, from which they had driven away the free citizens. An attempt was therefore made to rectify this evil, and by Caius Laelius[1]

Plutarch—Volume X, Loeb Classical Library, vol. 102, trans. B. Perrin (Cambridge: Harvard University Press, 1921), pp. 159–167.

[1]Caius Laelius Sapiens, a leading military hero in the Third Punic War and a close friend of Scipio Aemilianus, the conqueror of Carthage, attempted unsuccessfully to resettle the poor on public land.—Eds.

the comrade of Scipio; but the men of influence opposed his measures, and he, fearing the disturbance which might ensue, desisted, and received the surname of *Wise* or *Prudent* [for the Latin word *sapiens* would seem to have either meaning]. Tiberius, however, on being elected tribune of the people, took the matter directly in hand. . . .

He did not, however, draw up his law by himself, but took counsel with the citizens who were foremost in virtue and reputation. . . .

. . . And it is thought that a law dealing with injustice and rapacity so great was never drawn up in milder and gentler terms. For men who ought to have been punished for their disobedience and to have surrendered with payment of a fine the land which they were illegally enjoying, these men it merely ordered to abandon their injust acquisitions upon being paid their value, and to admit into ownership of them such citizens as needed assistance. But although the rectification of the wrong was so considerate, the people were satisfied to let bygones be bygones if they could be secure from such wrong in the future; the men of wealth and substance, however, were led by their greed to hate the law, and by their wrath and contentiousness to hate the law-giver, and tried to dissuade the people by alleging that Tiberius was introducing a re-distribution of land for the confusion of the body politic, and was stirring up a general revolution.

But they accomplished nothing; for Tiberius, striving to support a measure which was honourable and just with an eloquence that would have adorned even a meaner cause, was formidable and invincible, whenever, with the people crowding around the rostra [speaker's platforms], he took his stand there and pleaded for the poor. "The wild beasts that roam over Italy," he would say, "have every one of them a cave or lair to lurk in; but the men who fight and die for Italy enjoy the common air and light, indeed, but nothing else; houseless and homeless they wander about with their wives and children. And it is with lying lips that their imperators[2] exhort the soldiers in their battles to defend sepulchres and shrines from the enemy; for not a man of them has an hereditary altar, not one of all these many Romans an ancestral tomb, but they fight and die to support others in wealth and luxury, and though they are styled masters of the world, they have not a single clod of earth that is their own."

Such words as these, the product of a lofty spirit and genuine feeling, and falling upon the ears of a people profoundly moved and fully aroused to the speaker's support, no adversary of Tiberius could successfully withstand.

---

[2]First meaning a commander, general, or captain in the army, *imperator* later meant "emperor."—Eds.

Cicero
JUSTIFYING CAESAR'S ASSASSINATION

In the century following the assassination of Tiberius Gracchus in 133 B.C., the Roman Republic was torn by conspiracies to seize the state, civil wars, assassinations, mob violence, and confiscations of property by political opponents.

In 49 B.C., Julius Caesar (100–44 B.C.), a talented and ambitious commander, marched on Rome. After defeating the Senate's forces, he was appointed dictator for ten years. A creative statesman, Caesar introduced reforms to resolve the grievances of Romans and provincials. Some senators feared that Caesar aimed to establish a typical Hellenistic monarchy over Rome with himself as absolute king. The very word *king* was abhorrent to patriotic Romans, who gloried in their status as free citizens of a five-centuries-old republic. Finally, on the Ides (the fifteenth) of March, 44 B.C.,

Julius Caesar was slain by some sixty senators, who acted, they said, to restore the liberty of the Roman people. Their leaders were Marcus Junius Brutus (82–42 B.C.) and Gaius Cassius (d. 42 B.C.), both of whom Caesar had previously pardoned.

In the following reading from *On Duties*, Cicero, who was not one of the assassins, justifies the killing of Caesar.

Our tyrant deserved his death for having made an exception of the one thing that was the blackest crime of all. Why do we gather instances of petty crime—legacies criminally obtained and fraudulent buying and selling? Behold, here you have a man who was ambitious to be king of the Roman People and master of the whole world; and he achieved it! The man who maintains that such an ambition is morally right is a madman; for he justifies the destruction of law and liberty and thinks their hideous and detestable suppression glorious. But if anyone agrees that it is not morally right to be king in a state that once was free and that ought to be free now, and yet imagines that it is advantageous for him who can reach that position, with what remonstrance or rather with what appeal should I try to tear him away from so strange a delusion? For, oh ye immortal gods! can the most horrible and hideous of all murders—that of fatherland—bring advantage to anybody, even though he who has committed such a crime receives from his enslaved fellow-citizens the title of "Father of his Country"?

Cicero, *De Officiis*, Loeb Classical Library, trans. Walter Miller (Cambridge: Harvard University Press, 1913), p. 357.

Velleius Paterculus
THE TRIUMPH OF OCTAVIAN

The assassination of Julius Caesar plunged Rome into renewed civil war in which thousands more perished. Two of Caesar's trusted lieutenants, Mark Antony and Lepidus, joined with Octavian (Caesar's adopted son, who became Augustus) and defeated the armies of Brutus and Cassius, two principal conspirators in the plot against Caesar. After Lepidus was forced into political obscurity, Antony and Octavian fought each other, with Rome as the prize. In 31 B.C., at the naval battle of Actium in western Greece, Octavian crushed the forces of Antony and his wife, Egypt's Queen Cleopatra. Both Antony and Cleopatra had fled to Egypt prior to the battle. The following year Octavian pursued the couple to Egypt where both committed suicide. Following is Velleius Paterculus' (c. 19 B.C.–c. A.D. 31) account of Octavian's triumph.

Then, in the consulate of Cæsar and Corvinus Messala, the decisive contest was waged at Actium, where, long before the engagement, it was easy to foresee, that victory would attend the Julian party. On [Octavian's] side, both the soldiers and the commander were full of vigour; on [Anthony's], everything was feeble: on this, the seamen were in full strength; on the other,

M. Velleius Paterculus, *An Abridgement of the History of Rome*, trans. George Baker (London: T. Cadell and W. Davis, in the Strand, 1814), 155–159.

they were greatly reduced by want: on this, the ships were moderate in size and active; on the opposite, they were more formidable only in appearance. From this side not a man deserted to Anthony; from the other, deserters came daily to Cæsar....

At length arrived the day of the grand dispute, when Cæsar and Anthony, with their fleets in line of battle, came to a general engagement; one fighting for the preservation, the other for the destruction of the world....

When the engagement began, every thing on one side was complete, the commander, the seamen, the soldiers; on the other, nothing but the soldiers. Cleopatra first began the flight, and Anthony chose to accompany her, rather than remain with his men in battle. Thus a general, whose duty it had been to punish deserters, became a deserter of his own army. His men, though deprived of their chief, maintained the fight a long time with most determined resolution; and many, even when they despaired of victory, continued it to death. Cæsar, although he could have conquered them with the sword, wished rather to subdue them by words; and calling aloud, and pointing, shewed them that Anthony had fled; asking them for whom, and against whom, they fought. At last, after a long struggle in favour of their absent leader, they were with difficulty prevailed on to lay down their arms, and yield the victory; and Cæsar granted them life and pardon more readily than they were persuaded to ask them of him. It was universally allowed, that the soldiers acted the part of an excellent commander, and the commander that of a most dastardly soldier. So that you can easily

judge, whether, in case of success, he would have regulated his conduct by his own judgment, or by Cleopatra's, since by hers he was determined to fly. The army on land submitted in like manner, after [its commander] had precipitately fled to Anthony.

What blessings that day procured to the world, what an improvement it produced in the state of the public welfare, no man can attempt to recount in such a hasty narrative as this abridgment. The victory was attended with the greatest clemency: very few were put to death....

In the next year, Cæsar followed the Queen and Anthony to Alexandria, and brought the war to a final conclusion. Anthony killed himself courageously enough, so as to compensate by his death for many crimes of effeminacy. Cleopatra, eluding the vigilance of her guards, had an asp brought to her, and by its bite put an end to her life, without betraying any womanish fear. It reflected honour on Cæsar's success and his merciful disposition, that not one of who bore arms against him was put to death by him. Decimus Brutus perished by the cruelty of Anthony; and the same Anthony, when Sextus Pompey was conquered by him, although he had pledged his honour to secure even his dignity, yet he bereft him of that and life together. Brutus and Cassius died voluntary deaths, without making trial of the disposition of the conquerors. The end of Anthony and Cleopatra we have now related. Canidius died in a more cowardly manner than was consonant to his frequent professions. Of the murderers of Cæsar, Cassius Parmensis was the last victim of vengeance, as Trebonius had been the first.

Sallust
MORAL DETERIORATION

In the dark days of the Republic after the assassination of Julius Caesar in 44 B.C., the Roman politician and historian Sallust (Gaius Sallustius Crispus, 86–35 B.C.) reflected on the causes of the Republic's collapse. In his account of a failed coup d'état that occurred in 63 B.C., Sallust contrasted the virtues of the early Republic with the moral decline that set in after the destruction of Carthage. Having failed to be elected consul in 63 B.C., Catiline, a Roman noble, organized a conspiracy to seize the state. The coup d'état was thwarted by the vigorous action of the consul Cicero, who arrested the known conspirators and had them executed. Catiline, who led an army against the forces loyal to the government, was defeated and killed.

In peace and war [in the early Republic], as I have said, virtue was held in high esteem. The closest unity prevailed, and avarice was a thing almost unknown. Justice and righteousness were upheld not so much by law as by natural instinct. They quarrelled and fought with their country's foes; between themselves the citizens contended only for honour. In making offerings to the gods they spared no expense; at home they lived frugally and never betrayed a friend. By combining boldness in war with fair dealing when peace was restored, they protected themselves and the state. There are convincing proofs of this. In time of war, soldiers were often punished for attacking against orders or for being slow to obey a signal of recall from battle, whereas few ever ventured to desert their standards or to give ground when hard pressed. In peace, they governed by conferring benefits on their subjects, not by intimidation; and when wronged they would rather pardon than seek vengeance.

Thus by hard work and just dealing the power of the state increased. Mighty kings were vanquished, savage tribes and huge nations were brought to their knees; and when Carthage, Rome's rival in her quest for empire, had been annihilated [in 146 B.C.], every land and sea lay open to her. It was then that fortune turned unkind and confounded all her enterprises. To the men who had so easily endured toil and peril, anxiety and adversity, the leisure and riches which are generally regarded as so desirable proved a burden and a curse.

The Jugurthine War/The Conspiracy of Catiline by Sallust, translated by S.A. Handford, pp. 180–182, 203–204. © 1963. Reproduced by permission of Penguin Books Ltd.

Growing love of money, and the lust for power which followed it, engendered every kind of evil. Avarice destroyed honour, integrity, and every other virtue, and instead taught men to be proud and cruel, to neglect religion, and to hold nothing too sacred to sell. Ambition tempted many to be false, to have one thought hidden in their hearts, another ready on their tongues, to become a man's friend or enemy not because they judged him worthy or unworthy but because they thought it would pay them, and to put on the semblance of virtues that they had not. At first these vices grew slowly and sometimes met with punishment; later on, when the disease had spread like a plague, Rome changed: her government, once so just and admirable, became harsh and unendurable.

Reflecting on the last stages of the Republic's decline, Sallust believed that men had learned a most dangerous lesson: that they could gain power and wealth through violence and corruption rather than through virtue and self-restraint.

Never in its history—it seems to me—had the empire of Rome been in such a miserable plight. From east to west all the world had been vanquished by her armies and obeyed her will; at home there was profound peace and abundance of wealth, which mortal men esteem the chiefest of blessings. Yet there were Roman citizens obstinately determined to destroy both themselves and their country. In spite of two senatorial decrees, not one man among all the conspirators was induced by the promise of reward to betray their plans, and not one deserted from Catiline's camp. A deadly moral contagion had infected all their minds. And this madness was not confined to those actually implicated in the plot. The whole of the lower orders, impatient for a new régime, looked with favour on Catiline's enterprise.[1] In this they only did what might have been expected of them. In every country paupers envy respectable citizens and make heroes of unprincipled characters, hating the established order of things and hankering after innovation; discontented with their own lot, they are bent on general upheaval. Turmoil and rebellion bring them carefree profit, since poverty has nothing to lose.

The city populace were especially eager to fling themselves into a revolutionary adventure. There were several reasons for this. To begin with, those who had made themselves conspicuous anywhere by vice and shameless audacity, those who had wasted their substance by disgraceful excesses, and those whom scandalous or criminal conduct had exiled from their homes—all these had poured into Rome till it was like a sewer. Many, remembering Sulla's victory,[2] and seeing men who had served under him as common soldiers now risen to be senators, or so rich that they lived as luxuriously as kings, began to hope that they too, if they took up arms, might find victory a source of profit. Young men from the country, whose labour on the farms had barely kept them from starvation, had been attracted by the private and public doles available at Rome, and preferred an idle city life to such thankless toil. These, like all the rest, stood to gain by public calamities. It is no wonder, therefore, that these paupers,

devoid of moral scruple and incited by ambitious hopes, should have held their country as cheap as they held themselves. Those also to whom Sulla's victory had brought disaster by the proscription of their parents, the confiscation of their property, and the curtailment of their civil rights, looked forward with no less sanguine expectations to what might result from the coming struggle. Moreover, all the factions opposed to the Senate would rather see the state embroiled than accept their own exclusion from political power.

Such was the evil condition by which, after an interval of some years, Rome was once more afflicted. After the restoration of the power of the tribunes in the consulship of Pompey and Crassus,[3] this very important office was obtained by certain men whose youth intensified their natural aggressiveness. These tribunes began to rouse the mob by inveighing against the Senate, and then inflamed popular passion still further by handing out bribes and promises, whereby they won renown and influence for themselves. They were strenuously opposed by most of the nobility, who posed as defenders of the Senate but were really concerned to maintain their own privileged position. The whole truth—to put it in a word—is that although all disturbers of the peace in this period put forward specious pretexts, claiming either to be protecting the rights of the people or to be strengthening the authority of the Senate, this was mere pretence: in reality, every one of them was fighting for his personal aggrandizement. Lacking all self-restraint, they [stopped] at nothing to gain their ends, and both sides made ruthless use of any successes they won.

---

[1]This surely cannot have been true. Sallust must be exaggerating the popular support for the conspiracy.

[2]Lucius Cornelius Sulla (c. 138–78 B.C.) was a successful politician and general, whose rivalry with another politician and general, Gaius Marius (c. 155–86 B.C.), led to civil war. After seizing Rome and massacring his opponents, Sulla made himself dictator and increased the power of the aristocratic senate, suppressing the office of tribune of the people. The latter had been used by Tiberius and Gaius Gracchus, among others, to better the condition of the poorer classes.—Eds.

---

[3]Pompey (Gnaeus Pompeius, 106–48 B.C.) and Crassus (Marcus Licinius Crassus, c. 115–53 B.C.) held the office of consul in 55 B.C. In 59 B.C., together with Julius Caesar, they had formed a political alliance called a triumvirate (meaning "group of three men"), which dominated Roman government for the next decade.—Eds.

REVIEW QUESTIONS

1. What factors created a socioeconomic class struggle in the late Roman Republic?
2. According to Plutarch, what was the reaction of the senatorial order to the reforms proposed by Tiberius Gracchus?
3. Why did Cicero consider Caesar guilty of "the blackest crime of all"?
4. How did Octavian's triumph over Anthony and Cleopatra foreshadow the way he might govern the Roman Empire?
5. To what virtues did Sallust attribute the greatness of Rome?
6. What vices did Sallust believe could ruin a great state? Does his analysis have any contemporary significance?

CHAPTER 5
The Roman Empire

MARCUS AURELIUS, panel relief, c. A.D 176. The Roman emperor rides through the Roman Forum, having been accorded a triumph after defending the Empire against barbarian incursions. *(Erich Lessing / Art Resource, NY)*

In the chaotic years following Julius Caesar's assassination in 44 B.C., Augustus (formerly Octavian) emerged victorious over his rivals, becoming the unchallenged ruler of Rome. Although eager for personal power, Augustus was by no means a self-seeking tyrant; he was a creative statesman who prevented the renewal of civil war that had plagued the Roman Republic and introduced needed reforms in Italy and the provinces. His long reign, from 27 B.C. to A.D. 14, marks the beginning of the *Pax Romana*, the Roman Peace, which endured until A.D. 180.

The period of the Pax Romana was one of the finest in the ancient world. Revolts against Roman rule were few, and Roman legions ably defended the Empire's borders. The Mediterranean world had never enjoyed so many years of peace, effective government, and economic well-being. Stretching from Britain to the Arabian Desert and from the Danube River to the sands of the Sahara, the Roman Empire united some sixty million people. In many ways the Roman Empire was the fulfillment of the universalism and cosmopolitanism of the Hellenistic Age. The same law bound together Italians, Spaniards, North Africans, Greeks, Syrians, and other peoples. Although dissatisfaction was sometimes violently expressed and separatist tendencies persisted, notably in Judea and Gaul, people from diverse backgrounds viewed themselves as Romans even though they had never set foot in the capital city.

In the seventy years following Augustus' reign, political life was sometimes marred by conspiracies and assassinations, particularly after an emperor's death left the throne vacant. Marcus Cocceius Nerva, who reigned from A.D. 96 to 98, introduced a practice that led to orderly succession and gave Rome four exceptionally competent emperors. He adopted as his son and designated as his heir Trajan (Marcus Ulpius Traianus), a man of proven ability. From the accession of Nerva to the death of Marcus Aurelius Antoninus in A.D. 180, the Roman Empire was ruled by the "Five Good Emperors." Marcus Aurelius abandoned the use of adoption and allowed his son Commodus (Lucius Aelius Aurelius, A.D. 180–192) to succeed to the throne. An extravagant despot, Commodus was murdered in A.D. 192.

During the third century the Roman Empire suffered hard times, and the ordered civilization of the Pax Romana was shattered. The Empire was plunged into anarchy as generals vied for the throne. Taking advantage of the weakened border defenses, the barbarians (Germanic tribesmen) crossed the Danube frontier and pillaged Roman cities. Both civil war and barbarian attacks greatly disrupted the Roman economy, which even during good times suffered from basic weaknesses.

Two later emperors—Diocletian (G. Aurelius Valerius Diocletianus, A.D. 285–305) and Constantine (Flavius Valerius Constantinus,

A.D. 306–337)—tried to keep the Empire from dissolution by tightening control over the citizenry. Although heavy taxes, requisitioning of goods, and forced labor provided some stability, these measures also turned many citizens against the oppressive state. At the end of the fourth and the opening of the fifth century, several barbarian tribes poured into the weakened Empire in great numbers. In succeeding decades Germanic tribes overran Roman provinces and set up kingdoms on lands that had been Roman. The Roman Empire in the west fell; the eastern provinces, however, survived as the Byzantine Empire.

The history of the Roman Empire influenced Western civilization in many ways. From Latin, the language of Rome, came the Romance languages: French, Italian, Spanish, Portuguese, and Romanian. Roman law became the basis of the legal codes of most modern European states. Rome preserved Greek culture, the foundation of Western learning and aesthetics, and spread it to other lands. And Christianity, the religion of the West, was born in the Roman Empire.

1   The Imperial Office

The greatest achievement of Caesar Augustus (Octavian), grandnephew and adopted son of Julius Caesar, was undoubtedly the step-by-step building of a new constitutional structure for the Roman Empire. This political system, called by modern historians the Principate, has been described as a monarchy disguised as an oligarchical republic. The Roman antimonarchial tradition, nurtured for five centuries under the republican regime, had contributed directly to Julius Caesar's assassination. Augustus was wise enough, as he created a stable central executive office for the Empire, to camouflage the monarchial reality of his regime by maintaining the outer forms of the old Republic's constitution.

Augustus' chief innovation was creating the office of *Princeps* (first citizen), which combined a number of republican offices and powers and placed them at the disposal of one man. Desiring to maintain the appearance of traditional republican government, he refused to be called king. The Senate gave him the semireligious and revered name Augustus (venerable). In effect, however, he was the first Roman emperor. He cultivated the support of the traditional constituents of the Roman state—the senatorial nobility, knights (those who bid for the right to collect public revenues), public contractors, residents of the capital, soldiers and veterans, and the wealthy and politically useful provincial subjects of Rome. At the time of his death in A.D. 14, Augustus successfully passed on his imperial office to his chosen heir, his adopted son Tiberius.

Augustus
THE ACHIEVEMENTS OF THE DIVINE AUGUSTUS

In *Res gestae divi Augusti* (The Achievements of the Divine Augustus), a document composed shortly before his death and left to be published with his will, Augustus gave an account of those achievements for which he wanted to be remembered. A careful reading reveals the image Augustus chose to promote to justify his emperorship. It also describes the many responsibilities of holders of that office.

I drove into exile the murderers of my father [Julius Caesar], avenging their crime through tribunals established by law; and afterwards, when they made war on the republic, I twice defeated them in battle.

I undertook many civil and foreign wars by land and sea throughout the world, and as victor I spared the lives of all citizens who asked for mercy. When foreign peoples could safely be pardoned I preferred to preserve rather than to exterminate them. The Roman citizens who took the soldier's oath of obedience to me numbered about 500,000. I settled rather more than 300,000 of these in colonies or sent them back to their home towns after their period of service; to all these I assigned lands or gave money as rewards for their military service. . . .

The dictatorship was offered to me by both senate and people in my absence and when I was at Rome in the consulship of Marcus Marcellus and Lucius Arruntius, but I refused it. I did not decline in the great dearth of corn to undertake the charge of the corn-supply, which I so administered that within a few days I delivered the whole city from apprehension and immediate danger at my own cost and by my own efforts. . . . The senate and people of Rome agreed that I should be appointed supervisor of laws and morals without a colleague and with supreme power, but I would not accept any office inconsistent with the custom of our ancestors. The measures that the senate then desired me to take I carried out in virtue of my tribunician power. . . .

To each member of the Roman plebs [common populace] I paid under my father's will 300 sesterces,[1] and in my own name I gave them 400 each from the booty of war in my fifth consulship, and once again in my tenth consulship I paid out 400 sesterces as a largesse to each man from my own patrimony, and in my eleventh consulship I bought grain with my own money and distributed twelve rations apiece, and in the twelfth year of my tribunician power I gave every man 400 sesterces for the third time. These largesses of mine never reached fewer than 250,000 persons. . . .

. . . I paid monetary rewards to soldiers whom I settled in their home towns after completion of their service, and on this account I expended about 400,000,000 sesterces.

Four times I assisted the treasury with my own money, so that I transferred to the administrators of the treasury 150,000,000 sesterces. . . .

I restored the Capitol[2] and the theatre of Pompey, both works at great expense without

Augusti Res Gestae: The Achievements of The Divine Augustus (1967) edited by Brunt, P. A. & Moore, J. M. By permission of Oxford University Press.

[1]Sesterces, during the reign of Augustus, were small coins of bronze, each worth one-hundredth of a gold *aureus*, or one-quarter of a silver denarius, the basic coin of the Roman monetary system. Brunt (editor of source) notes that a Roman legionary soldier of this period earned 900 sesterces a year, out of which the cost of uniform, food, and arms was deducted. A Roman whose assessed wealth came to at least 400,000 sesterces qualified to enter the order of knights; to be a senator required one million sesterces. —Eds.
[2]Here "Capitol" refers to the temple of Jupiter, patron of Rome, on the Capitoline Hill. —Eds.

inscribing my own name on either. I restored the channels of the aqueducts, which in several places were falling into disrepair through age, and I brought water from a new spring into the aqueduct called Marcia, doubling the supply. I completed the Forum Julium[3] and the basilica between the temples of Castor and Saturn,[4] works begun and almost finished by my father. . . .

I gave three gladiatorial games in my own name and five in that of my sons or grandsons; at these games some 10,000 men took part in combat. Twice in my own name and a third time in that of my grandson I presented to the people displays by athletes summoned from all parts. I produced shows in my own name four times and in place of other magistrates twenty-three times. . . . I gave beast-hunts of African beasts in my own name or in that of my sons and grandsons in the circus or forum or amphitheatre on twenty-six occasions, on which about 3,500 beasts were destroyed.

I made the sea peaceful and freed it of pirates. In that war I captured about 30,000 slaves who had escaped from their masters and taken up arms against the republic, and I handed them over to their masters for punishment.

I extended the territory of all those provinces of the Roman people on whose borders lay peoples not subject to our government. I brought peace to the Gallic and Spanish provinces as well

as to Germany, throughout the area bordering on the [Atlantic] Ocean from Cadiz [in Spain] to the mouth of the Elbe [in northwestern Germany]. I secured the pacification of the Alps. . . . The Pannonian peoples [in western Hungary] . . . were conquered through the agency of Tiberius Nero[5] who was then my stepson and legate; I brought them into the empire of the Roman people, and extended the frontier of Illyricum[6] to the banks of the Danube. . . .

In my sixth and seventh consulships, after I had extinguished civil wars, and at a time when with universal consent I was in complete control of affairs, I transferred the republic from my power to the dominion of the senate and people of Rome. For this service of mine I was named Augustus by decree of the senate, and the doorposts of my house were publicly wreathed with bay leaves and a civic crown was fixed over my door and a golden shield was set in the Curia Julia,[7] which, as attested by the inscription thereon, was given me by the senate and people of Rome on account of my courage, clemency, justice and piety. After this time I excelled all in influence, although I possessed no more official power than others who were my colleagues in the several magistracies.

In my thirteenth consulship the senate, the equestrian order and the whole people of Rome gave me the title of Father of my Country. . . .

---

[3]The Forum (Square) Julium was surrounded by a covered portico. Begun by Julius Caesar, it was finished by Augustus. —Eds.

[4]Saturn was a Roman agricultural god associated with the Greek god Cronus. Castor, brother of Pollux and Helen of Troy, was the son of Jupiter by a mortal. The twins Castor and Pollux were deified in Rome for having helped the Romans in a battle. —Eds.

[5]Tiberius Nero, Augustus' adopted son and designated heir, reigned as emperor from A.D. 14 to 37. —Eds.

[6]Illyricum was a Roman province on the eastern coast of the Adriatic Sea. —Eds.

[7]The Curia Julia, also begun by Julius Caesar and completed by Augustus, was a courthouse. —Eds.

Tacitus
THE IMPOSITION OF ONE-MAN RULE

Not all Romans accepted Augustus' own evaluation of his achievements. In this reading, the Roman historian Cornelius Tacitus (A.D. c. 55–c. 117) described how Augustus seduced the Roman people into accepting monarchial rule.

[Augustus] seduced the army with bonuses, and his cheap food policy was successful bait for civilians. Indeed, he attracted everybody's goodwill by the enjoyable gift of peace. Then he gradually pushed ahead and absorbed the functions of the senate, the officials, and even the law. Opposition did not exist. War or judicial murder had disposed of all men of spirit. Upper-class survivors found that slavish obedience was the way to succeed, both politically and financially. They had profited from the revolution, and so now they liked the security of the existing arrangement better than the dangerous uncertainties of the old régime. Besides, the new order was popular in the provinces. There, government by Senate and People was looked upon sceptically as a matter of sparring dignitaries and extortionate officials. The legal system had provided no remedy against these, since it was wholly incapacitated by violence, favouritism, and—most of all—bribery.

To safeguard his domination Augustus made his sister's son Marcellus a priest and an aedile[1]—in spite of his extreme youth—and singled out Marcus Agrippa,[2] a commoner but a first-rate soldier who had helped to win his victories, by the award of two consecutive consulships; after the death of Marcellus, Agrippa was chosen by Augustus as his son-in-law. Next the emperor had his stepsons Tiberius and Nero Drusus[3] hailed publicly as victorious generals. . . .

At this time there was no longer any fighting—except a war against the Germans. . . . In the capital the situation was calm. The titles of officials remained the same. Actium[4] had been won before the younger men were born. Even most of the older generation had come into a world of civil wars. Practically no one had ever seen truly Republican government. The country had been transformed, and there was nothing left of the fine old Roman character. Political equality was a thing of the past; all eyes watched for imperial commands.

Tacitus, *The Annals of Imperial Rome,* translated by Michael Grant, pp. 29–31. (Penguin Classics, 1956, Sixth Revised Edition). Copyright © Michael Grant Publications Ltd., 1956, 1959, 1971, 1989. Reproduced by permission of Penguin Books Ltd.

[1]An aedile was a minor municipal magistrate, responsible for petty criminal cases and for the supervision of markets and public games—gladiator combats and chariot races.—Eds.

[2]Marcus Agrippa (c. 63–12 B.C.), Augustus' son-in-law, was his closest associate and virtually co-emperor; he predeceased Augustus.—Eds.

[3]Nero Drusus (38–9 B.C.), one of Augustus' stepsons, was the father of Emperor Claudius (ruled A.D. 41–54).—Eds.

[4]The Battle of Actium, fought in the sea off west-central Greece, pitted forces of Antony and Cleopatra against those of Octavian (Augustus). Octavian's victory gave him sole control of the Roman Empire.—Eds.

REVIEW QUESTIONS

1. Describe the functions of a Roman emperor as suggested by the career of Augustus.
2. What constituencies did Augustus have to serve?
3. How did Augustus disguise the monarchial character of his regime?

---

2   Imperial Culture

The reign of Augustus marks the golden age of Latin literature. This outpouring of literary works stemmed in part from the patronage of authors by Augustus and other prominent Romans. Roman poets and dramatists used Greek models, just as Roman philosophers, mathematicians, scientists, doctors, and geographers did. Not surprisingly, writers of the Augustan Age often expressed strong patriotic sentiments and were extravagant in their praise of Augustus.

Virgil
THE *AENEID*

The poet Virgil (Publius Vergilius Maro, 70–19 B.C.) admired Augustus, who was his patron, for ending the civil wars and bringing order to the Roman world. Augustus urged Virgil to compose a grand opus that would glorify Rome's imperial achievement—the emperor knew that he would find an honored place in such a work. It took Virgil ten years to produce the *Aeneid*, which was not fully completed when he died. Augustus disobeyed Virgil's deathbed request that the manuscript be destroyed, and the patriotic poem became Rome's national epic.

The *Aeneid* was greatly influenced by Homer's *Iliad* and *Odyssey*. In *The Iliad*, Homer dealt with the conflict between the early Greeks and the Trojans. Roman legend held that a Trojan remnant led by Prince Aeneas, son of Venus (the goddess of love) and a mortal father, Anchises, escaped the sacking of Troy. (Caesar Augustus claimed descent from the goddess Venus through Aeneas.) In book six, Aeneas, escorted by the Sybil, prophetess and priestess of Apollo, descends to the underworld in order to reach his father. There his father's soul describes the illustrious future that will be Rome's.

. . . Turn your two eyes
This way and see this people, your own Romans.
Here is Caesar, and all the line of Iulus
   [founder of the Julian family],
All who shall one day pass under the dome
Of the great sky: this is the man, this one,
Of whom so often you have heard the promise,
Caesar Augustus, son of the deified [Julius Caesar],
Who shall bring once again an Age of Gold
To Latium,[1] to the land where Saturn [Roman
   god] reigned
In early times. He will extend his power
Beyond the Garamants[2] and Indians,
Over far territories north and south

        . . .

Others will cast more tenderly in bronze
Their breathing figures, I can well believe,
And bring more lifelike portraits out of marble;
Argue more eloquently, use the pointer
To trace the paths of heaven accurately
And accurately foretell the rising stars.
Roman, remember by your strength to rule
Earth's peoples—for your arts are to be these:
To pacify, to impose the rule of law,
To spare the conquered, battle down the proud.

Virgil, *The Aeneid*, trans. Robert Fitzgerald (New York: Random House, 1983), pp. 187–188, 190.

[1]Latium was the ancient country in which stood the towns of Lavinium and Alba Longa; Rome was established in that region and became its most significant city.—Eds.
[2]The Garamants (Garamantes) were a warlike nomadic people living in the northwestern Sahara.—Eds.

Ovid
ART OF LOVE

The greatest of the Latin elegists during the golden age was Publius Ovidius Naso, or Ovid (43 B.C.–A.D. 17). Unlike Virgil, Ovid did not experience the civil wars during his adult years. Consequently, he was less inclined to praise the Augustan peace. He was married three times and supposedly had a mistress,

Corinna, to whom he wrote *Amores* (love letters). As a result of his marriages and affairs, Ovid's poetry reveals a preference for romance and humor and a fondness for love and sensual themes.

Ovid is best remembered for his advice to lovers contained in his most famous work—*Ars Amatoria* (Art of Love). Written when Ovid was fifty years old, the poem concerns itself with the art of seduction and is written in a worldly wise yet witty manner. It is divided into three books; the first and second tell how to attract and retain a woman who is the object of a man's desire.

Women can always be caught; that's the first
    rule of the game.
Sooner would birds in the spring be silent, or
    locusts in August,
Sooner would hounds run away when the fierce
    rabbits pursue,
Than would a woman, well-wooed, refuse to
    succumb to a lover;
She'll make you think she means No! while she
    is planning her Yes!
Love on the sly [stolen love] delights men; it is
    equally pleasing to women.
Men are poor at pretense; women can hide their
    desire.
It's a convention, no more [than that], that
    men play the part of pursuer.
Women don't run after us; mousetraps don't
    run after mice.

Play the role of the lover, give the impression
    of heartache;
No matter what your device, that you must
    make her believe,
Nor is it very hard—they all of them think
    that they're lovely,
Even the ugliest hag dotes on her beauty's appeal.
More than once, you will find, the pretense
    ends in conviction,
More than once the romance proves, after all, to
    be true.
So, girls, don't be too harsh on the men you
    suspect of pretending:
Some day the butterfly, Truth, breaks from the
    lying cocoon.

Flattery works on the mind as the waves on the
    bank of a river:
Praise her face and her hair; praise her fingers
    and toes.
Tears are a good thing, too; they move the most
    adamant natures.
Let her, if possible, see tears on your cheeks, in
    your eyes.
This is not easy: sometimes the eyes will not
    stream at your bidding.
What can be done about this?—get your hands
    wet, and apply.

What about sending her poems? A very
    difficult question.
Poems, I am sorry to say, aren't worth so much
    in this town.
Oh, they are praised, to be sure; but the girls
    want something more costly.
Even illiterates please, if they have money to burn.
Ours is a Golden Age, and gold can purchase
    you honors,
All the "Golden Mean" means is, gold is the end.
Homer himself, if he came attended by all of
    the Muses,
With no scrip in his purse, would be kicked
    out of the house.
There are a few, very few, bright girls with a
    real education,
Some (perhaps) here and there, willing to give
    it a try.
So, go ahead, praise both: the worth of the song
    matters little
Just so you make it sound lovely while reading
    aloud.
Whether or not she can tell one kind of verse
    from another,
If there's a line in her praise she will assume,
    "It's a gift!"

From *The Art of Love* by Ovid, translated by Rolfe Humphries (Bloomington: Indiana University Press, 1960), pp. 113, 124, 125, 138, 155, 156, 159, 161–162, 175. Reprinted with permission of Indiana University Press.

Juvenal
THE SATIRES

Juvenal (Decimus Junius Juvenalis, c. A.D. 60–c. 131), Rome's greatest satirical poet, found much fault with the Rome of his day. The streets were crowded, noisy, and unsafe; bullies itched to fight; criminals stole and murdered; the poor suffered even more than other Romans. The following excerpt from *The Satires* is Juvenal's account of the underside of life in Rome.

. . . A man's word
Is believed just to the extent of the
    wealth in his coffers stored.
Though he swear on all the altars from
    here to Samothrace,[1]
A poor man isn't believed. . . .

Anyway, a poor man's the butt of jokes if
    his cloak has a rip
Or is dirty, if his toga is slightly soiled, if a strip
Of leather is split in his shoes and gapes,
    if coarse thread shows
New stitches patching not one but many
    holes. Of the woes
Of unhappy poverty, none is more
    difficult to bear
Than that it heaps men with ridicule.
    Says an usher, "How dare
You sit there? Get out of the rows
    reserved for knights to share. . . ."

. . . What poor man ever inherits
A fortune or gets appointed as clerk to a
    magistrate?
Long ago the penniless Romans ought to
    have staged a great
Mass walkout. It's no easy job for a man
    to advance
When his talents are balked by his
    impoverished circumstance,
But in Rome it's harder than elsewhere. . . .
Here most of the sick die off because
    they get no sleep

(But the sickness is brought on by the
    undigested heap
Of sour food in their burning stomachs),
    for what rented flat
Allows you to sleep? Only rich men in
    this city have that.
There lies the root of the illness—carts
    rumbling in narrow streets
And cursing drivers stalled in a traffic
    jam—it defeats
All hope of rest. . . .

. . . Though we hurry, we merely crawl;
We're blocked by a surging mass ahead,
    a pushing wall
Of people behind. A man jabs me,
    elbowing through, one socks
A chair pole against me, one cracks my
    skull with a beam, one knocks
A wine cask against my ear. My legs are
    caked with splashing
Mud, from all sides the weight of
    enormous feet comes smashing
On mine, and a soldier stamps his
    hobnails through to my sole. . . .

. . . a piece of a pot
Falls down on my head, how often a
    broken vessel is shot
From the upper windows, with what a
    force it strikes and dints
The cobblestones! . . .

The Satires of Juvenal, translated by Hubert Creekmore, pp. 53–54 and 57–61. Permission granted courtesy of Schaffner Agency, Inc. for the estate of Hubert Creekmore.

[1]Samothrace, an island in the northern Aegean Sea, is best known today as the place where the famous statue of the Winged Victory (Nike) was found. —Eds.

The besotted bully, denied his chance in
   the shabby bars
Of killing somebody, suffers torments,
   itching to fight.
Like Achilles[2] bemoaning his friend, he
   tosses about all night,
Now flat on his face, now on his back—
   there's no way at all
He can rest, for some men can't sleep till
   after a bloody brawl.
But however rash and hot with youth
   and flushed with wine,
He avoids the noble whose crimson cloak
   and long double line
Of guards with brass lamps and torches
   show they're too much to handle.
But for me, whom the moon escorts, or
   the feeble light of a candle
Whose wick I husband and trim—he
   has no respect for me.
Now hear how the pitiful fight begins—
   if a fight it be,

When he delivers the punches and I am
   beaten to pulp.
He blocks my way and tells me to stop.
   I stop, with a gulp—
What else can you do when a madman
   stronger than you attacks? . . .

This is the poor man's freedom: having
   been soundly mauled
And cut to pieces by fists, he begs and
   prays, half dead,
To be allowed to go home with a few
   teeth still in his head.

But these aren't your only terrors. For
   you can never restrain
The criminal element. Lock up your
   house, put bolt and chain
On your shop, but when all's quiet,
   someone will rob you or he'll
Be a cutthroat perhaps and do you in
   quickly with cold steel. . . .

---

[2]Achilles, the Greeks' most formidable warrior in Homer's
Iliad, was torn by grief when his best friend Patroclus was
killed by the Trojans. —Eds.

REVIEW QUESTIONS

1. Why are some poems a valuable source for historians?
2. According to Virgil, what was Rome's destiny and the basis of its greatness?
3. Which of Ovid's suggestions do you consider very clever? Very foolish?
4. According to Juvenal, what were some of the hazards of urban life in ancient Rome?

3 Roman Stoicism

Stoicism, the leading school of thought in the Hellenistic world, appealed to
Roman thinkers. Founded by Zeno of Citium (335–267 B.C.), who established an
academy in Athens, Stoicism taught that universal principles, or natural law, un-
derlay the universe. Natural laws applied to all people and were grasped through
reason, which was common to all human beings. Stoicism gave expression to the
universalism of the Hellenistic Age; it held that all people—Greek and barbarian,

free and slave, rich and poor—were essentially equal, for they all had the capacity to reason and were all governed by the same universal laws. Living according to the law of reason that pervades the cosmos provides the individual with the inner fortitude to deal with life's misfortunes, said the Stoics; it is the path to virtue. In the tradition of Socrates, the Stoics regarded people as morally self-sufficient, capable of regulating their own lives. The Romans valued the Stoic emphasis on self-discipline and the molding of character according to worthy standards. The Stoic doctrine of natural law that applied to all peoples harmonized with the requirements of Rome's multinational empire.

Seneca
EPISTLES

Lucius Annaeus Seneca (4 B.C.–A.D. 65) was born at Cordoba (Cordova), Spain, into a highly educated family: his father, for example, was a distinguished rhetorician, politician, and historian. Sent to school in Rome, Seneca studied rhetoric and philosophy, particularly Stoicism. From A.D. 54 to 62, he was a key advisor to the emperor Nero (A.D. 54–68). Later, the notoriously unstable emperor accused Seneca of participating in a conspiracy against him and compelled him to commit suicide.

In traditional Stoic fashion, Seneca held that individuals belong to two commonwealths, the city where they are born and the kingdom of humanity, which is worldwide. In serving this superior commonwealth, individuals become aware of their moral potential. The virtuous tone of Seneca's writings (they had a great appeal to Christians) contrasted with the realities of his life, for Seneca used his political influence for self-enrichment and condoned murder to enhance his political power. Despite this discrepancy between Seneca's words and deeds, he was one of the few Romans to denounce the gladiatorial events as barbaric, and he urged humane treatment of slaves.

The sentiments expressed in these two moral essays, written in the form of epistles (letters) to his friend Lucilius, a prominent Roman civil servant, reveal Seneca's Stoic humanitarianism.

ON GLADIATORS

But nothing is more harmful to a good disposition than to while the time away at some public show. I return from such entertainments more greedy, more dissipated, nay, even more cruel and inhuman. By chance I fell in with a public show at midday, expecting some sport, buffoonery

Adapted from Seneca, *The Epistles*, trans. Thomas Morrell (London: W. Woodfall, 1786), vol. I, Epistles 7, 47.

[clownish amusement], or other relaxation, now that the spectators had seen their fill of human gore. All the bloody deeds of the morning were mere mercy: for now, all trifling apart, they commit downright murder. The combatants have nothing with which to shield the body; they are exposed to every stroke of their antagonist; and every stroke is a wound. And this some prefer to their fighting well armored! There is no helmet or shield to repel the blow; no defense, no art— for these are but so many balks and delays of death. In the morning men are exposed to lions and bears; at noon gladiators who fight to the death are ordered out against one another, and the conqueror is detained for another slaughter. Death alone puts an end to this business. "Kill, burn, scourge," is all they cry. "Why is he so afraid of the sword's point? Why is he so timorous to kill? Why does he not die more manfully?" They are urged on with floggings if they refuse to fight and are obliged to give and take wounds with an open breast. They are called upon to cut one another's throats.

ON SLAVERY

It by no means displeases me, Lucilius, to hear from those who confer with you, that you live on friendly terms with your slaves. This attests to your good sense and education. Are they slaves? No, they are men; they are comrades; they are humble friends. Nay, rather fellow-servants, if you reflect on the equal power of Fortune over both you and them. I therefore laugh at those who think it scandalous for a gentleman to permit, at times, his servant to sit down with him at supper. Why should he not? It is only proud custom that has ordained that a master dine surrounded by at least a dozen slaves and stuff himself, while the poor servants are not allowed to open their lips, even to speak. The slightest murmur is restrained by a rod; nor are mere accidents excused, such as a cough, a sneeze, or a hiccup. Silence interrupted by a word is sure to be punished severely. Thus the slaves must stand, perhaps the whole night, without taking a bit of food or drink or speaking a word. Whence it often happens that such as are not allowed to speak before their masters will speak disrespectfully of them behind their backs. In contrast, those slaves who have been allowed not only to speak before their masters, but sometimes with them, whose mouths were not sewed up, have been ready to incur the most imminent danger, even to the sacrificing of their lives, for their master's safety. Slaves are not naturally our enemies, but we make them such.

I pass by the more cruel and inhuman actions, wherein we treat slaves not as men but as beasts of burden. . . .

Were you to consider, that he whom you call your slave, is sprung from the same origin, enjoys the same climate, breathes the same air, and is subject to the same condition of life and death as yourself, you will think it possible to see him as a free-born person, as he is free to see you as a slave. After the fall of Marius,[1] how many people born of the most splendid parentage and not unjustly expecting a senatorial office for their exploits in war, did fortune cut down? She made one a shepherd, another a caretaker of a country cottage. Can you now despise the man whose fortune is such, into which, while you despise it, you may fall?

I will not discuss at length the treatment of slaves towards whom we behave cruelly and arrogantly. But this is the essence of what I would prescribe: treat your inferiors as you would have a superior treat you. As often as you think of the power that you have over a slave, reflect on the power that your master has over you. But you say, "I have no master." Be it so. The world goes well with you at present; it may not do so always. You may one day be a slave yourself. Do you know at what time Hecuba[2] became a slave, or Croesus,[3] or the mother of Darius,[4] or Plato[5], or Diogenes?[6] Live therefore courteously with your slave; talk with him, dine with him.

---

[1]Gaius Marius (c. 155–86 B.C.) was a famous Roman general.—Eds.

[2]In *The Iliad*, Hecuba, the wife of Priam, king of Troy, was enslaved by the Greeks after their conquest of Troy.—Eds.

[3]Croesus, king of Lydia in Asia Minor from 560 to 546 B.C., was famous for his wealth, but died in slavery after losing his kingdom in battle.—Eds.

[4]Darius III of Persia (336–330 B.C.) was defeated by Alexander the Great, who also captured Darius' mother, wives, and children.—Eds.

[5]Taken prisoner by a city at war at Athens, Plato was brought to the slave market, but was ransomed by a friend.—Eds.

[6]Diogenes (c. 412–323 B.C.), a famous Greek philosopher of the Cynic school, was captured by pirates and put up for sale in Crete. He is reported to have said, "Sell me to that man; he needs a master." He was bought by a wealthy Greek, who restored his freedom.—Eds.

Marcus Aurelius
MEDITATIONS

Emperor Marcus Aurelius Antoninus (ruled A.D. 161–180) was the last of the great Roman Stoics and the last of the so-called Five Good Emperors. His death brought an end to the Pax Romana. A gentle and peace-loving man, Marcus Aurelius was not spared violence and personal misfortune during his reign. Troops returning from Syria brought back a plague, which spread throughout the Empire. Marcus hurried to the East to quell an uprising by the commander of the forces in Asia, who declared himself emperor. Although the mutiny quickly died out, Marcus Aurelius' wife perished on the journey. Four of his five sons died young, and his fifth son, Commodus, who succeeded to the throne, was a cruel tyrant.

For the last fourteen years of his life, Marcus Aurelius had to deal with tribesmen from north of the Danube who broke through the defenses and plundered what is now the Balkan peninsula. Marcus took personal command of the hard-pressed legions on the frontier. During this period he wrote the *Meditations*, twelve books containing his reflections on duty, human dignity, the self-sufficiency of reason, and other themes traditionally discussed by Stoic thinkers. Written in Greek, this deeply personal expression of Stoic philosophy has been called "the highest ethical product of the ancient mind." Excerpts from the *Meditations* follow.

BOOK TWO

Begin each day by telling yourself: Today I shall be meeting with interference, ingratitude, insolence, disloyalty, ill-will, and selfishness—all of them due to the offenders' ignorance of what is good or evil. But for my part I have long perceived the nature of good and its nobility, the nature of evil and its meanness, and also the nature of the [evildoer] himself, who is my brother (not in the physical sense, but as a fellow-creature similarly endowed with reason and a share of the divine); therefore none of those things can injure me, for nobody can implicate me in what is degrading. Neither can I be angry with my brother or fall foul of him; for he and I were born to work together, like a man's two hands, feet, or eyelids, or like the upper and lower rows of his teeth. To obstruct each other is against Nature's law—and what is irritation or aversion but a form of obstruction?

A little flesh, a little breath, and a Reason to rule all—that is myself. . . . As one already on the threshold of death, think nothing of the first—of its viscid [thick] blood, its bones, its web of nerves and veins and arteries. The breath, too; what is that? A whiff of wind; and not even the same wind, but every moment puffed out and drawn in anew. But the third, the Reason, the master—on this you must concentrate. Now that your hairs are grey, let it play the part of a slave no more, twitching puppetwise at every pull of self-interest; and cease to fume at destiny by ever grumbling at today or lamenting over tomorrow. . . .

Hour by hour resolve firmly, like a Roman and a man, to do what comes to hand with correct and natural dignity, and with humanity,

Marcus Aurelius, *Meditations*, translated by Maxwell Staniforth, pp. 45–47, 57–58, 63, 65, 77. © 1964. Reproduced by permission of Penguin Books Ltd.

independence, and justice. Allow your mind freedom from all other considerations. This you can do, if you will approach each action as though it were your last, dismissing the wayward thought, the emotional recoil from the commands of reason, the desire to create an impression, the admiration of self, the discontent with your lot. See how little a man needs to master for his days to flow on in quietness and piety: he has but to observe these few counsels, and the gods will ask nothing more.

BOOK THREE

If mortal life can offer you anything better than justice and truth, self-control and courage—that is, peace of mind in the evident conformity of your actions to the laws of reason, and peace of mind under the visitations of a destiny you cannot control—if, I say, you can discern any higher ideal, why, turn to it with your whole soul, and rejoice in the prize you have found. . . .

Never value the advantages derived from anything involving breach of faith, loss of self-respect, hatred, suspicion, or execration of others, insincerity, or the desire for something which has to be veiled and curtained. One whose chief regard is for his own mind, and for the divinity within him and the service of its goodness, will strike no poses, utter no complaints, and crave neither for solitude nor yet for a crowd. . . . No other care has he in life but to keep his mind from straying into paths incompatible with those of an intelligent and social being. . . .

BOOK FOUR

Men seek for seclusion in the wilderness, by the seashore, or in the mountains—a dream you have cherished only too fondly yourself. But such fancies are wholly unworthy of a philosopher, since at any moment you choose you can retire within yourself. Nowhere can man find a quieter or more untroubled retreat than in his own soul; above all, he who possesses resources in himself, which he need only contemplate to secure immediate ease of mind—the ease that is but another word for a well-ordered spirit. Avail yourself often, then, of this retirement, and so continually renew yourself. Make your rules of life brief, yet so as to embrace the fundamentals; recurrence to them will then suffice to remove all vexation, and send you back without fretting to the duties to which you must return. . . .

If the power of thought is universal among mankind, so likewise is the possession of reason, making us rational creatures. It follows, therefore, that this reason speaks no less universally to us all with its "thou shalt" or "thou shalt not." So then there is a world-law; which in turn means that we are all fellow-citizens and share a common citizenship, and that the world is a single city. Is there any other common citizenship that can be claimed by all humanity? And it is from this world-polity that mind, reason, and law themselves derive. If not, whence else? As the earthy portion of me has its origin from earth, the watery from a different element, my breath from one source and my hot and fiery parts from another of their own elsewhere (for nothing comes from nothing, or can return to nothing), so too there must be an origin for the mind. . . .

BOOK FIVE

At day's first light have in readiness, against disinclination to leave your bed, the thought that "I am rising for the work of man." Must I grumble at setting out to do what I was born for, and for the sake of which I have been brought into the world? Is this the purpose of my creation, to lie here under the blankets and keep myself warm? "Ah, but it is a great deal more pleasant!" Was it for pleasure, then, that you were born, and not for work, not for effort? Look at the plants, the sparrows, ants, spiders, bees, all busy at their own tasks, each doing his part towards a coherent world-order; and will you refuse man's share of the work, instead of being prompt to carry out Nature's bidding? "Yes, but one must have some repose as well." Granted; but repose has its limits set by Nature, in the same way as food and drink have; and you overstep these limits, you go beyond the point of sufficiency; while on the other hand, when action is in question, you stop short of what you could well achieve.

Musonius Rufus
ENLIGHTENED LECTURES ON WOMEN

A major figure among the Roman Stoics, Gaius Musonius Rufus (c. A.D. 30–100) evidenced an enlightened view of women in his lectures.

BY MUSONIUS, FROM THE LECTURE SHOWING THAT WOMEN ALSO SHOULD STUDY PHILOSOPHY

(1) When someone asked him if women also should study philosophy, he began to teach, along lines like the following, how they should do it. For one thing, he said, women have received from the gods the same reasoning power as men—the power which we employ with each other and according to which we consider whether each action is good or bad, and honorable or shameful. Likewise the female has also the same senses as the male: seeing, hearing, ability to smell and the rest. . . . In addition, a desire for virtue and an affinity for it belong by nature not only to men but also to women: no less than men are they disposed by nature to be pleased by noble and just deeds and to censure things opposite these.

(2) Since this is so, why would it be appropriate for men but not women to seek to live honorably and consider how to do so, which is what studying philosophy is? Is it appropriate for men to be good, but not women? Let us also consider, one by one, each of the attributes which are appropriate for a woman who would be good, for it will be apparent that each one of these would come to her most easily from philosophy.

(3) To begin with, a woman must be able to manage an estate, to keep account of things beneficial to it, and to take charge of the household staff. I say that these things would be most characteristic of the woman who pursues philosophy, since each of these is a part of life, and knowledge concerning life is what philosophy is. Furthermore, as Socrates, quoting a verse from the *Odyssey,* used to say, the philosopher has as his goal investigating

What evil and good has been done in your halls.

But a woman must also be self-controlled: she must be free from sexual improprieties and must exercise self-control over other pleasures; she must not be a slave to desires; she must not be quarrelsome, extravagant, or vain. These are the characteristics of the self-controlled woman, as are the following: controlling anger, not being overcome by grief, and being stronger than every emotion.

(4) Philosophic study transmits these things: it seems to me that a person who has studied and practiced them would exhibit the most beautiful character, whether man or woman. What then? These things are so. Would not a

Musonius Rufus: Lectures & Sayings, trans. Cynthia King, published in 2011 by William B. Irvine at www.createspace.com, pp. 28–29, 31–33.

woman who studies philosophy be just? Would she not be a blameless partner in life, a good co-worker and like-minded one, a careful guardian of husband and children, entirely free from the love of gain or grasping for too much? And who, more than a female philosopher (and it is entirely necessary for her to think thus, if she were really a philosopher) would think it worse to do wrong (insofar as it is more shameful) than to be wronged? Likewise, who, more than a female philosopher, would think that suffering loss is better than taking more than one's share? And in addition, who, more than she, would love her children more than life? What woman would be more just than such a woman as this?

(5) Now surely it is appropriate for an educated woman to be braver than an uneducated woman and for a woman trained in philosophy to be braver than one untrained in it. Furthermore, it is appropriate for her not to submit to anything shameful because she fears death or is afraid of pain. It is also appropriate for her not to bow down to anyone, be he well-born, powerful, wealthy, or even, by Zeus, a tyrant.

BY MUSONIUS, FROM THE LECTURE ON WHETHER DAUGHTERS SHOULD GET THE SAME EDUCATION AS SONS

(1) One time in a discussion on whether sons and daughters should get the same education, he said that those who train horses and dogs deal with males no differently from females. Female dogs are trained to hunt in the same way as males. And if one wants female horses to perform well the tasks of horses, they should not be trained differently than the males. In the case of humans, will it really be necessary for males and not females to have something special in their education and upbringing? As if it were not necessary for both a man and a woman alike to have the same virtues, or as if it were possible to achieve the same virtues not through the same lessons, but through different ones!

(2) It is obvious that there is not one type of virtue for a man and another for a woman. To begin with, a man must have good sense, and so must a woman. What, after all, would be the usefulness of a foolish man or woman? Both men and women must live in accordance with justice. A man would not be a good citizen if he is unjust, and a woman would not manage her household well if she does not do it with justice. But if she is unjust, she will act unjustly towards her husband himself. . . . Furthermore, it is as right for a woman to be self-controlled as it is for a man. The laws punish equally a man who seduces and the woman who is seduced. Overeating, drinking too much, and other vices like these, which are acts of self-indulgence and which greatly shame those who are subject to them, show plainly that self-control is most essential for every human being, both female and male: through self-control alone and in no other way do we escape self-indulgence. . . .

(4) As far as the virtues of a man and a woman are concerned, it is entirely appropriate for both men and women to have the same upbringing and education. . . . If men and women must be equally good in the virtue appropriate for a human—must, that is, be wise and self-controlled, and share in courage and justice—will we not educate both alike, and teach both the same way the art by which a human would become good? We must do just that! . . .

(7) We must start by teaching infants that this thing is good and that thing is bad, that this thing is helpful and that thing is harmful, and that this thing must be done and that thing must not be done. As a result of this teaching, a like understanding arises in the girls and boys who master the lesson, and nothing is different for either group. Then we must instill in them shame towards everything base. When understanding and shame exist, both man and woman will obviously be self-controlled. . . .

(8) . . . Rather than educating men and women differently concerning the most important things in life, we should teach them the same. If anyone asks me what knowledge guides this education, I will say to him that just as no man would be properly educated without philosophy, so no woman would be either.

REVIEW QUESTIONS

1. What virtues did Stoics believe should guide human actions?
2. What Stoic philosophic principle influenced Seneca's view of the proper relationship between slaves and masters?
3. According to Marcus Aurelius, what was the purpose of human life?
4. How did a Stoic seek to achieve tranquillity of mind and spirit?
5. Musonius Rufus' lectures on women can be seen as a logical extension of Stoic philosophy. Explain.

4 Roman Law

One of the most significant legacies of Rome to Western civilization is the system of law developed by the Romans over many centuries. Roman law evolved into three distinct types: the civil law (*ius civile*), which was peculiar to the Roman state and applicable only to its citizens; the law of nature (*ius naturale*), an unchanging, everlasting, universal law that was binding on all persons by reason of their common humanity; the law of nations (*ius gentium*), an international law governing the relationship between Romans and other peoples. The law of nations was fashioned by Roman jurists as Rome came into contact with and conquered other cultures; it incorporated elements from Roman civil law and the legal traditions of the other peoples, particularly the Greeks. Roman jurists held that the law of nations accorded with natural law: that is, it rested upon principles of reason that were common to all humans.

Justinian
CORPUS IURIS CIVILIS

The principles of Roman law are drawn from many sources, from the statutes of emperors, edicts of magistrates, and commentaries of learned jurists, such as Ulpian (Domitius Ulpianus, d. A.D. 228), Gaius (A.D. c. 130–180), and Julius Paulus (second–third century A.D.). These past laws and judicial commentaries were culled and selectively incorporated in the *Corpus Iuris Civilis*, the imperial code drawn up by order of Emperor Justinian (A.D. 527–565) and promulgated in A.D. 534. It has been said that next to the Bible, no book has had a deeper impact on Western civilization than Justinian's code. It became the official body of laws of the eastern Roman (or Byzantine) Empire through the Middle Ages and was gradually reintroduced into Western Europe in the twelfth century. Roman law continued in the postmedieval world and formed the basis of common law in all Western lands except England and its dependencies, where its influence was less marked. Some principles of Roman law are readily recognizable in today's legal systems, as the following excerpts indicate.

- The Divine Trajan stated in a Rescript addressed to Julius Frontonus that anyone who is absent should not be convicted of crime. Likewise, no one should be convicted on suspicion; for the Divine Trajan stated in a Rescript to Assiduus Severus: "It is better to permit the crime of a guilty person to go unpunished than to condemn one who is innocent."

- No one suffers a penalty for merely thinking.

- Proof is incumbent upon the party who affirms a fact, not upon him who denies it.

- In inflicting penalties, the age and inexperience of the guilty party must always be taken into account.

- Nothing is so opposed to consent, which is the basis of *bona fide* contracts, as force and fear; and to approve anything of this kind is contrary to good morals.

- The crime or the punishment of a father can place no stigma upon his son; for each one is subjected to fate in accordance with his conduct, and no one is appointed the successor of the crime of another.

- Women are excluded from all civil or public employments; therefore they cannot be judges, or perform the duties of magistrates, or bring suits in court, or become sureties for others, or act as attorneys.

- A minor, also, must abstain from all civil employments.

- Every person should support his own offspring, and anyone who thinks that he can abandon his child shall be subjected to the penalty prescribed by law. We do not give any right to masters or to patrons to recover children who have been abandoned, when children exposed by them, as it were, to death, have been rescued through motives of pity, for no one can say that a child whom he has left to perish belongs to him.

- The authority and observance of long-established custom should not be treated with contempt, but it should not prevail to the extent of overcoming either reason or law.

Not all principles of Roman law have been incorporated into the legal codes of modern societies. One example is the use of torture to test the testimony of witnesses, particularly those of low social status. In those lands where Roman law remained in effect, torture was legal until the eighteenth century, when it was purged from European judicial systems.

- Torture is employed in the detection of crime, but a beginning should not be made with its application; and, therefore, in the first place, evidence should be resorted to, and if the party is liable to suspicion, he shall be compelled by torture to reveal his accomplices and crimes.

- Where several culprits are implicated in the same offence, they should be examined in such a way as to begin with the one who appears to be more timid than the others, and of tender age.

- Torture is not applied in [financial] matters, unless when an investigation is made with reference to property belonging to an estate; other things, however, are established by oath, or by the evidence of witnesses.

- Torture should not be inflicted upon a minor under fourteen years of age, as the Divine Pius stated in a Rescript addressed to Caecilius Jubentinus.

- All persons, however, without exception, shall be tortured in a case of high treason which has reference to princes, if their testimony is necessary, and circumstances demand it.

Justinian, *Corpus Iuris Civilis* (The Civil Law), trans. S. P. Scott, 17 vols. (Cincinnati: The Central Trust Company, 1932).

- Torture should not be applied to the extent that the accuser demands, but as reason and moderation may dictate.

- In questions where freedom is involved it is not necessary to seek for the truth by the torture of those whose status is in dispute.

- It was declared by the Imperial Constitutions that while confidence should not always be reposed in torture, it ought not to be rejected as absolutely unworthy of it, as the evidence obtained is weak and dangerous, and inimical to the truth; for most persons, either through their power of endurance, or through the severity of the torment, so despise suffering that the truth can in no way be extorted from them. Others are so little able to suffer that they prefer to lie rather than to endure the question, and hence it happens that they make confessions of different kinds, and they not only implicate themselves, but others as well.

- The Edict of the Divine Augustus, which he published during the Consulate of Vivius Avitus and Lucius Apronianus, is as follows: "I do not think that torture should be inflicted in every instance, and upon every person; but when capital and atrocious crimes cannot be detected and proved except by means of the torture of slaves, I hold that it is most effective for ascertaining the truth, and should be employed."

REVIEW QUESTIONS

1. What is the *ius naturale* and what are its implications when applied to particular legal cases?
2. What is the *ius gentium* and what were its origins?
3. What provisions of Justinian's code are reflected in present-day legal systems in Europe and America?
4. Why are both torture and slavery in the modern world seen as incompatible with the basic premises of natural law?

5 Provincial Administration

During the Pax Romana, Roman officials governed territories that extended from Britain, Spain, and present-day Morocco in the west to Mesopotamia and Armenia in the east; from the Rhine and Danube rivers in Western and Central Europe to the Sahara in northern Africa. The Roman Empire reached its greatest geographic extent under Emperor Trajan (A.D. 98–117), who conquered Dacia (heartland of modern Romania). The basic unit of political administration, the city, met most of the daily political and social needs of the population. Above the level of the city governments were the Roman provincial authorities, led by governors usually appointed by and responsible directly to the emperor. The Senate's role in governing the provinces gradually declined, and the burdens of ruling the vast territory fell largely on the emperor. This enormous task proved daunting for all but the most energetic and conscientious emperors.

CORRESPONDENCE BETWEEN PLINY THE YOUNGER AND EMPEROR TRAJAN

A series of letters exchanged between Emperor Trajan and Gaius Plinius Caecilius (Pliny the Younger, A.D. c. 61–c. 112), governor of the Roman province of Bithynia, located in the northwestern corner of Asia Minor, reveal the many problems Roman provincial officials faced. Given the highly personal character of the imperial office, provincial officials like Pliny, even when urged not to do so, tended to refer most problems directly to the emperor for policy guidance.

XXXIII

Pliny to the Emperor Trajan

While I was visiting another part of the province, a widespread fire broke out in Nicomedia[1] which destroyed many private houses and also two public buildings (the Elder Citizens' Club and the Temple of Isis)[2] although a road runs between them. It was fanned by the strong breeze in the early stages, but it would not have spread so far but for the apathy of the populace; for it is generally agreed that people stood watching the disaster without bestirring themselves to do anything to stop it. Apart from this, there is not a single fire engine anywhere in the town, not a bucket nor any apparatus for fighting a fire. These will now be provided on my instructions.

Will you, Sir, consider whether you think a company of firemen might be formed, limited to 150 members? I will see that no one shall be admitted who is not genuinely a fireman, and that the privileges granted shall not be abused: it will not be difficult to keep such small numbers under observation.

XXXIV

Trajan to Pliny

You may very well have had the idea that it should be possible to form a company of firemen

at Nicomedia on the model of those existing elsewhere, but we must remember that it is societies like these which have been responsible for the political disturbances in your province, particularly in its towns. If people assemble for a common purpose, whatever name we give them and for whatever reason, they soon turn into a political club. It is a better policy then to provide the equipment necessary for dealing with fires, and to instruct property owners to make use of it, calling on the help of the crowds which collect if they find it necessary.

XXXIX

Pliny to the Emperor Trajan

The theatre at Nicaea,[3] Sir, is more than half built but is still unfinished, and has already cost more than ten million sesterces,[4] or so I am told—I have not yet examined the relevant accounts. I am afraid it may be money wasted. The building is sinking and showing immense cracks, either because the soil is damp and soft or the stone used was poor and friable [crumbly]. We shall certainly have to consider whether it is

---

[1]Nicomedia was the capital city of the province of Bithynia (northern Turkey today). —Eds.
[2]Isis, the chief Egyptian goddess and consort of Osiris, was widely worshiped throughout the Roman Empire. —Eds.
[3]Nicaea was another city in Bithynia. The Roman theater was an open-air structure, consisting of the flat stage used by the performers, the orchestra (close to the stage, a place where senators and nobles sat), and the auditorium, a sloped stand or rows of stone benches on which the rest of the audience sat. Dramas and declamations of poetry were given in the theaters. —Eds.
[4]One sestertius (plural, *sesterces*) equals one-quarter of a silver denarius. —Eds.

to be finished or abandoned, or even demolished, as the foundations and substructure intended to hold up the building may have cost a lot but look none too solid to me. There are many additions to the theatre promised by private individuals, such as a colonnade on either side and a gallery above the auditorium,[5] but all these are now held up by the stoppage of work on the main building which must be finished first.

The citizens of Nicaea have also begun to rebuild their gymnasium[6] (which was destroyed by fire before my arrival) on a much larger and more extensive scale than before. They have already spent a large sum, which may be to little purpose, for the buildings are badly planned and too scattered. Moreover, an architect—admittedly a rival of the one who drew up the designs—has given the opinion that the walls cannot support the superstructure in spite of being twenty-two feet thick, as the rubble core has no facing of brick.

The people of Claudiopolis[7] are also building, or rather excavating, an enormous public bath in a hollow at the foot of a mountain. The money for this is coming either from the admission fees already paid by the new members of the town council elected by your gracious favour, or from what they will pay at my demand. So I am afraid there is misapplication of public funds at Nicaea....

...I am therefore compelled to ask you to send out an architect to inspect both theatre and bath and decide whether it will be more practicable, in view of what has already been spent, to keep to the original plans and finish both buildings as best we can, or to make any necessary alterations and changes of site so that we do not throw away more money in an attempt to make some use of the original outlay.

---

[5]The word *auditorium* was also used in the modern sense, a lecture room or courtroom; the word means "listening place." —Eds.
[6]As now, a gymnasium was a place where Greek and Roman wrestlers competed, and other small-scale athletic feats were performed. It was also a hall where citizens heard lectures or debates and socialized. —Eds.
[7]Claudiopolis was another city in the Roman province of Bithynia. —Eds.

XL
Trajan to Pliny

The future of the unfinished theatre at Nicaea can best be settled by you on the spot. It will be sufficient for me if you let me know your decision. But, once the main building is finished, you will have to see that private individuals carry out their promises of adding to the theatre.

These poor Greeks all love a gymnasium; so it may be that they were too ambitious in their plans at Nicaea. They will have to be content with one which suits their real needs.

As for the bath at Claudiopolis, which you say has been started in an unsuitable site, you must decide yourself what advice to give. You cannot lack architects: every province has skilled men trained for this work. It is a mistake to think they can be sent out more quickly from Rome when they usually come to us from Greece.

XXXI
Pliny to the Emperor Trajan

You may stoop when necessary, Sir, to give ear to my problems, without prejudice to your eminent position, seeing that I have your authority to refer to you when in doubt.

In several cities, notably Nicomedia and Nicaea, there are people who were sentenced to service in the mines or the arena, or to other similar punishments, but are now performing the duties of public slaves and receiving an annual salary for their work. Since this was told me I have long been debating what to do. I felt it was too hard on the men to send them back to work out their sentences after a lapse of many years, when most of them are old by now, and by all accounts are quietly leading honest lives, but I did not think it quite right to retain criminals in public service; and though I realized there was nothing to be gained by supporting these men at public expense if they did no work, they might be a potential danger if they were left to starve. I was therefore obliged to leave the whole question in suspense until I could consult you.

You may perhaps want to know how they came to be released from the sentences passed on them. I asked this question myself, but received no satisfactory answer to give you, and although the records of their sentences were produced, there were no documents to prove their release. But people have stated on their behalf that they had been released by order of the previous governors or their deputies, and this is confirmed by the unlikelihood that any unauthorized person would take this responsibility.

XXXII
Trajan to Pliny

Let us not forget that the chief reason for sending you to your province was the evident need for many reforms. Nothing in fact stands more in need of correction than the situation described in your letter, where criminals under sentence have not only been released without authority but are actually restored to the status of honest officials. Those among them who were sentenced within the last ten years and were released by no proper authority must therefore be sent back to work out their sentences. But if the men are elderly and have sentences dating back farther than ten years, they can be employed in work not far removed from penal labour, cleaning public baths and sewers, or repairing streets and highways, the usual employment for men of this type.

XXVI
Pliny to the Emperor Trajan

As a result of your generosity to me, Sir, Rosianus Germinus became one of my closest friends; for when I was consul he was my quaestor {financial officer}. I always found him devoted to my interests, and ever since then he has treated me with the greatest deference and increased the warmth of our public relations by many personal services. I therefore pray you to give your personal attention to my request

for his advancement; if you place any confidence in my advice you will bestow on him your favour. He will not fail to earn further promotion in whatever post you place him. I am sparing in my praises because I trust that his sincerity, integrity and application are well known to you already from the high offices he has held in Rome beneath your own eyes, as well as from his service in the army under your command.

I still feel that I have not given adequate expression to the warmth of my affection, and so once more I pray you, Sir, most urgently, to permit me to rejoice as soon as possible in the due promotion of my quaestor—that is to say, in my own advancement in his person.

LXV
Pliny to the Emperor Trajan

A very considerable question, Sir, in which the whole province is interested, has been lately started, concerning the state and maintenance of what are called *foundlings* {abandoned infants}. I have examined the rulings of former Princes upon this head, but not finding any thing in them either particular or general relating to the Bithynians, I thought it necessary to apply to you for your directions. For in a point which requires the special interposition of your authority, I could not content myself with following precedents.

An edict of the Emperor Augustus (as pretended) was read to me, concerning Asia[8]; also a letter from Vespasian to the Lacedaemonians, and another from Titus to the same, with one likewise from him to the Achaeans. Also a letter from Domitian to the Proconsuls Avidius Nigrinus and Armenius Brocchus, and another to the Lacedaemonians: but I have not transmitted them to you, as well because they were ill-copied (and some of them, too, of doubtful authority) as because I imagine the true copies are preserved in your Record Office.

---

[8] I.e., the Roman province so called.

LXVI
Trajan to Pliny

The question concerning free-born persons who have been exposed [abandoned] as infants and reared in slavery by those who took them up, has been frequently discussed; but I do not find in the archives of the Princes my predecessors, any general regulation upon this head, extending to all the provinces. There are, indeed, letters of Domitian to Avidius Nigrinus and Armenius Brocchus, which perhaps ought to be observed; but Bithynia is not comprehended in the provinces therein mentioned. I am of opinion, therefore, that those who desire emancipation upon this ground should not be debarred from publicly asserting their freedom, nor be obliged to purchase it by repaying the cost of their maintenance.

REVIEW QUESTION

What kinds of political and administrative problems in the Roman Empire are suggested by the letters of Trajan and Pliny?

---

6 The Roman Peace

The two-hundred-year period from Augustus' assumption of sole power in 27 B.C. to the death of Emperor Marcus Aurelius in A.D. 180 marks the Pax Romana, the Roman Peace. Roman poets and officials extolled the Roman achievement—the creation of a well-run world-state that brought order and stability to the different nations of the Mediterranean world.

Aelius Aristides
THE ROMAN ORATION
THE BLESSINGS OF THE PAX ROMANA

In the following reading, Aelius Aristides (A.D. 117–187), a Greek intellectual, glowingly praises the Pax Romana in an oration that was probably delivered in Rome. In the tradition of Roman orators, Aristides used hyperbole and exaggeration. Nevertheless, the oration does capture the universalism and cosmopolitanism that characterized the Roman Empire.

If one considers the vast extent of your empire he must be amazed that so small a fraction of it rules the world, but when he beholds the city and its spaciousness it is not astonishing that all the habitable world is ruled by such a capital. . . . Your possessions equal the sun's course. . . . You do not rule within fixed boundaries, nor can anyone dictate the limits of your sway. . . . Whatever any people produces can be found here, at all times and in abundance. . . . Egypt, Sicily, and the civilized part of Africa are your farms; ships are continually coming and going. . . .

Republished with permission of Elizabeth Hadas from *A History of Rome: From Its Origins to 529 A.D*, ed. Moses Hadas, 1956; permission conveyed through Copyright Clearance Center, Inc.

Vast as it is, your empire is more remarkable for its thoroughness than its scope: there are no dissident or rebellious enclaves. . . . The whole world prays in unison that your empire may endure forever.

Governors sent out to cities and peoples each rule their charges, but in their relations to each other they are equally subjects. The principal difference between governors and their charges is this—they demonstrate the proper way to be a subject. So great is their reverence for the great Ruler [the emperor], who administers all things. Him they believe to know their business better than they themselves do, and hence they respect and heed him more than one would a master overseeing a task and giving orders. No one is so self-assured that he can remain unmoved upon hearing the emperor's name; he rises in prayer and adoration and utters a twofold prayer—to the gods for the Ruler, and to the Ruler for himself. And if the governors are in the least doubt concerning the justice of claims or suits of the governed, public or private, they send to the Ruler for instructions at once and await his reply, as a chorus awaits its trainer's directions. Hence the Ruler need not exhaust himself by traveling to various parts to settle matters in person. It is easy for him to abide in his place and manage the world through letters; these arrive almost as soon as written, as if borne on wings.

But the most marvelous and admirable achievement of all, and the one deserving our fullest gratitude, is this. . . . You alone of the imperial powers of history rule over men who are free. You have not assigned this or that region to this nabob or that mogul. . . . But just as citizens in an individual city might designate magistrates, so you, whose city is the whole world, appoint governors to protect and provide for the governed, as if they were elective, not to lord it over their charges. As a result, so far from [treating] the office as if it were their own, governors make way for their successors readily when their term is up, and may not even await their coming. Appeals to a higher jurisdiction are as easy as appeals from parish to county. . . .

But the most notable and praiseworthy feature of all, a thing unparalleled, is your magnanimous conception of citizenship. All of your subjects (and this implies the whole world) you have divided into two parts: the better endowed and more virile, wherever they may be, you have granted citizenship and even kinship; the rest you govern as obedient subjects. Neither the seas nor expanse of land bars citizenship; Asia and Europe are not differentiated. Careers are open to talent. . . . Rich and poor find contentment and profit in your system; there is no other way of life. Your polity is a single and all-embracing harmony. . . .

You have not put walls around your city, as if you were hiding it or avoiding your subjects; to do so you considered ignoble and inconsistent with your principles, as if a master should show fear of his slaves. You did not overlook walls, however, but placed them round the empire, not the city. The splendid and distant walls you erected are worthy of you; to men within their circuit they are visible, but it requires a journey of months and years from the city to see them. Beyond the outermost ring of the civilized world you drew a second circle, larger in radius and easier to defend, like the outer fortifications of a city. Here you built walls and established cities in diverse parts. The cities you filled with colonists; you introduced arts and crafts and established an orderly culture. . . . Your military organization makes all others childish. Your soldiers and officers you train to prevail not only over the enemy but over themselves. The soldier lives under discipline daily, and none ever deserts the post assigned him.

You alone are, so to speak, natural rulers. Your predecessors were masters and slaves in turn; as rulers they were counterfeits, and reversed their positions like players in a ball game. . . . You have measured out the world, bridged rivers, cut roads through mountains, filled the wastes with posting stations, introduced orderly and refined modes of life. . . .

Be all gods and their offspring invoked to grant that this empire and this city flourish forever and never cease until stones float upon the sea and trees forbear to sprout in the springtide. May the great Ruler and his sons be preserved to administer all things well.

Tacitus
THE OTHER SIDE OF THE PAX ROMANA

Not all peoples in the Roman Empire welcomed Roman rule. Some nations, particularly Jews, Gauls, Britons, and Egyptians, saw themselves as victims of brutal domination and rose in revolt against their Roman governors. Our knowledge of their motives and grievances is usually secondhand, being found in the records of their enemies—the Romans and their collaborators.

Cornelius Tacitus (A.D. 56–117), Roman historian and orator, wrote a biography of his father-in-law, Agricola (A.D. 40–93), a general who completed the conquest of northern Britain. In this excerpt, Tacitus describes the character and motives of Roman imperialism from a Briton's viewpoint. The speech that follows is uttered by Calgacus, a leader of the northern, or Caledonian, tribes during the Roman campaign in the years A.D. 77–83. The ideas expressed, however, are those that Tacitus, a well-informed Roman of high social rank, believed the victims of Roman military conquest held about their situation.

"Whenever I consider why we are fighting and how we have reached this crisis, I have a strong sense that this day of your splendid rally may mean the dawn of liberty for the whole of Britain. You have mustered to a man, and to a man you are free. There are no lands behind us, and even the sea is menaced by the Roman fleet. The clash of battle—the hero's glory—has become the safest refuge for the coward. Battles against Rome have been lost and won before—but never without hope; we were always there in reserve. We, the choice flower of Britain, were treasured in her most secret places. Out of sight of subject shores, we kept even our eyes free from the defilement of tyranny. We, the last men on earth, the last of the free, have been shielded till today by the very remoteness and the seclusion for which we are famed. We have enjoyed the impressiveness of the unknown. But today the boundary of Britain is exposed; beyond us lies no nation, nothing but waves and rocks and the Romans, more deadly still than they, for you find in them an arrogance which no reasonable submission can elude. Brigands of the world, they have exhausted the land by their indiscriminate plunder, and now they ransack the sea. The wealth of an enemy excites their [greed], his poverty their lust of power. East and West have failed to glut their maw [stomach]. They are unique in being as violently tempted to attack the poor as the wealthy. Robbery, butchery, rapine, the liars call Empire; they create a desolation and call it peace.

"We instinctively love our children and our kinsmen above all else. These are torn from us by conscription to slave in other lands. Our wives and sisters, even if they are not raped by Roman enemies, are seduced by them in the guise of guests and friends. Our goods and fortunes are ground down to pay tribute, our land and its harvest to supply corn, our bodies and hands to build roads through woods and swamps—all under blows and insults. Slaves, born into slavery, once sold, get their keep from their masters. But as for Britain, never a day passes but she pays and feeds her enslavers. In a private household it is the latest arrival who is always the butt of his fellow-slaves; so, in this establishment, where all the world have long been slaves, it is we, the cheap new acquisitions, who are picked out for extirpation. You see, we have no fertile lands, no mines, no harbours, which we might be spared to work. Courage and martial spirit we have, but the master does not relish them in the subject. Even our remoteness and seclusion, while they protect, expose us to suspicion. Abandon, then, all hope of mercy and at last take courage, whether it is life or honour that you hold most dear. . . . Let us, then, uncorrupted, unconquered as we are, ready to fight for freedom but never to repent failure, prove at the first clash of arms what heroes Caledonia[1] has been holding in reserve. . . .

_____

[1]Caledonia was the name given by the Romans to the section of Scotland north of what is now the Firth of Forth. —Eds.

. . . Or can you seriously think that those Gauls or Germans[2]—and, to our bitter shame, many Britons too!— are bound to Rome by genuine loyalty or love? They may be lending their life-blood to foreign tyrants, but they were enemies of Rome much longer than they have been her slaves. Apprehension and terror are weak bonds of affection; once break them, and, where fear ends, hatred will begin. All that can goad men to victory is on our side. . . . In the ranks of our very enemies we shall find hands to help us. . . . They [the Romans] have nothing in reserve that need alarm us—only forts without garrisons, colonies of grey-beards, towns sick and distracted between rebel subjects and tyrant masters. Here before us is their general, here his army; behind are the tribute, the mines and all the other whips to scourge slaves. Whether you are to endure these for ever or take summary vengeance, this field must decide. On, then, into action and, as you go, think of those that went before you and of those that shall come after."

_____

[2]The Gauls consisted of several groups of tribes in modern Belgium, the Netherlands, France, and Switzerland. The Germani (Germans), who had been conquered by Rome, lived north of the Gauls, just south of the Rhine; the rest of the Germani occupied a large territory north and east of the Rhine. —Eds.

REVIEW QUESTIONS

1. According to Aelius Aristides, how did Roman rule benefit the peoples of the Roman Empire?
2. What views about Rome do you think Tacitus wishes to express through the speech he attributes to Calgacus the Briton?

7 Third-Century Crisis

An extravagant tyrant, Marcus Aurelius' son Commodus (Lucius Aelius Aurelius, A.D. 180–192) was an unworthy successor, and his reign marks the close of the Pax Romana. For the next hundred years the Roman Empire was burdened by economic, political, and military crises. For much of the third century, barbarian tribesmen broke through the northern frontier defenses and plundered the Balkans, Greece, Asia Minor, northern Italy, Gaul, and Spain; the Persians invaded the Empire from the east. The legions, consisting predominantly of the least Romanized provincials, used their weapons to place their own commanders on the throne. During the ensuing civil wars, the soldiers looted the towns as if they were an invading army. Rome was drifting into anarchy.

The devastations by barbarians and the soldiers wrecked the economy, which was further damaged by crushing taxes and requisitions of goods and by inflation caused by debased coinage. Everywhere, people were fleeing from plundering barbarians or soldiers, from warring armies, and from government officials who extorted taxes and goods and services from an already overburdened population.

Dio Cassius
CARACALLA'S EXTORTIONS

The reign (A.D. 211–217) of Caracalla provides an early example of the crushing demands imposed by the state on its citizenry. The following account comes from the *Roman History* of Dio Cassius (C. A.D. 150–235). In addition to writing history, Dio Cassius had an active career in public service, serving as a senator, governor, and consul.

[Caracalla] was fond of spending money upon the soldiers, great numbers of whom he kept in attendance upon him, alleging one excuse after another and one war after another; but he made it his business to strip, despoil, and grind down all the rest of mankind, and the senators by no means least. In the first place, there were the gold crowns that he was repeatedly demanding, on the constant pretext that he had conquered some enemy or other; and I am not referring, either, to the actual manufacture of the crowns—for what does that amount to?—but to the vast amount of money constantly being given under that name by the cities for the customary "crowning," as it is called, of the emperors. Then there were the provisions that we were required to furnish in great quantities on all occasions, and this without receiving any remuneration and sometimes actually at additional cost to ourselves—all of which supplies he either be-

stowed upon the soldiers or else peddled out; and there were the gifts which he demanded from the wealthy citizens and from the various communities; and the taxes, both the new ones which he promulgated and the ten percent tax that he instituted in place of the five percent tax applying to the emancipation of slaves, to bequests, and to all legacies. . . . But apart from all these burdens, we were also compelled to build at our own expense all sorts of houses for him whenever he set out from Rome, and costly lodgings in the middle of even the very shortest journeys; yet he not only never lived in them, but in some cases was not destined even to see them. Moreover, we constructed amphitheatres and race-courses wherever he spent the winter or expected to spend it, all without receiving any contribution from him; and they were all promptly demolished, the sole reason for their being built in the first place being, apparently, that we might become impoverished.

The emperor himself kept spending the money upon the soldiers, as we have said, and upon wild beasts and horses; for he was forever killing vast numbers of animals, both wild and domesticated, forcing us to furnish most of them, though he did buy a few. One day he slew a hundred boars at one time with his own hands. . . . In everything he was very hot-headed and very fickle, and he furthermore possessed the craftiness of his mother and the Syrians, to which race she belonged. He would appoint some freedman or other wealthy person to be director of the games in order that the man might spend money in this way also; and he would salute the spectators with his whip from the arena below and beg for gold pieces like a performer of the lowest class. . . . To such an extent was the entire world, so far as it owned his sway, devastated throughout his whole reign, that on one occasion the Romans at a horse-race shouted in unison this, among

other things: "We shall do the living to death,[1] that we may bury the dead." Indeed, he often used to say: "Nobody in the world should have money but me; and I want it to bestow upon the soldiers." Once when Julia [Domna, his mother] chided him for spending vast sums upon them and said, "There is no longer any source of revenue, either just or unjust, left to us," he replied, exhibiting his sword, "Be of good cheer, mother: for as long as we have this, we shall not run short of money."

Moreover to those who flattered him he distributed both money and goods.

―――――

[1]Or, "We are stripping the living. . . ."

PETITION TO EMPEROR PHILIP

A petition presented about A.D. 245 to Emperor Philip (M. Julius Philippus, A.D. 244–249) reveals the desperation of the peasants.

We who flee as suppliants to the refuge of your divinity are the entire population of your most sacred estate. We are suffering extortion and illegal exactions beyond all reason at the hands of those who ought to preserve the public welfare. . . . Military commanders, soldiers, and powerful and influential men in the city and your officials . . . swoop down upon us, take us away from our work, requisition our plow oxen, and illegally exact what is not due them. As a result we are suffering extraordinary injustice by this extortion. We wrote about all this to your majesty, Augustus,[1] when you held the prefecture of the Praetorian Guard[2] . . . and how your divinity

was moved [as] the rescript [emperor's official answer] quoted herewith makes clear: "We have transmitted the content of your petition to the governor, who will see to it that there is no further cause for complaint." But inasmuch as this rescript has brought us no aid, it has resulted that we are still suffering throughout the countryside illegal exactions of what is not owing, as certain parties assault us and trample upon us unjustly, and we are still suffering extraordinary extortion at the hands of the officials, and our resources have been exhausted and the estates deserted.

―――――

[1]The title Augustus was originally given by the Senate to Octavian, the first emperor. It later became the title of all his successors. —Eds.
[2]The Praetorian Guard, commanded by a prefect (*praefectus*), was the official troop of imperial bodyguards. —Eds.

Roman Civilization: Selected Readings, ed. Naphtali Lewis and Meyer Reinhold, Sourcebook 2: *The Empire* (New York: Columbia University Press, 1955), p. 454.

REVIEW QUESTIONS

1. How did the Roman emperors abuse their power?
2. What evidence do these documents provide of the citizens' growing hate for the Roman state?

8 The Demise of Rome

The conquest of the western provinces of the Roman Empire by various Germanic tribes in the fifth century A.D. was made easier by the apathy and frequent collaboration of Roman citizens themselves. Many Romans had grown to hate the bureaucratic oppressors who crushed them with constant demands for excessive and unfair taxes, forced labor on government projects, extortion, and all the evils of a police state. In some areas of Gaul and Spain, peasants had revolted and successfully defended their homes and farms against the Roman authorities. When such barbarians as the Visigoths, Vandals, and Ostrogoths entered the region, many Romans welcomed them as liberators and cooperated with them in establishing their new kingdoms.

Ammianus Marcellinus
THE BATTLE OF ADRIANOPLE

The problem of guarding the frontier became increasingly urgent in the last part of the fourth century. The Huns, a nomadic people from central Asia, swept across the plains of Russia with their armed cavalry. They subdued the Ostrogoths, a Germanic tribe in Ukraine, and put pressure on the Germanic Visigoths, who had migrated along the Danube into what is now Romania.

Encamped on the Danube, the Visigoths, desperate to escape from the Huns, petitioned the eastern emperor Valens to let them take refuge deeper within the Roman Empire. Not eager to resort to force to keep the Goths out and hoping that they would prove useful allies against other enemies, Valens permitted them to cross the Danube. But after imperial officials plundered their possessions and carried off some into slavery, the Visigoths took up arms against the Empire.

In A.D. 378, the Visigoths and the Romans fought each other in a historic battle at Adrianople. The Visigoths routed the Roman forces, killing or capturing perhaps as much as two-thirds of the Roman army. Emperor Valens perished in what was Rome's worst defeat since Cannae in the war with Hannibal. The Visigoths were on Roman territory to stay. The battle of Adrianople signified that Rome could no longer defend its borders. The Roman historian Ammianus Marcellinus (A.D. 330–c. 400) describes this historic battle in the following excerpts.

... In the meantime a report spread extensively through the nations of the Goths, that a race of men, hitherto unknown, had suddenly descended like a whirlwind from the lofty mountains, as if they had risen from some secret recess of the earth, and were ravaging and destroying everything which came in their way. And then the greater part of the population ... resolved to flee and to seek a home remote from all knowledge of the [Huns]; and after a long deliberation where to fix their abode, they resolved that a retreat into Thrace [within the Roman Empire] was the most suitable for these two reasons: first of all, because it is a district most fertile in grass; and

---

Ammianus Marcellinus, "So Destructive a Slaughter: The Battle of Adrianople," from *The Roman History*, trans. C. D. Yonge (Bohn's Classical Library, 1887).

also because by the great breadth of the Danube, it is wholly separated from the [Huns]. . . .

[Valens] sent forth several officers to bring this ferocious people and their wagons into our territory. And such great pains were taken to gratify this nation which was destined to overthrow the empire of Rome, that not one was left behind, not even of those who were stricken with mortal disease. Moreover, having obtained permission of the emperor to cross the Danube and to cultivate some districts in Thrace, they crossed the stream day and night, without ceasing, embarking in troops on board ships and rafts, and canoes made of the hollow trunks of trees, in which enterprise, as the Danube is the most difficult of all rivers to navigate, and was at that time swollen with continual rains, a great many were drowned, who, because they were too numerous for the vessels, tried to swim across, and in spite of all their exertions were swept away by the stream.

In this way, through the turbulent zeal of violent people, the ruin of the Roman empire was brought on. This, at all events, is neither obscure nor uncertain, that the unhappy officers who were intrusted with the charge of conducting the multitude of the barbarians across the river, though they repeatedly endeavoured to calculate their numbers, at last abandoned the attempt as hopeless; and the man who would wish to ascertain the number might as well (as the most illustrious of poets [Virgil] says) attempt to count the waves in the African sea, or the grains of sand tossed about by the zephyr. . . .

But after the innumerable multitudes of different nations, diffused over all our provinces, and spreading themselves over the vast expanse of our plains, filled all the champaign country and all the mountain ranges . . . the emperor assigned them a temporary provision for their immediate support, and ordered lands to be assigned them to cultivate.

At that time the defences of our provinces were much exposed and the armies of barbarians spread over them like the lava of Mount Etna. . . .

The barbarians, like beasts who had broken loose from their cages poured unrestrainedly over the vast extent of country. . . .

When the Visigoths proved to be enemies of Rome, the eastern emperor Valens led his army to Adrianople and pitched camp. As he waited impatiently for the arrival of Gratian, the western emperor, he took counsel with his officers.

Some, following the advice of Sebastian [Valens's nephew] recommended with urgency that he should at once go forth to battle; while Victor, master-general of the cavalry, a Sarmatian by birth, but a man of slow and cautious temper, recommended him to wait for his imperial colleague, and this advice was supported by several officers, who suggested that the reinforcement of [Gratian, the western emperor's] army would be likely to awe the fiery arrogance of the barbarians.

However, the fatal obstinacy of the emperor prevailed, fortified by the flattery of some of the princes, who advised him to hasten with all speed so that Gratian might have no share in a victory which, as they fancied, was already almost gained. . . .

The Roman army draws near the Visigoths, and the battle begins.

Then, having traversed the broken ground, which divided the two armies, as the burning day was progressing towards noon, at last, after marching eight miles, our men came in sight of the wagons of the enemy all arranged in a circle. According to their custom, the barbarian host raised a fierce and hideous yell, while the Roman generals marshalled their line of battle. The right wing of the cavalry was placed in front; the chief portion of the infantry was kept in reserve.

But the left wing of the cavalry, of which a considerable number were still straggling on the road, were advancing with speed, though with great difficulty. . . .

[I]n the meantime the cavalry of the Goths had returned . . . ; these descending from the mountains like a thunderbolt, spread confusion and slaughter among all whom in their rapid charge they came across.

And while arms and missiles of all kinds were meeting in fierce conflict, and Bellona [the goddess of war], blowing her mournful trumpet, was raging more fiercely than usual to inflict disaster on the Romans, our men began to retreat; but roused by the reproaches of their officers, they made a fresh stand, and the battle increased like a conflagration, terrifying our soldiers, numbers of whom were pierced by strokes from the javelins hurled at them, and from arrows.

Then the two lines of battle dashed against each other, like the rams of warships, and, thrusting with all their might, were tossed to and fro, like the waves of the sea. Our left wing had advanced actually up to the wagons, with the intent to push on still further if they were properly supported; but they were deserted by the rest of the cavalry, and so pressed upon by the superior numbers of the enemy, that they were overwhelmed and beaten down, like the ruin of a vast rampart. Presently our infantry also was left unsupported, while the different companies became so huddled together that a soldier could hardly draw his sword, or withdraw his hand after he had once stretched it out. And by this time such clouds of dust arose that it was scarcely possible to see the sky, which resounded with horrible cries; and in consequence, the darts, which were bearing death on every side, reached their mark, and fell with deadly effect because no one could see them beforehand so as to guard against them.

But when the barbarians, rushing on with their enormous host, beat down our horses and men, and left no spot to which our ranks could fall back to deploy, they were so closely packed that it was impossible to escape by forcing a way through them. Our men at last began to despise death, and again took to their swords, and slew all they encountered, while with mutual blows of battleaxes, helmets and breastplates were dashed in pieces.

Then you might see the barbarian towering in his fierceness, hissing or shouting, fall with his legs pierced through, or his right hand cut off, sword and all, or his side transfixed, and still, in the last gasp of life, casting round him defiant glances. The plain was covered with carcasses, strewing the mutual ruin of the combatants, while the groans of the dying, or of men fearfully wounded, were intense and caused great dismay all around.

Amidst all this great tumult and confusion our infantry were exhausted by toil and danger, till at last they had neither strength left to fight, nor spirits to plan anything; their spears were broken by the frequent collisions, so that they were forced to content themselves with their drawn swords, which they thrust into the dense battalions of the enemy, disregarding their own safety, and seeing that every possibility of escape was cut off from them.

The ground, covered with streams of blood, made their feet slip, so that all that they endeavoured to do was to sell their lives as dearly as possible; and with such vehemence did they resist their enemies who pressed on them, that some were even killed by their own weapons. At last one black pool of blood disfigured everything, and wherever the eye turned, it could see nothing but piled-up heaps of dead, and lifeless corpses trampled on without mercy.

The sun being now high in the heavens, having traversed the sign of Leo, and reached the abode of the heavenly Virgo, scorched the Romans, who were emaciated by hunger, worn out with toil, and scarcely able to support even the weight of their armour. At last our columns were entirely beaten back by the overpowering weight of the barbarians, and so they took to disorderly flight, which is the only resource in extremity, each man trying to save himself as well as he could.

While they were all flying and scattering themselves over roads with which they were unacquainted, the emperor, bewildered with terrible fear, made his way over heaps of dead, and fled to the battalions of the Lancearii [an elite force armed with spears] and the Mattiarii [infantrymen armed with lead-weighted darts], who, till the superior numbers of the enemy became wholly irresistible, stood firm and immovable. As soon as he saw him, Trajan [the Roman commander] exclaimed that all hope was lost, unless the emperor, thus deserted by his guards, could be protected by the aid of his foreign allies.

When this exclamation was heard, a count named Victor hastened to bring up with all speed the Batavians [German tribesmen in the service of Rome], who were placed in the reserve and who ought to have been near at hand, but as none of them could be found, he too retreated, and in a similar manner Richomeres and Saturninus [other Roman officers] saved themselves from danger.

So now, with rage flashing in their eyes, the barbarians pursued our men, who were in a state of torpor, the warmth of their veins having deserted them. Many were slain without knowing who smote them; some were overwhelmed by the mere weight of the crowd which pressed upon them; and some were slain by wounds—inflicted by their own comrades. The barbarians spared neither those who yielded nor those who resisted.

Besides these, many half-slain lay blocking up the roads, unable to endure the torture of their wounds; and heaps of dead horses were piled up and filled the plain with their carcasses. At last a dark moonless night put an end to the irremediable disaster which cost the Roman state so dear.

Just when it first became dark, the emperor being among a crowd of common soldiers, as it was believed—for no one said either that he had seen him, or been near him—was mortally wounded with an arrow, and, very shortly after, died, though his body was never found. For as some of the enemy loitered for a long time about the field in order to plunder the dead, none of the defeated army or of the inhabitants ventured to go to them. . . .

. . . Many illustrious men fell in this disastrous defeat. . . . Scarcely one-third of the whole army escaped. Nor, except the battle of Cannae, is so destructive a slaughter recorded in our annals.

After this disastrous battle, when night had veiled the earth in darkness, those who survived fled, some to the right, some to the left, or wherever fear guided them, each man seeking refuge among his relations, as no one could think of anything but himself, while all fancied the lances of the enemy sticking in their backs. And far off were heard the miserable wailings of those who were left behind—the sobs of the dying, and the agonizing groans of the wounded.

But when daylight returned, the conquerors, like wild beasts rendered still more savage by the blood they had tasted and allured by the temptations of groundless hope, marched in a dense column upon Adrianople.

Salvian
POLITICAL AND SOCIAL INJUSTICE

The growing hatred of citizens for the Roman state is well delineated in a book called *The Governance of God*, by Salvian (Salvianus) of Marseilles (A.D. c. 400–470). A Christian priest, Salvian was an eyewitness to the end of Roman rule in Gaul. He describes the political and moral causes of the collapse of the Roman state in the West in the following reading.

What towns, as well as what municipalities and villages are there in which there are not as many tyrants as *curiales*.[1] Perhaps they glory in this name of tyrant because it seems to be considered powerful and honored. For, almost all robbers rejoice and boast, if they are said to be more fierce than they really are. What place is there, as I have said, where the bowels of widows and orphans are not devoured by the leading men of the cities, and with them those of almost all holy men? . . . Not one of them [widows and orphans], therefore, is safe. In a manner, except for the very powerful, neither is anyone safe from the devastation of general brigandage, unless they are like the robbers themselves. To this state of affairs, indeed, to this crime has the world come that, unless one is bad, he cannot be safe. . . .

All the while, the poor are despoiled, the widows groan, the orphans are tread underfoot, so much so that many of them, and they are not of obscure birth and have received a liberal education, flee to the enemy lest they die from the pain of public persecution. They seek among the barbarians the dignity of the Roman because they cannot bear barbarous indignity among the Romans. Although these Romans differ in religion and language from the barbarians to whom they flee, and differ from them in respect to filthiness of body and clothing, nevertheless, as I have said, they prefer to bear among the barbarians a worship unlike their own rather than rampant injustice among the Romans.

Salvian tells how Roman citizens are deserting Rome to live under the rule of the Goths and other barbarian invaders. Moreover, in many parts of Spain and Gaul (France), peasants called *Bagaudae* have rebelled and established zones free from Roman authority.

Thus, far and wide, they migrate either to the Goths[2] or to the Bagaudae, or to other barbarians

---

The Writings of Salvian, The Presbyter, pp.134–138 and 141. Copyright ©1962 by The Catholic University of America Press. Used with permission.

everywhere in power; yet they do not repent having migrated. They prefer to live as freemen under an outward form of captivity than as captives under an appearance of liberty. Therefore, the name of Roman citizens, at one time not only greatly valued but dearly bought, is now repudiated and fled from, and it is almost considered not only base but even deserving of abhorrence.

And what can be a greater testimony of Roman wickedness than that many men, upright and noble and to whom the position of being a Roman citizen should be considered as of the highest splendor and dignity, have been driven by the cruelty of Roman wickedness to such a state of mind that they do not wish to be Romans? . . .

I am now about to speak of the Bagaudae [peasant insurgents] who were despoiled, oppressed and murdered by evil and cruel judges. After they had lost the right of Roman citizenship, they also lost the honor of bearing the Roman name. We blame their misfortunes on themselves. We ascribe to them a name which signifies their downfall. We give to them a name of which we ourselves are the cause. We call them rebels. We call those outlaws whom we compelled to be criminal.

For, by what other ways did they become Bagaudae, except by our wickedness, except by the wicked ways of judges, except by the proscription and pillage of those who have turned the assessments of public taxes into the benefit of their own gain and have made the tax levies their own booty? Like wild beasts, they did not rule but devoured their subjects, and feasted not only on the spoils of men, as most robbers are wont to do, but even on their torn flesh and, as I may say, on their blood.

---

[1]The *curiales* were members of the municipal councils. In the late years of the Roman Empire, they were forced to act as tax collectors for the central government and to pay from their own pockets whatever sums they could not collect from the overtaxed inhabitants. —Eds.

[2]The Goths were Germanic tribes that invaded Rome. The Visigoths invaded Italy in the early fifth century and seized Rome for a few days. This was the first time in eight centuries that a foreign enemy had entered the capital. Later the Visigoths occupied large areas of Spain and Gaul. In the late fifth century, the Ostrogoths invaded and conquered Italy, establishing a kingdom there. —Eds.

Thus it happened that men, strangled and killed by the robberies of judges, began to live as barbarians because they were not permitted to be Romans. They became satisfied to be what they were not, because they were not permitted to be what they were. They were compelled to defend their lives at least, because they saw that they had already completely lost their liberty. . . .

But what else can these wretched people wish for, they who suffer the incessant and even continuous destruction of public tax levies. To them there is always imminent a heavy and relentless proscription. They desert their homes, lest they be tortured in their very homes. They seek exile, lest they suffer torture. The enemy is more lenient to them than the tax collectors. This is proved by this very fact, that they flee to the enemy in order to avoid the full force of the heavy tax levy. This very tax levying, although hard and inhuman, would nevertheless be less heavy and harsh if all would bear it equally and

in common. Taxation is made more shameful and burdensome because all do not bear the burden of all. They extort tribute from the poor man for the taxes of the rich, and the weaker carry the load for the stronger. There is no other reason that they cannot bear all the taxation except that the burden imposed on the wretched is greater than their resources. . . .

Therefore, in the districts taken over by the barbarians, there is one desire among all the Romans, that they should never again find it necessary to pass under Roman jurisdiction. In those regions, it is the one and general prayer of the Roman people that they be allowed to carry on the life they lead with the barbarians. And we wonder why the Goths are not conquered by our portion of the population, when the Romans prefer to live among them rather than with us. Our brothers, therefore, are not only altogether unwilling to flee to us from them, but they even cast us aside in order to flee to them.

Saint Jerome
THE FATE OF ROME

Saint Jerome (Hieronymus, c. A.D. 340–420) was one of the major theologians and scriptural scholars of the late Roman period. He left Rome itself to join a monastery in Bethlehem in Judea, where he studied Hebrew and began work on a monumental new translation of the Hebrew and Christian scriptures into Latin. This new edition, called the Vulgate (written in the Latin of the common people), became the standard text of the Bible in the Western church for more than a thousand years. In the following letter to Agenuchia, a highborn lady of Gaul, Saint Jerome bemoans the fate of Rome, once so proud and powerful. The letter, dated A.D. 409, was written at a critical moment: the Visigoths had accepted a huge ransom to end their siege of Rome.

Nations innumerable and most savage have invaded all Gaul. The whole region between the

Readings in European History, vol. 1: *From the Breaking Up of the Roman Empire to the Protestant Revolt*, ed. James Harvey Robinson (Boston: Ginn and Company, 1904), pp. 44–45.

Alps and the Pyrenees, the ocean and the Rhine, has been devastated by the Quadi, the Vandals, the Sarmati, the Alani, the Gepidae, the hostile Heruli, the Saxons, the Burgundians, the Alemanni, and the Pannonians [barbarian tribes]. O wretched Empire! Mayence [Mainz], formerly so noble a city, has been taken and ruined, and in the church many thousands of men have been massacred. Worms has been destroyed after a long siege. Rheims, that powerful city, Amiens, Arras, Speyer, Strasburg,[1]—all have seen their citizens led away captive into Germany. Aquitaine and the provinces of Lyons and Narbonne, all save a few towns, have been depopulated; and these the sword threatens without, while hunger ravages within. I cannot speak without tears of Toulouse, which the merits of the holy Bishop Exuperius have prevailed so far to save from destruction. Spain, even, is in daily terror lest it perish, remembering the invasion of the Cimbri;[2] and whatsoever the other provinces have suffered once, they continue to suffer in their fear.

I will keep silence concerning the rest, lest I seem to despair of the mercy of God. For a long time, from the Black Sea to the Julian Alps,[3] those things which are ours have not been ours; and for thirty years, since the Danube boundary was broken, war has been waged in the very midst of the Roman Empire. Our tears are dried by old age. Except a few old men, all were born in captivity and siege, and do not desire the liberty they never knew. . . .

When the Visigoths led by Alaric sacked Rome in 410, Jerome lamented in another letter.

Who could believe that Rome, built upon the conquest of the whole world, would fall to the ground? that the mother herself would become the tomb of her peoples?

[1] The names of modern cities here used are not in all cases exact equivalents for the names of the regions mentioned by Jerome.
[2] The Cimbri, originally from what is now Denmark, spread southward to invade Spain, Gaul, and Italy in the late part of the second century B.C. They were defeated by the Roman general Marius (c. 157–86 B.C.). —Eds.

[3] The mountains called the Julian Alps are in northwest Slovenia. —Eds.

Pope Gregory I
THE END OF ROMAN GLORY

In the late sixth century, the Lombards, the last Germanic tribe to invade those lands that had once been Roman, swept down the Tiber valley and in A.D. 593 were at the gates of Rome. At that time, Pope Gregory I, "the Great" (reigned 590–604), descendant of a prominent and wealthy Roman senatorial family, reflected on Rome, once the "mistress of the world."

We see on all sides sorrows; we hear on all sides groans. Cities are destroyed, fortifications razed to the ground, fields devastated, the land reduced to solitude. No husbandman is left in

Gregory the Great, trans. F. Homes Dudden (New York: Longmans, Green and Co., 1905), vol. 2, pp. 18–20.

the field, few inhabitants remain in the cities, and yet these scanty remnants of the human race are still each day smitten without ceasing. . . . Some men are led away captive, others are mutilated, others slain before our eyes. What is there, then, my brethren to please us in this world?

What Rome herself, once deemed the Mistress of the World, has now become, we see—wasted away with afflictions, grievous and many, with the loss of citizens, the assaults of enemies, the frequent fall of ruined buildings. . . . For where is the Senate? Where is the People [the State]? The bones are dissolved, the flesh is consumed, all the pomp of the dignities of this world is gone. . . .

Yet even we who remain few as we are, still are daily smitten with the sword, still are daily crushed by innumerable afflictions. . . . For the Senate is no more, and the People has perished, yet sorrow and sighing are multiplied daily among the few that are left. Rome is, as it were, already empty and burning. . . . But where are they who once rejoiced in her glory? Where is their pomp? Where their pride? Where their constant and immediate joy? . . .

. . . The Sons of men of the world, when they wished for worldly advancement came together from all parts of the earth to this city. But now behold! she is desolate. Behold! she is wasted away. No one hastens to her for worldly advancement.

REVIEW QUESTIONS

1. How does Ammianus account for Rome's defeat at Adrianople?
2. What conditions in late Roman society undermined the social and political bonds between the rulers and the ruled?
3. What were the consequences of the Germanic invasions as depicted by Saint Jerome and Pope Gregory I?

CHAPTER 6
Early Christianity

FRENCH PSALTER, fourteenth century. This medieval illustration depicts monks singing.
(Bridgeman-Giraudon / Art Resource, NY)

Christianity, the core religion of Western civilization, emerged during the first century of the Roman Empire. The first Christians were followers of Jesus Christ, a Jew, who, in the tradition of the Hebrew prophets, called for a moral reformation of the individual. Jesus' life, teachings, crucifixion, and the belief that he had risen from the dead convinced his followers that Jesus was divine and had shown humanity the way to salvation. Dedicated disciples spread this message throughout the Mediterranean world.

Surviving persecution and gaining in numbers, Christianity appealed to all classes from slave to aristocrat and had become the state religion of Rome by the end of the fourth century. The reasons for the spread and triumph of Christianity are diverse. The poor and oppressed of the Roman world were drawn to Jesus' message of love and compassion, his concern for humanity; the promise of salvation had an immense attraction to people who were burdened with misfortune and fearful of death. Jesus' call for a moral transformation of the individual addressed itself to the inner conscience of men and women of all social classes.

The Judeo-Christian and Greco-Roman (classical humanist) traditions constitute the foundations of Western civilization. Nevertheless, they represent two contrasting views of the world. For classical humanists, the ultimate aim of life was the achievement of excellence in this world, the maximum cultivation of human talent; Christians subordinated this world to a higher reality. For Christians, the principal purpose of life was the attainment of salvation—entrance into a heavenly kingdom after death.

In the Greco-Roman tradition, reason was autonomous; that is, the intellect depended on its own powers and neither required nor accepted guidance from a supernatural authority. For example, Socrates held that ethical standards were arrived at through rational thought alone; they were not divine commandments revealed to human beings by a heavenly lawmaker. Conservative Christian churchmen, believing that Greek intellectualism posed a threat to Christian teachings, wanted nothing to do with Greek philosophy. But other Christians, recognizing the value of Greek philosophy, sought to integrate Greek learning into the Christian framework. Greek philosophy, they said, could help Christians clarify, organize, and explain their teachings. Those who advocated studying and utilizing Greek philosophy prevailed; thus Christianity preserved rational thought, the priceless achievement of the Greek mind. In the process, however, philosophy lost its autonomy, for Early Christian thinkers insisted that to reason properly one must first believe in God and his revelation, with the Bible as the ultimate authority. Without these prior conditions, the Christians argued, reason would lead to error. Thus, for Early Christian thinkers, unlike their Greek predecessors, reason was not autonomous: it was subject to divine authority as interpreted by the church.

In the late Roman Empire, when Roman institutions were breaking down and classical values were being discarded, Christianity was a dynamic movement. Surviving the barbarian invasions, the Christian church gave form and direction to the European culture that emerged in the Middle Ages.

---

1 The Teachings of Jesus

During the reign (A.D. 14–37) of the Emperor Tiberius, the Roman governor in Judea, Pontius Pilate, executed on charges of sedition an obscure Jewish religious teacher, Jesus of Nazareth. While performing healings and exorcisms, Jesus expounded a message of hope and salvation for sinners who repented. To the Jews who were attracted to Jesus' person and teachings, Jesus appeared to be a new prophet or even the long-awaited Messiah, the divinely promised leader who would restore Israel to freedom and usher in a new age.

Jesus made enemies among those powerful Jewish leaders who believed that the popular preacher was undermining their authority and weakening respect for their teachings on the requirements of Jewish law. The Romans viewed Jesus as a political agitator who might lead the Jews in a revolt against Roman rule. Some Jewish leaders denounced Jesus to the Roman authorities, who executed him.

After the death of Jesus, his loyal followers, who believed in his resurrection, continued to preach his teachings, forming small congregations of those faithful to his mission and words. They soon spread out as missionaries to Jewish and Gentile communities throughout the Roman Empire. These followers of Jesus, the Messiah, or in Greek, *Christos* (anointed one), were the founders of the Christian church.

Like Socrates, Jesus himself never wrote a book; all we know of his life and teachings are the recollections of his disciples, passed down orally until put in written form some thirty to seventy years after his death. These primary sources include the *gospels* (good news) attributed to the saints Mark, Matthew, Luke, and John; the letters of Saint Paul and others; the Acts of the Apostles, a historical account of their missionary work; and the book of Revelation, a prophetic portrayal of the coming messianic kingdom of Jesus and God's destruction of the powers of evil. These works, composed several decades and more after Jesus' death and collected together definitively in the fourth century, comprise the New Testament, the Christian sacred scriptures. They reflect the ways in which the Early Christians remembered Jesus' teachings and the meaning of his life and ministry.

THE GOSPEL ACCORDING TO SAINT MARK

In this reading from Saint Mark's gospel, Jesus stated in a few words the core of his ethical teaching.

28 And one of the scribes[A] came up and heard them disputing with one another, and seeing that he answered them well, asked him, "Which commandment is the first of all?" [29]Jesus answered, "The first is, 'Hear, O Israel: The Lord our God, the Lord is one;[B] [30]and you shall love the Lord your God with all your heart, and with all your soul, and with all your mind, and with all your strength.' [31]The second is this, 'You shall love your neighbor as yourself.' There is no other commandment greater than these." [32]And the scribe said to him, "You are right, Teacher;

you have truly said that he is one, and there is no other but he; [33]and to love him with all the heart, and with all the understanding, and with all the strength, and to love one's neighbor as oneself, is much more than all whole burnt offerings and sacrifices." [34]And when Jesus saw that he answered wisely, he said to him, "You are not far from the kingdom of God." And after that no one dared to ask him any question. [Mark 12]

[A]Scribes were not only copyists of the scrolls that contained Jewish law, but they were also students of that law.
[Editors' footnotes for Bible readings in this chapter are not numbered, to eliminate confusion with verse numbers. —Eds.]
[B]"Hear, O Israel" occurs in the Book of Deuteronomy in the Hebrew scriptures as the "first law," that of monotheism (one God). Here, as a Jew, Jesus was reminding his followers of this fact. —Eds.

THE GOSPEL ACCORDING TO SAINT MATTHEW

In the gospel of Saint Matthew, Jesus outlined to his disciples the attitudes pleasing to God; this is the famous Sermon on the Mount.

1 Seeing the crowds, he went up on the mountain, and when he sat down his disciples came to him. [2]And he opened his mouth and taught them, saying:

3 "Blessed are the poor in spirit, for theirs is the kingdom of heaven.

4 "Blessed are those who mourn, for they shall be comforted.

5 "Blessed are the meek, for they shall inherit the earth.

6 "Blessed are those who hunger and thirst for righteousness, for they shall be satisfied.

7 "Blessed are the merciful, for they shall obtain mercy.

8 "Blessed are the pure in heart, for they shall see God.

9 "Blessed are the peacemakers, for they shall be called sons of God.

10 "Blessed are those who are persecuted for righteousness' sake, for theirs is the kingdom of heaven.

11 "Blessed are you when men revile you and persecute you and utter all kinds of evil against you falsely on my account. [12]Rejoice and be glad, for your reward is great in heaven, for so men persecuted the prophets who were before you. . . ." [Matthew 5]

A characteristic feature of Jesus' teaching—one that angered the Jewish leaders—was a demand that his followers go beyond the letter of the Jewish law. In the tradition of the Hebrew prophets, Jesus stressed the ethical demands that underlie this law and urged a moral transformation of human character, based on a love of God and neighbor. In the following passage, Jesus reinterprets the Hebrew commandments on killing, adultery, divorce, vengeance, the definition of a neighbor, and almsgiving.

---

17 "Think not that I have come to abolish the law and the prophets; I have come not to abolish them but to fulfil them. . . .

21 "You have heard that it was said to the men of old, 'You shall not kill; and whoever kills shall be liable to judgment.' [22]But I say to you that every one who is angry with his brother shall be liable to judgment; whoever insults his brother shall be liable to the council, and whoever says, 'You fool!' shall be liable to the hell of fire. [23]So if you are offering your gift at the altar, and there remember that your brother has something against you, [24]leave your gift there before the altar and go; first be reconciled to your brother, and then come and offer your gift. [25]Make friends quickly with your accuser. . . .

27 "You have heard that it was said, 'You shall not commit adultery.' [28]But I say to you that every one who looks at a woman lustfully has already committed adultery with her in his heart. [29]If your right eye causes you to sin, pluck it out and throw it away; it is better that you lose one of your members than that your whole body be thrown into hell. [30]And if your right hand causes you to sin, cut it off and throw it away; it is better that you lose one of your members than that your whole body go into hell.

31 "It was also said, 'Whoever divorces his wife, let him give her a certificate of divorce.' [32]But I say to you that every one who divorces his wife, except on the ground of unchastity, makes her an adulteress; and whoever marries a divorced woman commits adultery. . . .

38 "You have heard that it was said, 'An eye for an eye and a tooth for a tooth.' [39]But I say to you, Do not resist one who is evil. But if any one strikes you on the right cheek, turn to him the other also; [40]and if any one would sue you and take your coat, let him have your cloak as well; [41]and if any one forces you to go one mile, go with him two miles. [42]Give to him who begs from you, and do not refuse him who would borrow from you.

43 "You have heard that it was said, 'You shall love your neighbor and hate your enemy.' [44]But I say to you, Love your enemies and pray for those who persecute you, [45]so that you may be sons of your Father who is in heaven. . . ." [Matthew 5]

— — —

1 "Beware of practicing your piety before men in order to be seen by them; for then you will have no reward from your Father who is in heaven.

2 "Thus, when you give alms, sound no trumpet before you, as the hypocrites do in the synagogues[A] and in the streets, that they may be praised by men. Truly, I say to you, they have their reward. [3]But when you give alms, do not let your left hand know what your right hand is doing, [4]so that your alms may be in secret; and your Father who sees in secret will reward you. . . ." [Matthew 6]

[A]Synagogues, originally a name given to substitutes outside Judea for the Temple in Jerusalem, coexisted with the Temple; they were places for public prayer and study of the Hebrew scriptures. —Eds.

REVIEW QUESTIONS

1. What did Jesus believe to be the basic tenets of his teachings?
2. Why might his message appeal to many people?

---

2 The Dead Sea Scrolls

Between 1947 and 1956 some 800 documents, written primarily in Hebrew but also in Aramaic and Greek, were discovered in eleven caves on the shore of the Dead Sea, thirteen miles east of Jerusalem. Relying on advanced radiocarbon dating tests and textual analysis, scholars conclude that the documents were written in stages between 200 B.C. and 70 A.D. The oldest copies of Old Testament writings ever found, these scrolls, many of them fragments but some intact manuscripts, are of considerable historical and religious importance. For example, the Isaiah Scroll, is a thousand years older than the earliest known surviving text. The scrolls also contain some previously unknown psalms and unknown stories about Joseph, Moses, and other biblical figures; commentaries on the Hebrew scriptures; wisdom writings; and rules for the Essenes, the Jewish sect that wrote the scrolls.

The Essenes were a devout Jewish sect that established a semimonastic community in the barren Judean Desert at Qumran to live more holy lives. Rejecting the Temple priests as corrupt—the "Sons of Darkness"—they were led by a priest called the "Teacher of Righteousness." Although the scrolls make no reference to Jesus or his followers, scholars do find parallels between the Qumran community and the Jesus movement. Like Jesus, for example, the community spoke of the end of days that they believed was imminent. Both the Qumran community and Jesus' early followers considered themselves the true Israel, referred to themselves as the "sons of light," and anticipated a coming messianic age.

Josephus
THE ESSENES

Flavius Josephus (A.D. C. 37–C. 100), originally Joseph Benb-Mathias, was a scholarly Jewish commander during the Jewish revolt against Rome (A.D. 66–70). Captured by Romans in 67, he became an active collaborator for the rest of the war.

His *The Jewish War*, an account of the conflict between the Jews of Palestine and their Roman rulers, also contains passages that describe the essential outlook of the Essenes.

Among the Jews there are three schools of thought, whose adherents are called Pharisees, Sadducees, and Essenes respectively. The Essenes profess a severer discipline: they are Jews by birth and are peculiarly attached to each other. They eschew pleasure-seeking as a vice and regard temperance and mastery of the passions as virtue. Scorning wedlock, they select other men's children while still pliable and teachable, and fashion them after their own pattern—not that they wish to do away with marriage as a means of continuing the race, but they are afraid of the promiscuity of women and convinced that none of the sex remains faithful to one man. Contemptuous of wealth, they are communists to perfection, and none of them will be found to be better off than the rest: their rule is that novices admitted to the sect must surrender their property to the order, so that among them all neither humiliating poverty nor excessive wealth is ever seen, but each man's possessions go into the pool and as with brothers their entire property belongs to them all. . . . Men to supervise the community's affairs are elected by show of hands, chosen for their tasks by universal suffrage. . . .

. . . Among themselves nothing is bought or sold: everyone gives what he has to anybody in need and receives from him in return something he himself can use; and even without giving anything in return they are free to share the possessions of anyone they choose. . . .

In general they take no action without orders from the supervisors, but two things are left entirely to them—personal aid and charity; they may of their own accord help any deserving person in need or supply the penniless with food. But gifts to their own kinsfolk require official sanction. Showing indignation only when justified, they keep their

Josephus, *The Jewish War*, translated by G. A. Williamson, pp. 133–135. (London: Penguin Books, 1970) © 1970. Reproduced by permission of Penguin Books Ltd.

tempers under control; they champion good faith and serve the cause of peace. Every word they speak is more binding than an oath; swearing they reject as something worse than perjury, for they say a man is already condemned if he cannot be believed without God being named. They are wonderfully devoted to the work of ancient writers, choosing mostly books that can help soul and body; from them in their anxiety to cure disease they learn all about medicinal roots and the properties of stones.

Persons desirous of joining the sect are not immediately admitted. For a whole year a candidate is excluded but is required to observe the same rule of life as the members, receiving from them a hatchet, the loin-cloth mentioned above, and white garments. When he has given proof of his temperance during this period, he is associated more closely with the rule and permitted to share the purer waters of sanctification, though not yet admitted to the communal life. He has demonstrated his strength of purpose, but for two more years his character is tested, and if he is then seen to be worthy, he is accepted into the society. But before touching the communal food he must swear terrible oaths, first that he will revere the Godhead, and secondly that he will deal justly with men, will injure no one either of his own accord or at another's bidding, will always hate the wicked and co-operate with the good, and will keep faith at all times and with all men—especially with rulers, since all power is conferred by God. If he himself receives power, he will never abuse his authority and never by dress or additional ornament outshine those under him; he will always love truth and seek to convict liars, will keep his hands from stealing and his soul innocent of unholy gain, and will never hide anything from members of the sect or reveal any of their secrets to others, even if brought by violence to the point of death. He further swears to impart their teaching to no man otherwise than as he himself received it, to take no part in armed robbery, and to preserve the books of the sect and in the same way the names of the angels. Such are the oaths by which they make sure of their converts.

The Qumran Community
THE COMMUNITY RULE

Found in the Dead Sea Scrolls is the Essenes' Community Rule, which shows the members' commitment to the Law of Moses with its command for righteous behavior.

And this is the Rule for the men of the Community who have freely pledged themselves to be converted from all evil and to cling to all His commandments according to His will.

They shall separate from the congregation of the men of injustice and shall unite, with respect to the Law and possessions, under the authority of the sons of Zadok, the Priests who keep the Covenant, and of the multitude of the men of the Community who hold fast to the Covenant. Every decision concerning doctrine, property, and justice shall be determined by them.

They shall practise truth and humility in common, and justice and uprightness and charity and modesty in all their ways. No man shall walk in the stubbornness of his heart so that he strays after his heart and eyes and evil inclination, but he shall circumcise in the Community the foreskin of evil inclination and of stiffness of neck that they may lay a foundation of truth for Israel, for the Community of the everlasting Covenant. They shall atone for all those in Aaron who have freely pledged themselves to holiness, and for those in Israel who have freely pledged themselves to the House of Truth, and for those

The Complete Dead Sea Scrolls in English, rev. ed. by Geza Vermes, pp. 103–105. Copyright © 2004. Reproduced by permission of Penguin Books Ltd.

who join them to live in community and to take part in the trial and judgement and condemnation of all those who transgress the precepts.

On joining the Community, this shall be their code of behaviour with respect to all these precepts.

Whoever approaches the Council of the Community shall enter the Covenant of God in the presence of all who have freely pledged themselves. He shall undertake by a binding oath to return with all his heart and soul to every commandment of the Law of Moses in accordance with all that has been revealed of it to the sons of Zadok, the Priests, Keepers of the Covenant and Seekers of His will, and to the multitude of the men of their Covenant who together have freely pledged themselves to His truth and to walking in the way of His delight. And he shall undertake by the Covenant to separate from all the men of injustice who walk in the way of wickedness.

For they are not reckoned in His Covenant. They have neither inquired nor sought after Him concerning His laws that they might know the hidden things in which they have sinfully erred; and matters revealed they have treated with insolence. Therefore Wrath shall rise up to condemn, and Vengeance shall be executed by the curses of the Covenant, and great chastisements of eternal destruction shall be visited on them, leaving no remnant. They shall not enter the water to partake of the pure Meal of the men of holiness, for they shall not be cleansed unless they turn from their wickedness: for all who transgress His word are unclean. Likewise, no man shall consort with him in regard to his work or property lest he be burdened with the guilt of his sin. He shall indeed keep away from him in all things: as it is written, *Keep away from all that is false* [Exod. 28:7]. No member of the Community shall follow them in matters of doctrine and justice, or eat or drink anything of theirs, or take anything from them except for a price; as it is written, *Keep away from the man in whose nostrils is breath, for wherein is he counted?* [Isa. 2:22]. For all those not reckoned in His Covenant are to be set apart, together with all that is theirs. None of the men of holiness shall lean upon works of vanity: for they are all vanity who know not His Covenant, and He will blot from the world all them that despise His word. All their deeds are defilement before Him, and all their property unclean.

But when a man enters the Covenant to walk according to all these precepts that he may be joined to the holy Congregation, they shall examine his spirit in community with respect to his understanding and practice of the Law, under the authority of the sons of Aaron who have freely pledged themselves in the Community to restore His Covenant and to heed all the precepts commanded by Him, and of the multitude of Israel who have freely pledged themselves in the Community to return to His Covenant. They shall inscribe them in order, one after another, according to their understanding and their deeds, that every one may obey his companion, the man of lesser rank obeying his superior. And they shall examine their spirit and deeds yearly, so that each man may be advanced in accordance with his understanding and perfection of way, or moved down in accordance with his distortions. They shall rebuke one another in truth, humility, and charity. Let no man address his companion with anger, or ill-temper, or obduracy, or with envy prompted by the spirit of wickedness. Let him not hate him [because of his uncircumcised] heart, but let him rebuke him on the very same day lest he incur guilt because of him. And furthermore, let no man accuse his companion before the Congregation without having admonished him in the presence of witnesses.

These are the ways in which all of them shall walk, each man with his companion, wherever they dwell. The man of lesser rank shall obey the greater in matters of work and money. They shall eat in common and bless in common and deliberate in common.

REVIEW QUESTIONS

1. What were the requirements for becoming an Essene?
2. Compare the ideas expressed in the Dead Sea Scrolls and attributed to the Essenes by Josephus with those in the gospels of St. Mark and St. Matthew.

3 Christianity and Greco-Roman Learning

Should the cultural inheritance of the Greco-Roman world be retained or discarded? This was a formidable problem for Early Christian thinkers. Those who urged abandoning Greco-Roman learning argued that such knowledge would corrupt the morality of the young and would lead Christians to doubt scripture. On the other hand, several Christian intellectuals, particularly those educated in the Greco-Roman classics, defended the study of pagan works. Their view ultimately prevailed.

Christians preserved the intellectual tradition of Greece. However, philosophy underwent a crucial change: philosophic thought among Christians had to be directed in accordance with the requirements of their faith. The intellect was not fully autonomous; it could not question or challenge Christian teachings but had to accept the church's dictums regarding God's existence, the creation of the universe, the mission of Jesus, and the purpose of life and death.

Tertullian
WHAT HAS JERUSALEM TO DO WITH ATHENS?

A native of Carthage, Tertullian (Quintus Septimus Florens Tertullianus, A.D. c. 160–c. 240) became a Christian about A.D. 190 and thereafter was a defender of Christian morals against both pagans and less rigorous Christians. He emphasized the sacredness of life and the Christian abhorrence of violence. His *Prescriptions against Heretics* reveals hostility toward Greco-Roman learning, an attitude shared by some other Early Christian thinkers.

. . . Worldly wisdom culminates in philosophy with its rash interpretation of God's nature and purpose. It is philosophy that supplies the heresies[1] with their equipment. . . . The idea of a mortal soul was picked up from the Epicureans, and the denial of the restitution of the flesh was taken from the common tradition of the philosophical schools. . . . Heretics and philosophers [ponder] the same themes and are caught up in the same discussions. What is the origin of evil and why? The origin of man, and how? . . . A plague on Aristotle, who taught them dialectic [logical argumentation], the art which destroys as much as it builds, which changes its opinions like a coat, forces its conjectures, is stubborn in argument, works hard at being contentious and is a burden even to itself. For it reconsiders every point to make sure it never finishes a discussion.

Early Latin Theology, trans. and ed. S. L. Greenslade (Volume V: The Library of Christian Classics, 1956), pp. 35–36. Published simultaneously in Great Britain and the USA by the SCM Press, Ltd., London, and the Westminster Press, Philadelphia.

[1]A heresy is any belief that differs from official or standard doctrine. —Eds.
[2]The Stoic philosophers took their name from the Greek word *stoa*, "porch," the place where Zeno, their founder, used to teach. *Porch of Solomon* is used to designate the teachings of King Solomon, who built the great Temple in Jerusalem. Tertullian makes it clear he follows Solomon's wisdom. —Eds.

From philosophy come those fables and . . . fruitless questionings, those "words that creep like as doth a canker." To hold us back from such things, the Apostle [Paul] testifies expressly in his letter to the Colossians [Colossians 2:8] that we should beware of philosophy. "Take heed lest any man [beguile] you through philosophy or vain deceit, after the tradition of men," against the providence of the Holy Ghost. He had been at Athens where he had come to grips with the human wisdom which attacks and perverts truth, being itself divided up into its own swarm of heresies by the variety of its mutually antagonistic sects. What has Jerusalem to do with Athens, the Church with [Plato's] Academy, the Christian with the heretic? Our principles come from the Porch of Solomon,[2] who had himself taught that the Lord is to be sought in simplicity of heart. I have no use for a Stoic or a Platonic or a dialectic Christianity. After Jesus Christ we have no need of speculation, after the Gospel no need of research. When we come to believe, we have no desire to believe anything else; for we begin by believing that there is nothing else which we have to believe.

Clement of Alexandria
IN DEFENSE OF GREEK LEARNING

In the following passage, Clement of Alexandria (A.D. c. 150–c. 220) expresses his admiration for Greek learning. A Greek Christian theologian, Clement combined Christianity with Platonism.

The Greeks should not be condemned by those who have merely glanced at their writings, for comprehension of these works requires careful investigation. Philosophy is not the originator of false practices and base deeds as some have calumniated it; nor does it beguile us and lead us away from faith.

Rather philosophy is a clear image of truth, a divine gift to the Greeks. Before the advent of the Lord, philosophy helped the Greeks to attain righteousness, and it is now conducive to piety; it supplies a preparatory teaching for those who will later embrace the faith. God is the cause of all good things: some given primarily in the form of the Old and the New Testament; others are the consequence of philosophy. Perchance too philosophy was given to the Greeks primarily till the Lord should call the Greeks to serve him. Thus philosophy acted as a schoolmaster to the Greeks, preparing them for Christ, as the laws of the Jews prepared them for Christ.

The way of truth is one. But into it, as into a perennial river, streams flow from all sides. We assert that philosophy, which is characterized by investigation into the form and nature of things, is the truth of which the Lord Himself said, "I am the truth." Thus Greek preparatory culture, including philosophy itself, is shown to have come down from God to men.

Some do not wish to touch either philosophy or logic or to learn natural science. They demand bare faith alone, as if they wished, without bestowing any care on the vine, straightway to gather clusters from the first. I call him truly learned who brings everything to bear on the truth; so that from geometry, music, grammar, and philosophy itself, he culls what is useful and guards the faith against assault. And he who brings everything to bear on a right life, learning from Greeks and non-Greeks, this man is an experienced searcher after truth. And

Clement of Alexandria, *Stromata (Miscellanies)*, trans. William Wilson in A. Roberts and James Donaldson, *Ante-Nicene Christian Library* (Edinburgh: T. & T. Clark, 1867), vol. 4, *The Writings of Clement of Alexandria*, pp. 303–305, 307–310, 318.

how necessary it is for him who desires to be partaker of the power of God to treat of intellectual subjects by philosophising.

According to some, Greek philosophy apprehended the truth accidentally, dimly, partially. Others will have it that Greek philosophy was instituted by the devil. Several hold that certain powers descending from heaven inspired the whole of philosophy. But if Greek philosophy does not comprehend the whole of truth and does not encompass God's commandments, yet it prepares the way for God's teachings; training in some way or other, molding character, and fitting him who believes in Providence for the reception of truth.

Saint Augustine
APPROPRIATING PAGAN LEARNING AND INSTITUTIONS FOR CHRISTIAN ENDS

Saint Augustine (see pages 190–193) also argued that pagan learning and institutions could be put to good use by Christians.

Any statements by those who are called philosophers, especially the Platonists, which happen to be true and consistent with our faith should not cause alarm, but be claimed for our own use, as it were from owners who have no right to them. Like the treasures of the ancient Egyptians, who possessed not only idols and heavy burdens, which the people of Israel hated and shunned, but also vessels and ornaments of silver and gold, and clothes, which on leaving Egypt the people of Israel, in order to make better use of them, surreptitiously claimed for themselves (they did this not on their own authority but at God's command) . . . similarly all the branches of pagan learning contain not only false and superstitious fantasies and bur-

densome studies that involve unnecessary effort, which each one of us must loathe and avoid as under Christ's guidance we abandon the company of pagans, but also studies for liberated minds which are more appropriate to the service of the truth, and some very useful moral instruction, as well as the various truths about monotheism to be found in their writers. These treasures . . . which were used wickedly and harmfully in the service of demons must be removed by Christians, as they separate themselves in spirit from the wretched company of pagans, and applied to their true function, that of preaching the gospel. As for their clothing—which corresponds to human institutions, but those appropriate to human society, which in this life we cannot do without—this may be accepted and kept for conversion to Christian purposes. This is exactly what many good and faithful Christians have done.

Saint Augustine: On Christian Teaching, trans. R. P. H. Green, with introduction and notes (London: Oxford University Press, 1997), pp. 64–65.

REVIEW QUESTIONS

1. Why did Tertullian object to Christians studying pagan literature?
2. Why did Clement of Alexandria favor the study of pagan learning? Why did Saint Augustine?
3. What might have been the consequences if the Christian church had followed the advice of Tertullian rather than that of Clement?

4   The Persecutions

Under Roman law, all cults had to be approved by the authorities, and religious associations were licensed by the state. At first, the Christians were assumed to be members of a Jewish sect, and as Judaism was a legal religion, the authorities did not intervene in the work of the Christian missionaries except as they were involved in disputes within the Jewish community. By the reign (A.D. 54–68) of Emperor Nero, Roman officials had become aware that the new Christian churches were composed of many Gentiles as well as Jews and could no longer reasonably be considered a legitimate part of the privileged Jewish religious community. The first major persecution broke out in the city of Rome when Nero, to put down a rumor that he had set afire a large section of the city, decided to focus blame for the disaster on the small Christian community. When the unpopular Christians were arrested, they pleaded guilty not to arson, but to the crime of being Christians: that is, to belonging to an illegal sect or association. The penalty for such unlicensed association was death. Those who denied they were Christians and agreed to offer sacrifice to the gods of Rome were released.

THE MARTYRDOM OF BLANDINA

During the second century A.D., Christians in the Roman Empire were at times victims of mob actions, usually stimulated by some disaster like an outbreak of disease, an earthquake, a drought, or other communal catastrophes attributed to the anger of the gods. Christians' pacifism and their refusal to participate in the worship of the state deities, in processions and festivals, and in theatrical performances and gladiatorial games, made them increasingly unpopular.

The next reading is a letter sent in A.D. 177 by the Christians of the cities of Lyons and Vienne in Gaul (France) to fellow Christians in Asia and Phrygia (both in modern Turkey). The letter describes a group of Christians arrested and reviled by enraged mobs.

First, indeed, they [the Christians] endured nobly the sufferings heaped upon them by the general populace, clamors, blows, being dragged along, robberies, stonings, imprisonments, and all that an enraged mob loves to inflict on opponents and enemies. Then they were taken to the forum by . . . the ordained authorities of the city and were examined in the presence of the whole multitude. Having confessed, they were imprisoned until the arrival of the governor. When

they were afterwards brought before him . . . he treated us with all manner of cruelty. . . .

. . . [Some refused to renounce their faith in Christ, but others] appeared unprepared and untrained and still weak, unable to endure the strain of a great contest. Of these about ten became apostates [renounced their religion], who caused us great pain and excessive sorrow, and weakened the zeal of the others who had not yet been seized, and who, although suffering all kinds of evil, were constantly with the martyrs and did not abandon them. . . . And some of our servants who were heathens were seized because the governor had ordered that we should all be examined in public.

Eusebius, *Ecclesiastical History,* book 5, ch. 1, in *Translation and Reprints from the Original Sources of European History,* vol. 4 (1897 series), ed. D. C. Munro and Edith Bramhall (Philadelphia: University of Pennsylvania Press, 1898), pp. 11–19.

These by the wiles of Satan, fearing the tortures which they saw the saints suffering and urged by the soldiers to do this, accused us falsely of Thyestean banquets[1] and Oedipodean incests[2] and of deeds which it is not lawful for us to speak of, or think of, and which we do not believe men ever committed. When these accusations were reported all raged like wild beasts against us. . . . Then finally the holy martyrs endured sufferings beyond all description and Satan strove earnestly that some blasphemies might be uttered by them also.

But the whole rage of the people, governor and soldiers was aroused exceedingly against Sanctus, deacon from Vienne, and against Maturus, a recent convert but a noble combatant, and against Attalus, a native of Pergamum [a city in Asia Minor], who had always been a pillar and a foundation in that place, and against Blandina [a slave] through whom Christ showed that what appears mean, deformed and contemptible to men is of great glory with God through love for Him, shown in power and not boasting in appearance. For while we all, together with her mistress on earth, who was herself also one of the combatants among the martyrs, feared lest in the strife she should be unable to make her confession on account of her bodily weakness, Blandina was filled with such power that she was delivered and raised above those who took turns in torturing her in every manner from dawn till evening; and they confessed that they were defeated and had nothing more which they could do to her. They marvelled at her endurance, for her whole body was mangled and broken; and they testified that one form of torture was sufficient to destroy life, to say nothing of so many and so great tortures. But the blessed one, like a noble athlete, renewed her strength . . . , and her comfort, refreshment and relief from suffering was in saying, "I am a Christian" and "Nothing vile is done by us."

. . . Maturus, Sanctus, Blandina and Attalus were therefore led to the wild beasts in the amphitheatre, and in order to give to the heathen public a spectacle of cruelty, a day was especially appointed for our people to fight with the wild beasts. Accordingly Maturus and Sanctus again passed through the whole torture in the amphitheatre, not as if they had suffered nothing at all before, but rather as if having overcome the adversary already in many kinds of contests they were now striving for the crown itself. They endured again the running the gauntlet customary in that place and the attacks from the wild beasts and everything that the raging multitude, who cried out from one place or another, desired, and at last the iron chair in which their bodies were roasted and tormented with the fumes. Not even with this did the tortures cease, but they raged still more, desiring to overcome their patience, and they did not hear a word from Sanctus except the confession [that he was a Christian] which he had made from the beginning. These accordingly, after their life had continued for a very long time through the great conflict, died at last, after having furnished a spectacle to the world throughout that day instead of all the varieties of gladiatorial combats.

But Blandina suspended on a stake was exposed as food for the wild beasts which should fall upon her. Because she seemed to be suspended in the manner of a cross and because of her earnest prayers, she encouraged the contestants greatly. They looking upon her in her conflict, beheld with their eyes, through their sister, Him who had suffered for them in order to persuade those who trust in Him that everyone who suffers for the glory of Christ has eternal fellowship with the living God. And as none of the beasts touched her at that time, she was taken down from the stake and led away again to the prison, to be preserved for another contest. . . .

---

[1]Thyestes, in Greek myth, was forced to eat his own sons at a banquet; the reference is to cannibalism. —Eds.
[2]Oedipus, the protagonist of several Greek dramas, unwittingly committed incest with his mother. —Eds.

The Roman authorities frequently set free anyone who denied his Christian faith and was willing to worship a Roman god, usually the divine emperor.

. . . For Caesar had written that these [Christians] should be put to death, but if any should deny they should be dismissed. At the beginning of the festival held there, which is attended by throngs of people from all nations, the governor had the blessed ones brought to the judgment-seat to be a show and spectacle for the multitude. Therefore he examined them again, and as many as seemed to be Roman citizens he had beheaded, the others he sent to the wild beasts.

Christ was glorified greatly in those who had previously denied him, for contrary to the expectation of the heathen, they confessed. For these were examined separately as about to be set free, and when they confessed, they were added to the number of the martyrs. But those who never had a particle of faith . . . or any thought of the fear of God . . . blasphemed the way [slandered Christianity] through their apostasy. . . .

. . . The bodies of the martyrs after having been exposed and exhibited in every manner for six days, were afterwards burned and reduced to ashes by the lawless men and thrown in the river Rhone which flows close by, so that no remnants of them might still be seen on the earth. And they did this as if they were able to overcome God and prevent their coming to life again, in order, as some said, "that they may have no hope of a resurrection, trusting in which they bring to us a certain foreign and strange religion, and despise awful punishments and are ready with joy to suffer death. Now let us see whether they will rise again, and if their God is able to aid them and rescue them from our hands."

REVIEW QUESTIONS

1. What do the stories of the martyrs tell us about the character of Roman society?
2. Tertullian claimed that "the blood of the martyrs was the seed of the faith." How did the persecutions strengthen Christianity?

---

5 Monastic Life

In the late third century A.D., inspired by Jesus' example of self-denial and seeking to escape from the distractions of worldly concerns, some zealous Christians withdrew to the deserts of Roman Egypt in search of peace and isolation. They turned their minds wholly to prayer, contemplation, and ascetic practices. These hermits, the "desert fathers," were the earliest Christian monks. In time, some hermits banded together to form monastic communities, living under written rules that established a form of monastic government and way of life.

The hermit or monk "took up the Cross"—that is, emulated the way of Christ through a life of prayer, introspective self-examination, hard work, and ascetic practices like fasting, sexual abstinence, physical deprivation, and poverty. The hermitage and the monastery were schools for sanctity; thus the hermits and monks have been the spiritual models for many male and female Christians from late Roman times down to the present age.

The many Early Christians who were drawn to the austerity of the African desert sought to escape the distractions of the world, to find religious insight, and to come closer to God. These hermits and mystics produced a vast body of literature describing their lives and experiences. Written first in Greek by the participants themselves, these accounts were translated into Latin in the fourth, fifth, and sixth centuries; they were finally collected into a comprehensive work, *Vitae Patrum* (Lives of the Fathers), in the seventeenth century.

Saint Jerome
THE AGONY OF SOLITUDE IN THE DESERT

The Christian ascetic's vision of the world was honed in the isolation of the desert. The price of such insight was the agony that came with self-denial and solitude. Saint Jerome (A.D. 374–419), who lived in the desert during the fourth century, vividly described this suffering in a letter written to his female pupil Eustochium. He recounts the effects of the desert's austerity, which debilitated his body and disoriented his mind with delirious memories of earlier years and "enchantments" in Rome.

Oh, how many times did I, set in the desert, in that vast solitude parched with the fires of the sun that offers a dread abiding to the monk, how often did I think myself back in the old Roman enchantments. There I sat solitary, full of bitterness; my disfigured limbs shuddered away from the sackcloth, my dirty skin was taking on the hue of the Ethiopian's flesh: every day tears, every day sighing: and if in spite of my struggles sleep would tower over and sink upon me, my battered body ached on the naked earth. Of food and drink I say nothing, since even a sick monk uses only cold water, and to take anything cooked is wanton luxury. Yet that same I, who for fear of hell condemned myself to such a prison, I, the comrade of scorpions and wild beasts, was there, watching the maidens in their dances: my face haggard with fasting, my mind burnt with desire in my frigid body, and the fires of lust alone leaped before a man prematurely dead. So, destitute of all aid, I used to lie at the feet of Christ, watering them with my tears, wiping them with my hair, struggling to subdue my rebellious flesh with seven days' fasting. I do not blush to confess the misery of my hapless days: rather could I weep that I am not what I was once. I remember crying out till day became one with night, nor ceasing to beat my breast until my Lord would chide and tranquillity return. I grew to dread even my cell, with its knowledge of my imaginings; and grim and angry with myself, would set out solitary to explore the desert: and wherever I would spy the depth of a valley or a mountainside or a precipitous rock, there was my place of prayer, there the torture-house of my unhappy flesh: and, the Lord Himself is witness, after many tears, and eyes that clung to heaven, I would sometimes seem to myself to be one with the angelic hosts.

Excerpted from *The Desert Fathers* by Helen Waddell, pp. 36–37. © 1936, with permission from Constable & Robinson.

Cassian of Marseilles
ON THE DANGERS AND FRUITS OF SOLITUDE

Cassian of Marseilles (A.D. c. 360–c. 435), who lived as an ascetic in the Egyptian desert and later founded monasteries in France, believed that the Christian hermit's most fearsome enemy was an emotional state that he called *accidie*. One of the dangers of solitude, *accidie* was a tedium or perturbation of the heart, an awesome apathy, boredom, and mental distraction, with which the desert fathers had forever to contend.

It is akin to dejection and especially felt by wandering monks and solitaries, a persistent and obnoxious enemy to such as dwell in the desert, disturbing the monk especially about midday, like a fever mounting at a regular time, and bringing its highest tide of inflammation at definite accustomed hours to the sick soul. And so some of the Fathers declare it to be the demon of noontide which is spoken of in the xcth Psalm.[1]

When this besieges the unhappy mind, it begets aversion from the place, boredom with one's cell, and scorn and contempt for one's brethren, whether they be dwelling with one or some way off, as careless and unspiritually minded persons. Also, towards any work that may be done within the enclosure of our own lair, we become listless and inert. It will not suffer us to stay in our cell, or to attend to our reading: we lament that in all this while, living in the same spot, we have made no progress, we sigh and complain that bereft of sympathetic fellowship we have no spiritual fruit; and bewail ourselves as empty of all spiritual profit, abiding vacant and useless in this place; and we that could guide others and be of value to multitudes have edified no man, enriched no man with our precept and example. We praise other and far distant monasteries, describing them as more helpful to one's progress, more congenial to one's soul's health. We paint the fellowship of the brethren there, its suavity, its richness in spiritual conversation, contrasting it with the harshness of all that is at hand, where not only is there no edification to be had from any of the brethren who dwell here, but where one cannot even procure one's victuals without enormous toil. Finally we conclude that there is no health for us so long as we stay in this place, short of abandoning that cell wherein to tarry further will be only to perish with it, and betaking ourselves elsewhere as quickly as possible.

And so the wise Fathers in Egypt would in no way suffer the monks, especially the younger, to be idle, measuring the state of their heart and their progress in patience and humility by their steadiness at work; and not only might they accept nothing from anyone towards their support, but out of their own toil they supplied such brethren as came by, or were from foreign parts, and did send huge stores of victuals and provisions throughout Libya, a barren and hungry land, and to those that pined in the squalor of the prisons in the towns. . . . There was a saying approved by the ancient Fathers in Egypt; that a busy monk is besieged by a single devil: but an idle one destroyed by spirits innumerable.

Excerpted from *The Desert Fathers* by Helen Waddell, pp. 229–232. © 1936, with permission from Constable & Robinson.

[1]Ps. 90 in the Douai Bible; Ps. 91 in most modern editions. —Eds.

REVIEW QUESTIONS

1. Why did the desert fathers feel that solitude and self-mortification were the best ways to serve Christ?
2. What would you recommend for a Christian today as the best way to serve God?

6 Christianity and Society

Although the principal concern of Jesus' followers was the attainment of salvation, Christians still had to deal with the world and its ways. In the process of doing so, they developed attitudes and customs that have had an enduring influence on Western culture.

Lactantius
ACQUISITIVENESS AS THE SOURCE OF EVIL

Early Christian theologians were concerned primarily with preparation for the afterlife, but they also aspired to shape a just social order on earth. For them devotion to God and neighbor, as Jesus had commanded, was the basis for achieving a just society. This meant having compassion for the poor and needy, distributing earthly goods more fairly, and eschewing greed.

A particularly insightful Early Christian view of social justice is found in *Divine Institutes*, written by the fourth-century Christian apologist L. Caecilius Firmianus Lactantius. Relying on classical themes rather than Genesis, Lactantius describes an early golden age in which people lived in peace and "without insatiable and obsessive greed laying claim to everything." It was a time in which no one went "short of what nature produced for all. . . . [The] haves bestowed their goods so plentifully upon the have-nots that all were equally well off." But when an evil king seized the throne, justice was extirpated, hatred and deceit flourished, and the worship of God disappeared. As concern for the common good dissipated, "So began conflict and treachery and pride in the shedding of human blood." In the following passages from *Divine Institutes*, Lactantius shows that greed is the source of evil and is the principal cause for the degeneration of society.

Acquisitiveness was the source of all these evils, acquisitiveness which sprang out of the contempt of true majesty. It was not simply that those who had plenty of something would not share it with others, but they actually got hold of others' goods and turned them all to their private profit; so that, whereas previously property had been a matter of one person

contributing his labor for the use of all, now it was the concentration of goods in a few wealthy households. First they began to accumulate and monopolize the necessaries of life and keep them inaccessible, to bring others under their power as slaves. The gifts of heaven they made out to be their own—not for humanity's sake, for they had none of that, but to sweep up every means that could serve their acquisitive greed. They had laws passed which represented as "justice" the grossest inequities and injustices, to protect their rapacious practice and purpose against mass resistance. So they laid claim to authority to sanction what force, resources, and sheer unscrupulousness had achieved for them. And since there was actually no trace of justice in them—which would have been expressed in humanity, equality, and compassion—they began to find satisfaction in arrogant and inegalitarian self-promotion, which put them on a higher rank than others, with retinues of staff, armed guards, and distinguishing dress. This is the origin of honors, marks of nobility, official status: relying on the terror of the axe and sword, they were to rule a cowed and craven people with the "right of masters." Such was the condition of human life introduced by the king who, after driving his father out by war, established not a kingdom but an unprincipled tyranny by force of arms, destroying that "golden age" of justice and forcing men to be harsh and conscienceless— all by the singular means of diverting worship from God to himself, a demand enforced by terror of his pitiless power. . . .

. . . For God who gives being and life to men wished us all to be equal, that is, alike. He laid down the same terms of life for us all, making us capable of wisdom and promising us immortality, excluding nobody from the benefits of heaven. And so, as he gives us all a place in the daylight, waters the earth for us all, provides nourishment and precious, relaxing sleep, no less does he endow us all with moral equality. With him there is no slave or master. Since we all have the same father, so we are all alike his freeborn children. No one is poor in his eyes, except for want of justice; no one is rich, except in moral qualities. No one is prominent, except in being incorruptible; no one is famous, except for works of mercy performed on a grand scale; no one has the title "Excellency" without accomplishing all the stages of moral growth. And that is why neither the Romans nor the Greeks could sustain justice, since they had so many levels of disparity in their societies, separating poorest from richest, powerless from powerful, the obscure from the most elevated dignities of royal state. Where all are not alike, there is no equality; and inequality is enough to

rule out justice, the very point of which is to afford like treatment to those who have entered this life on like terms. . . .

But someone will say, "Don't you have poor and rich, slaves and masters, in your community [of Christians]? Aren't there distinctions between one member and another?" Not at all! That is precisely the reason that we address one another as "Brother," since we believe we are one another's equals. Since human worth is measured in spiritual not in physical terms, we ignore our various physical situations; slaves are not slaves to us, but we treat them and address them as brothers in the spirit, fellow slaves in devotion to God. Wealth, too, is no ground of distinction, except insofar as it provides the opportunity for preeminence in good works. To be rich is not a matter of *having*, but of *using* riches for the tasks of justice; and those whom one would suppose poor are actually no less rich, in that they are short of nothing and hanker after nothing. Yet although our attitude of humility makes us one another's equals, free and slave, rich and poor, there are, in fact, distinctions which God makes, distinctions in virtue, that is: the juster, the higher. For if justice means behaving as the equal of inferiors, then, although it is *equality* that one excels in, yet by conducting oneself not merely as the equal of one's inferiors but as their subordinate, one will attain a far *higher* rank of dignity in God's sight. It is true, the brevity and fragility of everything in this transitory life makes men compete with one another for status—a most repellent, most self-assertive style of behavior, and entirely irrelevant to mature rationality, since this whole realm of earthly preoccupation runs counter to the values of heaven. For as "the wisdom of men is utter folly with God" [1 Cor. 3:19] . . . so it follows that one who achieves earthly prominence is insignificant and contemptible to God. Leaving aside all the highly regarded goods of this world that militate against virtue and weaken our mental resources, what security is there in rank, wealth, or power, when God can bring even kings lower than the low? And so among the commands which God took care to give us, he included this in particular: "Whoever exalts himself will be humbled, and whoever humbles himself will be exalted" [Matt. 23:12]. We learn from this wholesome prescription that whoever adopts a modest, unassuming style in the sight of men, stands out with distinction in the sight of God. There is truth in the quotation from Euripides, which goes: "What are taken here for evils may be known in heaven for goods."

Justin Martyr
CHRISTIAN MORALITY

Justin Martyr, a convert to Christianity, was martyred between A.D. 162 and 167. He is most remembered for his response to charges that Christians were immoral and disloyal to the emperor. In the following selection from *First Apology,* Justin recounts essential moral principles adopted by Early Christians.

For we warn you in advance to be on your guard, lest the demons whom we have previously accused should deceive you and divert you from reading and understanding what we say. For they strive to have you as their slaves and servants, and sometimes by appearances in dreams, sometimes by magical tricks, they subdue all who do not struggle to the utmost for their own salvation, as we do also who, after being persuaded by the Word, renounced them, and follow the only unbegotten. God through His Son. Those who formerly delighted in fornication now embrace chastity alone, those who formerly made use of magical arts have dedicated themselves to the good and unbegotten God, we who once valued above everything the gaining of wealth and possessions now bring what we have into a common stock, and share with everyone in need, we who hated and destroyed one another, and would not share the same hearth with people of a different tribe on account of their different customs, now since the coming of Christ, live familiarly with them, and pray for our enemies, and try to persuade those who unjustly hate us to live

according to the good advice of Christ, to the end that they may share with us the same joyful hope of a reward from God the Master of all. But lest we should seem to deceive, we consider it right, before embarking on our promised demonstration, to cite a few of the precepts given by Christ Himself. It is for you then, as powerful rulers, to find out whether we have been taught and do teach these things truly. Short and concise utterances come from Him, for He was no sophist, but His word was the power of God.

Concerning chastity he said this, "Whosoever looks upon a woman to lust after her has already committed adultery with her in his heart before God." And: "If your right eye offends you, cut it out; for it is better for you to enter into the Kingdom of Heaven with one eye, than with two eyes to be cast into eternal fire." And: "Whosoever shall marry her that is divorced from another husband, commits adultery." . . . So that all who according to human law make second marriages are sinners in the sight of our Master, as are those who look on a woman to lust after her. For not only the man who in act commits adultery is condemned by Him, but also the man who desires to commit adultery; since not only our deeds but also our thoughts are open before God. And many,

St. Justin Martyr: The First and Second Apologies, translated with notes by Leslie William Bernard (New York: Paulist Press, 1997), pp. 31–33.

both men and women, who have been Christ's disciples from childhood, have preserved their purity at the age of sixty or seventy years; and I am proud that I could produce such from every race of men and women. For what shall we say then of the countless multitude of those who have turned away from intemperance and learned these things? For Christ did not call the righteous and temperate to repentance, but the ungodly and licentious and unrighteous. So He said, "I came not to call the righteous, but sinners to repentance." For the Heavenly Father desires the repentance of a sinner, rather than his punishment. And concerning our affection for all people He taught so: "If you love those who love you, what new thing do you do? for

even the fornicators do this. But I say to you, Pray for your enemies, and love those who hate you, and bless those who curse you, and pray for those who despitefully use you." And that we should share with the needy, and do nothing for glory, He said these things; "Give to everyone who asks and turn not away from him who wishes to borrow." . . .

. . . And concerning our being long-suffering and servants to all and free from anger, this is what He said: "To him that smites you on the one cheek, offer also the other; and to him that takes away your shirt do not forbid your cloak also. . . . And let your good works shine before men, that they, seeing them, may wonder at your Father who is in heaven."

Saint Benedict of Nursia
THE CHRISTIAN WAY OF LIFE

In the following selection from his monastic book of rules, Saint Benedict of Nursia (A.D. C. 480–547) advises his monks on the attitudes and conduct necessary to live a virtuous Christian life.

WHAT ARE THE INSTRUMENTS OF GOOD WORKS?

In the first place, to love the Lord God with the whole heart, whole soul, whole strength, then his neighbor as himself.

Then not to kill, not to commit adultery, not to steal, not to covet, not to bear false witness, to honor all men, and what anyone would not have done to him, let him not do to another. To deny himself, that he may follow Christ, to chasten the body, to renounce luxuries, to love fasting. To relieve the poor, to clothe the naked, to visit the sick, to bury the dead, to help in tribulation, to console the afflicted.

Oliver J. Thatcher, *Library of Original Sources* (Milwaukee: University Research Extension Co., 1907), vol. 4, pp. 133–134.

To make himself a stranger to the affairs of the world, to prefer nothing before the love of Christ, not to give way to anger, not to bear any grudge, not to harbour deceit in the heart, not to forsake charity. Not to swear, lest haply he perjure himself, to utter truth from his heart and his mouth. Not to return evil for evil, not to do injuries, but rather to bear them patiently, to love his enemies, not to curse again those who curse him, but rather to bless them, to endure persecution for righteousness' sake. Not to be proud, not given to wine, not gluttonous, not addicted to sleep, not slothful, not given to murmur, not a slanderer. To commit his hope to God; when he sees anything good in himself to attribute it to God, and not to himself, but let him always know that which is evil is his own doing, and impute it to himself. To fear the day of judgment, to dread hell, to desire eternal life with all spiritual longing, to have the expectation of death every day before his eyes. To watch over his actions at all times, to know certainly that in all places the eye of God is upon him; those evil thoughts which come into his heart to dash to pieces on Christ, and to make them known to his spiritual senior. To keep his lips from evil and wicked discourse, not to be fond of much talking, not to speak vain words or such as provoke laughter, not to love much or violent laughter. To give willing attention to the sacred readings, to pray frequently every day, to confess his past sins to God, in prayer, with tears and groanings; from thence forward to reform as to those sins.

Not to fulfill the desires of the flesh, to hate his own will, in all things to obey the commands of the abbot, even though he himself (which God forbid) should do otherwise, remembering our Lord's commands: "What they say, do; but what they do, do ye not." Not to desire to be called a saint before he is one, but first to be one that he may be truly called one; every day to fulfill the commands of God in his deeds, to love chastity, to hate no one, not to have jealousy or envy, not to love contention, to avoid self-conceit; to reverence seniors, to love juniors, to pray for enemies in the love of Christ, to be reconciled with his adversary, before the going down of the sun, and never to despair of the mercy of God. . . .

The Apostle Paul
THE SUBMISSIVE ROLE OF WOMEN

After the execution of Jesus by the Roman authorities in Judea around A.D. 30, his disciples, believing that he had risen from the dead, sought a clearer understanding of his life and teachings. They became convinced that Jesus' mission, calling people to repent their sins and receive God's forgiveness and to conduct their lives according to a high code of ethics, must be carried on. They proceeded to spread the "good news" to their fellow Jews and eventually to other peoples throughout the Roman world.

The disciples of Jesus were soon joined in this great mission by a man known to us as Saint Paul, the first great theologian of the new Christian church. Saint Paul started his life as a pious Jew named Saul. Born around A.D. 5 in Tarsus, a Greek city in Asia Minor, Paul enjoyed Roman citizenship. He studied the Hebrew scriptures in Judea and joined in the early persecution of Jesus' followers. Yet through a visionary experience, Paul was converted to the belief that Jesus was the Messiah. He traveled widely throughout Syria, Asia Minor, and Greece, converting both Jews and non-Jews. He kept in touch with the new Christian communities by visits and letters. Several of the latter are included in the New Testament. He died around A.D. 65.

Passages in the New Testament concerning the role of women in Christian society have greatly affected the Western view of the relationship between the sexes. Paul's letter to the Ephesians and his first letter to Timothy contain passages emphasizing the traditional, submissive role of women in the Christian church. Although conservative theologians accept the Pauline authorship of these letters, liberal scholars date Ephesians about A.D. 95, thirty years after Paul's death, and 1 Timothy about A.D. 130. If the later dates are correct, the following passages reflect the attitude of the developing Christian church rather than Paul's own opinion. Nonetheless, these passages, and others like them, have had an enormous influence on Christian attitudes toward women.

THE MORALS OF THE HOME

Wives, be subject to your husbands, as to the Lord. For the husband is the head of the wife as Christ is the head of the church, his body, and is himself its Savior. As the church is subject to Christ, so let wives also be subject in everything to their husbands. Husbands, love your wives, as Christ loved the church and gave himself up for her, that he might sanctify her, having cleansed her by the washing of water with the word, that the church might be presented before him in splendor, without spot or wrinkle or any such thing, that she might be holy and without blemish. Even so husbands should love their wives as their own bodies. He who loves his wife loves himself. For no man ever hates his own flesh, but nourishes and cherishes it, as Christ does the church, because we are members of his body. "For this reason a man shall leave his father and mother and be joined to his wife, and the two shall become one." This is a great mystery, and I take it to mean Christ and the church; however, let each one of you love his wife as himself, and let the wife see that she respects her husband. [Ephesians 5:22–32]

WOMEN IN THE ASSEMBLY

I desire then that in every place the men should pray, lifting holy hands without anger or quarreling; also that women should adorn themselves modestly and sensibly in seemly apparel, not with braided hair or gold or pearls or costly attire but by good deeds, as befits women who profess religion. Let a woman learn in silence with all submissiveness. I permit no woman to teach or to have authority over men; she is to keep silent. For Adam was formed first, then Eve; and Adam was not deceived, but the woman was deceived and became a transgressor. Yet woman will be saved through bearing chidren, if she continues in faith and love and holiness, with modesty. [1 Timothy 2:8–15]

Revised Standard Version of the Bible, copyright 1952 [2nd edition, 1971] by the Division of Christian Education of the National Council of the Churches of Christ in the United States of America. Used by permission. All rights reserved.

REVIEW QUESTIONS

1. Lactantius assails human greed and social inequality as evil. What does he conceive as the natural condition of human beings, and how does he justify his assertion?
2. According to Justin Martyr, what sins were Christians now able to renounce?
3. How do you react to Justin Martyr's views on sexual matters?
4. Why would Benedict's message appeal to many people?
5. In your opinion, which of Paul's views have merit today? Which do you reject?

7 Jews in the Era of Early Christianity

Numerous links connect Early Christianity and Judaism. Jesus himself and his earliest followers, including the Twelve Apostles, were Jews who were faithful to Jewish law. Jesus' message was first spread in synagogues throughout the Roman Empire. Early Christianity's affirmation of the preciousness of the human being, created in God's image, its belief that God rules history, its awareness of human sinfulness, its call for repentance, and its appeal to God for forgiveness are rooted in Judaism. The Christian reference to God as a "merciful Father" derives from Jewish prayer. Also rooted in Judaism are the moral norms proclaimed by Jesus in the Sermon on the Mount and on other occasions. For example, "Thou shalt love thy neighbor as thyself" was the motto of the Jewish sage Hillel, a contemporary of Jesus, who founded a school. The great value that the Torah gives to charity was inherited by Christianity. Jesus' use of parables to convey his teachings, the concept of the Messiah, respect for the Sabbath, and congregational worship also stem from Judaism. And, of course, Christians viewed the Hebrew scriptures as God's word.

Over the years, however, Christians forgot or devalued this relationship to Judaism, and some thinkers began to show hostility toward Judaism and Jews that had tragic consequences in later centuries. Several factors fueled this anti-Judaism: resentment against Jews for their refusal to embrace Jesus; the polemics of the Jewish establishment against the followers of Jesus; the role in Jesus' death ascribed to Jews by the New Testament; resentment against those Christians who Judaized—that is, continued to observe Jewish festivals and the Jewish Sabbath, regard the synagogue as holy, and practice circumcision; and anger that Judaism remained a vital religion, for this undermined the conviction that Christianity was the fulfillment of Judaism and the one true faith.

What made Christian anti-Judaism particularly ominous was the effort of some theologians to demonize the Jewish people. The myth emerged that the Jews, murderers of the incarnate God who embodied all that was good, were a cursed people, children of the Devil, whose suffering was intended by God.

The diabolization of the Jew, which bore no relationship to the actual behavior of Jews or to their highly ethical religion, and the "theology of victimization," which held that the Jews were collectively and eternally cursed for denying Christ, became powerful myths, which, over the centuries, poisoned Christians' hearts and minds against Jews, spurring innumerable humiliations, persecutions, and massacres.

Saint John Chrysostom
CHRISTIAN DEMONIZATION OF JEWS

A particularly fierce attack on Jews was made by John Chrysostom (A.D. 347–407), a prominent church father. John sought to discourage Christians from participating in Jewish festivals, which still maintained their attraction for converts. In a series of sermons, he repeatedly castigated the Jews as demons and deicides. Since Jews are hated by God, he told the congregation, it is also a Christian's duty to hate these pitiable and miserable people.

What is this disease? The festivals of the pitiful and miserable Jews are soon to march upon us one after the other and in quick succession: the feast of Trumpets,[1] the feast of Tabernacles,[2] the fasts.[3] There are many in our ranks who say they think as we do. Yet some of these are going to watch the festivals and others will join the Jews in keeping their feasts and observing their fasts. I wish to drive this perverse custom from the Church right now. . . . But now that the Jewish festivals are close by and at the very door, if I should fail to cure those who are sick with the Judaizing disease, I am afraid that, because of their ill-suited association and deep ignorance, some Christians may partake in the Jews' transgressions; once they have done so, I fear my discourses on these transgressions will be in vain. For if they hear no word from me today, they will then join the Jews in their fasts; once they have committed this sin, it will be useless for me to apply the remedy.

And so it is that I hasten to anticipate this danger and prevent it. . . .

But do not be surprised that I called the Jews pitiable. They really are pitiable and miserable. When so many blessings from heaven came into their hands, they thrust them aside and were at great pains to reject them. . . . From their childhood they read the prophets, but they crucified him whom the prophets had foretold. We did not hear the divine prophecies but we did worship him of whom they prophesied. And so they are pitiful because they rejected the blessings which were sent to them, while others seized hold of these blessings and drew them to themselves. . . .

Many, I know, respect the Jews and think that their present way of life is a venerable one. This is why I hasten to uproot and tear out this deadly opinion. . . . [T]he synagogue is not only a brothel and a theater; it also is a den of robbers and a lodging for wild beasts. . . . [W]hen God forsakes a people, what hope of salvation is left? When God forsakes a place, that place becomes the dwelling of demons.

But at any rate the Jews say that they, too, adore God. God forbid that I say that. No Jew adores God! Who says so? The Son of God says so. For he said: "If you were to know my Father, you would also know me. But you neither know me nor do you know my Father" [John 8:19]. Could I produce a witness more trustworthy than the Son of God?

If, then, the Jews fail to know the Father, if they crucified the Son, if they thrust off the help of the Spirit, who should not make bold to declare plainly that the synagogue is a dwelling of demons? God is not worshipped there. Heaven forbid! From now on it remains a place of idolatry. But still some people pay it honor as a holy place. . . .

. . . In our churches we hear countless discourses on eternal punishments, on rivers of fire, on the venomous worm, on bonds that cannot be burst, on exterior darkness. But the Jews neither know nor dream of these things. They live for their bellies, they gape for the things of this world, their condition is no better than that of pigs or goats because of their wanton ways and excessive gluttony. They know but one thing: to fill their bellies and be drunk, to get all cut and bruised, to be hurt and wounded while fighting for their favorite charioteers. . . .

. . . Indeed the synagogue is less deserving of honor than any inn. It is not merely a lodging place for robbers and cheats but also for demons. This is true not only of the synagogues but also of the souls of the Jews, as I shall try to prove at the end of my discourse. . . .

From Saint John Chrysostom, *Discourses Against Judaizing Christians*, translated by Paul W. Harkins, pp. 3–5, 10–11, 15, 18–19, 21, 23–25, 28, 144–145. Copyright © 1979 by Catholic University of America Press. Reprinted by permission.

[1]This is the New Year, or Rosh Ha-Shanah, which falls on the first of Tishri (Sept.–Oct.).
[2]This falls on the fifteenth of Tishri and lasts a week, during which the Jews danced and "made merry before the Lord" (cf. Lev. 23:33–43).
[3]The fasts here referred to would seem to be the Ten Days of Penitence between Rosh Ha-Shanah and Yom Kippur (the Day of Atonement).

But I must get back again to those who are sick. Consider, then, with whom they are sharing their fasts. It is with those who shouted: "Crucify him, Crucify him" [Luke 23:21], with those who said: "His blood be upon us and upon our children."[4] . . . Is it not strange that those who worship the Crucified keep common festival with those who crucified him? Is it not a sign of folly and the worst madness?

Since there are some who think of the synagogue as a holy place, I must say a few words to them. Why do you reverence that place? Must you not despise it, hold it in abomination, run away from it? They answer that the Law and the books of the prophets are kept there. What is this? Will any place where these books are be a holy place? By no means! This is the reason above all others why I hate the synagogue and abhor it. They have the prophets but do not believe them; they read the sacred writings but reject their witness—and this is a mark of men guilty of the greatest outrage.

Tell me this. If you were to see a venerable man, illustrious and renowned, dragged off into a tavern or den of robbers: if you were to see him outraged, beaten, and subjected there to the worst violence, would you have held that tavern or den in high esteem because that great and esteemed man had been inside it while undergoing that violent treatment? I think not. Rather, for this very reason you would have hated and abhorred the place.

Let that be your judgment about the synagogue, too. For they brought the books of Moses and the prophets along with them into the synagogue, not to honor them but to outrage them with dishonor. When they say that Moses and the prophets knew not Christ and said nothing about his coming, what greater outrage could they do to those holy men than to accuse them of failing to recognize their Master, than to say that those saintly prophets are partners of their impiety? And so it is that we must hate both them and their synagogue all the more because of their offensive treatment of those holy men. . . .

Therefore, flee the gatherings and holy places of the Jews. Let no man venerate the synagogue because of the holy books; let him hate and avoid it because the Jews outrage and maltreat the holy ones, because they refuse to believe their words, because they accuse them of the ultimate impiety. . . .

Certainly it is the time for me to show that demons dwell in the synagogue, not only in the place itself but also in the souls of the Jews. . . . Do you see that demons dwell in their souls and that these demons are more dangerous than the ones of old? And this is very reasonable. In the old days the Jews acted impiously toward the prophets; now they outrage the Master of the prophets. Tell me this. Do you not shudder to come into the same place with men possessed, who have so many unclean spirits, who have been reared amid slaughter and bloodshed? Must you share a greeting with them and exchange a bare word? Must you not turn away from them since they are the common disgrace and infection of the whole world? Have they not come to every form of wickedness? Have not all the prophets spent themselves making many and long speeches of accusation against them?[5] . . .

Tell me this. If a man were to have slain your son, would you endure to look upon him, or to accept his greeting? Would you not shun him as a wicked demon, as the devil himself? They slew the Son of your Lord; do you have the boldness to enter with them under the same roof? After he was slain he heaped such honor upon

---

[4]Matt. 27:25. Chrysostom obviously holds the position, which was common for centuries, that all Jews are responsible for Christ's passion and death. Vatican II's "Declaration on the Relationship of the Church to Non-Christian Religions" states that these "cannot be blamed on all the Jews then living, without distinction, nor upon the Jews of today. Although the Church is the new people of God, the Jews should not be presented as repudiated or cursed by God, as if such views followed from the holy scriptures." A footnote at this point says that Cardinal Bea and others explained Matt. 27:25 as the cry of a Jerusalem crowd that had no right to speak for the whole Jewish people.

[5]Chrysostom argues from the guilt of their forebears to the guilt of contemporary Jews.

you that he made you his brother and coheir. But you dishonor him so much that you pay honor to those who slew him on the cross, that you observe with them the fellowship of the festivals, that you go to their profane places, enter their unclean doors, and share in the tables of demons. For I am persuaded to call the fasting of the Jews a table of demons because they slew God. If the Jews are acting against God, must they not be serving the demons? . . .

Meanwhile, I ask you to rescue your brothers, to set them free from their error, and to bring them back to the truth. . . . I want them to learn these facts from you and to free themselves from their wicked association with the Jews. I want them then to show themselves sincere and genuine Christians. I want them to shun the evil gatherings of the Jews and their synagogues, both in the city and in the suburbs, because these are robbers' dens and dwellings of demons.

Rabbinic Judaism
ETHICAL CONCERNS

Contrary to the hopes of Early Christian theologians, Jews generally did not convert to the new religion but preserved their ancient faith, which took the form called Rabbinic Judaism. Evolving in the centuries following the destruction of the Temple in Jerusalem, the center of Jewish religious life, by the Romans in A.D. 70, Rabbinic Judaism parallels the period of Early Christianity. The rabbis who shaped this development in Jewish thought maintained that to understand properly the written law, the Torah revealed at Sinai, it was necessary to study the oral tradition—that is, the wisdom transmitted over the centuries by word of mouth. Rabbinical writings interpreted the oral tradition to elucidate the behavior the Torah demanded of Jews. The Talmud, which is a compilation of the discussions and decisions of the rabbis during this period, provided Jews with an authoritative set of rules that governed every phase of Jewish life for centuries.

The rabbinical literature shows the rabbis' great concern with ethical considerations, as the following excerpts from the Talmud illustrate.

He who does charity and justice is as if he had filled the whole world with kindness. (*Sukkah, 49*)

Charity knows neither race nor creed. (*Gittin, 61a*)

He who gives charity serves the Holy One daily, and sanctifies His Name.

The Talmudic Anthology, selected and edited by Louis J. Newman in collaboration with Samuel Spitz (New York: Behrman House, 1945), pp. 49, 51, 116–118, 130, 146, 176, 301–302. Used by permission of Martha Newman.

The Good Impulse seeks the joy of the Torah; the Evil Impulse, the joy of women, wine and arrogance. (*Zohar, i, 202a*)

He is called a man who subdues his impulses. (*Zohar, ii, 128a*)

God created the Evil Impulse, but also the Torah as its antidote. (*Kiddushin, 30a*)

Upon the heart of man lies the stone of the Evil Inclination. (*Bereshit Rabbah, 70, 8*)

Rabbi Simeon ben Lakish said: "Man should always rouse his good impulse against the Evil, and he may thus succeed in overcoming it. But if not, more potent means are at his command, such as immersing himself in the study of the Torah." *(Berakot, 5a)*

When the wrong-doer makes amends (confesses and begs forgiveness), it is the duty of the injured party to forgive him: "When thou hast mercy upon thy fellow, thou hast One to have mercy on thee; but if thou hast not mercy upon thy fellow, thou hast none to have mercy on thee." *(Tanhuma, Buber, Wayyera, par. 30)*

R. Zeira said: "I was privileged to know a man with perfect trust in God. He set aside hours for the study of the Torah, and no matter how much he stood to lose, he would never desist from his period of study. He would say: 'If God desires to send me profit, He can do so after my time of study.'" *(Y. Sotah, 9)*

Judaism is not only ethical, but ethics constitutes its essence, its nature—"its beginning, its middle and its end." *(Midrash Tanhuma, Wayishlah)*

When man appears before the Throne of Judgment, the first question he is asked is not— "Have you believed in God," or, "Have you prayed or performed ritual acts," but "Have you dealt honorably, faithfully in all your dealings with your fellow-man?" *(Shabbat, 31a)*

The Rabbis have taught: "For the sake of peaceful intercourse or for the sake of the Torah whose ways are ways of peace, the non-Jewish poor may gather unharvested produce left over in Jewish fields, in the same fashion as the Jewish poor. The non-Jewish poor shall receive food and garments from Jewish charity funds the same as Jews. If the non-Jewish sick have no friends, they should be visited the same as the Jewish sick. If no one claims the body of the non-Jewish dead, they should be buried by Jews, the same as the Jewish dead. When a Jew sees a non-Jew at work in the field, he should greet him with words of blessing, even in the forbidden seventh year when a Jewish worker should be shunned." *(Gittin, 61)*

It is forbidden to rob the idolator. *(Y. Baba Metzia, 2, 5)*

Even an idolator can be a Zaddik [righteous person]. *(Bemidbar Rabbah, 8, 2)*

Even a non-Jew who speaks words of wisdom is called a wise man. *(Megillah, 16)*

The just among the Gentiles are priests of God. *(Eliyahu Zuta, 20)*

The righteous among the Gentiles will have a share in the World-to-Come. *(Yalkut Shimeoni, Prophets, Section 296)*

To rob or defraud a Gentile is worse than to rob an Israelite "on account of the profanation of the Name"—the Israelite lays the wrong to the individual; the Gentile blames the religion. *(Tosefta Baba Kamma, 10, 15)*

That man's life is indeed enriched who is wedded to a virtuous woman. *(Shabbat, 25b)*

A man without a wife lives without good, without help, without joy, without blessing and without forgiveness. *(Kohelet Rabbah, 9, 7)*

A man should be careful not to irritate his wife and cause her to weep. *(Baba Metzia, 59)*

REVIEW QUESTIONS

1. In what ways did John Chrysostom demonize the Jews?
2. What is the historical significance of this form of anti-Judaism?
3. Among the ethical considerations expressed in the Talmud, enumerate those that seem compatible with Early Christianity. Are any incompatible?

---

8   The Christian Worldview

Building on the life and teachings of Jesus as reported in the Gospels and apostolic letters collected in the New Testament, the Early Christian thinkers formulated a comprehensive worldview. The Christian view stressed the sinful nature of human beings—their almost unlimited capacity for evildoing. The church taught that only through the gift of God's grace could individuals overcome the consequences of sin and obtain salvation. Christian leaders drew a sharp distinction between a spiritual realm (called the "City of God" by Saint Augustine) and the secular world (the "city of the world" or the "city of man"), where Christians had to live out their earthly, material existence. Christians were urged to live in the world, but not to live by its values. Rather, they were to imitate the ways of Jesus in thought, word, and deed, as interpreted by the authorities of the church.

The task of living a Christian life in a secular world was not easy. Not the least of the problems was how Christians could relate to the political power structure of earthly societies. The task of finding a Christian basis for relations between church and state has been a continuous process since Early Christian times. It has had wide repercussions in creating a distinctive Christian view of the legitimate powers of the state.

Saint Augustine
THE CITY OF GOD

Augustine (Aurelius Augustinus, A.D. 354–430), bishop of Hippo (now Souk-Ahras in modern Algeria), was one of the great theologians of the Early Christian church. He formulated a view of life and of the individual that became definitive for Western Christians until it was partially superseded by the writings of Thomas Aquinas in the thirteenth century. Although Augustine admired the achievements of Socrates and Plato, he could not accept their central premise: that in the search for truth the individual relied on reason alone.

The sacking of Rome by the Visigoths in A.D. 410 shocked the entire Roman world. Pagans blamed the catastrophe on the Christians; by abandoning the old gods, said pagans, Christians had brought down the wrath of heaven on Rome. In reply to these charges, Saint Augustine wrote the *City of God*, setting forth the Christian view of the world and humanity.

The theme of the first group of passages from Augustine's *City of God* is a crucial element in the Christian outlook: that when human beings turn away from God to follow their own desires as Adam and Eve did—the original sin—they fall into evil and become afflicted with many miseries, which can be relieved only through God's grace.

I have already said, in previous Books, that God had two purposes in deriving all men from one man. His first purpose was to give unity to the human race by the likeness of nature. His second purpose was to bind mankind by the bond of peace, through blood relationship, into one harmonious whole. I have said further that no member of this race would ever have died had not the first two [Adam and Eve]—one created from nothing and the second from the first—merited this death by disobedience. The sin which they committed was so great that it impaired all human nature—in this sense, that the nature has been transmitted to posterity with a propensity to sin and a necessity to die. . . .

When a man lives "according to man" and not "according to God" he is like the Devil. . . .

When man lives according to himself, that is to say, according to human ways and not according to God's will, then surely he lives according to falsehood. Man himself, of course, is not a lie, since God who is his Author and Creator could not be the Author and Creator of a lie. Rather, man has been so constituted in truth that he was meant to live not according to himself but to Him who made him—that is, he was meant to do the will of God rather than his own. It is a lie not to live as a man was created to live.

Man indeed desires happiness even when he does so live as to make happiness impossible. . . . The happiness of man can come not from himself but only from God, and that to live according to oneself is to sin, and to sin is to lose God. . . .

Moreover, our first parents [Adam and Eve] only fell openly into the sin of disobedience

because, secretly, they had begun to be guilty. Actually, their bad deed could not have been done had not bad will preceded it; what is more, the root of their bad will was nothing else than pride. For, "pride is the beginning of all sin." And what is pride but an appetite for inordinate exaltation? Now, exaltation is inordinate when the soul cuts itself off from the very Source [God] to which it should keep close and somehow makes itself and becomes an end to itself. This takes place when the soul becomes inordinately pleased with itself, and such self-pleasing occurs when the soul falls away from the unchangeable Good which ought to please the soul far more than the soul can please itself. Now, this falling away is the soul's own doing, for, if the will had merely remained firm in the love of that higher immutable Good which lighted its mind into knowledge and warmed its will into love, it would not have turned away in search of satisfaction in itself and, by so doing, have lost that light and warmth. And thus Eve would not have believed that the serpent's lie was true, nor would Adam have preferred the will of his wife to the will of God. . . .

This life of ours—if a life so full of such great ills can properly be called a life—bears witness to the fact that, from its very start, the race of mortal men has been a race condemned. Think, first, of that dreadful abyss of ignorance from which all error flows and so engulfs the sons of Adam in a darksome pool that no one can escape without the toll of toils and tears and fears. Then, take our very love for all those things that prove so vain and poisonous and breed so many heartaches, troubles, griefs, and fears; such insane joys in discord, strife, and war; such wrath and plots of enemies, deceivers, sycophants; such fraud and theft and robbery; such perfidy and pride, envy and ambition, homicide and murder, cruelty and savagery,

St. Augustine, *The City of God,* pp. 295, 300–301, 308–309, 321, 507, 519–520, 522, 540–541. Copyright ©1958 by Catholic University Press of America. Used with permission.

lawlessness and lust; all the shameless passions of the impure—fornication and adultery, incest and unnatural sins, rape and countless other uncleannesses too nasty to be mentioned; the sins against religion—sacrilege and heresy, blasphemy and perjury; the iniquities against our neighbors—calumnies and cheating, lies and false witness, violence to persons and property; the injustices of the courts and the innumerable other miseries and maladies that fill the world, yet escape attention.

It is true that it is wicked men who do such things, but the source of all such sins is that radical canker [sinfulness] in the mind and will that is innate in every son of Adam. . . .

Yet, for all this blight of ignorance and folly, fallen man has not been left without some ministries of Providence, nor has God, in His anger, shut up His mercies. There are still within the reach of man himself, if only he will pay the price of toil and trouble, the twin resources of law and education. With the one, he can make war on human passion; with the other, he can keep the light of learning lit even in the darkness of our native ignorance. . . .

From this all but hell of unhappiness here on earth, nothing can save us but the grace of Jesus Christ, who is our Saviour, Lord and God. In fact, the very meaning of the name, Jesus, is Saviour, and when we say "save" we mean, especially, that He saves us from passing from the misery of this mortal life to a still more miserable condition, which is not so much a life as death. . . .

Augustine saw a conflict between the earthly city, visible, temporal, and corrupt, and the City of God, invisible, eternal, and perfect. Those Christians favored with God's grace lived in this earthly city as strangers and pilgrims passing through on their journey to their true homeland, the heavenly kingdom. The fate of the earthly city was of no ultimate concern to these Christians. For Augustine, this earthly world represented the forces of evil that would finally be destroyed at the end of time, when Christ would come again.

What we see, then, is that two societies have issued from two kinds of love. Worldly society has flowered from a selfish love which dared to despise even God, whereas the communion of saints is rooted in a love of God that is ready to trample on self. In a word, this latter relies on the Lord, whereas the other boasts that it can get along by itself. The city of man seeks the praise of men, whereas the height of glory for the other is to hear God in the witness of conscience. The one lifts up its head in its own boasting; the other says to God: "Thou art my glory, thou liftest up my head."

In the city of the world both the rulers themselves and the people they dominate are dominated by the lust for domination; whereas in the City of God all citizens serve one another in charity, whether they serve by the responsibilities of office or by the duties of obedience. The one city loves its leaders as symbols of its own strength; the other says to its God: "I love thee, O Lord, my strength." Hence, even the wise men in the city of man live according to man, and their only goal has been the goods of their bodies or of the mind or of both; though some of them have reached a knowledge of God, "they did not glorify him as God or give thanks but became vain in their reasonings, and their senseless minds have been darkened. For while professing to be wise" (that is to say, while glorying in their own wisdom, under the domination of pride), "they have become fools, and they have changed the glory of the incorruptible God for an image made like to corruptible man and to birds and four-footed beasts and creeping things" (meaning that they either led their people, or imitated them, in adoring idols shaped like these things), "and they worshiped and served the creature rather than the Creator who is blessed forever." In the City of God, on the contrary, there is no merely human wisdom, but there is a piety which worships the true God as He should be worshiped and has as its goal that reward of all holiness whether in the society of saints on earth or in that of angels of heaven, which is "that God may be all in all." . . .

Augustine says that history reveals the intermingling of the City of God and the City of Man in time and space, and the incessant combat between the partisans of these two cities. This struggle will continue until time itself is annulled by God when Christ returns and the saints are separated from sinners at the Last Judgment. Then the saints will join Jesus and be with him for eternity, and the sinners will be separated from God and confined to hell, also for eternity.

. . . In the eternal City of God, each and all of the citizens are personally immortal with an immortality which the holy angels never lost and which even human beings can come to share. This is to be achieved by the supreme omnipotence of the Creator, the Founder of the City. . . .

Who can measure the happiness of heaven, where no evil at all can touch us, no good will be out of reach; where life is to be one long laud extolling God, who will be all in all; where there will be no weariness to call for rest, no need to call for toil, no place for any energy but praise. . . .

. . . There will be such poise, such grace, such beauty as become a place where nothing unbecoming can be found. Wherever the spirit wills, there, in a flash, will the body be. Nor will the spirit ever will anything unbecoming either to itself or to the body.

In heaven, all glory will be true glory, since no one could ever err in praising too little or too much. True honor will never be denied where due, never be given where undeserved, and, since none but the worthy are permitted there, no one will unworthily [pursue] glory. Perfect peace will reign, since nothing in ourselves or in any others could disturb this peace.

REVIEW QUESTIONS

1. According to Augustine, what was the origin of the unity of the human race? What was the origin of human sinfulness?
2. Describe Augustine's conception of the two cities—of God and of man—and the radical implications of this teaching in shaping Christian culture.

CHAPTER 7

The Early Middle Ages

CORONATION OF CHARLEMAGNE, by David Aubert, vellum, 1462. The crowning of Charlemagne by the pope, on Christmas Eve, A.D 800, implied that the emperor had a spiritual responsibility to spread and defend the faith. *(Scala/Art Resource, NY)*

The establishment of Germanic kingdoms in the fifth and sixth centuries on Roman lands marked the end of the ancient world and the start of the Middle Ages, a period that spanned a thousand years. During the Middle Ages the center of Western civilization shifted northward from the lands bordering the Mediterranean Sea to parts of Europe that Greco-Roman civilization had barely penetrated.

The Early Middle Ages (500–1050) marked an age of transition. The humanist culture that characterized the Greco-Roman past had disintegrated, and a new civilization was emerging in Latin Christendom, which covered Western and Central Europe. Medieval civilization consisted of a blending of the remnants of Greco-Roman culture with Germanic customs and Christian principles. The central element was Christianity; the Christian view of a transcendent God and the quest for salvation pervaded the medieval outlook, and the church was the dominant institution.

During the Early Middle Ages, Latin Christendom was a pioneer society struggling to overcome invasions, a breakdown of central authority, a decline in trade and town life, and a deterioration of highly refined culture. The Latin Christian church, centered in Rome and headed by the pope, progressively gave form and unity to the new civilization. Christian clergy preserved some of the learning of the ancient world, which they incorporated into the Christian outlook. Dedicated missionaries converted various Germanic, Celtic, and Slavic peoples to Latin Christianity. From Italy to the North Sea and from Ireland to Poland, an emerging Christian tradition was providing unity to people with differing customs and beliefs.

The center of emerging medieval civilization was the kingdom of the Franks, located in Gaul (France) and western Germany. Migrating westward from their homeland in the valley of the Rhine River, the Germanic Franks conquered Roman Gaul in the fifth and sixth centuries. Charlemagne (ruled 768–814), the greatest of the Frankish rulers, added large areas of Germany and Italy to his kingdom. On Christmas Day in the year 800, Pope Leo III crowned Charlemagne "Emperor of the Romans," a sign that the memory of imperial Rome still persisted. (With the coronation of Otto the Great in 962, the German ruler was now referred to as Holy Roman Emperor.) Without Roman law, a professional civil service, and great cities serving as centers of trade, however, Charlemagne's Frankish Empire was only a pale shadow of the Roman Empire. Rather, the crowning of a German king as emperor of the Romans by the pope signified something new: the intermingling of Germanic, Christian, and Roman elements that came to characterize medieval Latin Christendom.

Charlemagne's empire rested more on the strength of the emperor's personality than it did on viable institutions. Charlemagne's heirs were unable to hold the empire together; power passed gradually into the hands of large landholders, who exercised governmental authority in their own regions. Also contributing to this decline in centralized authority were devastating raids by Muslims from Spain, North Africa, and Mediterranean islands; by Northmen from Scandinavia; and by Magyars from Western Asia. Europe had entered an age of feudalism, in which public authority was dispersed among lords and held as if it were private inheritable property.

Feudalism rested on an economic base known as manorialism. Although family farms owned by free peasants still existed, the essential agricultural arrangement in medieval society was the village community (manor), headed by a lord or his steward and farmed by serfs, who were bound to the land. A lord controlled at least one manorial village; great lords might possess scores. Much land was held by various clerical institutions; the church's manors were similar to those run by nonclerics.

Feudalism was an improvised response to the challenge posed by ineffectual central authority, and it provided some order and law during a period of breakdown. Medieval feudal practices were not uniform but differed from region to region. In later centuries, when kings reasserted their authority and fashioned strong central governments, the power of lords declined.

Latin Christendom (Western and Central Europe) was only one of three new civilizations based on religion that emerged after the decline of the Roman Empire; Byzantium and Islam were the other two. During the Early Middle Ages both of these eastern civilizations were far more advanced than Latin Christendom. And yet it was Latin Christendom, not Byzantine or Islamic civilizations, that eventually produced the modern world.

1 The Byzantine Cultural Achievement

During the Early Middle Ages, when learning was in retreat in Latin Christendom, Byzantine civilization preserved the intellectual tradition of ancient Greece. Although the western Roman Empire fell to the German tribes, the eastern provinces of the Empire survived. They did so because they were richer, more urbanized, and more populous and because the main thrust of the Germanic and Hunnish invaders had been directed at the western regions. In the eastern parts, Byzantine civilization took shape. Its religion was Christianity, its culture Greek, and its machinery of administration Roman. Contacts with Byzantine learning during the High Middle Ages stimulated learning in the Latin West.

Theophylact Simocattes
THE VALUE OF REASON AND HISTORY

In the following selection Theophylact Simocattes, a seventh-century Byzantine historian, shows respect for the tradition of reason that was inherited from the classical world and familiarity with Homer, the wellspring of Greek literature. Like Thucydides, he values history, considering it a far better avenue to knowledge than the myths and fables created or embellished by poets.

Man is adorned not only by the endowments of nature but also by the fruits of his own efforts. For reason, which he possesses, is an admirable and divine trait by which he renders to God his adoration and homage. Through reason he enters into knowledge of himself and does not remain ignorant of the ordering of his creation. Accordingly, through reason men come together with each other and, turning away from external considerations, they direct their thoughts toward the mystery of their own nature.

Reason has given many good things to men and is an excellent helpmate of nature. The things which nature has withheld from man, reason provides in the most effective manner, embellishing those things which are seen, adding spice to those that are tasted, roughening or softening things to the touch, composing poetry and music for the ear, soothing the soul by lessening discord, and bringing sounds into concord. Is not reason also the most persuasive master of the crafts?—reason which has made a well-woven tunic from wool, which from wood has constructed carts for farmers, oars for sailors, and small wicker shields for soldiers as protection against the dangers of the battlefield.

Most important of all, reason provides the hearer with that pleasure which reflects the greatest amount of experience, the study of history, which is the instructor of the spirit. Nothing can be more seductive than history for the minds of those who desire to learn. It is sufficient to cite an example from Homer to demonstrate

this: Soon after he had been thrown on the beach by violent waves of the sea, the son of Laertes, Odysseus, almost naked and with his body emaciated from the mishap of the shipwreck, was graciously received at the court of Alcinous. There he was clothed in a bright robe and given a place at the table of the king. Although only just arrived, he was granted permission to speak and an opportunity to relate his adventures. His recital pleased the Phocaeans so much that the banquet seemed to have changed into a theater. Indeed, they lent him an attention altogether remarkable, nor did they feel during his long narration any tedium, although he described the many misfortunes he had suffered. For listening brings an overwhelming desire (to hear more) and thus easily accepts a strange tale.

It is for this reason that in learning the poets are considered most estimable, for they realize that the spirits of men are fond of stories, always yearning to acquire knowledge and thirsty for strange narrations. Thus the poets create myths for men and clothe their phrases with adornments, fleshing out the fables with method, and embellishing their nonsense with meter as if with enchanted spells. This artifice has succeeded so well that poets are considered to be theologians, intimately associated with the gods. It is believed that through the poets' mouths the gods reveal their own personal affairs and also whether a felicitous or a calamitous event will happen to men in their lifetime.

This being so, one may term history the common teacher of all men: it shows which course to follow and which to avoid as profitless. The most competent generals are those who have been instructed by history, for history reveals how to draw up troops and by what means to outmaneuver the enemy through ambush. History renders these generals more prudent because they know about the misfortunes of others, and it directs them through observation of the mistakes of others. Similarly, it has shown that men become happier through good conduct, pushing men to higher peaks of virtue through gradual advances. For the old man history is his support and staff, while for the young, it is the fairest and wisest instructor,

applying (the fruit of) great experience to new situations and thus anticipating somewhat the lessons of time. I now dedicate my own zeal and efforts to history, although I know that I am undertaking a greater task than I am able to fulfill effectively, since I lack elegance of expression, profundity of thought, purity of syntax, and skill in composition. If any parts of my work should prove pleasing in any way, let this be ascribed rather to the result of chance than to my own skill.

REVIEW QUESTION

Why did Theophylact value reason? History? What is his debt to ancient Greece?

2 Islam

The vital new religion of Islam emerged in the seventh century among the Arabs of Arabia. Its founder was Muhammad (c. 570–632), a prosperous merchant in Mecca, a trading city near the Red Sea. When Muhammad was about forty, he believed that he was visited by the angel Gabriel, who ordered him to "recite in the name of the Lord!" Transformed by this vision, Muhammad was convinced that he had been chosen to serve as a prophet.

Although most desert Arabs worshiped tribal gods, in the towns and trading centers many Arabs were familiar with Judaism and Christianity, and some had accepted the idea of one God. Rejecting the many deities of the tribal religions, Muhammad offered the Arabs a new monotheistic faith, Islam, which means "surrender to Allah" (God).

THE KORAN

Islamic standards of morality and rules governing daily life are set by the Koran, the book that Muslims believe contains the words of Allah as revealed to Muhammad. Muslims see their religion as the completion and perfection of Judaism and Christianity. They regard the ancient Hebrew prophets as sent from God and value their messages about compassion and the oneness of humanity. Muslims also regard Jesus as a great prophet but do not consider him divine. They see Muhammad as the last and greatest of the prophets and believe that he was entirely human, not divine. Muslims worship only Allah, the creator and ruler of heaven and earth, a single, all-powerful God who is merciful, compassionate, and just. Following are excerpts from the Koran.

The Koran, translated by N. J. Dawood (New York: Penguin Books, 1995) pp. 27, 38, 46–47, 64–65, 78, 376, 378–379, 381.

Copyright © N.J. Dawood, 1956, 1959, 1966, 1968, 1974, 1990. Reproduced by permission of Penguin Books Ltd.

GOD

God: there is no god but Him, the Living, the Eternal One. Neither slumber nor sleep overtakes Him. His is what the heavens and the earth contain. Who can intercede with Him except by His permission? He knows what is before and behind men. They can grasp only that part of His knowledge which He wills. His throne is as vast as the heavens and the earth, and the preservation of both does not weary Him. He is the Exalted, the Immense One. [2:255]

———

In the Name of God, the Compassionate, the Merciful

It is the Merciful who has taught the Koran.

He created man and taught him articulate speech. The sun and the moon pursue their ordered course. The plants and the trees bow down in adoration.

He raised the heaven on high and set the balance of all things, that you might not transgress that balance. Give just weight and full measure.

He laid the earth for His creatures, with all its fruits and blossom-bearing palm, chaff-covered grain and scented herbs. Which of your Lord's blessings would you deny?

He created man from potter's clay, and the jinn [spirits that could be good or evil] from smokeless fire. Which of your Lord's blessings would you deny? [55:1–18]

———

All that is in the heavens and the earth gives glory to God. He is the Mighty, the Wise One.

It is He that has sovereignty over the heavens and the earth. He ordains life and death, and has power over all things.

He is the First and the Last, the Visible and the Unseen. He has knowledge of all things.

It was He who created the heavens and the earth in six days, and then mounted the throne. He knows all that goes into the earth and all that emerges from it, all that comes down from heaven and all that ascends to it. He is with you wherever you are. God is cognizant of all your actions.

He has sovereignty over the heavens and the earth. To God shall all things return. He causes the night to pass into the day, and causes the day to pass into the night. He has knowledge of the inmost thoughts of men. [57:1–6]

RIGHTEOUSNESS AND MERCY

Righteousness does not consist in whether you face towards the East or the West. The righteous man is he who believes in God and the Last Day, in the angels and the Book and the prophets; who, though he loves it dearly, gives away his wealth to kinsfolk, to orphans, to the destitute, to the traveller in need and to beggars, and for the redemption of captives; who attends to his prayers and renders the alms levy; who is true to his promises and steadfast in trial and adversity and in times of war. Such are the true believers; such are the God-fearing. [2:176–177]

———

Serve God and associate none with Him. Show kindness to parents and kindred, to orphans and to the destitute, to near and distant neighbours, to those that keep company with you, to the traveller in need, and to the slaves you own. God does not love arrogant and boastful men, who are themselves niggardly and enjoin others to be niggardly; who conceal the riches which God of His bounty has bestowed upon them (We have prepared a shameful punishment for the unbelievers); and who spend their wealth for the sake of ostentation, believing neither in God nor in the Last Day. He that chooses Satan for his friend, an evil friend has he. [4:36–39]

CHRISTIANITY

And remember the angels' words to Mary. They said: "God has chosen you. He has made you pure and exalted you above womankind.

Mary, be obedient to your Lord; bow down and worship with the worshippers".

This is an account of a divine secret. We reveal it to you.[1] You were not present when they cast lots to see which of them should have charge of Mary; nor were you present when they argued about her.

The angels said to Mary: "God bids you rejoice in a word from Him. His name is the Messiah, Jesus the son of Mary. He shall be noble in this world and in the hereafter, and shall be one of those who are favoured. He shall preach to men in his cradle and in the prime of manhood, and shall lead a righteous life."

"Lord," she said, "how can I bear a child when no man has touched me?"

He replied: "Even thus. God creates whom He will. When He decrees a thing He need only say: 'Be,' and it is. He will instruct him in the scriptures and in wisdom, in the Torah and in the Gospel, and send him forth as an apostle to the Israelites. He will say: 'I bring you a sign from your Lord. From clay I will make for you the likeness of a bird. I shall breathe into it and, by God's leave, it shall become a living bird. By God's leave I shall heal the blind man and the leper, and raise the dead to life. I shall tell you what to eat and what to store up in your houses. Surely that will be a sign for you, if you are true believers. I come to confirm the Torah which preceded me and to make lawful to you some of the things you are forbidden. I bring you a sign from your Lord: therefore fear God and obey me. God is my Lord and your Lord: therefore serve Him. That is a straight path.'" [3:42–51]

People of the Book,[2] do not transgress the bounds of your religion. Speak nothing but the truth about God. The Messiah, Jesus the son of Mary, was no more than God's apostle and His Word which He cast to Mary: a spirit from Him. So believe in God and His apostles and do not say: "Three" [a reference to the Trinity].

Forbear, and it shall be better for you. God is but one God. God forbid that He should have a son! His is all that the heavens and the earth contain. God is the all-sufficient protector. The Messiah does not disdain to be a servant of God, nor do the angels who are nearest to Him. Those who through arrogance disdain His service shall all be brought before Him. [4:171–172]

HEAVEN AND HELL

When that which is coming comes—and no soul shall then deny its coming—some shall be abased and others exalted.

When the earth shakes and quivers, and the mountains crumble away and scatter abroad into fine dust, you shall be divided into three multitudes: those on the right (blessed shall be those on the right); those on the left (damned shall be those on the left); and those to the fore (foremost shall be those). Such are they that shall be brought near to their Lord in the gardens of delight: a whole multitude from the men of old, but only a few from the latter generations.

They shall recline on jewelled couches face to face, and there shall wait on them immortal youths with bowls and ewers and a cup of purest wine (that will neither pain their heads nor take away their reason); with fruits of their own choice and flesh of fowls that they relish. And theirs shall be the dark-eyed houris [beautiful virgins], chaste as hidden pearls: a guerdon [reward] for their deeds.

There they shall hear no idle talk, no sinful speech, but only the greeting, "Peace! Peace!" Those on the right hand—happy shall be those on the right hand! They shall recline on couches raised on high in the shade of thornless [cedars] and clusters of talh;[3] amidst gushing waters and abundant fruits, unforbidden, neverending.

We created the houris and made them virgins, loving companions for those on the right

---

[1]Muhammad.
[2]Christians.

[3]Probably the banana fruit.

hand: a multitude from the men of old, and a multitude from the later generations.

As for those on the left hand (wretched shall be those on the left hand!) they shall dwell amidst scorching winds and seething water: in the shade of pitch-black smoke, neither cool nor refreshing. For they have lived in comfort and persisted in the heinous sin,[4] saying: "When we are once dead and turned to dust and bones, shall we be raised to life? And our forefathers, too?"

Say: "Those of old, and those of the present age, shall be brought together on an appointed day. As for you sinners who deny the truth, you shall eat the fruit of the Zaqqūm tree and fill your bellies with it. You shall drink scalding water: yet you shall drink it as the thirsty camel drinks." [56:1–56]

WOMEN

Men have authority over women because God has made the one superior to the other, and because they spend their wealth to maintain them. Good women are obedient. They guard their unseen parts because God has guarded them. As for those from whom you fear disobedience, admonish them and send them to beds apart and beat them. Then if they obey you, take no further action against them. Surely God is high, supreme.

If you fear a breach between a man and his wife, appoint an arbiter from his people and another from hers. If they wish to be reconciled God will bring them together again. Surely God is all-knowing and wise. [4:34–35]

----

[4]Idolatry.

REVIEW QUESTIONS

1. Compare and contrast the views of God and morality described in the Koran with those found in the Hebrew scriptures and the New Testament.
2. What advice does the Koran give to Christians?

3 Muslim Relations with Christians and Jews

The Koran regards Jesus as a righteous prophet who performed miracles but rejects his divinity and denounces as blasphemers those who believe in it. Muslims accept the Hebrew scriptures as God's revelation, but historically were often critical of Jews, probably because of their opposition to Muhammad in Medina. In Islamic lands both Christians and Jews were called the people of the Book and were granted the status of *dhimmis*—minorities who lived under the protection of Islamic authority. They were not required to convert and were free to practice their faith in private and to govern their own communities. For these privileges, they had to accept a subordinate status, which included payment of a poll tax and humiliating restrictions on their activities (described in the following documents). Despite these prohibitions, Christians and Jews generally enjoyed toleration and some rose to positions of prominence. Jews in particular lived in greater security than they did in Christian lands where, in the High and Late Middle Ages, they were subject to frequent persecution, including expulsion and massacre. Although some passages in the Koran disparage Jews, medieval Muslims, unlike Christians in the Latin West, did not teach that Jews were agents of Satan.

LEGAL TEXTS AND DECREES: RESTRICTIONS ON *DHIMMIS*

The first document describing restrictions on Jews and Christians is from a legal text drawn up in the eighth and ninth centuries. The second is a decree issued by a caliph in 1354. The Arabic terms in brackets were inserted by Bernard Lewis, the translator.

You will be subject to the authority of Islam and to no contrary authority. You will not refuse to carry out any obligation which we think fit to impose upon you by virtue of this authority.

If any one of you speaks improperly of Muhammad, may God bless and save him, the Book of God, or of His religion, he forfeits the protection [*dhimma*] of God, of the Commander of the Faithful, and of all the Muslims; he has contravened the conditions upon which he was given his safe-conduct; his property and his life are at the disposal of the Commander of the Faithful.

If one of them commits fornication with a Muslim woman or goes through a form of marriage with her or robs a Muslim on the highway or subverts a Muslim from his religion or gives aid to those who made war against the Muslims by fighting with them or by showing them the weak points of the Muslims, or by harboring their spies, he has contravened his pact [*'ahd*], and his life and his property are at the disposal of the Muslims.

If he commits some lesser offense against the property or the honor of a Muslim or against an infidel under Muslim protection, with a pact or safe-conduct, he shall be punished.

We shall supervise all your dealings with Muslims. If there is anything in which you are engaged which is not lawful for a Muslim, we shall reject it and punish you for it. If you sell a Muslim something we hold forbidden, such as wine, pig, blood, or carrion, and the like, we shall annul the sale, confiscate the price if it has

been paid, and not return the thing to you if it still exists, but pour it out if it is wine or blood and burn it if it is carrion; if the purchaser has already consumed it, we shall not oblige him to pay for it, but we shall punish you for it.

You shall not give a Muslim anything to eat or drink which is forbidden, nor marry him in the presence of witnesses chosen from among you nor by wedding rites we hold to be invalid. . . .

If any of you steals and the victim takes him before a judge, his hand shall be cut off if his crime is punishable by this penalty, and he shall make restitution. . . .

You may not display crosses in Muslim cities, nor proclaim polytheism, nor build churches or meeting places for your prayers, nor strike clappers, nor proclaim your polytheistic beliefs on the subject of Jesus, son of [Mary], or any other to a Muslim.

You shall wear the girdle [*zunnār*] over all your garments, your cloaks and the rest, so that the girdles are not hidden. You shall differentiate yourselves by your saddles and your mounts, and you shall distinguish your and their headgear [*qalansuwa*] by a mark which you shall place on your headgear. You shall not occupy the middle of the road or the seats in the market, obstructing Muslims.

Every free adult male of sound mind among you shall have to pay a poll tax [*jizya*] of one dinar, in good coin, at the beginning of each year. He shall not be able to leave his city until he pays his poll tax or appoints someone to pay it on his behalf, with no further liability until the beginning of the year. The poor among you is liable for the poll tax, which should be paid for him. Poverty does not free you from

Islam: From the Prophet Muhammad to the Capture of Constantinople, vol. 2, *Religion and Society*, ed. and trans. Bernard Lewis (1987), pp. 219–222, 234–235. Copyright © 1974 by Bernard Lewis. By permission of Oxford University Press, Inc.

any obligation, nor does it abrogate your pact [*dhimma*]. . . . You are subject to no taxes on your money other than the poll tax as long as you stay in your country or travel around in the lands of the Muslims otherwise than as a merchant. You may in no circumstances enter Mecca. If you travel for trade, you shall pay to the Muslims a tenth part of all your merchandise. You may go wherever you wish in the lands of the Muslims, except [holy] Mecca, and reside wherever you wish in the lands of the Muslims, except the Hijāz, where you may only stay for three days in any city, after which you must leave. . . .

We owe you protection, for yourselves and for property which it is lawful for you to hold according to our laws, against anybody, Muslim or other, who seeks to wrong you, as we would protect our own persons and property, and we administer justice to you in matters under our jurisdiction as we do with our own property. But no one among you can ask us to protect any forbidden thing which you own, such as blood, carrion, wine, or pigs, as we would protect lawful property. We shall not prevent you from having them, but we shall not allow you to display them in the cities of the Muslims. If a Muslim or any other buys such merchandise, we shall not compel him to pay the price, because these are forbidden things and therefore have no price which could be legally enforced. But we shall restrain him from troubling you in this, and if he persists he shall be punished, though not by enforcing payment for what he took from you.

You must observe all the conditions which we have imposed.

———

A noble decree, to the effect that all the communities of Jews, Christians, and Samaritans in the Egyptian lands and the God-guarded realms of Islam and their dependencies must conform to the covenant accorded by the Commander of the Faithful 'Umar ibn al-Khaṭṭāb, may God be pleased with him, to the members of these communities in bygone times, as follows: That they shall not build any new convent or church or hermitage in the lands of Islam, nor rebuild any such building which is destroyed; that they shall not harbor spies nor any who are suspect to the Muslims, nor shall they deceitfully plot against the Muslims; that they shall not teach their children the Qur'ān; that they shall not make public display of polytheism; that they shall not obstruct any of their relatives who wish to accept Islam; that they shall not dress like the Muslims, but shall wear blue and yellow distinguishing dress; that their women shall be prevented from dressing like Muslim women; that they shall not ride with stirrups nor gird a sword, nor ride on a horse or mule but only on donkeys, side-seat on litters; that they shall not sell intoxicating drinks; that they shall keep to their special dress wherever they are; that they shall wear girdles not made of silk around their waists; that the Christian woman who appears in public shall wear a cotton veil, dyed blue, and the Jewess a yellow veil; that none of them shall enter the bath except wearing a sign around his neck which distinguishes him from the Muslims, such as a ring made of iron or lead or some other material; that they shall not build themselves houses higher than the houses of the Muslims, nor equal to them, but only lower; that they shall knock lightly with their clappers and not raise their voices in their churches; that they shall not work in the service of our exalted state, may God strengthen its foundations, nor in the service of any of the amirs, may Almighty God strengthen them, nor shall any of them hold a position which would give him authority over any of the Muslims; that jurisdiction over the estates of the dead among them shall be according to the noble Muhammadan Holy Law and that the rules of administrative confiscation will be applied to them equally as to the Muslim dead; that the women of the protected communities shall not enter public bathhouses together with the Muslim women, but that separate bathhouses shall be made for them, into which they shall enter. All this is in accordance with the rulings of the doctors of the Holy Law, as has been explained.

REVIEW QUESTION

What was the purpose of the restrictions imposed on Christians and Jews?

4 Jihad

Muhammad had conveyed to his followers their religious obligation to perform *jihad*, a complex term whose two essential meanings are an internal striving by an individual for moral self-improvement (Greater Jihad) and a collective military struggle to defend Islam against its enemies and to extend Muslim power over other lands so that all people will be subject to Allah (Lesser Jihad). Historically the doctrine of jihad held that the Islamic community (*umma*), the recipient of Allah's revelation, is commanded to make Allah's directives supreme over the whole world. Either by conversion or conquest, infidels are destined to submit to Islamic jurisdiction.

Westerners, who are repulsed by the Islamic concept of jihad and feel threatened by jihadist terrorists, generally interpret jihad as a Muslim's fanatical duty to engage in holy war against the perceived enemies of Islam. Seeking to defend their faith against critics who attack contemporary Islam as an incubator of terrorism, some Muslim intellectuals and religious authorities often respond by stressing Islam's peaceful, tolerant, and humanitarian characteristics, its command to win converts by preaching and persuasion. Central to their argument is the traditional distinction in Islam between the lesser jihad and the greater jihad. Over the centuries, however, most classical Islamic theologians and jurists interpreted jihad as a military obligation to advance Islamic power. And that is how Islamic radicals interpret it today.

SAYINGS ATTRIBUTED TO THE PROPHET

Muhammad glorified jihad and criticized those who did not participate in it, calling them "hypocrites" and "sick in heart." The Koran states: "Those who are killed in the path of God, He does not let their good deeds go for nothing." The Hadith, which consists of an assemblage of sayings and actions attributed to Muhammad and is a major source of Islamic law, contains numerous passages prescribing and lauding jihad as the following excerpts indicate.

I asked Allah's Apostle, "O Allah's Apostle! What is the best deed?" He replied, "To offer the prayers at their early stated fixed times." I asked,

"What is next in goodness?" He replied, "To be good and dutiful to your parents." I further asked, what is next in goodness?" He replied, "To participate in Jihad in Allah's Cause."

Sayings Attributed to the Prophet, pp. 7–14–7–15 www.usc.edu/dept/MSA/fundamentals/hadithsunnah/b. University of Southern California.

A man came to Allah's Apostle and said, "Instruct me as to such a deed as equals Jihad (in reward)." He replied, "I do not find such a deed."

———

The Prophet said, "Last night two men came to me (in a dream) and made me ascend a tree and then admitted me into a better and superior house, better of which I have never seen. One of them said, 'This house is the house of martyrs.'"

———

The Prophet said, "A single endeavor (of fighting) in Allah's Cause in the forenoon or in the afternoon is better than the world and whatever is in it."

———

The Prophet said, "Nobody who dies and finds good from Allah (in the Hereafter) would wish to come back to this world even if he were given the whole world and whatever is in it, except the martyr who, on seeing the superiority of martyrdom, would like to come back to the world and get killed again (in Allah's Cause)."

Narrated Anas: The Prophet said, "A single endeavor (of fighting) in Allah's Cause in the afternoon or in the forenoon is better than all the world and whatever is in it. A place in Paradise as small as the bow or lash of one of you is better than all the world and whatever is in it."

———

A man whose face was covered with an iron mask (i.e., clad in armor) came to the Prophet and said, "O Allah's Apostle! Shall I fight or embrace Islam first?" The Prophet said, 'Embrace Islam first and then fight.' So he embraced Islam, and was martyred. Allah's Apostle said, "A little work, but a great reward." (He did very little (after embracing Islam), but he will be rewarded in abundance).

———

A man came to the Prophet and asked, "A man fights for war booty; another fights for fame and a third fights for showing off; which of them fights in Allah's Cause?" The Prophet said, "He who fights that Allah's Word (i.e., Islam) should be superior, fights in Allah's Cause."

———

Allah's Apostle said, "Anyone whose both feet get covered with dust in Allah's Cause will not be touched by the (Hell) fire."

Ibn Taymiyyah
THE RELIGIOUS AND MORAL DOCTRINE OF JIHAD

Present-day Islamists who advocate jihad against the enemies of Islam often quote extensively Shaykh ul-Islaam Taqi al-Din Ahmad ibn Taymiyyah (1263–1328), a Syrian theologian who regarded jihad as a Muslim's religious and moral duty as the following excerpt from his writings reveals.

The benefit of jihad is general, extending not only to the person who participates in it but also to others. . . . More than any other act it implies love and devotion for God, Who is exalted, trust in Him, the surrender of one's life and property to Him. . . . Any individual or community that participates in it, finds itself between two blissful outcomes: either victory and triumph or martyrdom and Paradise. . . . Now, it is in jihad that one can live and die in ultimate happiness, both in this world and in the hereafter. Abandoning it means losing

Jihad in Classical and Modern Times, ed. Rudolf Peters (Princeton: Markus Wiener, 1996), pp. 48–49. © 1996 by Markus Wiener Publications.

entirely or partially both kinds of happiness. There are people who want to perform religious and temporal deeds full of hardship in spite of their lack of benefit, whereas actually jihad is religiously and temporarily more beneficial than any other deed full of hardship. . . . The death of a martyr . . . is the best of all manners of dying.

REVIEW QUESTIONS

1. What is the meaning of jihad defined in the Hadith? What reasons led Muslims to perform jihad?
2. How, according to Ibn Taymiyyah, does jihad provide ultimate happiness?

5 Islam and Greek Learning

In the eighth and ninth centuries, Muslim civilization, which creatively integrated Arabic, Byzantine, Persian, and Indian cultural traditions, entered its golden age. Muslim science, philosophy, and mathematics, based largely on the achievements of the ancient Greeks, made brilliant contributions to the sum of knowledge at a time when Latin Christendom had lost much of Greco-Roman thought and culture. The Muslims had acquired Greek learning from the older Persian and Byzantine civilizations, which had kept alive the Greek inheritance. By translating Greek works into Arabic and commenting on them, Muslim scholars performed the great historical task of preserving the philosophical and scientific heritage of ancient Greece. Along with this heritage, the original contributions of Muslim scholars and scientists were also passed on to Christian Europe.

Avicenna
LOVE OF LEARNING

The most eminent Muslim thinker, Ibn Sina, known to the West as Avicenna (980–1037), was a poet, doctor, scientist, and philosopher who wrote on every field of knowledge. His philosophical works, which relied heavily on Aristotle, had an important influence on medieval Christian thinkers. In his autobiography, excerpted below, Avicenna describes his love for learning and his debt to ancient Greece.

[In] Bukhara [in present-day Uzbekistan] I was put under teachers of the Koran and of

Arthur J. Arberry, *Avicenna on Theology* (London: John Murray, 1951), pp. 9–13. Copyright © 1951 by John Murray Publishers.

letters. By the time I was ten I had mastered the Koran and a great deal of literature, so that I was marvelled at for my aptitude. . . . Then there came to Bukhara a man called Abū 'Abd Allāh al-Nātilī who claimed to be a philosopher; my father invited him to stay in our house. . . . I now commenced reading the *Isagoge* (of Porphyry)[1] with al-Nātilī. . . . He marvelled at me exceedingly, and warned my father that I should not engage in any other occupation but learning; whatever problem he stated to me, I showed a better mental conception of it than he. So I continued until I had read all the straightforward parts of Logic with him; as for the subtler points, he had no acquaintance with them.

From then onward I took to reading texts by myself; I studied the commentaries, until I had completely mastered the science of Logic. Similarly with Euclid[2] I read the first five or six figures with him, and thereafter undertook on my own account to solve the entire remainder of the book. Next I moved on to the *Almagest* (of

Ptolemy)[3]; when I had finished the prolegomena [introductory essay] and reached the geometrical figures, al-Nātilī told me to go on reading and to solve the problems by myself. . . .

I now occupied myself with mastering the various texts and commentaries on natural science and metaphysics, until all the gates of knowledge were open to me. Next I desired to study medicine, and proceeded to read all the books that have been written on this subject. . . .

The next eighteen months I devoted entirely to reading; I studied Logic once again, and all the parts of philosophy. During all this time I did not sleep one night through, nor devoted my attention to any other matter by day. . . . So I continued until I had made myself master of all the sciences; I now comprehended them to the limits of human possibility. . . .

I was now a master of Logic, natural sciences and mathematics. I therefore returned to metaphysics; I read the *Metaphysica* (of Aristotle). . . .

---

[1]Porphyry (A.D. 233–c. 305) wrote a history of philosophy and edited the lectures of Plotinus, the Neoplatonist. The *Isagoge* was Porphyry's introduction to the categories of Aristotle. —Eds.

[2]Euclid, an Alexandrian mathematician who lived around 300 B.C. He creatively synthesized earlier developments in geometry. —Eds.

[3]Ptolemy, a mathematician, geographer, and astronomer who worked at Alexandria in the second century A.D. His *Almagest*, a Greek-Arabic term meaning "the greatest," summed up antiquity's knowledge of astronomy and became the authoritative text during the Middle Ages. —Eds.

REVIEW QUESTION

Provide examples of Avicenna's familiarity with Greek learning.

---

6   Converting the Germanic Peoples to Christianity

From its beginnings, Christianity sought to carry to all peoples its offer of salvation through faith in Jesus. After Christianity had become the religion of the Roman state, pagan cults were suppressed. When the western Roman provinces fell under the power of invading Germanic tribes, Christian Romans faced the task of converting their new rulers to their religion.

The ability of the Christian religion to penetrate and absorb alien cultures while preserving its own core beliefs was continually tested in the Early Middle Ages. Roman Britain had been invaded in the fifth century by various tribes from northwestern Germany, Denmark, and the Netherlands. Among these tribes were the Angles (from which the word *English* is derived), the Saxons, and the Jutes. The Romano-Britons, who were Christians, were forced to retreat westward to occupy what became the Celtic-speaking Christian principalities of Cornwall, Wales, and Cumberland. Pagan Germans ruled the rest of England.

Bede
HISTORY OF THE ENGLISH CHURCH AND PEOPLE

The English monk called the Venerable Bede (673–735), in his *History of the English Church and People*, cites a letter from Pope Gregory I, "the Great," written in 601. In the letter, the pope forwarded instructions for Augustine of Canterbury, whom he had appointed leader of a mission to convert the English to Christianity. He wrote his emissary to tell Augustine to win the favor of the pagan English by accommodating the requirements of Christian beliefs to the existing non-Christian cultural practices, as the excerpt shows.

When these [missionaries] had left, the holy father Gregory sent after them letters worthy of our notice, which show most clearly his unwearying interest in the salvation of our nation. The letter runs as follows:

"To our well loved son Abbot[1] Mellitus: Gregory, servant of the servants of God.

"Since the departure of yourself and your companions, we have been somewhat anxious, because we have received no news of the success of your journey. Therefore, when by God's help you reach our most reverend brother, Bishop Augustine,[2] we wish you to inform him that we have been giving careful thought to the affairs of the English, and have come to the conclusion that the temples of the idols in that country should on no account be destroyed. He is to destroy the idols, but the temples themselves are to be aspersed [sprinkled] with holy water, altars set up, and relics enclosed in them. For if these temples are well built, they are to be purified from devil-worship,[3] and dedicated to the service of the true God. In this way, we hope that the people, seeing that its temples are not destroyed, may abandon idolatry and resort to these places as before, and may come to know and adore the true God. And since they have a custom of sacrificing many oxen to devils, let

---

Bede, *A History of the English Church and People*, trans. Leo Sherley-Price, pp. 86–87. Copyright © 1955, revised edition 1968. Reproduced by permission of Penguin Books Ltd.

---

[1]The elected head of a monastic community, the abbot was supposed to rule justly and paternally following the constitution (rule) of the community. —Eds.
[2]Augustine (not to be confused with Augustine of Hippo) was an Italian monk who was sent in 597 to convert the English to Christianity. He established his see (bishopric) at Canterbury and founded others at Rochester and London, successfully directing missionary activity in the southern part of what is now England. —Eds.
[3]As Christianity was monotheistic, it denied the validity of any other gods. Therefore, Christians customarily designated the pagan deities as "devils," or evil spirits. —Eds.

some other solemnity be substituted in its place, such as a day of Dedication[4] or the Festivals of the holy martyrs [saints' days] whose relics are enshrined there. On such occasions they might well construct shelters of boughs for themselves around the churches that were once temples, and celebrate the solemnity with devout feasting. They are no longer to sacrifice beasts to the Devil, but they may kill them for food to the praise of God, and give thanks to the Giver of all gifts for His bounty. If the people are allowed some worldly pleasures in this way, they will more readily come to desire the joys of the spirit. For it is certainly impossible to eradicate all errors from obstinate minds at one stroke, and whoever wishes to climb to a mountain top climbs gradually step by step, and not in one leap. It was in this way that God revealed Himself to the Israelite people in Egypt, permitting the sacrifices formerly offered to the Devil to be offered thenceforward to Himself instead. So He bade them sacrifice beasts to Him, so that, once they became enlightened, they might abandon a wrong conception of sacrifice, and adopt the right. For, while they were to continue to offer beasts as before, they were to offer them to God instead of to idols, thus transforming the idea of sacrifice. Of your kindness, you are to inform our brother Augustine of this policy, so that he may consider how he may best implement it on the spot. God keep you safe, my very dear son." . . .

---

[4]The anniversary of the dedication or consecration of a church was celebrated as a holiday. —Eds.

Einhard
FORCIBLE CONVERSION
UNDER CHARLEMAGNE

Although most conversions were based on peaceful persuasion or a voluntary act of consent, occasionally Christianity was imposed by force. Thus, after his long wars against the pagan Saxons, Charlemagne required the Saxons to adopt Christianity and be assimilated into the kingdom of the Franks. In his biography of Charlemagne, the Frankish historian Einhard (770–840) described this event.

No war ever undertaken by the Frank nation was carried on with such persistence and bitterness, or cost so much labor, because the Saxons,[1] like almost all the tribes of Germany, were a fierce people, given to the worship of devils, and hostile to our religion, and did not consider it dishonorable to transgress and violate all law, human and divine. Then there were peculiar circumstances that tended to cause a breach of peace every day. Except in a few places, where large forests or mountain ridges intervened and made the bounds certain, the line between ourselves and the Saxons passed almost in its whole extent through an open country, so that

---

Einhard, *Life of Charlemagne*, trans. Samuel E. Turner (Ann Arbor: University of Michigan Press, 1960), pp. 30–32.

[1]The Saxons were members of a Germanic tribe living between the Rhine and Elbe rivers. —Eds.

there was no end to the murders, thefts, and arsons on both sides. In this way the Franks became so embittered that they at last resolved to make reprisals no longer, but to come to open war with the Saxons [in 772]. Accordingly war was begun against them, and was waged for thirty-three successive years with great fury; more, however, to the disadvantage of the Saxons than of the Franks. It could doubtless have been brought to an end sooner, had it not been for the faithlessness of the Saxons. It is hard to say how often they were conquered, and humbly submitting to the King, promised to do what was enjoined upon them, gave without hesitation the required hostages, and received the officers sent them from the King. They were sometimes so much weakened and reduced that they promised to renounce the worship of devils, and to adopt Christianity, but they were no less ready to violate these terms than prompt to accept them, so that it is impossible to tell which came easier to them to do; scarcely a year passed from the beginning of the war without such changes on their part. But the King did not suffer his high purpose and steadfastness—firm

alike in good and evil fortune—to be wearied by any fickleness on their part, or to be turned from the task that he had undertaken; on the contrary, he never allowed their faithless behavior to go unpunished, but either took the field against them in person, or sent his counts[2] with an army to wreak vengeance and exact righteous satisfaction. At last, after conquering and subduing all who had offered resistance, he took ten thousand of those that lived on the banks of the Elbe,[3] and settled them, with their wives and children, in many different bodies here and there in Gaul and Germany. The war that had lasted so many years was at length ended by their acceding to the terms offered by the King; which were renunciation of their national religious customs and the worship of devils, acceptance of the sacraments of the Christian faith and religion, and union with the Franks to form one people.

---

[2]Counts were royal officials exercising the king's authority in districts called counties. —Eds.
[3]The Elbe River, in central Germany, flows northwestward into the North Sea. —Eds.

Martin of Braga
THE PERSISTENCE OF PAGANISM IN THE COUNTRYSIDE

The persistence of paganism in the countryside remained an ongoing and serious problem for the clergy. Bishop Martin of Braga (c. 520–580), in *On the Castigation of Rustics,* a letter to another bishop in Spain that he expected to be delivered as a sermon to peasants, denounced Christian converts for retaining traditional religious beliefs, practices, and cults despite the pact they had made with God in baptism. In particular, he railed against the peasants' worship of sacred trees and stones and their attempt to divine the future through magic. Following is an excerpt from *On the Castigation of Rustics.*

You promised to renounce the Devil and his angels and all his evil works. And you confessed you believed in Father, Son, and Holy Spirit, and hoped, at the end of the age, for the resurrection of the flesh and eternal life.

See what a bond and confession God holds from you! And how can any of you, who has renounced the Devil and his angels and his evil works, now return again to the worship of the Devil? For to burn candles at stones and trees and springs, and where three roads meet, what is it but the worship of the Devil? To observe divinations and auguries and the days of idols, what is it but worship of the Devil? To observe the "days" of Vulcan [August 23] and the first days of each month, to adorn tables and hang up laurels, to watch the foot, and to pour out fruit and wine over a log in the hearth, and to put bread in a spring, what is it but the worship of the Devil? For women to invoke Minerva in their weaving, to keep weddings for the "day" of Venus [Friday], and to consider which day one should set out on a journey, what is it but the worship of the Devil? To mutter spells over herbs and invoke the names of demons in incantations, what is it but the worship of the Devil? And many other things which it takes too long to say. And you do all these things *after* renouncing the Devil, after Baptism, and, returning to the worship of demons and to their evil works, you have betrayed your Faith and broken the pact you made with God. You have abandoned the Sign of the Cross you received in Baptism, and you give heed to signs of the Devil by little birds and sneezing and many other things. Why does no augury harm me or any other upright Christian? Because, where the Sign of the Cross has gone before, the sign of the Devil is nothing. Why does

it harm you? Because you despise the Sign of Cross and fear the sign you made for yourselves. Likewise you have abandoned the Holy Incantation, that is the Creed you received in Baptism, and the Lord's Prayer, and you cling to diabolical incantations and chants. Whoever, therefore, having despised the Sign of the Cross of Christ, turns to other signs, has lost the Sign of the Cross which he received in Baptism. So, too, he who has other incantations invented by magicians and enchanters, has lost the Creed and the Lord's Prayer, which he received in the Faith of Christ, and has trampled underfoot the Faith of Christ, for one cannot worship God and the Devil at once.

If, therefore, beloved sons, you acknowledge that all the things we have said are true, if a man knows he has done these things after Baptism, and has broken the Faith of Christ, let him not despair of himself, nor say in his heart, "Since I have done such great evil after Baptism, perhaps God will not forgive me my sins." Do not doubt the mercy of God. Only make such a pact in your heart with God that, from now onward, you will no longer worship demons, nor adore anything except the God of Heaven, nor commit murder, nor adultery nor fornication, nor steal nor perjure yourself. And when you have promised this to God of your whole heart, and, further, have ceased to commit these sins, trust in God's pardon, for thus says the Lord by the prophet: "In whatever day the unjust shall forget his iniquities and do justice, I also will forget all his iniquities" [Ezek. 18:21]. God, therefore, waits for repentance. But that repentance is true when a man no longer does the evil he did but both asks for pardon for his past [sins] and bewares lest he return again to them in the future, and, on the other hand, practices good, both providing alms for the hungry poor, refreshing the tired guest, and, whatever he does not wish another should do to him, not doing to another, for in this word the commandments of God are fulfilled.

REVIEW QUESTIONS

1. Give examples of the methods Pope Gregory I suggested for introducing Christianity in pagan England.
2. Compare the methods Charlemagne used to convert the Saxons with the instruction given by Pope Gregory I to Augustine of Canterbury.
3. What is Bishop Martin of Braga's concept of devil worship? How did he believe Christianity could overcome it?

---

7 The Transmission of Learning

Learning, which had been in retreat in the Late Roman Empire, continued its decline in the unsettled conditions following Rome's demise. The old Roman schools closed, and many scientific and literary works of the ancient world were either lost or neglected. Knowledge of the Greek language in Western Europe virtually disappeared, and except for clerics, few people could read or write Latin. The few learned people generally did not engage in original thought but preserved and transmitted surviving elements of the Greco-Roman past.

One such scholar was Cassiodorus (c. 490–575), who served three Ostrogothic kings in Italy. Cassiodorus wrote theological treatises and the twelve-volume *History of the Goths*, but his principal achievement was collecting Greek and Latin manuscripts. Like other Christian scholars before and after him, Cassiodorus maintained that the study of secular literature was an aid to understanding sacred writings. He retired to a monastery where he fostered the monastic practice of copying Christian and pagan manuscripts. Without this effort of monks, many important secular and Christian writings might have perished.

Cassiodorus
THE MONK AS SCRIBE

In the following reading from his introduction to *Divine and Human Readings*, Cassiodorus gave his views on the importance of the monastic scribe's vocation. Cassiodorus believed that through his pen the scribe preaches the word of God and is inspired by his text to know God more fully.

ON SCRIBES AND THE REMEMBERING OF CORRECT SPELLING

1. I admit that among those of your tasks which require physical effort that of the scribe,[1] if he writes correctly, appeals most to me; and it appeals, perhaps not without reason, for by reading the Divine scriptures he wholesomely instructs his own mind and by copying the precepts of the Lord he spreads them far and wide. Happy his

---

Cassiodorus Senator, *An Introduction to Divine and Human Readings*, trans. Leslie W. Jones, pp. 133–135. Copyright © 1946, renewed 1974, by Columbia University Press. Used with permission.

[1]Scribes were persons trained to copy by hand the texts of books, or to take dictation. —Eds.

design, praiseworthy his zeal, to preach to men with the hand alone, to unleash tongues with the fingers, to give salvation silently to mortals, and to fight against the illicit temptations of the devil with pen and ink. Every word of the Lord written by the scribe is a wound inflicted on Satan. And so, though seated in one spot, with the dissemination of his work he travels through different provinces. The product of his toil is read in holy places; people hear the means by which they may turn themselves away from base desire and serve the Lord with heart undefiled. Though absent, he labors at his task. I cannot deny that he may receive a renovation of life from these many blessings, if only he accomplishes things of this sort, not with a vain show of ambition, but with upright zeal. Man multiplies the heavenly words, and in a certain metaphorical sense, if one may so express himself, that which the virtue of the Holy Trinity utters is written by a trinity of fingers. O sight glorious to those who contemplate it carefully! With gliding pen the heavenly words are copied so that the devil's craft, by means of which he caused the head of the Lord to be struck during His passion, may be destroyed. They deserve praise too for seeming in some way to imitate the action of the Lord, who, though it was expressed figuratively, wrote His law with the use of His all-powerful finger. Much indeed is there to be said about such a distinguished art, but it is enough to mention the fact that those men are called scribes (*librarii*) who serve zealously the just scales (*libra*) of the Lord.

2. But lest in performing this great service copyists introduce faulty words with letters changed or lest an untutored corrector fail to know how to correct mistakes, let them read the works of ancient authors on orthography [spelling]. . . .

. . . I have collected as many of these works as possible with eager curiosity. . . . [If you] read [them] with unremitting zeal,

they will completely free you from the fog of ignorance, so that what was previously unknown may become for the most part very well known.

3. In addition to these things we have provided workers skilled in bookbinding, in order that a handsome external form may clothe the beauty of sacred letters; in some measure, perhaps, we imitate the example in the parable of the Lord [Matt. 22:11], who amid the glory of the heavenly banquet has clothed in wedding garments those whom He judges worthy of being invited to the table. And for the binders, in fitting manner, unless I err, we have represented various styles of binding in a single codex,[2] that he who so desires may choose for himself the type of cover he prefers.

4. We have also prepared cleverly constructed lamps which preserve their illuminating flames and feed their own fire and without human attendance abundantly maintain a very full clearness of most copious light; and the fat oil in them does not fail, although it is burned continually with a bright flame.

5. Nor have we by any means allowed you to be unacquainted with the hour meters which have been discovered to be very useful to the human race. I have provided a sundial for you for bright days and a water clock which points out the hour continually both day and night, since on some days the bright sun is frequently absent, and rain water passes in marvellous fashion into the ground, because the fiery force of the sun, regulated from above, fails. And so the art of man has brought into harmony elements which are naturally separated; the

---

[2]A codex consists of the rectangular sheets on which scribes have written, bound together on one side like a modern book. Invented in the late first century A.D., the codex gradually replaced scrolls as the predominant way to store written texts. —Eds.

hour meters are so reliable that you consider an act of either as having been arranged by messengers. These instruments, then, have been provided in order that the soldiers of Christ,[3] warned by most definite signs, may be summoned to the carrying out of their divine task as if by sounding trumpets.

_____

[3]"Soldiers of Christ" is a metaphor to describe the monks in their vocation. —Eds.

REVIEW QUESTIONS

1. What was the function of a scribe?
2. What contributions did the monasteries make in the development of medieval culture?

---

8 The Carolingian Renaissance

The Early Middle Ages witnessed a marked decline in learning and the arts. Patronage of both the liberal and the visual arts by the old Roman aristocracy was not widely copied by the Germanic ruling class that replaced the Romans. Support for learning and the arts shifted from secular to ecclesiastical patrons. Monasteries became the new centers for intellectual and artistic activities, and Christian themes and values almost entirely displaced the worldly values of Greco-Roman culture.

Under the patronage of Charlemagne (742–814), the great Frankish emperor, a conscious revival of classical Greek and Roman learning and the visual arts occurred. Charlemagne realized that his great empire could not be effectively governed without a cadre of literate clergy and administrators. To educate the leaders of the Frankish Empire, Charlemagne sponsored a number of reforms designed to improve the educational institutions and the quality of literacy and learning in his realm. At court, he completely reformed the school conducted for the children of his family and his courtiers and recruited the best scholars in Western Europe to staff it. Among these scholars was the English deacon Alcuin of York (735–804), who became his chief advisor on educational and religious affairs. They aimed at restoring classical learning to serve the needs of the new Christian culture.

Einhard
CHARLEMAGNE'S APPRECIATION OF LEARNING

The revival of classical learning and the visual arts under Charlemagne is called the Carolingian Renaissance, a cultural awakening that helped shape medieval civilization. One of Charlemagne's most significant decisions was ordering the making of copies of old manuscripts dating back to Roman times. Much of today's knowledge of Roman learning and literature comes from surviving Carolingian copies of older Latin texts that no longer exist. In the following reading, Charlemagne's biographer Einhard describes Western Europe's greatest royal patron of the liberal arts since the fall of the Roman Empire.

Charles [Charlemagne] had the gift of ready and fluent speech, and could express whatever he had to say with the utmost clearness. He was not satisfied with command of his native language merely, but gave attention to the study of foreign ones, and in particular was such a master of Latin that he could speak it as well as his native tongue; but he could understand Greek better than he could speak it. He was so eloquent, indeed, that he might have passed for a teacher of eloquence. He most zealously cultivated the liberal arts, held those who taught them in great esteem, and conferred great honors upon them. He took lessons in grammar of the deacon Peterof Pisa,[1] at that time an aged man. Another deacon, Albin of Britain, surnamed Alcuin, a man of Saxon extraction, who was the greatest scholar of the day, was his teacher in other branches of learning. The King spent much time and labor with him studying rhetoric, dialectics, and especially astronomy; he learned to reckon, and used to investigate the motions of the heavenly bodies most curiously, with an intelligent scrutiny. He also tried to write, and used to keep tablets and blanks in bed under his pillow, that at leisure hours he might accustom his hand to form the letters; however, as he did not begin his efforts in due season, but late in life, they met with ill success.

He cherished with the greatest fervor and devotion the principles of the Christian religion, which had been instilled into him from infancy. Hence it was that he built the beautiful basilica[2] at Aix-la-Chapelle,[3] which he adorned with gold and silver and lamps, and with rails and doors of solid brass. He had the columns and marbles for this structure brought from Rome and Ravenna,[4] for he could not find such as were suitable elsewhere. He was a constant worshipper at this church as long as his health permitted, going morning and evening, even after nightfall, besides attending mass; and he took care that all the services there conducted should be administered with the utmost possible propriety, very often warning the sextons not to let any improper or unclean thing be brought into the building or remain in it. He provided it with a great number of sacred vessels of gold and silver and with such a quantity of clerical robes that not even the doorkeepers who fill the humblest office in the church were obliged to wear their everyday clothes when in the exercise of their duties. He was at great pains to improve the church reading and psalmody [singing], for he was well skilled in both, although he neither read in public nor sang, except in a low tone and with others.

[1]Peter of Pisa, a famous grammarian (in Latin, the international language of the Middle Ages), was brought from Italy to teach at the school in Charlemagne's palace. He encouraged interest in pre-Christian classical writing, which influenced the court poets of that era. —Eds.

[2]A basilica is usually a rectangular-shaped church, whose main chamber is divided by columns into a central nave and side aisles. There was usually a semicircular apse at the narrow end facing the east, which was the visual focal point and the location of the main altar. —Eds.

[3]Aix-la-Chapelle, now Aachen, was Charlemagne's capital. It was located in what is now western Germany, near the Netherlands–Belgium frontier. —Eds.

[4]Ravenna, in northeastern Italy, was the final capital of the western Roman Empire in the fifth century; in the sixth and seventh centuries it was the capital of the Byzantine governors of Italy. Ravenna is famous for its magnificent sixth-century churches and mosaic art. —Eds.

Einhard, *Life of Charlemagne*, trans. Samuel E. Turner (Ann Arbor: University of Michigan Press, 1960), pp. 53–54.

He was very forward in succoring the poor, and in that gratuitous generosity which the Greeks call alms, so much so that he not only made a point of giving in his own country and his own kingdom, but when he discovered that there were Christians living in poverty in Syria, Egypt, and Africa, at Jerusalem, Alexandria, and Carthage, he had compassion on their wants, and used to send money over the seas to them. . . .

Charlemagne
AN INJUNCTION TO MONASTERIES
TO CULTIVATE LETTERS

In a letter to the Abbot Baugulf of Fulda (in Germany), Charlemagne announced his decision to use monasteries as schools for training future clergymen in grammar, writing, and rhetoric.

Charles, by the grace of God, King of the Franks and Lombards and Patrician of the Romans, to Abbot Baugulf and to all the congregation, also to the faithful committed to you, we have directed a loving greeting by our ambassadors in the name of omnipotent God.

Be it known, therefore, to your devotion pleasing to God, that we, together with our faithful, have considered it to be useful that the bishoprics and monasteries entrusted by the favor of Christ to our control, in addition to the [rule] of monastic life and the intercourse of holy religion, . . . also ought to be zealous in [the cultivation of letters], teaching those who by the gift of God are able to learn, according to the capacity of each individual, so that just as the observance of the rule imparts order and grace to honesty of morals, so also zeal in teaching and learning may do the same for sentences, so that those who desire to please God by living rightly should not neglect to please him also by speaking correctly. For it is written: "Either from thy words thou shalt be justified or from thy words thou shalt be condemned" [Matt. 12:37].

For although correct conduct may be better than knowledge, nevertheless knowledge precedes conduct. Therefore, each one ought to study what he desires to accomplish, so that . . . the mind may know more fully what ought to be done, as the tongue hastens in the praises of omnipotent God without the hindrances of errors. For since errors should be shunned by all men, . . . the more they ought to be avoided as far as possible by those who are chosen for this very purpose alone, so that they ought to be the especial servants of truth. For when in the years . . . [past], letters were often written to us from several monasteries in which it was stated that the brethren who dwelt there offered up in our behalf sacred and pious prayers, we have recognized in most of these letters both correct thoughts and uncouth expressions; because what pious devotion dictated faithfully to the mind, the tongue, uneducated on account of the neglect of study, was not able to express in the letter without error. . . . We began to fear lest perchance, as the skill in writing was less, so also the wisdom for understanding the Holy scriptures might be

Einhard, *Life of Charlemagne*, trans. Samuel E. Turner (Ann Arbor: University of Michigan Press, 1960), pp. 30–32, 53–54.

much less than it rightly ought to be. And we all know well that, although errors of speech are dangerous, far more dangerous are errors of the understanding. Therefore, we exhort you not only not to neglect the study of letters, but also with most humble mind, pleasing to God, to study earnestly in order that you may be able more easily and more correctly to penetrate the mysteries of the divine scriptures. Since, moreover, images . . . and similar figures are found in the sacred pages, no one doubts that each one in reading these will understand the spiritual sense more quickly if previously he shall have been fully instructed in the mastery of letters. Such men truly are to be chosen for this work as have both the will and the ability to learn and a desire to instruct others. And may this be done with a zeal as great as the earnestness with which we command it.

REVIEW QUESTION

Why was Charlemagne so anxious to raise the educational standards of both the clergy and laity of his empire? How did he go about doing it?

---

9   The Feudal Lord: Vassal and Warrior

In societies in which the state's role in regulating human relationships is minimal, law and order are maintained through custom and contract. This condition prevailed in the Early Middle Ages, particularly among the Germanic peoples. Laws were based on the community's assumptions about what was right and wrong, enforced by public opinion and community-approved use of force. To enforce law and to protect oneself and one's family, a person formed contractual ties with others and sought security and justice in mutual aid. A principal form of such a contract was called vassalage. By its terms, two free men of different means bound themselves to assistance and loyal support. The socially and economically superior man was called the lord; the man of inferior social status was called the vassal. The vassal pledged to be loyal and fight on behalf of his lord when called upon, in return for the lord's loyalty and protection when they were needed. The contract was lifelong and had deep emotional meaning in addition to the obvious self-interest of both parties.

Vassalage was a dynamic relationship, ever changing in content and meaning according to time, place, and circumstances. In the Carolingian Empire, vassalage was practiced by all members of the free class wealthy enough to afford weapons. Charlemagne and his successors tried to use vassalage as a means of controlling their warlike subjects and organizing them to serve more effectively for the defense of the royal family's realms. Eventually, the kings' vassals used their military skills, their own landed wealth, and their political power to diminish royal power. The royal vassals then became the true center of authority within medieval society.

An important part of the lord–vassal relationship was the lord's grant of a fief to his vassal. The fief might be any object of value that reflected the vassal's social status and the lord's respect for his services. A fief could be a warhorse, sword, and suit of armor; a public office; a right to collect a tax or toll; or authority to hold a court of justice in a specified district. The most sought-after fief was a land grant—one or more manors from which to draw income. Fiefs were held for the duration of the bond of vassalage. If the bond was broken by death or disloyalty, the fief was forfeited to its grantor. By the late ninth century, however, fiefs had become hereditary, as had the right to be a vassal to a specific lord.

Galbert of Bruges
COMMENDATION AND THE OATH OF FEALTY

This reading contains an eyewitness account of the ceremony of commendation, or investiture, in which vassals swore an oath of fealty (loyalty) to their new lord, William Clito, count of Flanders, in 1127, and were then invested with their fiefs. The account comes from an early twelfth-century chronicle written by a Flemish notary, Galbert of Bruges (a major medieval commercial city in Flanders, now part of Belgium).

Through the whole remaining part of the day those who had been previously enfeoffed [given fiefs] by the most pious count Charles,[1] did homage to the count, taking up now again their fiefs and offices and whatever they had before rightfully and legitimately obtained. On Thursday the seventh of April, homages were again made to the count being completed in the following order of faith and security.

First they did their homage thus: The count asked if he was willing to become completely his man, and the other replied, "I am willing"; and with clasped hands, surrounded by the hands of the count, they were bound together by a kiss. Secondly, he who had done homage gave his fealty to the representative of the count in these words, "I promise on my faith that I will in future be faithful to count William, and will observe my homage to him completely against all persons in good faith and without deceit," and thirdly, he took his oath to this upon the relics of the saints. Afterward, with a little rod which the count held in his hand, he gave investitures to all who by this agreement had given their security and homage and accompanying oath.

Translations and Reprints from the Original Sources of European History, ed. E. P. Cheyney (Philadelphia: University of Pennsylvania Press, 1895), vol. 4, no. 3, p. 18.

[1]Charles, count of Flanders, was murdered on March 2, 1127. —Eds.

Bishop Fulbert of Chartres
OBLIGATIONS OF LORDS AND VASSALS

In a letter written in 1020 to William, duke of Aquitaine, Bishop Fulbert (c. 962–1028) of Chartres summarizes the obligations of the lord and the vassal.

To William most glorious duke of the Aquitanians,[1] bishop Fulbert [asks] the favor of his prayers.

Asked to write something concerning the form of fealty, I have noted briefly for you on the authority of the books the things which follow. He who swears fealty to his lord ought always to have these six things in memory; what is harmless, safe, honorable, useful, easy, practicable. Harmless, that is to say that he should not be injurious to his lord in his body; safe, that he should not be injurious to him in his secrets or in the defences through which he is able to be secure; honorable, that he should not be injurious to him in his justice or in other matters that pertain to his honor; useful, that he should not be injurious to him in his possessions; easy or practicable, that that good which his lord is able to do easily, he make not difficult, nor that which is practicable he make impossible to him.

However, that the faithful vassal should avoid these injuries is proper, but not for this does he deserve his holding; for it is not sufficient to abstain from evil, unless what is good is done also. It remains, therefore, that in the same six things mentioned above he should faithfully counsel and aid his lord, if he wishes to be looked upon as worthy of his benefice and to be safe concerning the fealty which he has sworn.

The lord also ought to act toward his faithful vassal reciprocally in all these things. And if he does not do this he will be justly considered guilty of bad faith, just as the former, if he should be detected in the avoidance of or the doing of or the consenting to them, would be perfidious and perjured.

Translations and Reprints from the Original Sources of European History, ed. E. P. Cheney (Philadelphia: University of Pennsylvania Press, 1895), vol. 4, no. 3, pp. 23–24.

---

[1]The Aquitanians inhabited the kingdom of Aquitaine in southwestern France—later a province of France. —Eds.

Dhouda
LOYALTY TO LORD AND KING

In the middle of the ninth century, Dhouda, a Frankish noblewoman, wrote *Handbook for William*, for her eldest son, in which she instructed him in the proper behavior toward the king, Charles the Bald; other magnates; his father; and God. It is the only substantial work authored by a woman that survived the Carolingian era. Dhouda was familiar with several important Christian works of late antiquity and both New and Old Testaments. In the following passages from the handbook, Dhouda tells William that it is his Christian duty to be loyal to his king and his magnates.

DIRECTION ON YOUR COMPORTMENT TOWARD YOUR LORD

You have Charles as your lord; you have him as lord because, as I believe, God and your father,

---

Dhouda, *Handbook For William*, trans. Carol Neel (Washington, D.C.: The Catholic University of America Press, 1991), pp. 25–27, 31–32.

Bernard, have chosen him for you to serve at the beginning of your career, in the flower of your youth. Remember that he comes from a great and noble lineage on both sides of his family. Serve him not only so that you please him in obvious ways, but also as one clearheaded in matters of both body and soul. Be steadfastly and completely loyal to him in all things. . . .

What shall I say of the attitude of Joab, of Abner, and of many others toward the king David. Facing dangers on their king's behalf in many places, they desired with all their might to please their lord more than themselves. And what of those many others in holy scripture who faithfully obeyed their lords' commands? Because of their watchful strength they were found worthy to flourish in this world. For we know that, as scripture tells, all honor and authority are given by God. Therefore we should serve our lords faithfully, without ill will, without reluctance, and without sluggishness. As we read, *there is no power but from God: and he . . . that resisteth the power, resisteth the ordinance of God.*

That is why, my son, I urge you to keep this loyalty as long as you live, in your body and in your mind. For the advancement that it brings you will be of great value both to you and to those who in turn serve you. May the madness of treachery never, not once, make you offer an angry insult. May it never give rise in your heart to the idea of being disloyal to your lord. There is harsh and shameful talk about men who act in this fashion. I do not think that such will befall you or those who fight alongside you because such an attitude has never shown itself among your ancestors. It has not been seen among them, it is not seen now, and it will not be seen in the future.

Be truthful to your lord, my son William, child of their lineage. Be vigilant, energetic, and offer him ready assistance as I have said here. In every matter of importance to royal power take care to show yourself a man of good judgment—in your own thoughts and in public—to the extent that God gives you strength. Read the sayings and the lives of the holy Fathers who have gone before us. You will there discover how you may serve your lord and be faithful to him in all things. When you understand this, devote yourself

to the faithful execution of your lord's commands. Look around as well and observe those who fight for him loyally and constantly. Learn from them how you may serve him. Then, informed by their example, with the help and support of God you will easily reach the celestial goal I have mentioned above. And may your heavenly Lord God be generous and benevolent toward you. May he keep you safe, be your kind leader and your protector. May he deign to assist you in all your actions and be your constant defender. *As it shall be the will of God in heaven so be it done.* Amen. . . .

REGARDING YOUR LORD'S FAMILY

As for the great and famous relations and associates of your royal lord—those who are descended from his illustrious father's side as well as those related to him by marriage—fear, love, honor, and cherish them if you and those who fight alongside you are found worthy to serve them in the royal and imperial court or anywhere else you may act on their behalf. In all undertakings in their interest maintain a pure, fitting, and steadfast obedience to them, as well as good faith in the execution of your duties. . . .

So, my son William, bear patiently the yoke that governs a servant and be faithful to your lord Charles—whatever sort of lord he may be—and to his worthy, relations of both sexes and to all those of royal origins. It is fitting for you and for all those who fight under their royal power to do so, and I wish that you serve them to good ends, faithfully, with all your might. For as we believe, God chose them and established them in royal power, granting them glory almost as great in its likeness to the ancients' as that promised to Abraham, Isaac, and Jacob, and to their worthy children and descendants.

REVIEW QUESTIONS

1. In the Middle Ages, contracts were symbolized and publicly noted by the use of various ritual acts or gestures. Explain how the contract of vassalage was signified by specific rituals or actions.
2. What were some of the ethical and emotive dimensions of vassalage? Describe the mutual obligations of lords and vassals.
3. What were the prime virtues of a nobleman that Dhouda tried to convey to her son?

---

10 The Burdens of Serfdom

The feudal lord's way of life was made possible by the toil of the serfs who worked on the manors. Serfs, who were not free persons, had some rights but also many burdensome obligations. Unlike slaves, they could not be sold off the land or dispossessed from their landholdings. Their tenure on their farms was hereditary, but they owed heavy rent to the landlord in the form of labor and a share of their crops and livestock. There were many restrictions on their personal freedom: they needed the landlord's permission to leave the estate, to marry, or to pass on personal property to their heirs. In return, they received security; they were defended by the landlords against outside aggressors or fellow serfs.

The labor services usually took up one-half of the work week of the serf. He was required to plant, plow, and harvest the lord's fields, repair roads, fix fences, clear ditches, and cart goods to barns and markets. Although specific obligations varied from time to time and manor to manor, they were sufficiently onerous to encourage the serfs to seek freedom; in later centuries, when the opportunity presented itself, a serf might flee to a nearby town or to newly developed lands, or might purchase certain freedoms from the manorial lord. The serfs' struggle to rid themselves of the burdens of serfdom took centuries. It was largely successful in Western Europe by the fifteenth century. But in Eastern Europe, serfdom was imposed on the formerly free peasantry in the sixteenth and seventeenth centuries. Remnants of serfdom in Western Europe survived until the French Revolution. Serfdom was abolished in Central and Eastern Europe in the mid-nineteenth century.

Bishop Adalbero of Laon
THE TRIPARTITE SOCIETY

Medieval thinkers came to see their society divided into three different but complementary groups: clergy, lords, and serfs. Each group had its own responsibilities—priests guided the souls of the faithful; lords protected society from its enemies; and the serfs' toil provided sustenance for everyone. Written in about 1020, the following statement by Bishop Adalbero of Laon, France, illustrates the tripartite nature of medieval society, including the status of serfs.

The community of the faithful is a single body, but the condition of society is threefold in order. For human law distinguishes two classes. Nobles and serfs, indeed, are not governed by the same ordinance. . . . The former are the warriors and the protectors of the churches. They are the defenders of the people, of both great and small, in short, of everyone, and at the same time they ensure their own safety. The other class is that of the serfs. This luckless breed possesses nothing except at the cost of its own labour. Who could, reckoning with an abacus, add up the sum of the cares with which the peasants are occupied, of their journeys on foot, of their hard labours? The serfs provide money, clothes, and food, for the rest; no free man could exist without serfs. Is there a task to be done? Does anyone want to put himself out? We see kings and prelates make themselves the serfs of their serfs; [but in truth] the master, who claims to feed his serf, is fed by him. And the serf never sees an end to his tears and his sighs. God's house, which we think of as one, is thus divided into three; some pray, others fight, and yet others work. The three groups, which coexist, cannot bear to be separated; the services rendered by one are a precondition for the labours of the two others; each in his turn takes it upon himself to relieve the whole. Thus the threefold assembly is none the less united, and it is thus that law has been able to triumph, and that the world has been able to enjoy peace.

Jacques le Goff, *Medieval Civilization*, trans. Julia Barrow (London: Blackwell, 1988), p. 255. Copyright © 1977 by Blackwell Publishers Ltd.

Ralph Glaber, Monk of Cluny
FAMINE

Among the hardships burdening medieval peasants was famine, which particularly afflicted the poor. The following passage by Ralph Glaber, monk of Cluny in France, describes the terrible famine of 1032–1034.

The famine started to spread its ravages and one could have feared the disappearance of almost the entire human race. The atmospheric conditions became so unfavourable that no suitable time could be found to sow seed, and that, especially because of the floods, there was no means of reaping the harvest. . . . Continual rains had soaked into all the soil to the point where during three years no one could dig furrows capable of taking the seed. At harvest-time, weeds and ill-omened tares had covered the whole surface of the fields. A [half bushel] of grain sown, where it gave the best yields, . . . produced barely a fistful. If by chance one found some food for sale, the seller could charge an outrageous price just as he pleased. However, when they had eaten the wild beasts and birds, the people started, under the sway of a devouring hunger, to collect all sorts of carrion [decaying flesh] and other things which are horrible to mention to eat. Some in order to escape death had recourse to forest roots and water-weed. Finally, horror takes hold of us listening to the perversions which then reigned among the human race. Alas! O woe! Something rarely heard of throughout the ages: rabid hunger made men devour human flesh. Travellers were kidnapped by people stronger than they were, their limbs were cut off, cooked on the fire and eaten. Many people who moved from one place to another to flee the famine, and who

Jacques le Goff, *Medieval Civilization*, trans. Julia Barrow (London: Blackwell, 1988), pp. 236–237. Copyright © 1988 by Blackwell Publishers Ltd. Reproduced with permission of Blackwell Publishing Ltd.

had found hospitality on the way, were murdered in the night, and served as food for those who had welcomed them. Many showed a fruit or an egg to children, enticed them into out-of-the-way spots, killed them, and devoured them. Bodies of the dead were in many places torn out of the ground and equally served to appease hunger. . . . Then people tried an experiment in the region of Mâcon which had never before, to our knowledge, been tried anywhere. Many people took out of the ground a white soil which looked like clay, mixed it with what flour or bran they had, and made out of this mixture loaves with which, they reckoned, they would not die of hunger; this practice however brought only an illusory hope of rescue and an illusory relief. One only saw pale and emaciated faces; many people had a skin distended with swellings; the human voice itself became thin, like the little cries of dying birds. The corpses of the dead, who were so numerous that they had to lie scattered without burial, served as food for the wolves, who thereafter continued for a long time to seek their pittance among men. And since it was not possible, as we said, to bury each person individually because of the great number of the dead, in certain places men who feared God dug what were commonly called charnel pits, into which the bodies of the dead were thrown by the 500 or more, as many as there was space for, pellmell, half naked or without any covering; crossroads and the edges of fields served as cemeteries. Although some heard say that they would find it better to take themselves off to other regions, many were those who perished along the way of starvation.

William of Jumièges and Wace
FAILED REBELLION

Occasionally, peasant anger at their treatment at the hands of lords led to open rebellion as illustrated in the following account by a Norman monk of an uprising of Norman peasants in 977.

[Richard] had scarcely reigned or been duke for any length of time when there arose in that land a war which was to cause great misery. The peasants and villeins [partly freed serfs], those from the woodlands and those from the plains (I do not know through whose instigation it happened or who started it in the first place), held a number of councils in groups of twenty, thirty and a hundred. They were devising a plan such that, if they could succeed in it and bring it to fruition, harm would be done to the highest noblemen. They discussed this in private and many of them swore between themselves that never again would they willingly have a lord or a governor. Lords did them nothing but harm and they could get nothing out of them, from either their produce or their labours; each day they were experiencing great suffering. They were enduring pain and hardship. Things used to be bad, but now they were worse; every day their beasts were being taken to pay for aids and service. There were so many complaints and legal actions and so many old and new customs that they could not have an hour's peace. Every day they were subject to [unjust treatment by their lords]. . . .

There were so many provosts and beadles [lesser officials], so many bailiffs, old and new, that they had no peace for a single hour; all day long they descended on them. They could not

The History of the Norman People: Wace's Roman De Rou, trans. Glyn S. Burgess, pp. 100–102. Copyright © 2004 by Boydell & Brewer Ltd. Reprinted with permission.

defend themselves in court; each one of them wanted his due. These men had their beasts taken by force and they did not dare take a stand or defend themselves. They could not go on living like this; they would have to abandon their lands. They could get no protection against either their lord or his men, who did not keep any agreement with them.

"Son of a whore!" said some, "why do we put up with all the harm which is being done to us? Let us free ourselves from their control! We are men as they are; we have the same limbs as they do, we are their equal physically and are able to endure as much as they can. The only thing we lack is courage. Let us unite on oath, defend our goods and ourselves and stick together. If they wish to wage war on us, against one knight we have thirty or forty peasants, skilful and valiant. Thirty men in the flower of their youth will be cowardly and shameful if they cannot defend themselves against one man, providing they are willing to join forces. With clubs and large stakes, arrows and staffs, axes, bows and pikes, and stones for those who have no arms, let us defend ourselves against knights with the large number of men we have. In this way we can go into woods, cut down trees and take what we will, catch fish in the rivers and venison in the forests. We will do as we wish with everything, with the woods, the ponds and the meadows."

Lords generally crushed these rebellions with great ferocity.

With such talk and such words, and other even more foolish remarks, they all agreed on this plan and all swore they would join forces and defend themselves together. They chose I do not know which or how many of the most intelligent amongst them and the best speakers who would go round the country receiving oaths. But a plan transmitted to so many people could not be concealed for long. Whether it was from vassals or men-at-arms, women or children, through drunkenness or anger, Richard very soon heard that the peasants were forming a commune and would take away what was rightfully his, from him and the other lords who had peasants and [tenants]. He sent for his uncle Ralph and related the whole affair to him; Ralph was the very valiant count of Évreux and very skilled in many things.

"My lord," he said, "do not worry; leave the peasants to me, for you would only regret taking action yourself. But send me your household troops, send me your knights."

"Willingly," Richard replied to him. Then Ralph sent his spies and his couriers to many places. He did so much spying and had his spies make so many enquiries, with both the sick and the healthy, that he caught and captured the peasants who were arranging the meetings and receiving the oaths. Ralph was very angry and did not want to bring them to trial; he gave them all cause to feel sad and sorrowful. He had the teeth of many of them pulled out and others' feet cut off, their eyes put out and their hands cut off; yet others he had branded on the hamstrings. He did not care who died as a result. The others he had roasted alive and others plunged into molten lead. He had them all so well dealt with that they were hideous to behold. Henceforth, they were not seen anywhere without being easily recognised. Then the commune came to an end and the peasants made no more moves; they all withdrew and abandoned what they had undertaken, as a result of the fear caused by seeing their friends injured and maimed. The rich peasants paid for all this, but they settled their debt from their own purses; they were left with nothing which could be taken from them while they could still be put to ransom. They reached the best agreements they could with their lords.

REVIEW QUESTIONS

1. What hardships did medieval peasants face?
2. On the basis of these documents, how do you think lords viewed serfs?

CHAPTER 8

The High and Late Middle Ages

CHRISTINE DE PISAN, fifteenth century. This medieval illustration depicts de Pisan, who wrote in praise of the virtues, abilities, and accomplishments of women, presenting her manuscript to Isabel of Bavaria. *(Historical Picture Archive/Corbis)*

The High Middle Ages (1050–1300) were an era of growth and vitality in Latin Christendom. Improvements in technology and cultivation of new lands led to an increase in agricultural production; the growing food supply, in turn, reduced the number of deaths from starvation and malnutrition, and better cultivation methods freed more people to engage in nonagricultural pursuits, particularly commerce.

During the Early Middle Ages, Italian towns had maintained a weak link with the Byzantine lands in the eastern Mediterranean. In the eleventh century, the Italians gained ascendancy over Muslim fleets in the Mediterranean and rapidly expanded their trade with the Byzantine Empire and North Africa. The growing population provided a market for silk, sugar, spices, dyes, and other Eastern goods. Other mercantile avenues opened up between Scandinavia and the Atlantic coast; between northern France, Flanders, and England; and along the rivers between the Baltic Sea in the north and the Black Sea and Constantinople in the southeast.

The revival of trade and the improved production of food led to the rebirth of towns in the eleventh century. During the Early Middle Ages, urban life had largely disappeared in Latin Christendom except in Italy, and even Italian towns had declined since Roman times both in population and as centers of trade and culture. During the twelfth century, towns throughout Latin Christendom became active centers of commerce and intellectual life. The rebirth of town life made possible the rise of a new social class: the middle class, consisting of merchants and artisans. These townspeople differed significantly from the clergy, the nobles, and the serfs—the other social strata in medieval society. The world of the townspeople was the marketplace rather than the church, the castle, or the manorial village. These merchants and artisans resisted efforts by lords to impose obligations upon them, as their livelihood required freedom from such constraints. The middle class became a dynamic force for change.

The High Middle Ages were also characterized by political and religious vitality. Strong kings extended their authority over more and more territory, often at the expense of feudal lords; in the process, they laid the foundation of the modern European state system. By the eleventh century the autonomy of the church—its freedom to select its own leaders and to fulfill its moral responsibilities—was threatened by kings and lords who appointed bishops and abbots to ecclesiastical offices. In effect, the churches and monasteries were at the mercy of temporal rulers, who distributed church positions as patronage, awarding them to their families, vassals, and loyal servants. These political appointees often lacked the spiritual character to maintain high standards of discipline among the priests or monks they supervised. Many clergy resented the subordination of the church to the economic and political interests of kings and lords. They held that for the church to fulfill its spiritual mission, it must be free from lay control.

The crisis within the church was dramatically addressed by a small band of clergy, mostly monks, who managed to elect to the papacy a series of committed reformers. These popes condemned clerical marriages, deeming them uncanonical, because they risked subordinating the church's interests to those of the clergymen's wives and children. Priests were required to be celibate like bishops and monks. The reformers also pressed for the systematic exclusion of the laity from participation in the governing of the church. In calling for the abolition of lay investiture (that is, the formal installation of clergy to their office by temporal lords), the papacy encountered bitter opposition. As head of the church, charged with the mission of saving souls, the papacy refused to accept a subordinate position to temporal rulers.

Economic, political, and religious vitality was complemented by a cultural and intellectual awakening. The twelfth and thirteenth centuries marked the high point of medieval civilization. The Christian outlook, with its otherworldly emphasis, shaped and inspired this awakening. Christian scholars rediscovered the writings of ancient Greek thinkers, which they tried to harmonize with Christian teachings. In the process, they constructed an impressive philosophical system that integrated Greek rationalism into the Christian worldview. The study of Roman law was revived, and some of its elements were incorporated into church law. A varied literature expressed both secular and religious themes, and a distinctive form of architecture, the Gothic, conveyed the overriding Christian concern with things spiritual.

During the Late Middle Ages, roughly the fourteenth and early fifteenth centuries, medieval civilization declined. In contrast to the vigor of the twelfth and thirteenth centuries, the fourteenth century was burdened by crop failures, famine, plagues, and reduced population. The church also came under attack from reformers who challenged clerical authority and questioned church teachings; from powerful kings who resisted papal interference in the political life of their kingdoms; and from political theorists who asserted that the pope had no authority to intervene in matters of state. In the city-states of Italy, a growing secularism signified a break with medieval otherworldliness and heralded the emergence of the modern outlook. Known as the Renaissance, this development is discussed in chapter 9.

1 The Revival of Trade and the Growth of Towns

Several factors contributed to economic vitality in the High Middle Ages: the end of the Viking raids in northwestern Europe, greater political stability provided by kings and powerful lords, and increased agricultural productivity, which freed some people to work at other pursuits and facilitated a population increase. The prime movers in trade were the merchant adventurers, a new class of entrepreneurs. Neither bound to the soil nor obligated to lifelong military service, merchants traveled the sea lanes and land roads to distant places in search of goods that could profitably be traded in other markets.

HOW TO SUCCEED IN BUSINESS

In the following reading from *The King's Mirror*, an anonymous thirteenth-century Norseman outlined the characteristics and skills a merchant needed and described the hazards of the job. In typical medieval fashion, he emphasized the moral dimensions of commercial transactions.

The man who is to be a trader will have to brave many perils, sometimes at sea and sometimes in heathen lands, but nearly always among alien peoples; and it must be his constant purpose to act discreetly wherever he happens to be. On the sea he must be alert and fearless.

When you are in a market town, or wherever you are, be polite and agreeable; then you will secure the friendship of all good men. Make it a habit to rise early in the morning, and go first and immediately to church. . . .

. . . When the services are over, go out to look after your business affairs. If you are unacquainted with the traffic of the town, observe carefully how those who are reputed the best and most prominent merchants conduct their business. You must also be careful to examine the wares that you buy before the purchase is finally made to make sure that they are sound and flawless. And whenever you make a purchase, call in a few trusty men to serve as witnesses as to how the bargain was made.

You should keep occupied with your business till breakfast or, if necessity demands it, till midday; after that you should eat your meal. Keep your table well provided and set with a white cloth, clean victuals, and good drinks. Serve enjoyable meals, if you can afford it. After the meal you may either take a nap or stroll about a little while for pastime and to see what other good merchants are employed with, or whether any new wares have come to the borough which you ought to buy. On returning to your lodgings examine your wares, lest they suffer damage after coming into your hands. If they are found to be injured and you are about to dispose of them, do not conceal the flaws from the purchaser: show him what the defects are and make such a bargain as you can; then you cannot be called a deceiver. Also put a good price on your wares, though not too high, and yet very near what you see can be obtained; then you cannot be called a foister [trickster].

Finally, remember this, that whenever you have an hour to spare you should give thought to your studies, especially to the law books; for

Lawrence M. Larson, *The King's Mirror* (New York: The Scandinavian Foundation, 1917), pp. 79–85.

it is clear that those who gain knowledge from books have keener wits than others, since those who are the most learned have the best proofs for their knowledge. Make a study of all the laws. . . . If you are acquainted with the law, you will not be annoyed by quibbles when you have suits to bring against men of your own class, but will be able to plead according to law in every case.

But although I have most to say about laws, I regard no man perfect in knowledge unless he has thoroughly learned and mastered the customs of the place where he is sojourning. And if you wish to become perfect in knowledge, you must learn all the languages, first of all Latin and French, for these idioms are most widely used; and yet, do not neglect your native tongue or speech.

. . . Train yourself to be as active as possible, though not so as to injure your health. Strive never to be downcast, for a downcast mind is always morbid; try rather to be friendly and genial at all times, of an even temper and never moody. Be upright and teach the right to every man who wishes to learn from you; and always associate with the best men. Guard your tongue carefully; this is good counsel, for your tongue may honor you, but it may also condemn you. Though you be angry speak few words and never in passion; for unless one is careful, he may utter words in wrath that he would later give gold to have unspoken. On the whole, I know of no revenge, though many employ it, that profits a man less than to bandy heated words with another, even though he has a quarrel to settle with him. You shall know of a truth that no virtue is higher or stronger than the power to keep one's tongue from foul or profane speech, tattling, or slanderous talk in any form. If children be given to you, let them not grow up without learning a trade; for we may expect a man to keep closer to knowledge and business when he comes of age, if he is trained in youth while under control.

And further, there are certain things which you must beware of and shun like the devil himself: these are drinking, chess, harlots,

quarreling, and throwing dice for stakes. For upon such foundations the greatest calamities are built; and unless they strive to avoid these things, few only are able to live long without blame or sin.

Observe carefully how the sky is lighted, the course of the heavenly bodies, the grouping of the hours, and the points of the horizon. Learn also how to mark the movements of the ocean and to discern how its turmoil ebbs and swells; for that is knowledge which all must possess who wish to trade abroad. Learn arithmetic thoroughly, for merchants have great need of that.

If you come to a place where the king or some other chief who is in authority has his officials, seek to win their friendship; and if they demand any necessary fees on the ruler's behalf, be prompt to render all such payments, lest by holding too tightly to little things you lose the greater. . . . If you can dispose of your wares at suitable prices, do not hold them long; for it is the wont of merchants to buy constantly and to sell rapidly. . . .

. . . If you attend carefully to all these things, with God's mercy you may hope for success. This, too, you must keep constantly in mind, if you wish to be counted a wise man, that you ought never to let a day pass without learning something that will profit you. Be not like those who think it beneath their dignity to hear or learn from others such things even as might avail them much if they knew them. For a man must regard it as great an honor to learn as to teach, if he wishes to be considered thoroughly informed. . . .

. . . Always buy good clothes and eat good fare if your means permit; and never keep unruly or quarrelsome men as attendants or messmates. Keep your temper calm though not to the point of suffering abuse or bringing upon yourself the reproach of cowardice. Though necessity may force you into strife, be not in a hurry to take revenge; first make sure that your effort will succeed and strike where it ought. Never display a heated temper when you see that you are likely to fail, but be sure to maintain your honor at some later time, unless your opponent should offer a satisfactory atonement.

If your wealth takes on rapid growth, divide it and invest it in a partnership trade in fields where you do not yourself travel; but be cautious in selecting partners. Always let Almighty God, the holy Virgin Mary, and the saint whom you have most frequently called upon to intercede for you be counted among your partners. Watch with care over the property which the saints are to share with you and always bring it faithfully to the place to which it was originally promised.

ORDINANCES OF THE GUILD MERCHANTS OF SOUTHAMPTON

Along with revived trade and burgeoning towns in the High Middle Ages came the formation of businessmen's associations, called guilds. Merchant guilds encompassed all townspeople engaged in commerce. Carpenters, bakers, shoemakers, and other skilled craftsmen formed guilds that specialized in each occupation. Though women were employed in many trades, working under male guild masters, they were rarely admitted to full membership. Guilds composed exclusively of women existed in only a few places like Paris and Cologne. Guilds tried to eliminate competition by barring outsiders from doing business in the town, by limiting membership, by fixing the price of their goods, and by setting quality standards. Guilds provided for the social needs of their members, too, as the following selection of guild regulations for the seaport of Southampton, England, show. The document itself belongs to the fourteenth century, but several of the regulations had been framed earlier.

6. . . . And if a guildsman be ill and in town, one shall send to him two loaves and a gallon of wine, and one dish of cooked food; and two of the approved men of the guild shall go to visit him and look to his condition.

7. And when a guildsman dies, all those who are of the guild and in the town shall be at the service of the dead, and guildsmen shall carry the body, and bring it to the place of sepulture [burial]. And he who will not do this shall pay, on his oath, twopence to be given to the poor. And

The Oak Book of Southampton, transcribed and ed. Paul Studer, Publications of the Southampton Record Society (Southampton: Cox & Shorland, 1910), vol. 1, no. 10, pp. 21, 25, 29, 37, 51, 53.

those of the ward where the dead man shall be, shall find a man to watch with the body the night that the dead person shall lie in his house. . . .

9. And when a guildsman dies, his eldest-born son or his next heir shall have the seat of his father, or of his uncle, if his father was not a guildsman, but of no one else. Nor can any husband, by reason of his wife, either have a seat in the guild or demand it by any right of his wife's ancestors. . . .

10. And no one ought nor can lawfully sell or give his seat in the guild to any man. And the son of a guildsman, other than his eldest, shall be admitted to the guild on payment of ten shillings [120 pence], and shall take the oath.

11. And if any guildsman be imprisoned in England in time of peace, the alderman, with

the seneschal[1]. . . . shall go at the cost of the guild to procure the release of him that is in prison.

12. And if any guildsman strike another with his fist, and be thereof attainted [found guilty], he shall lose his guildship until he has purchased it again for ten shillings, and shall take the oath like a new member. And if a guildsman strike another with a stick or a knife, or any other weapon, whatever it may be, he shall lose his guildship and his franchise,[2] and shall be held a stranger, until he be reconciled to good people of the guild, and have made satisfaction to the person whom he has injured, and be fined to the guild twenty shillings, which shall not be [forgiven or refunded]. . . .

19. And no one shall buy anything in the town of Southampton to sell it again in the same town, unless he be of the guild merchant or of the franchise. And if any one do so and be attainted (thereof), all that he has so bought shall be forfeited to the king. And no one shall be quit of custom unless he has done so as to be of the guild or of the franchise, and this from year to year.

20. And no one shall buy honey, seim [lard], salt herring, or any kind of oil, or millstones, or fresh hides, or any kind of fresh skins, except a guildsman; nor keep a tavern for wine, or sell cloth by retail, except on a market day or fair day; nor keep above five quarters of corn in his granary to sell by retail, if he is not a guildsman; and whoever shall do this, and be attainted (thereof), shall forfeit all to the king.

---

[1]An alderman was the chief of the guild, and a seneschal acted as its treasurer and vice-president. —Eds.

[2]A person's franchise was the privilege of citizenship in the town. —Eds.

21. No one of the guild shall be partner or joint dealer in any of the foresaid merchandises with any person who is (not?) of the guild, by any manner of coverture [concealment], art, contrivance, collusion, or any other manner. And whosoever shall do this, and be attainted (thereof), the goods so bought shall be forfeited to the king, and the guildsman shall lose his guildship.

22. And if any guildsman fall into poverty and have not wherewith to live, and cannot work, he shall be provided for: when the guild shall be held he shall have one mark from the guild to relieve his condition. No one of the guild or franchise shall avow another's goods for his own, by which the custom of the town may be defrauded. And if any one so do, and be attainted (thereof), he shall lose the guildship and the franchise, and the merchandise so avowed shall be forfeited to the king. . . .

41. No butcher or cook shall sell to any man other than wholesome and clean provisions, and well cooked; and if any do, and he be thereof attainted, he shall be put in the pillory an hour of the day, or give two shillings to the town for the offence.

42. And that no butcher or cook throw into the street any filth or other matter whereby the town or the street become more dirty, filthy, or corrupt; and if any one do this, and be attainted, he shall pay a fine of twelve pence, as often as he shall offend in the manner aforesaid.

43. No man shall have any pigs going about in the street, or have before his door, or in the street, muck or dung beyond two nights; and if any one has, let whoever will take it away; and he who shall have acted contrary to this statute shall be grievously fined.

ALLIANCE OF GERMAN TOWNS TO PROTECT MERCHANTS, 1253

The following document relates how several German cities entered into an alliance to protect merchants who were exposed to frequent dangers to life and property. Federations like the one described below grew into the famed Hanseatic League, which in the fourteenth century had a membership of about one hundred towns, mainly German. The league actively combated pirates and brigands and built lighthouses to promote safe navigation.

In the name of the holy and indivisible Trinity, Amen. The magistrates, consuls, and the whole community of burghers and citizens in Münster, Dortmund, Soest, and Lippstadt, to all who may read this document, greeting:

We hereby make known to all men, now and in the future, that because of the manifold dangers to which we are constantly exposed, of capture, robbery, and many other injuries, we have, by common counsel and consent, decided to unite in a perpetual confederation under the following terms, and we have mutually given and received word and oath:

First, that if any man shall take captive one of our citizens or seize his goods without just cause, we will altogether deny to him opportunity to trade in all our cities aforesaid. And if the castellan of any lord shall be the author of an injury that has been done, the afore-mentioned privileges shall be altogether withheld from the lord of that castellan, and from all his soldiers

and servants, and all others dwelling with him in his castle. . . .

If any robber has taken goods from one of our citizens . . . and the injured man shall go to any one of our [federated] cities seeking counsel and aid, in order that justice may be done upon the malefactor, the citizens of that city shall act as they would be obliged to act if executing justice for a similar crime committed against one of their own fellow-citizens.

And if any of our burgesses shall chance to go to any of our cities and fear to go forth because of peril to life and property, the burgesses of that city shall conduct him to a place whence his fellow-citizens can receive him in safety.

If a knight shall be denounced to us on reasonable grounds as a violator of faith and honor, we will denounce him in all our cities, and will by mutual consent withhold from him all privileges in our cities until he shall pay the whole debt for which he broke his word.

If any one of us shall buy goods taken from any of our confederates by theft or robbery, . . . he shall not offer the goods at retail anywhere and shall be held guilty with the thief and robber.

Readings in European History, vol. 1: From the Breaking Up of the Roman Empire to the Protestant Revolt, ed. James Harvey Robinson (Boston: Ginn and Company, 1904), p. 413.

REVIEW QUESTIONS

1. What attitudes were merchants encouraged to cultivate when dealing with customers and fellow merchants? How did their outlook differ from that of medieval clergy and nobility?
2. What business practices were recommended to merchants?
3. What was a guild and how did it benefit its members?
4. What method does the document presenting the rules for the Hanseatic League employ for subduing pirates, brigands, kidnappers, and dishonored knights?

2 Papal Supremacy

As the sole interpreters of God's revelation and the sole ministers of his sacraments, the clergy imposed and supervised the moral standards of Christendom. Papal theory maintained that human society was part of a divinely ordered universe, governed by God's universal law, and as the supreme spiritual leader of Christendom, the pope was charged with the mission of establishing a Christian society on earth. Popes maintained that all kings came under their power. Disobeying the pope, God's viceroy on earth, constituted disobedience to God himself. Responsible for implementing God's law, the pope could never take a subordinate position to kings, an attitude that led to a conflict between church and state in the High and Late Middle Ages as the power of monarchs grew.

Pope Gregory VII
THE *DICTATUS PAPAE*

Like no other pope before him, Gregory VII (ruled 1073–1085) asserted the preeminence of the papacy over secular rulers. He declared that princes should "not seek to subdue or subject holy Church to themselves as a handmaiden; but indeed let them fittingly strive to honor her eyes, namely the priests of the Lord, by acknowledging them as masters and fathers." His exaltation of the spiritual authority of the church encouraged future popes to challenge the state whenever it threatened the supremacy of Christian moral teachings or the church's freedom to carry out its mission. The exalted conception of the papacy as the central authority in the Christian church was expressed in its most extreme and detailed form in a series of propositions called the *Dictatus papae* (Rules of the Pope), which appear as numbered paragraphs in the excerpt below. Drawn up by the papal government during the pontificate of Gregory VII, the *Dictatus papae* represents claims and ambitions that would inspire many popes and theologians throughout the Middle Ages.

1. That the Roman church was established by God alone.
2. That the Roman pontiff [bishop] alone is rightly called universal.
3. That he alone has the power to depose and reinstate bishops.
4. That his legate [emissary], even if he be of lower ecclesiastical rank, presides over

bishops in council, and has the power to give sentence of deposition against them.
5. That the pope has the power to depose those who are absent (*i.e.*, without giving them a hearing).
6. That, among other things, we ought not to remain in the same house with those whom he has excommunicated.
7. That he alone has the right, according to the necessity of the occasion, to make new laws, to create new bishoprics, to make a

Ephraim Emerton, ed. and trans., *The Correspondence of Pope Gregory VII*, pp. 166–170. Copyright © 1932, renewed 1960 Columbia University Press. Used with permission.

monastery of a chapter of canons,[1] and *vice versa*, and either to divide a rich bishopric or to unite several poor ones.

8. That he alone may use the imperial insignia.

9. That all princes shall kiss the foot of the pope alone.

10. That his name alone is to be recited in the churches.

11. That the name applied to him belongs to him alone.

12. That he has the power to depose emperors.

13. That he has the right to transfer bishops from one see to another when it becomes necessary.

14. That he has the right to ordain as a cleric anyone from any part of the church whatsoever.

15. That anyone ordained by him may rule (as bishop) over another church, but cannot serve (as priest) in it, and that such a cleric may not receive a higher rank from any other bishop.

16. That no general synod may be called without his order.

17. That no action of a synod and no book shall be regarded as canonical [official] without his authority.

18. That his decree can be annulled by no one, and that he can annul the decrees of anyone.

19. That he can be judged by no one.

20. That no one shall dare to condemn a person who has appealed to the apostolic seat.

21. That the important cases of any church whatsoever shall be referred to the Roman church (that is, to the pope).

22. That the Roman church has never erred and will never err to all eternity, according to the testimony of the holy scriptures.

23. That the Roman pontiff who has been canonically ordained is made holy by the merits of St. Peter, according to the testimony of St. Ennodius, bishop of Pavia, which is confirmed by many of the holy fathers, as is shown by the decrees of the blessed pope Symmachus.

24. That by his command or permission subjects may accuse their rulers.

25. That he can depose and reinstate bishops without the calling of a synod.

26. That no one can be regarded as catholic who does not agree with the Roman church.

27. That he has the power to absolve subjects from their oath of fidelity to wicked rulers.

---

[1]A chapter of canons is a corporate ecclesiastical body composed of clergy who administer cathedrals or monastic communities. —Eds.

Pope Innocent III
"ROYAL POWER DERIVES ITS DIGNITY FROM THE PONTIFICAL AUTHORITY"

In the tradition of Gregory VII, Innocent III (ruled 1198–1216), the most powerful of medieval popes, asserts the claim for papal supremacy.

Documents of the Christian Church, ed. Henry Bettenson and Chris Maunder (Oxford: Oxford University Press, 1999), p. 123.

The Creator of the universe set up two great luminaries in the firmament of heaven; the greater light to rule the day, the lesser light to rule the night. In the same way for the firmament of the universal Church, which is spoken of as heaven, he appointed two great dignities; the greater to bear rule over souls (these being, as it were, days), the lesser to bear rule over bodies (those being, as it were nights). These dignities are the pontifical authority and the royal power. Furthermore, the moon derives her light from the sun, and is in truth inferior to the sun in both size and quality, in position as well as effect. In the same way the royal power derives its dignity from the pontifical authority: and the more closely it cleaves to the sphere of that authority the less is the light with which it is adorned; the further it is removed, the more it increases in splendour.

REVIEW QUESTION

Why were papal claims likely to stir a conflict with secular rulers?

---

3   The Crusades

In the eleventh century the Seljuk Turks, recent converts to Islam, conquered vast regions of the Near East including most of Asia Minor, the heartland of the Byzantine Empire. When the Seljuk Empire crumbled, Byzantine emperor Alexius I Comnenus (ruled 1081–1118), seeing an opportunity to regain lost lands, appealed to Latin princes and the pope for assistance, an appeal answered by Pope Urban II (ruled 1088–1099).

In 1095 at the Council of Clermont, Urban II in a dramatic speech urged Frankish lords to take up the sword against the Muslims, an event that marked the beginning of the Crusades—the struggle to regain the Holy Land from Islam. A Christian army mobilized by the papacy to defend the Christian faith accorded with the papal concept of a just war. Moreover, Urban hoped that such a venture might bring the Byzantine church under papal authority. Nobles viewed Urban's appeal as a great adventure that held the promise of glory, wealth, and new lands; they were also motivated by religious reasons: recovery of Christian holy places and a church-approved way of doing penance for their sins.

The Crusades demonstrated the growing strength and confidence of Latin Christendom, which previously had been on the defensive against Islam; it was also part of a wider movement of expansion on the part of Latin Christians. In the eleventh century, Italians had already driven the Muslims from Sardinia; Normans had taken Sicily from the Muslims and southern Italy from Byzantium; and Christian knights, supported by the papacy, were engaged in a long struggle to expel the Muslim Moors from Spain.

The First Crusade demonstrated Christian fanaticism as well as idealism and growing power, as contingents of crusaders robbed and massacred thousands of Jews in the Rhineland. The First Crusade was climaxed by the storming of Jerusalem in June 1099 and the slaughter of the city's inhabitants.

Robert the Monk
APPEAL OF URBAN II TO THE FRANKS

Pope Urban's speech, as reported by Robert the Monk, shows how skillfully the pope appealed to the Frankish lords.

"O race of the Franks, O people who live beyond the mountains, O people loved and chosen of God, as is clear from your many deeds, distinguished over all other nations by the situation of your land, your catholic faith, and your regard for the holy church, we have a special message and exhortation for you. For we wish you to know what a grave matter has brought us to your country. The sad news has come from Jerusalem and Constantinople that the people of Persia, an accursed and foreign race [the Turks], enemies of God, 'a generation that set not their heart aright, and whose spirit was not steadfast with God' [Ps. 78:8], have invaded the lands of those Christians and devastated them with the sword, rapine, and fire. Some of the Christians they have carried away as slaves, others they have put to death. The churches they have either destroyed or turned into mosques. They desecrate and overthrow the altars. . . . They have taken from the Greek empire a tract of land so large that it takes more than two months to walk through it. Whose duty is it to avenge this and recover that land, if not yours? For to you more than to other nations the Lord has given the military spirit, courage, agile bodies, and the bravery to strike down those who resist you. Let your minds be stirred to bravery by the deeds of your forefathers, and by the efficiency and greatness of . . . [Charlemagne], and of . . . his son [Louis the Pious], and of the other kings who have destroyed [Muslim] kingdoms, and established Christianity in their lands. You should be moved especially by the holy grave of our Lord and Saviour which is now held by unclean peoples, and by the holy places which are treated with dishonor and irreverently befouled with their uncleanness.

"O bravest of knights, descendants of unconquered ancestors, do not be weaker than they, but remember their courage. . . . Let no possessions keep you back, no solicitude for your property. Your land [France] is shut in on all sides by the sea and mountains, and is too thickly populated. There is not much wealth here, and the soil scarcely yields enough to support you. On this account you kill and devour each other, and carry on war and mutually destroy each other. Let your hatred and quarrels cease, your civil wars come to an end, and all your dissensions stop. Set out on the road to the holy sepulchre [site of Jesus' burial], take the land from that wicked people, and make it your own. That land which, as the scripture says, is flowing with milk and honey, God gave to the children of Israel. Jerusalem is the best of all lands, more fruitful than all others, as it were a second Paradise of delights. This land our Saviour [Jesus] made illustrious by his birth, beautiful with his life, and sacred with his suffering; he redeemed it with his death and glorified it with his tomb. This royal city is now held captive by her enemies, and made pagan by those who know not God. She asks and longs to be liberated and does not cease to beg you to come to her aid. She asks aid especially from you because, as I have said, God has given more of the military spirit to you than to other nations. Set out on this journey and you will obtain the remission of your sins and be sure of the incorruptible glory of the kingdom of heaven."

When Pope Urban had said this and much more of the same sort, all who were present were moved to cry out with one accord, "It is the will

Translations and Reprints from the Original Sources of European History, ed. D. C. Munro (Philadelphia: University of Pennsylvania Press, 1897), vol. 1, no. 4 (1894 series), pp. 5–8.

of God, it is the will of God." When the pope heard this he raised his eyes to heaven and gave thanks to God, and, commanding silence with a gesture of his hand, he said: "My dear brethren. . . . [L]et these words be your battle cry, because God caused you to speak them. Whenever you meet the enemy in battle, you shall all cry out, 'It is the will of God, it is the will of God.' . . . Whoever therefore shall determine to make this journey and shall make a vow to God and shall offer himself as a living sacrifice, holy, acceptable to God [Rom. 12:1], shall wear a cross on his brow or on his breast. And when he returns after having fulfilled his vow he shall wear the cross on his back. In this way he will obey the command of the Lord, 'Whosoever doth not bear his cross and come after me is not worthy of me'" [Luke 14:27].

William of Tyre
THE CAPTURE OF JERUSALEM

Over the centuries, some have praised the Crusades for inspiring idealism and heroism. Others, however, have castigated the movement for corrupting the Christian spirit and unleashing intolerance and fanaticism, which resulted in the slaughter of Jews in the Rhineland and of Muslims and Jews in Jerusalem—all in the name of Christ.

The crusaders captured Jerusalem in 1099 after a difficult siege, overcoming its defenses and breaking into the city. The following account of the massacre in the Holy City was written by William of Tyre (c. 1130–c. 1184), archbishop of the Crusader kingdom established in Tyre.

It was a Friday at the ninth hour. Verily, it seemed divinely ordained that the faithful who were fighting for the glory of the Saviour should have obtained the consummation of their desires at the same hour and on the very day on which the Lord had suffered in that city for the salvation of the world. It was on that day, as we read, that the first man was created and the second was delivered over to death for the salvation of the first. It was fitting, therefore, that, at that very hour, those who were members of His body and imitators of Him should triumph in His name over His enemies. . . .

Emily Atwater Babcock and A. C. Krey, *A History of Deeds Done Beyond the Sea*, pp. 369–374. Copyright © 1943 by Columbia University Press. Reprinted with permission.

. . . Regardless of age and condition, they laid low, without distinction, every enemy encountered. Everywhere was frightful carnage, everywhere lay heaps of severed heads, so that soon it was impossible to pass or to go from one place to another except over the bodies of the slain. Already the leaders had forced their way by various routes almost to the center of the city and wrought unspeakable slaughter as they advanced. A host of people followed in their train, athirst for the blood of the enemy and wholly intent upon destruction. . . . So frightful was the massacre throughout the city, so terrible the shedding of blood, that even the victors experienced sensations of horror and loathing. . . .

. . . A crowd of knights and foot soldiers . . . massacred all those who had taken refuge [in the court of the Temple]. No mercy was shown to anyone, and the whole place was flooded with the blood of the victims.

It was indeed the righteous judgment of God which ordained that those who had profaned the sanctuary of the Lord by their superstitious rites and had caused it to be an alien place to His faithful people should expiate their sin by death and, by pouring out their own blood, purify the sacred precincts.

It was impossible to look upon the vast numbers of the slain without horror; everywhere lay fragments of human bodies, and the very ground was covered with the blood of the slain. It was not alone the spectacle of headless bodies and mutilated limbs strewn in all directions that roused horror in all who looked upon them. Still more dreadful was it to gaze upon the victors themselves, dripping with blood from head to foot, an ominous sight which brought terror to all who met them. It is reported that within the Temple enclosure alone about ten thousand infidels perished, in addition to those who lay slain everywhere throughout the city in the streets and squares, the number of whom was estimated as no less.

The rest of the soldiers roved through the city in search of wretched survivors who might be hiding in the narrow portals and byways to escape death. These were dragged out into public view and slain like sheep. Some formed into bands and broke into houses where they laid violent hands on heads of families, on their wives, children, and their entire households. These victims were either put to the sword or dashed headlong to the ground from some elevated place so that they perished miserably. Each marauder claimed as his own in perpetuity the particular house which he had entered, together with all it contained. For before the capture of the city the pilgrims had agreed that, after it had been taken by force, whatever each man might win for himself should be his forever by right of possession, without molestation. Consequently the pilgrims searched the city most carefully and boldly killed the citizens. They penetrated into the most retired and out-of-the-way places and broke open the most private apartments of the foe. At the entrance of each house, as it was taken, the victor hung up his shield and his arms, as a sign to all who approached not to pause there but to pass by that place as already in possession of another. . . .

When at last the city had been set in order in this way, arms were laid aside. Then, clad in fresh garments, with clean hands and bare feet, in humility and contrition, they began to make the rounds of the venerable places which the Saviour had deigned to sanctify and make glorious with His bodily presence. With tearful sighs and heartfelt emotion they pressed kisses upon these revered spots. With especial veneration they approached the church of the Passion and Resurrection of the Lord. Here the leaders were met by the clergy and the faithful citizens of Jerusalem. These Christians who for so many years had borne the heavy yoke of undeserved bondage were eager to show their gratitude to the Redeemer for their restoration to liberty. Bearing in their hands crosses and relics of the saints, they led the way into the church to the accompaniment of hymns and sacred songs.

It was a pleasant sight and a source of spiritual joy to witness the pious devotion and deep fervor with which the pilgrims drew near to the holy places, the exultation of heart and happiness of spirit with which they kissed the memorials of the Lord's sojourn upon earth. On all sides were tears, everywhere sighs, not such as grief and anxiety are wont to cause, but such as fervent devotion and the satisfaction of spiritual joy produce as an offering to the Lord. Not alone in the church but throughout all Jerusalem arose the voice of a people giving thanks unto the Lord until it seemed as if the sound must be borne to the very heavens. Verily, of them might it well be said, "The voice of rejoicing and salvation is in the tabernacles of the righteous" [Ps. 118:15].

James of Vitry
"THE REMISSION OF SINS AND THE REWARD OF ETERNAL LIFE"

Many nobles set off for the Holy Land seeking adventure and economic gain. But it is likely that a religious impulse was the principal motive for joining a crusader army. The following sermon by James of Vitry (1160/1170–1240), a French bishop who was a propagandist for the Fifth Crusade and accompanied the crusading army, appeals to the nobles' hope for remission of sins and entrance into heaven.

[T]hose crusaders who prepare themselves for the service of God, truly confessed and contrite, are considered true martyrs while they are in the service of Christ, freed from venial and also mortal sins,[1] from all the penitence enjoined upon them, absolved from the punishment for their sins in this world and the punishment of purgatory[2] in the next, safe from the tortures of hell, in the glory and honour of being crowned in eternal beatitude.

The spouses and children are included in these benefits in as much as they contribute to expenses. But [crusaders] can also greatly help their deceased parents who have left their goods to them, if [the crusaders] take the cross with the intention of helping [their parents]. If it is possible to come to the aid of the dead by giving alms and doing other good works, what greater alms are there but to offer oneself and one's belongings to God and pledge one's soul to Christ, to leave behind one's spouse, children,

relatives and birthplace for the service of Christ alone, to expose oneself to dangers on land, dangers on sea, the dangers of thieves, the dangers of predators, the dangers of battles for the love of the Crucified? Therefore, have no doubt at all that this pilgrimage affords not only you the remission of sins and the reward of eternal life, but that whatever good you do on this journey on behalf of your spouses, children and parents, whether living or dead, will profit them greatly.

This is the full and plenary indulgence[3] that the pope concedes to you according to the keys that were given to him by God. This is like *the fountain open to the house of David for washing away* all sins and acquiring heavenly rewards.

From Christoph T. Maier, *Crusade Propaganda and Ideology: Model Sermons for the Preaching of the Cross*, p. 113. © 2000 Cambridge University Press. Reprinted with the permission of Cambridge University Press.

---

[1] Venial sin: a minor transgression against God's laws that does not deprive the soul of divine grace or salvation; mortal sin: a deliberate and serious transgression of God's laws, such as murder, that deprives the soul of salvation and leads to eternal damnation. —Eds.

[2] Purgatory: a place where the soul spends time paying for the person's sins before it can be admitted into heaven. —Eds.

[3] Plenary indulgence: the complete remission of venial sins incurred by the sinner; the remission of mortal sins is dependent further on God's grace. —Eds.

REVIEW QUESTIONS

1. Modern political propaganda frequently uses popular fears, prejudices, moral idealism, and patriotic fervor to shape public opinion. Discuss the techniques used by Pope Urban II to create public support for the Crusade.
2. What types of people did Pope Urban II address and what were his motives?
3. Why did William of Tyre believe that the massacre in Jerusalem was an act of religious purification?
4. Why do you think James of Vitry's sermon appealed to his listeners?

4 Religious Dissent

Like many groups held together by common ideology, the medieval church wanted to protect its doctrines from novel, dissident, or erroneous interpretations. To ensure orthodoxy and competency, therefore, all preachers were licensed by the bishop; unlicensed preaching, especially by unschooled laymen, was forbidden. In the western church, heresy had not been a serious problem in the post-Roman period. But in the twelfth century, heretical movements attracted significant numbers of supporters among both the clergy and laity and cut across frontiers and social classes.

Thomas Aquinas
DEATH FOR UNREPENTANT HERETICS

In the following selection, Thomas Aquinas (see page 247), the leading theologian of the Middle Ages, argues that unrepentant heretics should be executed.

With regard to heretics two points must be observed: one, on their own side, the other, on the side of the Church. On their own side there is the sin, whereby they deserve not only to be separated from the Church by excommunication, but also to be severed from the world by death. For it is a much graver matter to corrupt the faith which quickens the soul, than to forge money, which supports temporal life. Wherefore if forgers of money and other evildoers are forthwith condemned to death by the secular authority, much more reason is there for heretics, as soon as they are convicted of heresy, to be not only excommunicated but even put to death.

On the part of the Church, however, there is mercy which looks to the conversion of the wanderer, wherefore she condemns not at once, but *after the first and second admonition,* as the Apostle directs: after that, if he is yet stubborn, the Church no longer hoping for his conversion, looks to the salvation of others, by excommunicating him and separating him from the Church, and furthermore delivers him to the secular tribunal to be exterminated thereby from the world by death.

The *"Summa Theologica"* of St. Thomas Aquinas, Part II literally translated by the Fathers of the English Dominican Province (New York: Benziger Brothers, 1917), p. 154.

Bernard Gui
THE WALDENSIAN HERESY

One major heretical movement was that of the Waldensians, or Poor Men of Lyons, founded about 1173 by Peter Waldo (d. 1217), a rich merchant of Lyons, France, who gave away his wealth to the poor and began to preach in villages in southeastern France. Neither a priest nor a theologian, Waldo had the Bible translated from Latin into the common language of the people and preached the gospel message without the consent of church authorities. Small groups of Waldo's converts soon were found in towns and villages throughout southeastern France, northern Italy, and Switzerland. Within less than a decade, the Waldensians had aroused the clergy's hostility and were condemned as heretics by Pope Lucius III (ruled 1181–1185) at a council in Verona in 1184. Gradually, influenced by other heretical groups, the Waldensians adopted a more radical stance toward the medieval church. In the following reading from *Manual of an Inquisitor*, a fourteenth-century Dominican friar, Bernard Gui, describes the origin and the teachings of the Waldensians. The Waldensian criticisms of the church would be echoed in the writings of the leading Protestant reformers of the sixteenth century.

The sect and heresy of the Waldenses or Poor of Lyons began about the year of our Lord 1170. Its moving spirit and founder was a certain citizen of Lyons named Waldes, or Waldens, from whom his followers received their name. He was a rich man who, having given up all his property, resolved to devote himself to poverty and to evangelical perfection, just as the apostles had done. He had procured for himself translations of the Gospels and some other books of the Bible in vernacular French, also some texts from St. Augustine, St. Jerome, St. Ambrose, and St. Gregory, arranged topically, which he and his adherents called "sentences." On frequently reading these over among themselves, although very seldom understanding them aright, they were carried away by their emotions and, although they had but little learning, they usurped the function of the apostles by daring to preach "in the streets and the broad ways."

This man Waldes, or Waldens, won over to a like presumption many people of both sexes, made men and women his accomplices, and sent them out to preach as his disciples. They, men and women alike, although they were stupid and uneducated, wandered through villages, entered homes, preached in the squares and even in churches, the men especially, and spread many errors everywhere. Moreover, when they were summoned by the archbishop of Lyons, John of the Fair Hands, and by him forbidden such audacity, they were not at all willing to obey, alleging as excuse for their madness that "we ought to obey God rather than men," Who had commanded His apostles to "preach the gospel to every creature." By virtue of a false profession of poverty and a feigned appearance of sanctity, they arrogated to themselves what had been said to the apostles. Boldly declaring that they were imitators and successors of these apostles, they cast aspersions upon prelates and clergy for abundant wealth and lives of luxury.

Thus, through presumptuously usurping the office of preaching, they became teachers of error. After they had been warned to desist, they rendered themselves disobedient and contumacious, for which they were excommunicated and driven from that city and their native land. Finally, indeed, because they remained obdurate, they were pronounced schismatics [rebels] at a certain council which was held at Rome . . . and were then condemned as heretics. And so, as they had grown in number on the earth, they scattered throughout that province and neighboring areas and into the region of Lombardy [northern Italy]. Separated and cut off from the Church, when they mingled with other heretics

Bernard Gui, "Manual of an Inquisitor," in *Heresies of the High Middle Ages: Selected Sources*, trans. W. L. Wakefield and A. P. Evans, pp. 368–390. Copyright © 1991 by Columbia University Press. Used with permission.

and imbibed their errors, they combined with their own fantasies the errors and heresies of heretics of earlier days. . . .

. . . Now, the principal heresy of the aforesaid Waldenses was and still continues to be contempt of ecclesiastical authority. Then, having been excommunicated for this and given over to Satan, they were plunged by him into countless errors, and they combined with their own fantasies the errors of heretics of an earlier day.

The foolish followers and impious teachers of this sect hold and teach that they are not subject to our lord pope, the Roman pontiff, or to other prelates of the Roman Church, for they declare that the Roman Church persecutes and censures them unjustly and unduly. Also, they declare positively that they cannot be excommunicated by the said Roman pontiff and prelates, to none of whom ought obedience be given should he enjoin or command the members and teachers of this sect to desert and abjure it—this despite the fact that it has been condemned as heretical by the Roman Church.

Also, they hold and teach that every oath, in or out of court, without exception or qualification, has been forbidden by God as unlawful and sinful. . . .

Also, out of the same font of error, the aforesaid sect and heresy declares that any judicial process is forbidden by God and is, consequently, a sin and that it is contrary to God's command for any judge, in any case or for any reason, to sentence a man to corporal punishment involving bloodshed, or to death. They seize on the words of the Holy Gospels—"Judge not that ye be not judged"; "Thou shalt not kill"; and other similar passages—without the proper explanation essential to their interpretation. This they do without understanding the sense or accepting the signification or explanation which the Holy Roman Church wisely perceives and transmits to the faithful in accordance with the teaching of the Fathers [early Christian theologians], the doctors, and the canonical decrees.

Also, as it strays from the way and the right path, this sect does not accept or consider valid, but despises, rejects, and damns the canonical decrees, the decretals [judgments] of the supreme pontiffs, the rules concerning observance of fasts and holy days, and the precepts of the Fathers.

Also, in a more pernicious error in respect of the sacrament of penance and the keys [papal powers to legislate] of the Church, these [Waldensians] hold, and teach that, just as the apostles had it from Christ, they have from God alone and from no other the power to hear confessions from men and women who wish to confess to them, to give absolution, and to impose penance. And they do hear the confessions of such persons, they do give absolution [forgiveness] and impose penance, although they are not priests or clerics ordained by any bishop of the Roman Church but are laymen and nothing more. They do not claim to have any such power from the Roman Church, but rather disclaim it. . . .

Also, this sect and heresy ridicules the indulgences [remissions of punishments due to sin] which are published and granted by prelates of the Church, asserting that they are of no value whatever.

In regard to the sacrament of the Eucharist [communion, celebration of the Last Supper] they err, saying, not publicly but in private among themselves, that if the priest who celebrates or consecrates the Mass is a sinner, the bread and wine do not change into the body and blood of Christ in the sacrament of the altar; and in their view anyone is a sinner who is not a member of their sect. Also, they say that any righteous person, even though he be a layman and not a cleric ordained by a Catholic bishop, can perform the consecration of the body and blood of Christ, provided only that he be a member of their sect. This they apply even to women, with the same proviso that they belong to their sect. Thus they teach that every holy person is a priest.

Peter of les Vaux-de-Cernay
EXTERMINATING THE CATHARS

Catharism (also known as Albegensianism) was the most radical heresy to confront the medieval church. This belief represented a curious mixture of Gnosticism and Manicheanism—Eastern religious movements that had competed with Christianity in the days of the Roman Empire—and of doctrines considered heretical by the early church. Carried to Italy and southern France by Bulgarian missionaries, Catharism gained followers in regions where opposition to the worldliness and wealth of the clergy was already strong.

Cathari tenets differed considerably from those of the church as the first selection from Peter of les Vaux-de Cernay's *Historia Albigensis* (History of the Albigensian Crusade), written between about 1212 and 1218, illustrates. The author, a Cistercian monk, witnessed many of the events described in his narration.

First it should be understood that the heretics maintained the existence of two creators, one of things invisible whom they called the "benign" God and one of the things visible whom they named the "malign" God. They attributed the New Testament to the benign God and the Old Testament to the malign God, and rejected the whole of the latter except for certain passages quoted in the New Testament. These they considered acceptable because of their respect for the New Testament. They maintained that the author of the Old Testament was a "liar"; he said to our first ancestors "on the day that ye eat of the tree of the knowledge of good and evil, ye shall surely die"; but they did not die after eating the fruit as he had predicted (although, of course, the real truth is that as soon as they had tasted the forbidden fruit they became subject to the misery of death). They also called him "murderer" because he exterminated the inhabitants of Sodom and Gomorrah by fire and destroyed the world by the waters of the flood; and because he drowned Pharaoh and the Egyptians in the sea. They declared that all the patriarchs of the Old Testament were damned; they asserted that St. John the Baptist was one of the chief devils.

Further, in their secret meetings they said that the Christ who was born in the earthly and visible Bethlehem and crucified at Jerusalem was "evil," and that Mary Magdalene was his concubine—and that she was the woman taken in adultery who is referred to in the scriptures; the "good" Christ, they said, neither ate nor drank nor assumed the true flesh and was never in this world, except spiritually in the body of Paul. I have used the term "the earthly and visible Bethlehem" because the heretics believed there is a different and invisible earth in which—according to some of them—the "good" Christ was born and crucified. Again, they said that the good God had two wives, Oolla and Ooliba, on whom he begat sons and daughters. There were other heretics who said that there was only one Creator, but that he had two sons, Christ and the Devil; they said moreover that all created beings had once been good, but that everything had been corrupted by the vials referred to in the Book of Revelations.

All these people, the limbs of the Antichrist, the first-born of Satan, the seed of evildoers, children that are corrupters, speaking lies in hypocrisy, the seducers of simple hearts, had infected almost the whole of the province of Narbonne with the poison of their perfidy. They said that the Roman Church was a den of thieves, and the harlot spoken of in the Book of Revelations. They ridiculed the sacraments of the Church,

The History of the Albigensian Crusade: Peter of les Vaux-de-Cernay's Historia Albigenis, trans. W. A. Sibly and M. D. Sibly (Suffolk, Great Britain: Boydell Press, 1998), pp. 11–13, 85. Reprinted with permission from Boydell & Brewer Ltd.

arguing publicly that the holy water of baptism was no better than river water, that the consecrated host of the holy body of Christ was no different from common bread; instilling into the ears of simple folk the blasphemy that the body of Christ, even if it had been large enough to contain the whole Alps, would by now be wholly consumed and reduced to nothing by those eating of it. They considered that confirmation, extreme unction and confession were trivial and empty ceremonies; they preached that holy matrimony was mere harlotry, and that no one could find salvation in it by begetting sons and daughters. They denied the resurrection of the body, and invented new myths, claiming that our souls are really those angelic spirits who were driven from heaven through their rebellious pride and then left their glorified bodies in the ether; and that these souls after successively inhabiting any seven earthly bodies will then return to their original bodies, as though they had then completed their long penance.

It should be understood that some of the heretics were called "perfected" heretics or "good men," others "believers of the heretics." The "perfected" heretics wore a black robe, claimed (falsely) to practice chastity, and renounced meat, eggs and cheese. They wished it to appear that they were not liars although they lied, especially about God, almost unceasingly! They also said that no one should take oaths for any reason. The term "believers" was applied to those who lived a secular existence and did not try to copy the way of life of the "perfected," but hoped that by following their faith they would attain salvation; they were separated in the way they lived, but united in their beliefs—or rather unbelief! Those called "believers" were dedicated to usury, robbery, murder and illicit love, and to all kinds of perjury and perversity; indeed they felt they could sin in safety and without restraint, because they believed they could be saved without restitution of what they had stolen and without confession and penitence, so long as they were able to recite the Lord's prayer and ensure a "laying-on of hands" by their masters, in the final moments of their lives.

To explain further, they selected from the "perfected" heretics officials whom they called "deacons" and "bishops," and the "believers" held that no one of them could attain salvation without the laying-on of hands by these clergy just before death; indeed, they considered that however sinful a man might have been, then provided he had undergone this laying-on of hands on his deathbed, and so long as he was able to recite the Lord's prayer, he would gain salvation and (to use their own expression) "consolation"; to the extent that he would immediately fly up to heaven without making any amends or reparations for wrongs he had committed.

When the Cathari did not submit to peaceful persuasion, Innocent III called on kings and lords to exterminate Catharism with the sword. Lasting from 1208 to 1229 the war against the Cathari in southern France was marked by brutality and fanaticism, as Peter describes in the passage below. Command of the crusading army soon passed to Simon de Montfort, a minor baron with great ambition. De Montfort's army slaughtered suspected heretics throughout the county of Toulouse, effectively breaking the power of the nobles who protected the heretics. Innocent III sent legates to the region to arrest and try the Cathari. Under his successor, Dominican and Franciscan inquisitors completed the task of extermination.

Our Count now entered Minerve and went to the place where the heretics were gathered. As a true Catholic he wished them all to win salvation and come to know the way of truth, and he began to urge them to be converted to the Catholic faith. When he could make no progress, he had them taken out of the *castrum*. There were at least a hundred and forty perfected heretics. A huge pyre was made ready, and all were thrown on it—indeed there was no need for our soldiers to throw them on, since they were so hardened in their wickedness that they rushed into the fire of their own accord. Three women only were rescued, whom the noble lady the mother of Bouchard de Marly snatched from the flames and reconciled to the Holy Church. So the heretics were burnt; all the other inhabitants renounced heresy and were reconciled to the Church.

REVIEW QUESTIONS

1. On what grounds does Aquinas argue that the crime of the heretic deserves excommunication and death? What kind of leniency could the heretic expect from the church?
2. What was the Waldensian attitude toward the wealth and the temporal powers exercised by the medieval church?
3. How did the Waldensians differ from the orthodox church on the role of the clergy and the administration of the sacraments?
4. What church doctrines did the proponents of Catharism repudiate?
5. How did the Cathars believe salvation could be achieved?
6. Why did the church call for the extermination of the Cathars?

5   Medieval Learning: Synthesis of Reason and Christian Faith

The twelfth century witnessed a revived interest in classical learning and the founding of universities. Traditional theology was broadened by the application of a new system of critical analysis, called scholasticism. Scholastic thinkers assumed that some teachings of Christianity, which they accepted as true by faith, could also be demonstrated to be true by reason. They sought to explain and clarify theological doctrines by subjecting them to logical analysis.

Peter Abelard
INQUIRY INTO DIVERGENT VIEWS OF CHURCH FATHERS

Dialectics, a method of logical analysis, applied to the Bible and the writings of early Christian thinkers, was brilliantly taught by Peter Abelard (1079–1142) in the cathedral school at Paris. In his book *Sic et Non* (Yes and No), Abelard listed some 150 questions on which the early church authorities had taken differing positions over the centuries. He suggested that these issues could be resolved by the careful application of the dialectical method to the language of the texts.

Although he never intended to challenge the Christian faith, Abelard raised, with his critical scrutiny, fears that the dialectical approach would undermine faith and foster heresy. Saint Bernard of Clairvaux, a Cistercian monk and mystic, challenged the new methods of the Parisian professor and sought to silence him. In 1141, Abelard was forced to quit his teaching post, and he retired to a monastery, where he died the following year. Despite Bernard's apparent victory, the new scholastic rationalistic approach swept the schools of Europe. In the following reading, the critical use of rational methods in textual analysis is described by Abelard.

We must be careful not to be led astray by attributing views to the [Church] Fathers which they did not hold. This may happen if a wrong author's name is given to a book or if a text is corrupt. For many works are falsely attributed to one of the Fathers to give them authority, and some passages, even in the Bible, are corrupt through the errors of copyists. . . . We must be equally careful to make sure that an opinion quoted from a Father was not withdrawn or corrected by him in the light of later and better knowledge. . . . Again the passage in question may not give the Father's own opinion, but that of some other writer whom he is quoting. . . .

We must also make a thorough inquiry when different decisions are given on the same matter under canon [church] law. We must discover the underlying purpose of the opinion, whether it is meant to grant an indulgence or exhort to some perfection. In this way we may clear up the apparent contradiction. . . . If the opinion is a definitive judgment, we must determine whether it is of general application or directed to a particular case. . . . The when and why of the order must

also be considered because what is allowed at one time is often forbidden at another, and what is often laid down as the strict letter of the law may be sometimes moderated by a dispensation. . . .

Furthermore we customarily talk of things as they appear to our bodily senses and not as they are in actual fact. So judging by what we see we say it is a starry sky or it is not, and that the sun is hot or has no heat at all, when these things though variable in appearance are ever constant. Can we be surprised, then, that some matters have been stated by the Fathers as opinions rather than the truth? Then again many controversies would be quickly settled if we could be on our guard against a particular word used in different senses by different authors. . . .

A careful reader will employ all these ways of reconciling contradictions in the writings of the Fathers. But if the contradictions are so glaring that they cannot be reconciled, then the rival authorities must be compared and the view that has the heaviest backing be adopted. . . .

By collecting contrasting divergent opinions I hope to provoke young readers to push themselves to the limit in the search for truth, so that their wits may be sharpened by their investigation. It is by doubting that we come to investigate, and by investigating that we recognise the truth.

David Ayerst and A. S. T. Fisher, eds., *Records of Christianity*, vol. 2: *Christendom* (Oxford: Basil Blackwell, 1971), pp. 196–197.

Thomas Aquinas
SUMMA THEOLOGICA

For most of the Middle Ages, religious thought was dominated by the influence of Saint Augustine (d. 430), the greatest of the Latin church fathers. Augustine placed little value on the study of nature; for him, the city of Man (the world) was a sinful place from which people tried to escape in order to enter the City of God (heaven). Regarding God as the source of knowing, he held that reason by itself was an inadequate guide to knowledge: without faith in revealed truth, there could be no understanding. An alternative approach to that of Augustine was provided by Thomas Aquinas (1225–1274), a friar of the Order of Preachers (Dominicans), who taught theology at Paris and later in Italy. Both Augustine and Aquinas believed that God was the source of all truth, that human nature was corrupted by the imprint of the original sin of Adam and Eve, and that God revealed himself through the Bible and in the person of Jesus Christ. But, in contrast to Augustine, Aquinas expressed great confidence in the power of reason and favored applying it to investigate the natural world.

Aquinas held that as both faith and reason came from God, they were not in opposition to each other; properly understood, they supported each other. Because reason was no enemy of faith, it should not be feared. In addition to showing renewed respect for reason, Aquinas—influenced by Aristotelian empiricism (the acquisition of knowledge of nature through experience)—valued knowledge of the natural world. He saw the natural and supernatural worlds not as irreconcilable and hostile to each other, but as a continuous ascending hierarchy of divinely created orders of being moving progressively toward the Supreme Being. In constructing a synthesis of Christianity and Aristotelianism, Aquinas gave renewed importance to the natural world, human reason, and the creative human spirit. Nevertheless, by holding that reason was subordinate to faith, he remained a typically medieval thinker.

In the opening reading from his most ambitious work, the *Summa Theologica* (Highest Theology) Thomas Aquinas asserts that reason by itself is insufficient to lead human beings to salvation.

WHETHER, BESIDES THE PHILOSOPHICAL SCIENCES, ANY FURTHER DOCTRINE IS REQUIRED?

It was necessary for man's salvation that there should be a knowledge revealed by God, besides the philosophical sciences investigated by human reason. First, because man is directed to God as to an end that surpasses the grasp of his reason. . . . But the end must first be known by men who are to direct their thoughts and actions to the end. Hence it was necessary for the salvation of man that certain truths which exceed human reason should be made known to him by divine revelation. Even as regards those truths about God which human reason can investigate, it was necessary that man be taught by a divine revelation. For the truth about God, such as reason can know it, would only be known by a few, and that after a long time, and with the admixture of many errors; whereas man's whole salvation, which is in God, depends upon the

knowledge of this truth. Therefore, in order that the salvation of men might be brought about more fitly and more surely, it was necessary that they be taught divine truths by divine revelation. It was therefore necessary that, besides the philosophical sciences investigated by reason, there should be a sacred science by way of revelation.

In the next selection, Aquinas uses the categories of Aristotelian philosophy to demonstrate through natural reason God's existence.

WHETHER GOD EXISTS?

The existence of God can be proved in five ways.

The first and more manifest way is the argument from motion. It is certain, and evident to our senses, that in the world some things are in motion. Now whatever is moved is moved by another, for nothing can be moved except it is in potentiality to that towards which it is moved; whereas a thing moves inasmuch as it is in act. For motion is nothing else than the reduction of something from potentiality to actuality. But nothing can be reduced from potentiality to actuality, except by something in

Summa Contra Gentiles, trans. and ed. Anton Pegis. Copyright © 1945 by Random House, Inc. Copyright renewed 1973 by Random House, Inc. Reprinted 1997 by Hackett Publishing Company. Reprinted by permission of Hackett Publishing Company, Inc. All rights reserved.

a state of actuality. Thus that which is actually hot, as fire, makes wood, which is potentially hot, to be actually hot, and thereby moves and changes it. Now it is not possible that the same thing should be at once in actuality and potentiality in the same respect, but only in different respects. For what is actually hot cannot simultaneously be potentially hot; but it is simultaneously potentially cold. It is therefore impossible that in the same respect and in the same way a thing should be both mover and moved, *i.e.*, that it should move itself. Therefore, whatever is moved must be moved by another. If that by which it is moved be itself moved, then this also must needs be moved by another, and that by another again. But this cannot go on to infinity, because then there would be no first mover, and, consequently, no other mover, seeing that subsequent movers move only inasmuch as they are moved by the first mover; as the staff moves only because it is moved by the hand. Therefore it is necessary to arrive at a first mover, moved by no other; and this everyone understands to be God.

The second way is from the nature of efficient cause. In the world of sensible things we find there is an order of efficient causes. There is no case known (neither is it, indeed, possible) in which a thing is found to be the efficient cause of itself; for so it would be prior to itself, which is impossible. Now in efficient causes it is not possible to go on to infinity, because in all efficient causes following in order, the first is the cause of the intermediate cause, and the intermediate is the cause of the ultimate cause, whether the intermediate cause be several, or one only. Now to take away the cause is to take away the effect. Therefore, if there be no first cause among efficient causes, there will be no ultimate, nor any intermediate, cause. But if in efficient causes it is possible to go on to infinity, there will be no first efficient cause, neither will there be an ultimate effect, nor any intermediate efficient causes; all of which is plainly false. Therefore it is necessary to admit a first efficient cause, to which everyone gives the name of God.

The third way is taken from possibility and necessity, and runs thus. We find in nature things that are possible to be and not to be,

since they are found to be generated, and to be corrupted, and consequently, it is possible for them to be and not to be. But it is impossible for these always to exist, for that which can not-be at some time is not. Therefore, if everything can not-be, then at one time there was nothing in existence. Now if this were true, even now there would be nothing in existence, because that which does not exist begins to exist only through something already existing. Therefore, if at one time nothing was in existence, it would have been impossible for anything to have begun to exist; and thus even now nothing would be in existence—which is absurd. Therefore, not all beings are merely possible, but there must exist something the existence of which is necessary. But every necessary thing either has its necessity caused by another, or not. Now it is impossible to go on to infinity in necessary things which have their necessity caused by another, as has been already proved in regard to efficient causes. Therefore we cannot but admit the existence of some being having of itself its own necessity, and not receiving it from another, but rather causing in others their necessity. This all men speak of as God.

The fourth way is taken from the graduation to be found in things. Among beings there are some more and some less good, true, noble, and the like. But *more* and *less* are predicated of different things according as they resemble in their different ways something which is the maximum, as a thing is said to be hotter according as it more nearly resembles that which is hottest; so that there is something which is truest, something best, something noblest, and, consequently, something which is most being, for those things that are greatest in truth are greatest in being. . . . Now the maximum in any genus is the cause of all in that genus, as fire, which is the maximum of heat, is the cause of all hot things. . . . Therefore there must also be something which is to all beings the cause of their being, goodness, and every other perfection; and this we call God.

The fifth way is taken from the governance of the world. We see that things which lack knowledge, such as natural bodies, act for an end, and this is evident from their acting always, or nearly always, in the same way, so as to obtain the best result. Hence it is plain that they achieve their end, not fortuitously, but designedly. Now whatever lacks knowledge cannot move towards an end, unless it be directed by some being endowed with knowledge and intelligence; as the arrow is directed by the archer. Therefore some intelligent being exists by whom all natural things are directed to their end; and this being we call God.

REVIEW QUESTIONS

1. What was Peter Abelard's method of coping with textual problems? Why did this method cause controversy?
2. According to Thomas Aquinas, when does a person require more than reason to arrive at truth?
3. Show how Aquinas used both logic and an empirical method to prove the existence of God.

6 Medieval Universities

The twelfth century witnessed a revival of classical learning and cultural creativity. During this period, called the Twelfth-Century Awakening, Gothic cathedrals, an enduring testament to the creativeness of the religious spirit, were erected throughout Europe. Roman authors were again read and their style imitated. Latin translations of Greek philosophical and scientific texts stimulated scholars; the reintroduction of the study of Roman law began to influence political theory and institutions. These were some of the major changes that would leave a permanent mark on subsequent Western culture.

A significant achievement of this age was the emergence of universities. Arising spontaneously among teachers of the liberal arts and students of the higher studies of law, theology, and medicine, the universities gave more formal and lasting institutional structure to the more advanced levels of schooling. The medieval universities were largely dedicated to educating young men for careers as lawyers, judges, teachers, diplomats, and administrators of both church and state. The educational foundation for such professional careers was the study of grammar, rhetoric, logic, mathematics, and theology.

Geoffrey Chaucer
AN OXFORD CLERIC

In his masterpiece, *The Canterbury Tales*, English poet and diplomat Geoffrey Chaucer (c. 1340–1400) describes a typical student on pilgrimage to the shrine of Saint Thomas à Becket in Canterbury.

An *Oxford Cleric*, still a student though,
One who had taken logic long ago,
Was there; his horse was thinner than a rake,

And he was not too fat, I undertake,
But had a hollow look, a sober stare.
The thread upon his overcoat was bare;

He had found no preferment [employment] in
the church
And he was too unworldly to make search
For secular employment. By his bed
He preferred having twenty books, in red
And black, of Aristotle's philosophy,
To having fine clothes, fiddle, or psaltery
[a book of Psalms used for daily prayer].
Though a philosopher, as I have told,
He had not found the stone for making gold.[1]

Geoffrey Chaucer, *The Canterbury Tales*, trans. Nevill Coghill,
Penguin Classics, 1951, Fourth Revised Edition, 1977, p. 27.
Copyright 1951 by Nevill Coghill, © The Estate of Nevill
Coghill, 1958, 1960, 1975.

Whatever money from his friends he took
He spent on learning or another book
And prayed for them most earnestly, returning
Thanks to them thus for paying for his learning.
His only care was study, and indeed
He never spoke a word more than was need,
Formal at that, respectful in the extreme,
Short, to the point, and lofty in this theme.
The thought of moral virtue filled his speech
And he would gladly learn, and gladly teach.

[1]The *philosopher's stone* was the name given to the mythical
substance, searched for by alchemists, that would turn base
metals into gold. —Eds.

STUDENT LETTERS

The relationship between fathers and their sons enrolled at universities has
not changed all that much since the Middle Ages, as the letters that follow
demonstrate.

FATHERS TO SONS

I

I have recently discovered that you live dissolutely
and slothfully, preferring license to restraint and
play to work and strumming a guitar while the
others are at their studies, whence it happens that
you have read but one volume of law while your
more industrious companions have read several.
Wherefore I have decided to exhort you herewith
to repent utterly of your dissolute and careless
ways, that you may no longer be called a waster
and your shame may be turned to good repute.

II

I have learned—not from your master, although
he ought not to hide such things from me, but
from a certain trustworthy source—that you do
not study in your room or act in the schools as a

good student should, but play and wander about,
disobedient to your master and indulging in
sport and in certain other dishonorable practices
which I do not now care to explain by letter.

SONS TO FATHERS

I

Well-beloved father, I have not a penny, nor
can I get any save through you, for all things
at the University are so dear: nor can I study in
my Code or my Digest, for they are all tattered.
Moreover, I owe ten crowns in dues to the Pro-
vost, and can find no man to lend them to me;
I send you word of greetings and of money.

The Student hath need of many things if he
will profit here; his father and his kin must needs
supply him freely, that he be not compelled to
pawn his books, but have ready money in his
purse, with gowns and furs and decent clothing,

Reprinted from Edwin H. Zeydel, *Vagabond Verse: Secular
Latin Poems in the Middle Ages*, pp. 61, 63, 65, 67. Copyright
© 1966 Wayne State University Press, with the permission
of Wayne State University Press.

G. G. Coulton, *Five Centuries of Religion* (Cambridge:
Cambridge University Press, 1928-1929), vol. 3, p. 113.

or he will be damned for a beggar; wherefore, that men may not take me for a beast, I send you word of greetings and of money.

Wines are dear, and hostels, and other good things; I owe in every street, and am hard bested to free myself from such snares. Dear father, deign to help me! I fear to be excommunicated; already have I been cited, and there is not even a dry bone in my larder. If I find not the money before this feast of Easter, the church door will be shut in my face: wherefore grant my supplication, for I send you word of greetings and of money.

L'ENVOY

Well-beloved father, to ease my debts contracted at the tavern, at the baker's, with the doctor and the bedells [a minor college official], and to pay my subscriptions to the laundress and the barber, I send you word of greetings and of money.

II

Sing unto the Lord a new song, praise him with stringed instruments and organs, rejoice upon the high-sounding cymbals, for your son has held a glorious disputation, which was attended by a great number of teachers and scholars. He answered all questions without a mistake, and no one could get the better of him or prevail against his arguments. Moreover he celebrated a famous banquet, at which both rich and poor were honoured as never before, and he has duly begun to give lectures which are already so popular that others' classrooms are deserted and his own are filled.

A Wandering Scholar
"IN THE TAVERN LET ME DIE"

During the Middle Ages, errant students and idle clerks roamed the highways as free spirits, searching for adventure or at least for diversion. Some had given up their studies for lack of funds; others were restless or unable to secure the position they desired. These vagabonds sometimes amused themselves by composing poetry that ridiculed clerics and sang the praises of wine, gambling, and women. The following poem was written in Latin by a poet known as the "Archpoeta," who lived in the twelfth century.

Down the highway broad I walk,
Like a youth in mind,
Implicate myself in vice,
Virtue stays behind,
Avid for the world's delight
More than for salvation,
Dead in soul, I care but for
Body's exultation.

Prelate, you most circumspect,
Grace I would entreat,
It's a good death that I die,
Such death is sweet,
O, my heart is wounded sore
When a lass comes near it,
If there's one I cannot touch,
Her I rape in spirit.

It is most difficult indeed
Overcoming Nature,
Keeping pure our mind and thought
Near a girlish creature.
Young like me, one can't observe

Rules that are unfeeling,
Can't ignore such shapes and curves
Tempting and appealing.

Who when into fire is pushed
Is by fire not scorched?
Whoso in Pavia[1] stayed
Has not been debauched,
Where Dame Venus with a sign
Gives young men a shake-up,
Snares them with her luring eyes,
With her tempting makeup?

Secondly I've been accused
That I yield to gambling,
Yet when gambling strips me bare,
Then I can't go rambling,
For outside I quake with cold
While my heart glows white,
In this state far better song,
Finer verse I write.

Thirdly to the tavern I
Must refer in turn,
This I've spurned not in the past
Nor will ever spurn,
Till the holy angels come
With a chant supernal,
Singing masses for the dead—
Requiem eternal.

In the tavern let me die,
That's my resolution,
Bring me wine for lips so dry
At life's dissolution.
Joyfully the angel's choir
Then will sing my glory:
"Sit deus propicius
Huic potatori."[2]

Through the cup new light bursts up
In my spirit's flare,
Nectar stimulates my heart
Etherward to fare.
Wine that in the tavern flows

Has a richer flavor
Than the watered stuff our lord's
Steward likes to savor.

———

Special gifts on every man
Mother Nature lavished;
I can never write a verse
When by hunger ravished,
If I'm famished, one small boy
Bests me in a trice,
Thirst and hunger I detest
Like my own demise.

Special gifts for every man
Nature will produce,
I, when I compose my verse,
Vintage wine must use,
All the best the cellar's casks
Hold of these libations.
Such a wine calls forth from me
Copious conversations.

My verse has the quality
Of the wine I sip,
I can not do much until
Food has passed my lip,
What I write when starved and parched
Is of lowest class,
When I'm tight, with verse I make
Ovid I surpass.[3]

As a poet ne'er can I
Be appreciated
Till my stomach has been well
Filled with food and sated,
When god Bacchus[4] gains my brain's
Lofty citadel,
Phoebus[5] rushes in to voice
Many a miracle.

---

[1]Pavia, a city in northern Italy, drew many students in the Middle Ages. —Eds.
[2]"May God be well-disposed to this toper [drunkard]."

[3]Ovid, a Roman poet (43 B.C.–A.D. 17) and author of the *Metanorphoses,* was considered a master of metrical form. —Eds.
[4]Bacchus is an alternative name for Dionysus, the Greek god of wine and ecstasy. —Eds.
[5]Phoebus is another name for Apollo, the Greek god who represented male beauty and moral excellence. —Eds.

See, my own depravity
I have now confessed,
Disapproval of my sins
Have my friends expressed.

Not a single one of these
His own sins confesses,
Though he also likes the dice,
Likes the world's excesses.

REVIEW QUESTIONS

1. How do medieval students resemble their modern counterparts? How do they differ?
2. What virtues did Archpoeta find in his vices?

---

7 The Jews in the Middle Ages

Toward the end of the eleventh century, small communities of Jews were living in many of the larger towns of Christian Europe. Most of these Jews were descended from Jewish inhabitants of the Roman Empire. Under the protection of the Roman law or of individual Germanic kings, they had managed to survive amid a sometimes hostile Christian population. But religious fanaticism unleashed by the call for the First Crusade undermined Christian–Jewish relations gravely. Bands of crusaders began systematically to attack and massacre the Jewish inhabitants of Rhineland towns. Thousands were killed—many because they refused to convert to Christianity—and their houses were looted and burned. Efforts by the bishops and civil authorities to protect their Jewish subjects were largely ineffective. After the First Crusade, anti-Semitism became endemic in Latin Christendom.

Albert of Aix-la-Chapelle
MASSACRE OF THE JEWS OF MAINZ

In this reading, Albert, a twelfth-century priest of the city of Aix-la-Chapelle (Aachen, in the western part of Germany), describes the massacre of Jews (1096) at the beginning of the First Crusade.

At the beginning of summer in the same year in which Peter [the Hermit] and Gottschalk,[1] after collecting an army, had set out, there assembled in like fashion a large and innumerable host of Christians from diverse kingdoms and lands; namely, from the realms of France,

England, Flanders, and Lorraine. . . . I know not whether by a judgment of the Lord, or by some

---

The First Crusade, ed. August C. Krey (Princeton: Princeton University Press, 1921), pp. 54–55. Copyright © 1921 by Princeton University Press.

---

[1]A brilliant propagandist, Peter the Hermit raised a large army of poor and sparsely armed Frenchmen, who marched to Cologne to begin a crusade to the Holy Land. Most of them were killed by Turkish forces after crossing into Asia Minor. Gottschalk was a German priest who gathered a band of undisciplined soldiers to join the First Crusade. His forces were killed by Hungarians defending their families and property from these crusaders. —Eds.

error of mind, they rose in a spirit of cruelty against the Jewish people scattered throughout these cities and slaughtered them without mercy, especially in the Kingdom of Lorraine,[2] asserting it to be the beginning of their expedition and their duty against the enemies of the Christian faith. This slaughter of Jews was done first by citizens of Cologne.[3] These suddenly fell upon a small band of Jews and severely wounded and killed many; they destroyed the houses and synagogues of the Jews and divided among themselves a very large amount of money. When the Jews saw this cruelty, about two hundred in the silence of the night began flight by boat to Neuss. The pilgrims and crusaders discovered them, and after taking away all their possessions, inflicted on them similar slaughter, leaving not even one alive.

Not long after this, they started upon their journey, as they had vowed, and arrived in a great multitude at the city of Mainz. There Count Emico, a nobleman, a very mighty man in this region, was awaiting, with a large band of Teutons [German soldiers], the arrival of the pilgrims who were coming thither from diverse lands by the King's highway.

The Jews of this city, knowing of the slaughter of their brethren, and that they themselves could not escape the hands of so many, fled in hope of safety to Bishop Rothard. They put an infinite treasure in his guard and trust, having much faith in his protection, because he was Bishop of the city. Then that excellent Bishop of the city cautiously set aside the incredible amount of money received from them. He placed the Jews in the very spacious hall of his own house, away from the sight of Count Emico and his followers, that they might remain safe and sound in a very secure and strong place.

But Emico and the rest of his band held a council and, after sunrise, attacked the Jews in the hall with arrows and lances. Breaking the bolts and doors, they killed the Jews, about seven hundred in number, who in vain resisted the force and attack of so many thousands. They killed the women, also, and with their swords pierced tender children of whatever age and sex. The Jews, seeing that their Christian enemies were attacking them and their children, and that they were sparing no age, likewise fell upon one another, brother, children, wives, and sisters, and thus they perished at each other's hands. Horrible to say, mothers cut the throats of nursing children with knives and stabbed others, preferring them to perish thus by their own hands rather than to be killed by the weapons of the uncircumcised.

From this cruel slaughter of the Jews a few escaped; and a few because of fear, rather than because of love of the Christian faith, were baptized. With very great spoils taken from these people, Count Emico, Clarebold, Thomas, and all that intolerable company of men and women then continued on their way to Jerusalem.

---

[2]Lorraine, a duchy in the western part of the Holy Roman Empire, is now part of France. —Eds.

[3]Cologne (Köln), founded by the Romans in the first century A.D., was the largest city in the Rhine valley, a center of commerce, industry, and learning. Its politically powerful archbishop was a prince of the Holy Roman Empire. —Eds.

Pope Innocent III
A DECREE ON THE JEWS

Regarding the Jews as wicked because they refused to accept Christ, the church wanted them to live in humiliation. However, the church did at times seek to protect them from violence.

The Fourth Lateran Council in 1215, which was organized by Innocent III (ruled 1198–1216), the most powerful of medieval popes, barred Jews from public office and required them to wear a distinguishing badge on their clothing, a sign of their degradation. Yet Innocent, as the following passage indicates, also cautioned against harming Jews. The passage, however, reveals some of the torments faced by Jews.

. . . We decree that no Christian shall use violence to compel the Jews to accept baptism. But if a Jew, of his own accord, because of a change in his faith, shall have taken refuge with Christians, after his wish has been made known, he may be made a Christian without any opposition. For anyone who has not of his own will sought Christian baptism cannot have the true Christian faith. No Christian shall do the Jews any personal injury, except in executing the judgments of a judge, or deprive them of their possessions, or change the rights and privileges which they have been accustomed to have. During the celebration of their festivals, no one shall disturb them by beating them with clubs or by throwing stones at them. No one shall compel them to render any services except those which they have been accustomed to render. And to prevent the baseness and avarice of wicked men we forbid anyone to deface or damage their cemeteries or to extort money from them by threatening to exhume the bodies of their dead. . . .

A Source Book for Medieval History, ed. Oliver J. Thatcher and Edgar H. McNeal (New York: Charles Scribner's Sons, 1905), pp. 212–213.

THE LIBEL OF RITUAL MURDER

Despite efforts by some popes to protect Jews, outbreaks of violence toward them persisted and bizarre myths about them emerged, often fomented by the clergy. Jews were seen as agents of Satan conspiring to destroy Christendom and as sorcerers employing black magic against Christians. Perhaps the most absurd (and dangerous) charge against the Jewish people was the accusation of ritual murder— that the Jews, requiring Christian blood for the Passover service, sacrificed a Christian child. Despite the vehement denials of Jews and the protests of some enlightened Christian leaders, hundreds of such libelous accusations were made, resulting in the torture, trials, murder, and expulsion of many Jews. Allegations of ritual murder and accompanying trials persisted into the twentieth century, to the consternation and anger of enlightened people who regarded the charge as so much nonsense, a lingering medieval fabrication and superstition.

In the next passage, an English chronicler reports on the death of one young Harold of Gloucester purported to be murdered by Jews in 1168.

. . . [The eight-year-old] boy Harold, who is buried in the Church of St. Peter the Apostle, at Gloucester . . ., is said to have been carried away secretly by Jews, in the opinion of many,[1] on Feb. 21, and by them hidden till March 16. On that night, on the sixth of the preceding feast, the Jews of all England coming together as if to circumcise a certain boy, pretend

Joseph Jacobs, *The Jews of Angevin England* (London: David Nutt, 1893), p. 45.

[1]Even the chronicler puts it doubly doubtfully.

deceitfully that they are about to celebrate the feast [Passover] appointed by law in such case, and deceiving the citizens of Gloucester with that fraud, they tortured the lad placed before them with immense tortures. It is true no Christian was present, or saw or heard the deed, nor have we found that anything was betrayed by any Jew. But a little while after when the whole convent of monks of Gloucester and almost all the citizens of that city, and innumerable persons coming to the spectacle, saw

the wounds of the dead body, scars of fire, the thorns fixed on his head, and liquid wax poured into the eyes and face, and touched it with the diligent examination of their hands, those tortures were believed or guessed to have been inflicted on him in that manner. It was clear that they had made him a glorious martyr to Christ, being slain without sin, and having bound his feet with his own girdle, threw him into the river Severn. (The body is taken to St. Peter's Church, and there performs miracles.)

Philip II Augustus
EXPULSION OF THE JEWS
FROM FRANCE

At various times in the Middle Ages and Early Modern times, monarchs and town authorities expelled Jews from their lands after first confiscating their property. So numerous were these expulsions that by 1541, virtually all of Western Europe and most of Central Europe were largely devoid of Jews.

In 1181, Philip II Augustus of France had Jews arrested in their synagogues on the Sabbath, extracted an enormous sum from them, and canceled all debts payable to Jews but made one-fifth payable to his treasury. A year later, he banished the Jews from his royal domain. The king filled his coffers by seizing and selling Jewish land, homes, barns, and other properties. Synagogues were converted into churches. Running out of money, Philip permitted the Jews to return a few years later but imposed heavy taxes on their economic activities, principally money-lending.

In succeeding years Jews would face additional expulsions from French lands. In 1306, Philip IV, "the Fair," seeking to replenish his treasury, condemned Jews to exile. All their property, except for a few coins and the clothes they were wearing, was forfeited to the king, and all loan records were transferred to the exchequer so that Philip could collect every penny of principal and interest. Other recalls and expulsions ensued in the fourteenth century, but a final expulsion in 1394 brought an end to France's thousand-year-old Jewish community.

Following is a contemporary account of Philip Augustus' banishment of the Jews from France in 1182. The author begins with the widely believed myth that Jews engaged in ritual murder.

[Philip Augustus had often heard] that the Jews who dwelt in Paris were wont every year

on Easter day, or during the sacred week of our Lord's Passion, to go down secretly into underground vaults and kill a Christian as a sort of sacrifice in contempt of the Christian religion. For a long time they had persisted in this wickedness, inspired by the devil, and in Philip's father's time many of them had been seized and burned with fire. St. Richard, whose body rests in the church of the Holy Innocents-in-the-Fields in Paris, was thus put to death and crucified by the Jews, and through martyrdom went in blessedness to God. Wherefore many miracles have been wrought by the hand of God through the prayers and intercessions of St. Richard, to the glory of God, as we have heard.

And because the most Christian King Philip inquired diligently, and came to know full well these and many other iniquities of the Jews in his forefathers' days, therefore he burned with zeal, and in the same year in which he was invested at Rheims with the holy governance of the kingdom of the French, upon a Sabbath, the first of March, by his command, the Jews throughout all France were seized in their synagogues and then bespoiled of their gold and silver and garments, as the Jews themselves had spoiled the Egyptians at their exodus from Egypt. This was a harbinger of their expulsion, which by God's will soon followed. . . .

At this time a great multitude of Jews had been dwelling in France for a long time past, for they had flocked thither from divers parts of the world, because peace abode among the French, and liberality; for the Jews had heard how the kings of the French were prompt to act against their enemies, and were very merciful toward their subjects. And therefore their elders and men wise in the law of Moses, who were called by the Jews *didascali,* made resolve to come to Paris.

When they had made a long sojourn there, they grew so rich that they claimed as their own almost half of the whole city, and had Christians in their houses as menservants and maidservants, who were open backsliders from the faith of Jesus Christ, and *judaized* with the Jews. And this was contrary to the decree of God and the law of the Church. And whereas the Lord had said by the mouth of Moses in Deuteronomy [23: 19, 20], "Thou shalt not lend upon usury to thy brother," but "to a stranger," the Jews in their wickedness understood by "stranger" every Christian, and they took from the Christians their money at usury. And so heavily burdened in this wise were citizens and soldiers and peasants in the suburbs, and in the various towns and villages, that many of them were constrained to part with their possessions. Others were bound under oath in houses of the Jews in Paris, held as if captives in prison.

The most Christian King Philip heard of these things, and compassion was stirred within him. He took counsel with a certain hermit, Bernard by name, a holy and religious man, who at that time dwelt in the forest of Vincennes, and asked him what he should do. By his advice the king released all Christians of his kingdom from their debts to the Jews, and kept a fifth part of the whole amount for himself.

Finally came the culmination of their wickedness. Certain ecclesiastical vessels consecrated to God—the chalices and crosses of gold and silver bearing the image of our Lord Jesus Christ crucified—had been pledged to the Jews by way of security when the need of the churches was pressing. These they used so vilely, in their impiety and scorn of the Christian religion, that from the cups in which the body and blood of our Lord Jesus Christ was consecrated they gave their children cakes soaked in wine. . . .

In the year of our Lord's Incarnation 1182, in the month of April, which is called by the Jews Nisan, an edict went forth from the most serene king, Philip Augustus, that all the Jews of his kingdom should be prepared to go forth by the coming feast of St. John the Baptist. And then the king gave them leave to sell each his movable goods before the time fixed, that is, the feast of St. John the Baptist. But their real estate, that is, houses, fields, vineyards, barns, winepresses, and such like, he reserved for himself and his successors, the kings of the French.

Readings in European History, vol. 1: *From the Breaking Up of the Roman Empire to the Protestant Revolt,* ed. James Harvey Robinson (Boston: Ginn and Company, 1904), pp. 426–428.

When the faithless Jews heard this edict some of them were born again of water and the Holy Spirit and converted to the Lord, remaining steadfast in the faith of our Lord Jesus Christ. To them the king, out of regard for the Christian religion, restored all their possessions in their entirety, and gave them perpetual liberty.

Others were blinded by their ancient error and persisted in their perfidy; and they sought to win with gifts and golden promises the great of the land,—counts, barons, archbishops, bishops,—that through their influence and advice, and through the promise of infinite wealth, they might turn the king's mind from his firm intention. But the merciful and compassionate God, who does not forsake those who put their hope in him and who doth humble those who glory in their strength, . . . so fortified the illustrious king that he could not be moved by prayers nor promises of temporal things. . . .

The infidel Jews, perceiving that the great of the land, through whom they had been accustomed easily to bend the king's predecessors to their will, had suffered repulse, and astonished and stupefied by the strength of mind of Philip the king and his constancy in the Lord, exclaimed, "Scema Israhel!"[1] and prepared to sell all their household goods. The time was now at hand when the king had ordered them to leave France altogether, and it could not be in any way prolonged. Then did the Jews sell all their movable possessions in great haste, while their landed property reverted to the crown. Thus the Jews, having sold their goods and taken the price for the expenses of their journey, departed with their wives and children and all their households in the aforesaid year of the Lord 1182.

———

[1] Or Sh'ma Yisrael, "Hear, Israel," the first two words of a section in Deoteronomy incorporated into Jewish prayer services.

Maimonides
JEWISH LEARNING

Medieval Jews, despite frequent persecution, carried on a rich cultural and intellectual life based on their ancestral religion. The foremost Jewish scholar of the Middle Ages was Moses ben Maimon, also called by the Greek name Maimonides (1135–1204), who was born in Córdoba, Spain, then under Muslim rule. After his family emigrated from Spain, Maimonides went to Egypt, where he became physician to the sultan. During his lifetime, Maimonides achieved fame as a philosopher, theologian, mathematician, and physician; he was recognized as the leading Jewish sage of his day, and his writings were respected by Christian and Muslim thinkers as well. Like Christian scholastics and Muslim philosophers, Maimonides tried to harmonize faith with reason, to reconcile the Hebrew scriptures and the Talmud (Jewish biblical commentary) with Greek philosophy. In his writings on ethical themes, Maimonides demonstrated piety, wisdom, and humanity. In the following passages, he discusses education and charity.

TORAH STUDY

Every man in Israel is obliged to study Torah, whether he be poor or rich, in sound health or ailing, in the vigor of youth or very old and of weakened vitality. Even a man so poor that he is maintained by charity or goes begging from door to door, as also a man with a wife and children to support, are obliged to set aside a definite period during the day and at night for the study of the Torah.

Among the great sages of Israel, some were hewers of wood, some, drawers of water, while others were blind. Nevertheless, they devoted themselves by day and by night to the study of the Torah. Moreover, they are included among the transmitters of the tradition in the direct line from Moses our master.

Until what period in life is one obliged to study Torah? Even until the day of one's death, as it is said, "And lest they (the precepts) depart from thy heart all the days of thy life" [Deut. 4:9]. Whenever one ceases to study, one forgets.

The time allotted to study should be divided into three parts. A third should be devoted to the Written Law; a third to the Oral Law; and the last third a person should spend thinking and reflecting so that he may understand the end of a thing from its beginning, and deduct one matter from another and compare one matter to another, and reason out by the . . . rules by which the Torah is interpreted till one knows which are the principal rules and how to deduce therefrom what is forbidden and what is permitted and other like matters which he has learnt from oral tradition. This is termed Talmud.

> In the following excerpts, Maimonides emphasizes building mutual respect between teacher and students. An effective teacher does not angrily scold students for not learning, but reprimands them only when they are negligent and lazy. And on his part, the student must realize that "just as a person is commanded to honor and revere his father, so he is under an obligation to honor

and revere his teacher . . . who instructs him in wisdom [and] secures for him life in the world to come."

If the teacher taught and his pupils did not understand, he should not be angry with them or fall into a rage, but should repeat the lesson again and again till they have grasped the full meaning of the *halakah* (rule) he is expounding. So also, the pupil should not say "I understand" when he has not understood, but should ask again and again. And if the master is angry with him and storms at him, he should say "Master, it is Torah. I need to learn, and my intellectual capacities are deficient.". . .

A disciple should not feel ashamed before his fellow-students who grasp the lesson after hearing it once or twice, while he needs to hear it several times before he knows it. For if this makes him feel ashamed, he will go through school without having learnt anything. The ancient sages accordingly said, "A bashful man cannot learn, nor . . . teach" [Ethics of Fathers 2:6]. These observations only apply when the students' lack of understanding is due to the difficulty of the subject or to their mental deficiency. But if the teacher clearly sees that they are negligent and indolent in their study of the Torah and that this is the cause of their failure to understand, it is his duty to scold them and shame them with words of reproach, and so stimulate them to be keen. And in this regard, the sages said "Arouse awe in the pupils." . . .

As pupils are bound to honor their teacher, so a teacher ought to show courtesy and friendliness to his pupils. The Sages said "Let the honor of thy disciples be as dear to thee as thine own" [Ethics of the Fathers 4:15]. A man should take an interest in his pupils and love them, for they are his spiritual children who will bring him happiness in this world and in the world hereafter. . . .

Disciples increase the teacher's wisdom and broaden his mind. The sages said, "Much wisdom I learnt from my teachers, more from my

----

The Judaic Tradition: Jewish Writings from Antiquity to the Modern Age, selected and translated by Nahum N. Glatzer (Northvale, New Jersey: Jason Aronson, 1961), p. 344.

Jacob S. Minkin, *The World of Moses Maimonides: with Selections from His Writings* (New York: Thomas Voseloff, 1957) pp. 288, 290.

colleagues; from my pupils, most of all." Even as a small piece of wood kindles a large log, so a pupil of small attainments sharpens the mind of his teacher, so that by his questions, he elicits glorious wisdom.

Care for the poor is ingrained in the Jewish tradition. Rabbis gave the highest value to assistance, given in secret, that helps a poor person to become self-supporting. Maimonides drew upon this rabbinical tradition in his discussion of charity.

CHARITY

There are eight degrees in the giving of charity, one higher than the other. The highest degree, than which there is nothing higher, is to take hold of a Jew who has been crushed and to give him a gift or a loan, or to enter into partnership with him, or to find work for him, and thus to put him on his feet so that he will not be dependent on his fellow-men. Concerning this it is said [Leviticus 25:35]: "Then shalt thou *uphold* him." *Uphold* him, so that he should not fall and become a dependant.

Lower in degree to this is the one who gives charity (in Hebrew, "righteousness") to the poor, but does not know to whom he gives it, nor does the poor man know from whom he receives it. This is an unselfish meritorious act comparable to what was done in the Chamber of the Secret in the Temple where the charitable would deposit (alms) secretly and the poor of

Jacob R. Marcus, *The Jew in the Medieval World: A Source Book: 315–1791* (New York: The World Publishing Co. and Philadelphia: The Jewish Publication Society of America, 1960), pp. 364–365.

better family would help themselves secretly. Related to this degree is the giving to the (public) alms-chest. One should not give to the alms-chest unless he knows that the officer in charge is reliable, wise, and a capable administrator, like Hananiah ben Teradion, for example. (This martyr, (d. about 135), was very scrupulous with charity funds.)

Lower in degree to this is when the giver knows to whom he gives, but the poor does not know from whom he receives. An example of this are the great scholars [of Talmudic times] who used to go about in secret and leave their money at the door of the poor. This is proper practice, particularly meritorious when the officers in charge of charity are not administering properly.

Lower in degree to this is when the poor knows from whom he receives but the giver does not know to whom he gives. An example of this are the great scholars who used to tic up their money in (the corner of) their cloaks and throw them back over their shoulders. The poor would then come and take it without being put to shame.

Lower in degree to this is when one gives even before he is asked.

Lower in degree to this is when one gives after he has been asked.

Lower in degree to this is when one gives less than he should, but graciously.

Lower in degree to this is when one gives grudgingly.

The great scholars used to give a coin to the poor before every prayer and then they would pray, for it is said in the Bible [Psalm 17:15]: "As for me, I shall behold Thy face in 'righteousness' (that is, through 'charity')."

REVIEW QUESTIONS

1. What were the apparent motives of those who attacked the Jews at Cologne and elsewhere at the time of the First Crusade?
2. What harassments and abuses were Jews likely to suffer in late medieval society?
3. What was the attitude of the papacy toward Jews?
4. Why were Christians prone to believe the absurd myth that Jews committed ritual murder?
5. Analyze the motives of Philip II Augustus for expelling the Jews from France. How might Jewish spokesmen respond to his accusations?
6. Discuss the roles of scholarship, education, and charity in medieval Jewish culture.

8 Troubadour Love Songs

In the late twelfth century, new kinds of poetry with a distinctive set of themes began to be created at the castles and courts in France, Italy, Spain, and Germany. The poets, or troubadors, were themselves knights or noblewomen who composed their poems to be sung or read aloud for the entertainment of fellow feudal nobles. The subject was always that of the love between man and woman.

The original inspiration for the new troubadour poetry was probably the Arab poetry of Spain and Sicily, where the theme of courtly love was developed earlier. What was revolutionary in later European poetry was its treatment of the relationship between men and women. The troubadours reversed the traditional view of men as superior and women as inferior and dependent in their relationships. They introduced what is called "courtly love," a love relationship in which the woman is the superior and dominant figure, the man inferior and dependent. The male courts the lady, paying homage to her beauty and virtue. He suffers humiliation and frustration at her will and expresses the erotic tensions that consume him.

LOVE AS JOYOUS, PAINFUL, AND HUMOROUS

The following poems were all composed by southern French troubadours. In the first selection a poet sings the praises of his beloved.

I wandered through a garden, 'twas
    filled with flowers the rarest,
And of all these brilliant blossoms
    I culled the very fairest;
So fine its shape, so sweet its scent, its
    hues so richly blent,
That heaven, I'm sure, created it itself
    to represent.
My lady is so charming, my lady is so
    meek,
Such tenderness is in her smile, such
    beauty in her cheek;
Such kisses blossom on her lip, such
    love illumines her, eye—
Oh, never was there neath the stars a
    man so blest as I!
I gaze, I thrill with joy, I weep, in song
    my feelings flow—

A song of hope, delight, desire, with
    passion all aglow—
A fervent song, a pleading song, a song
    in every line—
Of thanks and praise to her who lists no
    other songs but mine.
Oh, hear me sweet! Oh, kiss me sweet!
    Oh, clasp me tenderly!
Thy beauties many, many touch, but
    none that love like me.

The following two poems tell of a lover's failure to win the affections of his beloved.

Now that the air is fresher
and the world turned green,
I shall sing once more
of the one I love and desire,
but we are so far apart
that I cannot go and witness
how my words might please her.

Songs of the Troubadors, ed. and trans. Anthony Bonner (New York: Schocken Books, 1972), pp. 42–43. Copyright © 1972. Reprinted by permission of the author.

And nothing can console me
but death, for evil tongues
(may God curse them)
have made us part.
And alas, I so desired her
that now I moan and cry
half mad with grief.

I sing of her, yet her beauty
is greater than I can tell,
with her fresh color, lovely eyes,
and white skin, untanned
and untainted by rouge.
She is so pure and noble
that no one can speak ill of her.

But above all, one must praise,
it seems to me, her truthfulness,
her manners and her gracious speech,
for she never would betray a friend;
and I was mad to believe
what I heard tell of her
and thus cause her to be angry.

I never intended to complain;
and even now, if she so desires,
she could bring me happiness
by granting what I seek.
I cannot go on like this much longer,
for since she's been so far away
I've scarcely slept or eaten.

Love is sweet to look upon
but bitter upon parting;
one day it makes you weep
and another skip and dance,
for now I know that the more
one enters love's service,
the more fickle it becomes.

Messenger, go with Godspeed
and bring this to my lady,
for I cannot stay here much longer
and live, or be cured elsewhere,
unless I have her next to me,
naked, to kiss and embrace
within a curtained room.

———

I said my heart was like to break,
  And that my soul was cast,
By passion's tide, just like a wreck
  Disabled by the blast.

I swore an oath that what I felt
  Was like to turn my head;
I sighed—such sighs!—and then I knelt,
  But not a word she said!

I preached of Grace in moving strain;
  I told her she was fair;
I whispered what renown she'd gain,
  By listening to my prayer.

I spoke of needle and of pole,
  And other things I'd read;
But unto all my rigmarole—
  Why not a word she said!

I prayed her then my love to test,
  To send me near or far—
I'd squelch the dragon in his den,
  I'd yoke him to my car.

I'd risk for her, as faithful knight,
  My eyes, or limbs, or head,
Being quite prepared to fool or fight—
  But not a word she said!

I argued that, if poor in cash,
  Yet I was rich in mind;
Of rivals vowed to make a hash,
  When such I chanced to find.

I knit my brows, I clenched my hand,
  I tried to wake her dread;
In quiet wise, you'll understand—
  But not a word she said!

———

Troubadours could also be playful. Sometimes they mocked women who labored too hard to preserve a youthful beauty.

———

That creature so splendid is but an old jade;
Of ointment and padding her beauty is made;
Unpainted if you had the hap to behold her,
You'd find her all wrinkles from forehead to
  shoulder.

———

John Rutherford, *The Troubadours: Their Loves and Their Lyrics* (London: Smith Elder & Co., 1873).

What a shame for a woman who has lost all her
    grace
To waste thus her time in bedaubing
    her face!
To neglect her poor soul I am sure is not right
    of her,
For a body that's going to corruption
    in spite of her.

Sometimes they even mocked this obsession
with romance.

You say the moon is all aglow,
    The nightingale a-singing—
I'd rather watch the red wine flow,
    And hear the goblets ringing.

You say 'tis sweet to hear the gale
    Creep sighing through the willows—
I'd rather hear a merry tale,
    'Mid a group of jolly fellows!

You say 'tis sweet the stars to view
    Upon the waters gleaming—
I'd rather see, 'twixt me and you
    And the post, my supper steaming.

REVIEW QUESTION

What do these troubadours' love songs reveal about the tradition of courtly love?

9 The Status of Women in Medieval Society

The precise status of a woman in medieval society differed immensely
depending on the time, the place, and her class. The majority of women
managed families and households, often taking part in farm work or crafts
connected with the family livelihood. However, their legal rights, social
standing, and power were inferior to those of adult males in their own families. During the High Middle Ages, the Christian church increasingly supported a patriarchal structure of authority in church and civil society that left
women effectively under the domination of males, clerical and lay. Although
clerical teachings tended to demean women, several church doctrines also
recognized the inherent dignity of a woman. The church regarded marriage
as a sacrament, considered adultery a sin, and subjected men and women to
the same moral standards. Neither sex had any special advantage in attaining
salvation.

Despite legal, social, and economic handicaps imposed upon them by males,
some women successfully assumed positions of power and achievement. A few
ruled kingdoms and principalities or headed convents and religious orders.
Others organized guilds; founded nunneries; practiced various crafts; served
as teachers, physicians, and midwives; and operated small businesses. Some
showed talent as poets, dramatists, and artists.

Jacopone da Todi
PRAISE OF THE VIRGIN MARY
"O THOU MOTHER, FOUNT OF LOVE"

The ambivalence that medieval men, particularly intellectuals, expressed toward women arose from several sources. First, medieval authors, who highly esteemed the writings of the ancient Greeks and Romans, were influenced by the hostility of classical authors toward women who did not accept their position as subordinate and inferior to men. Classical writers maintained that women were less intelligent, more carnal, and more devious than men. Second, prejudice against women was fostered by the clerical insistence that celibacy was superior to marriage (because the former made it possible to escape the distractions of the flesh and family life and concentrate on spiritual matters). Third, the Christian view of men and women as equals in the sight of God was obscured by certain scriptural texts, such as Saint Paul's "Let your women keep silence in the churches: for it is not permitted unto them to speak" (1 Cor. 14:34); and "Wives, submit yourselves unto your own husbands, as unto the Lord" (Eph. 5:22). This negative view of women was symbolized by the Old Testament portrait of Eve as the archetypal temptress who led Adam to sin. One medieval writer expressed it this way: "Between Adam and God in paradise there was but one woman and she had no rest until she had succeeded in banishing her husband from the garden of delights and in condemning Christ to the torments of the cross."

Countering this negative image was the New Testament picture of Mary, whose acceptance of her role as the mother of Jesus made salvation possible for all people. The highest expression of devotion to the Virgin Mary was reached in the twelfth and thirteenth centuries with the growing notion that Mary was preserved from original sin and remained free of sin throughout her life. Moreover, medieval Christians believed that Mary, by devoting her entire life to her son in his work of redemption, cooperated with him in his ministry. Therefore, as the mother of God she was able to intercede with her son on behalf of individual Christians. The numerous artistic depictions of Mary as the Mother of God and the Queen of Heaven, as well as the multitude of churches named after the Virgin, are evidence of the popular piety that the cult of Mary generated throughout the Middle Ages.

The following poem by Italian religious poet Jacopone da Todi (c. 1230–1306) is a tribute to the Virgin Mary.

At the Cross her station keeping
Stood the mournful mother weeping,
  Close to Jesus to the last;
  Through her heart, His sorrow sharing,

All His bitter anguish bearing,
  Now at length the sword had passed.

O how sad and sore distressed
Was that mother highly blest
  Of the sole-begotten One!
Christ above in torment hangs:

Medieval Literature in Translation, ed. Charles W. Jones (New York: Longmans, Green and Co., 1950), pp. 904–906.

She beneath Him holds the pangs
Of her dying glorious Son.

Is there one who would not weep
Whelmed in miseries so deep
   Christ's dear mother to behold?
Can the human heart refrain
From partaking in her pain,
In that mother's pain untold?

Bruised, derided, cursed, defiled,
She held her tender Child
   All with bloody scourges rent;
For the sins of His own nation,
Saw Him hang in desolation,
   Till His spirit forth he sent.

O thou mother, fount of love,
Touch my spirit from above,
   Make my heart with thine accord!
Make me feel as thou hast felt;
Make my soul to glow and melt
   With the love of Christ my Lord.

Holy mother, pierce me through!
In my heart each wound renew
   Of my Saviour crucified;
Let me share with thee His pain,
Who for all my sins was slain,
   Who for me in torments died.

Let me mingle tears with thee,
Mourning Him who mourned for me,
   All the days that I may live;
By the Cross with thee to stay,
There with thee to weep and pray,
   Is all I ask of thee to give.

Virgin of all virgins blest!
Listen to my fond request:
   Let me share thy grief divine;
Let me, to my latest breath,
In my body bear the death
   Of that dying Son of thine.

Wounded with His every wound,
Steep my soul till it hath swooned
   In His very blood away;
Be to me, O virgin, nigh,
Lest in flames I burn and die
   In His awful judgment day:

Christ, when Thou shalt call me hence,
Be Thy mother my defence,
   Be Thy cross my victory
While my body here decays,
May my soul Thy goodness praise,
   Safe in paradise with Thee.

Christine de Pisan
THE CITY OF LADIES

In the Late Middle Ages (or early Renaissance), a remarkable woman took up the task of defending women from their many male detractors. Christine de Pisan (1364–c. 1429) was born in Venice but moved with her parents to Paris, where her father was court physician and astrologer. She married a court notary when she was fifteen, had three children, and was left a widow and penniless ten years later. She decided to use her unusually good education to become a professional writer, an unheard-of occupation for a woman at that time. She won the patronage and friendship of noble ladies at the French royal court and produced many poems and books, including a biography of King Charles V and several polemical attacks upon the poets who slandered womankind. The most famous of these is *The City of Ladies*, written in 1405. In it Christine de Pisan questioned three allegorical figures—Reason, Rectitude, and Justice—about the lies and slanders of males concerning the virtues and achievements of women. The book is really a history of famous women and their accomplishments in many fields of endeavour. In the following passages, she challenged the traditional medieval attitude toward women. In questioning Lady Reason about the alleged inferiority of women to men, de Pisan cleverly changes the subject to that of virtue, proclaiming the equality of the sexes in attaining it.

"My lady [Lady Reason], according to what I understand from you, woman is a most noble creature. But even so, Cicero [Roman statesman] says that a man should never serve any woman and that he who does so debases himself, for no man should ever serve anyone lower than him."

She replied, "The man or the woman in whom resides greater virtue is the higher; neither the loftiness nor the lowliness of a person lies in the body according to the sex, but in the perfection of conduct and virtues. And surely he is happy who serves the Virgin [Mary, the mother of Jesus], who is above all the angels."

"My lady, one of the Catos[1]—who was such a great orator—said, nevertheless, that if this world were without women, we would converse with the gods."

She replied, "You can now see the foolishness of the man who is considered wise, because, thanks to a woman, man reigns with God. And if anyone would say that man was banished because of Lady Eve, I tell you that he gained more through [the Virgin] Mary than he lost through Eve when humanity was conjoined to the Godhead,[2] which would never have taken place if Eve's misdeed [eating the forbidden fruit] had not occurred. Thus man and woman should be glad for this sin, through which such an honor has come about. For as low as human nature fell through this creature woman, was human nature lifted higher by this same creature. And as for conversing with the gods, as

this Cato has said, if there had been no woman, he spoke truer than he knew, for he was a pagan, and among those of this belief, gods were thought to reside in Hell as well as in Heaven, that is, the devils whom they called the gods of Hell—so that it is no lie that these gods would have conversed with men, if Mary had not lived."

In this next passage, de Pisan discusses the slander that women are not as intelligent as men.

". . . But please enlighten me again, whether it has ever pleased this God, who has bestowed so many favors on women, to honor the feminine sex with the privilege of the virtue of high understanding and great learning, and whether women ever have a clever enough mind for this. I wish very much to know this because men maintain that the mind of women can learn only a little."

She [Lady Reason] answered, "My daughter, since I told you before, you know quite well that the opposite of their opinion is true, and to show you this even more clearly, I will give you proof through examples. I tell you again—and don't doubt the contrary—if it were customary to send daughters to school like sons, and if they were then taught the natural sciences, they would learn as thoroughly and understand the subtleties of all the arts and sciences

---

Christine de Pisan, *The Book of the City of Ladies*, trans. Earl Jeffrey Richards, pp. 24, 63–64, 153–154. Copyright © 1982 by Persea Books, Inc. Reprinted by permission of Persea Books, Inc., New York. All rights reserved.

[1]Several Roman statesmen bore the name Cato. Cato the Censor (234–149 B.C.) was a vigorous critic of women. —Eds.
[2]This clause refers to the Christian belief that God became a human being in the person of Jesus Christ. —Eds.

as well as sons. And by chance there happen to be such women, for, as I touched on before, just as women have more delicate bodies than men, weaker and less able to perform many tasks, so do they have minds that are freer and sharper whenever they apply themselves."

"My lady, what are you saying? With all due respect, could you dwell longer on this point, please. Certainly men would never admit this answer is true, unless it is explained more plainly, for they believe that one normally sees that men know more than women do."

She answered, "Do you know why women know less?"

"Not unless you tell me, my lady."

"Without the slightest doubt, it is because they are not involved in many different things, but stay at home, where it is enough for them to run the household, and there is nothing which so instructs a reasonable creature as the exercise and experience of many different things."

"My lady, since they have minds skilled in conceptualizing and learning, just like men, why don't women learn more?"

She replied, "Because, my daughter, the public does not require them to get involved in the affairs which men are commissioned to execute, just as I told you before. It is enough for women to perform the usual duties to which they are ordained. As for judging from experience, since one sees that women usually know less than men, that therefore their capacity for understanding is less, look at men who farm the flatlands or who live in the mountains. You will find that in many countries they seem completely savage because they are so simpleminded. All the same, there is no doubt that Nature provided them with the qualities of body and mind found in the wisest and most learned men. . . ."

Next, de Pisan argues in favor of giving young women the same opportunities for learning as men.

Following these remarks, I, Christine, spoke, "My lady, I realize that women have accomplished many good things and that even if evil women have done evil, it seems to me, nevertheless, that the benefits accrued and still accruing because of good women—particularly the wise and literary ones and those educated in the natural sciences whom I mentioned above—outweigh the evil. Therefore, I am amazed by the opinion of some men who claim that they do not want their daughters, wives, or kinswomen to be educated because their mores would be ruined as a result."

She responded, "Here you can clearly see that not all opinions of men are based on reason and that these men are wrong. For it must not be presumed that mores necessarily grow worse from knowing the moral sciences, which teach the virtues, indeed, there is not the slightest doubt that moral education amends and ennobles them. How could anyone think or believe that whoever follows good teaching or doctrine is the worse for it? Such an opinion cannot be expressed or maintained. I do not mean that it would be good for a man or a woman to study the art of divination or those fields of learning which are forbidden—for the holy Church did not remove them from common use without good reason—but it should not be believed that women are the worse for knowing what is good. . . .

". . . To speak of more recent times, without searching for examples in ancient history, Giovanni Andrea, a solemn law professor in Bologna [Italy] not quite sixty years ago, was not of the opinion that it was bad for women to be educated. He had a fair and good daughter, named Novella, who was educated in the law to such an advanced degree that when he was occupied by some task and not at leisure to present his lectures to his students, he would send Novella, his daughter, in his place to lecture to the students from his chair. And to prevent her beauty from distracting the concentration of her audience, she had a little curtain drawn in front of her. In this manner she could on occasion supplement and lighten her father's occupation. . . ."

A Merchant of Paris
ON LOVE AND MARRIAGE

It is difficult to generalize about so intimate a relationship as marriage. It is too intensely individual, and marital love is seldom captured by words that are not either trite or highly poetic in character. But in the late fourteenth century (c. 1393), a merchant of Paris, a man of mature years and experience, tried to put in words for his fifteen-year-old child bride some practical advice as to what a good wife should be and should do for her loving husband. The young lady was of higher social status than her husband, and he clearly expected that she would marry again after his death. His instructions were for her eyes only, but the manuscript survived in at least three copies. Discovered and published in French in 1846, it offers a rare look at the marital values and expectations of a wealthy, pious, and practical businessman living in one of the largest and most cosmopolitan cities of late medieval Europe.

WHEN TWO GOOD AND HONEST PEOPLE ARE MARRIED

I believe that when two good and honest people are married, all other affections, except their love for each other, are withdrawn, annulled, and forgotten. It seems to me that when they are together they look at each other more than they look at others, they come together and embrace each other, and they would rather talk and communicate with each other than with anyone else. When they are separated, they think of each other and say in their hearts: "This is what I will do, this is what I will say, this is what I will ask him when I see him again." All their special pleasures, greatest desires, and perfect joys are in pleasing and obeying each other. But if they don't love one another, they have no more than a routine sense of duty and respect for each other, which is not enough between many couples.

A Medieval Home Companion: Housekeeping in the Fourteenth Century, trans. and ed. Tania Bayard. HarperCollins, 1991. Copyright © Tania Bayard 1991. Reprinted by permission of Tania Bayard.

BE VERY LOVING AND INTIMATE WITH YOUR HUSBAND

You ought to be very loving and intimate with your husband, more than with all other living creatures; moderately loving and intimate with your good and nearest kinsfolk and your husband's kinsfolk; very distant with all other men; and entirely aloof from conceited and idle young men who have more expenses than income, and who, without property or good lineage, go dancing; and also distant from courtiers of very great lords. Moreover, have nothing to do with men and women who are said to lead corrupt, amorous, or dissolute lives.

Concerning what I have said about being very loving to your husband, it is certainly true that every man ought to love and cherish his wife, and every woman should love and cherish her husband: for he is her beginning. I can prove this, for it is found in the second chapter of the first book of the Bible, called Genesis. . . .

Do not think that someone else will hide for you that which you yourself have not been able to conceal. Be secretive and discreet with everyone except your husband. For you should conceal nothing from him, but tell him everything, and he should also tell you everything. . . . You two, man and woman, ought to be as one, and at all times and in all places the one should act on the other's advice. This is how good and wise people act and ought to act. . . .

HOW GOOD WIVES ACT TOWARD THEIR HUSBANDS, AND GOOD HUSBANDS TOWARD THEIR WIVES, WHEN THEY GO ASTRAY

Husbands ought to hide and conceal the follies of their wives and lovingly protect them from future mistakes, as did an honorable man of Venice.

In that city there was a married couple with three children. As the wife lay on her deathbed, she confessed, among other things, that one of the children was not her husband's. The confessor at length told her that he would seek advice about how to counsel her and return. This confessor went to the doctor who was looking after her and asked the nature of her illness. The doctor said that she would not be able to recover from it. Then the confessor went to her and told her that he didn't see how God would give her salvation unless she begged her husband for forgiveness for the wrong she had done him. She summoned her husband; had everyone removed from the room except her mother and her confessor, who placed her, and held her, on her knees on the bed: and before her husband, with folded hands, humbly begged pardon for having sinned in the law of his marriage and having had one of her children with another man. She would have said more, but her husband cried out: "Stop! Stop! Stop! Don't say anything else." Then he kissed her and pardoned her, saying: "Say no more. Don't tell me or anyone else which of your children it is; for I want to love each as much as the other—so equally that you will not be blamed during your lifetime or after your death. For through your blame, I will be dishonored, and because of it, your children, and others through them—that is, our relations—will receive vile and everlasting reproach. Therefore, don't say anything. I don't want to know any more. So that no one can ever

say that I do wrong by the other two, whichever it is, I will give him in my lifetime what would come to him under our laws of succession."

So, dear sister, you see that the wise man bent his heart to save his wife's reputation, which would affect his children. This shows you what wise men and women ought to do for each other to save their honor.

CHERISH YOUR HUSBAND'S PERSON CAREFULLY

Dear sister, if you have another husband after me, be aware that you must take very good care of his person. For generally when a woman has lost her first husband and marriage, it is hard for her, depending on her social status, to find a second who is to her liking, and she remains forsaken and helpless for a long time, and even more so when she loses the second. Therefore, cherish your husband's person carefully.

I entreat you to keep his linen clean, for this is up to you. Because the care of outside affairs is men's work, a husband must look after these things, and go and come, run here and there in rain, wind, snow, and hail—sometimes wet, sometimes dry, sometimes sweating, other times shivering, badly fed, badly housed, badly shod, badly bedded—and nothing harms him because he is cheered by the anticipation of the care his wife will take of him on his return—of the pleasures, joys, and comforts she will provide, or have provided for him in her presence: to have his shoes off before a good fire, to have his feet washed, to have clean shoes and hose, to be well fed, provided with good drink, well served, well honored, well bedded in white sheets and white nightcaps, well covered with good furs, and comforted with other joys and amusements, intimacies, affections, and secrets about which I am silent. And on the next day fresh linen and garments.

Indeed, dear sister, these favors cause a man to love and desire the return home and the sight of his good wife, and to be reserved with others. And so I advise you to comfort your second husband on all his homecomings, and persevere in this.

Also keep peace with him. Remember the country proverb that says there are three things that drive a good man from his home: a house with a bad roof, a smoking chimney, and a quarrelsome woman. Dear sister, I beg you, in order to preserve your husband's love and good will, be loving, amiable, and sweet with him. . . . By my soul! I believe doing good is the only enchantment, and one can no better bewitch a man than by giving him what pleases him.

Therefore, dear sister, I pray you to bewitch and bewitch again the husband whom you will have, preserve him from a badly covered house and a smoky chimney, and be not quarrelsome with him, but be sweet, amiable, and peaceful. Mind that in winter he has a good fire without smoke, and that he is well couched and covered between your breasts, and there bewitch him.

REVIEW QUESTIONS

1. How does Jacopone da Todi's poem present a positive image of women through its depiction of Mary?
2. Evaluate the arguments used by Christine de Pisan in her defense of women.
3. What is the merchant's attitude toward women in general and marriage in particular?
4. Which of the merchant's instructions to his wife do you consider most valuable in a good marriage?

10 Sexual Nonconformity: Satan's Lures

The clergy sought to impose uniform sexual standards throughout Christendom. They regarded sexual practices that were not intended for procreation, including homosexuality and masturbation, as violations of natural law and God's will and as Satan's temptations that lead to eternal damnation.

Robert of Flamborough
PROHIBITION OF SEXUAL SINS

The Fourth Lateran Council (1215) decreed that it was necessary for a Christian to go to confession at least once a year. Not doing so could be interpreted as a sign of heresy, which the church might investigate. This requirement gave the clergy tremendous control over the moral outlook of Christians throughout Europe. The following "interview" was a creation of Robert of Flamborough, an English schoolman or scholar who heard confessions of clerics studying at the University of Paris in the early thirteenth century; it was designed as a model to be used by confessors. Although not an actual interview, it does reveal the sexual standards the clergy aspired to uphold and the sexual behavior they sought to suppress.

Other Middle Ages: Witnesses at the Margin of Medieval Society, ed. Michael Goodich (Philadelphia: University of Pennsylvania Press, 1998), pp. 112–115.

Have you been lustful? The following things pertain to lust: extravagance, shamelessness, licentiousness, impudence, hesitation, flattery, allurements, voluptuousness, dissoluteness, feebleness, scurrility, and coitus. Extravagance is clear; likewise shamelessness. Hesitation is when a man acts without confidence. Flattery is when a man flatters others and accepts flattery from others. Allurements are clear. Voluptuousnes is when a man follows his longings, his desires. Dissoluteness may be found in gestures, words, deeds and attire. Feebleness is clear. Scurrility is when a man acts like a clown. Concerning all these things, do you ask pardon, etc.?

PRIEST: Those things which you otherwise do, do with confidence . . . and patiently . . . and firmly . . . and with perseverance . . . and with a relaxed mind. . . .

There remains coitus (intercourse), which is lust in the strict sense of the word. Have you ever been polluted with lust?

PENITENT: Many times.
PRIEST: Ever against nature?
PENITENT: Many times.
PRIEST: Ever with a man?
PENITENT: Many times.
PRIEST: With clerics or laymen?
PENITENT: With both clerics and laymen.
PRIEST: Married or single laymen?
PENITENT: Both.
PRIEST: With how many married persons?
PENITENT: I don't know.
PRIEST: You therefore don't know how often?
PENITENT: Correct.
PRIEST: Let's try to find out what we can. How long were you with those persons?
PENITENT: For seven years.
PRIEST: In what (priestly) order?
PENITENT: In the priesthood for two years, in the diaconate for two years, in the sub-diaconate for two years, and as an acolyte for a year. I sinned with single persons, but I don't know how many or how often.
PRIEST: Did you sin with clerics?
PENITENT: I sinned with both secular clergy and religious (monastic clergy).

PRIEST: Tell me with how many secular and how many religious clergy, in which order you and they were in when you sinned together, and whether they possessed the office of archdeacon, dean, abbot, or bishop. Did you ever introduce some innocent person to that sin? Tell me how many and what order you were then in.

He may afterward be asked whether he ever sinned any more against nature, if he had anyone "in an extraordinary way." If he should ask in what "extraordinary way," I won't answer him; he'll see for himself. I never mention anything to him from which he might derive some reason to sin, but only speak in a general way about things which everyone knows are sins. I painfully wrench a confession of masturbation out of him and likewise from a woman, but the method of getting this out should not be written down. Just as I asked a man whether he has done anything against nature, so I ask a woman, and in fact about every kind of fornication. Second, I inquire about adultery, then about every kind of fornication; afterward I ask about incest in this way:

Did you approach your female cousins? Say how often and how they were related to you. Afterward I inquire as above. Did you approach two females related to you by blood? Say how many times and how they are related, and afterward as above. You had how many (such female relatives) after your male relatives (had them)? Say how they [the males] are related to you, and afterward as above.

Did you approach a nun or another *conversa?*[1] Say to which order they belonged, and afterward as above.

Did you ever deflower a virgin? Did you approach your godmother (*commater*)? Your aunt? Your daughter? Your father's daughter? Your godfather's daughter? A woman during menstruation? An infidel, Jew, Gentile, heretic? Say how many times and how much. A woman in childbirth? A woman who has not been purified?[2] You should inquire about all of this as above.

---

[1] A woman who has taken a vow. —Eds.
[2] Forty days after childbirth. —Eds.

Did you approach a pregnant woman? I ask this because many little children are weakened in this way, crippled and oppressed. If someone is oppressed by your having sexual relations you should in my opinion never serve as a minister in any order or be promoted without papal dispensation. During menstruation or childbirth many lepers, epileptics, and children with evil characteristics are conceived.

Have you committed fornication in a holy place or on a holy day? Ask where and how often this has happened, in what order, with whom and what kind of fornication it was. If you have fornicated in a holy place like a church which has been consecrated or a cemetery, the place itself is reconciled by a simple priest in a private capacity, or solemnly by a bishop. It is reconciled by a simple priest in a private capacity if the crime is hidden, and solemnly by a bishop if the crime becomes known. For this purpose a special office and special masses are held. The simple priest

ought to walk around the place and sprinkle water which has been blessed in a dedicated church, singing seven Psalms and a litany. It is reconciled as for homicide, for whatever kind of fornication, if blood was shed there during a quarrel, [but] as if for theft according to some.

Did you approach prostitutes? You should be afraid lest she be your cousin or related by marriage, or vowed to enter religion, or because one of your relatives had had her, or for some other reason.

Did you procure her not for yourself? Say how often. . . . From the aforesaid inquiries you should know well enough what is to be investigated. Have you ever solicited another person through someone else? Inquire as above.

Were you ever "infamous" due to fornication? Something was said above concerning infamy. Did you ever fail to confess and approach the altar without contrition after fornication or in hatred or with a desire to sin? . . .

Peter Damian
CONDEMNATION OF HOMOSEXUALITY

In the following selection, Peter Damian (1007–1072), a prominent cleric, denounces homosexuality and holds that clergy who engage in this behavior are unable to carry out their spiritual duties and should be dismissed from their positions.

XVI

A Deserving Condemnation of Abominable Shamefulness

Truly, this vice is never to be compared with any other vice because it surpasses the enormity of all vices. Indeed, this vice is the death of bodies, the destruction of souls. It pollutes the flesh, it

Peter Damian, *Book of Gomorrah: An Eleventh-Century Treatise Against Clerical Homosexual Practices*, trans. Pierre J. Payer, pp. 63–65, 72–73. Copyright © 1982 by Wilfrid Laurier University Press. Reprinted with permission.

extinguishes the light of the mind. It evicts the Holy Spirit from the temple of the human heart; it introduces the devil who incites to lust. It casts into error; it completely removes the truth from the mind that has been deceived. It prepares snares for those entering; it shuts up those who fall into the pit so they cannot get out. It opens hell; it closes the door of heaven. It makes a citizen of the heavenly Jerusalem into an heir of infernal Babylon. It makes of the star of heaven the stubble of eternal fire; it cuts off a member of the Church and casts it into the consuming fire of boiling Gehenna [Hell]. This vice tries to overturn the walls of the heavenly homeland and is busy repairing the renewed bulwarks of Sodom. For it is this which violates sobriety, kills modesty, strangles chastity, and butchers irreparable virginity with the dagger of unclean contagion. It defiles everything, stains everything, pollutes everything. And as for itself, it permits nothing pure, nothing clean, nothing other than filth....

This vice casts men from the choir of the ecclesiastical community and compels them to pray with the possessed and with those who work for the devil. It separates the soul from God to join it with devils. This most pestilential queen of the sodomists makes the followers of her tyrannical laws filthy to men and hateful to God. She commands to join in evil wars against God.... She humiliates in church, condemns in law, defiles in secret, shames in public, gnaws the conscience as though with worms, sears the flesh as though with fire.... A person who himself participates in a sinful act ought not to be a judge of the crime in confession as long as he hesitates in any way to confess that he has sinned himself by joining in the sin of another.... The miserable flesh burns with the heat of lust.... In fact, after this most poisonous serpent once sinks its fangs into the unhappy soul, sense is snatched away, memory is borne off, the sharpness of the mind is obscured. It becomes unmindful of God and even forgetful of itself. This plague undermines the foundation of faith, weakens the strength of hope, destroys the bond of charity; it takes away justice, subverts fortitude, banishes temperance, blunts the keenness of prudence.

And what more should I say since it expels the whole host of the virtues from the chamber of the human heart and introduces every barbarous vice as if the bolts of the doors were pulled out....

Indeed, whomever this most atrocious beast once seizes upon with bloodthirsty jaws, it restrains with its bonds from every form of good work and immediately unleashes him down the steep descent of the most evil depravity. In fact, when one has fallen into this abyss of extreme ruin he becomes an exile from the heavenly homeland, separated from the body of Christ, confounded by the authority of the whole Church, condemned by the judgment of all the holy fathers. He is despised among men on earth and rejected from the community of heavenly citizens.... Burdened with the weight of the crime, he cannot arise nor conceal his evil for long in the hiding-place of ignorance. He cannot rejoice here while he lives nor can he hope there when he dies, since he is compelled to bear the disgrace of human derision now and afterwards the torment of eternal damnation.

XIX

The Service of an Unworthy Priest Is the Ruin of the People

O guilty, carnal men, why do you desire the height of ecclesiastical dignity with so much burning ambition? Why is it that you try with such desire to ensnare the people of God in the bonds of your own ruin? Is it not enough for you to throw yourselves down the steep cliffs of outrageous crime without having to involve others in the peril of your own ruin? ...

Or how can anyone who does not know whether he himself is pleasing to God ask God for forgiveness for others? ...

Therefore, the person who is still bound by earthly desires should beware lest, by more gravely igniting the anger of the strict Judge, he become the author of the ruin of his subordinates while he takes pleasure in his exalted position. So, if culpable vice still rules over him, a person should prudently take stock of himself before he dares to assume the position of the sacerdotal office, lest one who is perverted by his own crime should desire to become the intercessor for the faults of others. Be careful, be careful, and be afraid of igniting inextinguishably God's fury towards you; fear lest you provoke more sharply by your very prayers the one you offend openly by acting evilly. Intent on your own ruin, beware of becoming responsible for the ruin of another.

REVIEW QUESTION

What do these documents tell you about medieval sexual standards and practices?

11 Medieval Contributions to the Tradition of Liberty

In several ways the Middle Ages contributed to the development of liberty in the Western world. Townsmen organized themselves into revolutionary associations called communes to demand freedom from the domination of feudal lords. They successfully won personal liberties, the end of feudal labor services and arbitrary tax levies, and a system of municipal self-government. Another development crucial to the tradition of liberty was the resistance of lords to kings who attempted to interfere with the lords' customary rights. These actions helped to establish the tradition that kings were not above the law and could not rule arbitrarily or absolutely. There is a direct link between modern parliaments and medieval representative institutions, particularly in the case of the English Parliament.

By justifying resistance to tyrannical authority, medieval theologians made a significant contribution to the growth of liberty. They held that a monarch's powers were limited by God's laws and by what was for the common good of Christian people. Some argued that a monarch who ignored or violated the laws and liberties of the people or the church became a tyrant and forfeited his right to be ruler. Such rulers could be, and some in fact were, deposed.

John of Salisbury
POLICRATICUS
A DEFENSE OF TYRANNICIDE

One prelate who opposed the rule of tyrants was an Englishman, John of Salisbury (c. 1115–1180), who became bishop of Chartres, France, in 1176. He composed a statesman's handbook, *Policraticus*, explicitly defending the assassination of tyrants. Paraphrasing the Roman statesman Cicero, John held that it was right, lawful, and just to slay a tyrant.

. . . A tyrant, then, as the philosophers have described him, is one who oppresses the people by the rulership based upon force, while he who rules in accordance with the laws is a prince. Law is the gift of God, the model of equity, a standard of justice, a likeness of the divine will, the guardian of well-being, a bond of union and solidarity between peoples, a rule defining duties, a barrier against the vices and the

destroyer thereof, a punishment of violence and all wrong-doing. The law is assailed by force or by fraud, and, as it were, either wrecked by the fury of the lion or undermined by the wiles of the serpent. In whatever way this comes to pass, it is plain that it is the grace of God which is being assailed and that it is God himself who in a sense is challenged to battle. The prince fights for the laws and the liberty of the people; the tyrant thinks nothing done unless he brings the laws to nought and reduces the people to slavery. Hence the prince is a kind of likeness of divinity; and the tyrant, on the contrary,

The Statesman's Book of John Salisbury, trans. John Dickenson (1955; New York: Russell and Russell, 1963), pp. 335–336. Copyright © 1963 by Russell & Russell.

a likeness of the boldness of the Adversary [the devil], even of the wickedness of Lucifer. . . . The prince, as the likeness of the Deity, is to be loved, worshipped and cherished; the tyrant, the likeness of wickedness, is generally to be even killed. The origin of tyranny is iniquity, and springing from a poisonous root, it is a tree which grows and sprouts into a baleful pestilent growth, and to which the axe must by all means be laid.

THE MAGNA CARTA

Feudal nobles sought to limit the arbitrary powers of kings by compelling them to issue written charters of liberties. These earliest constitutions spelled out the rights of subjects and the obligations of rulers. In 1215 King John of England (ruled 1199–1216) was compelled to recognize the liberties of his vassals, the clergy, and the towns in the Magna Carta (Great Charter). The king and his agents were forbidden to act arbitrarily, and the king swore to govern by due process of law. Similar written constitutions checking the powers of kings and princes were achieved in other parts of Europe.

The Magna Carta asserted the feudal rights of the subjects of a monarch who allegedly tried to rule by personal will rather than by law. Though many of its detailed clauses subsequently lost their significance, three notions embedded in the Magna Carta became rooted in English constitutional tradition: that the king cannot levy a tax without the consent of his feudal council (later Parliament); that no one may be imprisoned or otherwise damaged except through due process of law and trial by jury of his (or her) peers; and that the king himself is subject to the law, and if he violates the rights of his subjects, he may be legally disobeyed and deposed. Significant portions of the document follow.

1. In the first place [I, John] have granted to God and by this our present Charter have confirmed, for us and our heirs in perpetuity, that the English church shall be free, and shall have its rights undiminished and its liberties unimpaired. . . . We have also granted to all the free men of our realm for ourselves and our heirs for ever, all the liberties written below, to have and hold, them and their heirs from us and our heirs. . . .

12. No scutage[1] or aid[2] is to be levied in our realm except by the common counsel of our realm, unless it is for the ransom of our person, the knighting of our eldest son or the first marriage of our eldest daughter; and for these only a reasonable aid is to be levied. Aids from the city of London are to be treated likewise.

13. And the city of London is to have all its ancient liberties and free customs both by land and water. Furthermore, we will and grant that all other cities, boroughs, towns and ports shall have all their liberties and free customs.

14. And to obtain the common counsel of the realm for the assessment of an aid (except

J. C. Holt, ed., *Magna Carta*, pp. 317, 321–323, 327–329, 333–335. Copyright © 1976. Reprinted by permission of Cambridge University Press.

[1]Scutage was a tax paid by knights to the king of England, their feudal overlord, in place of performing actual military service. In the absence of danger of war, the levying of scutage was considered an abuse of the king's authority. —Eds.
[2]Aid, in this sense, was any obligation, usually financial, due from a vassal to his lord. The word was later used to indicate a tax on income or property paid by his subjects to the English king. —Eds.

in the three cases aforesaid) or a scutage, we will have archbishops, bishops, abbots, earls and greater barons[3] summoned individually by our letters; and we shall also have summoned generally through our sheriffs and bailiffs[4] all those who hold of us in chief [hold a fief from the king], with at least forty days' notice, and at a fixed place; and in all letters of summons we will state the reason for the summons. And when the summons has thus been made, the business shall go forward on the day arranged according to the counsel of those present, even if not all those summoned have come. . . .

20. A free man shall not be amerced [fined] for a trivial offence, except in accordance with the degree of the offence; and for a serious offence he shall be amerced according to its gravity, saving his livelihood; and a merchant likewise, saving his merchandise; in the same way a villein [serf] shall be amerced saving his wainage;[5] if they fall into our mercy. And none of the aforesaid amercements shall be imposed except by the testimony of reputable men of the neighbourhood.

---

[3]Barons were vassals holding fiefs directly from the king; earls ("counts" in other lands) were nobles who managed counties or shires. —Eds.

[4]The sheriff was a royal official responsible for the carrying out of laws in a shire or county; bailiffs were his assistants. —Eds.

[5]*Wainage* (or *gainage*) is a collective term meaning farming tools and implements, including such things as wagons (wains). —Eds.

21. Earls and barons shall not be amerced except by their peers and only in accordance with the nature of the offence. . . .

38. Henceforth no bailiff shall put anyone on trial by his own unsupported allegation, without bringing credible witnesses to the charge.

39. No free man shall be taken or imprisoned or disseised [dispossessed] or outlawed or exiled or in any way ruined, nor will we go or send against him, except by the lawful judgement of his peers or by the law of the land.

40. To no one will we sell, to no one will we deny or delay right or justice.

41. All merchants are to be safe and secure in leaving and entering England, and in staying and travelling in England, both by land and by water, to buy and sell free from all maletotes [unjust taxes] by the ancient and rightful customs, except, in time of war, such as come from an enemy country. And if such are found in our land at the outbreak of war they shall be detained without damage to their persons or goods, until we or our chief justiciar [legal official] know how the merchants of our land are treated in the enemy country; and if ours are safe there, the others shall be safe in our land.

42. Henceforth anyone, saving his allegiance due to us, may leave our realm and return safe and secure by land and water, save for a short period in time of war on account of the general interest of the realm and excepting those imprisoned and outlawed according to the law of the land, and natives of an enemy country, and merchants, who shall be treated as aforesaid. . . .

REVIEW QUESTIONS

1. How does John of Salisbury distinguish a legitimate king from a tyrant?
2. In the selected passages of the Magna Carta, what specific liberties were guaranteed by the king to his subjects?
3. Why is the Magna Carta considered a landmark in English history?

12 The Fourteenth Century: An Age of Adversity

During the Late Middle Ages, roughly the fourteenth and early fifteenth centuries, medieval civilization was in decline. The fourteenth century, an age of adversity, was marked by crop failures, famine, population decline, plagues, stagnating production, unemployment, inflation, devastating warfare, and abandoned villages. Violent rebellions by the poor of the towns and countryside were ruthlessly suppressed by the upper classes. The century witnessed flights into mysticism, outbreaks of mass hysteria, and massacres of Jews; it was an age of pessimism and general insecurity. The papacy declined in power, heresy proliferated, and the synthesis of faith and reason, erected by Christian thinkers during the High Middle Ages, began to disintegrate. These developments were signs that the stable and coherent civilization of the thirteenth century was drawing to a close.

Jean de Venette
THE BLACK DEATH

Until the fourteenth century, the population of Europe had increased steadily from its low point in the centuries immediately following the fall of the western Roman Empire. Particularly from the eleventh century on, landlords tried to raise their income by bringing new land into cultivation. By improving farming technology, building dikes, draining marshland, and clearing forests, European peasants produced much more food, which permitted more people to survive and multiply. That advance in population tapered off by the early fourteenth century due to many crop failures and wars, which wasted the countryside and led to economic stagnation. But the greatest catastrophe began in the fall of 1347, when sailors returning to Sicily from eastern Mediterranean ports brought with them a new disease, bubonic plague. Within the next three years, from one-quarter to one-third of the population of Europe died from what became known, because of some of its symptoms, as the Black Death. Most who caught the plague died, though some survived. No one knew its cause or cure. We now know that the bacteria were transmitted by fleas from infected rats. The unsanitary living conditions of medieval towns and low standards of personal cleanliness helped to spread the disease. The people were so terrified by the incomprehensible pattern of the disease's progress that superstition, hysteria, and breakdown of civility were common.

The progress of the plague as it made its way through Europe and speculation on its causes, the terrible toll of victims, and various moral responses to the crisis are described in the following reading from the chronicle of Jean de Venette (c. 1308–c. 1368), a French friar who lived through the events described.

In A.D. 1348, the people of France and of almost the whole world were struck by a blow other than war. For in addition to the famine which I described in the beginning and to the wars which I described in the course of this narrative, pestilence and its attendant tribulations appeared again in various parts of the world. . . . All this year and the next, the mortality of men and women, of the young even more than of the old, in Paris and in the kingdom of France, and also, it is said, in other parts of the world, was so great that it was almost impossible to bury the dead. People lay ill little more than two or three days and died suddenly, as it were in full health. He who was well one day was dead the next and being carried to his grave. Swellings appeared suddenly in the armpit or in the groin—in many cases both—and they were infallible signs of death. This sickness or pestilence was called an epidemic by the doctors. Nothing like the great numbers who died in the years 1348 and 1349 has been heard of or seen or read of in times past. This plague and disease came from *ymaginatione* or association and contagion, for if a well man visited the sick he only rarely evaded the risk of death. Wherefore in many towns timid priests withdrew, leaving the exercise of their ministry to such of the religious as were more daring. In many places not two out of twenty remained alive. So high was the mortality at the Hôtel-Dieu [an early hospital] in Paris that for a long time, more than five hundred dead were carried daily with great devotion in carts to the cemetery of the Holy Innocents in Paris for burial. A very great number of the saintly sisters of the Hôtel-Dieu who, not fearing to die, nursed the sick in all sweetness and humility, with no thought of honor, a number too often renewed by death, rest in peace with Christ, as we may piously believe.

This plague, it is said, began among the unbelievers [Muslims], came to Italy, and then crossing the Alps reached Avignon [site of the papacy in that period], where it attacked several cardinals and took from them their whole

household. Then it spread, unforeseen, to France, through Gascony [now part of the south of France] and Spain, little by little, from town to town, from village to village, from house to house, and finally from person to person. It even crossed over to Germany, though it was not so bad there as with us. During the epidemic, God of His accustomed goodness deigned to grant this grace, that however suddenly men died, almost all awaited death joyfully. Nor was there anyone who died without confessing his sins and receiving the holy viaticum [the Eucharistic bread given to the sick or dying]. . . .

Some said that this pestilence was caused by infection of the air and waters, since there was at this time no famine nor lack of food supplies, but on the contrary great abundance. As a result of this theory of infected water and air as the source of the plague the Jews were suddenly and violently charged with infecting wells and water and corrupting the air. The whole world rose up against them cruelly on this account. In Germany and other parts of the world where Jews lived, they were massacred and slaughtered by Christians, and many thousands were burned everywhere, indiscriminately. The unshaken, if fatuous, constancy of the [Jewish] men and their wives was remarkable. For mothers hurled their children first into the fire that they might not be baptized and then leaped in after them to burn with their husbands and children. It is said that many bad Christians were found who in a like manner put poison into wells. But in truth, such poisonings, granted that they actually were perpetrated, could not have caused so great a plague nor have infected so many people. There were other causes; for example, the will of God and the corrupt humors and evil inherent in air and earth. Perhaps the poisonings, if they actually took place in some localities, reenforced these causes. The plague lasted in France for the greater part of the years 1348 and 1349 and then ceased. Many country villages and many houses in good towns remained empty and deserted. Many houses, including some splendid dwellings, very soon fell into ruins. Even in Paris several houses were thus ruined, though fewer here than elsewhere.

R. A. Newhall, ed., *The Chronicle of Jean de Venette*, trans. Jean Birdsall (New York: Columbia University Press, 1953), pp. 48–52, 128–129. © 1953 Columbia University Press. Used with permission.

After the cessation of the epidemic, pestilence, or plague, the men and women who survived married each other. There was no sterility among the women, but on the contrary fertility beyond the ordinary. Pregnant women were seen on every side. . . . But woe is me! the world was not changed for the better but for the worse by this renewal of population. For men were more avaricious and grasping than before, even though they had far greater possessions. They were more covetous and disturbed each other more frequently with suits, brawls, disputes, and pleas. Nor by the mortality resulting from this terrible plague inflicted by God was peace between kings and lords established. On the contrary, the enemies of the king of France and of the Church were stronger and wickeder than before and stirred up wars on sea and on land. Greater evils than before [swarmed] everywhere in the world. And this fact was very remarkable. Although there was an abundance of all goods, yet everything was twice as dear, whether it were utensils, victuals, or merchandise, hired helpers or peasants and serfs, except for some hereditary domains which remained abundantly stocked with everything. Charity began to cool, and iniquity with ignorance and sin to abound, for few could be found in the good towns and castles who knew how or were willing to instruct children in the rudiments of grammar.

Jean de Venette vividly describes one of the more bizarre reactions to the terrible plague, the sudden appearance of the Flagellants. Marching like pilgrims across the countryside, the Flagellants were a group of laymen and laywomen who sought divine pardon for their sins by preaching repentance to others and scourging themselves in a quasi-liturgical ceremony in local churches or marketplaces. The movement foreshadowed events in which moral, social, and economic discontent would increasingly manifest itself in the form of religiously justified popular uprisings against civil and clerical authorities.

In the year 1349, while the plague was still active and spreading from town to town, men in Germany, Flanders, Hainaut [east of Flanders], and Lorraine uprose and began a new sect on their own authority. Stripped to the waist, they gathered in large groups and bands and marched in procession through the crossroads and squares of cities and good towns. There they formed circles and beat upon their backs with weighted scourges, rejoicing as they did so in loud voices and singing hymns suitable to their rite and newly composed for it. Thus for thirty-three days they marched through many towns doing their penance and affording a great spectacle to the wondering people. They flogged their shoulders and arms with scourges tipped with iron points so zealously as to draw blood. But they did not come to Paris nor to any part of France, for they were forbidden to do so by the king of France, who did not want them. He acted on the advice of the masters of theology of the University of Paris, who said that this new sect had been formed contrary to the will of God, to the rites of Holy Mother Church, and to the salvation of all their souls. That indeed this was and is true appeared shortly. For Pope Clement VI was fully informed concerning this fatuous new rite by the masters of Paris through emissaries reverently sent to him and, on the grounds that it had been damnably formed, contrary to law, he forbade the Flagellants under threat of anathema [excommunication] to practise in the future the public penance which they had so presumptuously undertaken. His prohibition was just, for the Flagellants, supported by certain fatuous priests and monks, were enunciating doctrines and opinions which were beyond measure evil, erroneous, and fallacious. For example, they said that their blood thus drawn by the scourge and poured out was mingled with the blood of Christ. Their many errors showed how little they knew of the Catholic faith. Wherefore, as they had begun fatuously of themselves and not of God, so in a short time they were reduced to nothing. On being warned, they desisted and humbly received absolution and penance at the hands of their prelates as the pope's representatives. Many honorable women and devout matrons, it must be added, had done this penance with scourges, marching and singing through towns and churches like the men, but after a little like the others they desisted.

Sir John Froissart
THE PEASANT REVOLT OF 1381

In 1381, a rebellion of peasants and poor artisans in England threatened the political power of the ruling class. The rebellion, which was crushed and whose leaders were betrayed and executed, revealed the massive discontent of the lower classes and the specter of social upheaval that hovered over late medieval society. The following account of the rebellion is by Sir John Froissart (c. 1337–c. 1410), a French historian and poet who chronicled the Hundred Years' War between France and England, which wreaked havoc in the countries concerned.

While these conferences [of English nobles] were going forward there happened great commotions among the lower orders in England, by which that country was nearly ruined. In order that this disastrous rebellion may serve as an example to mankind, I will speak of all that was done from the information I had at the time. It is customary in England, as well as in several other countries, for the nobility to have great privileges over the commonality; that is to say, the lower orders are bound by law to plough the lands of the gentry, to harvest their grain, to carry it home to the barn, to thrash and winnow it; they are also bound to harvest and carry home the hay. All these services the prelates and gentlemen exact of their inferiors; and in the counties of Kent, Essex, Sussex, and Bedford, these services are more oppressive than in other parts of the kingdom. In consequence of this the evil[ly] disposed in these districts began to murmur, saying, that in the beginning of the world there were no slaves, and that no one ought to be treated as such, unless he had committed treason against his lord, as Lucifer had done against God; but they had done no such thing, for they were neither angels nor spirits, but men formed after the same likeness as these lords who treated them as beasts. This they would bear no longer; they were determined to be free, and if they laboured or did any work, they would be paid for it.

A crazy priest in the county of Kent, called John Ball, who for his absurd preaching had thrice been confined in prison by the Archbishop of Canterbury, was greatly instrumental in exciting these rebellious ideas. Every Sunday after mass, as the people were coming out of church, this John Ball was accustomed to assemble a crowd around him in the marketplace and preach to them. On such occasions he would say, "My good friends, matters cannot go on well in England until all things shall be in common; when there shall be neither vassals nor lords; when the lords shall be no more masters than ourselves. How ill they behave to us! for what reason do they thus hold us in bondage? Are we not all descended from the same parents, Adam and Eve? And what can they show, or what reason can they give, why they should be more masters than ourselves? They are clothed in velvet and rich stuffs, ornamented with ermine and other furs, while we are forced to wear poor clothing. They have wines, spices, and fine bread, while we have only rye and the refuse of the straw; and when we drink, it must be water. They have handsome seats and manors, while we must brave the wind and rain in our labours in the field; and it is by our labour they have wherewith to support their pomp. We are called slaves, and if we do not perform our service we are beaten, and we have no sovereign to whom we can complain or who would be willing to hear us. Let us go to the king and remonstrate with him; he is young, and from

John Froissart, *The Chronicles of England, France and Spain*, trans. Thomas Johnes (London: J. M. Dent & Sons, 1906), pp. 207–208, 210-211, 214.

him we may obtain a favourable answer, and if not we must ourselves seek to amend our condition." With such language as this did John Ball harangue the people of his village every Sunday after mass. The archbishop, on being informed of it, had him arrested and imprisoned for two or three months by way of punishment; but the moment he was out of prison, he returned to his former course. Many in the city of London envious of the rich and noble, having heard of John Ball's preaching, said among themselves that the country was badly governed, and that the nobility had seized upon all the gold and silver. These wicked Londoners, therefore, began to assemble in parties, and to show signs of rebellion; they also invited all those who held like opinions in the adjoining counties to come to London; telling them that they would find the town open to them and the commonalty of the same way of thinking as themselves, and that they would so press the king, that there should no longer be a slave in England.

By this means the men of Kent, Essex, Sussex, Bedford, and the adjoining counties, in number about 60,000, were brought to London, under command of Wat Tyler, Jack Straw, and John Ball. This Wat Tyler, who was chief of the three, had been a tiler of houses—a bad man and a great enemy to the nobility. . . .

With regard to the common people of London, numbers entertained these rebellious opinions, and on assembling at the bridge asked of the guards, "Why will you refuse admittance to these honest men? they are our friends, and what they are doing is for our good." So urgent were they, that it was found necessary to open the gates, when crowds rushed in and took possession of those shops which seemed best stocked with provisions; indeed, wherever they went, meat and drink were placed before them, and nothing was refused in the hope of appeasing them. Their leaders, John Ball, Jack Straw, and Wat Tyler, then marched through London, attended by more than 20,000 men, to the palace of the Savoy, which is a handsome building belonging to the Duke of Lancaster

[the king's uncle], situated on the banks of the Thames on the road to Westminster: here they immediately killed the porters, pushed into the house, and set it on fire. Not content with this outrage, they went to the house of the Knight-hospitalers of Rhodes, dedicated to St. John of Mount Carmel, which they burnt together with their church and hospital.

After this they paraded the streets, and killed every Fleming [citizen of Flanders] they could find, whether in house, church, or hospital: they broke open several houses of the Lombards [Italian bankers], taking whatever money they could lay their hands upon. They murdered a rich citizen, by name Richard Lyon, to whom Wat Tyler had formerly been servant in France, but having once beaten him, the [scoundrel] had never forgotten it; and when he had carried his men to his house, he ordered his head to be cut off, placed upon a pike, and carried through the streets of London. Thus did these wicked people act, and on this Thursday they did much damage to the city of London. Towards evening they fixed their quarters in a square, called St. Catherine's, before the Tower, declaring that they would not depart until they had obtained from the king every thing they wanted—until the Chancellor [chief financial officer] of England had accounted to them, and shown how the great sums which were raised had been expended. Considering the mischief which the mob had already done, you may easily imagine how miserable, at this time, was the situation of the king and those who were with him. . . .

. . . Now observe how fortunately matters turned out, for had these scoundrels succeeded in their intentions, all the nobility of England would have been destroyed; and after such success as this the people of other nations would have rebelled also, taking example from those of Ghent and Flanders, who at the time were in actual rebellion against their lord; the Parisians indeed the same year acted in a somewhat similar manner; upwards of 20,000 of them armed themselves with leaden maces and caused a rebellion. . . .

John Bromyard
VIRULENT DENUCIATION
OF THE RICH AND POWERFUL

In his sermons, John Bromyard, a fourteenth-century English Dominican preacher, frequently castigated greedy, corrupt, and idle clergy. His most virulent criticisms were often directed against the wealthy and powerful nobility. While he was not advocating revolution, his sermons did highlight the misery and resentment of the poor. Frequently his sermons stressed Judgment Day, when, before God, the oppressed would indict their oppressors, causing nobles to "blush in deepest shame." Following is an excerpt from one of Bromyard's sermons.

And with boldness will they be able to put their plaint before God and seek justice, speaking with Christ the judge, and reciting each in turn the injury from which they specially suffered. Some of them are able to say, as the subjects of evil lords—"We have hungered. But those our lords standing over there were the cause of this, because they took from us our labours and our goods." Others—"We have hungered and died of famine, and those yonder did detain our goods that were owing to us." Others—"We have thirsted and been naked, because those standing opposite, each in his own way, so impoverished us that we were unable to buy drink and clothing." Others—"We were made infirm. Those yonder did it, who beat us and afflicted us with blows." Others—"We were without shelter. But those men were the cause of it, by driving us from our home and from our land; . . . or because they did not receive us into their own guest-houses." Others—"We were in prison. But those yonder were the cause, indicting us on false charges, and setting us in the stocks." Others—"Our bodies have not been buried in consecrated ground. Those yonder are

responsible for this, by slaying us in numerous ways and in various places. Avenge, O Lord, our blood that has been shed!". . . Our labours and goods. . . they took away, to satiate their greed. They afflicted us with hunger and labours, that they might live delicately upon our labours and our goods. We have laboured and lived so hard a life that scarce for half the year had we a good sufficiency, scarce nothing save bread and bran and water. Nay rather, what is worse, we died of hunger. And they were served with three or four courses out of our goods, which they took from us, that is to say, after their manner and denied to us in our necessity. We hungered and thirsted and were afflicted with cold and nakedness. And those robbers yonder gave not our own goods to us when we were in want, neither did they feed or clothe us out of them. But their hounds and horses and apes, the rich, the powerful, the abounding, the gluttons, the drunkards and their prostitutes they fed and clothed with them, and allowed us to languish in want. . . .

O just God, mighty judge, the game was not fairly divided between them and us. Their satiety was our famine; their merriment was our wretchedness; their jousts and tournaments were our torments, because with our oats and at our expense they did these things. Their plenty was our scarcity. Their feasts, delectations, pomps, vanities, excesses and superfluities were our

G. R. Owst, *Literature and Pulpit in Medieval England: A Neglected Chapter in the History of English Letters & of the English People* (2nd. rev. ed.; New York: Barnes and Noble, 1961), pp. 300–301.

fastings, penalties, wants, calamities and spo-
liation. The love-ditties and laughter of their
dances were our mockery, our groanings and

remonstrations. They used to sing—'Well
enough! Well enough!'—and we groaned,
saying—'Woe to us! Woe to us!'"

REVIEW QUESTIONS

1. In the absence of any scientific knowledge about the nature and causes of the
   bubonic plague, how did the populace react to the mysterious spread of the disease?
2. In the chronicler's opinion, what were some of the long-term moral, social, and
   economic consequences of the plague?
3. What specific grievances motivated uprisings in England in the late fourteenth
   century?
4. What political principles were invoked by the leaders of the rebellion of 1381 to
   justify their demands and actions?
5. List the several reasons John Bromyard gives for indicting the wealthy and powerful.

13 The Medieval Church in Crisis

A threat to papal power and to the medieval ideal of a universal Christian
community guided by the church came from radical reformers, who questioned
the function and authority of the entire church hierarchy. These heretics in the
Late Middle Ages were forerunners of the Protestant Reformation in the sixteenth
century. Also questioning church authority were political theorists who argued
that the church was a purely spiritual institution and should refrain from trying
to wield temporal power.

Marsilius of Padua
ATTACK ON THE WORLDLY POWER OF THE CHURCH

The fourteenth century brought a new crisis in church–state relations. King Philip
the Fair (ruled 1285–1314) tried to raise revenues for the French government
by taxing the property and income of the clergy without papal consent, efforts
that were resisted by Pope Boniface VIII (ruled 1294–1303). When Boniface
threatened to excommunicate all who cooperated in such tax collection, the
king cut off all papal revenue from France. The struggle continued throughout
Boniface's pontificate, ending in an attack in 1303 by French agents on the papal
residence in Anagni, Italy, during which the aged pope was physically assaulted.
The bitter struggle called forth a series of responses from both sides describing
their respective positions on the proper relationship between state and church.
Papal theorists, of course, emphasized the superiority of the spiritual power of

the church over the temporal power of the state, and insisted that it was the duty of earthly authority to aid the church in the performance of its spiritual duties.

In *The Defender of the Peace*, Marsilius of Padua (c. 1275–1342) made a radical break with traditional medieval political thought. Marsilius argued that Christ never intended that his apostles or their successors, the bishops, should exercise temporal power. Political life operated according to its own principles and required no guidance from a higher authority; therefore, he said that the state should not be made to conform to standards formulated by the church. For Marsilius, the church was solely a spiritual institution; it possessed no temporal power, and the clergy were not above the laws of the state. Pope John XXII (ruled 1316–1334) branded him a heretic for publishing this work, and Marsilius was forced to seek the protection of the German prince, Louis of Bavaria. In the following passage, Marsilius outlines the relationship between church and state established by Christ.

. . . I shall first show, that Christ himself came into the world not to dominate men, nor to judge them by [temporal] judgment . . . nor to wield temporal rule, but rather to be subject as regards the status of the present life; and moreover, that he wanted to and did exclude himself, his apostles and disciples, and their successors, the bishops and priests, from all such coercive authority or worldly rule, both by his example and by his words of counsel or command. I shall also show that the leading apostles, as Christ's true imitators, did this same thing and taught their successors to do likewise; and moreover, that both Christ and the apostles wanted to be and were continuously subject in property and in person to the coercive jurisdiction of secular rulers, and that they taught and commanded all others, to whom they preached or wrote the law of truth, to do likewise, under pain of eternal damnation. Then I shall write a chapter on the power or authority of the keys which Christ gave to the apostles and their successors in office, bishops and priests, so that it may be clear what is the nature, quality, and extent of such power, both of the Roman bishop and of the others.

For ignorance on this point has hitherto been and still is the source of many questions and damnable controversies among the Christian faithful, as was mentioned in the first chapter of this discourse.

And so in pursuit of these aims we wish to show that Christ, in his purposes or intentions, words, and deeds, wished to exclude and did exclude himself and the apostles from every office of rulership, contentious jurisdiction, government, or coercive judgment in this world. This is first shown clearly beyond any doubt by the passage in the eighteenth chapter of the gospel of John. For when Christ was brought before Pontius Pilate, vicar of the Roman ruler in Judea, and accused of having called himself king of the Jews, Pontius asked him whether he had said this, or whether he did call himself a king, and Christ's reply included these words, among others: "My kingdom is not of this world," that is, I have not come to reign by temporal rule or dominion, in the way in which worldly kings reign. And proof of this was given by Christ himself through an evident sign when he said: "If my kingdom were of this world, my servants would certainly fight, that I should not be delivered to the Jews," as if to argue as follows: If I had come into this world to reign by worldly or coercive rule, I would have ministers for this rule, namely, men to fight and to coerce transgressors, as the other kings have; but I do not have such ministers, as you can clearly see. . . .

. . . It now remains to show that not only did Christ himself refuse rulership or coercive judgment in this world, whereby he furnished an example for his apostles and disciples and their successors to do likewise, but also he taught by words and showed by example that all men, both priests and non-priests, should be subject in property and in person to the coercive judgment of the rulers of this world. By his word and example, then, Christ showed this first with respect to property, by what is written in the twenty-second chapter of Matthew. For when the Jews asked him: "Tell us therefore, what dost thou think? Is it lawful to give tribute to Caesar, or not?" Christ, after looking at the coin and its inscription, replied: "Render therefore to Caesar the things that are Caesar's, and to God the things that are God's." . . . So, then, we ought to be subject to Caesar in all things, so long only as they are not contrary to piety, that is, to divine worship or commandment. Therefore, Christ wanted us to be subject in property to the secular ruler. . . .

Like Christ and the apostles, then, the Roman bishops and priests and the whole clergy of Rome and the other provinces used to live under the coercive government of those who were the rulers by authority of the human legislator. But later on, certain Roman bishops succumbed to the persuasion and incitation of that ruler of this world, that first parent of arrogance and presumption, that inculcator of all vices, the devil; and they were led, or rather misled, to a path foreign to that of Christ and the apostles. For cupidity and avarice, invading their minds, expelled therefrom that supreme meritorious poverty which Christ had introduced and established in the church. . . . And again, pride and ambition for secular rule, invading their minds, expelled therefrom that supreme humility which Christ had enjoined and commanded the church or whole priesthood to maintain.

This, then, as we have said, is and was the primary source of the present strife and discord between the emperors and the Roman pontiffs, since the controversies over the divine law and over the heresies of certain rulers have died out entirely. For the Roman bishops wrongly wish to possess excessive temporal goods, and refuse to be subject to the laws and edicts of the rulers or the human legislator, thereby opposing the example and teaching of Christ and the apostles. . . .

REVIEW QUESTIONS

1. What arguments did Marsilius use to strip the church of its practice of holding or claiming temporal political authority?
2. In Marsilius' opinion, who or what was to blame for the church's claim to exercise temporal political authority?

---

14 The Medieval Worldview
—⁓—

The modern world is linked in many ways to the Middle Ages. European cities, the middle class, the state system, English common law, representative institutions, universities—all had their origins in the Middle Ages. Despite these elements of continuity, the characteristic outlook of medieval people is markedly different from that of people today. Whereas science and secularism shape the modern point of view, religion was the foundation of the Middle Ages. Christian beliefs as formulated by the church made life and death purposeful and intelligible.

Medieval thinkers drew a sharp distinction between a higher, spiritual world and a lower, material world. God, the creator of the universe and the source of moral values, dwelled in the higher celestial world, an abode of perfection. The universe was organized as a hierarchy with God at the summit and hell at the other extremity. Earth, composed of base matter, stood just above hell. By believing in Christ and adhering to God's commandments as taught by the church, people could overcome their sinful nature and ascend to God's world. Sinners, on the other hand, would descend to hell, a fearful place the existence of which medieval people never doubted.

Lothario dei Segni (Pope Innocent III)
ON THE MISERY OF THE HUMAN CONDITION

At the center of medieval belief was the image of a perfect God and a wretched and sinful human being. God had given Adam and Eve freedom to choose; rebellious and presumptuous, they had used their freedom to disobey God. In doing so, they made evil an intrinsic part of the human personality. But God, who had not stopped loving human beings, showed them the way out of sin. God became man and died so that human beings might be saved. Men and women were weak, egocentric, and sinful. With God's grace they could overcome their sinful nature and gain salvation; without grace they were utterly helpless. A classic expression of this pessimistic view of human nature was written in the late twelfth century by the Italian canon lawyer Lothario dei Segni (c. 1160–1216), who was later elected pope in 1198, taking the name Innocent III. His *On the Misery of the Human Condition* was enormously popular and inspired numerous rhetorical writings on the same theme as late as the seventeenth century. Scattered excerpts follow.

• For sure man was formed out of earth, conceived in guilt, born to punishment. What he does is depraved and illicit, is shameful and improper, vain and unprofitable. He will become fuel for the eternal fires, food for worms, a mass of rottenness.

I shall try to make my explanation clearer and my treatment fuller. Man was formed of dust, slime, and ashes; what is even more vile, of the filthiest seed. He was conceived from the itch of the flesh, in the heat of passion and the stench of lust, and worse yet, with the stain of sin. He was born to toil, dread, and trouble; and more wretched still, was born only to die. He commits depraved acts by which he offends God, his neighbor, and himself; shameful acts by which he defiles his name, his person, and his conscience; and vain acts by which he ignores all things important, useful, and necessary. He will become fuel for those fires which are forever hot and burn forever bright; food for the worm which forever nibbles and digests; a mass of rottenness which will forever stink and reek.

• A bird is born to fly; man is born to toil. All his days are full of toil and hardship, and at night his mind has no rest.

Adapted from *On the Misery of the Human Condition: Pope Innocent III*, trans. R. Donald Howard and Margaret Mary Dietz, pp. 6, 13, 16, 25, 29, 33, 54, 68. 1st Edition, © 1969. Reprinted by permission of Pearson Education, Inc., Upper Saddle River, NJ.

• How much anxiety tortures mortals! They suffer all kinds of cares, are burdened with worry, tremble and shrink with fears and terrors, are weighted down with sorrow. Their nervousness makes them depressed, and their depression makes them nervous. Rich or poor, master or slave, married or single, good and bad alike—all suffer worldly torments and are tormented by worldly vexations.

• For sudden sorrow always follows worldly joy: what begins in gaiety ends in grief. Worldly happiness is besprinkled indeed with much bitterness.

• Then, suddenly, when least expected, misfortune strikes, a calamity befalls us, disease attacks; or death, which no one can escape, carries us off.

• Men strive especially for three things: riches, pleasures, and honors. Riches lead to immorality, pleasures to shame, and honors to vanity.

• But suppose a man is lifted up high, suppose he is raised to the very peak. At once his cares grow heavy, his worries mount up, he eats less and cannot sleep. And so nature is corrupted, his spirit weakened, his sleep disturbed, his appetite lost; his strength is diminished, he loses weight. Exhausting himself, he scarcely lives half a lifetime and ends his wretched days with a more wretched death.

• Almost the whole life of mortals is full of mortal sin, so that one can scarcely find anyone who does not go astray, does not return to his own vomit and rot in his own dung. Instead they "are glad when they have done evil and rejoice in most wicked things." "Being filled with all iniquity, malice, fornication, avarice, wickedness, full of envy, murders, contention, deceit, evil, being whisperers, detractors, hateful to God, irreverent, proud, haughty, plotters of evil, disobedient to parents, foolish, dissolute, without affection, without fidelity, without mercy." This world is full of such and worse; it abounds in heretics and schismatics [Christians who reject the authority of the pope], traitors and tyrants, simonists [buyers or sellers of spiritual offices or sacred items] and hypocrites; the ambitious and the covetous, robbers and brigands, violent men, extortionists, usurers, forgers; the impious and sacreligious, the betrayers and liars, the flatterers and deceivers; gossips, tricksters, gluttons, drunkards; adulterers, incestuous men, deviates, and the dirty-minded; the lazy, the careless, the vain, the prodigal, the impetuous, the irascible, the impatient and inconstant; poisoners, fortune tellers, perjurers, cursers; men who are presumptuous and arrogant, unbelieving and desperate; and finally those ensnared in all vices together.

"THE VANITY OF THIS WORLD"

The following poem, written in Latin by an unknown thirteenth-century author, expresses the medieval rejection of earthly pursuits and preoccupation with the world to come.

Why does the world war for glory that's vain?
All its successes wax only to wane;

Quickly its triumphs are frittered away,
Like vessels the potter casts out of frail clay.

As well trust to letters imprinted in ice
As trust the frail world with its treacherous
  device,

Twenty-One Medieval Latin Poems, ed. Edward James Martin (London: The Scholartis Press, 1931), pp. 53, 55.

Its prizes a fraud and its values all wrong;
Who would put faith in its promise for
long?

Rather in hardship's uncertain distress
Trust than in this world's unhappy success;
With dreams and with shadows it leads men
astray,
A cheat in our work and a cheat at our play.
Where now is Samson's invincible arm,
And where is Jonathan's sweet-natured charm?
Once-famous Solomon, where now is he
Or the fair Absolom, so good to see?[1]

Whither is Caesar the great Emperor fled,
Or Croesus whose show on his table was
spread?
Cicero's eloquence now is in vain;[2]
Where's Aristotle's magnificent brain?

All those great noblemen, all those past days,
All kings' achievements and all prelates' praise,

All the world's princes in all their array—
In the flash of an eye comes the end of the play.

Short is the season of all earthly fame;
Man's shadow, man's pleasure, they both are the
same,
And the prizes eternal he gives in exchange
For the pleasure that leads to a land that is
strange.

Food for the worms, dust and ashes, O why,
Bubble on water, be lifted so high?
Do good unto all men as long as ye may;
Ye know not your life will last after to-day.

This pride of the flesh which so dearly ye prize,
Like the flower of the grass (says the scripture),
it dies,
Or as the dry leaf which the wind whirls away,
Man's life is swept out from the light
of the day.

Call not your own what one day ye may lose;
The world will take back all it gives you
to use.
Let your hearts be in heaven, your thoughts in
the skies;
Happy is he who the world can despise.

---

[1]In the Old Testament, Samson was the warrior hero of the Israelites; Jonathan was the son of King Saul and the loving friend of David; Solomon was the king of Israel, famous for his wisdom; and Absalom was the most beloved son of David. —Eds.
[2]Croesus was a king of ancient Lydia renowned for his wealth. For Cicero, see chapter 4. —Eds.

Dante Alighieri
THE DIVINE COMEDY

Scholastic philosophy, which sought to demonstrate through reason the truth of Christian doctrines, and the Gothic cathedral, which seemed to soar from the material world to heaven, were two great expressions of the medieval mind. A third was *The Divine Comedy* (composed c. 1310–c. 1321) of Dante Alighieri, the greatest literary figure of the Middle Ages.

Dante Alighieri was a poet, political philosopher, soldier, and politician. Born in 1265 in Florence, Italy, he died in exile in 1321. *The Divine Comedy*, his greatest work, was composed of one hundred cantos (individual poems) and written not in Latin, the language of learning, but in the Tuscan Italian dialect of the common people.

The poem is an elaborate allegory in which each character and event can be understood on two or more levels—for example, a literal description of the levels of hell and Dante's (and every Christian's) struggle to overcome a flawed human nature and to ward off worldly sin. Dante, representing all human beings, is guided through the afterworlds: hell (inferno), purgatory, and heaven (paradise). The Roman poet Virgil (see page 133) conducts him through hell and purgatory; Beatrice, his long-dead beloved, leads him through heaven to the point where he sees God in all his glory.

In the descent through the nine concentric circles of hell, Virgil describes the nature and significance of each region through which they pass. In each section of hell, sinners are punished in proportion to their earthly sins. Over the entrance gate to hell, Dante reads these words:

THROUGH ME YOU GO INTO THE CITY OF
    GRIEF,
THROUGH ME YOU GO INTO THE PAIN THAT
    IS ETERNAL,
THROUGH ME YOU GO AMONG PEOPLE LOST.

JUSTICE MOVED MY EXALTED CREATOR;
THE DIVINE POWER MADE ME,
THE SUPREME WISDOM, AND THE PRIMAL
    LOVE.

BEFORE ME ALL CREATED THINGS WERE
    ETERNAL,
AND ETERNAL I WILL LAST.
ABANDON EVERY HOPE, YOU WHO ENTER
    HERE.

Dante descends from the first circle to the second circle, where he finds the souls of those who had been guilty of sins of the flesh.

Now I begin to hear the sad notes of pain,
now I have come to where
loud cries beat upon my ears.

I have reached a place mute of all light
which roars like the sea in a tempest
when beaten by conflicting winds.

Dante Alighieri, *The Divine Comedy*, trans. H. R. Huse (New York; Toronto: Rinehart & Co., 1954), pp. 17, 28, 162–164, 478–481.

The infernal storm which never stops
drives the spirit in its blast;
whirling and beating, it torments them.

When they come in front of the landslide,
they utter laments, moans, and shrieks;
there they curse the Divine Power.

I learned that to such a torment
carnal sinners are condemned
who subject their reason to desire.

And, as starlings are borne by their wings
in the cold season, in a broad and dense flock,
so that blast carries the evil spirits.

Here, there, up, and down, it blows them;
no hope ever comforts them
of rest or even of less pain.

And as cranes go chanting their lays,
making a long line of themselves in the air,
so I saw coming, uttering laments,
shades borne by that strife of winds.

Finally the two poets reach the ninth and lowest circle, a frozen wasteland reserved for Satan and traitors.

". . . look ahead,"
my master [Virgil] said, "and try to
discern him."

As, when a thick mist covers the land
or when night darkens our hemisphere,
a windmill, turning, appears from afar,

so now I seemed to see such a structure;
then because of the wind, I drew back
behind my guide, for there was no other
    protection.

Already—and with fear I put it into verse—
I was where the shades are covered in the ice
and show through like bits of straw in glass.

Some were lying, some standing erect,
some on their heads, others on their feet,
still others like a bow bent face to toes.

When we had gone so far ahead
that my master was pleased to show me
the creature (Lucifer)[1] that once had been so fair,

he stood from in front of me, and made me
    stop,
saying, "Behold, Dis![2] Here is the place
where you must arm yourself with courage."

How faint and frozen I then became,
do not ask, Reader, for I do not write it down,
since all words would be inadequate.

I did not die and did not stay alive:
think now for yourself, if you have the wit,
how I became, without life or death.

The emperor of the dolorous realm
from mid-breast protruded from the ice,
and I compare better in size

with the giants than they do with his arms.
Consider how big the whole must be,
proportioned as it is to such a part.

If he were once as handsome as he is ugly now,
and still presumed to lift his hand against his
    Maker,
all affliction must indeed come from him.

Oh, how great a marvel appeared to me
when I saw three faces on his head!
The one in front (hatred) was fiery red;

the two others which were joined to it
over the middle of each shoulder
were fused together at the top.

The right one (impotence) seemed between
    white and yellow;
the left (ignorance) was in color like those
who come from where the Nile rises.

Under each two great wings spread
of a size fitting to such a bird;
I have never seen such sails on the sea.

They had no feathers, and seemed
like those of a bat, and they flapped,
so that three blasts came from them.

Thence all Cocytus[3] was frozen.
With six eyes he wept, and over his three chins
he let tears drip and bloody foam.

In each mouth he chewed a sinner with
    his teeth
in the manner of a hemp brake,[4]
so that he kept three in pain.

To the one in front the biting was nothing
compared to the scratching, for at times,
his back was stripped of skin.

"The soul up there with the greatest
    punishment,"
said my master, "is Judas Iscariot.[5] His head
is inside the mouth, and he kicks with his legs.

Of the other two whose heads are down,
the one hanging from the black face is Brutus;[6]
see how he twists and says nothing.

The other who seems so heavy set is Cassius.[7]
But night is rising again now,
and it is time to leave, for we have seen all."

---

[1]Lucifer (light-bringer) was an archangel who led a rebellion against God and was cast into hell for punishment. He was identified with Satan. —Eds.

[2]Dis was another name for Pluto or Hades, the god of the dead and ruler of the underworld. —Eds.

[3]The Cocytus, a river in western Greece, was alleged to lead to the underworld. —Eds.

[4]A hemp brake was a tool used to break up hemp fibers so that they could be made into rope. —Eds.

[5]Judas Iscariot was the disciple who betrayed Jesus to the authorities. —Eds.

[6]Brutus, a first-century Roman statesman, conspired to murder Julius Caesar. —Eds.

[7]Cassius, another Roman statesman, was a co-conspirator with Brutus. —Eds.

Dante and Beatrice make the ascent to the highest heaven, the Empyrean, which is located beyond Saturn, the last of the seven planets, beyond the circle of stars that encloses the planets, and above the Primum Mobile—the outermost sphere revolving around the earth. Here at the summit of the universe is a realm of pure light that radiates truth, goodness, and happiness, where God is found. Dante is permitted to look at God, but words cannot describe "the glory of Him who moves us all."

For my sight, growing pure, penetrated
ever deeper into the rays
of the Light [God] which is true in Itself.

From then on my vision was greater
than our speech which fails at such a sight,
just as memory is overcome by the excess.

As one who in a dream sees clearly,
and the feeling impressed remains afterward,
although nothing else comes back to mind,

so am I; for my vision disappears
almost wholly, and yet the sweetness
caused by it is still distilled within my heart.

Thus, in sunlight, the snow melts away;
thus the sayings of the Sibyl [a Roman oracle], written
on light leaves, were lost in the wind.

O Supreme Light that risest so high
above mortal concepts, give back to my mind
a little of what Thou didst appear,

and make my tongue strong,
so that it may leave to future peoples
at least a spark of Thy glory!

For, by returning to my memory
and by sounding a little in these verses
more of Thy victory will be conceived.

By the keenness of the living ray I endured
I believe I would have been dazed
if my eyes had turned away from it;

and I remember that I was bolder
because of that to sustain the view
until my sight *attained* the Infinite Worth [God].

O abundant grace through which I presumed
to fix my eyes on the Eternal Light
so long that I consumed my vision on it!

In its depths I saw contained, bound with love
in one volume, what is scattered
on leaves throughout the world—

substances (things) and accidents (qualities) and their modes
as if fused together in such a way
that what I speak of is a single light.

The universal form (principle) of this unity
I believe I saw, because more abundantly
in saying this I feel that I rejoice.

One moment obscures more for me than twenty-five centuries
have clouded since the adventure which made Neptune [the sea god]
wonder at the shadow of the Argo (the first ship).[8]

Thus my mind with rapt attention
gazed fixedly, motionless and attentive,
continually enflamed by its very gazing.

In that light we become such
that we can never consent
to turn from it for another sight,

inasmuch as the good which is the object
of the will is all in it, and outside of it
whatever is perfect there is defective.

Now my speech, even for what I remember,
will be shorter than that of an infant
who still bathes his tongue at the breast.

---

[8]The *Argo*, in Greek legends, was the ship in which the hero Jason and his companions sailed in search of the Golden Fleece. A Greek poet, Apollonius of Rhodes, wrote an epic poem, the *Argonautica*, about it in the mid-third century B.C. —Eds.

Not that more than a single semblance
was in the living light I gazed upon
(for it is always as it was before),

but in my vision which gained strength
as I looked the single appearance,
through a change in me, was transformed.

Within the deep and clear subsistence
of the great light three circles of three colors
and of one dimension (the Trinity) appeared
    to me,

and one (the Son) seemed reflected from the
    other (the Father)
as Iris by Iris,[9] and the third (the Holy
    Spirit)
seemed fire emanating equally from both.

O how poor our speech is and how feeble
for my conception! Compared to what I saw
to say its power is "little" is to say too
    much.

O Eternal Light (Father), abiding in Thyself
    alone,
Thou (Son) alone understanding Thyself, and
    Thou (Holy Spirit)

understood only by Thee, Thou dost love and
    smile!

The circle which appeared in Thee
as a reflected light (the Son)
when contemplated a while

seemed depicted with our image within
    itself
and of its own (the Circle's) color,
so that my eyes were wholly fixed on it.

Like the geometer who strives
to square the circle and cannot find
by thinking the principle he needs

I was at that new sight. I wanted to see
how the (human) image was conformed
to the (divine) circle and has a place in it,

but my own wings were not enough for
    that—
except that my mind was illuminated by
    a flash
(of Grace) through which its wish was
    realized.

For the great imagination here power failed;
but already my desire and will (in harmony)
were turning like a wheel moved evenly

by the Love which turns the sun and the other
    stars.

---

[9]Iris, goddess of the rainbow, was the messenger of the gods. —Eds.

REVIEW QUESTIONS

1. Compare Innocent III's view of the human condition with that of ancient Greeks such as Homer, Pindar, and Sophocles (see chapter 1). What comfort did each offer for the tragic nature of the human condition?
2. Why does the author of "The Vanity of This World" assert that "happy is he who the world can despise"?
3. How did Dante conceive the nature of evil and the moral ordering of specific sins?
4. What was the medieval view of the human condition and its relation to the idea of God? Cite at least two sources from your reading to illustrate your viewpoint.

CHAPTER 9

The Renaissance

THE TRIUMPH OF GALATEA, by Raphael, 1513. This fresco from the Palazzo della Farnesina in Rome exemplifies the Renaissance artist's elevation of the human form. The mythological subject is also humanistic in its evocation of the ancient Greek tradition. (© Giraudon/The Bridgeman Art Library International)

From the fifteenth through the seventeenth centuries, medieval attitudes and institutions broke down, and distinctly modern cultural, economic, and political forms emerged. For many historians, the Renaissance, which originated in the city-states of Italy, marks the starting point of the modern era. The Renaissance was characterized by a rebirth of interest in the humanist culture and outlook of ancient Greece and Rome. Although Renaissance individuals did not repudiate Christianity, they valued worldly activities and interests to a much greater degree than did the people of the Middle Ages, whose outlook was dominated by Christian otherworldliness. Renaissance individuals were fascinated by *this* world and by life's possibilities; they aspired to live a rich and creative life on earth and to fulfill themselves through artistic and literary activity. The most admired person during the Renaissance was the multitalented individual, the "universal man," who distinguished himself as a writer, artist, linguist, athlete.

During the High Middle Ages there had been a revival of Greek and Roman learning. Yet there were two important differences between the period called the Twelfth-Century Awakening and the Renaissance. First, many more ancient works were restored to circulation during the Renaissance than during the cultural revival of the Middle Ages. Second, medieval scholastics had tried to fit the ideas of the ancients into a Christian framework; they used Greek philosophy to explain and demonstrate the truth of Christian teachings. Renaissance scholars, on the other hand, valued ancient works for their own sake, believing that Greek and Roman authors could teach much about the art of living.

A distinguishing feature of the Renaissance period was the humanist movement, an educational and cultural program based on the study of ancient Greek and Latin literature. By studying the humanities—history, literature, rhetoric, moral and political philosophy—humanists aimed to revive the worldly spirit of the ancient Greeks and Romans, which they believed had been lost in the Middle Ages.

Humanists were thus fascinated by the writings of the ancients. From the works of Thucydides, Plato, Cicero, Seneca, and other ancient authors, humanists sought guidelines for living life well in this world and looked for stylistic models for their own literary efforts. To the humanists, the ancients had written brilliantly, in an incomparable literary style, on friendship, citizenship, love, bravery, statesmanship, beauty, excellence, and every other topic devoted to the enrichment of human life.

Like the humanist movement, Renaissance art also marked a break with medieval culture. The art of the Middle Ages had served a religious function; its purpose was to lift the mind to God. It depicted a spiritual universe in which the supernatural was the supreme reality. The Gothic cathedral, with its flying buttresses, soared toward heaven, rising in ascending tiers; it reflected the medieval conception of a hierarchical universe with God at its apex. Painting also expressed gradations of spiritual values. Traditionally, the left side of a painting portrayed the damned, the right side the saved; dark colors expressed evil, light colors good. Spatial proportion was relative to spirituality—the less spiritually valuable a thing was, the less form it had (or the more deformed it was). Medieval art perfectly expressed the Christian view of the universe and the individual. The Renaissance shattered the dominance of religion over art, shifting attention from heaven to the natural world and to the human being; Renaissance artists often dealt with religious themes, but they placed their subjects in a naturalistic setting. Renaissance art also developed a new concept of visual space—perspective—that was defined from the standpoint of the individual observer. It was a quantitative space in which the artist, employing reason and mathematics, portrayed the essential form of the object as it appeared in three dimensions to the human eye; that is, it depicted the object in perspective.

The Renaissance began in the late fourteenth century in the northern Italian city-states, which had grown prosperous from the revival of trade in the Middle Ages. Italian merchants and bankers had the wealth to acquire libraries and fine works of art and to support art, literature, and scholarship. Surrounded by reminders of ancient Rome—amphitheaters, monuments, and sculpture—the well-to-do took an interest in classical culture and thought. In the late fifteenth and the sixteenth centuries, Renaissance ideas spread to Germany, France, Spain, and England through books available in great numbers due to the invention of the printing press in Germany in the mid-fifteenth century.

1 The Humanists' Fascination with Antiquity

Humanists believed that a refined person must know the literature of Greece and Rome. They strove to imitate the style of the ancients, to speak and write as eloquently as the Greeks and Romans. Toward these ends, they sought to read, print, and restore to circulation every scrap of ancient literature that could still be found.

Petrarch
THE FATHER OF HUMANISM

During his lifetime, Francesco Petrarca, or Petrarch (1304–1374), had an astounding reputation as a poet and scholar. Often called the "father of humanism," he inspired other humanists through his love for classical learning; his criticism of medieval Latin as barbaric in contrast to the style of Cicero, Seneca, and other Romans; and his literary works based on classical models. Petrarch saw his own age as a restoration of classical brilliance after an interval of medieval darkness.

A distinctly modern element in Petrarch's thought is the subjective and individualistic character of his writing. In talking about himself and probing his own feelings, Petrarch demonstrates a self-consciousness characteristic of the modern outlook.

Like many other humanists, Petrarch remained devoted to Christianity: "When it comes to thinking or speaking of religion, that is, of the highest truth, of true happiness and eternal salvation," he declared, "I certainly am not a Ciceronian or a Platonist but a Christian." Petrarch was a forerunner of the Christian humanism best represented by Erasmus (see page 326). Christian humanists combined an intense devotion to Christianity with a great love for classical literature, which they much preferred to the dull and turgid treatises written by scholastic philosophers and theologians. In the following passage, Petrarch criticizes his contemporaries for their ignorance of ancient writers and shows his commitment to classical learning.

. . . O inglorious age! that scorns antiquity, its mother, to whom it owes every noble art—that dares to declare itself not only equal but superior to the glorious past. I say nothing of the vulgar, the dregs of mankind, whose sayings and opinions may raise a laugh but hardly merit serious censure. . . .

. . . But what can be said in defense of men of education who ought not to be ignorant of antiquity and yet are plunged in this same darkness and delusion?

You see that I cannot speak of these matters without the greatest irritation and indignation. There has arisen of late a set of dialecticians [experts in logical argument], who are not only ignorant but demented. Like a black army of ants from some old rotten oak, they swarm forth from their hiding places and devastate the fields of sound learning. They condemn

Plato and Aristotle, and laugh at Socrates and Pythagoras.[1] And, good God! under what silly and incompetent leaders these opinions are put forth. . . . What shall we say of men who scorn Marcus Tullius Cicero,[2] the bright sun of eloquence? Of those who scoff at Varro and Seneca,[3] and are scandalized at what they choose

---

[1]The work of Aristotle (384–322 B.C.), a leading Greek philosopher, had an enormous influence among medieval and Renaissance scholars. A student of the philosopher Socrates, Plato (c. 427–347 B.C.) was one of the greatest philosophers of ancient Greece (see chapter 3). His work grew to be extremely influential in the Latin West during the Renaissance period, as new texts of his writings were discovered and translated into Latin and more people could read the originals in Greek. Pythagoras (c. 582–c. 507 B.C.) was a Greek philosopher whose work influenced both Socrates and Plato.—Eds.

[2]Cicero (106–43 B.C.) was a Roman statesman and rhetorician. His Latin style was especially admired and emulated during the Renaissance (see page 107).—Eds.

[3]Varro (116–27 B.C.) was a Roman scholar and historian. Seneca (4 B.C.–A.D. 65) was a Roman statesman, dramatist, and Stoic philosopher whose literary style was greatly admired during the Renaissance (see page 137).—Eds.

Petrarch: The First Modern Scholar and Man of Letters, trans. H. J. Robinson and H. W. Rolfe (New York: G. P. Putnam's Sons, 1909), pp. 208, 210, 213.

to call the crude, unfinished style of Livy and Sallust [Roman historians]? . . .

Such are the times, my friend, upon which we have fallen; such is the period in which we live and are growing old. Such are the critics of today, as I so often have occasion to lament and complain—men who are innocent of knowledge and virtue, and yet harbour the most exalted opinion of themselves. Not content with losing the words of the ancients, they must attack their genius and their ashes. They rejoice in their ignorance, as if what they did not know were not worth knowing. They give full rein to their license and conceit, and freely introduce among us new authors and outlandish teachings.

Leonardo Bruni
STUDY OF GREEK LITERATURE AND A HUMANIST EDUCATIONAL PROGRAM

Leonardo Bruni (1374–1444) was a Florentine humanist who extolled both intellectual study and active involvement in public affairs, an outlook called civic humanism. In the first reading from his *History of His Own Times in Italy*, Bruni expresses the humanist's love for ancient Greek literature and language.

Then first came a knowledge of Greek, which had not been in use among us for seven hundred years. Chrysoloras the Byzantine,[1] a man of noble birth and well versed in Greek letters, brought Greek learning to us. When his country was invaded by the Turks, he came by sea, first to Venice. The report of him soon spread, and he was cordially invited and besought and promised a public stipend, to come to Florence and open his store of riches to the youth. I was then studying Civil Law,[2] but . . . I burned with love of academic studies, and had spent no little pains on dialectic and rhetoric. At the coming of Chrysoloras I was torn in mind, deeming it shameful to desert the law, and yet a crime to lose such a chance of studying Greek literature; and often with youthful impulse I would say to myself: "Thou, when it is permitted thee to gaze on

Homer, Plato and Demosthenes,[3] and the other [Greek] poets, philosophers, orators, of whom such glorious things are spread abroad, and speak with them and be instructed in their admirable teaching, wilt thou desert and rob thyself? Wilt thou neglect this opportunity so divinely offered? For seven hundred years, no one in Italy has possessed Greek letters; and yet we confess that all knowledge is derived from them. How great advantage to your knowledge, enhancement of your fame, increase of your pleasure, will come from an understanding of this tongue? There are doctors of civil law everywhere; and the chance of learning will not fail thee. But if

---

Leonardo Bruni, *History of His Own Times in Italy* and *De Studiis et Literis* in Henry Osborn Taylor, *Thought and Expression in the Sixteenth Century*, 2nd rev. ed., vol. 1 (New York: Frederick Unger, 1930; republished 1959), pp. 36–37.

[1]Chrysoloras (c. 1355–1415), a Byzantine writer and teacher, introduced the study of Greek literature to the Italians, helping to open a new age of Western humanistic learning.—Eds.
[2]Civil law refers to the Roman law as codified by Emperor Justinian in the early sixth century A.D. and studied in medieval law schools (see page 143).—Eds.
[3]Demosthenes (384–322 B.C.) was an Athenian statesman and orator whose oratorical style was much admired by Renaissance humanists.—Eds.

this one and only doctor of Greek letters disappears, no one can be found to teach thee." Overcome at length by these reasons, I gave myself to Chrysoloras, with such zeal to learn, that what through the wakeful day I gathered, I followed after in the night, even when asleep.

In a treatise, *De Studiis et Literis* (On Learning and Literature), written around 1405 and addressed to the noble lady Baptista di Montefeltro (1383–1450), daughter of the count of Urbino, Bruni outlines the basic course of studies that the humanists recommended as the best preparation for a life of wisdom and virtue. In addition to the study of Christian literature, Bruni encourages a wide familiarity with the best minds and stylists of ancient Greek and Latin cultures.

. . . The foundations of all true learning must be laid in the sound and thorough knowledge of Latin: which implies study marked by a broad spirit, accurate scholarship, and careful attention to details. Unless this solid basis be secured it is useless to attempt to rear an enduring edifice. Without it the great monuments of literature are unintelligible, and the art of composition impossible. To attain this essential knowledge we must never relax our careful attention to the grammar of the language, but perpetually confirm and extend our acquaintance with it until it is thoroughly our own. . . . To this end we must be supremely careful in our choice of authors, lest an inartistic and debased style infect our own writing and degrade our taste; which danger is best avoided by bringing a keen, critical sense to bear upon select works, observing the sense of each passage, the structure of the sentence, the force of every word down to the least important particle. In this way our reading reacts directly upon our style. . . .

But we must not forget that true distinction is to be gained by a wide and varied range of such studies as conduce to the profitable enjoyment of life, in which, however, we must observe due proportion in the attention and time we devote to them.

First amongst such studies I place History: a subject which must not on any account be neglected by one who aspires to true cultivation. For it is our duty to understand the origins of our own history and its development; and the achievements of Peoples and of Kings.

For the careful study of the past enlarges our foresight in contemporary affairs and affords to citizens and to monarchs lessons of incitement or warning in the ordering of public policy. From History, also, we draw our store of examples of moral precepts.

In the monuments of ancient literature which have come down to us History holds a position of great distinction. We specially prize such [Roman] authors as Livy, Sallust and Curtius;[4] and, perhaps even above these, Julius Caesar; the style of whose Commentaries, so elegant and so limpid, entitles them to our warm admiration. . . .

The great Orators of antiquity must by all means be included. Nowhere do we find the virtues more warmly extolled, the vices so fiercely decried. From them we may learn, also, how to express consolation, encouragement, dissuasion or advice. If the principles which orators set forth are portrayed for us by philosophers, it is from the former that we learn how to employ the emotions—such as indignation, or pity—in driving home their application in individual cases. Further, from oratory we derive our store of those elegant or striking turns of expression which are used with so much effect in literary compositions. Lastly, in oratory we find that wealth of vocabulary, that clear easy-flowing style, that verve and force, which are invaluable to us both in writing and in conversation.

I come now to Poetry and the Poets. . . . For we cannot point to any great mind of the past for whom the Poets had not a powerful attraction. Aristotle, in constantly quoting Homer, Hesiod, Pindar, Euripides and other [Greek]

---

[4]Q. Curtius Rufus, a Roman historian and rhetorician of the mid-first century A.D., composed a biography of Alexander the Great. —Eds.

poets, proves that he knew their works hardly less intimately than those of the philosophers. Plato, also, frequently appeals to them, and in this way covers them with his approval. If we turn to Cicero, we find him not content with quoting Ennius, Accius,[5] and others of the Latins, but rendering poems from the Greek and employing them habitually. . . . Hence my view that familiarity with the great poets of antiquity is essential to any claim to true education. For in their writings we find deep speculations upon Nature, and upon the Causes and Origins of things, which must carry weight with us both from their antiquity and from their authorship. Besides these, many important truths upon matters of daily life are suggested or illustrated. All this is expressed with such grace and dignity as demands our admiration. . . . To sum up what I have endeavoured to set forth. That high standard of education to which I referred at the outset is only to be reached by one who has seen many things and read much.

---

[5]Ennius (239–169 B.C.) wrote the first great Latin epic poem, which was based on the legends of Rome's founding and its early history. Accius (c. 170–c. 90 B.C.), also a Roman, authored a history of Greek and Latin literature. —Eds.

Poet, Orator, Historian, and the rest, all must be studied, each must contribute a share. Our learning thus becomes full, ready, varied and elegant, available for action or for discourse in all subjects. But to enable us to make effectual use of what we know we must add to our knowledge the power of expression. These two sides of learning, indeed, should not be separated: they afford mutual aid and distinction. Proficiency in literary form, not accompanied by broad acquaintance with facts and truths, is a barren attainment; whilst information, however vast, which lacks all grace of expression, would seem to be put under a bushel or partly thrown away. Indeed, one may fairly ask what advantage it is to possess profound and varied learning if one cannot convey it in language worthy of the subject. Where, however, this double capacity exists—breadth of learning and grace of style— we allow the highest title to distinction and to abiding fame. If we review the great names of ancient [Greek and Roman] literature, Plato, Democritus, Aristotle, Theophrastus, Varro, Cicero, Seneca, Augustine, Jerome, Lactantius, we shall find it hard to say whether we admire more their attainments or their literary power.

Petrus Paulus Vergerius
THE IMPORTANCE OF LIBERAL STUDIES

In *On the Manners of a Gentleman and Liberal Studies,* written in 1392, Petrus Paulus Vergerius (1370–1444), a prominent Paduan scholar, upheld the importance of classical study and made astute observations regarding the educational process. He urged teachers to provide "examples of living men known and respected for their worth" for students to imitate. At an early age, students should learn moral discipline: they should be taught to disdain "arrogance or intolerable self-conceit," "untruthfulness," "idleness of mind," and overindulgence in food, drink, and sleep. They should also be imbued with respect for elders and the ceremonies of the church.

In the following passage from his education treatise, Vergerius discusses the nature and value of a liberal education.

We call those studies *liberal* which are worthy of a free man; those studies by which we attain and practise virtue and wisdom; that education which calls forth, trains and develops those highest gifts of body and of mind which ennoble men, and which are rightly judged to rank next in dignity to virtue only. For to a vulgar temper gain and pleasure are the one aim of existence, to a lofty nature, moral worth and fame. It is, then, of the highest importance that even from infancy this aim, this effort, should constantly be kept alive in growing minds. For I may affirm with fullest conviction that we shall not have attained wisdom in our later years unless in our earliest we have sincerely entered on its search. . . .

{My father}, Jacopo da Carrara, who, though a patron of learning, was not himself versed in Letters, died regretting that opportunity of acquiring a knowledge of higher studies had not been given him in youth; which shews us that, although we may in old age long for it, only in early years can we be sure of attaining that learning which we desire. So that it is no light motive to youthful diligence that we thereby provide ourselves with precious advantages against on-coming age, a spring of interest for a leisured life, a recreation for a busy one. Consider the necessity of the literary art to one immersed in reading and speculation: and its importance to one absorbed in affairs. To be able to speak and write with elegance is no slight advantage in negotiation, whether in public or private concerns. Especially in administration of the State, when intervals of rest and privacy are accorded to a prince, how must he value those means of occupying them wisely which the knowledge of literature affords to him! Think of [Roman emperor] Domitian: the son of Vespasian though he was, and brother of Titus, he was driven to occupy his leisure by *killing flies!* . . .

Indeed the power which good books have of diverting our thoughts from unworthy or distressing themes is another support to my arguement for the study of letters. Add to this their helpfulness on those occasions when we find ourselves alone, without companions and without preoccupations—what can we do better than gather our books around us? In them we see unfolded before us vast stores of knowledge, for our delight, it may be, or for our inspiration. In them are contained the records of the great achievements of men; the wonders of Nature; the works of Providence in the past, the key to her secrets of the future. And, most important of all, this Knowledge is not liable to decay. With a picture, an inscription, a coin, books share a kind of immortality. In all these memory is, as it were, made permanent; although, in its freedom from accidental risks, Literature surpasses every other form of record.

Literature indeed exhibits not facts alone, but thoughts, and their expression. Provided such thoughts be worthy, and worthily expressed, we feel assured that they will not die: although I do not think that thoughts without style will be likely to attract much notice or secure a sure survival. What greater charm can life offer than this power of making the past, the present, and even the future, our own by means of literature? How bright a household is the family of books! we may cry, with Cicero. In their company is no noise, no greed, no self-will: at a word they speak to you, at a word they are still: to all our requests their response is ever ready and to the point. Books indeed are a higher—a wider, more tenacious—memory, a store-house which is the common property of us all.

I attach great weight to the duty of handing down this priceless treasure to our sons. . . .

We come now to the consideration of the various subjects which may rightly be included under the name of "Liberal Studies." Amongst these I accord the first place to History, on grounds both of its attractiveness and of its utility, qualities which appeal equally to the scholar and to the statesman. Next in importance ranks Moral Philosophy, which indeed is, in a peculiar sense, a "Liberal Art," in that its purpose is to teach men the secret of true freedom. History, then, gives us the concrete examples of the precepts inculcated by philosophy.

William Harrison Woodward, *Vittorino Da Feltre and Other Humanist Educators* (Cambridge: Cambridge University Press, 1897), pp. 124, 127–129, 132–133.

The one shews what men should do, the other what men have said and done in the past, and what practical lessons we may draw there from for the present day. I would indicate as the third main branch of study, Eloquence, which indeed holds a place of distinction amongst the refined Arts. By philosophy we learn the essential truth of things, which by eloquence we so exhibit in orderly adornment as to bring conviction to differing minds. And history provides the light of experience—a cumulative wisdom fit to supplement the force of reason and the persuasion of eloquence. For we allow that soundness of judgment, wisdom of speech, integrity of conduct are the marks of a truly liberal temper. . . .

The Art of Letters . . . is a study adapted to all times and to all circumstances, to the investigation of fresh knowledge or to the re-casting and application of old. Hence the importance of grammar and of the rules of composition must be recognized at the outset, as the foundation on which the whole study of Literature must rest: and closely associated with these rudiments, the art of Disputation or Logical argument. The function of this is to enable us to discern fallacy from truth in discussion. Logic, indeed, as setting forth the true method of learning, is the guide to the acquisition of knowledge in whatever subject. Rhetoric comes next, and is strictly speaking the formal study by which we attain the art of eloquence; which, as we have just stated, takes the third place amongst the studies specially important in public life. . . .

After Eloquence we place Poetry and the Poetic Art, which though not without their value

in daily life and as an aid to oratory, have nevertheless their main concern for the leisure side of existence.

As to Music, the Greeks refused the title of "Educated" to anyone who could not sing or play. Socrates set an example to the Athenian youth, by himself learning to play in his old age; urging the pursuit of music not as a sensuous indulgence, but as an aid to the inner harmony of the soul. In so far as it is taught as a healthy recreation for the moral and spiritual nature, music is a truly liberal art, and, both as regards its theory and its practice, should find a place in education.

Arithmetic, which treats of the properties of numbers, Geometry, which treats of the properties of dimensions, lines, surfaces, and solid bodies, are weighty studies because they possess a peculiar element of certainty. The science of the Stars, their motions, magnitudes and distances, lifts us into the clear calm of the upper air. There we may contemplate the fixed stars, or the conjunctions of the planets, and predict the eclipses of the sun and the moon. The knowledge of Nature—animate and inanimate—the laws and the properties of things in heaven and in earth, their causes, mutations and effects, especially the explanation of their wonders (as they are popularly supposed) by the unravelling of their causes—this is a most delightful, and at the same time most profitable, study for youth. With these may be joined investigations concerning the weight of bodies, and those relative to the subject which mathematicians call "Perspective."

Lorenzo de' Medici
THE PURSUIT OF FAME AND GLORY

Another reason why Renaissance humanists admired antiquity was the praise Greek and Roman writers and artists received from their compatriots. The craving for fame and glory was a predominant feature of the Renaissance outlook. Breaking with the general medieval view that the pursuit of celebrity was sinful and a barrier to salvation, Renaissance humanists and artists longed for recognition, and bankers, generals, and princes wanted humanists to eulogize their accomplishments in words and sculptors to honor them in marble. In the following selection, Lorenzo de' Medici (1449–1492), ruler of the Florentine Republic, in a letter to Prince Federigo, son of the King of Naples, unabashedly expresses this quest for celebrity.

It has always been a matter of surprise to me that no great and fine work was originated in ancient times, either of hands or head, which did not receive private and public recognition and reward. So as all rivers and springs are said to have their origin from the great Ocean, all the famous deeds and marvellous works of bygone men may be said to derive from this laudable habit. The nutriment of every art is honour, and by the desire of glory alone are men's minds spurred to produce admirable works. Thus in Rome we see magnificent triumphal entries, in Greece the famous Olympian games, and both are celebrated by poets and orators with infinite mastery. For this alone were the chariot and the triumphal arch, the highly decorated theatres, the statues, the palm branches, the garlands, the funereal honours; for this alone were devised other splendid ornaments, and thus were encouraged high and noble deeds of the intellect and of the sword, all the marvellous works of the great men of ancient days, who assuredly (as our Tuscan poet says) will never lack fame so long as this world lasts. These of a truth were great and divine men, desirous of enduring fame and supremely grateful to those who, by celebrating the valour and noble deeds of great men in fine poetry, made their names immortal. Inflamed by such desire, Alexander the Great

on seeing the tomb of the famous Achilles with a sigh uttered those memorable words: "Fortunate art thou to have so glorious a sepulchre and to have been sung by such a pen." Fortunate indeed. For without the divine poet Homer Achilles' body and fame would have been buried in one tomb together. And even this poet, excellent above all others, would not have attained such honour and glory had he not been so admired by a learned Athenian, almost one may say raised from death to life. For after his death the great poet's noble work was scattered and dismembered until Pisistratus, prince of Athens, a man endowed with many virtues and of noble presence, offered large rewards to whosoever brought him verses by Homer. Thus with great diligence and care he collected and reconstructed the glorious poem, giving to it eternal life and to himself everlasting glory. For this reason the only epitaph on his statue is the record that he collected the poems of the great Homer. Oh, truly divine men, born for the good of humanity and of the world. The prince knew that his other deeds, however admirable, were as nothing compared with this one poem. Such were these antique men, whose deeds are not to be equalled in later times, and indeed are hardly believed. For as rewards for noble deeds no longer exist the flame of courage is extinguished; and as men do nothing worthy of praise the singers of great deeds are despised. If this had not been the case we should not now mourn the loss of so many Greek and Latin writers.

Lives of the Early Medici as Told in Their Correspondence, trans. and ed. Janet Ross (London: Chatto & Windos, 1910), pp. 88–90.

REVIEW QUESTIONS

1. What do historians mean by the term "Renaissance humanism"?
2. What made Petrarch aware that a *renaissance*, or rebirth, of classical learning was necessary in his time?

3. Why did Leonardo Bruni abandon his earlier course of studies to pursue the study of Greek literature?
4. What subjects made up the basic course of studies advocated by Bruni?
5. For Vergerius, what is the value of a liberal education?
6. How, according the Vergerius, do history, moral philosophy, and eloquence complement each other?
7. How do you interpret the desire of Renaissance figures for recognition and fame?

2 Human Dignity

In his short lifetime, Giovanni Pico della Mirandola (1463–1494) mastered Greek, Latin, Hebrew, and Arabic and aspired to synthesize the Hebrew, Greek, and Christian traditions. His most renowned work, *Oration on the Dignity of Man* (1486), has been called the humanist manifesto.

Pico della Mirandola
ORATION ON THE DIGNITY OF MAN

In the opening section of the *Oration*, Pico declares that unlike other creatures, human beings have not been assigned a fixed place in the universe. Our destiny is not determined by anything outside us. Rather, God has bestowed upon us a unique distinction: the liberty to determine the form and value our lives shall acquire. The notion that people have the power to shape their own lives is a key element in the emergence of the modern outlook.

I have read in the records of the Arabians, reverend Fathers, that Abdala the Saracen,[1] when questioned as to what on this stage of the world, as it were, could be seen most worthy of wonder, replied: "There is nothing to be seen more wonderful than man." In agreement with this opinion is the saying of Hermes Trismegistus: "A great miracle, Asclepius, is man."[2] But when I weighed the reason for these maxims, the many grounds for the excellence of human nature reported by many men failed to satisfy me—that man is the intermediary between creatures, the intimate of the gods, the king of the lower beings, by the acuteness of his senses, by the discernment of his reason, and by the light of his intelligence the interpreter of nature, the interval between fixed eternity and fleeting time, and (as the Persians say) the

Pico della Mirandola, "Oration on the Dignity of Man," trans. Elizabeth L. Forbes, from *The Renaissance Philosophy of Man*, ed. Ernst Cassirer, Paul Oskar Kristeller, and John H. Randall, Jr., pp. 223–225. Copyright © 1948 by the University of Chicago Press. Reprinted by permission.

[1]Abdala the Saracen possibly refers to the eighth-century A.D. writer Abd-Allah Ibn al-Muqaffa. —Eds.
[2]Ancient writings dealing with magic, alchemy, astrology, and occult philosophy were erroneously attributed to an assumed Egyptian priest, Hermes Trismegistus. Asclepius was a Greek god of healing. —Eds.

bond, nay, rather, the marriage song of the world, on David's [biblical king] testimony but little lower than the angels. Admittedly great though these reasons be, they are not the principal grounds, that is, those which may rightfully claim for themselves the privilege of the highest admiration. For why should we not admire more the angels themselves and the blessed choirs of heaven? At last it seems to me I have come to understand why man is the most fortunate of creatures and consequently worthy of all admiration and what precisely is that rank which is his lot in the universal chain of Being—a rank to be envied not only by brutes but even by the stars and by minds beyond this world. It is a matter past faith and a wondrous one. Why should it not be? For it is on this very account that man is rightly called and judged a great miracle and a wonderful creature indeed. . . .

. . . God the Father, the supreme Architect, had already built this cosmic home we behold, the most sacred temple of His godhead, by the laws of His mysterious wisdom. The region above the heavens He had adorned with Intelligences, the heavenly spheres He had quickened with eternal souls, and the excrementary and filthy parts of the lower world He had filled with a multitude of animals of every kind. But, when the work was finished, the Craftsman kept wishing that there were someone to ponder the plan of so great a work, to love its beauty, and to wonder at its vastness. Therefore, when everything was done (as Moses and Timaeus[3] bear witness), He finally took thought concerning the creation of man. But there was not among His archetypes that from which He could fashion a new offspring, nor was there in His treasure houses anything which He might bestow on His new son as an inheritance, nor was there in the seats of all the world a place where the latter might sit to contemplate the universe. All was now complete;

all things had been assigned to the highest, the middle, and the lowest orders. But in its final creation it was not the part of the Father's power to fail as though exhausted. It was not the part of His wisdom to waver in a needful matter through poverty of counsel. It was not the part of His kindly love that he who was to praise God's divine generosity in regard to others should be compelled to condemn it in regard to himself.

At last the best of artisans [God] ordained that that creature to whom He had been able to give nothing proper to himself should have joint possession of whatever had been peculiar to each of the different kinds of being. He therefore took man as a creature of indeterminate nature and, assigning him a place in the middle of the world, addressed him thus: "Neither a fixed abode nor a form that is thine alone nor any function peculiar to thyself have we given thee, Adam, to the end that according to thy longing and according to thy judgment thou mayest have and possess what abode, what form, and what functions thou thyself shalt desire. The nature of all other beings is limited and constrained within the bounds of laws prescribed by Us. Thou, constrained by no limits, in accordance with thine own free will, in whose hand We have placed thee, shalt ordain for thyself the limits of thy nature. We have set thee at the world's center that thou mayest from thence more easily observe whatever is in the world. We have made thee neither of heaven nor of earth, neither mortal nor immortal, so that with freedom of choice and with honor, as though the maker and molder of thyself, thou mayest fashion thyself in whatever shape thou shalt prefer. Thou shalt have the power to degenerate into the lower forms of life, which are brutish. Thou shalt have the power, out of thy soul's judgment, to be reborn into the higher forms, which are divine."

O supreme generosity of God the Father, O highest and most marvelous felicity of man! To him it is granted to have whatever he chooses, to be whatever he wills. Beasts as soon as they

---

[3]Timaeus, a Greek Pythagorean philosopher, was a central character in Plato's famous dialogue *Timaeus*. —Eds.

are born (so says Lucilius)[4] bring with them from their mother's womb all they will ever possess. Spiritual beings [angels], either from the beginning or soon thereafter, become what they are to be for ever and ever. On man when he came into life the Father conferred the seeds of all kinds and the germs of every way of life.

---

[4]Lucilius, a first-century A.D. Roman poet and Stoic philosopher, was a close friend of Seneca, the philosopher-dramatist. —Eds.

Whatever seeds each man cultivates will grow to maturity and bear in him their own fruit. If they be vegetative, he will be like a plant. If sensitive, he will become brutish. If rational, he will grow into a heavenly being. If intellectual, he will be an angel and the son of God. And if, happy in the lot of no created thing, he withdraws into the center of his own unity, his spirit, made one with God, in the solitary darkness of God, who is set above all things, shall surpass them all.

REVIEW QUESTIONS

1. According to Pico della Mirandola, what quality did humans alone possess? What did its possession allow them to do?
2. Compare Pico's view of the individual with that of Saint Augustine (page 173) and Pope Innocent III (page 287).

---

3 Individualism

Individualism was a hallmark of the Renaissance. The urban elite sought to demonstrate their unique talents, to assert their personalities, and to gain recognition for their accomplishments. Disdaining Christian humility, Renaissance individuals took pride in their talents and worldly accomplishments—"I can work miracles," said the great Leonardo da Vinci. Renaissance artists affixed their own signatures to their works.

Montaigne
ESSAYS

Another expression of Renaissance individualism was the effort of writers to explore their own lives, thoughts, and feelings. "I study myself more than any other subject." wrote the French Renaissance thinker Michel Eyguem de Montaigne (1533–1592) in his *Essays*. In this work, Montaigne attempted to study himself by reflecting on his personal experiences and judgments. In striving for self-understanding, Montaigne provides astute observations of human nature in general, as the following excerpts from *Essays* indicate.

. . . I would rather understand myself well by self-study than by reading Cicero. In the experience that I have of myself I find enough to make me wise, if I were a good scholar. Anyone who recalls the violence of his past anger, and to what a pitch his excitement carried him, will see its ugliness better than in Aristotle, and will conceive a juster hatred for it. Anyone who remembers the ills he has undergone and those that have threatened him, and the trivial happenings that have brought him from one state to another, thereby prepares himself for future changes and for the understanding of his condition.

Caesar's life has no more examples for us than our own; whether an emperor's or a common man's, it is still a life subject to all human accidents. Let us but listen to it, and we will tell ourselves all that we chiefly need to know. If a man remembers how very many times he has been wrong in his judgement, will it not be foolish of him not to mistrust it ever after? When I find myself convinced by another's argument that I have held a false opinion, I do not learn so much from the new fact he has taught me and from my ignorance on this particular point—this would be a small gain—as about my own weakness in general and the untrustworthiness of my understanding. From this I proceed to some reformation of the whole mass. With all my other errors I do the same, and find that my life greatly benefits by this rule. I do not look on the species and the individual as a stone over which I have stumbled; I learn to suspect my steps everywhere, and try to regulate them. To learn that one has said or done a foolish thing, that is nothing; one must learn that one is nothing but a fool, a much more comprehensive and important lesson. . . .

. . . So, in this matter of self-knowledge, the fact that everyone appears so decided and self-satisfied that everyone thinks he understands himself well enough, shows that nobody knows anything about himself, as Socrates pointed out. . . . I, who pretend to nothing else, find in myself such an infinite depth and variety that the sole fruit of my study is to make me feel how much I have still to learn. To this weakness of mine,

which I so often admit, I owe my tendency to be modest, to accept the beliefs laid down for me, and to be consistently cool and moderate in my opinions. I also owe to it my hatred for that tiresome and wrangling arrogance which believes and trusts entirely in itself, and is the chief enemy of learning and truth.

Listen to them laying down the law: the first stupidities they utter are in the style men use to proclaim religions and laws. "Nothing is more discreditable [said Cicero] than to assert and agree to something before we know and understand it." . . . Have we not even more reason to say this of our own? Assertion and dogmatism are positive signs of stupidity. . . .

This long attention that I give to self-study fits me to make very fair judgements of others; and there are few subjects of which I speak more happily and with better excuse. I am often able to see and distinguish my friends' nature more accurately than they do themselves.

One result of Montaigne's self-examination was to acquire an appreciation of physical pleasures which Christian theorists often disparaged.

I, who am a very earthy person, loathe that inhuman teaching which would make us despise and dislike the care of the body. I consider it just as wrong to reject natural pleasures as to set too much store by them. Xerxes was a fool when, lapped in all human delights, he offered a reward to anyone who would invent others. But hardly less of a fool is the man who curtails those pleasures which nature has found him. They should neither be pursued nor shunned; they should just be accepted. I accept them a little more liberally and kindly, and very readily let myself follow my natural inclination. . . . There are some who out of savage stupidity, as Aristotle says, despise [bodily delights].

Michel de Montaigne, *Essays*, trans. J. M. Cohen, pp. 354–357, 394–395. Copyright © J. M. Cohen, 1958. Used by permission of Penguin Books Ltd.

REVIEW QUESTIONS

1. For Montaigne, what is the value of self-study?
2. Have you ever benefited from self-study?

4 Break with Medieval Political Theory

Turning away from the religious orientation of the Middle Ages, Renaissance thinkers discussed the human condition in secular terms and opened up possibilities for thinking about moral and political problems in new ways. Thus, Niccolò Machiavelli (1469–1527), a Florentine statesman and political theorist, broke with medieval political theory. Medieval political thinkers held that the ruler derived power from God and had a religious obligation to rule in accordance with God's precepts. Machiavelli, though, ascribed no divine origin to kingship, nor did he attribute events to the mysterious will of God; and he explicitly rejected the principle that kings should adhere to Christian moral teachings. For Machiavelli, the state was a purely human creation. Successful kings or princes, he asserted, should be concerned only with preserving and strengthening the state's power and must ignore questions of good and evil, morality and immorality. Machiavelli did not assert that religion was supernatural in origin and rejected the prevailing belief that Christian morality should guide political life. For him, religion's value derived from other factors: a ruler could utilize religion to unite his subjects and to foster obedience to law.

Niccolò Machiavelli
THE PRINCE

In contrast to medieval thinkers, Machiavelli did not seek to construct an ideal Christian community but to discover how politics was *really* conducted. In *The Prince*, written in 1513 and published posthumously in 1532, he studied politics in the cold light of reason, as the following passage illustrates.

It now remains to be seen what are the methods and rules for a prince as regards his subjects and friends. And as I know that many have written of this, I fear that my writing about it may be deemed presumptuous, differing as I do, especially in this matter, from the opinions of others. But my intention being to write something of use to those who understand, it appears to me more proper to go to the real truth of the matter than to its imagination; and many have imagined republics and principalities which have never been seen or known to exist in reality; for how we live is so far removed from how we ought to live, that he who abandons what is done for what ought to be done, will rather learn to bring about his own ruin than his preservation.

Machiavelli removed ethics from political thinking. A successful ruler, he contended, is indifferent to moral and religious considerations. But will not the prince be punished on the Day of Judgment for violating Christian teachings? In startling contrast to medieval theorists, Machiavelli simply ignored the question. The action of a prince, he said, should be governed solely by necessity.

Excerpted from Niccolò Machiavelli, *The Prince*, trans. Luigi Ricci, rev. E. R. P. Vincent (1935), pp. 92–93, 97, 98–99, 101–103. By permission of Oxford University Press.

A man who wishes to make a profession of goodness in everything must necessarily come to grief among so many who are not good. Therefore it is necessary for a prince, who wishes to maintain himself, to learn how not to be good, and to use this knowledge and not use it, according to the necessity of the case.

Leaving on one side, then, those things which concern only an imaginary prince, and speaking of those that are real, I state that all men, and especially princes, who are placed at a greater height, are reputed for certain qualities which bring them either praise or blame. Thus one is considered liberal, another . . . miserly; . . . one a free giver, another rapacious; one cruel, another merciful; one a breaker of his word, another trustworthy; one effeminate and pusillanimous, another fierce and high-spirited; one humane, another haughty; one lascivious, another chaste; one frank, another astute; one hard, another easy; one serious, another frivolous; one religious, another an unbeliever, and so on. I know that every one will admit that it would be highly praiseworthy in a prince to possess all the above-named qualities that are reputed good, but as they cannot all be possessed or observed, human conditions not permitting of it, it is necessary that he should be prudent enough to avoid the scandal of those vices which would lose him the state, and guard himself if possible against those which will not lose it [for] him, but if not able to, he can indulge them with less scruple. And yet he must not mind incurring the scandal of those vices, without which it would be difficult to save the state, for if one considers well, it will be found that some things which seem virtues would, if followed, lead to one's ruin, and some others which appear vices result in one's greater security and wellbeing. . . .

. . . I say that every prince must desire to be considered merciful and not cruel. He must, however, take care not to misuse this mercifulness. Cesare Borgia was considered cruel, but his cruelty had brought order to the Romagna,[1]

united it, and reduced it to peace and fealty. If this is considered well, it will be seen that he was really much more merciful than the Florentine people, who, to avoid the name of cruelty, allowed Pistoia[2] to be destroyed. A prince, therefore, must not mind incurring the charge of cruelty for the purpose of keeping his subjects united and faithful; for, with a very few examples, he will be more merciful than those who, from excess of tenderness, allow disorders to arise, from whence spring bloodshed and rapine; for these as a rule injure the whole community, while the executions carried out by the prince injure only individuals. . . .

Machiavelli's rigorous investigation of politics led him to view human nature from the standpoint of its limitations and imperfections. The astute prince, he said, recognizes that human beings are by nature selfish, cowardly, and dishonest, and regulates his political strategy accordingly.

From this arises the question whether it is better to be loved more than feared, or feared more than loved. The reply is, that one ought to be both feared and loved, but as it is difficult for the two to go together, it is much safer to be feared than loved, if one of the two has to be wanting. For it may be said of men in general that they are ungrateful, voluble, dissemblers, anxious to avoid danger, and covetous of gain; as long as you benefit them, they are entirely yours; they offer you their blood, their goods, their life, and their children, as I have before said, when the necessity is remote; but when it approaches, they revolt. And the prince who has relied solely on their words, without making other preparations, is ruined; for the

---

[1]Cesare Borgia (c. 1476–1507) was the bastard son of Rodrigo Borgia, then a Spanish cardinal, and later Pope

Alexander VI (ruled 1492–1503). With his father's aid he attempted to carve out for himself an independent duchy in north-central Italy, with Romagna as its heart. Through cruelty, violence, and treachery, he succeeded at first in his ambition, but ultimately his principality collapsed. Romagna was eventually incorporated into the Papal State under Pope Julius II (ruled 1503–1513). —Eds.

[2]Pistoia, a small Italian city in Tuscany, came under the control of Florence in the fourteenth century. —Eds.

friendship which is gained by purchase and not through grandeur and nobility of spirit is bought but not secured, and at a pinch is not to be expended in your service. And men have less scruple in offending one who makes himself loved than one who makes himself feared; for love is held by a chain of obligation which, men being selfish, is broken whenever it serves their purpose; but fear is maintained by a dread of punishment which never fails.

Still, a prince should make himself feared in such a way that if he does not gain love, he at any rate avoids hatred; for fear and the absence of hatred may well go together, and will be always attained by one who abstains from interfering with the property of his citizens and subjects or with their women. And when he is obliged to take the life of any one, let him do so when there is a proper justification and manifest reason for it; but above all he must abstain from taking the property of others, for men forget more easily the death of their father than the loss of their patrimony. Then also pretexts for seizing property are never wanting, and one who begins to live by rapine will always find some reason for taking the goods of others, whereas causes for taking life are rarer and more fleeting.

But when the prince is with his army and has a large number of soldiers under his control, then it is extremely necessary that he should not mind being thought cruel; for without this reputation he could not keep an army united or disposed to any duty. Among the noteworthy actions of Hannibal[3] is numbered this, that although he had an enormous army, composed of men of all nations and fighting in foreign countries, there never arose any dissension either among them or against the prince, either in good fortune or in bad. This could not be due to anything but his inhuman cruelty, which together with his infinite other virtues, made him always venerated and terrible in the sight of his soldiers, and without

it his other virtues would not have sufficed to produce that effect. Thoughtless writers admire on the one hand his actions, and on the other blame the principal cause of them. . . .

> Again in marked contrast to the teachings of Christian (and ancient) moralists, Machiavelli said that the successful prince will use any means to achieve and sustain political power. If the end is desirable, all means are justified.

How laudable it is for a prince to keep good faith and live with integrity, and not with astuteness, every one knows. Still the experience of our times shows those princes to have done great things who have had little regard for good faith, and have been able by astuteness to confuse men's brains, and who have ultimately overcome those who have made loyalty their foundation.

You must know, then, that there are two methods of fighting, the one by law, the other by force: the first method is that of men, the second of beasts; but as the first method is often insufficient, one must have recourse to the second. It is therefore necessary for a prince to know well how to use both the beast and the man. . . .

A prince being thus obliged to know well how to act as a beast must imitate the fox and the lion, for the lion cannot protect himself from traps, and the fox cannot defend himself from wolves. One must therefore be a fox to recognise traps, and a lion to frighten wolves. Those that wish to be only lions do not understand this. Therefore, a prudent ruler ought not to keep faith when by so doing it would be against his interest, and when the reasons which made him bind himself no longer exist. If men were all good, this precept would not be a good one; but as they are bad, and would not observe their faith with you, so you are not bound to keep faith with them. Nor have legitimate grounds ever failed a prince who wished to show [plausible] excuse for the non-fulfilment of his promise. Of this one could furnish an infinite number of modern examples,

---

[3]Hannibal (247–182 B.C.) was a brilliant Carthaginian general whose military victories almost destroyed Roman power. He was finally defeated at the battle of Zama in 202 B.C. by the Roman general Scipio Africanus.—Eds.

and show how many times peace has been broken, and how many promises rendered worthless, by the faithlessness of princes, and those that have been best able to imitate the fox have succeeded best. But it is necessary to be able to disguise this character well, and to be a great feigner and dissembler; and men are so simple and so ready to obey present necessities, that one who deceives will always find those who allow themselves to be deceived. . . .

. . . Thus it is well to seem merciful, faithful, humane, sincere, religious, and also to be so; but you must have the mind so disposed that when it is needful to be otherwise you may be able to change to the opposite qualities. And it must be understood that a prince, and especially a new prince, cannot observe all those things which are considered good in men, being often obliged, in order to maintain the state, to act against faith, against charity, against humanity, and against religion. And, therefore, he must have a mind disposed to adapt itself according to the wind, and as the variations of fortune dictate, and, as I said before, not deviate from what is good, if possible, but be able to do evil if constrained.

A prince must take great care that nothing goes out of his mouth which is not full of the above-named five qualities, and, to see and hear him, he should seem to be all mercy, faith, integrity, humanity, and religion. And nothing is more necessary than to seem to have this last quality, for men in general judge more by the eyes than by the hands, for every one can see, but very few have to feel. Everybody sees what you appear to be, few feel what you are, and those few will not dare to oppose themselves to the many, who have the majesty of the state to defend them; and in the actions of men, and especially of princes, from which there is no appeal, the end justifies the means. Let a prince therefore aim at conquering and maintaining the state, and the means will always be judged honourable and praised by every one, for the vulgar is always taken by appearances and the issue of the event; and the world consists only of the vulgar, and the few who are not vulgar are isolated when the many have a rallying point in the prince. A certain prince of the present time, whom it is well not to name, never does anything but preach peace and good faith, but he is really a great enemy to both, and either of them, had he observed them, would have lost him state or reputation on many occasions.

REVIEW QUESTIONS

1. In what ways was Niccolò Machiavelli's advice to princes a break from the teachings of medieval political and moral philosophers?
2. How does Machiavelli's image of human nature compare with that of Pico della Mirandola, of Pope Gregory VII (page 234), and of Innocent III (page 287)?
3. Would Machiavelli's political advice help or hurt a politician in a modern democratic society?

5   The Ideal Gentleman

By the early sixteenth century, the era of the republics had come to an end in Italy, and the princely courts were the new social and political ideal. At the same time that Machiavelli was defining the new *political* ideal in his *Prince*, Baldassare Castiglione (1478–1529) was describing the new *social* ideal—the Renaissance courtier who served princes—in his *Book of the Courtier* (1528). Born into an illustrious Lombard family near Mantua, Castiglione received a humanist education in Latin and Greek and had a distinguished career serving in the courts of Italian dukes and Charles V in Spain. Castiglione's handbook became one of the most influential books of the day, providing instruction to aristocrats and nonaristocrats alike about how to be the perfect courtier or court lady. By the end of the sixteenth century, it had been translated into every major European language, making Castiglione the arbiter of aristocratic manners throughout Europe.

Like Greco-Roman moralists, Castiglione sought to overcome brutish elements in human nature and to shape a higher type of individual through reason. To structure the self artistically, to live life with verve and style, and to achieve a personal dignity were the humanist values that Castiglione's work spread beyond Italy.

Baldassare Castiglione
THE BOOK OF THE COURTIER

Castiglione chose the court of Urbino as the setting for his *Book of the Courtier,* which he wrote in the form of a conversation among the courtiers and ladies of the court. The participants—such as Guidobaldo, duke of Urbino; the duchess, Elisabetta Gonzaga; Count Ludovico da Canossa; and Cardinal Pietro Bembo— were all real people who in Castiglione's day had actual conversations at the court. In the first two books of *The Courtier,* Castiglione describes the ideal courtier as an example of the Renaissance "universal man," a well-rounded person with breadth of interest and versatility of accomplishment. For Castiglione, the courtier is a person of noble birth who is skilled in weaponry, an expert horseman, and adept at all sorts of games. And not only should the courtier be physically gifted, but he should be well educated. In the following passages, Count Ludovico declares that he should be learned in the humanities, the new educational curriculum of the Renaissance humanists. Moreover, in the spirit of the "universal man," he should be a musician, and he should display a knowledge of drawing and painting.

"I would have him more than passably learned in letters, at least in those studies which we call the humanities. Let him be conversant not only with the Latin language, but with Greek as well, because of the abundance and variety of things that are so divinely written therein.

Baldassare Castiglione, *The Book of the Courtier,* ed. Edgar Mayhew, trans. Charles Singleton, pp. 28–30, 32, 36–39, 70, 74, 77, 206–209. Copyright © 1959 by Charles S. Singleton and Edgar de N. Mayhew. Used by permission of Doubleday, a division of Random House, Inc.

Let him be versed in the poets, as well as in the orators and historians, and let him be practiced also in writing verse and prose, especially in our own vernacular; for, besides the personal satisfaction he will take in this, in this way he will never want for pleasant entertainment with the ladies, who are usually fond of such things. And if, because of other occupations or lack of study, he does not attain to such a perfection that his writings should merit great praise, let him take care to keep them under cover so that others will not laugh at him, and let him show them only to a friend who can be trusted; because at least they will be of profit to him in that, through such exercise, he will be capable of judging the writing of others. For it very rarely happens that a man who is unpracticed in writing, however learned he may be, can ever wholly understand the toils and industry of writers, or taste the sweetness and excellence of styles, and those intrinsic niceties that are often found in the ancients. . . .

"Gentlemen, you must know that I am not satisfied with our Courtier unless he also be a musician, and unless, besides understanding and being able to read music, he can play various instruments. For, if we rightly consider, no rest from toil and no medicine for ailing spirits can be found more decorous or praiseworthy in time of leisure than this; and especially in courts where, besides the release from vexations which music gives to all, many things are done to please the ladies, whose tender and delicate spirits are readily penetrated with harmony and filled with sweetness. Hence, it is no wonder that in both ancient and modern times they have always been particularly fond of musicians, finding the music a most welcome food for the spirit." . . .

Then the Count said: "Before we enter upon that subject, I would discuss another matter which I consider to be of great importance and which I think must therefore, in no way be neglected by our Courtier: and this is a knowledge of how to draw and an acquaintance with the art of painting itself."

REVIEW QUESTIONS

1. How does Castiglione's ideal gentleman reflect the spirit of Renaissance humanism and art?
2. Compare and contrast Castiglione's ideal courtier with what would be regarded as an ideal type during the Middle Ages.

---

6   The Genius of Leonardo da Vinci

Leonardo da Vinci (1452–1519) possessed extraordinary creative powers that awed his contemporaries. The Renaissance painter and art historian Giorgio Vasari said that Leonardo had "so rare a gift of talent and ability that to whatever subject he turned his attention, no matter how difficult, he presently made himself absolute master of it." His drawings, paintings, sculpture, innumerable inventions, and copious writings — exemplify the Renaissance spirit. They announced a new way of looking at nature and the individual. Leonardo examined objects in all their diversity and represented them realistically. For Leonardo, visual art was a means of arriving at nature's truths. Truth was attained when the artist brought both human reason and human creative capacity to bear on the direct experiences of the senses. Leonardo visually delineated the natural world with unprecedented scientific precision and simultaneously asserted his spiritual and intellectual freedom to do so. Through his art, Leonardo helped lay the foundations for modern science.

LEONARDO ON PAINTING

In his notebooks, Leonardo sketched an infinite variety of objects—inorganic, organic, human—and recorded fragmentary thoughts about them. Everywhere, he demonstrated a concern for the concrete specificity of things, which he depicted in minute detail. In the following excerpts on how the painter should represent a battle scene, Leonardo reveals his rigorous concern for accuracy.

The smoke [of artillery] which is mingled with the dust-laden air will as it rises to a certain height have more and more the appearance of a dark cloud, at the summit of which the smoke will be more distinctly visible than the dust. The smoke will assume a bluish tinge, and the dust will keep its natural colour. From the side whence the light comes this mixture of air and smoke and dust will seem far brighter than on the opposite side.

As for the combatants the more they are in the midst of this turmoil the less they will be visible, and the less will be the contrast between their lights and shadows.

You should give a ruddy glow to the faces and the figures and the air around them, and to the gunners and those near to them, and this glow should grow fainter as it is farther away from its cause. The figures which are between you and the light, if far away, will appear dark against a light background, and the nearer their limbs are to the ground the less will they be visible, for there the dust is greater and thicker. And if you make horses galloping away from the throng, make little clouds of dust as far distant one from another as is the space between the strides made by the horse, and that cloud which is farthest away from the horse should be the least visible, for it should be high and spread out and thin, while that which is nearest should be most conspicuous and smallest and most compact.

Let the air be full of arrows going in various directions, some mounting upwards, others falling, others flying horizontally; and let the balls shot from the guns have a train of smoke following their course. Show the figures in the foreground covered with dust on their hair and eyebrows and such other level parts as afford the dust a space to lodge.

Make the conquerors running, with their hair and other light things streaming in the wind, and with brows bent down; and they should be thrusting forward opposite limbs, that is, if a man advances the right foot, the left arm should also come forward. If you represent anyone fallen you should show the mark where he has been dragged through the dust which has become changed to blood-stained mire, and round about in the half-liquid earth you should show the marks of the trampling of men and horses who have passed over it.

Make a horse dragging the dead body of his master, and leaving behind him in the dust and mud the track of where the body was dragged along.

Make the beaten and conquered pallid, with brows raised and knit together, and let the skin above the brows be all full of lines of pain; at the sides of the nose show the furrows going in an arch from the nostrils and ending where the eye begins, and show the dilatation of the nostrils which is the cause of these lines; and let the lips be arched displaying the upper row of teeth, and let the teeth be parted after the manner of such as cry in lamentation. Show someone using his hand as a shield for his terrified eyes, turning the palm of it towards the enemy, and having the other resting on the ground to support the weight of his body; let others be crying out with their mouths wide open, and fleeing away. Put all sorts of armour lying between the feet of the combatants, such as broken shields, lances, swords, and other things like these. Make the dead, some half-buried in dust, others with

The Notebooks of Leonardo da Vinci, ed. Edward MacCurdy (New York: George Braziller, 1954), pp. 894–896. Jonathan Cape Ltd., an imprint of Random House Ltd. and used with permission.

the dust all mingled with the oozing blood and changing into crimson mud; and let the line of the blood be discerned by its colour, flowing in a sinuous stream from the corpse to the dust. Show others in the death agony grinding their teeth and rolling their eyes, with clenched fists grinding against their bodies and with legs distorted. Then you might show one, disarmed and struck down by the enemy, turning on him with teeth and nails to take fierce and inhuman vengeance; and let a riderless horse be seen galloping with mane streaming in the wind, charging among the enemy and doing them great mischief with his hoofs.

You may see there one of the combatants, maimed and fallen on the ground, protecting himself with his shield, and the enemy bending down over him and striving to give him the fatal stroke; there might also be seen many men fallen in a heap on top of a dead horse; . . . see that you make no level spot of ground that is not trampled over with blood.

LEONARDO ON HIS OWN GENIUS

In the following application for a position with Ludovico Sforza, duke of Milan, Leonardo lists his many talents.

Most Illustrious Lord: Having now sufficiently considered the specimens of all those who proclaim themselves skilled [designers] of instruments of war, . . . I shall endeavor, without prejudice to anyone else, to explain myself to your Excellency, showing your Lordship my secrets, and then offering them to your best pleasure and [approval] to work with effect at opportune moments on all those things which, in part, shall be briefly noted below.

1. I have a sort of extremely light and strong bridges, adapted to be most easily carried, and with them you may pursue and at any time flee from the enemy; and others, secure and indestructible by fire and battle, easy and convenient to lift and place. Also methods of burning and destroying those of the enemy.

2. I know how, when a place is besieged, to take the water out of the trenches, and make endless variety of bridges and covered ways and ladders, and other machines pertaining to such expeditions.

3. Item. If, by reason of the height of the banks, or the strength of the place and its position, it is impossible, when besieging a place, to avail oneself of the plan of bombardment, I have methods for destroying every rock or other fortress, even if it were founded on a rock. . . .

4. Again, I have kinds of mortars; most convenient and easy to carry; and with these I can fling small stones almost resembling a storm. . . .

5. Item. I have means by secret and [winding] mines and ways, made without noise, to reach a designated [spot], even if it were needed to pass under a trench or a river.

6. Item. I will make covered chariots, safe and unattackable. . . . And behind these, infantry could follow quite unhurt and without any hindrance.

7. Item. In case of need I will make big guns, mortars, and light ordnance of fine and useful forms, out of the common type.

8. Where the operation of bombardment should fail, I would contrive catapults . . . and other machines of marvellous efficacy and not in common use. . . .

The Literary Works of Leonardo da Vinci, compiled and ed. J. P. Richter (London: Sampson Low, et al., 1883), vol. 2, pt. 2, pp. 395–398.

9. And when the fight should be at sea I have kinds of many machines most efficient for offense and defense, and vessels which will resist the attack of the largest guns and powder and fumes.

10. In time of peace I believe I can give perfect satisfaction and to the equal of any other in architecture and the composition of buildings public and private; and in guiding water from one place to another.

11. Item. Also I can carry out sculpture in marble, bronze, or clay, and also I can do in painting whatever may be done, as well as any other, be he who he may. . . .

And if any one of the above-named things seem to anyone to be impossible, . . . I am most ready to make the experiment . . . in whatever place may please your Excellency.

REVIEW QUESTIONS

1. What does Leonardo da Vinci's advice on how to represent a battle scene reveal about his, artistic talents?
2. Which one of Leonardo's claims impressed you the most? Why?

---

7 Learned Renaissance Women

Except for nuns, few medieval women were literate. In Renaissance Italy, however, some upper- and middle-class girls did attend elementary school, where they learned to read and write and in some instances even studied Latin. Believing that learned daughters brought prestige to the family, some fathers hired tutors to instruct their daughters in the classics. Many female humanists had been taught by their enlightened humanist fathers who wanted their daughters to share in the richness of classical culture, which they perceived as training in virtue. Often, however, fathers perceived that education for females would simply make them better wives and household managers. Educated women often displayed a passion for studying literature. However, even educated and talented women were barred from entering the professions, including law and teaching in universities and upper-level boys' schools. A number of these women wrote works calling for equal education for women and the right to engage in the same scholarly pursuits as men.

Moderata Fonte
THE WORTH OF WOMEN

Moderata Fonte, a wealthy Venetian, completed the *Worth of Women* just before she died in childbirth in 1592 at the age of thirty-seven. The book's subtitle—*Wherein Is Clearly Revealed their Nobility and Their Superiority to Men*—shows the author's intent. The work consists of a dialogue among intelligent and articulate noble Venetian ladies who rail against men's behavior, particularly their determination to subjugate women. Following are excerpts from this feminist classic.

"We are not speaking ill of them out of envy." Leonora said, "but out of respect for the truth. For if a man steals (to take an example), he must be called a thief. If men usurp our rights, should we not complain and declare that they have wronged us? For if we are their inferiors in status, but not in worth, this is an abuse that has been introduced into the world and that men have then, over time, gradually translated into law and custom, and it has become so entrenched that they claim (and even actually believe) that the status they have gained through their bullying is theirs by right. And we women, who, among our other good qualities, are eminently mild, peaceable, and benign by nature, are prepared to put up even with an offense of this magnitude for the sake of a peaceful life. And we would suffer it still more willingly if they would just be reasonable and allow things to be equal and there to be some parity; if they did not insist on exerting such absolute control over us and in such an arrogant manner, treating us like slaves who cannot take a step without asking their permission or say a word without their jumping down our throats. Does this seem a matter of such little interest to us that we should be quiet and let things pass in silence?" . . .

"But we should not think that they behave like this only toward our sex [interjected Cornelia] for even among themselves they deceive one another, rob one another, destroy one another, and try to do each other down. Just think of all the assassinations, usurpations, perjuries, the blasphemy, gaming, gluttony, and other such vicious deeds they commit all the time. Not to mention the murders, assaults, and thefts, and other dissolute acts, all proceeding from men! And if they have so few scruples about committing these kind of excesses, think of what they are like where more minor

vices are concerned: just give a thought to their ingratitude, faithlessness, falsity, cruelty, arrogance, lust, and dishonesty!" . . .

"So, if, as I have shown, even amongst themselves they cannot show any mercy but rather despise one other and seek to harm one another, just consider how they will behave toward us. As fathers, as brothers, as sons or husbands or lovers or whatever other relationship they have to us, they all abuse us, humiliate us, and do all they can to harm . . . us. . . ."

But at that point Cornelia, interrupting their argument, continued, "Women who are married—or martyred, more accurately—have endless sources of misery. First there are those husbands who keep their wives on so tight a leash that they almost object to the air itself coming near them; so that the poor things, thinking that by marrying they are winning for themselves a certain womanly freedom to enjoy some respectable pastimes, find themselves more constricted than ever before, kept like animals within four walls and subjected to a hateful guardian rather than an affectionate husband. And it cannot be doubted that husbands such as these, through this kind of contemptuous treatment, cause the downfall of countless women who would be better behaved if their husbands were more kind and loving."

"You might add that there are some men," said Leonora, "who convince themselves that being so jealous and making life so unpleasant for their wives is the best way to keep them in line. Little do they know, poor fools, that their wives, seeing how little they are respected and how little faith their husbands have in them, finish up behaving as badly as they can! Whereas when a wife can see that her husband trusts her and is not going to interfere with her freedom, then she takes the yoke on her shoulders of her own free will and becomes jealous of herself. Because, quite apart from the respect she gains through her behavior, when a wife is treated so well by her husband,

Moderata Fonte, *The Worth of Women,* ed. and trans. Viginia Cox (Chicago: The University of Chicago Press, 1997), pp. 61–62, 68–71, 82. Reprinted by permission of The University of Chicago Press.

it would never occur to her to repay him so badly for his kind . . .

Cornelia then discusses three specific male vices

". . . Think of all those men who have wives as young and beautiful as angels and who, even so, neglect them and make fools of themselves over some shameless woman (for inevitably you do find a few such amid the masses of virtuous women), who may even be getting on in years and have very little going for her. Such men inflict endless sufferings on their wives, even stripping them of their most treasured things to give them to prostitutes, besides which, they very often make mistresses of their servants and fill the house with bastards and expect their wives to keep quiet and bring them up for them, so that the poor wives see themselves turned from the mistresses of a household into the prioresses of an orphanage. . . .

". . . They get so wrapped up in that cursed game of theirs that they stay out all day and all night with their gambling companions and leave their poor wives at home, so that instead of enjoying their nights in bed with their dear husbands, they have to spend their time sitting by the fire, counting the hours passing, like the watchmen on guard at the Arsenal, and waiting until dawn for their reprobate husbands finally to come home. And when they do come home, if by some unlucky chance they have lost, it's the wives who have to suffer for it, because the scoundrels take out all their anger on them, poor wretches. That's quite apart from the fact that they use up and squander all their wives' resources with this kind of perverse and vicious habit.

"Then there are those husbands who spend all their time shouting at their wives and who, if they don't find everything done just as they like it, abuse the poor creatures or even beat them over the most trivial matters, and who are always picking fault with the way in which the household is run, as though their wives were completely useless. And the poor women who are married to men like this gradually come to realize that they haven't, as they'd thought, left their childhood home to go and run their own household (which is the office of a wife, just as it is the husband's task to bring in the money and deal with the world outside); instead, it's as though they'd been sent to a strict schoolmaster. In fact, the poor things are so cowed and angered by the fury and nagging of their overbearing husbands that rather than loving them and longing to spend time with them, they find them irksome and want them to spend as much time as possible out of the house and out of their sight. You can tell from that quite how much pleasure the poor things get out of their husbands' bullying, to which they are condemned for life! And you can find endless examples of husbands who are irascible and intolerable in this way, though there may be different reasons why they are like that: some are bad by nature, while others undergo some kind of humiliation outside the home and then come home and try to give vent to their frustration by taking it out on their hapless wives." . . .

"But we women are so trusting, so kind and sensitive by nature [declared Leonora] that we are quick to trust; and then, since we are also compassionate and warmhearted, we cannot help loving in return (though in a sincere and virtuous manner). For we assume that men are like us, both in truthfulness and in purity of motives; and this tendency to judge men by ourselves is the cause of our downfall."

REVIEW QUESTION

Several of the ladies' complaints against men are also voiced by women today. Explain.

8   The Spread of the Renaissance

The Renaissance spread from Italy to Germany, France, England, and Spain. Exemplifying the Renaissance spirit in France was François Rabelais (c. 1495–c. 1553), a Benedictine monk (until he resigned from the order), a physician, and a humanist scholar. *Gargantua and Pantagruel*, Rabelais's satirical epic, attacked clerical education and monastic orders and expressed an appreciation for secular learning and a confidence in human nature. Like other Renaissance humanists, Rabelais criticized medieval philosophy for its overriding concern with obscure, confused, and irrelevant questions and censured a narrow-minded clergy who deprived people of life's joys. Expressing his aversion to medieval asceticism, he attacked monasticism as life-denying and extolled worldly pleasure as a legitimate need and aim of human nature.

François Rabelais
CELEBRATION OF THE WORLDLY LIFE

The following reading from *Gargantua and Pantagruel* contains a description of life at an imagined monastery, the abbey of Thélème, whose rules differed markedly from those of traditional medieval monasteries. Here Rabelais expressed the Renaissance celebration of the worldly life.

THE RULES ACCORDING TO WHICH THE THÉLÈMITES LIVED

All their life was regulated not by laws, statutes, or rules, but according to their free will and pleasure. They rose from bed when they pleased, and drank, ate, worked, and slept when the fancy seized them. Nobody woke them; nobody compelled them either to eat or to drink, or to do anything else whatever. So it was that Gargantua has established it. In their rules there was only one clause:

DO WHAT YOU WILL

because people who are free, well-born, well-bred, and easy in honest company have a natural spur and instinct which drives them to virtuous deeds and deflects them from vice; and this they called honour. When these same men are depressed and enslaved by vile constraint and subjection, they use this noble quality which once impelled them freely towards virtue, to throw off and break this yoke of slavery. For we always strive after things forbidden and covet what is denied us.

Making use of this liberty, they most laudably rivalled one another in all of them doing what they saw pleased one. If some man or woman said, "Let us drink," they all drank; if he or she said, "Let us play," they all played; if it was "Let us go and amuse ourselves in the fields," everyone went there. If it were for hawking or hunting, the ladies, mounted on fine mares, with their grand palfreys following, each carried on their daintily gloved wrists a

François Rabelais, *The Histories of Gargantua and Pantagruel*, trans. J. M. Cohen (Penguin Classics, 1955), pp. 194–195. Copyright © 1955 J. M. Cohen. Reproduced by permission of Penguin Books Ltd.

sparrow-hawk, a lanneret, or a merlin, the men carrying the other birds.[1]

So nobly were they instructed that there was not a man or woman among them who could not read, write, sing, play musical instruments, speak five or six languages, and compose in them both verse and prose. Never were seen such worthy knights, so valiant, so nimble both on foot and horse; knights more vigorous, more agile, handier with all weapons than they were. Never were seen ladies so good-looking, so dainty, less tiresome, more skilled with the fingers and the needle, and in every free and honest womanly pursuit than they were. . . .

Gargantua writes to his son Pantagruel, studying in Paris; in the letter, he describes a truly liberal education, one befitting a Renaissance humanist.

Now every method of teaching has been restored, and the study of languages has been revived: of Greek, without which it is disgraceful for a man to call himself a scholar, and of Hebrew, [other ancient Semitic languages], and Latin. The elegant and accurate art of printing, which is now in use, was invented in my time, by divine inspiration; as, by contrast, artillery was inspired by diabolical suggestion. The whole world is full of learned men, of very erudite tutors, and of most extensive libraries, and it is my opinion that neither in the time of Plato, of Cicero, nor of Papinian[2] were there such facilities for study as one finds today. No one, in future, will risk appearing in public or in any company, who is not well polished in Minerva's [Roman goddess of wisdom]

workshop. I find robbers, hangmen, freebooters, and grooms nowadays more learned than the doctors and preachers were in my time.

Why, the very women and girls aspire to the glory and reach out for the celestial manna[3] of sound learning. So much so that at my present age I have been compelled to learn Greek, which I had not despised like Cato,[4] but which I had not the leisure to learn in my youth. Indeed I find great delight in reading the *Morals* of Plutarch, Plato's magnificent *Dialogues*, the *Monuments* of Pausanias, and the *Antiquities* of Athenaeus,[5] while I wait for the hour when it will please God, my Creator, to call me and bid me leave this earth.

Therefore, my son, I beg you to devote your youth to the firm pursuit of your studies and to the attainment of virtue. You are in Paris. There you will find many praiseworthy examples to follow. You have Epistemon for your tutor, and he can give you living instruction by word of mouth. It is my earnest wish that you shall become a perfect master of languages. First of Greek, as Quintilian [Roman educational theorist] advises; secondly, of Latin; and then of Hebrew, on account of the Holy scriptures; also of Chaldean and Arabic, for the same reason; and I would have you model your Greek style on Plato's and your Latin on that of Cicero. Keep your memory well stocked with every tale from history, and here you will find help in the Cosmographes[6] of the historians. Of the liberal arts, geometry, arithmetic, and music, I gave you some smattering when you were still small, at the age of five or six. Go on

---

[1]*Palfreys* and *lanneret*, archaic terms, refer respectively to a saddle horse usually ridden by women and to a small male falcon native to the Mediterranean area. A merlin is a small black and white European falcon, now also called a pigeon hawk. —Eds.

[2]Papinian was a Roman jurist of the late second to early third century A.D. whose legal opinions were considered authoritative in late Roman law. —Eds.

[3]*Manna* refers to a food miraculously provided by God for the Hebrews during their exodus out of Egypt during Moses' time. —Eds.

[4]Cato the Elder (234–149 B.C.), a Roman statesman, was noted for his conservative morals and hostility to Greek influences in Roman society (see page 109). —Eds.

[5]Pausanias was a travel writer famous for his guides to the ancient monuments of Greece, and Athenaeus was a compiler of literary and philosophical writings. Both were Greeks of the second century A.D. —Eds.

[6]Cosmographes are books on geography, geology, and astronomy. —Eds.

and learn the rest, also the rules of astronomy. But leave divinatory astrology and Lully's[7] art alone, I beg of you, for they are frauds and vanities. Of Civil Law I would have you learn the best texts by heart, and relate them to the art of philosophy. And as for the knowledge of Nature's works, I should like you to give careful attention to that too; so that there may be no sea, river, or spring of which you do not know the fish. All the birds of the air, all the trees, shrubs, and bushes of the forest, all the herbs of the field, all the metals deep in the bowels of the earth, the precious stones of the whole East and the South—let none of them be unknown to you.

Then scrupulously peruse the books of the Greek, Arabian, and Latin doctors once more, not omitting the Talmudists and Cabalists,[8] and by frequent dissections gain a perfect knowledge of that other world which is man. At some hours of the day also, begin to examine the Holy scriptures. First the New Testament and the Epistles of the Apostles in Greek; and then the Old Testament, in Hebrew. In short, let me find you a veritable abyss of knowledge. For, later, when you have grown into a man, you will have to leave this quiet and repose of study, to learn chivalry and warfare, to defend my house, and to help our friends in every emergency against the attacks of evildoers.

---

[7]Lully alludes to Ramon Lull (c. 1236–1315), a Franciscan friar, a mystic, and a philosopher, who was falsely reputed to have authored various books on magic and alchemy. —Eds.

[8]Talmudists are students of the collection of writings on Jewish civil and religious laws, and Cabalists refers to students of a medieval Jewish occult tradition based on a mystical interpretation of the Hebrew scriptures. —Eds.

REVIEW QUESTIONS

1. In what ways did the curriculum recommended by Gargantua reflect the teachings of the Renaissance humanists?
2. How does the humanist educational program continue to influence the course of studies in modern universities?

CHAPTER 10

The Reformation

MARTIN LUTHER AND THE WITTENBERG REFORMERS, by Lucas Cranach the Younger, oil on wood panel, c. 1543. With Luther (left) are Frederick of Saxony, Luther's protector, who dominates the painting, and the Swiss reformer Huldreich Zwingli (to the right of Frederick). *(The Toledo Museum of Art; Gift of Edward Drummond Libbey)*

The reformation of the church in the sixteenth century was rooted in demands for spiritual renewal and institutional change. These pressures began as early as the late fourteenth century and came from many sources.

The papacy and orthodox Catholic theology were challenged by English theologian John Wycliffe (c. 1320–1384) and Czech theologian John Huss (c. 1369–1415). Both attacked the bishops' involvement in temporal politics and urged a return to the simple practices of the early apostolic church; and both, claiming that the Bible alone—not the church hierarchy—was the highest authority for Christians, emphasized study of the Holy scriptures by the laity and sermons in the common language of the people. Wycliffe, though not Huss, also undermined the clergy's authority by denying the priests' power to change the bread and wine into Christ's body and blood during the Mass. Despite severe persecution by church and state, followers of Wycliffe's and Huss' beliefs continued to exist and participated in the sixteenth-century Protestant movement.

Institutional reform from within was attempted through the Conciliar movement, which endeavored to restrict the pope's power through regular meetings of general councils of bishops. The Council of Constance (1414–1418) declared that a general council, not the papacy, was the supreme authority within the church and called for regular assemblies of bishops to consider the church's problems and initiate necessary reforms.

By the mid-fifteenth century, the Conciliar movement had collapsed, and the papacy, unreformed, freely exercised its supremacy. Fearful of losing its autonomy and power, the papacy resisted calling a new council from 1437 until 1512, when the Fifth Lateran Council met in Rome under close papal supervision. The council issued decrees aimed at improving education of the clergy, eliminating many abuses in church administration, and summoning a church council every five years. But the council's decrees were not implemented after the last session ended in 1517, the same year Martin Luther first challenged the papacy, thus starting the Protestant reform movement.

The principal source of the reform spirit was a widespread popular yearning for a more genuine spirituality. It took many forms: the rise of new pious practices; greater interest in mystical experiences and in the study of the Bible; the development of communal ways for lay people to live and work following the apostles' example; and a heightened search for ways within secular society to imitate more perfectly the life of Christ—called the New Devotion movement.

Several secular factors contributed to this heightening of spiritual feeling. The many wars, famines, and plagues of the late fourteenth and the fifteenth centuries had traumatized Europe. The increasing educational level of the urban middle class and skilled laborers and the invention of the printing press allowed the rapid and relatively inexpensive spread of captivating and controversial religious ideas. Finally, there was the influence of the humanist movement, particularly in northern Europe and Spain. Many humanists dedicated themselves to promoting higher levels of religious education. They stimulated public interest in biblical study by publishing new editions of the Holy scriptures and the writings of the church fathers, along with new devotional literature. Nearly all the religious reformers of the sixteenth century were deeply influenced by the ideals and methods of the Christian humanist movement.

In Germany, a spirit of discontent with social and economic conditions coincided with the demand for reform of the church and religious life. For several decades before Luther's revolt against the papacy, the economic conditions of the knights, the peasants, and the lower-class urban workers had deteriorated. The knights' grievances included loss of their political power to the centralizing governments of the German princes and increasing restrictions on their customary feudal privileges. Peasants protested that lords had steadily withdrawn certain of their customary rights and had added burdens, increasing the lords' income and control over their estates. The knights and peasants were squeezed into an ever-worsening social and economic niche. In the cities, the lower-class artisans and laborers were similarly oppressed. Those in the urban upper classes, who controlled town governments, enhanced their own economic privileges at the expense of lower-class citizens. The church, which was a major landowner and active in commercial enterprises in the towns, played an important role in these conflicts. All these grievances formed the explosive background to Martin Luther's challenge to the authority of the church and the Holy Roman Emperor, Charles V.

The success of the reformers, both Protestant and Catholic, depended on support from the ruling political forces in the various kingdoms, principalities, and city-states of Europe. Usually, the rulers' religious preference determined whether the church in that area remained Catholic or became Lutheran, Calvinist, or some combination of all three, as in England. The rulers of large parts of Germany, especially the imperial city-states, and of the Scandinavian kingdoms adopted the Lutheran reform. The Austrian and Spanish Hapsburg emperors and the French kings remained Catholic, although Calvinism had many adherents in France. In Eastern Europe, Protestantism was successful at first, but, under the influence of the Catholic reform movement, Catholicism later recovered its dominance. In Switzerland, allegiance was divided among Catholics and the followers of John Calvin, reformer of the church in Geneva, and of Ulrich Zwingli, reformer of the church in Zurich. Calvinism took root in Scotland, and its influence also grew in England, where it inspired the Puritan movement.

These divisions in the Christian church marked a turning point in European history and culture, ending forever the coherent worldview of medieval Christendom. The Reformation split the peoples of Europe into two broad political, intellectual, and spiritual camps: Protestant and Catholic. With the moral, political, and ideological power of the church significantly diminished, post-Reformation society was open to increasing secularization on all fronts. By ending the religious unity of the Middle Ages and weakening the authority of the Roman Catholic Church, the Reformation contributed significantly to the rise of modernity.

1 A Catholic Critic of the Church

The greatest scholar and most popular humanist author of the early sixteenth century was the Dutch priest Desiderius Erasmus (1466–1536). Educated under the influence of the New Devotion and well trained in the new humanistic studies, Erasmus dedicated his life to purifying the Latin and Greek texts of the Bible and those of the early fathers of the church. He used his wit and humanistic learning in his preaching to advocate a simpler yet more intense Christian life modeled on Christ. Erasmus castigated those who pandered to the superstitions of people by encouraging magical beliefs about relics, the cults of the saints, indulgences (see the next section), and other abuses of pious practices. He also was hostile to the excessive influence of scholastic philosophers on the church's theology, believing that in their quibbling over obscure philosophical-theological issues, they mocked the Christian faith as revealed in the New Testament. An Augustinian monk who preferred to live outside the monastery, Erasmus severely criticized the lax practices of monks and clergy. He argued, too, that salvation was not based on ascetic and ceremonial acts, but on deeds of love.

Although Erasmus at first welcomed Martin Luther's call for reform, he quickly discerned that Luther was going far beyond what he, Erasmus, felt was wise or necessary. He urged, instead, reform within the church's framework. Although scandalized by a pope leading armies and engaging in international war against other Christians, Erasmus clung loyally to the hierarchical church. He urged peace and civility on all parties, condemned extremist positions, and tried to work for peaceful reconciliation and reform. In 1524, Erasmus wrote a reasoned defense of the role of free will in the process of salvation, taking a Catholic position on this difficult theological problem. Luther was furious with Erasmus for not supporting him, and Erasmus found himself abused by zealots from both camps. To the end, he remained a devout, loyal, but critical Catholic reformer. His preaching, piety, and literary scholarship exemplified the ideals of Christian humanism.

Desiderius Erasmus
IN PRAISE OF FOLLY

Erasmus's most famous work was *In Praise of Folly*, written in 1509, before Luther's first challenge to the church. In the following passages, speaking through the voice of Folly, Erasmus castigates monks, theologians, and other Christians for failing to discern the true purpose of the Christian life: the imitation of Christ. It was said of Erasmus that he laid the egg Luther hatched—a judgment Erasmus did not acknowledge.

As for the theologians, perhaps it would be better to pass them over in silence, "*not stirring up the hornets' nest*" and "not laying a finger on the stinkweed," since this race of men is incredibly arrogant and touchy. For they might rise up en masse and march in ranks against me with six hundred conclusions and force me to recant. And if I should refuse, they would immediately shout "heretic." For this is the thunderbolt they always keep ready at a moment's notice to terrify anyone to whom they are not very favorably inclined. . . .

. . . They are so blessed by their Selflove as to be fully persuaded that they themselves dwell in the third heaven, looking down from high above on all other mortals as if they were earth-creeping vermin almost worthy of their pity. They are so closely hedged in by rows of magistral definitions, conclusions, corollaries, explicit and implicit propositions, they have so many *"holes they can run to,"* that Vulcan [Roman god of fire] himself couldn't net them tightly enough to keep them from escaping by means of distinctions, with which they cut all knots as cleanly as the fine-honed edge of "the headsman's axe"— so many new terms have they thought up and such monstrous jargon have they coined. . . .

In all of these there is so much erudition, so much difficulty, that I think the apostles themselves would need to be inspired by a different spirit if they were forced to match wits on such points with this new breed of theologians. Paul could provide a living example of faith, but when he said "Faith is the substance of things to be hoped for and the evidence of things not seen," his definition was not sufficiently magisterial. So, too, he lived a life of perfect charity, but he neither distinguished it nor defined it with sufficient dialectical precision in the first epistle to the Corinthians, chapter 13. . . .

. . . But Christ, interrupting their boasts (which would otherwise never come to an end), will say, "Where did this new race of Jews [quibbling theologians] come from? The only law I recognize as truly mine is the only one I hear nothing about. Long ago, not speaking obliquely in

parables but quite openly, I promised my Father's inheritance not to hoods [worn by monks], or trifling prayers, or fasts, but rather deeds of faith and charity. Nor do I acknowledge those who too readily acknowledge their own deeds: those who want to appear even holier than I am can go dwell in the heavens of the Abraxasians[1] if they like, or they can order that a new heaven be built for them by the men whose petty traditions they have placed before my precepts." When they hear this and see sailors and teamsters chosen in preference to them, how do you suppose their faces will look as they stare at each other? . . .

Almost as happy as the theologians are those men who are commonly called "religious" and "monks"—though both names are quite incorrect, since a good part of them are very far removed from religion and no one is encountered more frequently everywhere you go. I cannot imagine how anything could be more wretched than these men. . . . For even though everyone despises this breed of men so thoroughly that even a chance meeting with one of them is considered unlucky, still they maintain a splendid opinion of themselves. First of all, they consider it the very height of piety to have so little to do with literature as not even to be able to read. Moreover, when they roar out their psalms in church like braying asses (counting their prayers indeed, but understanding them not at all), then (of all things!) they imagine that the listening saints are soothed and caressed with manifold delight. Among them are some who make a great thing out of their squalor and beggary, who stand at the door bawling out their demands for bread—(indeed there is no inn or coach or ship where they do not make a disturbance), depriving other beggars of no small share of their income. And in this manner these most agreeable fellows, with their filth, ignorance, coarseness, impudence, recreate for us, as they say, an image of the apostles. . . .

Closely related to such men are those who have adopted the very foolish (but nevertheless quite

Excerpted from Desiderius Erasmus, *In Praise of Folly*, trans. Clarence H. Miller, pp. 63, 87–88, 90, 98–99, 100–101. Copyright © 1979. Reprinted by permission from Yale University Press.

[1]A heretical sect that believed there were 365 "heavens."—Eds.

agreeable) belief that if they look at a painting or statue of that huge . . . Christopher, they will not die on that day; or, if they address a statue of Barbara with the prescribed words, they will return from battle unharmed, or, if they accost Erasmus on certain days, with certain wax tapers, and in certain little formulas of prayer, they will soon become rich.[2] Moreover, in George they have discovered a new Hercules. . . .[3] They all but worship George's horse, most religiously decked out in breastplates and bosses [ornaments], and from time to time oblige him with some little gift. To swear by his bronze helmet is thought to be an oath fit for a king.

Now what shall I [Folly] say about those who find great comfort in soothing self-delusions about fictitious pardons for their sins, measuring out the times in purgatory down to the droplets of a waterclock, parceling out centuries, years, months, days, hours, as if they were using mathematical tables. Or what about those who rely on certain little magical tokens and prayers thought up by some pious impostor for his own amusement or profit? They promise themselves anything and everything: wealth, honor, pleasure, an abundance of everything, perpetual health, a long life, flourishing old age, and finally a seat next to Christ among the saints, though this last they don't want for quite a while yet—that is, when the pleasures of this life, to which they cling with all their might, have finally slipped through their fingers, then it will be soon enough to enter into the joys of the saints. Imagine here, if you please, some businessman or soldier or judge who thinks that if he throws into the collection basket one coin from all his plunder, the whole cesspool of his

sinful life will be immediately wiped out. He thinks all his acts of perjury, lust, drunkenness, quarreling, murder, deception, dishonesty, betrayal are paid off like a mortgage, and paid off in such a way that he can start off once more on a whole new round of sinful pleasures.

Now who could be more foolish—rather, who could be happier—than those who assure themselves they will have the very ultimate felicity because they have recited daily those seven little verses from the holy psalms? A certain devil—certainly a merry one, but too loose-lipped to be very clever—is believed to have mentioned them to St. Bernard,[4] but the poor devil was cheated by a clever trick. Such absurdities are so foolish that even I am almost ashamed of them, but still they are approved not only by the common people but even by learned teachers of religion. . . .

But why have I embarked on this vast sea of superstitions?

Not if I had a hundred tongues, a hundred
    mouths,
A voice of iron, could I survey all kinds
Of fools, or run through all the forms of folly.[5]

So rife, so teeming with such delusions is the entire life of all Christians everywhere. And yet priests are not unwilling to allow and even foster such delusions because they are not unaware of how many emoluments accumulate from this source. In the midst of all this, if some odious wiseman should stand up and sing out the true state of affairs: "You will not die badly if you live well. You redeem your sins if to the coin you add a hatred of evil deeds, then tears, vigils, prayers, fasts, and if you change your whole way of life. This saint will help you if you imitate his life"—if that wiseman were to growl out such assertions and more like them, look how much happiness he would immediately take away from the minds of mortals, look at the confusion he would throw them into!

---

[2]Christopher refers to Saint Christopher, a popular legendary giant and the patron saint of travelers. Barbara was a widely venerated but legendary early Christian martyr and saint. Erasmus, an Italian bishop and also a saint, was martyred in about A.D. 303. —Eds.

[3]George, the patron saint of England and of the crusaders, was believed to have been martyred in about A.D. 300. Saint George's battle with a dragon was a popular legend. Hercules, a Greek hero, performed twelve difficult tasks that won him immortality as a gift of the gods. He was himself worshiped as a god by later Greeks and Romans. —Eds.

---

[4]Saint Bernard (1091–1153) was a leading theologian, Cistercian monk, and preacher. —Eds.
[5]Virgil's *Aeneid* 6.625–627. —Eds.

REVIEW QUESTIONS

1. What criticisms did Desiderius Erasmus make of the institutional church?
2. What did he see as the solution to the ills afflicting the church?

2 The Lutheran Reformation

The reformation of the western Christian church in the sixteenth century was precipitated by Martin Luther (1483–1546). A pious German Augustinian monk and theologian, Luther had no intention of founding a new church or overthrowing the political and ecclesiastical order of late medieval Europe. He was educated in the tradition of the New Devotion, and as a theology professor at the university in Wittenberg, Germany, he opposed rationalistic, scholastic theology. Sympathetic at first to the ideas of Christian humanists like Erasmus, Luther too sought a reform of morals and an end to abusive practices within the church. But a visit to the papal court in Rome in 1510 left him profoundly shocked at its worldliness and disillusioned with the papacy's role in the church's governance.

Martin Luther
CRITIQUE OF CHURCH DOCTRINES

To finance the rebuilding of the church of St. Peter in Rome, the papacy in 1515 offered indulgences to those who gave alms for this pious work. An indulgence was a mitigation or remission of the penance imposed by a priest in absolving a penitent who confessed a sin and indicated remorse. Indulgences were granted by papal decrees for those who agreed to perform some act of charity, alms-giving, prayer, pilgrimage, or other pious work. Some preachers of this particular papal indulgence deceived people into believing that a "purchase" of this indulgence would win them, or even the dead, a secure place in heaven.

In 1517, Luther denounced the abuses connected with the preaching of papal indulgences. The quarrel led quickly to other and more profound theological issues. His opponents defended the use of indulgences on the basis of papal authority, shifting the debate to questions about the nature of papal power within the church. Luther responded with a vigorous attack on the whole system of papal governance. The principal points of his criticism were set out in his *Address to the Christian Nobility of the German Nation Concerning the Reform of the Christian Estate*, published in August 1520. In the first excerpt that follows, Luther argued that the papacy was blocking any reform of the church and appealed to the nobility of Germany to intervene by summoning a "free council" to reform the church.

A central point of contention between Luther and Catholic critics was his theological teaching on justification (salvation) by faith and on the role of good works in the scheme of salvation. Luther had suffered anguish about his unworthiness before God. Then, during a mystical experience, Luther suddenly perceived that his salvation came not because of his good works but as a free gift from God due to Luther's faith in Jesus Christ.

Thus, while never denying that a Christian was obliged to perform good works, Luther argued that such pious acts were not helpful in achieving salvation. His claim that salvation, or justification, was attained through faith in Jesus Christ as Lord and Savior, and through that act of faith alone, became the rallying point of the Protestant reformers.

The Catholic position, not authoritatively clarified until the Council of Trent (1545–1563), argued that justification came not only through faith, but through hope and love as well, obeying God's commandments and doing good works. In *The Freedom of a Christian*, published in 1520, Luther outlined his teaching on justification by faith and on the inefficacy of good works; the second excerpt is from this work.

Another dispute between Luther and papal theologians was the question of interpretation of the Bible. In the medieval church, the final authority in any dispute over the meaning of scriptural texts or church doctrine was ordinarily the pope alone, speaking as supreme head of the church or in concert with the bishops in an ecumenical council. The doctrine of papal infallibility (that the pope could not err in teaching matters of faith and morals) was already well known, but belief in this doctrine had not been formally required. Luther argued that the literal text of scripture was alone the foundation of Christian truth, not the teaching of popes or councils. Moreover, Luther said that all believers were priests, and the clergy did not hold any power beyond that of the laity; therefore the special privileges of the clergy were unjustified. The third excerpt contains Luther's views on the interpretation of scripture and the nature of priestly offices.

ON PAPAL POWER

The Romanists [traditional Catholics loyal to the papacy] have very cleverly built three walls around themselves. Hitherto they have protected themselves by these walls in such a way that no one has been able to reform them. As a result, the whole of Christendom has fallen abominably.

In the first place, when pressed by the temporal power they have made decrees and declared that the temporal power had no jurisdiction over them, but that, on the contrary, the spiritual power is above the temporal. In the second place, when the attempt is made to reprove them with the scriptures, they raise the objection that only the pope may interpret the scriptures. In the third place, if threatened with a council, their story is that no one may summon a council but the pope.

In this way they have cunningly stolen our three rods from us, that they may go unpunished. They have [settled] themselves within the safe stronghold of these three walls so that they can practice all the knavery and wickedness which we see today. Even when they have been compelled to hold a council they have weakened its power in advance by putting the princes

Martin Luther, *Luther's Works,* vol. 44: *The Christian in Society I,* ed. James Atkinson (55 volumes; Philadelphia: Concordia Publishing House, Muhlenberg Press, and Fortress Press, 1955–1986), pp. 126–127, 136–137. Copyright © 1966 by Augsburg Fortress Publishers. Used by permission.

under oath to let them remain as they were. In addition, they have given the pope full authority over all decisions of a council, so that it is all the same whether there are many councils or no councils. They only deceive us with puppet shows and sham fights. They fear terribly for their skin in a really free council! They have so intimidated kings and princes with this technique that they believe it would be an offense against God not to be obedient to the Romanists in all their knavish and ghoulish deceits. . . .

The Romanists have no basis in scripture for their claim that the pope alone has the right to call or confirm a council. This is just their own ruling, and it is only valid as long as it is not harmful to Christendom or contrary to the laws of God. Now when the pope deserves punishment, this ruling no longer obtains, for not to punish him by authority of a council is harmful to Christendom. . . .

Therefore, when necessity demands it, and the pope is an offense to Christendom, the first man who is able should, as a true member of the whole body, do what he can to bring about a truly free council. No one can do this so well as the temporal authorities, especially since they are also fellow-Christians, fellow-priests, fellow-members of the spiritual estate, fellow-lords over all things. Whenever it is necessary or profitable they ought to exercise the office and work which they have received from God over everyone.

JUSTIFICATION BY FAITH

You may ask, "What then is the Word of God, and how shall it be used, since there are so many words of God?" I answer: The Apostle explains this in Romans 1. The Word is the gospel of God concerning his Son, who was made flesh, suffered, rose from the dead, and was glorified

Martin Luther, *Luther's Works*, vol. 31: *Career of the Reformer I*, ed. Harold J. Grimm, gen. eds. Jaroslav Pelican and Helmut T. Lehmann (55 volumes; Philadelphia: Concordia Publishing House, Muhlenberg Press, and Fortress Press, 1955–1986), pp. 346–347, 372–373. Copyright © 1966 by Augsburg Fortress Publishers. Used by permission.

through the Spirit who sanctifies. To preach Christ means to feed the soul, make it righteous, set it free, and save it, provided it believes the preaching. Faith alone is the saving and efficacious use of the Word of God, according to Rom. 10[:9]: "If you confess with your lips that Jesus is Lord and believe in your heart that God raised him from the dead, you will be saved." Furthermore, "Christ is the end of the law, that every one who has faith may be justified" [Rom. 10:4]. Again, in Rom. 1[:17], "He who through faith is righteous shall live." The Word of God cannot be received and cherished by any works whatever but only by faith. Therefore it is clear that, as the soul needs only the Word of God for its life and righteousness, so it is justified by faith alone and not any works; for if it could be justified by anything else, it would not need the Word, and consequently it would not need faith.

This faith cannot exist in connection with works—that is to say, if you at the same time claim to be justified by works, whatever their character—for that would be the same as "limping with two different opinions" [1 Kings 18:21], as worshiping Baal and kissing one's own hand [Job 31:27–28], which, as Job says, is a very great iniquity. Therefore the moment you begin to have faith you learn that all things in you are altogether blameworthy, sinful, and damnable, as the Apostle says in Rom. 3[:23], "Since all have sinned and fall short of the glory of God," and, "None is righteous, no, not one: . . . all have turned aside, together they have gone wrong" [Rom. 3:10–12]. When you have learned this you will know that you need Christ, who suffered and rose again for you so that, if you believe in him, you may through this faith become a new man in so far as your sins are forgiven and you are justified by the merits of another, namely, of Christ alone.

Since, therefore, this faith can rule only in the inner man, as Rom. 10[:10] says, "For man believes with his heart and so is justified," and since faith alone justifies, it is clear that the inner man cannot be justified, freed, or saved by any outer work or action at all, and that these works, whatever their character, have nothing to do with this inner man.

On the other hand, only ungodliness and unbelief of heart, and no outer work, make him guilty and a damnable servant of sin. Wherefore it ought to be the first concern of every Christian to lay aside all confidence in works and increasingly to strengthen faith alone and through faith to grow in the knowledge, not of works, but of Christ Jesus, who suffered and rose for him, as Peter teaches in the last chapter of his first Epistle [1 Pet. 5:10]. No other work makes a Christian. . . .

Our faith in Christ does not free us from works but from false opinions concerning works, that is, from the foolish presumption that justification is acquired by works. Faith redeems, corrects, and preserves our consciences so that we know that righteousness does not consist in works, although works neither can nor ought to be wanting; just as we cannot be without food and drink and all the works of this mortal body, yet our righteousness is not in them, but in faith; and yet those works of the body are not to be despised or neglected on that account. In this world we are bound by the needs of our bodily life, but we are not righteous because of them. "My kingship is not of this world" [John 18:36], says Christ. He does not, however, say, "My kingship is not here, that is, in this world." And Paul says, "Though we live in the world we are not carrying on a worldly war" [2 Cor. 10:3], and in Gal. 2[:20], "The life I now live in the flesh I live by faith in the Son of God." Thus what we do, live, and are in works and ceremonies, we do because of the necessities of this life and of the effort to rule our body. Nevertheless we are righteous, not in these, but in the faith of the Son of God.

THE INTERPRETATION OF THE BIBLE AND THE NATURE OF THE CLERGY

They (the Roman Catholic Popes) want to be the only masters of scriptures. . . . They assume

What Luther Says: An Anthology, compiled by Ewald M. Plass (3 vols.; Saint Louis, Missouri: Concordia Publishing House, 1959), vol. 2, pp. 1062, 1063; vol. 3, pp. 1139, 1140; vol. 2, p. 943.

sole authority for themselves and would persuade us with insolent juggling of words that the Pope, whether he be bad or good, cannot err in matters of faith. . . .

. . . They cannot produce a letter to prove that the interpretation of scripture . . . belongs to the Pope alone. They themselves have usurped this power . . . and though they allege that this power was conferred on Peter when the keys were given to him, it is plain enough that the keys were not given to Peter alone but to the entire body of Christians [Matt. 16:19; 18:18]. . . .

. . . Every baptized Christian is a priest already, not by appointment or ordination from the Pope or any other man, but because Christ Himself has begotten him as a priest . . . in baptism. . . .

The Pope has usurped the term "priest" for his anointed and tonsured hordes [clergy and monks]. By this means they have separated themselves from the ordinary Christians and have called themselves uniquely the "clergy of God," God's heritage and chosen people who must help other Christians by their sacrifice and worship. . . . Therefore the Pope argues that he alone has the right and power to ordain and do what he will. . . .

[But] the preaching office is no more than a public service which happens to be conferred on someone by the entire congregation all the members of which are priests. . . .

. . . The fact that a pope or bishop anoints, makes tonsures, ordains, consecrates [makes holy], and prescribes garb different from those of the laity . . . nevermore makes a Christian and a spiritual man. Accordingly, through baptism all of us are consecrated to the priesthood, as St. Peter says . . . [1 Pet. 2:9].

To make it still clearer, if a small group of pious Christian laymen were taken captive and settled in a wilderness and had among them no priest consecrated by a bishop, if they were to agree to choose one from their midst, married or unmarried, and were to charge him with the office of baptizing, saying Mass, absolving [forgiving of sins], and preaching, such a man would be as truly a priest as he would if all bishops and popes had consecrated him.

Ulrich von Hutten
RESENTMENT OF ROME

Many Germans were drawn to Luther's message, for it signified a return to the spiritual purity of the first Christians, which had been undermined by a wealthy and corrupt church. Most historians agree that religious considerations—people's yearning for greater holiness and communion with God—were the principal reasons Luther attracted a following. But economic and political factors also drew Germans to him. The urban middle class, in particular, greatly resented the draining of money from German lands in order to provide a luxurious lifestyle for the Roman upper clergy. In a letter written in 1520 to the Elector Frederick of Saxony, Ulrich von Hutten (1488–1523), a distinguished humanist and supporter of Luther, angrily denounced the Roman church for plundering German lands. Hutten's words, excerpted below, also reveal an emerging sense of German national feeling.

We see that there is no gold and almost no silver in our German land. What little may perhaps be left is drawn away daily by the new schemes invented by the council of the most holy members of the Roman curia. What is thus squeezed out of us is put to the most shameful uses. Would you know, dear Germans, what employment I have myself seen that they make at Rome of our money? It does not lie idle! Leo the Tenth gives a part to nephews and relatives (these are so numerous that there is a proverb at Rome, "As thick as Leo's relations"). A portion is consumed by so many most reverend cardinals (of which the holy father created no less than one and thirty in a single day), as well as to support innumerable [auditors, personal secretaries, palace managers, and other high officials] forming the élite of the great head church. These in turn draw after them at untold expense copyists, beadles, messengers, servants, scullions [kitchen help], mule drivers, grooms and an innumerable army of prostitutes and of the most degraded followers. They maintain dogs, horses, monkeys, long-tailed apes and many more such creatures for their pleasure. They construct houses all of marble. They have precious

Translations and Reprints from the Original Sources of European History, ed. and trans. James Harvey Robinson and Merrick Whitcomb (Philadelphia: University of Pennsylvania Press, 1897), vol. 2, no. 6, pp.13–14.

stones, are clothed in purple and fine linen and dine sumptuously, frivolously indulging themselves in every species of luxury. In short, a vast number of the worst of men are supported in Rome in idle indulgence by means of our money. . . . Does not Your Grace perceive how many bold robbers, how many cunning hypocrites commit repeatedly the greatest crimes under the monk's cowl, and how many crafty hawks feign the simplicity of doves, and how many ravening wolves simulate the innocence of lambs? And although there be a few truly pious among them, even they cling to superstition and pervert the law of life which Christ laid down for us.

Now, if all these who devastate Germany and continue to devour everything might once be driven out, and an end made of their unbridled plundering, swindling and deception, with which the Romans have overwhelmed us, we should again have gold and silver in sufficient quantities and should be able to keep it. And then this money, in such supply and value as it may be present, might be put to better uses, for example: to put on foot great armaments and extend the boundaries of the [Holy Roman] Empire; also that the Turks may be conquered, if this seems desirable; that many who, because of poverty, steal and rob, may honestly earn their living once more, and that those who otherwise must starve may receive from the state contributions to mitigate their need; that scholars may be helped and the study of the arts and sciences, and of good literature advanced; above all that every virtue may receive its reward; want to be relieved at home; indolence banished and deceit killed.

REVIEW QUESTIONS

1. Why did Martin Luther see the papacy as the crucial block to any meaningful reform of the church?
2. How did Luther's teaching undermine the power of the clergy and traditional forms of piety?
3. According to Ulrich von Hutten, why were Germans distressed with the Roman church?

3 The German Peasants' Revolt

After Luther was outlawed as a heretic by the Imperial Diet (parliament) at Worms in 1521, economic and political grievances among the knights, peasants, and lower-class urban workers fostered a series of rebellions. The uprisings were largely local affairs, mostly in southwestern Germany. When the knights revolted against their lords in 1523, they were quickly crushed. A more widespread peasant revolt followed in 1525, accompanied in some places by sympathetic rebellions among the lower-class artisans and laborers of nearby towns. Driven to a frenzy by their grievances and religious enthusiasm, the German peasants seized lords' estates and pillaged churches and monasteries in a rebellion covering a third of the country. Lacking effective training and leaders, however, they were soon crushed by the vengeful lords' armies.

Although Luther was not primarily responsible for the peasants' revolt, his attacks on the abuses of the ruling nobles and the clergy coincided with the growing anger and resentment among knights, peasants, and lower-class townspeople. The peasants had hoped that Luther, who had denounced the lords' cruelty and oppression, would endorse if not lead their revolt. They were completely mistaken. Luther was preoccupied with the individual's relationship with God and with attaining salvation through faith. He did not intend to initiate social revolution and regarded rebellion against the constituted authority of the state as contrary to the Gospel's spirit. To Luther, subjects had the duty to obey state authority, since it was ordained by God.

Anonymous
TO THE ASSEMBLY OF THE COMMON PEASANTRY

In May 1525, at the time of the peasant rebellion, a pamphlet, *To the Assembly of the Common Peasantry*, whose author is unknown, was printed in Nuremberg. The work, excerpted below, clearly states the peasants' grievances.

CHAPTER FOUR

On false and unlimited power,
which one is not obliged to obey.

All the popes, emperors, kings, etc. who puff themselves up in their own estimation above other pious poor Christians, claiming to be a better kind of human—as if their lordship and authority to rule others were innate—do not want to recognize that they are God's stewards and officials. And they do not govern according to his commandment to maintain the common good and brotherly unity among us. God has established and ordained authority for this reason alone, and no other. . . .

Therefore whichever prince or lord invents and sets up his own self-serving burdens and commands, rules falsely, and he dares impudently to deceive God, his own lord. Where are you, you werewolves, with your financial tricks which impose one burden after another on the poor people? This year a labor service is voluntary, next year it becomes compulsory. In most cases this is how your old customary law has grown. In what dementia or camouflage did God, your lord, give you such power that we poor people have to cultivate your lands with labor services? But only in good weather, for on rainy days we poor people see the fruits of our sweat rot in the fields. May God, in his justice, not tolerate the terrible Babylonian captivity in which we poor people are driven to mow the lords' mead-

ows, to make hay, to cultivate the fields, to sow flax in them, to cut it, comb it, heat it, wash it, pound it, and spin it—yes, even to sew their underpants on their arses. We also have to pick peas and harvest carrots and asparagus.

Help us, God! Where has such misery ever been heard of! They tax and tear out the marrow of the poor people's bones, and we have to pay interest on that! Where are they, with their hired murderers and horsemen, the gamblers and whoremasters, who are stuffed fuller than puking dogs? In addition, we poor people have to give them taxes, payments, and interest. And at home [they assume that] the poor should have neither bread, salt nor lard for their wives and small children. Where are they, with their entry fines and heriot dues? Yes, damn their disgraceful fines and robber's dues! Where are the tyrants and raging ones, who appropriate taxes, customs, and user fees, and waste them so shamefully and wantonly, and lose what should go into the common chest or purse to serve the needs of the territory. . . .

God can and will no longer tolerate this great misery and wantonness, which is now found everywhere. May God enlighten his poor lambs through divine grace and with true Christian faith, and protect them against these ravaging wolves. . . .

CHAPTER SEVEN

Whether a community may depose its
authorities or not? . . .

I will speak only briefly about this. All the lords who issue selfish commands stemming from the desires of their hearts and their willful, unjust

Michael G. Baylor, ed., *The Radical Reformation*, pp. 107–110, 118, 122–124. Copyright © 1991 Cambridge University Press. Reprinted with the permission of Cambridge University Press.

heads, and who appropriate for themselves—I will remain silent about their plunder—taxes, customs, payments, and what similarly serves the common fund for the protection and maintenance of the common territory, these lords are in truth the real robbers and the declared enemies of their own territory. . . .

CHAPTER EIGHT

In what form a community may depose its lords. . . .

But if the lords always want to be lords and to treat you poor people in the most arbitrary way, contrary to the divine laws which I have discussed above, then follow Solomon and bravely assemble now! Arm yourselves in the spirit of the bold oxen and steers, who gather together staunchly in a ring with their horns outward, not with the intention of rebelling, but only to defend themselves against the ravaging wolves. . . .

After you have assembled, if your opponents still want to have a war, and they pursue this crazy idea of disputing the gospel with lances, halberds, guns, and armor, then it is God's will. Then let happen what cannot happen differently. Their sacrilegious attacks are hated by God. But you trust in God! Be firm in faith! You are not your own but God's warriors to uphold the gospel and to tear down the Babylonian prison! Each of you should make every effort to deal with the others in all fidelity and love! Do not quarrel among yourselves and be strict with one another! Let each tolerate the others with the greatest discipline and goodness; maintain the fear of God; and do not tolerate any drinkers! In no case allow blasphemers with their damned tongues among you! Then God will surely be your general.

CHAPTER NINE

Who should be blamed for being a rebel?

Some, along with their bloody band, blame you and cry out that you are deviant, treacherous rogues [who have betrayed] your hereditary and natural lords. But do not let yourselves be led astray and do not worry about what they jabber.

Yes, they scream, rant, and curse rebellion so violently, seeking to damn it completely. And in doing this they never think about the cause of the disturbance, which is themselves and their godless nature.

Martin Luther
AGAINST THE THIEVISH, MURDEROUS HORDES OF PEASANTS

A manifesto, the Twelve Articles, was drawn up by the leaders of the peasants of Swabia in southwestern Germany. It blended Lutheran reform ideas with the peasants' demands for relief from their landlords' domination. In a pamphlet published just prior to the peasants' uprising, Martin Luther criticized the Twelve Articles, opposing what he feared was an egalitarian social revolution that threatened the hierarchical order of society and the legitimate property rights of the lords and clergy. He urged peaceful resolution of the crisis, pointing out the just grievances of the peasants.

When in the spring of 1525 the peasants finally took up arms against their manorial lords, they were joined by the lower-class artisans and workers in many towns. In a pamphlet entitled *Against the Thievish, Murderous Hordes of Peasants,* Luther reacted sternly, urging the princes to repress the rebels with every power at their command.

. . . They are starting a rebellion, and are violently robbing and plundering monasteries and castles which are not theirs; by this they have doubly deserved death in body and soul as highwaymen and murderers. Furthermore, anyone who can be proved to be a seditious person is an outlaw before God and the emperor; and whoever is the first to put him to death does right and well. For if a man is in open rebellion, everyone is both his judge and his executioner; just as when a fire starts, the first man who can put it out is the best man to do the job. For rebellion is not just simple murder; it is like a great fire, which attacks and devastates a whole land. Thus rebellion brings with it a land filled with murder and bloodshed; it makes widows and orphans, and turns everything upside down, like the worst disaster. Therefore let everyone who can, smite, slay, and stab, secretly or openly, remembering that nothing can be more poisonous, hurtful, or devilish than a rebel. It is just as when one must kill a mad dog; if you do not strike him, he will strike you, and a whole land with you.

It does not help the peasants when they pretend that according to Genesis 1 and 2 all things were created free and common, and that all of us alike have been baptized. For under the New Testament, Moses does not count; for there stands our Master, Christ, and subjects us, along with our bodies and our property, to the emperor and the law of this world, when he says, "Render to

Caesar the things that are Caesar's" [Luke 20:25]. Paul, too, speaking in Romans 12[13:1] to all baptized Christians, says, "Let every person be subject to the governing authorities." And Peter says, "Be subject to every ordinance of man" [1 Pet. 2:13]. We are bound to live according to this teaching of Christ, as the Father commands from heaven, saying, "This is my beloved Son, listen to him" [Matt. 17:5].

For baptism does not make men free in body and property, but in soul; and the gospel does not make goods common, except in the case of those who, of their own free will, do what the apostles and disciples did in Acts 4[:32–37]. They did not demand, as do our insane peasants in their raging, that the goods of others— of Pilate and Herod—should be common, but only their own goods. Our peasants, however, want to make the goods of other men common, and keep their own for themselves. Fine Christians they are! I think there is not a devil left in hell; they have all gone into the peasants. Their raving has gone beyond all measure. . . .

. . . I will not oppose a ruler who, even though he does not tolerate the gospel, will smite and punish these peasants without first offering to submit the case to judgment. He is within his rights, since the peasants are not contending any longer for the gospel, but have become faithless, perjured, disobedient, rebellious murderers, robbers, and blasphemers, whom even a heathen ruler has the right and authority to punish. Indeed, it is his duty to punish such scoundrels, for this is why he bears the sword and is "the servant of God to execute his wrath on the wrongdoer," Romans 13[:4].

Martin Luther, *Luther's Works,* vol. 46: *The Christian in Society III,* ed. Robert C. Schultz (55 volumes; Philadelphia: Concordia Publishing House, Muhlenberg Press, and Fortress Press, 1955–1986), pp. 50–52. Copyright © 1967 by Augsburg Fortress Publishers. Used by permission.

REVIEW QUESTIONS

1. In referring to the "terrible Babylonian captivity" of the peasants, what afflictions did the anonymous pamphleteer describe?
2. On what grounds did he condemn those responsible for the peasants' misery?
3. What did he propose the peasants should do? How did he justify it?
4. How did Martin Luther use the scriptures to respond to the peasants' claims?

4   Luther and the Jews

Initially, Luther hoped to attract Jews to his vision of reformed Christianity. In *That Jesus Was Born a Jew* (1523), the young Luther expressed sympathy for Jewish sufferings and denounced persecution as a barrier to conversion. He declared, "I hope that if one deals in a kindly way with the Jews and instructs them carefully from the Holy scripture, many of them will become genuine Christians. . . . We [Christians] are aliens and in-laws; they are blood relatives, cousins, and brothers of our Lord." When the Jews did not abandon their faith, however, Luther launched a diatribe against them.

Martin Luther
ON THE JEWS AND THEIR LIES

In *On the Jews and Their Lies* (1543), Martin Luther accepted at face value hateful medieval myths about the Jews: that they engaged in sorcery and magic, poisoned the wells of Christians, desecrated the Eucharistic host, and ritually murdered Christian children. In the concluding section, excerpted here, Luther advises civil and clerical authorities to treat the Jews harshly. The authorities did not heed Luther's proposals to raze synagogues and homes—although some anti-Jewish measures were introduced—and for several centuries Lutheran theologians paid little mind to Luther's anti-Judaism. In the late nineteenth century, German nationalists revived Luther's treatise, and the Nazis gleefully circulated his words as an authoritative endorsement of their anti-Semitic ideology.[1]

. . . [D]ear Christian, be on your guard against the Jews, who, as you discover here, are consigned by the wrath of God to the devil, who has not only robbed them of a proper understanding of scripture, but also of ordinary human reason, shame, and sense, and only works mischief with Holy scriptures through them. Therefore they cannot be trusted and believed in any other matter either, even though a truthful word may drop from their lips occasionally. For anyone who dares to juggle the awesome word of God so frivolously and shamefully . . . cannot have a good spirit dwelling in him. Therefore, wherever you see a genuine Jew, you may with a good conscience cross yourself and bluntly say: "There goes a devil incarnate." . . .

. . . [D]ear Christian, be advised and do not doubt that next to the devil, you have no more bitter, venomous, and vehement foe than a real Jew who earnestly seeks to be a Jew. . . . Therefore the history books often accuse them of contaminating wells, of kidnaping and piercing children, as for example at Trent, Weissensee, etc. They, of course, deny this. Whether it is

Martin Luther, *Luther's Works,* vol. 47: *The Christian in Society IV,* ed. Franklin Sherman (55 volumes; Philadelphia: Concordia Publishing House, Muhlenberg Press, and Fortress Press, 1955–1986), pp. 213–214, 217, 242, 253, 256, 264–265, 268–270, 273–274. Copyright © 1967 by Augsburg Fortress Publishers. Used by permission.

[1]In 1994 the Church Council of the Evangelical Lutheran Church in America acknowledged "with pain . . . Luther's anti-Judaic diatribes and violent recommendations . . . against Jews. . . . [W]e reject this violent invective, and yet more do we express our deep and abiding sorrow over its tragic effects on subsequent generations. In concert with the Lutheran World Federation, we particularly deplore the appropriation of Luther's words by modern antisemites for the teaching of hatred toward Judaism or toward Jewish people in our day."—Eds.

true or not, I do know that they do not lack the complete, full, and ready will to do such things either secretly or openly where possible. This you can assuredly expect from them, and you must govern yourself accordingly. . . .

. . . [T]heir own vile external life . . . abounds with witchcraft, conjuring signs, figures, . . . idolatry, envy, and conceit. Moreover, they are nothing but thieves and robbers who daily eat no morsel and wear no thread of clothing which they have not stolen and pilfered from us by means of their accursed usury. Thus they live from day to day, together with wife and child, by theft and robbery, as archthieves and robbers, in the most impenitent security. . . .

But for us Christians they stand as a terrifying example of God's wrath. . . . The example of the Jews demonstrates clearly how easily the devil can mislead people, after they once have digressed from the proper understanding of scripture, into such blindness and darkness that it can be readily grasped and perceived simply by natural reason, yes, even by irrational beasts. And yet they who daily teach and hear God's word do not recognize this darkness but regard it as the true light. O Lord God, have mercy on us! . . .

. . . It serves them right that, rejecting the truth of God, they have to believe instead such abominable, stupid, inane lies, and that instead of the beautiful face of the divine word, they have to look into the devil's black, dark, lying behind, and worship his stench. . . .

. . . [The Jews wish to] lay their hands on the land, the goods, and the government of the whole world. . . . And now a storm breaks over us with curses, defamation, and derision that cannot be expressed with words. They wish that sword and war, distress and every misfortune may overtake us accursed Goyim. They vent their curses on us openly every Saturday in their synagogues and daily in their homes. They teach, urge, and train their children from infancy to remain the bitter, virulent, and wrathful enemies of the Christians. . . .

. . . They have been bloodthirsty bloodhounds and murderers of all Christendom for more than fourteen hundred years in their intentions, and would undoubtedly prefer to be such with their deeds. Thus they have been accused[2] of poisoning water and wells, of kidnapping children, of piercing them through with an awl, of hacking them in pieces, and in that way secretly cooling their wrath with the blood of Christians, for all of which they have often been condemned to death by fire. . . .

. . . Furthermore, we do not know to the present day which devil brought them into our country. We surely did not bring them from Jerusalem. . . . For they are a heavy burden, a plague, a pestilence, a sheer misfortune for our country. Proof for this is found in the fact that they have often been expelled forcibly from a country. . . .

What shall we Christians do with this rejected and condemned people, the Jews? Since they live among us, we dare not tolerate their conduct, now that we are aware of their lying and reviling and blaspheming. If we do, we become sharers in their lies, cursing, and blasphemy. . . . I shall give you my sincere advice:

First, to set fire to their synagogues or schools and to bury and cover with dirt whatever will not burn, so that no man will ever again see a stone or cinder of them. This is to be done in honor of our Lord and of Christendom, so that God might see that we are Christians, and do not condone or knowingly tolerate such public lying, cursing, and blaspheming of his Son and of his Christians. . . .

Second, I advise that their houses also be razed and destroyed. For they pursue in them the same aims as in their synagogues. Instead they might be lodged under a roof or in a barn, like the gypsies. This will bring home to them the fact that they are not masters in our country, as they boast, but that they are living in exile and in captivity, as they incessantly wail and lament about us before God.

---

[2]The element of caution in Luther's phraseology here perhaps indicates some awareness on his part of the unsupported character of such accusations. In 1510, for example, thirty-eight Jews had been executed in Berlin on a charge of desecration of the host. In 1539, however, in the context of a debate on policy toward the Jews at the assembly of Protestant estates at Frankfurt, Philip Melanchthon presented convincing evidence that they had been innocent.

Third, I advise that all their prayer books and Talmudic writings, in which such idolatry, lies, cursing, and blasphemy are taught, be taken from them.

Fourth, I advise that their rabbis be forbidden to teach henceforth on pain of loss of life and limb. . . .

Fifth, I advise that safe-conduct on the highways be abolished completely for the Jews. For they have no business in the countryside, since they are not lords, officials, tradesmen, or the like. Let them stay at home. . . .

Sixth, I advise that usury be prohibited to them, and that all cash and treasure of silver and gold be taken from them and put aside for safekeeping. The reason for such a measure is that, as said above, they have no other means of earning a livelihood than usury, and by it they have stolen and robbed from us all they possess. . . .

In brief, dear princes and lords, those of you who have Jews under your rule—if my counsel does not please you, find better advice, so that you and we all can be rid of the unbearable devilish burden of the Jews, lest we become guilty sharers before God in the lies, the blasphemy, the defamation, and the curses which the mad Jews indulge in so freely and wantonly against the person of our Lord Jesus Christ, his dear mother, all Christians, all authority, and ourselves.

REVIEW QUESTIONS

1. What factors seemed to motivate Martin Luther's attack against the Jews?
2. What steps did Luther advocate to reduce the role of the Jews in German society?

5 The Calvinist Reformation

In the first decade of the Lutheran movement, Protestant reform had not spread significantly outside Germany due to suppression by the royal governments in France, Spain, and England. But in 1534 a French clergyman, John Calvin (1509–1564), resigned his church offices and fled to Basel, a Swiss city that had accepted Protestant reforms. There he composed a summary of the new Protestant theology, *The Institutes of the Christian Religion*, which was to be revised four times before his death. Written in the elegant Latin style favored by humanists, the work was translated into French and soon became the principal theological text for French, Swiss, Dutch, Scottish, and English Protestant reformers. Calvin himself settled in Geneva, Switzerland, where his influence dominated the civil and religious life of the townspeople. From Geneva, Calvin carried on an active mission, spreading his reformed faith throughout his native France and elsewhere.

In 1536, the newly Protestant-controlled government of Geneva asked Calvin to draw up a public confession of the reformed faith, a catechism, and rules for liturgical worship. But the Council of Geneva's demand that all citizens be forced to subscribe to the new confession resulted in a change of government at the elections in 1538. Calvin withdrew to Basel. By 1541, the political situation had changed again; Calvin was recalled, and his recommendations for a new government for the church were put into law. He remained the spiritual leader of Geneva and of many reformed Protestants elsewhere until his death. Calvinism was especially influential in England and Scotland, giving rise to the Puritan movement in seventeenth-century England and the Presbyterian churches in Scotland and Ireland. Both of these religious traditions exercised great influence on the settlers of the English colonies in North America.

John Calvin
THE INSTITUTES OF THE
CHRISTIAN RELIGION

One doctrine that assumed greater and greater importance in the four separate revised editions of Calvin's *Institutes* was predestination: the belief that each person's salvation or damnation was already decided before birth. This doctrine raised a question about whether Christ offered salvation for all human beings or only for the elect—a chosen few who were predestined to be saved by God's sovereign will. Some argued that the latter interpretation, one strongly articulated by Saint Augustine, implied that God was a tyrant who created human beings to be damned and that they were not free to acquire salvation by faith. In effect, salvation and damnation were foreordained. To many Christians, this doctrine diminished the justice and mercy of God, made meaningless the idea of freedom of choice in the process of salvation, and stripped good works of any role in gaining salvation. In the following excerpt (from *The Institutes of the Christian Religion*), Calvin offered his definition of predestination and cited Saint Paul as an authority.

The covenant of life is not preached equally to all, and among those to whom it is preached, does not always meet with the same reception. This diversity displays the unsearchable depth of the divine judgment, and is without doubt subordinate to God's purpose of eternal election. But if it is plainly owing to the mere pleasure of God that salvation is spontaneously offered to some, while others have no access to it, great and difficult questions immediately arise, questions which are inexplicable, when just views are not entertained concerning election and predestination. To many this seems a perplexing subject, because they deem it most incongruous that of the great body of mankind some should be predestinated to salvation, and others to destruction. . . .

. . . By predestination we mean the eternal decree of God, by which he determined with

himself whatever he wished to happen with regard to every man. All are not created on equal terms, but some are preordained to eternal life, others to eternal damnation; and, accordingly, as each has been created for one or other of these ends, we say that he has been predestinated to life or to death. . . .

. . . We say, then, that scripture clearly proves this much, that God by his eternal and immutable counsel determined once for all those whom it was his pleasure one day to admit to salvation, and those whom, on the other hand, it was his pleasure to doom to destruction. We maintain that this counsel, as regards the elect, is founded on his free mercy, without any respect to human worth, while those whom he dooms to destruction are excluded from access to life by a just and blameless, but at the same time incomprehensible judgment. In regard to the elect, we regard calling as the evidence of election, and justification as another symbol of its manifestation, until it is fully

John Calvin, *Institutes of the Christian Religion*, vol. 2, trans. Henry Beveridge (Edinburgh: T. and T. Clark, 1869), pp. 202, 206, 210–212, 215–217, 219.

accomplished by the attainment of glory. But as the Lord seals his elect by calling and justification, so by excluding the reprobate either from the knowledge of his name or the sanctification of his Spirit, he by these marks in a manner discloses the judgment which awaits them. . . .

Many controvert all the positions which we have laid down, especially the gratuitous election of believers, which however cannot be overthrown. For they commonly imagine that God distinguishes between men according to the merits which he foresees that each individual is to have, giving the adoption of sons to those whom he foreknows will not be unworthy of his grace, and dooming those to destruction whose dispositions he perceives will be prone to mischief and wickedness. . . .

. . . Assuredly divine grace would not deserve all the praise of election, were not election gratuitous; and it would not be gratuitous, did God in electing any individual pay regard to his future works. Hence, what Christ said to his disciples is found to be universally applicable to all believers, "Ye have not chosen me, but I have chosen you" [John 15:16]. Here he not only excludes past merits, but declares that they had nothing in themselves for which they could be chosen, except in so far as his mercy anticipated. And how are we to understand the words of Paul, "Who hath first given to him, and it shall be recompensed unto him again?" [Rom. 6:35]. His meaning obviously is, that

men are altogether indebted to the preventing goodness of God, there being nothing in them, either past or future, to conciliate his favour.

[T]he Apostle [Paul] goes on to show, that the adoption of Jacob proceeded not on works but on the calling of God. In works he makes no mention of past or future, but distinctly opposes them to the calling of God, intimating, that when place is given to the one the other is overthrown; as if he had said, The only thing to be considered is what pleased God, not what men furnished of themselves. . . .

. . . We learn from the Apostle's words, that the salvation of believers is founded entirely on the decree of divine election, that the privilege is procured not by works but free calling. . . .

. . . Meanwhile, though Christ interpose as a Mediator, yet he claims the right of electing in common with the Father, "I speak not of you all: I know whom I have chosen" [John 13:18]. If it is asked whence he hath chosen them, he answers in another passage, "Out of the world;" which he excludes from his prayers when he commits his disciples to the Father [John 15:19]. We must indeed hold, when he affirms that he knows whom he has chosen, first, that some individuals of the human race are denoted; and, secondly, that they are not distinguished by the quality of their virtues, but by a heavenly decree. Hence it follows, that since Christ makes himself the author of election, none excel by their own strength or industry.

REVIEW QUESTION

Why was the doctrine of predestination so troublesome to many Christian theologians?

---

6 The Catholic Response to Protestantism

The criticisms of Catholic beliefs and practices by Luther, Calvin, and other Protestant reformers generated a host of theological defenses of traditional Catholicism. However, there was a general admission that grave abuses in Catholic clerical morals and discipline had been allowed to go uncorrected. Almost everyone agreed that a new general council of the church was necessary to clarify and affirm Catholic doctrine and institute reforms in clerical discipline and practices. Despite many promises to summon such a council, the popes delayed. Political conditions never seemed right, and the papacy, remembering the challenge to its power attempted by the Conciliar movement in the fifteenth century, feared that prematurely summoning a council could be a disaster for papal authority.

The council was finally convoked in 1545 at the Alpine city of Trent, on the borders between the German lands and Italy. The papacy was firmly in control, and no Protestant theologians participated in the conciliar sessions. The Council of Trent was suspended several times, the longest hiatus lasting for ten years (1552–1562); it concluded its work in 1563.

The council fathers confessed their responsibility for the evils that had grown up in the church and committed themselves to institutional reforms that would raise the standards of morality and learning among future bishops and other clergy. The most significant pastoral reforms included creating an official catechism outlining the orthodox beliefs of the Roman church, establishing seminaries to direct the education of future clergy, and reforming the bishop's office by increasing his responsibilities for the pastoral life of his diocese.

CANONS AND DECREES OF THE COUNCIL OF TRENT

On doctrinal matters, the Council of Trent (1545–1563) gave an authoritative Catholic response to Protestant teachings on a host of issues. In the following excerpt from its decrees, the council condemns the Protestant view that faith alone is necessary for salvation and insists on the integration of both faith and good works in the process of salvation. This position allowed the council to defend such traditional Catholic practices as monasticism, indulgences, mass for the dead, almsgiving, pilgrimages, veneration of saints, and other pious works.

THE NECESSITY OF PREPARATION FOR JUSTIFICATION [SALVATION] IN ADULTS, AND WHENCE IT PROCEEDS

It is furthermore declared that in adults the beginning of that justification must proceed from the predisposing grace of God through Jesus Christ, that is, from His vocation, whereby, without any merits on their part, they are

From *Canons and Decrees of the Council of Trent,* trans. H. J. Schroeder (Rockford, Ill.: Tan Books, 1979), pp. 18–19, 31–32, 33–35, 51–52, 162–163, 215.

called; that they who by sin had been cut off from God, may be disposed through His quickening and helping grace to convert themselves to their own justification by freely assenting to and cooperating with that grace; so that, while God touches the heart of man through the illumination of the Holy Ghost, man himself neither does absolutely nothing while receiving that inspiration, since he can also reject it, nor yet is he able by his own free will and without the grace of God to move himself to justice in His sight. Hence, when it is said in the sacred writings: *Turn ye to me, and I will turn to you* [Zech. 1:3], we are reminded of our liberty; and when we reply: *Convert us, O Lord, to thee, and we shall be converted* [Lam. 5:21], we confess that we need the grace of God. . . .

HOW THE GRATUITOUS JUSTIFICATION OF THE SINNER BY FAITH IS TO BE UNDERSTOOD

But when the Apostle [Paul] says that man is justified by faith and freely, these words are to be understood in that sense in which the uninterrupted unanimity of the Catholic Church has held and expressed them, namely, that we are therefore said to be justified by faith, because faith is the beginning of human salvation, the foundation and root of all justification, *without which it is impossible to please God* [Heb. 11:6] and to come to the fellowship of His sons; and we are therefore said to be justified gratuitously [unearned, as a freely given gift], because none of those things that precede justification, whether faith or works, merit the grace of justification. For, *if by grace, it is not now by works, otherwise*, as the Apostle says, *grace is no more grace* [Rom. 11:6]. . . .

IN WHAT THE JUSTIFICATION OF THE SINNER CONSISTS, AND WHAT ARE ITS CAUSES

. . . For though no one can be just except he to whom the merits of the passion of our Lord Jesus Christ are communicated, yet this takes place in that justification of the sinner, when by the merit of the most holy passion, *the charity of God is poured forth by the Holy Ghost in the hearts* [Rom. 5:5] of those who are justified and inheres in them; whence man through Jesus Christ, [with] whom he is [now one], receives in that justification, together with the remission of sins, all these infused at the same time, namely, faith, hope and charity. For faith, unless hope and charity be added to it, neither unites man perfectly with Christ nor makes him a living member of His body. For which reason it is most truly said that *faith without works is dead* [James 2:17, 20] and of no profit, and *in Christ Jesus neither*

circumcision availeth anything nor uncircumcision, but faith that worketh by charity [Gal. 5:6, 6:15]. This faith, conformably to Apostolic tradition, catechumens [candidates for baptism] ask of the Church before the sacrament of baptism, when they ask for the faith that gives eternal life, which without hope and charity faith cannot give. Whence also they hear immediately the word of Christ: *If thou wilt enter into life, keep the commandments* [Matt. 19:17]. . . .

The Council of Trent also condemned individual interpretation of the Bible and set up controls over the publication and sale of unauthorized religious books. It approved the cult of the saints and the use of images—practices condemned by Calvin and the Anabaptists.

Furthermore, to check unbridled spirits, it [the council] decrees that no one relying on his own judgment shall, in matters of faith and morals pertaining to the edification of Christian doctrine, distorting the Holy scriptures in accordance with his own conceptions, presume to interpret them contrary to that sense which holy mother Church, to whom it belongs to judge of their true sense and interpretation, has held and holds, or even contrary to the unanimous teaching of the [church] Fathers, even though such interpretations should never at any time be published. Those who act contrary to this shall be made known by the ordinaries [bishops] and punished in accordance with the penalties prescribed by the law.

And wishing, as is proper, to impose a restraint in this matter on printers also, who, now without restraint, thinking what pleases them is permitted them, print without the permission of ecclesiastical superiors the books of the Holy scriptures and the notes and commentaries thereon of all persons indiscriminately, often with the name of the press omitted, often also under a fictitious press-name, and what is worse, without the name of the author, and also indiscreetly have for sale such books printed elsewhere, (this council) decrees and ordains that in the future the Holy scriptures, especially the old

Vulgate [Latin] Edition, be printed in the most correct manner possible, and that it shall not be lawful for anyone to print or to have printed any books whatsoever dealing with sacred doctrinal matters without the name of the author, or in the future to sell them, or even to have them in possession, unless they have first been examined and approved by the ordinary [the local bishop], under penalty of anathema [condemnation and excommunication] and fine. . . .

ON THE INVOCATION, VENERATION, AND RELICS OF SAINTS, AND ON SACRED IMAGES

The holy council commands all bishops and others who hold the office of teaching and have charge of the *cura animarum* [care of souls], that in accordance with the usage of the Catholic and Apostolic Church, received from the primitive times of the Christian religion, and with the unanimous teaching of the holy Fathers and the decrees of sacred councils, they above all instruct the faithful diligently in matters relating to intercession and invocation of the saints, the veneration of relics, and the legitimate use of images, teaching them that the saints who reign together with Christ offer up their prayers to God for men, that it is good and beneficial suppliantly to invoke them and to have recourse to their prayers, assistance and support in order to obtain favors from God through His Son, Jesus Christ our Lord, who alone is our redeemer and savior. . . . Also, that the holy bodies of the holy martyrs and of others living with Christ, which were the living members of Christ and the temple of the Holy Ghost, to be awakened by Him to eternal life and to be glorified, are to be venerated by the faithful, through which many benefits are bestowed by God on men. . . . Moreover, that the images of Christ, of the Virgin Mother of God, and of the other saints are to be placed and retained especially in the churches, and that due honor and veneration is to be given them. . . .

The Council of Trent condemned the Protestant view that clergy were no different than lay people and reaffirmed the Catholic belief that the clergy are specially ordained intermediaries between God and human beings and are responsible for the administration of the church's sacraments. Whereas Luther admitted only three sacraments — (baptism, the Eucharist, and penance or confession) — and Calvin only two — (baptism and the Eucharist), the Council of Trent decreed that there were seven sacraments in the Catholic Church, including ordination of the clergy.

CANONS ON THE SACRAMENTS IN GENERAL

Canon 1. If anyone says that the sacraments of the New Law were not all instituted by our Lord Jesus Christ, or that there are more or less than seven, namely, baptism, confirmation, Eucharist, penance, extreme unction, order and matrimony, or that any one of these seven is not truly and intrinsically a sacrament, let him be anathema [cursed]. . . .

Can. 10. If anyone says that all Christians have the power to administer the word and all the sacraments, let him be anathema. . . .

CANONS ON THE SACRAMENT OF ORDER

Canon 1. If anyone says that there is not in the New Testament a visible and external priesthood, or that there is no power of consecrating and offering the true body and blood of the Lord and of forgiving . . . sins, but only the office and bare ministry of preaching the Gospel; or that those who do not preach are not priests at all, let him be anathema. . . .

Can. 4. If anyone says that by sacred ordination the Holy [Spirit] is not imparted and that therefore the bishops say in vain: *Receive ye the Holy [Spirit]*, or that by it a character is not imprinted, or that he who has once been a priest can again become a layman, let him be anathema.

Can. 5. If anyone says that the holy unction which the Church uses in ordination is not only not required but is detestable and pernicious, as also are the other ceremonies of order, let him be anathema.

Can. 6. If anyone says that in the Catholic Church there is not instituted a hierarchy by divine ordinance, which consists of bishops, priests and ministers, let him be anathema.

Can. 7. If anyone says that bishops are not superior to priests, or that they have not the power to confirm and ordain, or that the power which they have is common to them and to priests, or that orders conferred by them without the consent or call of the people or of the secular power are invalid, or that those who have been neither rightly ordained nor sent by ecclesiastical and canonical authority, but come from elsewhere, are lawful ministers of the word and of the sacraments, let him be anathema.

REVIEW QUESTIONS

1. What was the Catholic doctrine on justification by faith defined by the Council of Trent, and how did it differ from the views of Luther and Calvin?
2. How did the Council of Trent approach the problem of authoritative interpretation of the scriptures and of church doctrines?

7 Religious Persecution

The passions aroused by the Reformation culminated in vicious religious persecution. Regarding Protestants as dangerous heretics who had affronted God and threatened his church, Catholic clergy and rulers tried to eliminate them, often by fire and sword. Protestants also engaged in persecution, principally against the Anabaptists, a Protestant sect that deviated from the teachings of the main Protestant reformers.

Chronicle of King Francis I
BURNING OF PROTESTANTS IN PARIS

One day in the autumn of 1534 Protestants in several French cities plastered walls and doors with anti-church tracts. Fearing that Protestant heresy would prove calamitous to his realm and undermine his authority, Francis I (1515–1547) in 1535, after an elaborate ceremony, had Protestants publicly burned in Paris as a warning to Protestant dissenters. Following is a contemporary account of the spectacle.

The most Christian king [Francis I], our sovereign lord, knowing that certain damnable heresies and blasphemies swarmed in his kingdom and desiring with the aid of God to extirpate the same decreed that a sacred procession should be held in this city of Paris on the twenty-first day [actually the twenty-ninth] of January 1535. The streets were adorned with gorgeous tapestries and the crowds held in order by archers in uniform. First came the crosses and banners of the Diocese of Paris followed by citizens and merchants carrying torches, then the four monastic orders with relics, next priests and canons of the parochial churches with relics, and the monks

Roland Bainton, *The Age of the Reformation* (New York: D. Van Nostrand, 1956), pp. 180–181. Reprinted by permission of Krieger Publishing.

of Saint Martin with the head of that saint. Another carried the head of Saint Philip, one of the most precious relics in Paris. The body of Madame Saincte Geneviève was borne by six citizens in their shirts. Then followed the Canons of Notre Dame, the Rector of the University, and the Swiss Guard with their band of violins, trumpets, and cornets. Among the relics were the true cross of Christ and the crown of thorns and the lance that pierced his side. Then came a great number of the archbishops and bishops with the blood of our Saviour, the rod of Moses, and the head of John the Baptist. Next the cardinals. The precious body of our Lord was carried by the archdeacons on a velvet cushion of violet adorned with *fluers de lys.* Following the Holy Sacrament came the King alone with bare head carrying a lighted taper. After him marched Monseigneur the Cardinal of Lorraine, then all the princes and knights and members of the *Parlement*, etc. The Holy Sacrament was taken to the church of Notre Dame and there deposited with great reverence by the Bishop of Paris. Then the King and his children, the Queen and her attendants and many notables had dinner with the Bishop of Paris. After dinner the King made a speech against the execrable and damnable opinions dispersed throughout his kingdom. While the King, the Queen, and their court were with the Bishop of Paris, into their presence were brought six of the said heretics and in front of the church of Notre Dame they were burned alive. A number of other heretics went to the stake during the days following so that all over Paris one saw gibbets [gallows] by which the people were filled with terror.

THE PERSECUTION OF ANABAPTISTS: THE EXAMINATION OF ELIZABETH DIRKS

The break with the Roman church and the rapid growth of a reformed church party in Germany under Luther's leadership was soon complicated by the appearance of other anti-Roman Protestants who differed with both the papacy and Luther on questions of theology and church discipline. In the Swiss city of Zurich, enthusiastic reformers like Ulrich Zwingli (1484–1531) and Conrad Grebel (c. 1500–1526) overthrew the local Catholic authorities but failed to agree fully with Luther or with each other on several theological matters. Grebel and his supporters, called Anabaptists, held that admission to membership in the church must be a voluntary act by adults, and condemned the practice of baptizing infants. When Zwingli insisted that no reforms in ecclesiastical practices should be undertaken without permission of the public authorities, the Zurich Anabaptists refused to comply, declaring the complete freedom of the church from state control. Condemned by Zwingli and forced into exile, the Zurich Anabaptists soon spread their ideas throughout the German-speaking lands.

Although the majority of Anabaptists renounced the use of force to impose any religious practice, the Anabaptist reformers in Münster, a city in northwestern Germany, did not. After winning control of the city council, they expelled all citizens who refused to become Anabaptists. Under the influence of "prophets," some Münster Anabaptists adopted practicing polygamy, communal ownership of property, and violence in anticipation of the imminent end of the world. In 1535, the forces of neighboring German princes captured Münster, slaughtering the Anabaptists.

The excesses of the Münster sect caused both Protestant and Catholic authorities to persecute more peaceful and orthodox Anabaptists wherever they were discovered. Fervent, but oppressed, the movement remained small and confined to an underground existence. Modern Christian churches that acknowledge the sixteenth-century Anabaptists as their spiritual forebears are the Mennonites and Amish, the Plymouth (Pilgrim) Separatists, and the English and American Baptists.

In January 1549, Elizabeth Dirks was arrested in Holland, at that time under Catholic control. A former nun, she had come to doubt whether monastic life was truly Christian and fled the convent. Following is a verbatim account of her trial before Catholic examiners. Condemned to death, Elizabeth Dirks was drowned in a sack.

EXAMINERS: We understand that you are a teacher and have led many astray. We want to know who your friends are.

ELIZABETH: I am commanded to love the Lord my God and honor my parents. Therefore I will not tell you who my parents are. That I suffer for Christ is damaging to my friends.

EXAMINERS: We will let that rest for the present, but we want to know whom you have taught.

ELIZABETH: No, my Lords, do not press me on this point. Ask me about my faith and I will answer you gladly.

EXAMINERS: We will make it so tough that you will tell us.

ELIZABETH: I hope through the grace of God to guard my tongue that I shall not be a traitor and deliver my brother to death.

EXAMINERS: What persons were with you when you were baptized?

ELIZABETH: Christ said, "Ask those who were present" [John 18:21].

EXAMINERS: Now we see that you are a teacher because you make yourself equal to Christ.

ELIZABETH: No indeed. Far be it from me, for I count myself no better than the [lowest] from the house of the Lord.

EXAMINERS: What do you mean by the house of the Lord? Don't you consider our church to be the house of the Lord?

ELIZABETH: I do not, my Lords. For it is written, "You are the temple of the living God" [2 Cor. 6:16]. As God said, "I will dwell with you" [Lev. 26:11].

EXAMINERS: What do you think of our Mass?

ELIZABETH: My Lords, I have no faith in your Mass but only in that which is in the Word of God.

EXAMINERS: What do you believe about the Holy Sacrament?

ELIZABETH: I have never in my life read in scripture about a Holy Sacrament, but only of the Supper of the Lord.

EXAMINERS: Shut your mouth. The devil speaks through it.

ELIZABETH: Yes, my Lords, this is a little matter, for the servant is not greater than his Lord [Matt. 10:24].

EXAMINERS: You speak with a haughty tongue.

ELIZABETH: No, my Lords, I speak with a free tongue.

EXAMINERS: What did the Lord say when he gave the supper to his disciples?

ELIZABETH: What did he give them, flesh or bread?

EXAMINERS: He gave them bread.

ELIZABETH: Did not the Lord continue to sit there? How then could they eat his flesh?

EXAMINERS: What do you believe about the baptism of children, seeing that you have had yourself baptized again?

Roland H. Bainton, *Women of the Reformation in Germany and Italy*, pp. 145–149. Copyright © 1971 by Augsburg Fortress Publishers. Used by permission.

ELIZABETH: No, my Lords, I have not had myself baptized again. I have been baptized once on my faith, because it is written, "Baptism belongs to believers." [She deduces this from Peter's confession, Matt. 16:15-16.]

EXAMINERS: Are our children then damned because they are baptized?

ELIZABETH: No, my Lords. Far be it from me to judge the children.

EXAMINERS: Do you not think that you are saved by baptism?

ELIZABETH: No, my Lords. All the water in the sea cannot save me. All my salvation is in Christ, who has commanded me to love the Lord, my God, and my neighbor as myself.

EXAMINERS: Do priests have the power to forgive sins?

ELIZABETH: No, my Lords. How should I believe that? I say that Christ is the only priest through whom sins are forgiven.

EXAMINERS: You say that you accept everything in accord with Holy scripture. Do you not then hold to the word of James?

ELIZABETH: How can I not hold to it?

EXAMINERS: Did he not say, "Go to the elders of the congregation that they should anoint you and pray for you" [James 5:13]?

ELIZABETH: Yes, but would you say, my Lords, that you are such a congregation?

EXAMINERS: The Holy Ghost has made you so holy that you don't need penance or the sacrament.

ELIZABETH: No, my Lords. I freely confess that I have transgressed the ordinances of the pope which the emperor has confirmed with placards. But if you can show me that in any articles I have transgressed against the Lord, my God, I will wail over myself as a miserable sinner.

This was her first hearing.

Then they took her again before the council and brought her to the torture room. Hans, the executioner, was there. The Lords said, "So far we have treated you gently. Since you won't confess we will put you to the torture." The Procurator General said, "Mr. Hans, take hold of her." Mr. Hans answered, "Oh no, my Lords, she will confess voluntarily." But since she would not, he put screws on her thumbs and on two forefingers till the blood spurted from the nails.

EXAMINERS: Confess and we will ease your pain. We told you to confess and not to call upon the Lord, your God!

But she held steadfastly to the Lord, her God, as above related. Then they eased her pain and she said, "Ask me. I will answer, for I feel no pain any more at all as I did."

EXAMINERS: Then won't you confess?

ELIZABETH: No, my Lords.

Then they put two screws on her legs and she said, "Oh my Lords, do not put me to shame. No man has ever touched my bare body." The Procurator General said, "Miss Elizabeth, we will not treat you dishonorably." Then she fainted and one said, "Maybe she's dead." Reviving she said, "I'm alive. I'm not dead." Then they took off the screws and tried to bend her by blandishments.

ELIZABETH: Why do you try me with candied speech as one does with children?

So they could get from her not a word against her brothers in the faith, nor against any one.

EXAMINERS: Will you recant everything you have said?

ELIZABETH: No, my Lords. I will not, but I will seal it with my blood.

EXAMINERS: We will not torture you any more. Will you now tell us in good faith who baptized you?

ELIZABETH: Oh no, my Lords. I have told you all along that I will not do it.

Then, on March 27, 1549, Elizabeth was condemned to death and drowned in a sack. And thus she offered up her life to God.

Menno Simons
AN ANABAPTIST REJECTION
OF THE USE OF FORCE

Menno Simons (c. 1496–1561), a Dutch priest who converted to Anabaptism in 1536, is considered the founder of the Mennonite church. In the following passages from his collected theological writings, Simons offered a biblical justification for the Anabaptist rejection of using force or state power to impose religious beliefs or practices.

Say, my dear people, where do the holy scriptures teach that in Christ's kingdom and church we shall proceed with the magistrate, with the sword, and with physical force and tyranny over a man's conscience and faith, things subject to the judgment of God alone? Where have Christ and the apostles acted thus, advised thus, commanded thus? Ah, Christ says merely, Beware of false prophets; and Paul ordains that we shall avoid a heretical person after he has been admonished once or twice. John teaches that we shall not greet nor receive into the house the man who goes onward and does not bring the doctrine of Christ. But they do not write, Away with those heretics, Report them to the authorities, Lock them up, Expel them out of the city and the country, Throw them into the fire, the water, as the Catholics have done for many years, and as is still found to a great extent with you—you who make yourselves believe that you teach the word of God! . . .

Peter was commanded to sheathe his sword. All Christians are commanded to love their enemies: to do good unto those who abuse and persecute them; to give the mantle when the cloak is taken, the other cheek when one is struck. Tell me, how can a Christian defend Scripturally retaliation, rebellion, war, striking, slaying, torturing, stealing, robbing and plundering and burning cities, and conquering countries?

The great Lord who has created you and us, who has placed our hearts within us knows, and He only knows that our hearts and hands are clear of all sedition and murderous mutiny. By His grace we will ever remain clear. For we truly confess that all rebellion is of the flesh and of the devil.

O beloved reader, our weapons are not swords and spears, but patience, silence, and hope, and the Word of God. With these we must maintain our heavy warfare and fight our battle. Paul says, The weapons of our warfare are not carnal; but mighty through God. With these we intend and desire to storm the kingdom of the devil; and not with sword, spears, cannon, and coats of mail. For He esteemeth iron as straw, and brass as rotten wood. Thus may we with our Prince, Teacher, and Example Christ Jesus, raise the father against the son, and the son against the father, and may we cast down imagination and every high thing that exalteth itself against the knowledge of God, and bring into captivity every thought in obedience to Christ.

True Christians do not know vengeance, no matter how they are mistreated. In patience they possess their souls. Luke 21:18. And they do not break their peace, even if they should be tempted by bondage, torture, poverty, and besides, by the sword and fire. They do not cry, Vengeance, vengeance, as does the world; but

The Complete Works of Menno Simons, ed. John C. Wanger, trans. Leonard Verduin (1956), pp. 537, 550, 555, and 779. Used by permission of Menno Media.

with Christ they supplicate and pray: Father, forgive them; for they know not what they do. Luke 23:34; Acts 7:60.

According to the declaration of the prophets they have beaten their swords into plowshares and their spears into pruning hooks. They shall sit every man under his vine and under his fig-tree, Christ; neither shall they learn war any more. Isa[iah] 2:4; Mic[ah] 4:3. . . .

Behold, beloved rulers and judges, if you take to heart these scriptures and diligently ponder them, then you will observe, first, that your of-fice is not your own but God's, so that you may bend your knees before His majesty; fear His great and adorable name, and rightly and rea-sonably execute your ordained office. Then you will not so freely with your perishable earthly power invade and transgress against Christ, the Lord of lords in His kingdom, power, and ju-risdiction, and with your iron sword adjudicate in that which belongs exclusively to the eter-nal judgment of the Most High God, such as in faith and matters pertaining to faith. In the same vein Luther and others wrote in the begin-ning, but after they came to greater and higher estate they forgot it all. . . .

. . . If he is a preacher called by the Spirit of God, then let him show a single letter in all the New Testament that Christ or the apostles have ever called on the magistrates to defend and protect the true church against the attack of the wicked, as, alas, he calls us. No, no. Christ Jesus and His pow-erful Word and the Holy Spirit are the protectors and defenders of the church, and not, eternally not, the emperor, king, or any worldly potentate! The kingdom of the Spirit must be protected and defended by the sword of the Spirit, and not by the sword of the world. This, in the light of the doctrine and example of Christ and His apostles, is too plain to be defended.

I would say further, if the magistracy rightly understood Christ and His kingdom, they would in my opinion rather choose death than to meddle with their worldly power and sword in spiritual matters which are reserved not to the judgment of man but to the judgment of the great and Almighty God alone. But they are taught by those who have the care of their souls that they may proscribe, imprison, torture, and slay those who are not obedient to their doctrine, as may, alas, be seen in many different cities and countries.

REVIEW QUESTIONS

1. Why was the burning of heretics treated as a public festival?
2. Why were Anabaptists like Elizabeth Dirks considered dangerous to both Catholic and Protestant authorities?
3. What were Simons' reasons for rejecting the use of state power to impose religious belief or practices?
4. What would Simons have thought of Luther's support of state authority on behalf of the church?

CHAPTER 11

Early Modern Society and Politics

HERNÁN CORTÉS. The Spanish explorer and conqueror of Mexico meets the Aztec emperor Montezuma. *(HIP/Art Resource, NY)*

The period from the Renaissance through the Scientific Revolution in the sixteenth and seventeenth centuries saw the breakdown of distinctively medieval cultural, political, and economic forms. The Renaissance produced a more secular attitude and expressed confidence in human capacities. Shortly afterward, the Protestant Reformation ended the religious unity of medieval Latin Christendom and weakened the political power of the church. At the same time the discovery of new trade routes to East Asia and of new lands across the Atlantic widened the imagination and ambitions of Christian Europeans and precipitated a commercial revolution. This great expansion of economic activity furthered capitalism and initiated a global economy—two developments associated with the modern world.

In the late fifteenth century, many Europeans encountered peoples whose cultures markedly differed from their own. The Portuguese, trying to break the Muslim monopoly over trade between Europe and eastern Asia, explored along the Atlantic coast of Africa, establishing their first links with the peoples and kingdoms of the sub-Saharan regions of modern Guinea, Ghana, Dahomey, and the Congo. Setting up fortified trading posts along the way, they eventually sailed around the Cape of Good Hope at the tip of Africa and reached India in 1498. By 1516, Portuguese merchants had reached the port of Canton in southern China. The Portuguese established fortified trading posts in India and Southeast Asia, some of which (Goa, Timor, Macao) they continued to hold into the late twentieth century.

In India, China, and Japan, the Portuguese found highly advanced civilizations that were able to resist European political and cultural domination fairly effectively. In contrast, the Spaniards, with the discovery of the Caribbean islands by Christopher Columbus in 1492, encountered a local population living in a Stone Age culture. There were no cities, no state structures, no significant architecture or art; technology was primitive, and contacts with other peoples limited. However, after 1518, when the Spaniards landed on the American mainland, they found in Mexico and Peru advanced civilizations with great cities, well-developed governments, monumental architecture, and extensive commercial networks. The vast regions and diverse peoples of the Americas were gradually linked to Europe's Christian culture and expanding economy during the sixteenth and seventeenth centuries.

Exploration and commercial expansion created the foundations of a global economy in which the European economy was tied to Asian spices, African slaves, and American silver. A wide variety of goods circulated all over the globe. From the West Indies and East Asia, sugar, rice, tea, cacao, and tobacco flowed into Europe. From the Americas, potatoes, corn, sweet potatoes, and manioc (from which tapioca is made) spread to the rest of the world. Europeans paid for Asian silks and spices with American silver.

The increasing demand for goods and a rise in prices produced more opportunities for the accumulation and investment of capital by private individuals, which is the essence of capitalism. State policies designed to increase national wealth and power also stimulated the growth of capitalism. Governments subsidized new industries, chartered joint-stock companies to engage in overseas trade, and struck at internal tariffs and guild regulations that hampered domestic economic growth. Improvements in banking, shipbuilding, mining, and manufacturing further stimulated economic growth.

In the sixteenth and seventeenth centuries the old medieval political order dissolved, and the modern state began to emerge. The modern state has a strong central government that issues laws that apply throughout the land and a permanent army of professional soldiers paid by the state. Trained bureaucrats, responsible to the central government, collect taxes, enforce laws, and administer justice. The modern state has a secular character; promotion of religion is not the state's concern, and churches do not determine state policy. These features of the modern state were generally not prevalent in the Middle Ages, when the nobles, church, and towns possessed powers and privileges that impeded central authority, and kings were expected to rule in accordance with Christian principles. In the sixteenth and seventeenth centuries, monarchs were exercising central authority with ever-greater effectiveness at the expense of nobles and clergy. The secularization of the state became firmly established after the Thirty Years' War (1618–1648); with their states worn out by Catholic–Protestant conflicts, kings came to act less for religious motives than for reasons of national security and power.

Historically, the modern state has been characterized by a devotion to the nation and by feelings of national pride. There is a national language that is used throughout the land, and the people have a sense of sharing a common culture and history, of being distinct from other peoples. There were some signs of growing national feeling during the sixteenth and seventeenth centuries, but this feature of the modern state did not become a major part of European political life until the nineteenth century. During the early modern period, loyalty was largely given to a town, to a province, to a noble, or to the person of the king rather than to the nation, the people as a whole.

---

1   The Age of Exploration and Conquest

In 1498, a Portuguese explorer, Vasco da Gama (c. 1460–1524), sailed a fleet of four ships around Africa into the Indian Ocean and landed at the Indian port of Calicut. His voyage marked the first step in the creation of a Portuguese commercial empire in East Asia. For centuries afterward, Europeans competed by fair means and foul for access to and control of the Asian trade. The Dutch, English, and

French eventually established trading posts and colonies along the same routes pioneered by the Portuguese. Meanwhile, the Spaniards, following the initial discovery of the Caribbean islands by Columbus in 1492, proceeded to explore, conquer, and settle the mainland of Central, South, and North America.

Bernal Díaz del Castillo
THE DISCOVERY AND CONQUEST OF MEXICO

In 1518, Spanish ships explored the mainland coast along the Gulf of Mexico near the Yucatán Peninsula. The following year an expedition under the leadership of Hernando Cortés (1485–1547) landed at the site of modern Veracruz to explore the newly discovered country. There the Spaniards were unexpectedly confronted with ambassadors from Montezuma (ruled c. 1502–1520), the ruler of an extensive Aztec empire; the Aztecs presented Cortés with gifts made of jade, gold, and silver and with rich textiles, and urged that the Spaniards depart—Montezuma feared Cortés was the Aztec god Quetzalcoatl who had come to reclaim his kingdom. Having 555 troops together with 16 horses and some cannons, Cortés refused and announced that he was sent by his king to speak directly with Montezuma. Sinking his ships to prevent his troops from deserting, Cortés marched inland to the Aztec capital, Tenochtitlán, the site of today's Mexico City; the Spaniards found a civilization with a high level of social and political organization and advanced techniques of engineering, architecture, writing, astronomy, painting, and ceramics. Located on islands in the midst of a lake, Tenochtitlán was approached by three stone causeways that converged in a great central square, dominated by a high pyramidal temple. Other magnificent stone temples and palaces, paved marketplaces, canals with boats carrying products needed by the busy inhabitants, and cultivated gardens with aviaries presented impressive urban scenes. Thousands of priests, soldiers, civil servants, artisans, and laborers filled the streets and houses.

The following excerpts are from *The Discovery and Conquest of Mexico*, the personal memoir of Bernal Díaz del Castillo (c. 1492–1581). Díaz accompanied Cortés and wrote an eyewitness account of this first confrontation between Christian and Aztec civilizations. In the following passage Díaz described Montezuma and his courtiers. Although generally favorable in his account of Montezuma, Díaz reported a rumor that the Aztec emperor ate human flesh for dinner. Whether the Aztecs were cannibals is still disputed among scholars.

The Great Montezuma was about forty years old, of good height and well proportioned, slender

Bernal Díaz del Castillo, *The Discovery and Conquest of Mexico*, trans. A. P. Maudslay (New York: Farrar, Straus and Cudahy, 1956; reprinted in 1984 by Farrar, Straus and Giroux), pp. 208–209, 211, 213–216, 219–220, 225–226.

and spare of flesh, not very swarthy, but of the natural colour and shade of an Indian. He did not wear his hair long, but so as just to cover his ears, his scanty black beard was well shaped and thin. His face was somewhat long, but cheerful, and he had good eyes and showed in his appearance and manner both tenderness and, when necessary, gravity. He was very neat and clean and bathed once every day in the afternoon. He had many women as mistresses, daughters of Chieftains, and he had two great Cacicas [noblewomen] as his legitimate wives. He was free from unnatural offences. The clothes that he wore one day, he did not put on again until four days later. He had over two hundred Chieftains in his guard, in other rooms close to his own, not that all were meant to converse with him, but only one or another, and when they went to speak to him they were obliged to take off their rich mantles [cloaks] and put on others of little worth, but they had to be clean, and they had to enter barefoot with their eyes lowered to the ground, and not to look up in his face. And they made him three obeisances [bows], and said: "Lord, my Lord, my Great Lord," before they came up to him, and then they made their report and with few words he dismissed them, and on taking leave they did not turn their backs, but kept their faces towards him with their eyes to the ground, and they did not turn their backs until they left the room. I noticed another thing, that when other great chiefs came from distant lands about disputes or business, when they reached the apartments of the Great Montezuma, they had to come barefoot and with poor mantles, and they might not enter directly into the Palace, but had to loiter about a little on one side of the Palace door, for to enter hurriedly was considered to be disrespectful. . . .

I have heard it said that they were wont to cook for him the flesh of young boys, but as he had such a variety of dishes, made of so many things, we could not succeed in seeing if they were of human flesh or of other things, for they daily cooked fowls, turkeys, pheasants, native partridges, quail, tame and wild ducks, venison, wild boar, reed birds, pigeons, hares and rabbits, and many sorts of birds and other things which are bred in this country, and they are so numerous that I cannot finish naming them in a hurry; so we had no insight into it; but I know for certain that after our

Captain [Cortés] censured the sacrifice of human beings, and the eating of their flesh, he ordered that such food should not be prepared for him thenceforth. . . .

. . . While Montezuma was at table eating, as I have described, there were waiting on him two other graceful women to bring him tortillas, kneaded with eggs and other sustaining ingredients, and these tortillas were very white, and they were brought on plates covered with clean napkins, and they also brought him another kind of bread, like long balls kneaded with other kinds of sustaining food, and *pan pachol*, for so they call it in this country, which is a sort of wafer. There were also placed on the table three tubes much painted and gilded, which held *liquidambar* [a sort of sweet gum] mixed with certain herbs which they call *tabaco*, and when he had finished eating, after they had danced before him and sung and the table was removed, he inhaled the smoke from one of those tubes, but he took very little of it and with that he fell asleep. . . .

Let us leave this and go on to another great house, where they keep many Idols, and they say that they are their fierce gods, and with them many kinds of carnivorous beasts of prey, tigers and two kinds of lions, and animals something like wolves and foxes, and other smaller carnivorous animals, and all these carnivores they feed with flesh, and the greater number of them breed in the house. They give them as food deer and fowls, dogs and other things which they are used to hunt, and I have heard it said that they feed them on the bodies of the Indians who have been sacrificed. It is in this way; you have already heard me say that when they sacrifice a wretched Indian they saw open the chest with stone knives and hasten to tear out the palpitating heart and blood, and offer it to their Idols, in whose name the sacrifice is made. Then they cut off the thighs, arms and head and eat the former at feasts and banquets, and the head they hang up on some beams, and the body of the man sacrificed is not eaten but given to these fierce animals. They also have in that cursed house many vipers and poisonous snakes which carry on their tails things that sound like bells. These are the worst vipers of all, and they keep them in jars and great pottery vessels with many feathers, and there they lay their eggs and rear their young, and they give them to eat the bodies of the Indians who have been sacrificed, and the flesh of dogs which they are in the habit of breeding.

Let me speak now of the infernal noise when the lions and tigers roared and the jackals and foxes howled and the serpents hissed, it was horrible to listen to and it seemed like a hell. Let us go on and speak of the skilled workmen Montezuma employed in every craft that was practised among them. We will begin with lapidaries [gem cutters] and workers in gold and silver and all the hollow work, which even the great goldsmiths in Spain were forced to admire. . . . Let us go on to the great craftsmen in feather work, and painters and sculptors who were most refined; then to the Indian women who did the weaving and the washing, who made such an immense quantity of fine fabrics with wonderful featherwork designs; the greater part of it was brought daily from some towns of the province on the north coast near Vera Cruz called Cotaxtla.

Díaz records with amazement the great central marketplace with its merchants and myriad products.

. . . When we arrived at the great market place, called Tlaltelolco, we were astounded at the number of people and the quantity of merchandise that it contained, and at the good order and control that was maintained, for we had never seen such a thing before. The chieftains who accompanied us acted as guides. Each kind of merchandise was kept by itself and had its fixed place marked out. Let us begin with the dealers in gold, silver, and precious stones, feathers, mantles, and embroidered goods. Then there were other wares consisting of Indian slaves both men and women; and I say that they bring as many of them to that great market for sale as the Portuguese bring negroes from Guinea; and they brought them along tied to long poles, with collars round their necks so that they could not escape, and others they left free. Next there were other traders who sold great pieces of cloth and cotton, and articles of twisted thread, and there were *cacahuateros* who sold cacao. In this way one could see every sort of merchandise that is to be found in the whole of New Spain [Spain's name for Mexico]. . . .

. . . And we saw the fresh water that comes from Chapultepec [a wooded area near Tenochtitlán] which supplies the city, and we saw the bridges on the three causeways which were built at certain distances apart through which the water of the lake flowed in and out from one side to the other, and we beheld on that great lake a great multitude of canoes, some coming with supplies of food and others returning loaded with cargoes of merchandise; and we saw that from every house of that great city and of all the other cities that were built in the water it was impossible to pass from house to house, except by drawbridges which were made of wood or in canoes; and we saw in those cities Cues [pyramidal temples] and oratories like towers and fortresses and all gleaming white, and it was a wonderful thing to behold; then the houses with flat roofs, and on the causeways other small towers and oratories which were like fortresses.

After having examined and considered all that we had seen we turned to look at the great market place and the crowds of people that were in it, some buying and others selling, so that the murmur and hum of their voices and words that they used could be heard more than a league off. Some of the soldiers among us who had been in many parts of the world, in Constantinople, and all over Italy, and in Rome, said that so large a market place and so full of people, and so well regulated and arranged, they had never beheld before. . . .

When Cortés mocks the Aztec ruler's religious devotion to his gods and proposes setting up the Christian cross and image of the Virgin Mary, Montezuma reproaches him.

. . . Our Captain said to Montezuma through our interpreter, half laughing: "Señor Montezuma, I do not understand how such a great Prince and wise man as you are has not come to the conclusion, in your mind, that these idols of yours are not gods, but evil things that are called devils, and so that you may know it and all your priests may see it clearly, do me the favour to approve of my placing a cross here on the top of this tower, and that in one part of these oratories where your Huichilobos and Tezcatepuca [Aztec gods] stand we may divide off a space where we can set up an image of Our Lady (an image which Montezuma had already seen) and you will see by the fear in which these Idols hold it that they are deceiving you."

Montezuma replied half angrily (and the two priests who were with him showed great annoyance), and said: "Señor Malinche [Aztec name for Cortés], if I had known that you would have said such defamatory things I would not have shown you my gods, we consider them to be very good, for they give us health and rains and good seed times and seasons and as many victories as we desire, and we are obliged to worship them and make sacrifices, and I pray you not to say another word to their dishonour." . . .

The Spaniards decide to build a Christian chapel within the walls of the huge Aztec palace

in which they are quartered, hoping to convert the Aztecs by the example of their own Christian religious devotions. By chance, they discover a secret door to a room filled with treasure.

. . . Now as there was a rumour and we had heard the story that Montezuma kept the treasure of his father Axayaca in that building, it was suspected that it might be in this chamber which had been closed up and cemented only a few days before. Yañes spoke about it to Juan Valásquez de Leon and Francisco de Lugo, and those Captains told the story to Cortés, and the door was secretly opened. When it was opened Cortés and some of his Captains went in first, and they saw such a number of jewels and slabs and plates of gold and chalchihuites [figures of goddesses] and other great riches, that they were quite carried away and did not know what to say about such wealth. The news soon spread among all the other Captains and soldiers, and very secretly we went in to see it. When I saw it I marvelled, and as at that time I was a youth and had never seen such riches as those in my life before, I took it for certain that there could not be another such store of wealth in the whole world. It was decided by all our captains and soldiers, that we should not dream of touching a particle of it, but that the stones should immediately be put back in the doorway and it should be sealed up and cemented just as we found it, and that it should not be spoken about, lest it should reach Montezuma's ears, until times should alter.

REVIEW QUESTIONS

1. What evidence did Bernal Díaz del Castillo offer to show that the Aztecs were a highly civilized people?
2. What moral and religious practices of the Aztecs did the Spaniards find strange and contrary to Christian beliefs?

2 Spanish Oppression of Amerindians

To work the mines and large estates they established in the New World, the Spanish conquistadors reduced the Amerindians to servitude. Outraged by the inhumane treatment of the Amerindians, Spanish missionaries, principally Dominicans, condemned the settlers in fiery sermons and appealed to the Spanish throne to intervene. In a sermon preached on the island of Hispaniola (today the Dominican Republic and Haiti), a Dominican missionary said angrily, "Are these Indians not men? Do they not have rational souls? Are you not obliged to love them as you love yourselves?"

Juan Lopez de Palacios Rubios
JUSTIFYING SPANISH DOMINATION OF AMERINDIANS

The *Requerimiento* (Requirement), drafted in 1513 by Juan Lopez de Palacios Rubios, Spain's chief crown jurist, provided legal and theological justification for Spanish domination of Amerindians. In effect the document, reproduced below, asserted that it was God's will that Amerindians submit to both Catholicism and Spanish rule, that in subduing native people the Spaniards were engaged in a just war. Before launching an attack, the Spaniards read the document aloud to Amerindians who, of course, could not understand Spanish.

On the part of the King, Don Fernando, and of Doña Juana, his daughter, Queen of Castille and León, subduers of the barbarous nations, we their servants notify and make known to you, as best we can, that the Lord our God, Living and Eternal, created the Heaven and the Earth, and one man and one woman, of whom you and we, all the men of the world, were and are descendants, and all those who came after us. But, on account of the multitude which has sprung from this man and woman in the five thousand years since the world was created, it was necessary that some men should go one way and some another, and that they should be divided into many kingdoms and provinces, for in one alone they could not be sustained.

Of all these nations God our Lord gave charge to one man, called St. Peter, that he should be Lord and Superior of all the men in the world, that all should obey him, and that he should be the head of the whole human race, wherever men should live, and under whatever law, sect, or belief they should be; and he gave him the world for his kingdom and jurisdiction.

And he commanded him to place his seat in Rome, as the spot most fitting to rule the world from; but also he permitted him to have his seat in any other part of the world, and to judge and govern all Christians, Moors, Jews, Gentiles, and all other sects. This man was called Pope, as if to say, Admirable Great Father and Governor of men. The men who lived in that time obeyed

Juan Lopez de Palacios Rubios, http://users.dickinson.edu/~borges/Resources-Requerimiento.htm

that St. Peter, and took him for Lord, King, and Superior of the universe; so also they have regarded the others who after him have been elected to the pontificate, and so has it been continued even till now, and will continue till the end of the world.

One of these Pontiffs, who succeeded that St. Peter as Lord of the world, in the dignity and seat which I have before mentioned, made donation of these isles and Tierra-firme to the aforesaid King and Queen and to their successors, our lords, with all that there are in these territories, as is contained in certain writings which passed upon the subject as aforesaid, which you can see if you wish.

So their Highnesses are kings and lords of these islands and land of Tierra-firme by virtue of this donation: and some islands, and indeed almost all those to whom this has been notified, have received and served their Highnesses, as lords and kings, in the way that subjects ought to do, with good will, without any resistance, immediately, without delay, when they were informed of the aforesaid facts. And also they received and obeyed the priests whom their Highnesses sent to preach to them and to teach them our Holy Faith; and all these, of their own free will, without any reward or condition, have become Christians, and are so, and their Highnesses have joyfully and benignantly received them, and also have commanded them to be treated as their subjects and vassals; and you too are held and obliged to do the same. Wherefore, as best we can, we ask and require you that you consider what we have said to you, and that you take the time that shall be necessary to understand and deliberate upon it, and that you acknowledge the Church as the Ruler and Superior of the whole world, and the high priest called Pope, and in his name the King and Queen Doña Juana our lords, in his place, as superiors and lords and kings of these islands

and this Tierra-firme by virtue of the said donation, and that you consent and give place that these religious fathers should declare and preach to you the aforesaid.

If you do so, you will do well, and that which you are obliged to do to their Highnesses, and we in their name shall receive you in all love and charity, and shall leave you, your wives, and your children, and your lands, free without servitude, that you may do with them and with yourselves freely that which you like and think best, and they shall not compel you to turn Christians, unless you yourselves, when informed of the truth, should wish to be converted to our Holy Catholic Faith, as almost all the inhabitants of the rest of the islands have done. And, besides this, their Highnesses award you many privileges and exemptions and will grant you many benefits.

But, if you do not do this, and maliciously make delay in it, I certify to you that, with the help of God, we shall powerfully enter into your country, and shall make war against you in all ways and manners that we can, and shall subject you to the yoke and obedience of the Church and of their Highnesses; we shall take you and your wives and your children, and shall make slaves of them, and as such shall sell and dispose of them as their Highnesses may command; and we shall take away your goods, and shall do you all the mischief and damage that we can, as to vassals who do not obey, and refuse to receive their lord, and resist and contradict him; and we protest that the deaths and losses which shall accrue from this are your fault, and not that of their Highnesses, or ours, nor of these cavaliers who come with us. And that we have said this to you and made this Requisition, we request the notary here present to give us his testimony in writing, and we ask the rest who are present that they should be witnesses of this Requisition.

Bartolomé de Las Casas
THE TEARS OF THE INDIANS

A particularly eloquent defender of the Amerindians was Bartolomé de Las Casas (1474–1566), who spent most of his long life in Spanish America. In *The Tears of the Indians*, also published as *A Short History of the Destruction of the Indies*, Las Casas described in graphic detail the atrocities inflicted on the Amerindians. His account greatly exaggerated the number of Amerindians killed by the Spaniards; disease, for which the Amerindians had no immunity, not Spanish mistreatment, was the principal reason for the decimation of the native population. Las Casas' appeals were instrumental in stimulating reforms by the Spanish throne, but the distance separating Spain from her possessions in the New World often prevented effective enforcement of these reforms. In the following excerpt from *The Tears of the Indians*, Las Casas recounts the brutal behavior of the Spaniards toward the native inhabitants of Hispaniola whom he described as a people "devoid of wickedness and duplicity . . . or desire for vengeance."

On the Island Hispaniola was where the Spaniards first landed, as I have said. Here those Christians perpetrated their first ravages and oppressions against the native peoples. This was the first land in the New World to be destroyed and depopulated by the Christians, and here they began their subjection of the women and children, taking them away from the Indians to use them and ill use them, eating the food they provided with their sweat and toil. The Spaniards did not content themselves with what the Indians gave them of their own free will, according to their ability, which was always too little to satisfy enormous appetites, for a Christian eats and consumes in one day an amount of food that would suffice to feed three houses inhabited by ten Indians for one month. And they committed other acts of force and violence and oppression which made the Indians realize that these men had not come from Heaven. And some of the Indians concealed their foods while others concealed their wives and children and

still others fled to the mountains to avoid the terrible transactions of the Christians.

And the Christians attacked them with buffets and beatings, until finally they laid hands on the nobles of the villages. Then they behaved with such temerity and shamelessness that the most powerful ruler of the islands had to see his own wife raped by a Christian officer.

From that time onward the Indians began to seek ways to throw the Christians out of their lands. They took up arms, but their weapons were very weak and of little service in offense and still less in defense. (Because of this, the wars of the Indians against each other are little more than games played by children.) And the Christians, with their horses and swords and pikes began to carry out massacres and strange cruelties against them. They attacked the towns and spared neither the children nor the aged nor pregnant women nor women in childbed, not only stabbing them and dismembering them but cutting them to pieces as if dealing with sheep in the slaughter house. They laid bets as to who, with one stroke of the sword, could split a man in two or could cut off his head or spill out his entrails with a single stroke of the pike. They took infants from their mothers' breasts,

The Devastation of the Indies: A Brief Account, trans. Herma Briffault (Continuum International Publishing Group, 1992), pp. 32–34. © 1992 Continuum International Publishing Company.

snatching them by the legs and pitching them headfirst against the crags or snatched them by the arms and threw them into the rivers, roaring with laughter and saying as the babies fell into the water, "Boil there, you offspring of the devil!" Other infants they put to the sword along with their mothers and anyone else who happened to be nearby. They made some low wide gallows on which the hanged victim's feet almost touched the ground, stringing up their victims in lots of thirteen, in memory of Our Redeemer and His twelve Apostles, then set burning wood at their feet and thus burned them alive. To others they attached straw or wrapped their whole bodies in straw and set them afire. With still others, all those they wanted to capture alive, they cut off their hands and hung them round the victim's neck, saying, "Go now, carry the message," meaning, Take the news to the Indians who have fled to the mountains. They usually dealt with the chieftains and nobles in the following way: they made a grid of rods which they placed on forked sticks, then lashed the victims to the grid and lighted a smoldering fire underneath, so that little by little, as those captives screamed in despair and torment, their souls would leave them.

I once saw this, when there were four or five nobles lashed on grids and burning; I seem even to recall that there were two or three pairs of grids where others were burning, and because they uttered such loud screams that they disturbed the captain's sleep, he ordered them to be strangled. And the constable, who was worse than an executioner, did not want to obey that order (and I know the name of that constable and know his relatives in Seville), but instead put a stick over the victims' tongues, so they could not make a sound, and he stirred up the fire, but not too much, so that they roasted slowly, as he liked. I saw all these things I have described, and countless others.

And because all the people who could do so fled to the mountains to escape these inhuman, ruthless, and ferocious acts, the Spanish captains, enemies of the human race, pursued them with the fierce dogs they kept which attacked the Indians, tearing them to pieces and devouring them. And because on few and far between occasions, the Indians justifiably killed some Christians, the Spaniards made a rule among themselves that for every Christian slain by the Indians, they would slay a hundred Indians.

REVIEW QUESTIONS

1. How did the author of the *Requerimiento* justify the subjugation of the Amerindians?
2. How do you explain the cruelty of the Spaniards?

---

3   Toward the Modern Economy:
The Example of Holland

The Spanish and Portuguese monopoly of trade was challenged in the late sixteenth century, first by English privateers who preyed on the Spanish fleets crossing the Atlantic and then by the Dutch who were in revolt against their sovereign, the Spanish king Philip II (ruled 1556–1598). Earlier, the Dutch had traded with both Spanish and Portuguese ports, but were not allowed to seek markets directly with the Americas or the East Indies. When Philip II, who was also king of Portugal from 1580, excluded the rebellious Dutch from trading in his ports—a policy that was renewed by his son, Philip III (ruled 1598–1621)—Dutch merchants decided to break the Portuguese monopoly over trade with the East Indies.

In doing so, they launched the first of many commercial wars designed to win control over world trade markets.

To encourage trade with the East Indies, the Dutch government established a private limited stockholding company, the East India Company, and granted it a monopoly over trade and colonization anywhere east of the Cape of Good Hope or beyond the Straits of Magellan at the southern tip of South America. The company was granted the right to build fortresses, to raise armies, to establish laws and courts in territories it captured from the Spanish or the Portuguese, and to enter into diplomatic alliances with other princes. The East India Company was the foundation on which the Dutch built their colonial empire. Other European states established similar corporations to further trade and colonization.

William Carr
THE DUTCH EAST INDIA COMPANY

In 1693, William Carr, the English consul at Amsterdam, wrote a travelers' guide to the leading cities of Holland, Flanders, northern Germany, and Scandinavia. Of these, the largest and wealthiest was Amsterdam in Holland. In less than a century, this once small medieval city had grown to become the most important commercial port in the West and the center of European financial capitalism. In the following selection, Carr describes the commercial trading system of the famous Dutch East India Company, which established trading posts in South Africa, the Persian Gulf area, India, Ceylon, Bangladesh, Indonesia, China, and Japan. Although not mentioned by Carr, the Dutch West India Company conducted similar operations in the Caribbean and North America. The Dutch trading post of New Amsterdam at the mouth of the Hudson River would become the city of New York, the world center of finance capitalism in the twentieth century.

. . . The East India Company of the Netherlands is said to be a commonwealth within a commonwealth, and this is true when you consider the sovereign power and privileges the company has been granted by the States General [the ruling council of the Dutch Republic] and also consider its riches and vast number of subjects, and the many territories and colonies it possesses in the East Indies. The company is said to have 30,000 men in its constant employ and more than 200 capital ships, in addition to its sloops, ketches, and yachts. The company possesses many colonies formerly belonging to Spain,

Portugal, and various Indian princes, and as good Christians company members have spread the Gospel of Christ in these lands, printing the Bible, prayer books, and catechisms in Indian languages and maintaining ministers and teachers to instruct those that are converted to the faith. Having said that this company is so extensive—as it were a commonwealth apart—I will demonstrate that it is a commonwealth first by its power, riches, and strength in the East Indies, and second, by its position in Europe. . . . But I will begin at the Cape of Good Hope [Africa] where the company has built a fort where it maintains a garrison to defend its ships when they stop there for fresh water. From there let us view the company on the island of Java, where it has built a fair city

William Carr, *Travels Through Holland, Germany, Sweden and Denmark by an English Gentleman* (London: Randal Taylor, 1693), pp. 14–18, 33–34, 60–64.

called Batavia and fortified it with bastions like those in Amsterdam. This city is the residence of the company's grand minister of state, called the General of the Indies. He has six privy counsellors (ordinary) and two extraordinary; they oversee the concerns of the company throughout the Indies, including matters of war and peace. . . . The General of the Indies has horse and foot soldiers, officers, and servants—as if he were a sovereign prince—all paid for by the company. . . . So formidable is the company in the East Indies that it looks as though it aims to rule the South Seas. It also has a great trade with China and Japan. . . . With Persia also it has great commerce and is so confident that it wages war with the Persian monarch if he

wrongs it in trade. It also has several colonies on the coast of Malabar and Coromandel [west coast of India] and in the country of the Great Mogul. . . . But especially let us examine the company on the rich island of Ceylon [Sri Lanka] where it controls the plains, so the king of the island is forced to live in the mountains while the company possesses the city of Colombo. . . . I will say no more of the company's power in the Indies, but let us examine its position in Europe. To begin with, in Amsterdam the company has two large stately palaces, one being in the old part of the city, and the other in the new; in the old part it keeps its court—where the Resident Committee of the company sits— and sells the company's goods.

REVIEW QUESTION

What evidence of the Dutch East India Company's power does Carr provide?

---

4   The Jews of Spain and Portugal: Expulsion, Forced Conversion, Inquisition

For centuries the Jewish community in Spain had distinguished itself in commerce and intellectual pursuits, and Jews had served Spanish kings as ministers and physicians. However, the five-hundred-year struggle, seen as a crusade, to drive the Muslims out of Spain and the vitriolic preachings of clerics, particularly Dominican friars, exacerbated anti-Jewish feelings. In a three-month period in 1391, mobs slew some 50,000 Jews and prompted many others to join the growing number of *conversos* (converts). A century later, in 1492, the Spanish monarchs Ferdinand and Isabella, fearing that converted Jews were being encouraged by their relatives and erstwhile co-religionists to return to Judaism, ordered the expulsion of those Spanish Jews who would not convert to Catholicism. Perhaps as many as 150,000 Jews fled; it is not known how many remained and converted.

Old Christians disdained the *conversos,* or New Christians. They accused the converts of secretly practicing Judaism and resented their rise to positions of eminence in business, the professions, government service, and even the church. The hostility to *conversos* also had a racial component, as Old Christians insisted, contrary to Catholic theology, that baptism would not cleanse the bad blood of Jews. Old Christians were obsessed with racial purity, refusing to intermarry with New Christians, even if the family had been faithful Catholics for generations, and barring their entry into certain military and religious orders. For social acceptance, one had to prove a lineage that had no Jewish blood.

Andrés Bernáldez
AN EARLY ACCOUNT OF THE SPANISH INQUISITION

For centuries the Spanish Inquisition, established to guard against religious backsliding by New Christians and run by clergy motivated by church doctrines that denigrated Jews and Judaism, relentlessly hounded the converts' descendants. Those *conversos* who showed signs of Judaizing, such as not eating pork, putting on clean clothes on Saturday, the Jewish Sabbath, or celebrating Jewish holidays, were considered heretics and put on trial. If found guilty, they could be turned over to the secular authorities and burned at the stake, often in front of a large crowd. At times cruel torture was applied to gain a confession. Suspects who confessed their heresy were considered to be "reconciled" to the church. They escaped excommunication but faced other punishments, including wearing the *sambenitos*, a yellow smock with red crosses, in public for a specified length of time.

The following account of the Spanish Inquisition was written in the early sixteenth century by Andrés Bernáldez, a priest and chronicler.

CHAPTER 43

On the beginning of the heresy and the beginning of the Inquisition, and when Mosaic depravity and the punishment of Jewish ceremonies had its climax

Heretical Mosaic depravity reigned for a long time, hidden away in corners, not daring to show itself; and it was allowed to exist through the negligence of the prelates—namely, the archbishops and bishops of Spain—who never acknowledged or denounced it to the kings or the popes as they were obliged to do.

This Mosaic heresy had its start in the year of Our Lord 1390, at the beginning of the

reign of King Henry III of Castile, when the plundering of the Jewish quarter occurred as a result of the preaching of Friar Vincent Ferrér, a holy, Catholic, and learned man, of the Order of St. Dominic. At that time, Ferrer wanted to convert all the Jews of Spain through preaching and proofs from the Holy Law and scripture, and to put an end to that obstinate, stinking synagogue. He and other preachers preached a great deal to the Jews in the synagogues, churches, and fields. . . .

[But] Friar Vincent Ferrér could convert only a few Jews, and the people spitefully put the Jews in Castile to the sword and killed many, and this occurred all over Castile in a single day, Tuesday. Then the Jews themselves came to the churches to be baptized, and so they were; and very many in Castile were made into Christians. After their baptism, some went to Portugal and to other kingdoms to be Jews; others, after

The Spanish Inquisition 1478–1614: An Anthology of Sources, edited and translated by Lu Ann Homza (Indianapolis, Indiana: Hackett Publishing Co., 2006), pp. 1–3, 5–8. Reprinted by permission of Hackett Publishing Company, Inc. All rights reserved.

some time had passed, returned to being Jews in places where they were not known. Many unbaptized Jews and synagogues still remained in Castile. . . .

The baptized Jews who stayed were called *conversos*; this is the origin of the name "*converso*," which means those converted to the Holy Catholic Faith. The *conversos* observed the Faith very badly . . . for the most part they were secret Jews. . . . Those who could avoid baptizing their children, did so; and those who did baptize them, washed them in their houses as soon as they brought them home. . . . You also have to know that before the Inquisition arrived, the customs of ordinary *conversos* were the same as the same stinking Jews', which was why they continually talked to each other. . . . They did not eat pork except by force. . . . They observed Passover and Saturdays as best they could: . . . they had Jews who preached to them in their houses, in secret, especially to the women. . . . They . . . secretly performed all the Jewish ceremonies as best they could, the men as well as the women. They always avoided receiving the Sacraments of the Holy Church, except when they were constrained by the Church's constitutions. They never confessed the truth. . . .

The King and Queen were simultaneously informed that this monstrous affliction ran through all of Castile. They obtained a bull from Pope Sixtus IV to proceed against this heresy and to punish it with fire. The papal bull was conceded and the inquisition ordered in 1480.

CHAPTER 44

How they began to seize, burn, and reconcile Jewish heretics in Seville. And the great pestilence of 1481

Their Highnesses having obtained the bull for the Inquisition . . . the first inquisitors came to Seville: two Dominican monks, a provincial and a vicar, one named Friar Miguel [de Morillo] and the other Friar Juan [de San Martin]. Accompanying them was Dr. Medina, a cleric of San Pedro. The three, working as one, began their inquisition with great diligence, at the start of 1481.

In a very few days, through various ways and means, these three men knew the truth of this wicked heretical depravity, and began to seize the guiltiest men and women. . . . They began to sentence people to death by fire.

After this burning, all the *conversos* who had confessed were terrified . . . and they fled the city and the archbishopric. A penalty was imposed upon them, that they could not flee the city under pain of death, and guards were put at the city gates; so many were seized that there was no place to put them. . . .

That year, after the plague ended, the inquisitors returned to Seville and continued their inquisition. And over the next eight years, until 1488, they burned more than six hundred people and reconciled more than five thousand, whom they put into perpetual prisons. Some people were in those prisons for four or five years or more. And the inquisitors would take people out of prison and put *sanbenitos* on them—with red crosses in front and behind—and they had to walk around in those *sanbenitos* for a long time. Afterward the *sanbenitos* were removed.

Among those burned in those eight years were three ordained clerics and three or four monks, all of *converso* lineage. The inquisitors also burned a doctor, a monk of the Trinitarian order called Savariego, who was a great preacher and a great liar, a trickster heretic. . . . Many of the heretics who were reconciled to the Church returned afterward to judaizing, and they were burned through the same sort of prosecution in Seville and in parts of Castile.

Damião de Gois
THE FORCED CONVERSION
OF PORTUGUESE JEWS

Influenced by the recent expulsion of the Spanish Jews, in 1497 King Manuel of Portugal (ruled 1495–1521) also demanded the expulsion or conversion of the Jews in his own country. Making the event more harrowing for the unfortunate Jews was the king's order to wrest Jewish children aged fourteen or younger from their parents, baptize them, and place them in Christian homes. This wave of persecution was not confined to those who actively practiced the Jewish faith. The recent converts, or New Christians, free of the barriers that had been placed on them as Jews, were rising rapidly in the professions, government service, and business. In 1506, Old Christians, driven by fear and hate and aroused by friars shouting heresy, massacred New Christians. Damião de Gois, a contemporary Christian chronicler, reported that the mob dragged the victims

> through the streets with their sons, wives and daughters [and] threw them indiscriminately, dead and alive onto the bonfires, without any mercy. And so great was the cruelty that they even executed children and babies in the cradle, taking them by the legs, cutting them into pieces and smashing them against walls. In these cruelties, they did not forget to sack the houses and steal all the gold, silver and jewels which they found in them, the matter reaching such a frenzy that they dragged [even] from the churches many men, women, boys and girls, tearing them away from . . . the images of our Lord and Our Lady and the other saints, which they had embraced for fear of death, killing and burning without distinction, [and] without fear of God, both women and men.

In the following selection, Damião de Gois describes the events surrounding the forced conversion of Portuguese Jews.

Many of the Jews born in the kingdom [of Portugal] and of those who came from Castile received the water of baptism, and those who did not want to convert then began to arrange matters suitably for their embarkation. At this time the king, for reasons that moved him thus, ordered that on a certain day their sons and

J. H. Edwards, ed. and trans., *The Jews in Western Europe, 1400–1600*, pp. 61, 63. Copyright © 1994 by J. H. Edwards. Reprinted by permission of the author.

daughters, aged fourteen and below, should be taken from them and distributed among the towns and villages of the kingdom, where at his own expense [the king] ordered that they should be brought up and indoctrinated in the faith of our saviour Jesus Christ. This was agreed by the king with his council of state in Estremoz, and from there he went to Evora at the beginning of Lent in the year 1497, where he announced that the appointed day would be Easter Sunday.

Because there was less secrecy among the members of the [royal] council than had been expected, concerning what had been ordered in this matter, on the day on which [this] was to happen, it was necessary for the king to command that the execution of this order should be implemented at once throughout the kingdom, before by means and devices the Jews might have sent their children abroad. This action was the cause, not only of great terror, mixed with many tears, pain and sadness among the Jews, but also of much fright and surprise among the Christians, because no [human] creature ought to suffer or endure having his children forcibly separated from him. And [even] among foreigners [perhaps the native population of Portugal's colonies] virtually the same feeling exists by natural communication [i.e. without Christianity], principally among the rational ones, because with them Nature communicates the effects of her law more freely than with irrational beasts.

This same law compelled many of the "old" Christians to be so moved to pity and mercy by the angry cries, weeping and wailing of the fathers and mothers from whom their children were forcibly taken, that they themselves hid [Jewish children] in their houses so that [the Jews] should not see them snatched from their hands. Those [Christians] saved them, knowing that they were thus acting against the law and the pragmatic of their king and lord, and that this same natural law made the Jews themselves use such cruelty that many of them killed their children, by suffocating them and drowning them in wells and rivers, as well as other methods, preferring to see them die in this way rather than be separated from them, without hope that they would ever see them again; and, for the same reason, many of [the parents] killed themselves.

While these actions were being carried out, the king never ceased to concern himself with what was necessary for the salvation of these people's souls, so that, moved by piety, he played a trick on them, by ordering them to be allowed to embark. Of the three ports of the kingdom that were designated for this, he forbade them two and commanded that they should all go to Lisbon to embark, giving them the [quarter of] the Estaos in which to shelter, and more than twenty thousand souls gathered there. Because of these delays, the time that the king had fixed for their departure went by, and thus they all remained as captives. Finding themselves in so wretched a state, many of them placed themselves at the mercy of the king. He returned their children to them and promised them that for twenty years he would inflict no harm upon them and that they would become Christians; [all of] which the king conceded to them, together with many other privileges that he gave them. As for those who did not want to be Christians, he ordered immediate embarkation to be granted to them, thus freeing them from the captivity in which they found themselves; and they all passed over to the lands of the Moors [North Africa].

Now it appears that we might be regarded as neglectful if we did not state the reason why the king ordered the children of the Jews to be taken from them, but not those of the Moors, because they too left the kingdom because they did not wish to receive the water of baptism and believe what the Catholic Church believes. The reason was that from the seizure of the Jews' children no harm could result for the Christians dispersed throughout the world, in which the Jews, because of their sins, do not have kingdoms or lordships, cities and towns, but rather, everywhere they live they are pilgrims and taxpayers, without having power or authority to carry out their wishes against the injuries and evils which are done to them. But for *our* sins and punishment, God allows the Moors to occupy the greater part of Asia and Africa and a great part of Europe, where they have empires and kingdoms and great lordships, in which many

Christians are under tribute to them, as well as many whom they hold as captives. For all these [reasons], it would be very prejudicial to take the Moors' children away from them, because it is clear that they would not hesitate to avenge those to whom such an injury was done on the Christians living in the lands of other Moors, once they found out about it, and above all on the Portuguese, against whom they would have a particular grievance in this regard. And this was the reason why [the Muslims] were allowed to leave the kingdom with their children and the Jews were not, to all of whom God permitted through his mercy to know the way of truth, so that they might be saved in it.

REVIEW QUESTIONS

1. Why did Christians persecute Jews and New Christians with a clear conscience?
2. Why didn't the Portuguese take away the children of Muslims the way they did Jewish children?

5 The Atlantic Slave Trade

As the first Portuguese merchants began to penetrate southward along the coast of Western Africa, they found that the local African societies engaged in an extensive trade in slave laborers. African slavers brought their captives, generally prisoners of war and kidnap victims, to coastal slave markets where they were purchased by Europeans. Some slaves were taken back to Europe, but after 1500 the trade shifted largely to the Portuguese colony in Brazil and the Spanish colonies in the West Indies. In addition, Arabs and Portuguese competed in conveying slaves from East Africa to the markets of the Middle East. The widespread use of African slaves marked a new stage in the history of slavery. In the Western world slavery became identified with race; the myth emerged that blacks were slaves by nature.

In the seventeenth century, the Dutch and English entered the West African slave trade, ousting the Portuguese as the principal slave traders to the West Indies and North America. The supply of laborers from Africa was essential to the New World's successful economic development. The Africans proved themselves to be skilled farmers and artisans who could endure the heavy labor of plantation life without the high rate of sickness and death that afflicted the local Native American populations. The Atlantic slave trade continued for more than three hundred years until finally suppressed by European governments in the nineteenth century. During that period, it is estimated that between 9.5 and 12 million African men, women, and children were shipped to the New World as slaves.

Seventeenth-Century Slave Traders
BUYING AND TRANSPORTING
AFRICANS

Dealing in slaves was a profitable business that attracted numerous entrepreneurs. Following are two accounts written by slave traders in the seventeenth century.

As the slaves come down to Fida from the inland country, they are put into a booth, or prison, built for that purpose, near the beach, all of them together; and when the Europeans are to receive them, they are brought out into a large plain, where the surgeons examine every part of every one of them, to the smallest member, men and women being all stark naked. Such as are allowed good and sound, are set on the one side, and the others by themselves; which slaves so rejected are there called Mackrons, being above thirty five years of age, or defective in their limbs, eyes or teeth; or grown grey, or that have the venereal disease, or any other imperfection. These being so set aside, each of the others, which have passed as good, is marked on the breast, with a red-hot iron, imprinting the mark of the French, English, or Dutch companies, that so each nation may distinguish their own, and to prevent their being chang'd by the natives for worse, as they are apt enough to do. In this particular, care is taken that the women, as tenderest, be not burnt too hard.

The branded slaves, after this, are returned to their former booth, where the factor [buyer] is to subsist them at his own charge, which amounts to about two-pence a day for each of them, with bread and water, which is all their allowance. There they continue sometimes ten or fifteen days, till the sea is still enough to send them aboard; for very often it continues too

boisterous for so long a time, unless in January, February and March, which is commonly the calmest season: and when it is so, the slaves are carried off by parcels, in bar-canoes, and put aboard the ships in the road. Before they enter the canoes, or come out of the booth, their former Black masters strip them of every rag they have, without distinction of men or women; to supply which, in orderly ships, each of them as they come aboard is allowed a piece of canvas, to wrap around their waist, which is very acceptable to those poor wretches. . . . in the aforesaid months of January, February and March, which are the good season, ships are for the most part soon dispatched, if there be a good number of slaves at hand; so that they need not stay above four weeks for their cargo, and sometimes it is done in a fortnight.

The Blacks of Fida are so expeditious at this trade of slaves that they can deliver a thousand every month. . . . If there happens to be no stock of slaves at Fida, the factor must trust the Blacks with his goods, to the value of a hundred and fifty, or two hundred slaves; which goods they carry up into the inland, to buy slaves, at all the markets, for above two hundred leagues up the country, where they are kept like cattle [are kept] in Europe; the slaves sold there being generally prisoners of war, taken from their enemies, like other booty, and perhaps some few sold by their own countrymen, in extreme want, or upon a famine; as also some as a punishment of heinous crimes: tho' many Europeans believe that parents sell their own children, men their wives and relations, which, if it ever happens, is so seldom, that it cannot justly be charged upon a whole nation, as a custom and common practice.

Documents Illustrative of the History of the Slave Trade to America, vol. 1, ed. Elizabeth Donnan (Washington, D.C.: Carnegie Institution, 1935), pp. 293–294, 402–403, 406, 407–408. Copyright © 1935 by the Carnegie Institution. Reprinted by permission of Carnegie Institution of Washington.

A second slaver describes the loading and transporting of the newly acquired slaves.

When our slaves were come to the seaside, our canoes were ready to carry them off to the long-boat, if the sea permitted, and she convey'd them aboard ship, where the men were all put in irons, two and two shackled together, to prevent their mutiny, or swimming ashore.

The negroes are so wilful and loth to leave their own country, that they have often leap'd out of the canoes, boat and ship, into the sea, and kept under water till they were drowned, to avoid being taken up and saved by our boats, which pursued them; they having a more dreadful apprehension of Barbadoes than we can have of hell, tho' in reality they live much better there than in their own country; but home is home, etc: we have likewise seen [many] of them eaten by the sharks, of which a prodigious number [swam] about the ships in this place, and I have been told will follow her hence to Barbadoes, for the dead negroes that are thrown over-board in the passage. I am certain in our voyage there we did not [lack] the sight of some every day, but that they were the same I can't affirm.

We had about 12 negroes did wilfully drown themselves, and others starv'd themselves to death; for 'tis their belief that when they die they return home to their own country and friends again.

I have been inform'd that some commanders have cut off the legs and arms of the most wilful, to terrify the rest, for they believe if they lose a member, they cannot return home again: I was advis'd by some of my officers to do the same, but I could not be perswaded to entertain the least thought of it, much less put in practice such barbarity and cruelty to poor creatures, who, excepting their want of christianity and true religion (their misfortune more than fault) are as much the works of God's hands, and no doubt as dear to him as ourselves; nor can I imagine why they should be despis'd for

their colour, being what they cannot help, and the effect of the climate it has pleas'd God to appoint them. I can't think there is any intrinsick value in one colour more than another, nor that white is better than black, only we think so because we are so, and are prone to judge favourably in our own case, as well as the blacks, who in odium of the colour, say, the devil is white, and so paint him. . . .

When our slaves are aboard we shackle the men two and two, while we lie in port, and in sight of their own country, for 'tis then they attempt to make their escape, and mutiny; to prevent which we always keep centinels upon the hatchways, and have a chest full of small arms, ready loaden and prim'd, constantly lying at hand upon the quarter-deck, together with some granada shells; and two of our quarter-deck guns, pointing on the deck thence, and two more out of the steerage, the door of which is always kept shut, and well barr'd; they are fed twice a day, at 10 in the morning, and 4 in the evening, which is the time they are aptest to mutiny, being all upon deck; therefore all that time [those] of our men are not employ'd in distributing their victuals to them, and settling them, stand to their arms; and some with lighted matches at the great guns that yaun upon them . . . till they have done and gone down to their kennels between decks. . . .

When we come to sea we let them all out of irons, they never attempting then to rebel, considering that should they kill or master us, they could not tell how to manage the ship, or must trust us, who would carry them where we pleas'd; therefore the only danger is while we are in sight of their own country, which they are loth to part with; but once out of sight out of mind: I never heard that they mutiny'd in any ships of consequence, that had a good number of men, and the least care; but in small tools [vessels] where they had but few men, and those negligent or drunk, then they surpriz'd and butcher'd them, cut the cables, and let the vessel drive ashore, and every one shift for himself. However, we have some 30 or 40 gold coast[1] negroes, which we buy, and are procur'd us there by our factors, to make guardians and overseers of the Whidaw negroes, and sleep among them to keep them from quarrelling; and in order, as well as to give us notice, if they can discover any caballing or plotting among them, which trust they will discharge with great diligence: they also take care to make the negroes scrape the decks where they lodge every morning very clean, to eschew any distempers that may engender from filth and nastiness; when we constitute a guardian, we give him a cat of nine tails [whip] as a badge

of his office, which he is not a little proud of, and will exercise with great authority. We often at sea in the evenings would let the slaves come up into the sun to air themselves, and make them jump and dance for an hour or two to our bag-pipes, harp, and fiddle, by which exercise to preserve them in health; but notwithstanding all our endeavour, 'twas my hard fortune to have great sickness and mortality among them.

Having bought my compliment of 700 slaves, *viz.* 480 men and 220 women, and finish'd all my business at Whidaw, I took my leave of the old king . . . and parted, with many affectionate expressions on both sides, being forced to promise him that I would return again the next year, with several things he desired me to bring him from England. . . .

---

[1]The Gold Coast was a section of coastal western Africa along the Gulf of Guinea, known for its trade in gold. —Eds.

John Newton
THOUGHTS UPON THE AFRICAN SLAVE TRADE

For several years in the mid-eighteenth century, Englishman John Newton was involved in the forcible transporting of Africans to the New World. In time he began to question the morality of slavery. Ordained as a minister—he wrote the words to "Amazing Grace," the famous Christian hymn—Newton came to support abolitionism. In *Thoughts upon the African Slave Trade* (1788), he resolutely condemned the slave trade: "I know no method of getting money, not even that of robbing for it upon the highway, which has so direct a tendency to efface the moral sense, to rob the heart of every gentle and humane disposition, and to harden it, like steel, against all impressions of sensibility."

In the following excerpts from this pamphlet, Newton tells of Africans attacking the ship's crew in a desperate bid for freedom and recalls the abuse of female captives by "white savages."

Usually, about two-thirds of a cargo of slaves are males. When a hundred and fifty or two

---

John Newton, *Thoughts Upon the African Slave Trade* (London: J. Buckland, 1788), pp. 103–106.

hundred stout men, torn from their native land, many of whom never saw the sea, much less a ship, till a short space before they had embarked; who have, probably, the same natural prejudice against a white man, as we have against a black; and who often bring with them an apprehension they are bought to be eaten: I say, when thus circumstanced, it is not to be expected that they will tamely resign themselves to their situation. It is always taken for granted, that they will attempt to gain their liberty if possible. Accordingly, as we dare not trust them, we receive them on board, from the first as enemies; and, before their number exceeds, perhaps, ten or fifteen, they are all put in irons; in most ships, two and two together. . . .

. . . One unguarded hour, or minute, is sufficient to give the slaves the opportunity they are always waiting for. An attempt to rise upon the ship's company, brings on instantaneous and horrid war: for, when they are once in motion, they are desperate; and where they do not conquer, they are seldom quelled without much mischief and bloodshed on both sides. . . .

. . . The patriots, who formed and animated the plan, if they can be found out, must be treated as villains, and punished, to intimidate the rest. These punishments, in their nature and degree, depend upon the sovereign will of the captain. Some are content with inflicting such moderate punishment as may suffice for an example. But unlimited power, instigated by revenge, and where the heart, by a long familiarity with the sufferings of slaves is become callous, and insensible to the pleadings of humanity, is terrible!

I have seen them sentenced to unmerciful whippings, continued till the poor creatures have not had power to groan under their misery, and hardly a sign of life has remained. I have seen them agonizing for hours, I believe for days together, under the torture of the thumbscrews; a dreadful engine, which, if the screw be turned by an unrelenting hand, can give intolerable anguish. There have been instances in which cruelty has proceeded still further; but, as I hope they are few, and I can mention but one from my own knowledge, I shall but mention it.

I have often heard a captain, who has been long since been dead, boast of his conduct in a former voyage, when his slaves attempted to rise upon him. After he had suppressed the insurrection, he sat in judgment upon the insurgents; and

not only, in cold blood, adjudged several of them, I know not how many, to die, but studied, with no small attention, how to make death as excruciating as possible. For my reader's sake, I suppress the recital of particulars.

. . . When the women and girls are taken on board a ship, naked, trembling, terrified, perhaps almost exhausted with cold, fatigue, and hunger, they are often exposed to the wanton rudeness of white savages. The poor creatures cannot understand the language they hear, but the looks and manner of the speakers are sufficiently intelligible. In imagination, the prey is divided, upon the spot, and only reserved till opportunity offers. Where resistance or refusal, would be utterly in vain, even the solicitation of consent is seldom thought of. But I forbear.— This is not a subject for declamation. Facts like these, so certain and so numerous, speak for themselves. Surely, if the advocates for the Slave Trade attempt to plead for it, before the wives and daughters of our happy land, or before those who have wives or daughters of their own, they must lose their cause.

Perhaps some hard-hearted pleader may suggest, that such treatment would indeed be cruel, in Europe: but the African women are negroes, savages, who have no idea of the nicer sensations which obtain among civilized people. I dare contradict chem in the strongest terms. I have lived long, and conversed much, amongst these supposed savages. I have often slept in their towns, in a house filled with goods for trade, with no person in the house but myself, and with no other door than a mat; in that security, which no man in his senses would expect in this civilized nation, especially in this metropolis, without the precaution of having strong doors, strongly locked and bolted. And with regard to the women, in Sherbro [island off the coast of West Africa], where I was most acquainted, I have seen many instances of modesty, and even delicacy, which would not disgrace an English woman. Yet, such is the treatment which I have known permitted, if not encouraged, in many of our ships—they have been abandoned, without restraint, to the lawless will of the first comer.

Malachy Postlethwayt
SLAVERY DEFENDED

While some people attacked African bondage as morally repugnant, its proponents argued that it was a boon to shipping and manufacturing and also benefited Africans by liberating them from oppressive African rulers, who had captured and enslaved them, and placing them in the care of more humane Christian masters, who instructed them in Christian ideals. Malachy Postlethwayt (c. 1707–1767), an English economist, defended slavery in the following excerpt written in 1746.

The most approved judges of the commercial interests of these Kingdoms have ever been of the opinion, that our West-India and African trades are the most nationally beneficial of any we carry on. It is also allowed on all hands, that the trade to Africa is the Branch which renders our American colonies and plantations so advantageous to Great Britain, that traffic only affording our planters a constant supply of negro servants for the culture of their lands in the produce of sugars, tobacco, rice, rum, cotton, pimento, and all other our plantation-produce: so that the extensive employment of our shipping in, to, and from America, the great brood of Seamen consequent thereupon, and the daily bread of the most considerable part of our British manufactures, are owing primarily to the labours of Negroes; who, as they were the first happy instruments of raising our plantations; so their labour only can support and preserve them, and render them still more and more profitable to their mother-kingdom.

The negro-trade, therefore, and the national consequences resulting from it, may be justly esteemed an inexhaustible fund of wealth and naval power to this nation. And by the surplus of negroes above what have served our own plantations, we have drawn likewise no inconsiderable quantities of treasure from the Spaniards, who are settled on the continent of America, . . . for Negroes furnished them from Jamaica. . . .

What renders the negro trade still more estimable and important, is, that near nine-tenths of those negroes are paid for in Africa with British produce and manufactures only; and the remainder with East-India commodities. We send no specie or bullion [coined money] to pay for the products of Africa but, 'tis certain, we bring from thence very large quantities of gold. . . .

And it may be worth consideration that while our plantations depend only on planting by negro servants, they will neither depopulate our own country, become independent of her dominion, or any way interfere with the interests of the British manufacturer, merchant, or landed gentleman: whereas were we under the necessity of supplying our colonies with white-men instead of blacks, they could not fail being in a capacity to interfere with the manufactures of this nation, in time to shake off their dependency thereon, and prove as injurious to the landed, and trading interests as ever they have hitherto been beneficial.

Many are prepossessed against this trade, thinking it a barbarous, inhuman and unlawful traffic for a Christian country to trade in Blacks; to which I would beg leave to observe; that though the odious appellation of slaves is

Malachy Postlethwayt, *The Nature and Private Advantages of the African Trade Considered: Being an Enquiry How Far it Concerns the Trading Interest of Great Britain, Effectually to Support and Maintain the Forts and Settlements in Africa Belonging to the Royal African Company of England* (London: John and Paul Knapton, 1746), pp. 1–6, 40–41.

annexed to this trade, it being called by some the slave-trade, yet it does not appear from the best enquiry I have been able to make, that the state of those people is changed for the worse, by being servants to our British planters in America; they are certainly treated with great lenity and humanity: and as the improvement of the planter's estates depends upon due care being taken of their healths and lives, I cannot but think their condition is much bettered to what it was in their own country.

Besides, the negro princes in Africa, 'tis well known, are in perpetual war with each other, and since before they had this method of disposing of their prisoners of war to Christian merchants, they were wont not only to be applied to inhuman sacrifices, but to extreme torture and barbarity, their transportation must certainly be a melioration [improvement] of their condition; provided living in a civilized Christian country, is better than living among savages: Nay, if life be preferable to torment and cruel death, their state cannot, with any color of reason, be presumed to be worsened. . . .

As the present prosperity and splendor of the British colonies have been owing to negro labor, so not only their future advancement, but even their very being depends [on it]. That our colonies are capable of very great improvements, by the proper application of the labour of blacks, has been urged by the most experienced judges of commerce.

The negro princes and chiefs in Africa are generally at war with each other on the continent; and the prisoners of war, instead of being slain, or applied to inhuman sacrifices, are carefully preserved and sold to those Europeans only, who have established interest and power among the natives, by means of forts and settlements; or to such who are admitted to traffic with the natives, by virtue, and under the sanction and protection of such European settlements; which is the case of all the British merchants who trade to Africa at present, at full liberty, under the authority and protection of our Royal African Company's rights and privileges, interest and power among the natives. . . .

John Wesley
SLAVERY ATTACKED

John Wesley (1703–1791) was, with his brother Charles, the founder of the evangelical Methodist movement in England. Inspired by the Great Awakening in the American colonies, he launched a successful revival of Christianity in England in 1739. The rest of his long life was devoted to leadership of the Methodist movement.

Wesley's eyes were opened to the evils of slavery by reading an indictment of the slave trade by a French Quaker, Anthony Benezet. In 1774 he published the tract *Thoughts Upon Slavery*, from which the extracts below are taken. Wesley drew heavily on Benezet's writings for his facts, but in warning participants in the slave trade of divine retribution, he spoke in the cadences of the inspired evangelical preacher.

Wesley became one of the leaders in the movement against slavery and his pioneering work, in which he was supported by the Methodist movement, helped bring about the abolition of slavery in England in 1807.

I would inquire whether [the abuses of slavery] can be defended on the principles of even heathen honesty, whether they can be reconciled (setting the Bible out of question) with any degree of either justice or mercy.

The grand plea is, "They are authorized by law." But can law, human law, change the nature of things? Can it turn darkness into light or evil into good? By no means. Notwithstanding ten thousand laws, right is right, and wrong is wrong still. There must still remain an essential [difference] between justice and injustice, cruelty and mercy. So that I still ask, who can reconcile this treatment of the Negroes first and last, with either mercy or justice? . . . Yea, where is the justice of taking away the lives of innocent, inoffensive men, murdering thousands of them in their own land, by the hands of their own countrymen, many thousands year after year on shipboard, and then casting them like dung into the sea and tens of thousands in that cruel slavery to which they are so unjustly reduced? . . .

But if this manner of procuring and treating Negroes is not consistent either with mercy or justice, yet there is a plea for it which every man of business will acknowledge to be quite sufficient. . . . "D—n justice, it is necessity. . . . It is necessary that we should procure slaves, and when we have procured them, it is necessary to use them with severity, considering their stupidity, stubbornness and wickedness."

I answer you stumble at the threshold. I deny that villainy is ever necessary. It is impossible that it should ever be necessary for any reasonable creature to violate all the laws of justice, mercy, and truth. No circumstances can make it necessary for a man to burst in sunder all the ties of humanity. It can never be necessary for a rational being to sink himself below a brute. A man can be under no necessity of degrading himself into a wolf. The absurdity of the supposition is so glaring that one would wonder anyone can help seeing it. . . .

"But the furnishing us with slaves is necessary for the trade, and wealth, and glory of our nation." Here are several mistakes. For first wealth is not necessary to the glory of any nation, but wisdom, virtue, justice, mercy, generosity, public spirit, love of our country. These are necessary to the real glory of a nation, but abundance of wealth is not.

. . . But, secondly, it is not clear that we should have either less money or trade (only less of that detestable trade of man-stealing), if there was not a Negro in all our islands or in all English America. It is demonstrable, white men inured to it by degrees can work as well as they, and they would do it, were Negroes out of the way, and proper encouragement given them. However, thirdly, I come back to the same point: Better no trade than trade procured by villainy. It is far better to have no wealth than to gain wealth at the expense of virtue. Better is honest poverty than all the riches bought by the tears, and sweat, and blood of our fellow creatures.

"However this be, it is necessary, when we have slaves, to use them with severity." What, to whip them for every petty offence, till they are all in gore blood? To take that opportunity of rubbing pepper and salt into their raw flesh? To drop burning wax upon their skin? To castrate them? To cut off half their foot with an axe? To hang them on gibbets, that they may die by inches with heat, and hunger, and thirst? To pin them down to the ground, and then burn them by degrees from the feet to the head? To roast them alive? When did a Turk or heathen find it necessary to use a fellow-creature thus?

I pray, to what end is this usage necessary? "Why to prevent their running away, and to keep them constantly to their labour, that they may not idle away their time. So miserably stupid is this race of men, yea, so stupid and so wicked." Allowing them to be as stupid as you say, to whom is that stupidity owing? Without question it lies at the door of their inhuman masters who give them no means, no opportunity of improving their understanding. . . . Consequently it is not their fault but yours: you must answer for it before God and man. . . .

John Wesley, *Thoughts Upon Slavery* (London: R. Hawes, 1774), pp. 29–30, 34–35, 38–44, 47–49, 52–53.

And what pains have you taken, what method have you used, to reclaim them from their wickedness? Have you carefully taught them, "That there is a God, a wise, powerful, merciful being, the creator and governor of heaven and earth? That he has appointed a day wherein he will judge the world, will take account of all our thoughts, words and actions? That in that day he will reward every child of man according to his works: that 'Then the righteous shall inherit the kingdom prepared for them from the foundation of the world: and the wicked shall be cast into everlasting fire, prepared for the devil and his angels.' " If you have not done this, if you have taken no pains or thought about the matter, can you wonder at their wickedness? What wonder if they should cut your throat? And if they did, whom could you thank for it but yourself? You first acted the villain in making them slaves (whether you stole them or bought them). You kept them stupid and wicked by cutting them off from all opportunities of improving either in knowledge or virtue. And now you assign their want of wisdom and goodness as the reason for using them worse than brute beasts. . . .

It remains only to make a little application of the preceding observations . . . I therefore add a few words to those who are more immediately concerned, . . . and first to the captains employed in this trade. . . .

Is there a God? You know there is. Is he a just God? Then there must be a state of retribution; a state wherein the just God will reward every man according to his works. Then what reward will he render to you? O think betimes! Before you drop into eternity! Think now: he shall have judgment without mercy, that showed no mercy.

Are you a man? . . . Have you no sympathy? No sense of human woe? No pity for the miserable? . . . When you squeezed the agonizing creatures down in the ship, or when you threw their poor mangled remains into the sea, had you no relenting? Did not one tear drop from your eye, one sigh escape from your breast? Do you feel no relenting now? If you do not, you must go on till the measure of your iniquities is full. Then will the great God deal with *you*, as you have dealt with *them*, and require all their blood at your hands. . . .

Today resolve, God being your helper, to escape for your life. Regard not money! All that a man hath will he give for his life! Whatever you lose, lose not your soul; nothing can countervail that loss. Immediately quit the horrid trade. At all events, be an honest man.

This equally concerns every merchant who is engaged in the slave-trade. It is you that induce the African villain, to sell his countrymen, and in order thereto, to steal, rob, murder men, women and children without number. By enabling the English villain to pay him for so doing, whom you overpay for his execrable labour. It is your money that is the spring of all, that impowers him to go on. . . . And is your conscience quite reconciled to this? Does it never reproach you at all? Has gold entirely blinded your eyes, and stupefied your heart? . . . Have no more part in this detestable business. Be you a man! Not a wolf, a devourer of the human species. Be merciful that you may obtain mercy.

And this equally concerns every gentleman that has an estate in our African plantations. Yea, all slave-holders of whatever rank and degree, seeing men-buyers are exactly at a level with men-sellers. Indeed you say, "I pay honestly for my goods, and am not concerned to know how they are come by." Nay, but . . . you know they are not honestly come by. . . .

If therefore you have any regard to justice (to say nothing of mercy, nor of the revealed law of God) render unto all their due. Give liberty to whom liberty is due, that is, to every child of man, to every partaker of human nature. Let none serve you but by his own act and deed, by his own voluntary choice. Away with all whips, all chains, all compulsion. Be gentle toward all men. And see that you invariably do unto every one, as you would he should do unto you.

O thou God of love, thou who art loving to every man, and whose mercy is over all thy works: Thou who art the father of the spirits of all flesh, and who art rich in mercy unto all: Thou who hast mingled in one blood all the nations upon earth: have compassion upon these outcasts of men, who are trodden down as dung upon the earth. Arise and help these who have no helper, whose blood is spilt upon the ground like water! Are not these also the work of thine own hands, the purchase of thy Son's blood? Stir them up to cry unto thee in the land of their captivity; and let their complaint come up before thee; let it enter into thine ears! Make even those that lead them away captive to pity them. . . . O burst thou all their chains in sunder; more especially the chains of their sins: Thou, Saviour of all, make them free, that they may be free indeed!

REVIEW QUESTIONS

1. When were the African slaves most likely to try to escape? How did the slave traders try to prevent this?
2. Did either of the two seventeenth-century slave traders express any humane feelings toward the captive Africans?
3. According to John Newton, what kind of treatment was given to Africans on slave ships? What did Newton think of this treatment?
4. What was Malachy Postlethwayt's argument in defense of slavery? How would John Newton respond to it? What is your response?
5. To whom did John Wesley address his arguments against the slave trade?
6. What were the commercial justifications for slavery that Wesley disputed? How did he account for the seeming inferiority of the slaves?

6 The Witch Craze

In both ancient and medieval times, it was widely believed that certain persons, called sorcerers or witches, had supernatural powers over both nature and human beings and that these powers enabled witches to harm people through magical practices. Those suspected of sorcery were greatly feared and were subject to execution. In the Late Middle Ages, Europeans began to view suspected witches as having entered into a pact with the devil. The church began to treat them as devil worshipers, heretics, rebels against the church, and threats to society.

During the sixteenth and seventeenth centuries, both Roman Catholics and Protestants intensified the struggle to destroy alleged witches; thousands were questioned under torture and, if convicted of witchcraft, were put to death, a sentence justified by both the Old Testament and Roman law. Belief in witches was not limited to superstitious peasants and fanatics. Prominent intellectuals, theologians, philosophers, and scientists either supported the prosecution of witches or remained silent. Few doubted the existence of witches, and forced confessions were accepted as proof of sorcery; the idea of witchcraft offered credible explanations for otherwise inexplicable human experiences. Although the number of females accused of witchcraft outnumbered the males, during these times persons of all ages, social classes, education, and occupations could find themselves facing the charge of witchcraft. The regular use of torture during interrogation of suspects probably accounted for most confessions, and the alleged bizarre and sometimes lurid practices of suspects seem to have been the products of mental disorders and popular beliefs in occult powers.

Heinrich Krämer and Jakob Sprenger
THE HAMMER OF WITCHES

Written in 1487 by Heinrich Krämer and Jakob Sprenger, both Dominican inquisitors in Germany, *The Hammer of Witches* became a standard reference work for the beliefs and practices of witches. The work, excerpted below, tells us much about the mindset of early modern Europeans committed to a belief in witches who served the devil.

And this class [of witches] is made up of those who, against every instinct of human or animal nature, are in the habit of eating and devouring the children of their own species. And this is the most powerful class of witches, who practise innumerable other harms also. For they raise hailstorms and hurtful tempests and lightnings; cause sterility in men and animals; offer to devils, or otherwise kill, the children whom they do not devour. But these are only the children who have not been re-born by baptism at the font, for they cannot devour those who have been baptized, nor any without God's permission. They can also, before the eyes of their parents, and when no one is in sight, throw into the water children walking by the water side; they make horses go mad under their riders; they can transport themselves from place to place through the air, either in body or in imagination; they can affect Judges and Magistrates so that they cannot hurt them; they can cause themselves and others to keep silence under torture; they can bring about a great trembling in the hands and horror in the minds

of those who would arrest them. . . . [T]hey can at times strike whom they will with lightning, and even kill some men and animals; they can make of no effect the generative desires, and even the power of copulation, cause abortion, kill infants in the mother's womb by a mere exterior touch; they can at times bewitch men and animals with a mere look, without touching them, and cause death; they dedicate their own children to devils; and in short, as has been said, they can cause all the plagues. . . . [I]t is common to all of them to practise carnal copulation with devils. . . .

[T]here are now [such witches], some in the country of Lombardy [in northern Italy], in the domains of the Duke of Austria, where the Inquisitor of Como, as we told in the former Part, caused forty-one witches to be burned in one year; and he was fifty-five years old, and still continues to labour in the Inquisition.

Now the method of profession is twofold. One is a solemn ceremony, like a solemn vow. The other is private, and can be made to the devil at any hour alone. The first method is when witches meet together in conclave on a set day, and the devil appears to them in the assumed body of a man, and urges them to keep faith with him, promising them worldly prosperity and length of life; and they

Heinrich Krämer and Jakob Sprenger, *The Malleus Maleficarum,* trans. Montague Summers (London: John Rodker, 1928), pp. 99–101. Dover Publications, 1971.

recommend a novice to his acceptance. And the devil asks whether she will abjure the Faith, and forsake the holy Christian religion and the worship of the Anomalous Woman (for so they call the Most Blessed Virgin Mary), and never venerate the Sacraments; and if he finds the novice or disciple willing, then the devil stretches out his hand, and so does the novice, and she swears with upraised hand to keep that covenant. And when this is done, the devil at once adds that this is not enough; and when the disciple asks what more must be done, the devil demands the following oath of homage to himself: that she give herself to him, body and soul, for ever, and do her utmost to bring others of both sexes into his power. He adds, finally, that she is to make certain unguents [ointments] from the bones and limbs of children, especially those who have been baptized; by all which means she will be able to fulfil all her wishes with his help.

We Inquisitors had credible experience of this method in the town of Breisach in the diocese of Basel [in Switzerland], receiving full information from a young girl witch who had been converted, whose aunt also had been burned in the diocese of Strasburg [in Germany]. And she added that she had become a witch by the method in which her aunt had first tried to seduce her. . . .

She said also that the greatest injuries were inflicted by midwives, because they were under an obligation to kill or offer to devils as many children as possible; and that she had been severely beaten by her aunt because she had opened a secret pot and found the heads of a great many children. And much more she told us, having first, as was proper, taken an oath to speak the truth.

And her account of the method of professing the devil's faith undoubtedly agrees with what has been written by that most eminent Doctor, John Nider, who even in our times has written very illuminatingly; and it may be especially remarked that he tells us the following, which

he had from an Inquisitor of the diocese of Edua, who held many inquisitions on witches in that diocese, and caused many to be burned.

For he says that this Inquisitor told him that in the Duchy of Lausanne [in Switzerland] certain witches had cooked and eaten their own children, and that the following was the method in which they became initiated into such practices. The witches met together and, by their art, summoned a devil in the form of a man, to whom the novice was compelled to swear to deny the Christian religion, never to adore the Eucharist, and to tread the Cross underfoot whenever she could do so secretly.

Here is another example from the same source. There was lately a general report, brought to the notice of Peter the Judge in Boltingen, that thirteen infants had been devoured in the State of Berne [in Switzerland]; and public justice exacted full vengeance on the murderers. And when Peter asked one of the captive witches in what manner they ate children, she replied: "This is the manner of it. We set our snares chiefly for unbaptized children, and even for those that have been baptized, especially when they have not been protected by the sign of the Cross and prayers" (reader, notice that, at the devil's command, they take the unbaptized chiefly, in order that they may not be baptized), "and with our spells we kill them in their cradles or even when they are sleeping by their parents' side, in such a way that they afterwards are thought to have been overlain or to have died some other natural death. Then we secretly take them from their graves, and cook them in a cauldron, until the whole flesh comes away from the bones to make a soup which may easily be drunk. Of the more solid matter we make an unguent which is of virtue to help us in our arts and pleasures and our transportations; and with the liquid we fill a flask or skin, whoever drinks from which, with the addition of a few other ceremonies, immediately acquires much knowledge and becomes a leader in our sect."

Johannes Junius
A CONFESSION OF WITCHCRAFT EXPLAINED

In 1628 Johannes Junius, lord mayor of Bamberg, a city in Bavaria, Germany, was accused of practicing witchcraft. When Junius denied the charge, he was tortured. He then confessed to having become a witch and was burned at the stake. The reasons for his confession are revealed in a letter he secretly sent to his daughter.

Many hundred thousand good-nights, dearly beloved daughter Veronica. Innocent have I come into prison, innocent have I been tortured, innocent must I die. For whoever comes into the witch prison must become a witch or be tortured until he invents something out of his head and—God pity him—bethinks him of something. I will tell you how it has gone with me. When I was the first time put to the torture, Dr. Braun, Dr. Kötzendörffer, and two strange doctors were there. Then Dr. Braun asks me, "Kinsman, how come you here?" I answer, "Through falsehood, through misfortune." "Hear, you," he says, "you are a witch; will you confess it voluntarily? If not, we'll bring in witnesses and the executioner for you." I said "I am no witch, I have a pure conscience in the matter; if there are a thousand witnesses, I am not anxious, but I'll gladly hear the witnesses." Now the chancellor's son was set before me . . . and afterward Hoppfen Elss. She had seen me dance on Haupts-moor. . . . I answered: "I have never renounced God, and will never do it—God graciously keep me from it. I'll rather bear whatever I must." And then came also—God in highest Heaven have mercy—the executioner, and put the thumbscrews on me, both hands bound together, so that the blood ran out at the nails and everywhere, so that for four weeks

I could not use my hands, as you can see from the writing. . . . Thereafter they first stripped me, bound my hands behind me, and drew me up in the torture. Then I thought heaven and earth were at an end; eight times did they draw me up and let me fall again, so that I suffered terrible agony. . . .[1]

. . . When at last the executioner led me back into the prison, he said to me: "Sir, I beg you, for God's sake confess something, whether it be true or not. Invent something, for you cannot endure the torture which you will be put to; and, even if you bear it all, yet you will not escape, not even if you were an earl [high nobleman], but one torture will follow after another until you say you are a witch. Not before that," he said, "will they let you go, as you may see by all their trials, for one is just like another." . . .

And so I begged, since I was in wretched plight, to be given one day for thought and a priest. The priest was refused me, but the time for thought was given. Now, my dear child, see in what hazard I stood and still stand. I must say that I am a witch, though I am not,—must now renounce God, though I have never done it

Translations and Reprints from the Original Sources of European History, ed. George L. Burr (Philadelphia: University of Pennsylvania Press, 1907), vol. 3, no. 4, pp. 26–28.

[1]This torture of the strappado, which was that in most common use by the courts, consisted of a rope, attached to the hands of the prisoner (bound behind his back) and carried over a pulley at the ceiling. By this he was drawn up and left hanging. To increase the pain, weights were attached to his feet or he was suddenly jerked up and let drop.

before. Day and night I was deeply troubled, but at last there came to me a new idea. I would not be anxious, but, since I had been given no priest with whom I could take counsel, I would myself think of something and say it. It were surely better that I just say it with mouth and words, even though I had not really done it; and afterwards I would confess it to the priest, and let those answer for it who compel me to do it. . . . And so I made my confession, . . . but it was all a lie.

Now follows, dear child, what I confessed in order to escape that great anguish and bitter torture, which it was impossible for me longer to bear. [He then describes his confession] . . .

Now, dear child, here you have all my confession, for which I must die. And they are sheer lies and made-up things, so help me God. For all this I was forced to say through fear of the torture which was threatened beyond what I had already endured. For they never leave off with the torture till one confesses something be he ever so good, he must be a witch. Nobody escapes, though he were an earl. . . .

Dear child, keep this letter secret so that people do not find it, else I shall be tortured most piteously and the jailers will be beheaded. So strictly is it forbidden. . . . Dear child, pay this man a dollar. . . . I have taken several days to write this: my hands are both lame. I am in a sad plight. . . .

Good night, for your father Johannes Junius will never see you more. July 24, 1628.

[And on the margin of the letter he adds:]

Dear child, six have confessed against me at once: the Chancellor, his son, Neudecker, Zaner, Hoffmaisters Ursel, and Hoppfen Elss—all false, through compulsion, as they have all told me, and begged my forgiveness in God's name before they were executed. . . . They know nothing but good of me. They were forced to say it, just as I myself was. . . .

Nicholas Malebranche
SEARCH AFTER TRUTH

Greatly influenced by Descartes (see page 414), the French thinker Nicholas Malebranche (1638–1715) supplemented his training in philosophy and theology with the study of mathematics and natural science. His most important work, *Search After Truth*, which appeared in two volumes in 1674 and 1675, treated many technical, philosophical, and theological issues. In this work, from which an excerpt follows, he also analyzed the belief in witchcraft, attributing it to the unchecked power of people's imagination. Malebranche attempted a rational explanation of the witch craze and wanted the courts to dismiss charges of witchcraft. Nevertheless, he still believed that although "true witches are very rare," they do exist.

The strangest effect of the power of imagination is the disorderly fear of the apparition of spirits, of enchantments, of symbols, of the charms of Lycanthropes or Werewolves, and generally of everything which is supposed to depend upon the demon's power.

Nothing is more terrible or more frightening to the mind, or produces deeper vestiges on the brain, than the idea of an invisible power which thinks only about harming us and which is irresistible. Speeches which reveal this idea are always heard with fear and curiosity. Holding on to everything extraordinary, men take bizarre pleasure in recounting these surprising and prodigious stories about the power and malice of Witches, in order to frighten both others and themselves. So it is not astonishing if Witches are so common in some countries, where belief in the Sabbat [a secret meeting of witches where they engage in orgiastic rites] is too deeply rooted; where the most absurd stories about spells are listened to as authentic; and where madmen and seers whose imagination has become disordered. . . . from telling these stories . . . are burned as real Witches.

I well know that some people will take exception to my attributing most witchcraft to the power of imagination, because I know that men want to be made afraid, that they become angry with those who want to demystify them. . . .

Superstitions are not easily destroyed, and they cannot be attacked without finding a large number of defenders. It is easy enough to prove that the inclination to believe blindly all the dreams of Demonographers [those who study demons] is produced and maintained by the same cause which makes superstitious men stubborn. Nevertheless, that will not prevent me from describing in a few words how, I believe, such opinions get established.

A shepherd in his fold after dinner tells his wife and children about the adventures of the Sabbat. As his imagination is moderately inspired by vapours from wine, and since he believes that he has attended that imaginary assembly several times, he does not fail to speak about it in a strong and lively manner. His natural eloquence, together with the disposition of his entire family to hear such a new and terrible subject discussed, should doubtlessly produce strange traces in weak imaginations. It is naturally impossible that a woman and her children not remain completely

frightened, full, and convinced of what they have heard said. This is a husband, a father, who is speaking about what he has seen and done; he is loved and respected; why should he not be believed? This Shepherd repeats it on different days. Little by little the mother's and children's imagination receives deeper traces from it. They grow used to it, the fears pass, and the conviction remains. . . .

Several times Witches of good faith have been found, who generally tell everybody that they have gone to the Sabbat, and who are so convinced of it, that although several persons watched them and assured them that they had not left their beds, they could not agree with their testimony. . . . So we should not be astonished if a man who thinks he has been to the Sabbat, and consequently talks about it in a firm voice and with an assured countenance, easily persuades some people who listen to him respectfully about all the circumstances which he describes, and thus transmits in their imagination traces similar to those which deceive him.

When men talk to us, they engrave in our brain traces similar to those which they possess. When they have deep traces, they talk to us in a manner which engraves deep ones in us; for they cannot speak without making us in some way similar to them. Children at their mother's breast only see what their mother sees. Even when they have become worldly-wise, they imagine few things of which their parents are not the cause, since even the wisest men conduct themselves more by the imagination of others, *i.e.*, by opinion and custom, [than] by the rules of reason. Thus in places where Witches are burned, a great number of them are found. Because in places where they are condemned to fire, men truly believe that they commit witchcraft, and this belief is fortified by the speeches which are made about it. If one were to stop punishing them and were to treat them like madmen, then it would be seen in time that there would no longer be any Witches, because those who do it only in imagination (who are surely the greater number) would then abandon their errors.

In Nicolas Malebranche, *Recherche de la Vérité, Oeuvres Complites*, published under the direction of Audré Robinet, Volume I, pages 370 to 376, VRIN, Paris, 1962.

It is indubitable that real Witches deserve death. . . . But by punishing all [those who believe themselves or are believed by others to be witches] common opinion is strengthened, imaginary Witches are multiplied, and so an infinity of people are lost and damned. It is thus right that many Parlements [French courts] no longer punish Witches. There are many fewer of them in the lands of their jurisdictions; and the envy, hatred, or malice of evil men cannot use this pretext to destroy the innocent. . . .

It is ordinary enough for some people to have fairly lively dreams at night and to be able to remember them exactly when awake, although the subject of their dream is not in itself very terrible. Thus it is not difficult for people to persuade themselves that they have been at the Sabbat, for that merely requires that their brain preserves the traces made there during sleep.

The chief reason which prevents us from taking our dreams for realities is that we cannot link our dreams with the things we have done during our wakefulness. By that we recognize that they were only dreams. But Witches cannot recognize in this way that their imaginary Sabbat is a dream. . . .

I am persuaded that true Witches are very rare, that the Sabbat is only a dream, and that the Parlements who dismiss accusations of witchcraft are the most equitable. However, I do not doubt that Witches, charms, enchantments, etc., could exist, and that the demon sometimes exercises his malice upon men by special permission of a superior power.

REVIEW QUESTIONS

1. According to *The Hammer of Witches*, what anti-Christian practices did witches engage in?
2. According to Johannes Junius, how were apparently innocent people successfully prosecuted for practicing witchcraft? What did the victims of the witch craze and the Inquisition have in common?
3. To what did Malebranche attribute a belief in witchcraft?

7 The Court of Louis XIV

During his seventy-two-year reign (1643–1715), Louis XIV, the "Sun King," gave France greater unity and central authority than it had ever known. To prevent the great nobles from challenging royal authority, Louis XIV chose many of his ministers and provincial administrators from the middle class. The great nobles, "princes of the blood," enjoyed considerable social prestige but exercised no real power in the government. The king encouraged these "people of quality" to live at court where they contended with each other for his favor.

As the symbol of France and the greatest ruler of Europe, Louis insisted that the social life at Versailles provide an appropriate setting for his exalted person. During his long reign, France set the style for the whole of Europe. The splendor of Versailles was the talk of Europe, and other monarchs sought to imitate the fashions and manners of the Sun King's court.

Duc de Saint-Simon
AN ASSESSMENT OF LOUIS XIV

Louis de Rouvroi, duc de Saint-Simon (1675–1755), was an astute observer of Louis XIV and his court. The following description of Louis XIV comes from Saint-Simon's extensive *Memoirs.*

Louis XIV was made for a brilliant Court. In the midst of other men, his figure, his courage, his grace, his beauty, his grand mien, even the tone of his voice and the majestic and natural charm of all his person, distinguished him till his death. . . . The superior ability of his early ministers and his early generals soon wearied him. He liked nobody to be in any way superior to him. Thus he chose his ministers, not for their knowledge, but for their ignorance; not for their capacity, but for their want of it. He liked to form them, as he said; liked to teach them even the most trifling things. It was the same with his generals. He took credit to himself for instructing them; wished it to be thought that from his cabinet he commanded and directed all his armies. Naturally fond of trifles, he unceasingly occupied himself with the most petty details of his troops, his household, his mansions. This vanity, this unmeasured and unreasonable love of admiration, was his ruin. His ministers, his generals, his mistresses, his courtiers, soon perceived his weakness. They praised him with emulation and spoiled him. Those whom he liked owed his affection for them to their untiring flatteries. This is what gave his ministers so much authority, and the opportunities they had for adulating him, of attributing everything to him, and of pretending to learn everything from him. Suppleness, meanness, an admiring, dependent, cringing manner—above all, an air of nothingness—were the sole means of pleasing him.

Though his intellect, as I have said, was beneath mediocrity, it was capable of being formed. He loved glory, was fond of order and regularity; was by disposition prudent, moderate, discreet, master of his movements and his tongue. Will it be believed? He was also by disposition good and just! God had sufficiently gifted him to enable him to be a good King; perhaps even *a tolerably great King*! All the evil came to him from elsewhere. His early education was . . . neglected. He was scarcely taught how to read or write, and remained so ignorant, that the most familiar historical and other facts were utterly unknown to him! He fell, accordingly, and sometimes even in public, into the grossest absurdities.

He was exceedingly jealous of the attention paid him. Not only did he notice the presence of the most distinguished courtiers, but those of inferior degree also. He looked to the right and to the left, not only upon rising but upon going to bed, at his meals, in passing through his apartments, or his gardens of Versailles, where alone the courtiers were allowed to follow him; he saw and noticed everybody; not one escaped him, not even those who hoped to remain unnoticed. He marked well all absentees from the court, found out the reason of their absence, and never lost an opportunity of acting towards them as the occasion might seem to justify. With some of the courtiers (the most distinguished), it was a demerit not to make the court their ordinary abode; with others 'twas a fault to come but rarely; for those who never or scarcely ever came it was certain disgrace. When their names were in any way mentioned, "I do not know them," the King would reply haughtily. Those who presented themselves but

Memoirs of the Duc de Saint-Simon, ed. W. H. Lewis, trans. Bayle St. John (London: Batsford, 1964), pp. 129, 130, 131, 132, 133, 140, 144, 145. Copyright © 1964 Batsford, Ltd. Used by permission of Anova Books.

seldom were thus characterised: "They are people I never see"; these decrees were irrevocable. He could not bear people who liked Paris [better than Versailles].

Louis XIV took great pains to be well informed of all that passed everywhere; in the public places, in the private houses, in society and familiar intercourse. His spies and tell-tales were infinite. He had them of all species; many who were ignorant that their information reached him; others who knew it; others who wrote to him direct, sending their letters through channels he indicated; and all these letters were seen by him alone, and always before everything else; others who sometimes spoke to him secretly in his cabinet, entering by the back stairs. These unknown means ruined an infinite number of people of all classes, who never could discover the cause; often ruined them very unjustly; for the King, once prejudiced, never altered his opinion, or so rarely, that nothing was more rare. He had, too, another fault, very dangerous for others and often for himself, since it deprived him of good subjects. He had an excellent memory; in this way, that if he saw a man who, twenty years before, perhaps, had in some manner offended him, he did not forget the man, though he might forget the offence. This was enough, however, to exclude the person from all favour. The representations of a minister, of a general, of his confessor even, could not move the King. He would not yield.

The most cruel means by which the King was informed of what was passing—for many years before anybody knew it—was that of opening letters. The prompitude and dexterity with which they were opened passes understanding. He saw extracts from all the letters in which there were passages that the chiefs of the post-office, and then the minister who governed it, thought ought to go before him; entire letters, too, were sent to him, when their contents seemed to justify the sending. Thus the chiefs of the post, nay, the principal clerks were in a position to suppose what they pleased and against whom they pleased. A word of contempt against the King or the government, a joke, a detached phrase, was enough. It is incredible how many people, justly or unjustly, were more or less ruined, always without resource, without trial, and without knowing why. . . .

Never was man so naturally polite, or of a politeness so measured, so graduated, so adapted to person, time, and place. Towards women his politeness was without parallel. Never did he pass the humblest petticoat without raising his hat; even to chambermaids, that he knew to be such, as often happened at Marly. For ladies he took his hat off completely. . . . He took it off for the princes of the blood, as for the ladies. If he accosted ladies he did not cover himself until he had quitted them. All this was out of doors, for in the house he was never covered. . . .

The King loved air and exercise very much, as long as he could make use of them. He had excelled in dancing, and at tennis and mall [a lawn game]. On horseback he was admirable, even at a late age. He liked to see everything done with grace and address. To acquit yourself well or ill before him was a merit or a fault. . . . He was very fond of shooting, and there was not a better or more graceful shot than he. He had always in his cabinet seven or eight pointer bitches, and was fond of feeding them, to make himself known to them. He was very fond, too, of stag hunting. . . .

He liked splendour, magnificence, and profusion in everything: you pleased him if you shone through the brilliancy of your houses, your clothes, your table, your equipages.

As for the King himself, nobody ever approached his magnificence. His buildings, who could number them? At the same time, who was there who did not deplore the pride, the caprice, the bad taste seen in them? St. Germains, a lovely spot, with a marvellous view, rich forest, terraces, gardens, and water he abandoned for Versailles; the dullest and most ungrateful of all places, without prospect, without wood, without water, without soil; for the ground is all shifting sand or swamp, the air accordingly bad. . . .

Let me now speak of the amours of the King which were even more fatal to the state than his building mania.

Louis XIV in his youth more made for love than any of his subjects—being tired of gathering passing sweets, fixed himself at last upon La Vallière.[1] The progress and the result of his love are well known. . . .

When the King travelled his coach was always full of women; his mistresses, afterwards his bastards, his daughters-in-law, sometimes *Madame*, and other ladies when there was room. In the coach, during his journeys, there were always all sorts of things to eat, as meat, pastry, fruit. A quarter of a league was not passed over before the King asked if somebody would not eat. He never ate anything between meals himself, not even fruit; but he amused himself by seeing others do so, aye, and to bursting. You were obliged to be hungry, merry, and to eat with appetite, otherwise he was displeased and even showed it. And yet after this, if you supped with him at table the same day, you were compelled to eat with as good a countenance as though you had tasted nothing since the previous night. He was as inconsiderate in other and more delicate matters; and ladies, in his long drives and stations, had often occasion to curse him. The Duchesse de Chevreuse once rode all the way from Versailles to Fontainbleau in such extremity, that several times she was well-nigh losing consciousness. . . .

At ten o'clock his supper was served. The captain of the guard announced this to him. A quarter of an hour after the King came to supper, and from the ante-chamber of Madame de Maintenon[2] to the table again, any one spoke to him who wished. This supper was always on a grand scale, the royal household (that is, the sons and daughters of France), at table, and a large number of courtiers and ladies present, sitting or standing. . . .

During all his life, the King failed only once in his attendance at mass. It was with the army, during a forced march; he missed no fast day, unless really indisposed. Some days before Lent, he publicly declared that he should be very much displeased if any one ate meat or gave it to others, under any pretext.

---

[1]Françoise-Louise de La Vallière was Louis XIV's mistress from 1661 to 1667; she held great influence over him and was the mother of four of his children. After being discarded as his mistress, she retired to a convent in 1674.—Eds.

[2]Françoise d'Aubigné (Madame de Maintenon) was the widow of a celebrated poet when she became governess to two of the king's children in 1669. He provided her with an estate and later married her secretly.—Eds.

Liselotte von der Pfalz (Elizabeth Charlotte d'Orleans) A SKETCH OF COURT LIFE

Deprived of power and usefulness, many great nobles lived a frivolous, if not debauched, existence at Versailles. The letters of Elizabeth Charlotte, duchesse d'Orleans (1652–1722)—her German name was Liselotte von der Pfalz—describe this lifestyle. A native of Germany, the duchesse was married to Louis XIV's only brother and spent fifty years at the king's court. During this period she wrote extensive letters, some of which are reproduced below, to her German relatives.

Versailles, 13 February 1695

Where in the world does one find a husband who loves only his spouse and does not have someone, be it mistresses or boys, on the side? If for this reason wives were to go in for the same behavior one could never be sure, as Godfather so rightly says, that the children of the house are the rightful heirs. Does the young duchess[1] not know that a woman's honor consists of having commerce with no one but her husband, and that for a man it is not shameful to have mistresses but shameful indeed to be a cuckold? . . . .

Your Grace would not believe how coarse and unmannerly French men have become in the last twelve or thirteen years. One would be hard put to find two young men of quality who know how to behave properly either in what they say or in what they do. There are two very different causes for this: namely, all the piety at court and the debauchery among men. Because of the first, men and women are not allowed to speak to each other in public, which used to be a way to give young gentlemen polish. And secondly, because they love the boys, they no longer want to please anyone but one another, and the most popular among them is the one who knows best how to be debauched, coarse, and insolent. This habit has become so ingrained that no one knows how to live properly any longer, and they are worse than peasants behind the plough. . . .

It is a great honor to sit next to the King during the sermon, but I would be happy to cede this honor to someone else, for His Majesty will not permit me to sleep. As soon as I go to sleep, the King nudges me with his elbow and wakes me up; thus I can never really go to sleep nor really stay awake. And that gives one a headache.

―――――

Paris, 14 May 1695

At every gathering here in France people do nothing but play *lansquenet.* This game is all the rage now. . . . The stakes are horrendously high here, and the people act like madmen when they are playing. One bawls, another hits the table with his fist so hard that the whole room shakes, and a third one blasphemes to make one's hair stand on end; in short, they show such despair that one is frightened even to look at them.

―――――

Saint Cloud, 15 September 1695

The story of Saint Cyr is worse than it is written in the book,[2] and funnier, too. The young maids there fell in love with each other and were caught in committing indecencies together. They say that Madame de Maintenon wept bitter tears about this and had all the relics exposed in order to drive out the demon of lewdness. Also, a preacher was dispatched to preach against lewdness. But he himself said such filthy things that the good and modest girls could not stand it and walked out of the church, while the others, the guilty ones, were so taken by the giggles that they could not hold them in.

―――――

Versailles, 7 March 1696

I will tell . . . how everything is here, and I will begin with Monsieur. All he has in his head are his young fellows, with whom he wants to gorge and guzzle all night long, and he gives them huge sums of money; nothing is too much or too costly for these boys. Meanwhile, his children and I barely have what we need. Whenever I need shirts or sheets it means no end of begging, yet at the same time he gives 10,000 *talers* to La Carte[3] so that he can buy his linens in

―――――

Liselotte von der Pfalz, *A Woman's Life in the Court of the Sun King: Letters of Liselotte von der Pfalz, Elisabeth Charlotte, Duchesse d'Orleans, 1652–1722,* trans. Elborg Forster, pp. 87–88, 90–92, 106–107, 111–112. Copyright © 1984 by The Johns Hopkins University Press. Reprinted with permission of The Johns Hopkins University Press.

[1]Electress Sophie's daughter-in-law, who was caught in a scandalous adultery with Count Christoph von Koenigsmarck.
[2]A book that had been sent to Madame by her aunt: among other things, it contained negative accounts of the convent school of Saint-Cyr, which had been founded by Madame de Maintenon.
[3]One of Monsieur's favorites, a particularly greedy character.

Flanders. And since he knows that I am bound to find out where all the money goes, he is wary of me, afraid that I might speak about it to the King, who might chase the boys away. Whatever I may do or say to show that I do not object to his life, he still does not trust me and makes trouble for me with the King every day; even says that I hate the King. If there is any bad gossip, Monsieur tells the King that I have started it and even adds a few stout lies of his own, and sometimes he himself tells me about the terrible things he has said about me. Thereby he so turns the King against me that I can never be in his good graces. Monsieur also continually stirs up my children against me; since he does not want my son to realize how little is being done for his future, he always indulges him in his debaucheries and encourages them. Then if I suggest to my son that he should try to please the King more and abstain from vice, Monsieur and my son laugh in my face, and in Paris both of them lead an absolutely shameful life. My son's inclinations are good, and he could make something of himself if he were not corrupted by Monsieur. My daughter, thank God, he does not drag into debauchery, and to tell the truth, the girl does not have the slightest propensity for *galanterie* [flirtations and love affairs]. But Monsieur does not let me have control over her, always takes her places where I am not, and surrounds her with such rabble that it is a miracle that she has not been corrupted. Moreover, he is inculcating her with such hatred of the Germans that she can barely stand to be with me because I am German, and that makes me feel that she will end up like my son. . . . It is true that in public Monsieur is polite to me, but in fact he cannot stand me. As soon as he sees that any of my servants, be they male or female, become attached to me, he conceives an utter dislike for them and does them harm whenever he can; those who despise me, on the other hand, have all his favor. Monsieur is doing everything he can to make me hated, not only by the King, but also by Monsieur Le Dauphin, and everyone else too. . . . Indeed, the King is so well aware that Monsieur likes me to be treated with contempt

that whenever there is trouble between them, the reconciliation always amounts to extra favors for Monsieur's beloved boys and bad treatment for me. All the silverware that came from the Palatinate Monsieur has melted down and sold, and all the proceeds were given to the boys; every day new ones show up, and all of his jewelry is being sold, pawned, pledged, and given to the young men so that if—God forbid—Monsieur should die today, tomorrow I would be thrown upon the King's mercy and not know where to find my daily bread. Monsieur says quite loudly and does not conceal from his daughter and from me that since he is getting old now, he feels that there is no time to lose and that he means to spare no expense to have a merry time until his end: he also says that those who will live longer than he will just have to see how they can get along and that he loves himself more than he loves me and his children. And indeed he practices what he preaches. If I were to tell Your Grace all the details, I would have to write a whole book. Everything here [at court] is pure self-interest and deviousness, and that makes life most unpleasant. If one does not want to get involved in intrigues and *galanteries*, one must live by oneself, which is also quite boring. In order to clear my head of these dismal reflections, I go hunting as often as possible, but this will come to an end as soon as my poor horses can no longer walk, for Monsieur has never bought me any new ones and is not likely to do so now. In the past the King used to give them to me, but now times are bad. . . . The young people are so brutal that he has to be afraid of them and does not feel like having anything to do with them: the old ones are full of politics and only seek one's company after they see that one has the King's good graces.

———

Versailles, 2 February 1698

I firmly believe that the wild life that my son leads, carousing all night long and not going to bed until eight in the morning, will do him in before long. He often looks as if he had been pulled out of the grave: this is sure to kill him, but his father never wants to reprimand him. But since nothing I could say would do any good I will be quiet, although I do want to add that it is truly a shame that my son is being dragged into this profligate life, for if he had been accustomed to better and more honorable ways, he would have become a better person. He is not lacking in wit, nor is he ignorant, and from his youth he had every inclination for that which is good, commendable and befitting his rank; but ever since he has become his own master, a lot of contemptible wretches have attached themselves to him, making him keep company with, begging your leave, the vilest kinds of common whores, and he has changed so much that one does not recognize either his face or his temperament, and since he leads this life he no longer takes pleasure in anything; his pleasure in music, which used to be a passion, is gone too. In short, he has become quite insufferable, and I fear that in the end he will lose his very life over it.

———

Versailles, 16 March 1698

Monsieur is keener than ever on the boys and now takes lackeys out of the antechambers; every last penny he has is squandered in this way, and some day his children will be complete beggars, but he does not care about anything but providing for these pleasures of his. He opposes me in everything and avoids me at all times; he lets himself be ruled completely by these rakes and everything in his and my house is being sold for the benefit of these fellows. It is shameful what goes on here. My son has been completely captivated by Monsieur's favorites; since he loves women, they act as his pimps, sponge off him, gorge and guzzle with him, and drag him so deeply into debauchery that he cannot seem to get out of it; and since he knows that I do not approve of his ways, he avoids me and does not like me at all. Monsieur is glad that my son likes his favorites and not me and therefore puts up with everything from him. My son's wife does not love her husband; just as long as he is away from her, she is content, and

in this respect they are well matched; all she cares about is her brothers' and sisters' grandeur. That is how things are here; so Your Grace can imagine what a pleasant life it is for me.

———

Versailles, 8 March 1699

Yesterday at table we talked about the Duchesse de Lesdiguières, who certainly has a strange temperament. All day long she does nothing but drink coffee or tea; she never reads or writes, nor does she do needlework or play cards. When she takes coffee, her chambermaids and herself must be dressed in the Turkish manner; when she takes tea, the servants who bring it must be dressed in the Indian manner. The chambermaids often weep bitter tears that they must change their clothes two or three times a day. If anyone comes to call on the lady, her antechamber is full of pages, lackeys, and noblemen; then one comes to a locked door, and when one knocks, a great big Moor wearing a silver turban and a big sabre comes to open up and lets the lady or gentleman, whoever it may be, enter, but all alone. He leads the caller to a second door, which is also locked, and it is opened by another Moor who bolts it after the people have gone through, just as the first one had done. The same thing happens in the third room. In the fourth one there are two valets who lead the caller to the fifth room, where one finds the Duchess all by herself. All the portraits in her room are of her coach horses, which she had painted. These she has led one by one into the courtyard every morning and watches them from the window wearing spectacles, for she does not see well. In her room she also has a painting of the conclave, done in an unusual manner: the Pope and all the cardinals are depicted as Moors, and she also has a piece of yellow silk embroidered with a whole lot of Moors. In her garden, which is very beautiful, there is a marble column with an epitaph to one of her deceased cats which she had loved very much. If her son wants to see her, he must ask for an audience, and so must his wife: after they have inquired six or seven times whether they might be permitted to see her, she receives them, but with the same ceremonies as if they were strangers.

REVIEW QUESTIONS

1. According to Saint-Simon, what were Louis XIV's likes and dislikes?
2. What were the duchesse d'Orleans' major complaints about her life at court?

---

8 Justification of Absolute Monarchy by Divine Right

Effectively blocking royal absolutism in the Middle Ages were the dispersion of power between kings and feudal lords, the vigorous sense of personal freedom and urban autonomy of the townspeople, and the limitations on royal power imposed by the church. However, by the late sixteenth century, monarchs were asserting their authority over competing groups with ever-greater effectiveness. In the seventeenth century, European kings implemented their claim to absolute power as monarchs chosen by and responsible to God alone. This theory, called the divine right of kings, became the dominant political ideology of seventeenth-century Europe.

Bishop Jacques-Benigne Bossuet *POLITICS DRAWN FROM THE VERY WORDS OF HOLY SCRIPTURE*

Louis XIV was the symbol of *absolutism*, a term applied to those early modern states where monarchs exercised power free of constitutional restraints. Theorists of absolutism like Bishop Jacques-Benigne Bossuet (1627–1704) argued that monarchs received their authority directly from God. Following are excerpts from Bossuet's *Politics Drawn from the Very Words of Holy scripture*, published posthumously in 1709.

THIRD BOOK, IN WHICH ONE BEGINS TO EXPLAIN THE NATURE AND THE PROPERTIES OF ROYAL AUTHORITY

Article II, Royal Authority is Sacred

1st Proposition, God establishes kings as his ministers, and reigns through them over the peoples   We have already seen that all power comes from God.

Bishop Jaques-Benigne Bossuet, *Politics Drawn from the Very Words of Holy scripture,* trans. and ed. Patrick Riley, pp. 57–61, 81–83. Copyright © 1990. Reprinted by permission of Cambridge University Press.

"The prince, St. Paul adds, is God's minister to thee for good. But if thou do that which is evil, fear: for he beareth not the sword in vain. For he is God's minister: an avenger to execute wrath upon him that doth evil."

Thus princes act as ministers of God, and his lieutenants on earth. It is through them that he exercises his Empire. . . .

It is in this way that we have seen that the royal throne is not the throne of a man, but the throne of God himself. "God hath chosen Solomon my son, to sit upon the throne of the kingdom of the Lord over Israel." And again: "Solomon sat on the throne of the Lord."

And in order that no one believe that it was peculiar to the Israelites to have kings established by God, here is what Ecclesiasticus says: "Over every nation he set a ruler." . . .

Thus he governs all peoples, and gives them, all of them, their kings; though he governs Israel in a more particular and announced fashion.

2nd Proposition, The person of kings is sacred It appears from all this that the person of kings is sacred, and that to attempt anything against them is a sacrilege. . . . [T]hey are sacred through their charge, as being the representatives of divine majesty, deputized by his providence for the execution of his plans. It is thus that God calls Cyrus his anointed. . . .

One must protect kings as sacred things; and whoever neglects to guard them is worthy of death. . . .

3rd Proposition, One must obey the prince by reason of religion and conscience . . . Even if rulers do not acquit themselves of this duty [punishment of evildoers and praise of the good], one must respect in them their charge and their ministry. "Servants, be subject to your masters with all fear, not only to the good and gentle, but also to the angry and unjust."

There is thus something religious in the respect one gives to the prince. The service of God and respect for kings are inseparable things, and St. Peter places these two duties together: "Fear God, Honor the King."

God, moreover, has put something divine into kings. "I have said: You are Gods, and all of you the sons of the most High." It is God himself whom David makes speak in this way. . . .

4th Proposition, Kings should respect their own power, and use it only for the public good Their power coming from on high, as has been said, they must not believe that they are the owners of it, to use it as they please; rather must they use it with fear and restraint, as something which comes to them from God, and for which God will ask an accounting of them.

FOURTH BOOK, ON THE CHARACTERISTICS OF ROYALTY (CONTINUATION)

First Article, Royal Authority is Absolute

1st Proposition, The prince need account to no one for what he ordains . . . Without this absolute authority, he can neither do good nor suppress evil: his power must be such that no one can hope to escape him; and, in fine, the sole defense of individuals against the public power, must be their innocence. . . .

2nd Proposition, When the prince has decided, there can be no other decision The judgments of sovereigns are attributed to God himself. . . .

[N]o one has the right to judge or to review after him.

One must, then, obey princes as if they were justice itself, without which there is neither order nor justice in affairs.

They are gods, and share in some way in divine independence. "I have said: You are gods, and all of you the sons of the most High."

Only God can judge their judgments and their persons. . . .

It follows from this that he who does not want to obey the prince, is . . . condemned irremissibly to death as an enemy of public peace and of human society. . . .

The prince can correct himself when he knows that he has done badly; but against his authority there can be no remedy except his authority.

3rd Proposition, There is no co-active force against the prince One calls co-active [coercive] force a power to constrain and to execute what is legitimately ordained. To the prince alone belongs legitimate command; to him alone belongs co-active force as well.

It is for that reason also that St. Paul gives the sword to him alone. "If thou do that which is evil, fear; for he beareth not the sword in vain."

In the state only the prince should be armed: otherwise everything is in confusion, and the state falls back into anarchy.

He who creates a sovereign prince puts everything together into his hands, both the sovereign authority to judge and all the power of the state.

REVIEW QUESTION

According to Bossuet, why do kings merit absolute obedience, and what duty do they owe to God?

9 A Secular Defense of Absolutism

Thomas Hobbes (1588–1679), a British philosopher and political theorist, witnessed the agonies of the English civil war, including the execution of Charles I in 1649. These developments fortified Hobbes's conviction that absolutism was the most desirable and logical form of government. Only the unlimited power of a sovereign, said Hobbes, could contain human passions that disrupt the social order and threaten civilized life; only absolute rule could provide an environment secure enough for people to pursue their individual interests.

Leviathan (1651), Hobbes's principal work of political thought, broke with medieval political theory. Medieval thinkers assigned each group of people—clergy, lords, serfs, guildsmen—a place in a fixed social order; an individual's social duties were set by ancient traditions believed to have been ordained by God. During early modern times, the great expansion of commerce and capitalism spurred the new individualism already pronounced in Renaissance culture; group ties were shattered by competition and accelerating social mobility. Hobbes gave expression to a society where people confronted each other as competing individuals.

Thomas Hobbes
LEVIATHAN

Hobbes was influenced by the new scientific thought that saw mathematical knowledge as the avenue to truth. Using geometry as a model, Hobbes began with what he believed were self-evident axioms regarding human nature, from which he deduced other truths. He aimed at constructing political philosophy on a scientific foundation and rejected the authority of tradition and religion as inconsistent with a science of politics. Thus, although Hobbes supported absolutism, he dismissed the idea advanced by other theorists of absolutism that the monarch's power derived from God. He also rejected the idea that the state should not be obeyed when it violated God's law. *Leviathan* is a rational and secular political statement. In this modern approach, rather than in Hobbes' justification of absolutism, lies the work's significance.

Hobbes had a pessimistic view of human nature. Believing that people are innately selfish and grasping, he maintained that competition and dissension, rather than cooperation, characterize human relations. Even when reason teaches that cooperation is more advantageous than competition, Hobbes observed that people are reluctant to alter their ways, because passion, not reason, governs their behavior. In the following passages from *Leviathan*, Hobbes describes the causes of human conflicts.

Nature hath made men so equall, in the faculties of body, and mind; as that though there bee found one man sometimes manifestly stronger in body, or of quicker mind than another; yet when all is reckoned together, the difference between man, and man, is not so considerable, as that one man can thereupon claim to himselfe any benefit, to which another may not pretend, as well as he. For as to the strength of body, the weakest has strength enough to kill the strongest, either by secret machination, or by confederacy with others, that are in the same danger with himselfe. . . .

And as to the faculties of the mind . . . men are . . . [more] equall than unequall. . . .

From this equality of ability, ariseth equality of hope in the attaining of our Ends. And therefore if any two men desire the same thing, which neverthelesse they cannot both enjoy, they become enemies; and in the way to their End, . . . endeavour to destroy, or subdue one another. . . . If one plant, sow, build, or possesse a convenient Seat, others may probably be expected to come prepared with forces united, to dispossesse, and deprive him, not only of the fruit of his labour, but also of his life, or liberty. . . .

So that in the nature of man, we find three principall causes of quarrell. First, Competition; Secondly, Diffidence; Thirdly, Glory.

The first, maketh men invade for Gain; the second, for Safety; and the third, for Reputation. The first use Violence, to make themselves Masters of other men's persons, wives, children, and cattell; the second, to defend them; the

third, for trifles, as a word, a smile, a different opinion, and any other signe of undervalue, either direct in their Persons, or by reflexion in their Kindred, their Friends, their Nation, their Profession, or their Name.

Hereby it is manifest, that during the time men live without a common Power to keep them all in awe, they are in that condition which is called Warre; and such a warre, as is of every man, against every man. . . .

Hobbes then describes a state of nature—the hypothetical condition of humanity prior to the formation of the state—as a war of all against all. For Hobbes, the state of nature is a logical abstraction, a device employed to make his point. Only a strong ruling entity—the state—will end the perpetual strife and provide security. For Hobbes, the state is merely a useful arrangement that permits individuals to exchange goods and services in a secure environment. The ruling authority in the state, the sovereign, must have supreme power, or society will collapse and the anarchy of the state of nature will return.

Whatsoever therefore is consequent to a time of Warre, where every man is Enemy to every man; the same is consequent to the time, wherein men live without other security, than what their own strength, and their own invention shall furnish them withall. In such condition, there is no place for Industry; because the fruit thereof is uncertain: and consequently no Culture of the Earth; no Navigation, nor use of the commodities that may be imported by Sea; no commodious Building; no Instruments of moving, and removing such things as require much force; no Knowledge of the face of the Earth; no account

The English Works of Thomas Hobbes of Malmesbury, vol. 3, *Leviathan,* ed. William Molesworth (London: J. Bohn, 1839), pp. 110–113, 116–117, 154, 157–158, 160–161.

of Time; no Arts; no Letters; no Society; and which is worst of all, continuall feare, and danger of violent death; And the life of man, solitary, poore, nasty, brutish, and short. . . .

The Passions that encline men to Peace, are Feare of Death; Desire of such things as are necessary to commodious living; and a Hope by their Industry to obtain them. And Reason suggesteth convenient Articles of Peace, upon which men may be drawn to agreement. . . .

And because the condition of Man, (as hath been declared in the precedent Chapter) is a condition of Warre of every one against every one; in which case every one is governed by his own Reason; and there is nothing he can make use of, that may not be a help unto him, in preserving his life against his enemyes; It followeth, that in such a condition, every man has a Right to every thing; even to one another's body. And therefore, as long as this naturall Right of every man to every thing endureth, there can be no security to any man, (how strong or wise soever he be,) of living out the time, which Nature ordinarily alloweth men to live. . . .

. . . If there be no Power erected, or not great enough for our security; every man will and may lawfully rely on his own strength and art, for caution against all other men. . . .

The only way to erect . . . a Common Power, as may be able to defend them from the invasion of [foreigners] and the injuries of one another, and thereby to secure them in such sort, as that by their owne industrie, and by the fruites of the Earth, they may nourish themselves and live contentedly; is, to conferre all their power and strength upon one Man, or upon one Assembly of men, that may reduce all their Wills, by plurality of voices, unto one Will . . . and therein to submit their Wills, every one to his Will, and their Judgements, to his Judgment. This is more than Consent, or Concord; it is a reall Unitie of them all, in one and the same Person, made by Covenant of every man with every man, in such manner, as if every man should say to every man, *I Authorise and give up my Right of Governing my selfe, to this Man, or to this Assembly of men, on this condition, that thou give up thy*

Right to him, and Authorise all his Actions in like manner. This done, the Multitude so united in one Person, is called a COMMON-WEALTH. . . . For by this Authorite, given him by every particular man in the Common-wealth, he hath the use of so much Power and Strength . . . conferred on him, that by terror thereof, he is inabled to forme the wills of them all, to Peace at home, and mutuall [aid] against their enemies abroad. And in him consisteth the Essence of the Common-wealth; which (to define it,) is *One Person, of whose Acts a great Multitude, by mutuall Covenants one with another, have made themselves every one the Author, to the end he may use the strength and means of them all, as he shall think expedient, for their Peace and Common Defence.*

And he that carryeth this Person, is called SOVERAIGNE, and said to have *Soveraigne Power*; and every one besides, his SUBJECT. . . .

. . . They that have already Instituted a Common-wealth, being thereby bound by Covenant . . . cannot lawfully make a new Covenant, amongst themselves, to be obedient to any other, in any thing whatsoever, without his permission. And therefore, they that are subjects to a Monarch, cannot without his leave cast off Monarchy, and return to the confusion of a disunited Multitude; nor transferre their Person from him that beareth it, to another Man, or other Assembly of men: for they . . . are bound, every man to every man, to [acknowledge] . . . that he that already is their Soveraigne, shall do, and judge fit to be done; so that [those who do not obey] break their Covenant made to that man, which is injustice: and they have also every man given the Soveraignty to him that beareth their Person; and therefore if they depose him, they take from him that which is his own, and so again it is injustice. . . . And whereas some men have pretended for their disobedience to their Soveraign, a new Covenant, made, not with men, but with God; this also is unjust: for there is no Covenant with God, but by mediation of some body that representeth God's Person; which none doth but God's Lieutenant, who hath the Soveraignty under God. But this pretence of Covenant with God, is so evident a [lie], even in the pretenders own consciences, that it is not onely an act of an unjust, but also of a vile, and unmanly disposition. . . .

. . . Consequently none of [the sovereign's] Subjects, by any pretence of forfeiture, can be freed from his Subjection.

REVIEW QUESTIONS

1. What was Thomas Hobbes' view of human nature and what conclusions did he draw from it about the best form of government?
2. What has been the political legacy of Hobbes' notion of the state?

10 The Triumph of Constitutional Monarchy in England: The Glorious Revolution

The struggle against absolute monarchy in England during the early seventeenth century reached a climax during the reign (1625–1649) of Charles I. Parliament raised its own army as civil war broke out between its supporters and those of the king. Captured by the Scottish Presbyterian rebels in 1646 and turned over to the English parliamentary army in 1647, Charles was held prisoner for two years until the Puritan parliamentary general Oliver Cromwell (1599–1658) decided to put him on trial for treason. The king was found guilty and executed in 1649.

The revolutionary parliamentary regime evolved into a military dictatorship headed by Cromwell. After Cromwell's death, Parliament in 1660 restored the monarchy and invited the late king's heir to end his exile and take the throne. Charles II (ruled 1660–1685), by discretion and skillful statesmanship, managed to evade many difficulties caused by the hostility of those who opposed his policies. He attempted to ease religious discrimination by ending the laws that penalized dissenters who rejected the official Church of England. But the religious prejudices of Parliament forced the king to desist, and the laws penalizing both Protestant dissenters and Roman Catholics remained in force. The king's motives for establishing religious toleration were suspect, since he himself was married to a French Catholic and his brother and heir James, duke of York, was also a staunch Catholic.

When James II succeeded to the throne in 1685, he tried unsuccessfully to get Parliament to repeal the Test Act, a law that forbade anyone to hold a civil or military office or to enter a university unless he was a member in good standing of the Church of England. This law effectively barred both Catholics and Protestant dissenters from serving in the king's government. When Parliament refused to act, James got the legal Court of the King's Bench to approve his decree suspending the Test Act. The court affirmed that the king, due to his sovereign authority, had absolute power to suspend any law at his sole discretion. The prerogatives claimed by the king were seen by many as an attempt to impose absolute monarchy on the English people.

King James further roused enemies by appointing many Catholics to high government posts and by issuing his Declaration of Indulgence for Liberty of Conscience on April 4, 1687. This declaration established complete freedom of worship for all

Englishmen, ending all civil penalties and discriminations based on religious dissent. Instead of hailing the declaration as a step forward in solving the religious quarrels within the kingdom, many persons viewed this suspension of the laws as a further act of absolutism because James acted unilaterally without consulting Parliament. This act united the king's enemies and alienated his former supporters.

When the king's wife gave birth to a son in 1688, making the heir to the throne another Catholic, almost all factions (except the Catholics) abandoned James II and in 1689 invited the Dutch Protestant Prince William of Orange and his wife, Mary, James II's Protestant daughter, to come to England. James and his Catholic family and friends fled to France. Parliament declared the throne vacant and offered it to William and Mary as joint sovereigns. As a result of the "Glorious Revolution," the English monarchy became clearly limited by the will of Parliament.

THE ENGLISH DECLARATION OF RIGHTS

In depriving James II of the throne, Parliament had destroyed forever in Britain the theory of divine right as an operating principle of government and had firmly established a limited constitutional monarchy. The appointment of William and Mary was accompanied by a declaration of rights (later enacted as the Bill of Rights), which enumerated and declared illegal James II's arbitrary acts. The English Declaration of Rights, excerpted below, compelled William and Mary and future monarchs to recognize the right of the people's representatives to dispose of the royal office and to set limits on its powers. These rights were subsequently formulated into laws passed by Parliament. Prior to the American Revolution, colonists protested that British actions in the American colonies violated certain rights guaranteed in the English Bill of Rights. Several of these rights were later included in the Constitution of the United States.

And whereas the said late king James the Second having abdicated the government and the throne being thereby vacant, His Highness the prince of Orange (whom it hath pleased Almighty God to make the glorious instrument of delivering this kingdom from popery and arbitrary power) did (by the advice of the lords spiritual and temporal and divers principal persons of the commons)[1] cause letters to be written to the lords spiritual and temporal, being Protestants; and other letters to the several counties, cities, universities, boroughs and Cinque ports[2]

for the choosing of such persons to represent them, as were of right to be sent to parliament, to meet and sit at Westminster upon the two and twentieth day of January in this year one thousand six hundred eighty and eight,[3] in order to [guarantee] . . . that their religion, laws and liberties might not again be in danger

Select Documents of English Constitutional History, ed. George Burton Adams and H. Morse Stephen (London: Macmillan Co., 1902).

[1]"The lords spiritual" refers to the bishops of the Church of England who sat in the House of Lords, and "the lords temporal" refers to the nobility entitled to sit in the House of Lords. The commons refers to the elected representatives in the House of Commons. —Eds.
[2]The Cinque ports along England's southeastern coast (originally five in number) enjoyed special privileges because of their military duties in providing for coastal defense. —Eds.
[3]The year was in fact 1689 because until 1752, the English used March 25 as the beginning of the new year. —Eds.

of being subverted; upon which letters elections having been accordingly made.

And thereupon the said lords spiritual and temporal and commons pursuant to their respective letters and elections being now assembled in a full and free representative of this nation, taking into their most serious consideration the best means for attaining the ends aforesaid, do in the first place (as their ancestors in like case have usually done) for the vindicating and asserting their ancient rights and liberties, declare:

That the pretended power of suspending of laws or the execution of laws by regal authority without consent of parliament is illegal.

That the pretended power of dispensing with laws or the execution of laws by regal authority as it hath been assumed and exercised of late is illegal.

That the commission for erecting the late court of commissioners for ecclesiastical causes and all other commissions and courts of like nature are illegal and pernicious.

That the levying money for or to the use of the crown by pretence of prerogative without grant of parliament for a longer time or in other manner than the same is or shall be granted is illegal.

That it is the right of the subjects to petition the king and all commitments and prosecutions for such petitioning are illegal.

That the raising or keeping a standing army within the kingdom in time of peace unless it be with consent of parliament is against the law.

That the subjects which are Protestants may have arms for their defence suitable to their conditions and as allowed by law.

That election of members of parliament ought to be free.

That the freedom of speech and debates or proceedings in parliament ought not to be impeached or questioned in any court or place out of parliament.

That excessive bail ought not to be required nor excessive fines imposed nor cruel and unusual punishments inflicted.

That jurors ought to be duly impanelled and returned and jurors which pass upon men in trials for high treason ought to be freeholders.

That all grants and promises of fines and forfeitures of particular persons before conviction are illegal and void.

And that for redress of all grievances and for the amending, strengthening and preserving of the laws parliaments ought to be held frequently.

And they do claim, demand and insist upon all and singular the premises as their undoubted rights and liberties and that no declarations, judgments, doings or proceedings to the prejudice of the people in any of the said premises ought in any wise to be drawn hereafter into consequence or example.

REVIEW QUESTIONS

1. How did the English Declaration of Rights limit royal authority? With what result?
2. In what ways did the Glorious Revolution impact the American rebellion in the 1770s?

CHAPTER 12

The Scientific Revolution

GALILEO GALILEI, by Samuel Sartain, 1852. Galileo's support of the Copernican system and rejection of the medieval division of the universe into higher and lower realms make him a principal shaper of modern science. *(The Granger Collection, New York)*

The Scientific Revolution of the sixteenth and seventeenth centuries replaced the medieval view of the universe with a new cosmology and produced a new way of investigating nature. It overthrew the medieval conception of nature as a hierarchical order ascending toward a realm of perfection. Rejecting reliance on authority, the thinkers of the Scientific Revolution affirmed the individual's ability to know the natural world through the method of mathematical reasoning, the direct observation of nature, and carefully controlled experiments.

The medieval view of the universe had blended the theories of Aristotle and Ptolemy, two ancient Greek thinkers, with Christian teachings. In that view, a stationary earth stood in the center of the universe just above hell. Revolving around the earth were seven planets: the moon, Mercury, Venus, the sun, Mars, Jupiter, and Saturn. Because people believed that earth did not move, it was not considered a planet. Each planet was attached to a transparent sphere that turned around the earth. Encompassing the universe was a sphere of fixed stars; beyond the stars lay three heavenly spheres, the outermost of which was the abode of God. An earth-centered universe accorded with the Christian idea that God had created the universe for men and women and that salvation was the aim of life.

Also agreeable to the medieval Christian view was Aristotle's division of the universe into a lower, earthly realm and a higher realm beyond the moon. Two sets of laws operated in the universe, one on earth and the other in the celestial realm. Earthly objects were composed of four elements: earth, water, fire, and air; celestial objects were composed of the divine ether—a substance too pure, too clear, too fine, too spiritual to be found on earth. Celestial objects naturally moved in perfectly circular orbits around the earth; earthly objects, composed mainly of the heavy elements of earth and water, naturally fell downward, whereas objects made of the lighter elements of air and fire naturally flew upward toward the sky.

The destruction of the medieval world picture began with the publication in 1543 of *On the Revolutions of the Heavenly Spheres*, by Nicolaus Copernicus, a Polish mathematician, astronomer, and clergyman. In Copernicus' system, the sun was in the center of the universe, and the earth was another planet that moved around the sun. Most thinkers of the time, committed to the Aristotelian–Ptolemaic system and to the biblical statements that seemed to support it, rejected Copernicus' helioentric conclusions.

The work of Galileo Galilei, an Italian mathematician, astronomer, and physicist, was decisive in the shattering of the medieval cosmos and the shaping of the modern scientific outlook. Galileo advanced the modern view that knowledge of nature derives from direct observation and from mathematics. For Galileo, the universe was a "grand book which . . . is written in the language of mathematics, and its characters are triangles, circles, and other geometric figures without which it is humanly impossible to understand a single word of it." Galileo also pioneered experimental physics, advanced the modern idea that nature is uniform throughout the universe, and attacked reliance on scholastic authority rather than on experimentation in resolving scientific controversies.

Johannes Kepler (1571–1630), a contemporary of Galileo, discovered three laws of planetary motion that greatly advanced astronomical knowledge. Kepler showed that the path of a planet was an ellipse, not a circle as Ptolemy (and Copernicus) had believed, and that planets do not move at uniform speed but accelerate as they near the sun. He devised formulas to calculate accurately both a planet's speed at each point in its orbit around the sun and a planet's location at a particular time. Kepler's laws provided further evidence that Copernicus had been right, for they made sense only in a sun-centered universe, but Kepler could not explain why planets stayed in their orbits rather than flying off into space or crashing into the sun. The resolution of that question was left to Sir Isaac Newton.

Newton's great achievement was integrating the findings of Copernicus, Galileo, and Kepler into a single theoretical system. In *Principia Mathematica* (1687), he formulated the mechanical laws of motion and attraction that govern celestial and terrestrial objects.

The creation of a new model of the universe was one great achievement of the Scientific Revolution; another accomplishment was the formulation of the scientific method. The scientific method encompasses two approaches to knowledge, which usually complement each other: the empirical (inductive) and the rational (deductive). Although all sciences use both approaches, the inductive method is generally more applicable in such descriptive sciences as biology, anatomy, and geology, which rely on the accumulation of data. In the inductive approach, general principles are derived from analyzing external experiences—observations and the results of experiments. In the deductive approach, used in mathematics and theoretical physics, truths are derived in successive steps from indubitable axioms. Whereas the inductive method builds its concepts from an analysis of sense experience, the deductive approach constructs its ideas from self-evident principles that are conceived by the mind itself without external experience. The deductive and inductive approaches to knowledge, and their interplay, have been a constantly recurring feature in Western intellectual history since the rationalism of Plato and the empiricism of Aristotle. The success of the scientific method in modern times arose from the skillful synchronization of induction and deduction by such giants as Leonardo da Vinci, Copernicus, Kepler, Galileo, and Newton.

The Scientific Revolution was instrumental in shaping the modern outlook. It destroyed the medieval conception of the universe and established the scientific method as the means for investigating nature and acquiring knowledge, even in areas having little to do with the study of the physical world. By demonstrating the powers of the human mind, the Scientific Revolution gave thinkers great confidence in reason and led eventually to a rejection of traditional beliefs in magic, astrology, and witches. In the eighteenth century, this growing skepticism led thinkers to question miracles and other Christian beliefs that seemed contrary to reason and natural law.

---

1   The Copernican Revolution

In proclaiming that the earth was not stationary but revolved around the sun, Nicolaus Copernicus (1473–1543) revolutionized the science of astronomy. Fearing controversy and scorn, Copernicus long refused to publish his great work, *On the Revolutions of the Heavenly Spheres* (1543). However, persuaded by friends, he finally relented and permitted publication; a copy of his book reached him on his deathbed. As Copernicus anticipated, his ideas aroused the ire of many thinkers.

Both Catholic and Protestant philosophers and theologians, including Martin Luther, attacked Copernicus for contradicting the Bible and Aristotle and Ptolemy, and they raised several specific objections. First, certain passages in the Bible imply a stationary earth and a sun that moves (for example, Psalm 93 says, "Yea, the world is established; it shall never be moved"; and in attacking Copernicus, Luther pointed out that "sacred scripture tells us that Joshua commanded the sun to stand still, and not the earth"). Second, a body as heavy as the earth cannot move through space at such speed as Copernicus suggested. Third, if the earth spins on its axis, why does a stone dropped from a height land directly below instead of at a point behind where it was dropped? Fourth, if the earth moved, objects would fly off it. And finally, the moon cannot orbit both the earth and the sun at the same time.

Nicolaus Copernicus
ON THE REVOLUTIONS OF THE HEAVENLY SPHERES

On the Revolutions of the Heavenly Spheres was dedicated to Pope Paul III, whom Copernicus asked to protect him from vilification. In the dedication, Copernicus explains his reason for delaying publication of *Revolutions*.

To His Holiness, Pope Paul III, Nicholas Copernicus' Preface to His Books on the Revolutions

I can readily imagine, Holy Father, that as soon as some people hear that in this volume, which I have written about the revolutions of the spheres of the universe, I ascribe certain motions to the terrestrial globe, they will shout that I must be immediately repudiated together with this belief. For I am not so enamored of my own opinions that I disregard what others may think of them. I am aware that a philosopher's ideas are not subject to the judgement of ordinary persons, because it is his endeavor to seek the truth in all things, to the extent permitted to human reason by God. Yet I hold that completely erroneous views should be shunned. Those who know that the consensus of many centuries has sanctioned the conception that the earth remains at rest in the middle of the heaven as its center would, I reflected, regard it as an insane pronouncement if I made the opposite assertion that the earth moves. Therefore I debated with myself for a long time whether to publish the volume which I wrote to prove the earth's motion or rather to follow the example of the Pythagoreans[1] and certain others, who used to transmit philosophy's secrets only to kinsmen and friends, not in writing but by word of mouth. . . . And they did so, it seems to me, not, as some suppose, because they were in some way jealous about their teachings, which would be spread around; on the contrary, they wanted the very beautiful thoughts attained by great men of deep devotion not to be ridiculed by those who are reluctant to exert themselves vigorously in any literary pursuit unless it is lucrative; or if they are stimulated to the nonacquisitive study of philosophy by the exhortation and example of others, yet because of their dullness of mind they play the same part among philosophers as drones among bees. When I weighed these considerations, the scorn which I had reason to fear on account of the novelty and unconventionality of my opinion almost induced me to abandon completely the work which I had undertaken.

But while I hesitated for a long time and even resisted, my friends [encouraged me]. . . . Foremost among them was the cardinal of Capua [a city in southern Italy], Nicholas Schönberg, renowned in every field of learning.

Next to him was a man who loves me dearly, Tiedemann Giese, bishop of Chelmno [a city in northern Poland], a close student of sacred letters as well as of all good literature. For he repeatedly encouraged me and, sometimes adding reproaches, urgently requested me to publish this volume and finally permit it to appear after being buried among my papers and lying concealed not merely until the ninth year[2] but by now the fourth period of nine years. The same conduct was recommended to me by not a few other very eminent scholars. They exhorted me no longer to refuse, on account of the fear which I felt, to make my work available for the general use of students of astronomy. The crazier my doctrine of the earth's motion now appeared to most people, the argument ran, so much the more admiration and thanks would it gain after they saw the publication of my writings dispel the fog of absurdity by most luminous proofs. Influenced therefore by these persuasive men and by this hope, in the end I allowed my friends to bring out an edition of the volume, as they had long besought me to do. . . .

But you [your Holiness] are rather waiting to hear from me how it occurred to me to venture to conceive any motion of the earth, against the traditional opinion of astronomers and almost against common sense. . . . [Copernicus then describes some of the problems connected with the Ptolemaic system.]

For a long time, then, I reflected on this confusion in the astronomical traditions concerning the derivation of the motions of the universe's spheres. I began to be annoyed that the movements of the world machine, created for our sake by the best and most systematic

---

Nicolaus Copernicus, *On the Revolutions*, trans. Edward Rosen, ed. Jerzy Dobrzycki. Reprinted by permission of the Estate of Edward Rosen.

---

[1]Pythagoreans were followers of Pythagoras, a Greek mathematician and philosopher of the sixth century B.C.; they were particularly interested in cosmology. —Eds.

[2]The Roman poet Horace, who lived in the first century B.C., suggested in *Ars Poetica* that writers should keep a new manuscript in a cupboard "until the ninth year" before publishing it. Only then, he argued, would they have enough objectivity to judge its value. Copernicus is referring to this famous piece of advice. —Eds.

Artisan of all [God], were not understood with greater certainty by the philosophers, who otherwise examined so precisely the most insignificant trifles of this world. For this reason I undertook the task of rereading the works of all the philosophers which I could obtain to learn whether anyone had ever proposed other motions of the universe's spheres than those expounded by the teachers of astronomy in the schools. And in fact first I found in Cicero that Hicetas supposed the earth to move. Later I also discovered in Plutarch[3] that certain others were of this opinion. . . .

Therefore, having obtained the opportunity from these sources, I too began to consider the mobility of the earth. . . . I thought that I too would be readily permitted to ascertain whether explanations sounder than those of my predecessors could be found for the revolution of the celestial spheres on the assumption of some motion of the earth.

Having thus assumed the motions which I ascribe to the earth later on in the volume, by long and intense study I finally found that if the motions of the other planets are correlated with the orbiting of the earth, and are computed for the revolution of each planet, not only do their phenomena follow therefrom but also the order and size of all the planets and spheres, and heaven itself is so linked together that in no portion of it can anything be shifted without disrupting the remaining parts and the universe as a whole. Accordingly in the arrangement of the volume too I have adopted the following order. In the first book I set forth the entire distribution of the spheres together with the motions which I attribute to the earth, so that this book contains, as it were, the general

structure of the universe. Then in the remaining books I correlate the motions of the other planets and of all the spheres with the movement of the earth so that I may thereby determine to what extent the motions and appearances of the other planets and spheres can be saved if they are correlated with the earth's motions. I have no doubt that acute and learned astronomers will agree with me if, as this discipline especially requires, they are willing to examine and consider, not superficially but thoroughly, what I adduce in this volume in proof of these matters. However, in order that the educated and uneducated alike may see that I do not run away from the judgement of anybody at all, I have preferred dedicating my studies to Your Holiness rather than to anyone else. For even in this very remote corner of the earth where I live you are considered the highest authority by virtue of the loftiness of your office and your love for all literature and astronomy too. Hence by your prestige and judgement you can easily suppress calumnious attacks although, as the proverb has it, there is no remedy for a backbite.

Perhaps there will be babblers who claim to be judges of astronomy although completely ignorant of the subject and, badly distorting some passage of scripture to their purpose, will dare to find fault with my undertaking and censure it. I disregard them even to the extent of despising their criticism as unfounded. For it is not unknown that Lactantius,[4] otherwise an illustrious writer but hardly an astronomer, speaks quite childishly about the earth's shape, when he mocks those who declared that the earth has the form of a globe. Hence scholars need not be surprised if any such persons will likewise ridicule me. Astronomy is written for astronomers. To them my work too will seem, unless I am mistaken, to make some contribution.

---

[3]Hicetas, a Pythagorean philosopher of the fourth century B.C., taught that the earth rotated on its axis while the other heavenly bodies were at rest. Cicero was a Roman statesman of the first century B.C. Plutarch (A.D. c. 50– c. 120) was a Greek moral philosopher and biographer whose works were especially popular among Renaissance humanists. —Eds.

---

[4]Renaissance humanists admired Lactantius (c. 240– c. 320), a Latin rhetorician and Christian apologist, for his classical, Ciceronian literary style. —Eds.

Cardinal Bellarmine
ATTACK ON THE COPERNICAN THEORY

In 1615, Cardinal Bellarmine, who in the name of the Inquisition warned Galileo not to defend the Copernican theory, expressed his displeasure with heliocentrism in a letter to Paolo Antonio Foscarini. Foscarini, head of the Carmelites, an order of mendicant friars in Calabria, and professor of theology, had tried to show that the earth's motion was not incompatible with biblical statements.

Cardinal Bellarmine to Foscarini (12 April 1615)

My Very Reverend Father,

I have read with interest the letter in Italian and the essay in Latin which Your [Reverence] sent me; I thank you for the one and for the other and confess that they are full of intelligence and erudition. You ask for my opinion, and so I shall give it to you, but very briefly, since now you have little time for reading and I for writing.

First, . . . to [I] want to affirm that in reality the sun is at the center of the world and only turns on itself without moving from east to west, and the earth . . . revolves with great speed around the sun . . . is a very dangerous thing, likely not only to irritate all scholastic philosophers and theologians, but also to harm the Holy Faith by rendering Holy scripture false. For your [Reverence] has well shown many ways of interpreting Holy scripture, but has not applied them to particular cases; without a doubt you would have encountered very great difficulties if you had wanted to interpret all those passages you yourself cited.

Second, I say that, as you know, the Council [of Trent] prohibits interpreting scripture against the common consensus of the Holy

Maurice A. Finocchiaro, ed., *The Galileo Affair: A Documentary History*, pp. 67–68. Copyright © 1989 by The Regents of the University of California. Reprinted by permission of the University of California Press.

Fathers; and if Your [Reverence] wants to read not only the Holy Fathers, but also the modern commentaries on Genesis, the Psalms, Ecclesiastes, and Joshua, you will find all agreeing in the literal interpretation that the sun is in heaven and turns around the earth with great speed, and that the earth is very far from heaven and sits motionless at the center of the world. Consider now, with your sense of prudence, whether the Church can tolerate giving scripture a meaning contrary to the Holy Fathers and to all the Greek and Latin commentators. Nor can one answer that this is not a matter of faith, since if it is not a matter of faith "as regards the topic," it is a matter of faith "as regards the speaker"; and so it would be heretical to say that Abraham did not have two children and Jacob twelve, as well as to say that Christ was not born of a virgin, because both are said by the Holy Spirit through the mouth of the prophets and the apostles.

Third, I say that if there were a true demonstration that the sun is at the center of the world and the earth in the third heaven, and that the sun does not circle the earth but the earth circles the sun, then one would have to proceed with great care in explaining the scriptures that appear contrary, and say rather that we do not understand them than that what is demonstrated is false. But I will not believe that there is such a demonstration, until it is shown to me. . . . and in case of doubt one must not abandon the Holy scripture as interpreted by the Holy Fathers. I add that the one who wrote, "The sun also ariseth, and the sun goeth down, and hasteth to his place where he arose," was Solomon [King of ancient Israel], who not only spoke inspired by God, but was a man above all others wise and learned in the human sciences and in the knowledge of created things; he received all this wisdom from God; therefore it is not likely that he was affirming something that was contrary to truth already demonstrated or capable of being demonstrated.

REVIEW QUESTIONS

1. What led Nicolaus Copernicus to investigate the motions of the universe's spheres?
2. Why did he fear to publish this theory about the earth's motion?
3. On what grounds did Cardinal Bellarmine reject the Copernican theory?

2 Galileo: Confirming the Copernican System

The brilliant Italian scientist Galileo Galilei (1564–1642) rejected the medieval division of the universe into higher and lower realms and proclaimed the modern idea of nature's uniformity. Learning that a telescope had been invented in Holland, Galileo built one for himself and used it to investigate the heavens. Through his telescope, Galileo saw craters and mountains on the moon; he concluded that celestial bodies were not pure, perfect, and immutable, as had been believed. There was no difference in quality between heavenly and earthly bodies; nature was the same throughout.

With his telescope, Galileo discovered four moons orbiting Jupiter, an observation that overcame a principal objection to the Copernican system. Galileo showed that a celestial body could indeed move around a center other than the earth; that earth was not the common center for all celestial bodies; that a celestial body (earth's moon or Jupiter's moons) could orbit a planet at the same time that the planet revolved around another body (namely, the sun).

Galileo appealed to the Roman Catholic authorities asking them to halt their actions against the theories of Copernicus, but was unsuccessful. His support of Copernicus aroused the ire of both clergy and scholastic philosophers. In 1616, the church placed Copernicus's book on the index of forbidden books, and Galileo was ordered to cease his defense of the Copernican theory. In 1632, Galileo published *Dialogue Concerning the Two Chief World Systems* in which he upheld the Copernican view. Widely distributed and acclaimed, the book antagonized Galileo's enemies, who succeeded in halting further printing. Summoned to Rome, the aging and infirm scientist was put on trial by the Inquisition and ordered to renounce the Copernican theory. Galileo bowed to the Inquisition, which condemned the *Dialogue* and sentenced him to life imprisonment—largely house arrest at his own villa near Florence, where he was treated humanely.

Galileo Galilei
LETTER TO THE GRAND DUCHESS CHRISTINA AND *DIALOGUE CONCERNING THE TWO CHIEF WORLD SYSTEMS— PTOLEMAIC AND COPERNICAN*

The first reading illustrates Galileo's active involvement in a struggle for freedom of inquiry many years before the *Dialogue* was published. In 1615, in a letter addressed to Grand Duchess Christina of Tuscany, Galileo argued that passages from the Bible had no authority in scientific disputes.

The second reading (from the *Dialogue*) reveals Galileo's views on Aristotle. Medieval scholastics regarded Aristotle as the supreme authority on questions concerning nature, an attitude that was perpetuated by early modern scholastics. Galileo insisted that such reliance on authority was a hindrance to scientific investigation, that it is through observation, experiment, and reason that one arrives at physical truth.

BIBLICAL AUTHORITY

Some years ago, as Your Serene Highness well knows, I discovered in the heavens many things that had not been seen before our own age. The novelty of these things, as well as some consequences which followed from them in contradiction to the physical notions commonly held among academic philosophers, stirred up against me no small number of professors—as if I had placed these things in the sky with my own hands in order to upset nature and overturn the sciences. They seemed to forget that the increase of known truths stimulates the investigation, establishment, and growth of the arts; not their diminution or destruction.

Showing a greater fondness for their own opinions than for truth, they sought to deny and disprove the new things which, if they had cared to look for themselves, their own senses would

Galileo Galilei, *Dialogue Concerning the Two Chief World Systems*, trans. Stillman Drake, pp. 107–112, 112–113, 175–177, 179–184. © 1962, University of California Press. Reprinted by permission of University of California Press.

have demonstrated to them. To this end they hurled various charges and published numerous writings filled with vain arguments, and they made the grave mistake of sprinkling these with passages taken from places in the Bible which they had failed to understand properly, and which were ill suited to their purposes. . . .

. . . Men who were well grounded in astronomical and physical science were persuaded as soon as they received my first message. There were others who denied them or remained in doubt only because of their novel and unexpected character, and because they had not yet had the opportunity to see for themselves. These men have by degrees come to be satisfied. But some, besides allegiance to their original error, possess I know not what fanciful interest in remaining hostile not so much toward the things in question as toward their discoverer. No longer being able to deny them, these men now take refuge in obstinate silence, but being more than ever exasperated by that which has pacified and quieted other men, they divert their thoughts to other fancies and seek new ways to damage me. . . .

. . . Possibly because they are disturbed by the known truth of other propositions of mine which differ from those commonly held, and therefore mistrusting their defense so long as they confine themselves to the field of philosophy, these men have resolved to fabricate a shield for their fallacies out of the mantle of pretended religion and the authority of the Bible. These they apply, with little judgment, to the refutation of arguments that they do not understand and have not even listened to.

First they have endeavored to spread the opinion that such propositions in general are contrary to the Bible and are consequently damnable and heretical. . . . Hence they have had no trouble in finding men who would preach the damnability and heresy of the new doctrine from their very pulpits with unwonted confidence, thus doing impious and inconsiderate injury not only to that doctrine and its followers but to all mathematics and mathematicians in general. . . .

. . . They go about invoking the Bible, which they would have minister to their deceitful purposes. Contrary to the sense of the Bible and the intention of the holy [Church] Fathers, if I am not mistaken, they would extend such authorities until even in purely physical matters—where faith is not involved—they would have us altogether abandon reason and the evidence of our senses in favor of some biblical passage, though under the surface meaning of its words this passage may contain a different sense.

I hope to show that I proceed with much greater piety than they do, when I argue not against condemning [Copernicus'] book, but against condemning it in the way they suggest—that is, without understanding it, weighing it, or so much as reading it. For Copernicus never discusses matters of religion or faith, nor does he use arguments that depend in any way upon the authority of sacred writings which he might have interpreted erroneously. He stands always upon physical conclusions pertaining to the celestial motions, and deals with them by astronomical and geometrical demonstrations, founded primarily upon sense experiences and very exact observations. He did not ignore the Bible, but he knew very well that if his doctrine were proved, then it could not

contradict the scriptures when they were rightly understood. . . .

The reason produced for condemning the opinion that the earth moves and the sun stands still is that in many places in the Bible one may read that the sun moves and the earth stands still. Since the Bible cannot err, it follows as a necessary consequence that anyone takes an erroneous and heretical position who maintains that the sun is inherently motionless and the earth movable.

With regard to this argument, I think in the first place that it is very pious to say and prudent to affirm that the holy Bible can never speak untruth—whenever its true meaning is understood. But I believe nobody will deny that it is often very abstruse, and may say things which are quite different from what its bare words signify. Hence in expounding the Bible if one were always to confine oneself to the unadorned grammatical meaning, one might fall into error. . . .

. . . Now the Bible, merely to condescend to popular capacity, has not hesitated to obscure some very important pronouncements, attributing to God himself some qualities extremely remote from (and even contrary to) His essence. Who, then, would positively declare that this principle has been set aside, and the Bible has confined itself rigorously to the bare and restricted sense of its words, when speaking but casually of the earth, of water, of the sun, or of any other created thing? Especially in view of the fact that these things in no way concern the primary purpose of the sacred writings, which is the service of God and the salvation of souls—matters infinitely beyond the comprehension of the common people.

This being granted, I think that in discussions of physical problems we ought to begin not from the authority of scriptural passages, but from sense-experiences and necessary demonstrations. . . . Nothing physical which sense-experience sets before our eyes, or which necessary demonstrations prove to us, ought to be called in question (much less condemned) upon the testimony of biblical passages which may have some different meaning beneath their words. . . .

. . . I do not feel obliged to believe that that same God who has endowed us with senses, reason, and intellect has intended to forgo their use and by some other means to give us knowledge which we can attain by them. He would not require us to deny sense and reason in physical matters which are set before our eyes and minds by direct experience or necessary demonstrations. . . .

It is obvious that such [anti-Copernican] authors, not having penetrated the true senses of scripture, would impose upon others an obligation to subscribe to conclusions that are repugnant to manifest reason and sense, if they had any authority to do so. God forbid that this sort of abuse should gain countenance and authority, for then in a short time it would be necessary to proscribe all the contemplative sciences. People who are unable to understand perfectly both the Bible and the sciences far outnumber those who do understand. The former, glancing superficially through the Bible, would arrogate to themselves the authority to decree upon every question of physics on the strength of some word which they have misunderstood, and which was employed by the sacred authors for some different purpose. And the smaller number of understanding men could not dam up the furious torrent of such people, who would gain the majority of followers simply because it is much more pleasant to gain a reputation for wisdom without effort or study than to consume oneself tirelessly in the most laborious disciplines.

Galileo attacked the unquestioning acceptance of Aristotle's teachings in his *Dialogue Concerning the Two Chief World Systems—Ptolemaic and Copernican.* In the *Dialogue,* Simplicio is an Aristotelian and Salviati is a spokesman for Galileo; Sagredo, a third participant, introduces the problem of relying on the authority of Aristotle.

ARISTOTELIAN AUTHORITY

SAGREDO One day I was at the home of a very famous doctor in Venice, where many persons came on account of their studies, and others occasionally came out of curiosity to see some anatomical dissection performed by a man who was truly no less learned than he was a careful and expert anatomist. It happened on this day that he was investigating the source and origin of the nerves, about which there exists a notorious controversy between the Galenist and Peripatetic doctors.[1] The anatomist showed that the great trunk of nerves, leaving the brain and passing through the nape, extended on down the spine and then branched out through the whole body, and that only a single strand as fine as a thread arrived at the heart. Turning to a gentleman whom we knew to be a Peripatetic philosopher, and on whose account he had been exhibiting and demonstrating everything with unusual care, he asked this man whether he was at last satisfied and convinced that the nerves originated in the brain and not in the heart. The philosopher, after considering for awhile, answered: "You have made me see this matter so plainly and palpably that if Aristotle's text were not contrary to it, stating clearly that the nerves originate in the heart, I should be forced to admit it to be true." . . .

SIMPLICIO But if Aristotle is to be abandoned, whom shall we have for a guide in philosophy? Suppose you name some author.

SALVIATI We need guides in forests and in unknown lands, but on plains and in open places only the blind need guides. It is better for such people to stay at home, but anyone with eyes in his head and his wits about him could serve as a guide for them. In saying this, I do not mean that a person should not listen to Aristotle; indeed, I applaud the reading and careful study of

---

[1]Galenist doctors followed the medical theories of Galen (A.D. c. 130–c. 200), a Greek anatomist and physician whose writings had great authority among medieval and early modern physicians. Peripatetic doctors followed Aristotle's teachings.—Eds.

his works, and I reproach only those who give themselves up as slaves to him in such a way as to subscribe blindly to everything he says and take it as an inviolable decree without looking for any other reasons. This abuse carries with it another profound disorder, that other people do not try harder to comprehend the strength of his demonstrations. And what is more revolting in a public dispute, when someone is deal-ing with demonstrable conclusions, than to hear him interrupted by a text (often written to some quite different purpose) thrown into his teeth by an opponent? If, indeed, you wish to continue in this method of studying, then put aside the name of philosophers and call yourselves historians, or memory experts; for it is not proper that those who never philosophize should usurp the honorable title of philosopher.

GALILEO CONDEMNED BY THE INQUISITION

The following selection is drawn from the records of the Inquisition, which found Galileo guilty of teaching Copernicanism.

Whereas you, Galileo, son of the late Vincenzo Galilei, Florentine, aged seventy years, were in the year 1615 denounced to this Holy Office for holding as true the false doctrine taught by some that the Sun is the center of the world and immovable and that the Earth moves, and also with a diurnal [daily] motion; for having disciples to whom you taught the same doctrine; for holding correspondence with certain mathematicians of Germany concerning the same; for having printed certain letters, entitled "On the Sunspots," wherein you developed the same doctrine as true; and for replying to the objections from the Holy scriptures, which from time to time were urged against it, by glossing the said scriptures according to your own meaning: and whereas there was thereupon produced the copy of a document in the form of a letter, purporting to be written by you to one formerly your disciple, and in this divers propositions are set forth, following the position of Copernicus, which are contrary to the true sense and authority of Holy scripture:

This Holy Tribunal being therefore of intention to proceed against the disorder and mischief thence resulting, which went on increasing to the prejudice of the Holy Faith, by command of His Holiness and of the Most Eminent Lords Cardinals of this supreme and universal Inquisition, the two propositions of the stability of the Sun and the motion of the Earth were by the theological Qualifiers qualified as follows:

The proposition that the Sun is the center of the world and does not move from its place is absurd and false philosophically and formally heretical, because it is expressly contrary to the Holy scripture.

The proposition that the Earth is not the center of the world and immovable but that it moves, and also with a diurnal motion, is equally absurd and false philosophically and theologically considered at least erroneous in faith.

But whereas it was desired at that time to deal leniently with you, it was decreed at the Holy Congregation held before His Holiness on the twenty-fifth of February, 1616, that his Eminence the Lord Cardinal Bellarmine should order you

"Galileo Before the Inquisition," in Giorgio de Santillana, *The Crime of Galileo,* pp. 306–308, 310. Copyright © 1955 by the University of Chicago Press. Reprinted by permission.

to abandon altogether the said false doctrine and, in the event of your refusal, that an injunction should be imposed upon you by the Commissary of the Holy Office to give up the said doctrine and not to teach it to others, not to defend it, nor even discuss it; and failing your acquiescence in this injunction, that you should be imprisoned.

And, in order that a doctrine so pernicious might be wholly rooted out and not insinuate itself further to the grave prejudice of Catholic truth, a decree was issued by the Holy Congregation of the Index prohibiting the books which treat of this doctrine and declaring the doctrine itself to be false and wholly contrary to the sacred and divine scripture.

And whereas a book appeared here recently, printed last year at Florence, the title of which shows that you were the author, this title being: "Dialogue of Galileo Galilei on the Great World Systems"; and whereas the Holy Congregation was afterward informed that through the publication of the said book the false opinion of the motion of the Earth and the stability of the Sun was daily gaining ground, the said book was taken into careful consideration, and in it there was discovered a patent violation of the aforesaid injunction that had been imposed upon you, for in this book you have defended the said opinion previously condemned and to your face declared to be so, although in the said book you strive by various devices to produce the impression that you leave it undecided, and in express terms as probable: which, however, is a most grievous error, as an opinion can in no wise be probable which has been declared and defined to be contrary to divine scripture.

Therefore by our order you were cited before this Holy Office, where, being examined upon your oath, you acknowledged the book to be written and published by you. You confessed that you began to write the said book about ten or twelve years ago, after the command had been imposed upon you as above; that you requested license to print it without, however, intimating to those who granted you this license that you had been commanded not to hold, defend, or teach the doctrine in question in any way whatever.

We say, pronounce, sentence, and declare that you, the said Galileo, by reason of the matters adduced in trial, and by you confessed as above, have rendered yourself in the judgment of this Holy Office vehemently suspected of heresy, namely, of having believed and held the doctrine—which is false and contrary to the sacred and divine scriptures—that the Sun is the center of the world and does not move from east to west and that the Earth moves and is not the center of the world; and that an opinion may be held and defended as probable after it has been declared and defined to be contrary to the Holy scripture; and that consequently you have incurred all the censures and penalties imposed and promulgated in the sacred canons and other constitutions, general and particular, against such delinquents. From which we are content that you be absolved, provided that, first, with a sincere heart and unfeigned faith, you abjure, curse, and detest before us the aforesaid errors and heresies and every other error and heresy contrary to the Catholic and Apostolic Roman Church in the form to be prescribed by us for you.

And, in order that this your grave and pernicious error and transgression may not remain altogether unpunished and that you may be more cautious in the future and an example to others that they may abstain from similar delinquencies, we ordain that the book of the "Dialogue of Galileo Galilei" be prohibited by public edict. . . .

REVIEW QUESTIONS

1. What was Galileo Galilei's objection to using the Bible as a source of knowledge of physical things? According to him, how did one acquire knowledge of nature?
2. What point was Galileo making in telling the story of the anatomical dissection?
3. What was Galileo's view on the use of Aristotle's works as a basis for scientific endeavors?
4. Why did the Inquisition regard the teaching of Copernicanism as dangerous?

3 Prophet of Modern Science

Sir Francis Bacon (1561–1626), an English statesman and philosopher, vigorously supported the advancement of science and the scientific method. He believed that increased comprehension and mastery of nature would improve living conditions for people and therefore wanted science to encompass systematic research; toward this end, he urged the state to fund scientific institutions. Bacon denounced universities for merely repeating Aristotelian concepts and discussing abstruse problems—Is matter formless? Are all natural substances composed of matter?—that did not increase understanding of nature or contribute to human betterment. The webs spun by these scholastics, he said, were ingenious but valueless. Bacon wanted an educational program that stressed direct contact with nature and fostered new discoveries.

Bacon was among the first to appreciate the new science's value and to explain its method clearly. Like Leonardo da Vinci, Bacon gave supreme value to the direct observation of nature; for this reason he is one of the founders of the empirical tradition in modern philosophy. Bacon upheld the inductive approach—careful investigation of nature, accumulation of data, and experimentation—as the way to truth and useful knowledge. Because he wanted science to serve a practical function, Bacon praised artisans and technicians who improved technology.

Francis Bacon
ATTACK ON AUTHORITY
AND ADVOCACY OF
EXPERIMENTAL SCIENCE

Bacon was not himself a scientist; he made no discoveries and had no laboratory. Nevertheless, for his advocacy of the scientific method, Bacon is deservedly regarded as a prophet of modern science.

During the seventeenth and eighteenth centuries, the experimental method advocated by Bacon was increasingly employed in the various sciences. For example, experimenting with bodies in motion, Galileo formulated a law of falling bodies that he expressed mathematically. By "having frequent recourse to vivisections employing a variety of animals . . . and collating numerous observations," wrote William Harvey, he was able to demonstrate that all blood passes through a central organ, the heart, flowing away from the heart through the arteries and back to it through the veins, and that this constant, rotating circulation is caused by the rhythmic contractions of the heart muscle acting as a pump. In 1741, Herman Boerhaave wrote that the truths of chemistry are not deduced from pure thought but are arrived at through innumerable experiments: "We allow of no other theory in chemistry except which is built on general laws, which must originally have been deduced from a multitude of common incontestable facts always happening in the same manner, so as to authorize the enacting them into a general rule."

In the first passage from *Redargutio Philosophiarum* (The Refutation of Philosophies), written in 1609, a treatise on the "idols of the theater"—fallacious ways of thinking based on given systems of philosophy—Bacon attacks the slavish reliance on Aristotle.

But even though Aristotle were the man he is thought to be I should still warn you against receiving as oracles the thoughts and opinions of one man. What justification can there be for this self-imposed servitude [that] . . . you are content to repeat Aristotle after two thousand [years]? . . . But if you will be guided by me you will deny, not only to this man but to any mortal now living or who shall live hereafter, the right to dictate your opinions. . . . You will never be sorry for trusting your own strength, if you but once make trial of it. You may be inferior to Aristotle on the whole, but not in everything. Finally, and this is the head and front of the whole matter, there is at least one thing in which you are far ahead of him—in precedents, in experience, in the lessons of time. Aristotle, it is said, wrote a book in which he gathered together the laws and institutions of two hundred and fifty-five cities; yet I have no doubt that the customs of Rome are worth more than all of them combined so far as military and political science are concerned. The position is the same in natural philosophy. Are you of a mind to cast aside not only your own endowments but the gifts of time? Assert yourselves before it is too late. Apply yourselves to the study of things themselves. Be not for ever the property of one man.

In these excerpts from *The New Organon* (New System of Logic), in 1620 Bacon criticizes contemporary methods used to inquire into nature. He expresses his ideas in the form of aphorisms—concise statements of principles or general truths.

I.   Man, being the servant and interpreter of Nature, can do and understand so much and so much only as he has observed in fact or in thought of the course of nature: beyond this he neither knows anything nor can do anything.

VIII.   . . . The sciences we now possess are merely systems for the nice ordering and setting forth of things already invented; not methods of invention or directions for new works.

XII.   The logic now in use serves rather to fix and give stability to the errors which have their foundation in commonly received notions than to help the search after truth. So it does more harm than good.

XIX.   There are and can be only two ways of searching into and discovering truth. The one [begins with] the . . . most general axioms, and from these principles, the truth of which it takes for settled and immoveable, proceeds to judgment and to the discovery of middle axioms. And this way is now in fashion. The other derives axioms from the senses and particulars, rising by a gradual and unbroken ascent, so that it arrives at the most general axioms last of all. This is the true way, but as yet untried.

XXIII.   There is a great difference between . . . certain empty dogmas, and the true signatures and marks set upon the works of creation as they are found in nature.

XXIV.   It cannot be that axioms established by argumentation should avail for the discovery of new works; since the subtlety of nature is greater many times over than the subtlety of argument. But axioms duly and orderly formed from particulars easily discover the way to new particulars, and thus render sciences active.

The Philosophy of Francis Bacon, ed. and trans. Benjamin Farrington, pp. 114–115. Copyright © 1970 by Liverpool University Press. Reprinted with permission.

Novum Organum in *The Works of Francis Bacon*, vol. III, coll., ed., and trans. by James Spedding, Robert Leslie Ellis, and Douglas Dennon Heath (Boston: Taggard and Thompson, 1863), pp. 67–69, 71–72, 135–136, 142.

XXXI.   It is idle to expect any great advancement in science from the superinducing [adding] and engrafting of new things upon old. We must begin anew from the very foundations, unless we would revolve for ever in a circle with mean and contemptible progress.

CIX.   There is therefore much ground for hoping that there are still laid up in the womb of nature many secrets of excellent use, having no affinity or parallelism with anything that is now known, but lying entirely out of the beat of the imagination, which have not yet been found out. They too no doubt will some time or other, in the course and revolution of many ages, come to light of themselves, just as the others did; only by the method of which we are now treating they can be speedily and suddenly and simultaneously presented and anticipated.

REVIEW QUESTIONS

1. What intellectual attitude did Francis Bacon believe obstructed new scientific discoveries in his time?
2. What method of scientific inquiry did Bacon advocate?

---

4 The Autonomy of the Mind

René Descartes (1596–1650), a French mathematician and philosopher, united the new currents of thought initiated during the Renaissance and the Scientific Revolution. Descartes said that the universe was a mechanical system whose inner laws could be discovered through mathematical thinking and formulated in mathematical terms. With Descartes' assertions on the power of thought, human beings became fully aware of their capacity to comprehend the world through their mental powers. For this reason he is regarded as the founder of modern philosophy.

The deductive approach stressed by Descartes presumes that inherent in the mind are mathematical principles, logical relationships, the principle of cause and effect, concepts of size and motion, and so on—ideas that exist independently of human experience with the external world. Descartes, for example, would say that the properties of a right-angle triangle ($a^2 + b^2 = c^2$) are implicit in human consciousness prior to any experience one might have with a triangle. These innate ideas, said Descartes, permit the mind to give order and coherence to the physical world. Descartes held that the mind arrives at truth when it "intuits" or comprehends the logical necessity of its own ideas and expresses these ideas with clarity, certainty, and precision.

René Descartes
DISCOURSE ON METHOD

In the *Discourse on Method* (1637), Descartes proclaimed the mind's autonomy and importance, and its ability and right to comprehend truth. In this work he offered a method whereby one could achieve certainty and thereby produce a comprehensive understanding of nature and human culture. In the following passage from the *Discourse on Method*, he explained the purpose of his inquiry. How he did so is almost as revolutionary as the ideas he wished to express. He spoke in the first person, autobiographically, as an individual employing his own reason, and he addressed himself to other individuals, inviting them to use their reason. He brought to his narrative an unprecedented confidence in the power of his own judgment and a deep disenchantment with the learning of his times.

PART ONE

From my childhood I lived in a world of books, and since I was taught that by their help I could gain a clear and assured knowledge of everything useful in life, I was eager to learn from them. But as soon as I had finished the course of studies which usually admits one to the ranks of the learned, I changed my opinion completely. For I found myself saddled with so many doubts and errors that I seemed to have gained nothing in trying to educate myself unless it was to discover more and more fully how ignorant I was.

Nevertheless I had been in one of the most celebrated schools in Europe, where I thought there should be wise men if wise men existed anywhere on earth. I had learned there everything that others learned, and, not satisfied with merely the knowledge that was taught, I had perused as many books as I could find which contained more unusual and recondite knowledge. . . . And finally, it did not seem to me that our times were less flourishing and fertile than were any of the earlier periods. All this led me to conclude that I could judge others by myself, and to decide that there was no such wisdom in the world as I had previously hoped to find. . . .

I revered our theology, and hoped as much as anyone else to get to heaven, but having learned on great authority that the road was just as open to the most ignorant as to the most learned, and that the truths of revelation which lead thereto are beyond our understanding, I would not have dared to submit them to the weakness of my reasonings. I thought that to succeed in their examination it would be necessary to have some extraordinary assistance from heaven, and to be more than a man.

I will say nothing of philosophy except that it has been studied for many centuries by the most outstanding minds without having produced anything which is not in dispute and consequently doubtful. I did not have enough presumption to hope to succeed better than the others; and when I noticed how many different opinions learned men may hold on the same subject, despite the fact that no more than one of them can ever be right, I resolved to consider almost as false any opinion which was merely plausible. . . .

This is why I gave up my studies entirely as soon as I reached the age when I was no longer under the control of my teachers. I resolved to seek no other knowledge than that which I might find within myself, or perhaps in the great book of nature. I spent a few years of my adolescence traveling, seeing courts and armies, living with people of diverse types and stations of life, acquiring varied experience, testing myself in the episodes which fortune sent me, and, above all, thinking about the things around me so that I could derive some profit from them. For it seemed to me that I might find much more of the truth in the cogitations [reflections] which each man made on things which were important to him, and where he would be the loser if he judged badly, than in the cogitations of a man of letters in his study, concerned with speculations which produce no effect, and which have no consequences to him. . . .

. . . After spending several years in thus studying the book of nature and acquiring experience, I eventually reached the decision to study my own self, and to employ all my abilities to try to choose the right path.

René Descartes, *Discourse on Method*, trans. Laurence J. Lafleur (New York: Macmillan Publishing Company, 1956), pp. 3–7, 9–12, 14, 20–21.

This produced much better results in my case, I think, than would have been produced if I had never left my books and my country. . . .

PART TWO

. . . As far as the opinions which I had been receiving since my birth were concerned, I could not do better than to reject them completely for once in my lifetime, and to resume them afterwards, or perhaps accept better ones in their place, when I had determined how they fitted into a rational scheme. And I firmly believed that by this means I would succeed in conducting my life much better than if I built only upon the old foundations and gave credence to the principles which I had acquired in my childhood without ever having examined them to see whether they were true or not. . . .

. . . Never has my intention been more than to try to reform my own ideas, and rebuild them on foundations that would be wholly mine. . . . The decision to abandon all one's preconceived notions is not an example for all to follow. . . .

As for myself, I should no doubt have . . . [never attempted it] if I had had but a single teacher or if I had not known the differences which have always existed among the most learned. I had discovered in college that one cannot imagine anything so strange and unbelievable but that it has been upheld by some philosopher; and in my travels I had found that those who held opinions contrary to ours were neither barbarians nor savages, but that many of them were at least as reasonable as ourselves. I had considered how the same man, with the same capacity for reason, becomes different as a result of being brought up among Frenchmen or Germans than he would be if he had been brought up among Chinese or cannibals; and how, in our fashions, the thing which pleased us ten years ago, and perhaps will please us again ten years in the future, now seems extravagant and ridiculous; and I felt that in all these ways we are much more greatly influenced by custom and example than by any certain knowledge. Faced with this divergence of opinion, I could

not accept the testimony of the majority, for I thought it worthless as a proof of anything somewhat difficult to discover, since it is much more likely that a single man will have discovered it than a whole people. Nor, on the other hand, could I select anyone whose opinions seemed to me to be preferable to those of others, and I was thus constrained to embark on the investigation for myself.

Nevertheless, like a man who walks alone in the darkness, I resolved to go so slowly and circumspectly that if I did not get ahead very rapidly I was at least safe from falling. Also, I did not want to reject all the opinions which had slipped irrationally into my consciousness since birth, until I had first spent enough time planning how to accomplish the task which I was then undertaking, and seeking the true method of obtaining knowledge of everything which my mind was capable of understanding. . . .

Descartes' method consists of four principles that place the capacity to arrive at truth entirely within the province of the human mind. One finds a self-evident principle, such as a geometric axiom. From this general principle, other truths are deduced through logical reasoning. This is accomplished by breaking a problem down into its elementary components and then, step by step, moving toward more complex knowledge.

. . . I thought that some other method [besides that of logic, algebra, and geometry] must be found to combine the advantages of these three and to escape their faults. Finally, just as the multitude of laws frequently furnishes an excuse for vice, and a state is much better governed with a few laws which are strictly adhered to, so I thought that instead of the great number of precepts of which logic is composed, I would have enough with the four following ones, provided that I made a firm and unalterable resolution not to violate them even in a single instance.

The first rule was never to accept anything as true unless I recognized it to be evidently such: that is, carefully to avoid precipitation and prejudgment, and to include nothing in my conclusions unless it presented itself so clearly and distinctly to my mind that there was no occasion to doubt it.

The second was to divide each of the difficulties which I encountered into as many parts as possible, and as might be required for an easier solution.

The third was to think in an orderly fashion, beginning with the things which were simplest and easiest to understand, and gradually and by degrees reaching toward more complex knowledge, even treating as though ordered materials which were not necessarily so.

The last was always to make enumerations so complete, and reviews so general, that I would be certain that nothing was omitted. . . .

What pleased me most about this method was that it enabled me to reason in all things, if not perfectly, at least as well as was in my power. In addition, I felt that in practicing it my mind was gradually becoming accustomed to conceive its objects more clearly and distinctly. . . .

Descartes was searching for an incontrovertible truth that could serve as the first principle of philosophy. His arrival at the famous dictum "I think, therefore I am" marks the beginning of modern philosophy.

PART FOUR

. . . As I desired to devote myself wholly to the search for truth, I thought that I should . . . reject as absolutely false anything of which I could have the least doubt, in order to see whether anything would be left after this procedure which could be called wholly certain. Thus, as our senses deceive us at times, I was ready to suppose that nothing was at all the way our senses represented them to be. As there are men who make mistakes in reasoning even on the simplest topics in geometry, I judged that I was as liable to error as any other, and rejected as false all the reasoning which I had previously accepted as valid demonstration. Finally, as the same precepts which we have when awake may come to us when asleep without their being true, I decided to suppose that nothing that had ever entered my mind was more real than the illusions of my dreams. But I soon noticed that while I thus wished to think everything false, it was necessarily true that I who thought so was something. Since this truth, *I think, therefore I am*, was so firm and assured that all the most extravagant suppositions of the sceptics[1] were unable to shake it, I judged that I could safely accept it as the first principle of the philosophy I was seeking.

---

[1]The skeptics belonged to the ancient Greek philosophic school that held true knowledge to be beyond human grasp and treated all knowledge as uncertain. —Eds.

REVIEW QUESTIONS

1. Why was René Descartes critical of the learning of his day?
2. What are the implications of Descartes' famous words: "I think, therefore I am"?
3. Compare Descartes' method with the approach advocated by Francis Bacon.

---

5 The Mechanical Universe

By demonstrating that all bodies in the universe—earthly objects as well as moons, planets, and stars—obey the same laws of motion and gravitation, Sir Isaac Newton (1646–1723) completed the destruction of the medieval view of the universe. The idea that the same laws governed the movement of earthly and heavenly bodies was completely foreign to medieval thinkers, who drew a sharp division between a higher celestial world and a lower terrestrial one. In the *Principia Mathematica* (1687), Newton showed that the same forces that hold celestial bodies in their orbits around the sun make apples fall to the ground. For Newton, the universe was like a giant clock, all of whose parts obeyed strict mechanical principles and worked together in perfect precision. To Newton's contemporaries, it seemed as if mystery had been banished from the universe.

Isaac Newton
PRINCIPIA MATHEMATICA

In the first of the following passages from *Principia Mathematica*, Newton states the principle of universal law and lauds the experimental method as the means of acquiring knowledge.

RULES OF REASONING IN PHILOSOPHY

Rule I.   We are to admit no more causes of natural things than such as are both true and sufficient to explain their appearances.

To this purpose the philosophers say that Nature does nothing in vain, and more is in vain when less will serve; for Nature is pleased with simplicity, and affects not the pomp of superfluous causes.

Rule II.   Therefore to the same natural effects we must, as far as possible, assign the same causes.

As to respiration in a man and in a beast; the descent of stones [meteorites] in *Europe* and in *America*; the light of our culinary fire and of the sun; the reflection of light in the earth, and in the planets.

Rule III.   The qualities of bodies, which . . . are found to belong to all bodies within the reach of our experiments, are to be esteemed the universal qualities of all bodies whatsoever.

For since the qualities of bodies are only known to us by experiments, we are to hold for universal all such as universally agree

with experiments. . . . We are certainly not to relinquish the evidence of experiments for the sake of dreams and vain fictions of our own devising; nor are we to recede from the analogy of Nature, which [is] . . . simple, and always consonant to itself. We no other way know the extension of bodies than by our senses, nor do these reach it in all bodies; but because we perceive extension in all that are sensible, therefore, we ascribe it universally to all others also. That abundance of bodies are hard, we learn by experience; and because the hardness of the whole arises from the hardness of the parts, we, therefore, justly infer the hardness of the undivided particles not only of the bodies we feel but of all others. That all bodies are impenetrable, we gather not from reason, but from sensation. The bodies which we handle we find impenetrable, and thence, conclude impenetrability to be an universal property of all bodies whatsoever. That all bodies are moveable, and endowed with certain powers (which we call . . . {*inertia*}) of persevering in their motion, or in their rest, we only infer from the like properties observed in the bodies which we have seen. The extension, hardness, impenetrability, mobility, . . . of the whole, result from the extension, hardness, impenetrability, mobility, . . . of the parts; and thence we conclude the least particles of all bodies to be also all extended, and hard and impenetrable, and moveable, . . . And this is the foundation of all philosophy. . . .

Sir Isaac Newton, *The Mathematical Principles of Natural Philosophy*, Book III, trans. Andrew Motte (London: H. D. Symonds, 1803), II, pp. 160–162, 310–314.

Lastly, if it universally appears, by experiments and astronomical observations, that all bodies about the earth gravitate towards the earth, and that in proportion to the quantity of matter which they severally contain; that the moon likewise, according to the quantity of its matter, gravitates towards the earth; that, on the other hand, our sea gravitates towards the moon; and all the planets mutually one towards another; and the comets in like manner towards the sun; we must, in consequence of this rule, universally allow that all bodies whatsoever are endowed with a principle of mutual gravitation. . . .

Rule IV.   In experimental philosophy we are to look upon propositions collected by general induction from phenomena as accurately or very nearly true, notwithstanding any contrary hypotheses that may be imagined, till such time as other phenomena occur, by which they may either be made more accurate, or liable to exceptions.

This rule we must follow, that the argument of induction may not be evaded by hypotheses.

Newton describes further his concepts of gravity and scientific methodology.

GRAVITY

Hitherto, we have explained the phenomena of the heavens and of our sea by the power of gravity, but have not yet assigned the cause of this power. This is certain, that it must proceed from a cause that penetrates to the very centres of the sun and planets, without suffering the least diminution of its force; that operates not according to the quantity of the surfaces of the particles upon which it acts (as mechanical causes used to do) but according to the quantity of the solid matter which they contain, and propagates its virtue on all sides to immense distances, decreasing always in the duplicate portion of the distances. . . .

Hitherto I have not been able to discover the cause of those properties of gravity from the phenomena, and I frame no hypothesis; for whatever is not deduced from the phenomena is to be called an hypothesis; and hypotheses, whether metaphysical or physical, whether of occult qualities or mechanical, have no place in experimental philosophy. In this philosophy particular propositions are inferred from the phenomena, and afterward rendered general by induction. Thus it was the impenetrability, the mobility, and the impulsive forces of bodies, and the laws of motion and of gravitation were discovered. And to us it is enough that gravity does really exist, and acts according to the laws which we have explained, and abundantly serves to account for all the motions of the celestial bodies, and of our sea.

A devout Anglican, Newton believed that God had created this superbly organized universe.

GOD AND THE UNIVERSE

This most beautiful system of the sun, planets, and comets could only proceed from the counsel and dominion of an intelligent and powerful Being. And if the fixed stars are the centers of other like systems, these, being formed by the like wise counsel, must be all subject to the dominion of One, especially since the light of the fixed stars is of the same nature with the light of the sun and from every system light passes into all the other systems; and lest the systems of the fixed stars should, by their gravity, fall on each other mutually, he hath placed those systems at immense distances from one another.

This Being governs all things not as the soul of the world, but as Lord over all; and on account of his dominion he is wont to be called "Lord God" . . . or "Universal Ruler." . . . It is the dominion of a spiritual being which constitutes a God. . . . And from his true dominion it follows that the true God is a living, intelligent and powerful Being. . . . he governs all things, and knows all things that are or can be done. . . . He endures for ever, and is every where present; and by existing always and every where, he constitutes duration and space. . . .

In him are all things contained and moved; yet neither affects the other: God suffers nothing from the motion of bodies; bodies find no resistance from the omnipresence of God. . . . As a blind man has no idea of colors so we have no idea of the manner by which the all-wise God preserves and understands all things. He is utterly void of all body and bodily figure, and can therefore neither be seen, nor heard, nor touched; nor ought to be worshipped under the representation of any corporeal thing. We have ideas of his attributes, but what the real substance of any thing is we know not. . . . Much less, then, have we any idea of the substance of God. We know him only by his most wise and excellent contrivances of things. . . . [W]e reverence and adore him as his servants; and a god without dominion, providence, and final causes, is nothing else but Fate and Nature. Blind metaphysical necessity, which is certainly the same always and everywhere, could produce no variety of things. All that diversity of natural things which we find suited to different times and places could arise from nothing but the ideas and will of a Being necessarily existing. . . . And thus much concerning God; to discourse of whom from the appearances of things does certainly belong to Natural Philosophy.

REVIEW QUESTIONS

1. What did Isaac Newton mean by universal law? What examples of universal law did he provide?
2. What method for investigating nature did Newton advocate?
3. Summarize Newton's arguments for God's existence.
4. For Newton, what is God's relationship to the universe?

6 The Limitations of Science

Most seventeenth- and eighteenth-century thinkers regarded the discoveries of Newton and others as a great triumph for civilization. These discoveries uncovered nature's mysteries, provided a method for exploring nature further, and demonstated the capacity of the human mind.

In later centuries, further implications of the new cosmology caused great anguish. The conviction that God had created the universe for them, that the earth was fixed beneath their feet, and that God had given the earth the central position in his creation had brought medieval people a profound sense of security. They knew why they were here, and they never doubted that heaven was the final resting place for the faithful. Copernican astronomy dethroned the earth, expelled human beings from their central position, and implied an infinite universe. In the sixteenth and seventeenth centuries, few thinkers grasped the full significance of this displacement. However, in succeeding centuries, this radical cosmological transformation proved as traumatic for the modern mind as did Adam and Eve's expulsion from the Garden of Eden for the medieval mind. Today we know that the earth is one of billions and billions of celestial bodies, a tiny speck in an endless cosmic ocean, and that the universe is some twelve billion years old. Could such a universe have been created just for human beings? Could it contain a heaven that assures eternal life for the faithful and a hell with eternal fires and torments for sinners?

Blaise Pascal
PENSÉES

Few people at the time were aware of the full implications of the new cosmology. One who did understand was Blaise Pascal (1623–1662), a French scientist and mathematician. A devout Catholic, Pascal was frightened by what he called "the eternal silence of these infinite spaces" and realized that the new science could stir doubt, uncertainty, and anxiety, which threatened belief—as the following excerpts from his *Pensées* illustrate.

67.   *The vanity of the sciences.*—Physical science will not console me for the ignorance of morality in the time of affliction. But the science of ethics will always console me for the ignorance of the physical sciences.

76.   To write against those who made too profound a study of science: Descartes.

77.   I cannot forgive Descartes. In all his philosophy he would have been quite willing to dispense with God. But he had to make Him give a fillip to set the world in motion; beyond this he has no further need of God.

83.   *We must thus begin the chapter on the deceptive powers.* Man is only a subject full of error, natural and ineffaceable, without grace. Nothing shows him the truth. Everything deceives him. These two sources of truth, reason and the senses, besides being both wanting in sincerity, deceive each other in turn. The senses mislead the reason with false appearances, and receive from reason in their turn the same trickery which they apply to her; reason has her revenge. The passions of the soul trouble the senses, and

make false impressions upon them. They rival each other in falsehood and deception.

194.   I see those frightful spaces of the universe which surround me, and I find myself tied to one corner of this vast expanse, without knowing why I am put in this place rather than in another, nor why the short time which is given me to live is assigned to me at this point rather than at another of the whole eternity which was before me or which shall come after me. I see nothing but infinites on all sides, which surround me as an atom, and as a shadow which endures only for an instant and returns no more. All I know is that I must soon die, but what I know least is this very death which I cannot escape.

205.   When I consider the short duration of my life, swallowed up in the eternity before and after, the little space which I fill, and even can see, engulfed in the infinite immensity of spaces of which I am ignorant, and which know me not, I am frightened, and am astonished at being here rather than there; for there is no reason why here rather than there, why now rather than then. Who has put me here? By whose order and direction have this place and time been allotted to me?

206.   The eternal silence of these infinite spaces frightens me.

Pascal's Pensées, introduction by T. S. Eliot (New York: E. P. Dutton & Co., 1958), pp. 15, 23, 27, 55, 61.

REVIEW QUESTIONS

1. What was Pascal's reaction to the new directions in science?
2. In today's world, what developments in science and technology cause great concern?

CHAPTER 13

The Enlightenment

Isaac Newton and Voltaire, frontispiece to *Elémens de la philosophie de Neuton*, Voltaire's interpretation of Newton's work, 1738. The philosophe sits translating the inspired work of Newton; Voltaire's manuscript is illuminated by seemingly divine light coming from Newton himself, reflected down to Voltaire by a muse, representing Voltaire's lover Émilie du Châtelet—who actually translated Newton and collaborated with Voltaire to make sense of Newton's work. *(Marie Arouet de Voltaire)*

The Enlightenment of the eighteenth century culminated the movement toward modernity that started in the Renaissance era. The thinkers of the Enlightenment, called *philosophes*, attacked medieval otherworldliness, dethroned theology from its once-proud position as queen of the sciences, and based their understanding of nature and society on reason alone, unaided by revelation or priestly authority.

From the broad spectrum of Western history, several traditions flowed into the Enlightenment: the rational spirit born in classical Greece, the Stoic emphasis on natural law that applies to all human beings, and the Christian belief that all individuals are equal in God's eyes. A more immediate influence on the Enlightenment was Renaissance humanism, which focused on the individual and worldly human accomplishments and which criticized medieval theology-philosophy for its preoccupation with questions that seemed unrelated to the human condition. In many ways, the Enlightenment grew directly out of the Scientific Revolution. The philosophes praised both Newton's discovery of the mechanical laws that govern the universe and the scientific method that made this discovery possible. They wanted to transfer the scientific method—the reliance on experience and the critical use of the intellect—to the realm of society. They maintained that independent of clerical authority, human beings through reason could grasp the natural laws that govern the social world, just as Newton had uncovered the laws of nature that operate in the physical world. The philosophes said that those institutions and traditions that could not meet the test of reason, because they were based on authority, ignorance, or superstition, had to be reformed or dispensed with.

For medieval philosophers, reason had been subordinate to revelation; the Christian outlook determined the medieval concept of nature, morality, government, law, and life's purpose. During the Renaissance and Scientific Revolution, reason increasingly asserted its autonomy. For example, Machiavelli rejected the principle that politics should be based on Christian teachings; he recognized no higher world as the source of a higher truth. Galileo held that on questions regarding nature, one should trust to observation, experimentation, and mathematical reasoning and should not rely on scripture. Descartes rejected reliance on past authority and maintained that through thought alone one could attain knowledge that has absolute certainty. Agreeing with Descartes that the mind is self-sufficient, the philosophes rejected the guidance of revelation and its priestly interpreters. They believed that through the use of reason, individuals could comprehend and reform society.

The Enlightenment philosophes articulated basic principles of the modern outlook: confidence in the self-sufficiency of the human mind, belief that individuals possess natural rights that governments should not violate, and the desire to reform society in accordance with rational principles. Their views influenced the reformers of the French Revolution, the Founding Fathers of the United States, and modern liberalism.

1 The Enlightenment Outlook

The critical use of the intellect was the central principle of the Enlightenment. The philosophes rejected beliefs and traditions that seemed to conflict with reason and attacked clerical and political authorities for interfering with the free use of the intellect.

Immanuel Kant
"WHAT IS ENLIGHTENMENT?"

The German philosopher Immanuel Kant (1724–1804) is a giant in the history of modern philosophy. Several twentieth-century philosophic movements have their origins in Kantian thought, and many issues raised by Kant still retain their importance. For example, in *Metaphysical Foundations of Morals* (1785), Kant set forth the categorical imperative that remains a crucial principle in moral philosophy. Kant asserted that when confronted with a moral choice, people should ask themselves: "Canst thou also will that thy maxim should be a universal law?" By this, Kant meant that people should ponder whether they would want the moral principle underlying their action to be elevated to a universal law that would govern others in similar circumstances. If they concluded that it should not, then the maxim should be rejected and the action avoided.

Kant valued the essential ideals of the Enlightenment and viewed the French Revolution, which put these ideals into law, as the triumph of liberty over despotism. In an essay entitled "What Is Enlightenment?" (1784), he contended that the Enlightenment marked a new way of thinking and eloquently affirmed the Enlightenment's confidence in and commitment to reason.

Enlightenment is man's leaving his self-caused immaturity. Immaturity is the incapacity to use one's intelligence without the guidance of another. Such immaturity is self-caused if it is not caused by lack of intelligence, but by lack of determination and courage to use one's intelligence without being guided by another. *Sapere Aude!* [Dare to know!] Have the courage to use your own intelligence! is therefore the motto of the enlightenment.

Through laziness and cowardice a large part of mankind, even after nature has freed them from alien guidance, gladly remain immature. It is because of laziness and cowardice that it is so easy for others to usurp the role of guardians. It is so comfortable to be a minor! If I have a book which provides meaning for me, a pastor who has conscience for me, a doctor who will judge my diet for me and so on, then I do not need to exert myself. I do not have any need to think; if I can pay, others will take over the tedious job for me. The guardians who have kindly undertaken the supervision will see to it that by far the largest part of mankind, including the entire "beautiful sex," should consider the step into maturity, not only as difficult but as very dangerous.

Immanuel Kant, *The Philosophy of Kant*, trans. Carl Friedrich. Copyright © 1949 by Random House, Inc. Used by permission of Random House, Inc.

After having made their domestic animals dumb and having carefully prevented these quiet creatures from daring to take any step beyond the lead-strings to which they have fastened them, these guardians then show them the danger which threatens them, should they attempt to walk alone. Now this danger is not really so very great; for they would presumably learn to walk after some stumbling. However, an example of this kind intimidates and frightens people out of all further attempts.

It is difficult for the isolated individual to work himself out of the immaturity which has become almost natural for him. He has even become fond of it and for the time being is incapable of employing his own intelligence, because he has never been allowed to make the attempt. Statutes and formulas, these mechanical tools of a serviceable use, or rather misuse, of his natural faculties, are the ankle-chains of a continuous immaturity. Whoever threw it off would make an uncertain jump over the smallest trench because he is not accustomed to such free movement. Therefore there are only a few who have pursued a firm path and have succeeded in escaping from immaturity by their own cultivation of the mind.

But it is more nearly possible for a public to enlighten itself: this is even inescapable if only the public is given its freedom. For there will always be some people who think for themselves, even among the self-appointed guardians of the great mass who, after having thrown off the yoke of immaturity themselves, will spread about them the spirit of a reasonable estimate of their own value and of the need for every man to think for himself. . . . [A] public can only arrive at enlightenment slowly. Through revolution, the abandonment of personal despotism may be engendered and the end of profit-seeking and domineering oppression may occur, but never a true reform of the state of mind. Instead, new prejudices, just like the old ones, will serve as the guiding reins of the great, unthinking mass. . . .

All that is required for this enlightenment is *freedom*; and particularly the least harmful of all that may be called freedom, namely, the freedom for man to make *public use* of his reason in all matters. But I hear people clamor on all sides: Don't argue! The officer says: Don't argue, drill! The tax collector: Don't argue, pay! The pastor: Don't argue, believe! . . . Here we have restrictions on freedom everywhere. Which restriction is hampering enlightenment, and which does not, or even promotes it? I answer: The *public use* of a man's reason must be free at all times, and this alone can bring enlightenment among men. . . .

I mean by the public use of one's reason, the use which a scholar makes of it before the entire reading public. . . .

The question may now be put: Do we live at present in an enlightened age? The answer is: No, but in an age of enlightenment. Much still prevents men from being placed in a position. . . to use their own minds securely and well in matters of religion. But we do have very definite indications that this field of endeavor is being opened up for men to work freely and reduce gradually the hindrances preventing a general enlightenment and an escape from self-caused immaturity.

REVIEW QUESTIONS

1. What did Immanuel Kant mean by the terms *enlightenment* and *freedom?*
2. In Kant's view, what factors delayed the progress of human enlightenment?
3. What are the political implications of Kant's views?

2   Political Liberty

John Locke (1632–1704), a British statesman, philosopher, and political theorist, was a principal source of the Enlightenment. Eighteenth-century thinkers were particularly influenced by Locke's advocacy of religious toleration, his reliance on experience as the source of knowledge, and his concern for liberty. In his first *Letter Concerning Toleration* (1689), Locke declared that Christians who persecute others in the name of religion vitiate Christ's teachings. Locke's political philosophy as formulated in the *Two Treatises on Government* (1690) complements his theory of knowledge (see page 435); both were rational and secular attempts to understand and improve the human condition. The Lockean spirit pervades the American Declaration of Independence and the U.S. Constitution and Bill of Rights; it is the basis of the liberal tradition that aims to protect individual liberty from despotic state authority.

Viewing human beings as brutish and selfish, Thomas Hobbes (see page 393) in *Leviathan* (1651) had prescribed a state with unlimited power; only in this way, he said, could people be protected from each other and civilized life preserved. Locke, regarding people as essentially good and humane, developed a conception of the state differing fundamentally from Hobbes'. Locke held that human beings are born with natural rights of life, liberty, and property; they establish the state to protect these rights. Consequently, neither executive nor legislature, neither king nor assembly has the authority to deprive individuals of their natural rights. Whereas Hobbes justified absolute monarchy, Locke explicitly endorsed constitutional government in which the power to govern derives from the consent of the governed and the state's authority is limited by agreement.

John Locke
SECOND TREATISE ON GOVERNMENT

Locke said that originally, in establishing a government, human beings had never agreed to surrender their natural rights to any state authority. The state's founders intended the new polity to preserve these natural rights and to implement the people's will. Therefore, as the following passage from Locke's *Second Treatise on Government* illustrates, the power exercised by magistrates cannot be absolute or arbitrary.

. . . *Political power* is that power, which every man having in the state of nature, has given up into the hands of the society, and therein to the governors, whom the society hath set over itself, with this express or tacit trust, that it shall be employed for their good, and the preservation of their property: now this *power*, which every man has *in the state of nature*, and which he parts with to the society in all such cases where the society can secure him, is to use such means, for the preserving of his own property, as he thinks good, and nature allows him; and to punish the breach

John Locke, *Two Treatises on Civil Government* (London: 1688, 7th reprinting by J. Whiston et al., 1772), pp. 292, 315–316, 354–355, 358–359, 361–362.

of the law of nature in others, so as (according to the best of his reason) may most conduce to the preservation of himself, and the rest of mankind. So that the *end and measure of this power*, when in every man's hands in the state of nature, being the preservation of all of his society, that is, all mankind in general, it can have no other *end or measure*, when in the hands of the magistrate, but to preserve the members of that society in their lives, liberties, and possessions; and so cannot be an absolute, arbitrary power over their lives and fortunes, which are as much as possible to be preserved; but a *power to make laws*, and annex such *penalties* to them, as may tend to the preservation of the whole, by cutting off those parts, and those only, which are so corrupt, that they threaten the sound and healthy, without which no severity is lawful. And this *power has its original only from compact*, and agreement, and the mutual consent of those who make up the community. . . .

These are the *bounds*, which the trust, that is put in them by the society, and the law of God and nature, have *set to the legislative* power of every common-wealth, in all forms of government.

First, They are to govern by *promulgated established laws*, not to be varied in particular cases, but to have one rule for rich and poor, for the favourite at court, and the country man at plough.

Secondly, These *laws* also ought to be designed *for* no other end ultimately, but *the good of the people.*

Thirdly, They must *not raise taxes* on the *property of the people, without the consent of the people,* given by themselves, or their deputies. And this properly concerns only such governments, where the *legislative* is always in being, or at least where the people have not reserved any part of the legislative to deputies, to be from time to time chosen by themselves.

Fourthly, The *legislative* neither must *nor can transfer the power of making laws* to any body else, or place it any where, but where the people have. . . .

If government fails to fulfill the end for which it was established—the preservation of the individual's right to life, liberty,

and property—the people have a right to dissolve that government.

. . . The *legislative acts against the trust* reposed in them, when they endeavour to invade the property of the subject, and to make themselves, or any part of the community, masters, or arbitrary disposers of the lives, liberties, or fortunes of the people.

The reason why men enter into society, is the preservation of their property; and the end why they chuse and authorize a legislative, is, that there may be laws made, and rules set, as guards and fences to the properties of all the members of the society, to limit the power, and moderate the dominion of every part and member of the society: for since it can never be supposed to be the will of the society, that the legislative should have a power to destroy that which every one designs to secure, by entering into society, and for which the people submitted themselves to legislators of their own making; whenever the *legislators endeavour to take away, and destroy the property of the people*, or to reduce them to slavery under arbitrary power, they put themselves into a state of war with the people, who are thereupon absolved from any farther obedience, and are left to the common refuge, which God hath provided for all men, against force and violence. Whensoever therefore the *legislative* shall transgress this fundamental rule of society; and either by ambition, fear, folly or corruption, *endeavour to grasp* themselves, *or put into the hands of any other, an absolute power* over the lives, liberties, and estates of the people; by this breach of trust they *forfeit the power* the people had put into their hands for quite contrary ends, and it devolves to the people, who have a right to resume their original liberty, and, by the establishment of a new legislative, (such as they shall think fit) provide for their own safety and security, which is the end for which they are in society. What I have said here, concerning the legislative in general, holds true also concerning the supreme executor, who having a double trust put in him, both to have a part in the legislative, and the supreme execution of the law, acts against both, when he goes about to set up his own arbitrary will as the law of the society. He *acts* also *contrary to his trust*, when he either employs the force, treasure, and offices of the society, to corrupt the *representatives*, and gain them to his purposes; or openly pre-engages the *electors,* and prescribes to their choice, such, whom he has, by sollicitations, threats, promises, or otherwise, won to his designs; and employs them to bring in such, who have promised beforehand what to vote, and what to enact. . . .

Locke responds to the charge that his theory will produce "frequent rebellion." Indeed, says Locke, the true rebels are the magistrates who, acting contrary to the trust granted them, violate the people's rights.

. . . Such *revolutions happen* not upon every little mismanagement in public affairs. *Great mistakes* in the ruling part, many wrong and inconvenient laws, and all the *slips* of human frailty, will be *borne by the people* without mutiny or murmur. But if a long train of abuses, prevarications and artifices, all tending the same way, make the design visible to the people, and they cannot but feel what they lie under, and see whither they are going; it is not to be wondered at, that they should then rouze themselves, and endeavour to put the rule into such hands which may secure to them the ends for which government was at first erected. . . .

. . . I answer, that *this doctrine* of a power in the people of providing for their safety a-new, by a new legislative, when their legislators have acted contrary to their trust, by invading their property, is *the best defence against rebellion*, and the probablest means to hinder it: for *rebellion* being an opposition, not to persons, but authority, which is founded only in the constitutions and laws of the government; those, whoever they be, who by force break through, and by force justify their violation of them, are truly and properly *rebels*: for when men, by entering into society and civil government, have excluded force, and introduced laws for the preservation of property, peace, and unity amongst themselves, those who set up force again in opposition to the laws, do [rebel], that is, bring back again the state of war, and are properly rebels: which they who are in power, (by the pretence they have to authority, the temptation of force they have in their hands, and the flattery of those about them) being likeliest to do; the properest way to prevent the evil, is to shew them the danger and injustice of it, who are under the greatest temptation to run into it.

The end of government is the good of mankind; and which is *best for mankind*, that the people should always be exposed to the boundless will of tyranny, or that the rulers should be sometimes liable to be opposed, when they grow exorbitant in the use of their power, and employ it for the destruction, and not the preservation of the properties of their people?

Thomas Jefferson
DECLARATION OF INDEPENDENCE

Written in 1776 by Thomas Jefferson (1743–1826) to justify the American colonists' break with Britain, the Declaration of Independence enumerated principles that were quite familiar to English statesmen and intellectuals. The preamble to the Declaration, excerpted below, articulated clearly Locke's philosophy of natural rights. Locke had viewed life, liberty, and property as the individual's essential natural rights; Jefferson substituted the "pursuit of happiness" for property.

A DECLARATION BY THE REPRESENTATIVES OF THE UNITED STATES OF AMERICA, IN GENERAL CONGRESS ASSEMBLED

When in the Course of human Events, it becomes necessary for one People to dissolve the Political Bands which have connected them with another, and to assume among the Powers of the Earth, the separate and equal Station to which the Laws of Nature and of Nature's God entitle them, a decent Respect to the Opinions of Mankind requires that they should declare the causes which impel them to the Separation.

We hold these Truths to be self-evident, that all Men are created equal, that they are endowed by their Creator with certain unalienable Rights, that among these are Life, Liberty, and the Pursuit of Happiness—That to secure these Rights, Governments are instituted among Men, deriving their just Powers from the Consent of the Governed, That whenever any Form

of Government becomes destructive of these Ends, it is the Right of the People to alter or to abolish it, and to institute new Government, laying its Foundation on such Principles, and organizing its Powers in such Form, as to them shall seem most likely to effect their Safety and Happiness. Prudence, indeed, will dictate that Governments long established should not be changed for light and transient Causes; and accordingly all Experience hath shewn, that Mankind are more disposed to suffer, while Evils are sufferable, than to right themselves by abolishing the Forms to which they are accustomed. But when a long Train of Abuses and Usurpations, pursuing invariably the same Object, evinces a Design to reduce them under absolute Despotism, it is their right, it is their duty, to throw off such Government, and to provide new Guards for their future Security. Such has been the patient Sufferance of these Colonies; and such is now the Necessity which constrains them to alter their former Systems of Government. The History of the present King of Great-Britain is a History of repeated Injuries and Usurpations, all having in direct Object the Establishment of an absolute Tyranny over these States. . . .

First printing of the Declaration of Independence, July 4, 1776, Papers of the Continental Congress No. 1, Rough Journal of Congress, III.

REVIEW QUESTIONS

1. Compare the views of John Locke with those of Thomas Hobbes regarding the character of human nature, political authority, and the right to rebellion.
2. Compare Locke's theory of natural rights with the principles stated in the American Declaration of Independence.

---

3 Attack on Religion

Christianity came under severe attack during the eighteenth century. The philosophes rejected Christian doctrines that seemed contrary to reason. Deism, the dominant religious outlook of the philosophes, taught that religion should accord with reason and natural law. To deists, it seemed reasonable to believe in God, for this superbly constructed universe required a creator in the same manner that a watch required a watchmaker. But, said the deists, after God had constructed the universe, he did not interfere in its operations; the universe was governed by mechanical laws. Deists denied that the Bible was God's work, rejected clerical authority, and dismissed miracles—like Jesus walking on water—as incompatible with natural law. To them, Jesus was not divine but an inspired teacher of morality. Many deists still considered themselves Christians; the clergy, however, viewed the deists' religious views with horror.

Voltaire
A PLEA FOR TOLERANCE AND REASON

François Marie Arouet (1694–1778), known to the world as Voltaire, was the recognized leader of the French Enlightenment. Few of the philosophes had a better mind, and none had a sharper wit. A relentless critic of the Old Regime (the social structure in prerevolutionary France), Voltaire attacked superstition, religious fanaticism and persecution, censorship, and other abuses of eighteenth-century French society. Spending more than two years in Great Britain, Voltaire acquired a great admiration for English liberty, toleration, commerce, and science. In *Letters Concerning the English Nation* (1733), he drew unfavorable comparisons between a progressive Britain and a reactionary France.

Voltaire's angriest words were directed against established Christianity, to which he attributed many of the ills of modern society. Voltaire regarded Christianity as "the Christ-worshiping superstition" that someday would be destroyed "by the weapons of reason." He rejected revelation and the church hierarchy and was repulsed by Christian intolerance, but he accepted Christian morality and believed in God as the prime mover who set the universe in motion.

The following passages compiled from Voltaire's works—grouped according to topic—provide insight into the outlook of the philosophes. The excerpts come from sources that include his *Treatise on Tolerance* (1763), *The Philosophical Dictionary* (1764), and *Commentary on the Book of Crime and Punishments* (1766).

TOLERANCE

It does not require any great art or studied elocution to prove that Christians ought to tolerate one another. I will go even further and say that we ought to look upon all men as our brothers. What! call a Turk, a Jew, and a Siamese, my brother? Yes, of course; for are we not all children of the same father, and the creatures of the same God?

———

What is tolerance? . . . We are all full of weakness and errors; let us mutually pardon our follies. This is the last law of nature. . . .

It is clear that every private individual who persecutes a man, his brother, because he is not of the same opinion, is a monster. . . .

Of all religions, the Christian ought doubtless to inspire the most tolerance, although hitherto the Christians have been the most intolerant of all men.

———

. . . Tolerance has never brought civil war; intolerance has covered the earth with carnage. . . .

What! Is each citizen to be permitted to believe and to think that which his reason

———

Voltaire, *Candide and Other Writings*, ed. Haskell M. Block, pp. 368, 374–375, 385, 406–407, 428–429, 441, 443–444, 525. (Random House, 1956).

———

The section above that begins ". . .Tolerance has never brought. . ." is from E. L. Higgins, ed., *The French Revolution As Told By Contemporaries* (Boston: Houghton Mifflin, 1938), pp. 35–36. All other sections in this reading are from the Block text referenced at left. —Eds.

rightly or wrongly dictates? He should indeed, provided that he does not disturb the public order; for it is not contingent on man to believe or not to believe; but it is contingent on him to respect the usages of his country; and if you say that it is a crime not to believe in the dominant religion, you accuse then yourself the first Christians, your ancestors, and you justify those whom you accuse of having martyred them.

You reply that there is a great difference, that all religions are the work of men, and that the Apostolic Roman Catholic Church is alone the work of God. But in good faith, ought our religion because it is divine reign through hate, violence, exiles, usurpation of property, prisons, tortures, murders, and thanksgivings to God for these murders? The more the Christian religion is divine, the less it pertains to man to require it; if God made it, God will sustain it without you. You know that intolerance produces only hypocrites or rebels; what distressing alternatives! In short, do you want to sustain through executioners the religion of a God whom executioners have put to death and who taught only gentleness and patience?

———

I shall never cease, my dear sir, to preach tolerance from the housetops, despite the complaints of your priests and the outcries of ours, until persecution is no more. The progress of reason is slow, the roots of prejudice lie deep. Doubtless, I shall never see the fruits of my efforts, but they are seeds which may one day germinate.

DOGMA

. . . Is Jesus the Word? If He be the Word, did He emanate from God in time or before time? If He emanated from God, is He co-eternal and consubstantial with Him, or is He of a similar substance? Is He distinct from Him, or is He not? Is He made or begotten? Can He beget in His turn? Has He paternity? or productive virtue without paternity? Is the Holy Ghost made? or begotten? or produced? or proceeding from the Father? or proceeding from the Son? or proceeding from both? Can He beget? can He produce? is His hypostasis consubstantial with the hypostasis of the Father and

the Son? and how is it that, having the same nature—the same essence as the Father and the Son, He cannot do the same things done by these persons who are Himself?

Assuredly, I understand nothing of this; no one has ever understood any of it, and that is why we have slaughtered one another.

The Christians tricked, cavilled, hated, and excommunicated one another, for some of these dogmas inaccessible to human intellect.

FANATICISM

Fanaticism is to superstition what delirium is to fever, what rage is to anger. He who has ecstasies and visions, who takes dreams for realities, and his own imaginations for prophecies is an enthusiast; he who reinforces his madness by murder is a fanatic. . . .

The most detestable example of fanaticism is that exhibited on the night of St. Bartholomew,[1] when the people of Paris rushed from house to house to stab, slaughter, throw out of the window, and tear in pieces their fellow citizens who did not go to mass.

There are some cold-blooded fanatics; such as those judges who sentence men to death for no other crime than that of thinking differently from themselves. . . .

Once fanaticism has infected a brain, the disease is almost incurable. I have seen convulsionaries who, while speaking of the miracles of Saint Paris [a fourth-century Italian bishop], gradually grew heated in spite of themselves. Their eyes became inflamed, their limbs shook, fury disfigured their face, and they would have killed anyone who contradicted them.

There is no other remedy for this epidemic malady than that philosophical spirit which, extending itself from one to another, at length softens the manners of men and prevents the access of the disease. For when the disorder has made any progress, we should, without loss of time, flee from it, and wait till the air has become purified.

———

[1]"St. Bartholomew" refers to the day of August 24, 1572, when the populace of Paris, instigated by King Charles IX at his mother's urging, began a week-long slaughter of Protestants. —Eds.

PERSECUTION

What is a persecutor? He whose wounded pride and furious fanaticism arouse princes and magistrates against innocent men, whose only crime is that of being of a different opinion. "Impudent man! you have worshipped God; you have preached and practiced virtue; you have served man; you have protected the orphan, have helped the poor; you have changed deserts, in which slaves dragged on a miserable existence, into fertile lands peopled by happy families; but I have discovered that you despise me, and have never read my controversial work. You know that I am a rogue; that I have forged G[od]'s signature, that I have stolen. You might tell these things; I must anticipate you. I will, therefore, go to the confessor [spiritual counselor] of the prime minister, or the magistrate; I will show them, with outstretched neck and twisted mouth, that you hold an erroneous opinion in relation to the cells in which the Septuagint was studied; that you have even spoken disrespectfully ten years ago of Tobit's dog,[2] which you asserted to have been a spaniel, while I proved that it was a greyhound. I will denounce you as the enemy of God and man!" Such is the language of the persecutor; and if precisely these words do not issue from his lips, they are engraven on his heart with the pointed steel of fanaticism steeped in the bitterness of envy. . . .

O God of mercy! If any man can resemble that evil being who is described as ceaselessly employed in the destruction of your works, is it not the persecutor?

SUPERSTITION

In 1749 a woman was burned in the Bishopric of Würzburg [a city in central Germany], convicted of being a witch. This is an extraordinary phe-

nomenon in the age in which we live. Is it possible that people who boast of their reformation and of trampling superstition under foot, who indeed supposed that they had reached the perfection of reason, could nevertheless believe in witchcraft, and this more than a hundred years after the so-called reformation of their reason?

In 1652 a peasant woman named Michelle Chaudron, living in the little territory of Geneva [a major city in Switzerland], met the devil going out of the city. The devil gave her a kiss, received her homage, and imprinted on her upper lip and right breast the mark that he customarily bestows on all whom he recognizes as his favorites. This seal of the devil is a little mark which makes the skin insensitive, as all the demonographical jurists of those times affirm.

The devil ordered Michelle Chaudron to bewitch two girls. She obeyed her master punctually. The girls' parents accused her of witchcraft before the law. The girls were questioned and confronted with the accused. They declared that they felt a continual pricking in certain parts of their bodies and that they were possessed. Doctors were called, or at least, those who passed for doctors at that time. They examined the girls. They looked for the devil's seal on Michelle's body—what the statement of the case called *satanic marks.* Into them they drove a long needle, already a painful torture. Blood flowed out, and Michelle made it known, by her cries, that satanic marks certainly do not make one insensitive. The judges, seeing no definite proof that Michelle Chaudron was a witch, proceeded to torture her, a method that infallibly produces the necessary proofs: this wretched woman, yielding to the violence of torture, at last confessed every thing they desired.

The doctors again looked for the satanic mark. They found a little black spot on one of her thighs. They drove in the needle. The torment of the torture had been so horrible that the poor creature hardly felt the needle; thus the crime was established. But as customs were becoming somewhat mild at that time, she was burned only after being hanged and strangled.

---

[2]The Septuagint, the version of the Hebrew scriptures used by Saint Paul and other early Christians, was a Greek translation done by Hellenized Jews in Alexandria sometime in the late third or the second century B.C. *Tobit's dog* appears in the book of Tobit, a Hebrew book contained in the Catholic version of the Bible. —Eds.

In those days every tribunal of Christian Europe resounded with similar arrests. The [twigs] were lit everywhere for witches, as for heretics. People reproached the Turks most for having neither witches nor demons among them. This absence of demons was considered an infallible proof of the falseness of a religion.

A zealous friend of public welfare, of humanity, of true religion, has stated in one of his writings on behalf of innocence, that Christian tribunals have condemned to death over a hundred thousand accused witches. If to these judicial murders are added the infinitely superior number of massacred heretics, that part of the world will seem to be nothing but a vast scaffold covered with torturers and victims, surrounded by judges, guards and spectators.

Thomas Paine
THE AGE OF REASON

Exemplifying the deist outlook was Thomas Paine (1737–1809), an Englishman who moved to America in 1774. Paine's *Common Sense* (1776) was an eloquent appeal for American independence. Paine is also famous for *The Rights of Man* (1791–1792), in which he defended the French Revolution. In *The Age of Reason* (1794–1796), he denounced Christian mysteries, miracles, and prophecies as superstition and called for a natural religion that accorded with reason and science.

I believe in one God, and no more; and I hope for happiness beyond this life.

I believe in the equality of man; and I believe that religious duties consist in doing justice, loving mercy, and endeavoring to make our fellow-creatures happy.

But, lest it should be supposed that I believe many other things in addition to these, I shall, in the progress of this work, declare the things I do not believe, and my reasons for not believing them.

I do not believe in the creed professed by the Jewish church, by the Roman church, by the Greek church, by the Turkish church, by the Protestant church, nor by any church that I know of. My own mind is my own church. . . .

When Moses told the children of Israel that he received the two tablets of the [Ten] commandments from the hands of God, they were not obliged to believe him, because they had no other authority for it than his telling them so; and I have no other authority for it than some historian telling me so. The commandments carry no internal evidence of divinity with them; they contain some good moral precepts, such as any man qualified to be a lawgiver, or a legislator, could produce himself, without having recourse to supernatural intervention. . . .

When also I am told that a woman called the Virgin Mary, said, or gave out, that she was with child without any cohabitation with a man, and that her betrothed husband, Joseph, said that an angel told him so, I have a right to believe them or not; such a circumstance required a much stronger evidence than their bare word for it; but we have not even this—for neither Joseph nor Mary wrote any such matter themselves; it is only reported by others that *they said so*—it is hearsay upon hearsay, and I do not choose to rest my belief upon such evidence.

Thomas Paine, *Age of Reason Being an Investigation of the True and Fabulous Theology* (New York: Peter Eckler, 1892), pp. 5–11.

It is, however, not difficult to account for the credit that was given to the story of Jesus Christ being the son of God. He was born when the heathen mythology had still some fashion and repute in the world, and that mythology had prepared the people for the belief of such a story. Almost all the extraordinary men that lived under the heathen mythology were reputed to be the sons of some of their gods. It was not a new thing, at that time, to believe a man to have been celestially begotten; the intercourse of gods with women was then a matter of familiar opinion. Their Jupiter [chief Roman god], according to their accounts, had cohabited with hundreds: the story, therefore, had nothing in it either new, wonderful, or obscene; it was conformable to the opinions that then prevailed among the people called Gentiles, or Mythologists, and it was those people only that believed it. The Jews who had kept strictly to the belief of one God, and no more, and who had always rejected the heathen mythology, never credited the story. . . .

Nothing that is here said can apply, even with the most distant disrespect, to the real character of Jesus Christ. He was a virtuous and an amiable man. The morality that he preached and practised was of the most benevolent kind; and though similar systems of morality had been preached by Confucius [Chinese philosopher], and by some of the Greek philosophers, many years before; by the Quakers [members of the Society of Friends] since; and by many good men in all ages, it has not been exceeded by any. . . .

. . . The resurrection and ascension [of Jesus Christ], supposing them to have taken place, admitted of public and ocular demonstration, like that of the ascension of a balloon, or the sun at noon-day, to all Jerusalem at least. A thing which everybody is required to believe, requires that the proof and evidence of it should be equal to all, and universal; and as the public visibility of this last related act was the only evidence that could give sanction to the former part, the whole of it falls to the ground, because that evidence never was given. Instead of this, a small number of persons, not more than eight or nine, are introduced as proxies for the whole world, to say they saw it, and all the rest of the world are called upon to believe it. But it appears that Thomas [one of Jesus' disciples] did not believe the resurrection, and, as they say, would not believe without having ocular and manual demonstration himself. *So neither will I*, and the reason is equally as good for me, and for every other person, as for Thomas.

It is in vain to attempt to palliate or disguise this matter. The story, so far as relates to the supernatural part, has every mark of fraud and imposition stamped upon the face of it. Who were the authors of it is as impossible for us now to know, as it is for us to be assured that the books in which the account is related were written by the persons whose names they bear; the best surviving evidence we now have respecting this affair is the Jews. They are regularly descended from the people who lived in the times this resurrection and ascension is said to have happened, and they say, *it is not true*.

REVIEW QUESTIONS

1. What arguments did Voltaire offer in favor of religious toleration?
2. Why did Voltaire ridicule Christian theological disputation?
3. What did Voltaire mean by the term *fanaticism*? What examples did he provide? How was it to be cured?
4. What Christian beliefs did Thomas Paine reject? Why?

4 Epistemology

The philosophes sought a naturalistic understanding of the human condition, one that examined human nature and society without reference to God's will. Toward this end, they sought to explain how the mind acquires knowledge; and as reformers, they stressed the importance of education in shaping a better person and a better society.

John Locke
ESSAY CONCERNING HUMAN UNDERSTANDING

In his *Essay Concerning Human Understanding* (1690), a work of immense significance in the history of philosophy, John Locke argued that human beings are not born with innate ideas (the idea of God and principles of good and evil, for example) divinely implanted in their minds. Rather, said Locke, the human mind at birth is a blank slate upon which are imprinted sensations derived from contact with the world. These sensations, combined with the mind's reflections on them, are the source of ideas. In effect, knowledge is derived from experience. In the tradition of Francis Bacon, Locke's epistemology (theory of knowledge) implied that people should not dwell on insoluble questions, particularly sterile theological issues, but should seek practical knowledge that promotes human happiness and enlightens human beings and gives them control over their environment.

Locke's empiricism, which aspired to useful knowledge and stimulated an interest in political and ethical questions that focused on human concerns, helped to mold the utilitarian and reformist spirit of the Enlightenment. If there are no innate ideas, said the philosophes, then human beings are not born with original sin, contrary to what Christians believed. All that individuals are derives from their particular experiences. If people are provided with a proper environment and education, they will become intelligent and productive citizens. "[O]f all the Men we meet with," wrote Locke, "Nine Parts of Ten are what they are, Good or Evil, useful or not, by their Education. 'Tis that which makes the great Difference in Mankind." This was how the reform-minded philosophes interpreted Locke. They preferred to believe that evil stemmed from faulty institutions and poor education, both of which could be remedied, rather than from a defective human nature. Excerpts from *Essay Concerning Human Understanding* follow.

Let us then suppose the mind to be, as we say, white paper, void of all characters, without any ideas:—How comes it to be furnished? Whence comes it by that vast store which the busy and boundless fancy of man has painted on it with an almost endless variety?

Whence has it all the *materials* of reason and knowledge? To this I answer, in one word, from EXPERIENCE. In that all our knowledge is founded; and from that it ultimately derives itself. Our observation employed either, about external sensible objects or about the internal operations of our minds perceived and reflected on by ourselves, is that which supplies our understandings with all the *materials* of thinking. These two are the fountains of knowledge, from whence all the ideas we have, or can naturally have, do spring.

First, our Senses, conversant about particular sensible objects, do convey into the mind several distinct perceptions of things, according to those various ways wherein those objects do affect them. And thus we come by those *ideas* we have of *yellow, white, heat, cold, soft, hard, bitter, sweet*, and all those which we call sensible qualities; which when I say the senses convey into the mind, I mean, they from external objects convey into the mind what produces there those perceptions. This great source of most of the ideas we have, depending wholly upon our senses, and derived by them to the understanding, I call SENSATION.

Secondly, the other fountain from which experience furnisheth the understanding with ideas is,—the perception of the operations of our own mind within us, as it is employed about the ideas it has got. . . .

And such are *perception, thinking, doubting, believing, reasoning, knowing, willing*, and all the different actings of our own minds;—which we being conscious of, and observing in ourselves, do from these receive into our understandings as distinct ideas as we do from bodies affecting our senses. This source of ideas every man has wholly in himself; and though it be not sense, as having nothing to do with external objects, yet it is very like it, and might properly enough be called *internal sense*. But as I call

the other Sensation, so I call this REFLECTION, the ideas it affords being such only as the mind gets by reflecting on its own operations within itself. By reflection then, in the following part of this discourse, I would be understood to mean, that notice which the mind takes of its own operations, and the manner of them, by reason whereof there come to be ideas of these operations in the understanding. These two, I say, viz. external material things, as the objects of SENSATION, and the operations of our own minds within, as the objects of REFLECTION, are to me the only originals from whence all our ideas take their beginnings. . . .

The understanding seems to me not to have the least glimmering of any ideas which it doth not receive from one of these two. *External objects* furnish the mind with the ideas of sensible qualities, which are all those different perceptions they produce in us; and *the mind* furnishes the understanding with ideas of its own operations.

These, when we have taken a full survey of them, and their several modes, (combinations, and relations,) we shall find to contain all our whole stock of ideas; and that we have nothing in our minds which did not come in one of these two ways. Let any one examine his own thoughts, and thoroughly search into his understanding; and then let him tell me, whether all the original ideas he has there, are any other than of the objects of his senses, or of the operations of his mind, considered as objects of his reflection. And how great a mass of knowledge soever he imagines to be lodged there, he will, upon taking a strict view, see that he has not any idea in his mind but what one of these two have imprinted;—though perhaps, with infinite variety compounded and enlarged by the understanding, as we shall see hereafter.

He that attentively considers the state of a child, at his first coming into the world, will have little reason to think him stored with plenty of ideas, that are to be the matter of his future knowledge. It is *by degrees* he comes to be furnished with them.

John Locke, *An Essay Concerning Human Understanding*, vol. 1, ed. Alexander Campbell Fraser (Oxford: Clarendon Press, 1894), pp. 121–125.

Claude-Adrien Helvétius
ESSAYS ON THE MIND AND A TREATISE ON MAN

Even more than did Locke, Claude-Adrien Helvétius (1715–1777) emphasized the importance of the environment in shaping the human mind. Disparities in intelligence and talent, said Helvétius, are due entirely to environmental conditions and not to inborn qualities. Since human beings are malleable and perfectible, their moral and intellectual growth depends on proper conditioning. For this reason he called for political reforms, particularly the implementation of a program of enlightened public education.

In 1758 Helvétius published *Essays on the Mind*, which treated ethics in a purely naturalistic way. Shocked by his separation of morality from God's commands and from fear of divine punishment as well as by his attacks on the clergy, the authorities suppressed the book. His second major work, *A Treatise on Man*, was published posthumously in 1777. Apparently Helvétius wanted to avoid another controversy. The following passages from both works illustrate Helvétius' belief that "education makes us what we are."

ESSAYS ON THE MIND

The general conclusion of this discourse is, that genius is common, and the circumstances, proper to unfold it, very extraordinary. If we may compare what is profane to what is sacred, we may say in this respect, Many are called, but few are chosen.

The inequality observable among men, therefore, depends on the government under which they lie; on the greater or less happiness of the age in which they are born; on the education; on their desire of improvement, and on the importance of the ideas that are the subject of their contemplations.

The man of genius is then only produced by the circumstances in which he is placed.[1] Thus all the art of education consists in placing young men in such a concurrence of circumstances as are proper to unfold the buds of genius and virtue. [I am led to this conclusion by] the desire of promoting the happiness of mankind. I am convinced that a good education would diffuse light, virtue, and consequently, happiness in society; and that the opinion, that geniuses and virtue are merely gifts of nature, is a great obstacle to making any farther progress in the science of education, and in this respect is the great favourer of idleness and negligence. With this view, examining the effects which nature and education may have upon us, I have perceived that education makes us what we are; in consequence of which I have thought that

[1] The opinion I advance must appear very pleasing to the vanity of the greatest part of mankind, and therefore, ought to meet with a favourable reception. According to my principles, they ought not to attribute the inferiority of their abilities to the humbling cause of a less perfect [endowment], but to the education they have received, as well as to the circumstances in which they have been placed. Every man of moderate abilities, in conformity with my principles, has a right to think, that if he had been more favoured by fortune, if he had been born in a certain age or country, he [would have] himself been like the great men whose genius he is forced to admire.

Claude Helvétius, *Essay on the Mind and its Several Faculties*, trans. from the French (London: J. M. Richardson, 1809).

it was the duty of a citizen to make known a truth proper to awaken the attention, with respect to the means of carrying this education to perfection.

A TREATISE ON MAN

Some maintain that, *The understanding is the effect of a certain sort of interior temperament and organization.*

Locke and I say: *The inequality in minds or understandings, is the effect of a known cause, and this cause is the difference of education. . . .*

Among the great number of questions treated of in this work, one of the most important was to determine whether genius, virtue, and talents, to which nations owe their grandeur and felicity, were the effect of the difference of . . . the organs of the five senses [that is, differences due to birth] . . . or if the same genius, the same virtues, and the same talents were the effect of education, over which the laws and the form of government are all powerful.

If I have proved the truth of the latter assertion, it must be allowed that the happiness of nations is in their own hands, and that it entirely depends on the greater or less interest they take in improving the science of education.

REVIEW QUESTIONS

1. According to John Locke, knowledge originates in experience and has two sources—sensation and reflection. What does this mean, and what makes this view of knowledge so revolutionary?

2. How does Locke's view of the origin of knowledge compare to that of René Descartes (see chapter 12)? Which view do you favor, or can you suggest another alternative?

3. What is the relationship between Locke's theory of knowledge and his conceptions of human nature and politics?

4. In what way may Claude Helvétius be regarded as a disciple of John Locke, and how did he expand the significance of Locke's ideas?

5 Compendium of Knowledge

The 38-volume *Encyclopedia*, whose 150 or more contributors included leading Enlightenment thinkers, was undertaken in Paris during the 1740s as a monumental effort to bring together all human knowledge and to propagate Enlightenment ideas. The *Encyclopedia*'s numerous articles on science and technology and its limited coverage of theological questions attest to the new interests of eighteenth-century intellectuals. Serving as principal editor, Denis Diderot (1713–1784) steered the project through difficult periods, including the suspension of publication by French authorities. After the first two volumes were published, the authorities denounced the work for containing "maxims that would tend to destroy royal authority, foment a spirit of independence and revolt, . . . and lay the foundations for the corruption of morals and religion." In 1759, Pope Clement XIII condemned the *Encyclopedia* for having "scandalous doctrines [and] inducing scorn for religion." It required careful diplomacy and

clever ruses to finish the project and still incorporate ideas considered dangerous by religious and governmental authorities. With the project's completion in
1772, Diderot and Enlightenment opinion triumphed over clerical censors and
powerful elements at the French court.

Denis Diderot
ENCYCLOPEDIA

The *Encyclopedia* was a monument to the Enlightenment, as Diderot himself
recognized. "This work will surely produce in time a revolution in the minds
of man, and I hope that tyrants, oppressors, fanatics, and the intolerant will
not gain thereby. We shall have served humanity." Some articles from the
Encyclopedia follow.

ENCYCLOPEDIA   . . . In truth, the aim of an
encyclopedia is to collect all the knowledge scattered over the face of the earth, to present its
general outlines and structure to the men with
whom we live, and to transmit this to those
who will come after us, so that the work of past
centuries may be useful to the following centuries, that our children, by becoming more
educated, may at the same time become more
virtuous and happier, and that we may not die
without having deserved well of the human
race. . . .

. . . We have seen that our *Encyclopedia* could
only have been the endeavor of a philosophical
century. . . .

I have said that it could only belong to a
philosophical age to attempt an *encyclopedia*; and
I have said this because such a work constantly
demands more intellectual daring than is commonly found in [less courageous periods]. All
things must be examined, debated, investigated
without exception and without regard for anyone's feelings. . . . We must ride roughshod over
all these ancient puerilities, overturn the barriers that reason never erected, give back to the
arts and sciences the liberty that is so precious to

them. . . . We have for quite some time needed
a reasoning age when men would no longer seek
the rules in classical authors but in nature. . . .

FANATICISM   . . . is blind and passionate zeal
born of superstitious opinions, causing people to
commit ridiculous, unjust, and cruel actions, not
only without any shame or remorse, but even
with a kind of joy and comfort. *Fanaticism,* therefore, is only superstition put into practice. . . .

Fanaticism has done much more harm to the
world than impiety. What do impious people claim? To free themselves of a yoke, while
fanatics want to extend their chains over all the
earth. Infernal zealomania! . . .

GOVERNMENT   . . . The good of the people
must be the great purpose of the *government.* The
governors are appointed to fulfill it; and the
civil constitution that invests them with this
power is bound therein by the laws of nature
and by the law of reason, which has determined
that purpose in any form of *government* as the
cause of its welfare. The greatest good of the
people is its liberty. Liberty is to the body of the
state what health is to each individual; without health man cannot enjoy pleasure; without
liberty the state of welfare is excluded from nations. A patriotic governor will therefore see
that the right to defend and to maintain liberty
is the most sacred of his duties. . . .

Denis Diderot, *The Encyclopedia: Selections*, ed. and trans.
Stephen J. Gendzier, pp. 92–93, 105–106, 124–125,
134, 136, 153, 156, 183–187, 199. Copyright © 1967 by
Harper & Row. Used by permission of the author.

If it happens that those who hold the reins of *government* find some resistance when they use their power for the destruction and not the conservation of things that rightfully belong to the people, they must blame themselves, because the public good and the advantage of society are the purposes of establishing a *government.* Hence it necessarily follows that power cannot be arbitrary and that it must be exercised according to the established laws so that the people may know its duty and be secure within the shelter of laws, and so that governors at the same time should be held within just limits and not be tempted to employ the power they have in hand to do harmful things to the body politic. . . .

HISTORY   . . . *On the usefullness of history.* The advantage consists of the comparison that a statesman or a citizen can make of foreign laws, morals, and customs with those of his country. This is what stimulates modern nations to surpass one another in the arts, in commerce, and in agriculture. The great mistakes of the past are useful in all areas. We cannot describe too often the crimes and misfortunes caused by absurd quarrels. It is certain that by refreshing our memory of these quarrels, we prevent a repetition of them. . . .

HUMANITY   . . . is a benevolent feeling for all men, which hardly inflames anyone without a great and sensitive soul. This sublime and noble enthusiasm is troubled by the pains of other people and by the necessity to alleviate them. With these sentiments an individual would wish to cover the entire universe in order to abolish slavery, superstition, vice, and misfortune. . . .

INTOLERANCE   . . . Any method that would tend to stir up men, to arm nations, and to soak the earth with blood is impious.

It is impious to want to impose laws upon man's conscience: this is a universal rule of conduct. People must be enlightened and not constrained. . . .

What did Christ recommend to his disciples when he sent them among the Gentiles? Was it to kill or to die? Was it to persecute or to suffer? . . .

Which is the true voice of humanity, the persecutor who strikes or the persecuted who moans?

PEACE   . . . War is the fruit of man's depravity; it is a convulsive and violent sickness of the body politic. . . .

If reason governed men and had the influence over the heads of nations that it deserves, we would never see them inconsiderately surrender themselves to the fury of war; they would not show that ferocity that characterizes wild beasts. . . .

POLITICAL AUTHORITY   No man has received from nature the right to command others. Liberty is a gift from heaven, and each individual of the same species has the right to enjoy it as soon as he enjoys the use of reason. . . .

The prince owes to his very subjects the *authority* that he has over them; and this *authority* is limited by the laws of nature and the state. The laws of nature and the state are the conditions under which they have submitted or are supposed to have submitted to its government. . . .

Moreover the government, although hereditary in a family and placed in the hands of one person, is not private property, but public property that consequently can never be taken from the people, to whom it belongs exclusively, fundamentally, and as a freehold. Consequently it is always the people who make the lease or the agreement: they always intervene in the contract that adjudges its exercise. It is not the state that belongs to the prince, it is the prince who belongs to the state: but it does rest with the prince to govern in the state, because the state has chosen him for that purpose: he has bound himself to the people and the administration of affairs, and they in their turn are bound to obey him according to the laws. . . .

THE PRESS   [which includes newspapers, magazines, books, and so forth] . . . People ask if freedom of the *press* is advantageous or prejudicial to a state. The answer is not difficult. It is of the greatest importance to conserve this practice in all states founded on liberty. I would even say that the disadvantages of this liberty are so inconsiderable compared to its advantages that this ought to be the common right of the universe, and it is certainly advisable to authorize its practice in all governments. . . .

REVIEW QUESTIONS

1. Why was the publication of the *Encyclopedia* a vital step in the philosophes' hopes for reform?
2. To what extent were John Locke's political ideals reflected in the *Encyclopedia*?
3. Why was freedom of the press of such significance to the philosophes?

6 Rousseau: Political Reform

To the philosophes, advances in the arts were hallmarks of progress. However, Jean Jacques Rousseau argued that the accumulation of knowledge improved human understanding but corrupted the morals of human beings. In *A Discourse on the Arts and Sciences* (1750) and *A Discourse on the Origin of Inequality* (1755), Rousseau diagnosed the illnesses of modern civilization. He said that human nature, which was originally good, had been corrupted by society. As a result, he stated at the beginning of *The Social Contract* (1762), "Man is born free; and everywhere he is in chains." How can humanity be made moral and free again? In *The Social Contract*, Rousseau suggested one cure: reforming the political system. He argued that in the existing civil society the rich and powerful who controlled the state oppressed the majority. Rousseau admired the small, ancient Greek city-state (polis), where citizens participated actively and directly in public affairs. A small state modeled after the ancient Greek polis, said Rousseau, would be best able to resolve the tensions between individual freedom and the requirements of the collective community.

Jean Jacques Rousseau
THE SOCIAL CONTRACT

In the opening chapters of *The Social Contract*, Rousseau rejected the principle that one person has a natural authority over others. All legitimate authority, he said, stemmed from human traditions, not from nature. Rousseau had only contempt for absolute monarchy and in *The Social Contract* sought to provide a theoretical foundation for political liberty.

[To rulers who argued that they provided security for their subjects, Rousseau responded as follows:]

It will be said that the despot assures his subjects civil tranquillity. Granted; but what do they gain, if the wars his ambition brings down upon them, his insatiable avidity, and the vexatious conduct of his ministers press harder on them than their own dissensions would have done? What do they gain, if the very tranquillity they enjoy is one of their miseries? Tranquillity is found also in dungeons; but is that enough to make them desirable places to live in? The Greeks imprisoned in the cave of the Cyclops lived there very tranquilly, while they were awaiting their turn to be devoured. . . .

Even if each man could alienate himself [relinquish his freedom], he could not alienate his children: they are born men and free; their liberty belongs to them, and no one but they has the right to dispose of it. Before they come to years of discretion, the father can, in their name, lay down conditions for their preservation and well-being, but he cannot give them irrevocably and without conditions: such a gift is contrary to the ends of nature, and exceeds the rights of paternity. It would therefore be necessary, in order to legitimize an arbitrary government, that in every generation the people should be in a position to accept or reject it; but, were this so, the government would be no longer arbitrary.

To renounce liberty is to renounce being a man, to surrender the rights of humanity and even its duties. For him who renounces everything no indemnity is possible. Such a renunciation is incompatible with man's nature; to remove all liberty from his will is to remove all morality from his acts.

Like Hobbes and Locke, Rousseau refers to an original social contract that terminates the state of nature and establishes the civil state. The clash of particular interests in the state of nature necessitates the creation of civil authority.

Jean Jacques Rousseau, *The Social Contract and Discourses*, trans. G. D. H. Cole, Everyman's Library (London: J. H. Dent, 1991), pp. 8–9, 13–15, 18–19, 23, and 26–28.

I suppose men to have reached the point at which the obstacles in the way of their preservation in the state of nature [are] greater than the resources at the disposal of each individual for his maintenance in that state. That primitive condition can then subsist no longer; and the human race would perish unless it changed its manner of existence. . . .

This sum of forces can arise only where several persons come together: but, as the force and liberty of each man are the chief instruments of his self-preservation, how can he pledge them without harming his own interests, and neglecting the care he owes to himself? This difficulty, in its bearing on my present subject, may be stated in the following terms:

"The problem is to find a form of association which will defend and protect with the whole common force the person and goods of each associate, and in which each, while uniting himself with all, may still obey himself alone, and remain as free as before." This is the fundamental problem of which the *Social Contract* provides the solution.

In entering into the social contract, the individual surrenders his rights to the community as a whole, which governs in accordance with the general will—an underlying principle that expresses what is best for the community. The general will is a plainly visible truth that is easily discerned by reason and common sense purged of self-interest and unworthy motives. For Rousseau, the general will by definition is always right and always works to the community's advantage. True freedom consists of obedience to laws that coincide with the general will. Obedience to the general will transforms an individual motivated by self-interest, appetites, and passions into a higher type of person—a citizen committed to the general good. What happens, however, if a person's private will—that is, expressions of particular, selfish interests—clashes with the general will? As private interests could ruin the body politic, says Rousseau, "whoever refuses to obey the general will shall be compelled to do so by the whole body." Thus Rousseau rejects entirely the Lockean principle that citizens possess rights independently of and against the state. Because Rousseau grants the sovereign (the people constituted as a corporate body) virtually unlimited authority over the citizenry, some critics view him as a precursor of modern dictatorship.

The clauses of this contract . . . properly understood, may be reduced to one—the total alienation of each associate, together with all his rights, to the whole community; for, in the first place, as each gives himself absolutely, the conditions are the same for all; and, this being so, no one has any interest in making them burdensome to others.

Moreover, the alienation being without reserve, the union is as perfect as it can be, and no associate has anything more to demand: for, if the individuals retained certain rights, as there would be no common superior to decide between them and the public, each, being on one point his own judge, would ask to be so on all; the state of nature would thus continue, and the association would necessarily become inoperative or tyrannical.

Finally, each man, in giving himself to all, gives himself to nobody; and as there is no associate over which he does not acquire the same right as he yields others over himself, he gains an equivalent for everything he loses, and an increase of force for the preservation of what he has.

If then we discard from the social compact what is not of its essence, we shall find that it reduces itself to the following terms:

"Each of us puts his person and all his power in common under the supreme direction of the general will, and, in our corporate capacity, we receive each member as an indivisible part of the whole."

At once, in place of the individual personality of each contracting party, this act of association creates a moral and collective body, composed of as many members as the assembly contains voters, and receiving from this act its unity, its common identity, its life, and its will. . . .

In order then that the social compact may not be an empty formula, it tacitly includes the undertaking, which alone can give force to the rest, that whoever refuses to obey the general will shall be compelled to do so by the whole body. This means nothing less than that he will be forced to be free; for this is the condition which, by giving each citizen to his country, secures him against all personal dependence. In this lies the key to the working of the political machine; this alone legitimizes civil undertakings, which, without it, would be absurd, tyrannical, and liable to the most frightful abuses.

The passage from the state of nature to the civil state produces a very remarkable change in man, by substituting justice for instinct in his conduct, and giving his actions the morality they had formerly lacked. Then only, when the voice of duty takes the place of physical impulses and right of appetite, does man, who so far had considered only himself, find that he is forced to act on different principles, and to consult his reason before listening to his inclinations. Although, in this state, he deprives himself of some advantages which he got from nature, he gains in return others so great, his faculties are so stimulated and developed, his ideas so extended, his feelings so ennobled, and his whole soul so uplifted, that, did not the abuses of this new condition often degrade him below that which he left, he would be bound to bless continually the happy moment which took him from it forever, and, instead of a stupid and unimaginative animal, made him an intelligent being and a man.

Let us draw up the whole account in terms easily commensurable. What man loses by the social contract is his natural liberty and an unlimited right to everything he tries to get and succeeds in getting; what he gains is civil liberty and the proprietorship of all he possesses. If we are to avoid mistake in weighing one against the other, we must clearly distinguish natural liberty, which is bounded only by the strength of the individual, from civil liberty, which is limited by the general will; and possession, which is merely the effect of force or the right of the first occupier, from property, which can be founded only on a positive title.

We might, over and above all this, add, to what man acquires in the civil state, moral liberty, which alone makes him truly master of himself; for the mere impulse of appetite is slavery, while obedience to a law which we prescribe to ourselves is liberty. . . .

The first and most important deduction from the principles we have so far laid down is that the general will alone can direct the State according to the object for which it was instituted, i.e. the common good: for if the clashing of particular interests made the establishment of societies necessary, the agreement of these very interests made it possible. The common element in these different interests is what forms the social tie; and, were there no point of agreement between them all, no society could exist. It is solely on the basis of this common interest that every society should be governed. . . .

It follows from what has gone before that the general will is always right and tends to the public advantage; but it does not follow that the deliberations of the people are always equally correct. Our will is always for our own good, but we do not always see what that is; the people is never corrupted, but it is often deceived, and on such occasions only does it seem to will what is bad.

There is often a great deal of difference between the will of all and the general will; the latter considers only the common interest, while the former takes private interest into account, and is no more than a sum of particular

wills: but take away from these same wills the pluses and minuses that cancel one another, and the general will remains as the sum of the differences.

If, when the people, being furnished with adequate information, held its deliberations, the citizens had no communication one with another, the grand total of the small differences would always give the general will, and the decision would always be good. But when factions arise, and partial associations are formed at the expense of the great association, the will of each of these associations becomes general in relation to its members, while it remains particular in relation to the State: it may then be said that there are no longer as many votes as there are men, but only as many as there are associations. The differences become less numerous and give a less general result. Lastly, when one of these associations is so great as to prevail over all the rest, the result is no longer a sum of small differences, but a single difference; in this case there is no longer a general will, and the opinion which prevails is purely particular.

It is therefore essential, if the general will is to be able to express itself, that there should be no partial society [factions] within the State, and that each citizen should think only his own thoughts. . . . But if there are partial societies, it is best to have as many as possible and to prevent them from being unequal. . . . These precautions are the only ones that can guarantee that the general will shall be always enlightened, and that the people shall in no way deceive itself.

REVIEW QUESTIONS

1. What did Jean Jacques Rousseau mean by the "general will"? What function did it serve in his political theory?
2. Why do some thinkers view Rousseau as a champion of democracy, whereas others see him as a spiritual precursor of totalitarianism?

7 Humanitarianism

A humanitarian spirit pervaded the philosophes' outlook. Showing a warm concern for humanity, they attacked militarism, slavery, religious persecution, torture, and other violations of human dignity, as can be seen in passages from the *Encyclopedia* and Voltaire's works earlier in this chapter. Through reasoned arguments they sought to make humankind recognize and renounce its own barbarity. In the following selections, other eighteenth-century reformers denounce judicial torture, the abuse of prisoners, and slavery.

Caesare Beccaria
ON CRIMES AND PUNISHMENTS

In *On Crimes and Punishments* (1764), Caesare Beccaria (1738–1794), an Italian economist and criminologist, condemned torture, commonly used to obtain confessions in many European countries, as irrational and inhuman.

The true relations between sovereigns and their subjects, and between nations, have been discovered. Commerce has been reanimated by the common knowledge of philosophical truths diffused by the art of printing, and there has sprung up among nations a tacit rivalry of industriousness that is most humane and truly worthy of rational beings. Such good things we owe to the productive enlightenment of this age. But very few persons have studied and fought against the cruelty of punishments and the irregularities of criminal procedures, a part of legislation that is as fundamental as it is widely neglected in almost all of Europe. Very few persons have undertaken to demolish the accumulated errors of centuries by rising to general principles, curbing, at least, with the sole force that acknowledged truths possess, the unbounded course of ill-directed power which has continually produced a long and authorized

Cesare Beccaria, *On Crimes and Punishments*, 1st edition, trans. H. Paolucci, pp. 8–10, 30, 32–33. Copyright © 1963. Reprinted by permission of Pearson Education, Upper Saddle River, New Jersey.

example of the most cold-blooded barbarity. And yet the groans of the weak, sacrificed to cruel ignorance and to opulent indolence; the barbarous torments, multiplied with lavish and useless severity, for crimes either not proved or wholly imaginary; the filth and horrors of a prison, intensified by that cruellest tormentor of the miserable, uncertainty—all these ought to have roused that breed of magistrates who direct the opinions of men. . . .

But what are to be the proper punishments for such crimes?

Is the death-penalty really *useful* and *necessary* for the security and good order of society? Are torture and torments *just*, and do they attain the *end* for which laws are instituted? What is the best way to prevent crimes? Are the same punishments equally effective for all times? What influence have they on customary behavior? These problems deserve to be analyzed with that geometric precision which the mist of sophisms, seductive eloquence, and timorous doubt cannot withstand. If I could boast only of having been the first to present to Italy, with a little more clarity, what other nations have boldly written and are beginning to practice, I would account myself fortunate. But if, by defending the rights of man and of unconquerable truth, I should help to save from the spasm and agonies of death some wretched victim of tyranny or of no less fatal ignorance, the thanks and tears of one innocent mortal in his transports of joy would console me for the contempt of all mankind. . . .

A cruelty consecrated by the practice of most nations is torture of the accused during his trial, either to make him confess the crime or to clear up contradictory statements, or to discover accomplices, or to purge him of infamy in some metaphysical and incomprehensible way, or, finally, to discover other crimes of which he might be guilty but of which he is not accused.

No man can be called *guilty* before a judge has sentenced him, nor can society deprive him of public protection before it has been decided that he has in fact violated the conditions under which such protection was accorded him. What right is it, then, if not simply that of might, which empowers a judge to inflict punishment on a citizen while doubt still remains as to his guilt or innocence? Here is the dilemma, which is nothing new: the fact of the crime is either certain or uncertain; if certain, all that is due is the punishment established by the laws, and tortures are useless because the criminal's confession is useless; if uncertain, then one must not torture the innocent, for such, according to the laws, is a man whose crimes are not yet proved. . . .

. . . The impression of pain may become so great that, filling the entire sensory capacity of the tortured person, it leaves him free only to choose what for the moment is the shortest way of escape from pain. The response of the accused is then as inevitable as the impressions of fire and water. The sensitive innocent man will then confess himself guilty when he believes that, by so doing, he can put an end to his torment. Every difference between guilt and innocence disappears by virtue of the very means one pretends to be using to discover it. (Torture) is an infallible means indeed—for absolving robust scoundrels and for condemning innocent persons who happen to be weak. Such are the fatal defects of this so-called criterion of truth, a criterion fit for a cannibal. . . .

Of two men, equally innocent or equally guilty, the strong and courageous will be acquitted, the weak and timid condemned, by virtue of this rigorous rational argument: "I, the judge, was supposed to find you guilty of such and such a crime; you, the strong, have been able to resist the pain, and I therefore absolve you; you, the weak, have yielded, and I therefore condemn you. I am aware that a confession wrenched forth by torments ought to be of no weight whatsoever, but I'll torment you again if you don't confirm what you have confessed."

A strange consequence that necessarily follows from the use of torture is that the innocent person is placed in a condition worse than that of the guilty, for if both are tortured, the circumstances are all against the former. Either he confesses the crime and is condemned, or he is declared innocent and has suffered a punishment he did not deserve. The guilty man, on the contrary, finds himself in a favorable situation; that is, if, as a consequence of having firmly resisted the torture, he is absolved as innocent, he will have escaped a greater punishment by enduring a lesser one. Thus the innocent cannot but lose, whereas the guilty may gain. . . .

It would be superfluous to [cite] . . . the innumerable examples of innocent persons who have confessed themselves criminals because of the agonies of torture; there is no nation, there is no age that does not have its own to cite.

John Howard
STATE OF THE PRISONS IN ENGLAND AND WALES

In 1777 John Howard (1726–1790), a British philanthropist, published *State of the Prisons in England and Wales*. Howard's publicizing of the terrible conditions in prisons led Parliament to enact penal reforms. Following are excerpts from Howard's influential book.

There are prisons, into which whoever looks will, at first sight of the people confined there, be convinced, that there is some great error in the management of them: the sallow meagre countenances declare, without words, that they are very miserable: many who went in healthy, are in a few months changed to emaciated dejected objects. Some are seen pining under diseases, "*sick and in prison;*" expiring on the floors, in loathsome cells, of pestilential fevers, and . . . small-pox: victims, I must not say to the cruelty, but I will say to the inattention, of sheriffs, and gentlemen in the commission of the peace.

The cause of this distress is, that many prisons are scantily supplied, and some almost totally unprovided with the necessaries of life.

There are several Bridewells [prisons for those convicted of lesser crimes such as vagrancy and disorderly conduct] (to begin with them) in which prisoners have no allowance of FOOD at all. In some, the keeper farms what little is allowed them: and where he engages to supply each prisoner with one or two pennyworth of bread a day, I have known this shrunk to half, sometimes less than half the quantity, cut or broken from his own loaf.

It will perhaps be asked, does not their work maintain them? for every one knows that those offenders are committed to *hard labour*. The answer to that question, though true, will hardly be believed. There are very few Bridewells in which any work is done, or can be done. The prisoners have neither tools, nor materials of any kind; but spend their time in sloth, profaneness and debauchery, to a degree which, in some of those houses that I have seen, is extremely shocking. . . .

I have asked some keepers, since the late act for preserving the health of prisoners, why no care is taken of their sick: and have been answered, that the magistrates tell them *the act does not extend to Bridewells.*

In consequence of this, at the quarter sessions you see prisoners, covered (hardly covered) with rags; almost famished; and sick of diseases, which the discharged spread wherever they go, and with which those who are sent to the County-Gaols infect these prisons. . . .

Felons have in some Gaols two pennyworth of bread a day; in some three halfpennyworth; in some a pennyworth; in some a shilling a week. . . . I often weighed the bread in different prisons, and found the penny loaf 7½ to 8½ ounces, the other loaves in proportion. It is probable that when this allowance was fixed by its value, near double the quantity that the money will now purchase, might be bought for it: yet the allowance continues unaltered. . . .

This allowance being so far short of the cravings of nature, and in some prisons lessened by farming to the gaoler, many criminals are half starved: such of them as at their commitment were in health, come out almost famished, scarce able to move, and for weeks incapable of any labour.

John Howard, *The State of Prisons in England and Wales with Preliminary Observations and an Account of Some Foreign Prisons* (London: Warrington, 1777).

Many prisons have NO WATER. This defect is frequent in Bridewells, and Town-Gaols. In the felons courts of some County-Gaols there is no water: in some places where there is water, prisoners are always locked up within doors, and have no more than the keeper or his servants think fit to bring them: in one place they are limited to three pints a day each—a scanty provision for drink and cleanliness! . . .

From hence any one may judge of the probability there is against the health and life of prisoners, crowded in close rooms, cells, and subterraneous dungeons, for fourteen or sixteen hours out of the four and twenty. In some of those caverns the floor is very damp: in others there is sometimes an inch or two of water; and the straw, or bedding is laid on such floors, seldom on barrack bedsteads. . . . Some Gaols have no SEWERS; and in those that have, if they be not properly attended to, they are, even to a visitant, offensive beyond expression: how noxious then to people constantly confined in those prisons!

In many Gaols, and in most Bridewells, there is no allowance of STRAW for prisoners to sleep on; and if by any means they get a little, it is not changed for months together, so that it is almost worn to dust. Some lie upon rags, others upon the bare floors. When I have complained of this to the keepers, their justification has been, "The county allows no straw; the prisoners have none but at my cost."

The evils mentioned hitherto affect the *health* and *life* of prisoners: I have now to complain of what is pernicious to their MORALS; and that is, the confining all sorts of prisoners together: debtors and felons; men and women; the young beginner and the old offender: and with all these, in some counties, such as are guilty of misdemeanors only. . . .

In some Gaols you see (and who can see it without pain?) boys of twelve or fourteen eagerly listening to the stories told by practised and experienced criminals, of their adventures, successes, stratagems, and escapes.

I must here add, that in some few Gaols are confined idiots and lunatics. . . . The insane, where they are not kept separate, disturb and terrify other prisoners. No care is taken of them, although it is probable that by medicines, and proper regimen, some of them might be restored to their senses, and to usefulness in life. . . .

A cruel custom obtains in most of our Gaols, which is that of the prisoners demanding of a new comer GARNISH, FOOTING, or (as it is called in some London Gaols) CHUMMAGE. "Pay or strip," are the fatal words. I say *fatal*, for they are so to some; who having no money, are obliged to give up part of their scanty apparel; and if they have no bedding or straw to sleep on, contract diseases, which I have known to prove mortal.

Loading prisoners with HEAVY IRONS, which make their walking, and even lying down to sleep, difficult and painful, is another custom which I cannot but condemn. In some County-Gaols the *women* do not escape this severity.

Denis Diderot
ENCYCLOPEDIA
"MEN AND THEIR LIBERTY ARE NOT OBJECTS OF COMMERCE. . . ."

Montesquieu, Voltaire, David Hume, Benjamin Franklin, Thomas Paine, and several other philosophes condemned slavery and the slave trade. In Book 15 of *The Spirit of the Laws* (1748), Montesquieu scornfully refuted all justifications for slavery. Ultimately, he said, slavery, which violates the fundamental principle of justice underlying the universe, derived from base human desires to dominate and exploit other human beings. In 1780, Paine helped draft the act abolishing slavery in Pennsylvania. Five years earlier, he wrote:

> Our Traders in Men . . . must know the wickedness of that SLAVETRADE, if they attend to reasoning, or the dictates of their own hearts, and {those who} shun and stifle all these willfully sacrifice Conscience, and the character of integrity to that Golden Idol. . . . Most shocking of all is the alleging the sacred scriptures to favour this wicked practice.

The *Encyclopedia* denounced slavery as a violation of the individual's natural rights.

[This trade] is the buying of unfortunate Negroes by Europeans on the coast of Africa to use as slaves in their colonies. This buying of Negroes, to reduce them to slavery, is one business that violates religion, morality, natural laws, and all the rights of human nature.

Negroes, says a modern Englishman full of enlightenment and humanity, have not become slaves by the right of war; neither do they deliver themselves voluntarily into bondage, and consequently their children are not born slaves. Nobody is unaware that they are bought from their own princes, who claim to have the right to dispose of their liberty, and that traders have them transported in the same way as their other goods, either in their colonies or in America, where they are displayed for sale.

If commerce of this kind can be justified by a moral principle, there is no crime, however atrocious it may be, that cannot be made legitimate. Kings, princes, and magistrates are not the proprietors of their subjects: they do not, therefore, have the right to dispose of their liberty and to sell them as slaves.

On the other hand, no man has the right to buy them or to make himself their master. Men and their liberty are not objects of commerce; they can be neither sold nor bought nor paid for at any price. We must conclude from this that a man whose slave has run away should only blame himself, since he had acquired for money illicit goods whose acquisition is prohibited by all the laws of humanity and equity.

There is not, therefore, a single one of these unfortunate people regarded only as slaves who does not have the right to be declared free, since he has never lost his freedom, which he could not lose and which his prince, his father, and any person whatsoever in the world had not the power to dispose of. Consequently the sale that has been completed is invalid in itself. This Negro does not divest himself and can never divest himself of his natural right; he carries it everywhere with him, and he can demand everywhere that he be allowed to enjoy it. It is, therefore, patent inhumanity on the part of judges in free countries where he is transported, not to emancipate him immediately by declaring him free, since he is their fellow man, having a soul like them.

Denis Diderot, *The Encyclopedia: Selections*, ed. and trans. Stephen J. Gendzier, pp. 229–231. Copyright © 1967 by Harper & Row. Used by permission of the author.

REVIEW QUESTIONS

1. What were Caesare Beccaria's arguments against the use of torture in judicial proceedings? In your opinion, can torture ever be justified?
2. What ideals of the Enlightenment philosophes are reflected in Beccaria's arguments?
3. List the abuses in British jails that John Howard disclosed.
4. Why did the author of the *Encyclopedia* article regard slavery as a crime? How did he react to the argument that slaves are property?

8   Literature as Satire: Critiques of European Society

The French philosophes, particularly Voltaire, Diderot, and Montesquieu (see page 456), often used the medium of literature to decry the ills of their society and advance Enlightenment values. In the process they wrote satires that are still read and admired for their literary merits and insights into human nature and society. The eighteenth century also saw the publication of Jonathan Swift's *Gulliver's Travels* (1726), one of the greatest satirical works written in English.

Voltaire
CANDIDE

In *Candide* (1759), Voltaire's most important work of fiction, he explored the question: Why do the innocent suffer? And because Voltaire delved into this mystery with wit, irony, satire, and wisdom, the work continues to be hailed as a literary masterpiece.

The illegitimate Candide (son of the sister of the baron in whose castle he lives in Westphalia) is tutored by the philosopher Pangloss, a teacher of "metaphysico-theologo-cosmolonigology": that is, a person who speaks nonsense. The naive Pangloss clings steadfastly to the belief that all that happens, even the worst misfortunes, are for the best.

Candide falls in love with Cunegund, the beautiful daughter of the baron of the castle; but the baron forcibly removes Candide from the castle when he discovers their love. Candide subsequently suffers a series of disastrous misfortunes, but he continues to adhere to the belief firmly instilled in him by Pangloss, that everything happens for the best and that this is the best of all possible worlds. Later, he meets an old beggar, who turns out to be his former teacher, Pangloss, who tells Candide that the Bulgarians have destroyed the castle and killed Cunegund and her family. Candide and Pangloss then travel together to Lisbon, where they survive the terrible earthquake, only to have Pangloss hanged (but he escapes death) by the Inquisition. Soon thereafter, Candide is reunited with Cunegund, who, despite having been raped and sold into prostitution, has not been killed. Following further adventures and misfortunes, the lovers are again separated when Cunegund is captured by pirates.

After experiencing more episodes of human wickedness and natural disasters, Candide abandons the philosophy of optimism, declaring "that we must cultivate our gardens." By this Voltaire meant that we can never achieve utopia, but neither should we descend to the level of brutes. Through purposeful and honest work, and the deliberate pursuit of virtue, we can improve, however modestly, the quality of human existence.

The following excerpt from Candide starts with Candide's first misfortune after being driven out of the castle at Westphalia. In addition to ridiculing philosophical optimism, Voltaire expresses his revulsion for militarism.

CHAPTER II

What Befell Candide Among the Bulgarians

Candide, thus driven out of this terrestrial paradise, wandered a long time, without knowing where he went; sometimes he raised his eyes, all bedewed with tears, toward Heaven, and sometimes he cast a melancholy look toward the magnificent castle where dwelt the fairest of young baronesses. He laid himself down to sleep in a furrow, heartbroken and supperless. The snow fell in great flakes, and, in the morning when he awoke, he was almost frozen to death; however, he made shift to crawl to the next town, which was called Waldberghoff-trarbk-dikdorff, without a penny in his pocket, and half dead with hunger and fatigue. He took up his stand at the door of an inn. He had not been long there before two men dressed in blue fixed their eyes steadfastly upon him.

"Faith, comrade," said one of them to the other, "yonder is a well-made young fellow, and of the right size."

Thereupon they went up to Candide, and with the greatest civility and politeness invited him to dine with them.

"Gentlemen," replied Candide, with a most engaging modesty, "you do me much honor, but, upon my word, I have no money."

"Money, sir!" said one of the men in blue to him. "Young persons of your appearance and merit never pay anything. Why, are you not five feet five inches high?"

"Yes, gentlemen, that is really my size," replied he with a low bow.

"Come then, sir, sit down along with us. We will not only pay your reckoning, but will never suffer such a clever young fellow as you to want money. Mankind were born to assist one another."

"You are perfectly right, gentlemen," said Candide; "that is precisely the doctrine of Master Pangloss; and I am convinced that everything is for the best."

His generous companions next entreated him to accept a few crowns, which he readily complied with, at the same time offering them his note for the payment, which they refused, and sat down to table.

"Have you not a great affection for—"

"Oh, yes!" he replied. "I have a great affection for the lovely Miss Cunegund."

"Maybe so," replied one of the men, "but that is not the question! We are asking you whether you have not a great affection for the King of the Bulgarians?"[1]

"For the King of the Bulgarians?" said Candide. "Not at all. Why, I never saw him in my life."

"Is it possible! Oh, he is a most charming king! Come, we must drink his health."

"With all my heart, gentlemen," Candide said, and he tossed off his glass.

"Bravo!" cried the blues. "You are now the support, the defender, the hero of the Bulgarians; your fortune is made; you are on the high road to glory."

So saying, they put him in irons and carried him away to the regiment. There he was made to wheel about to the right, to the left, to draw his ramrod, to return his ramrod, to present, to fire, to march, and they gave him thirty blows with a cane. The next day he performed his exercise a little better, and they gave him but twenty. The day following he came with ten and was looked upon as a young fellow of surprising genius by all his comrades.

Candide was struck with amazement and could not for the soul of him conceive how he came to be a hero. One fine spring morning, he took it into his head to take a walk, and he marched straight forward, conceiving it to be a privilege of the human species, as well as of the brute creation, to make use of their legs how and when they pleased. He had not gone above two leagues when he was overtaken by four other heroes, six feet high, who bound him neck and

---

Voltaire, *Candide and Zadig*, trans. Tobias George Smollett, ed. Lester G. Crocker (New York: Washington Square Press and Pocket Books, 1962), pp. 6–15, 20–21.

[1]I.e., Prussians.

heels, and carried him to a dungeon. A court-martial sat upon him, and he was asked which he liked best, either to run the gauntlet six and thirty times through the whole regiment, or to have his brains blown out with a dozen musket balls. In vain did he remonstrate to them that the human will is free, and that he chose neither. They obliged him to make a choice, and he determined, in virtue of that divine gift called free will, to run the gauntlet six and thirty times. He had gone through his discipline twice, and the regiment being composed of two thousand men, they composed for him exactly four thousand strokes, which laid bare all his muscles and nerves, from the nape of his neck to his rump. As they were preparing to make him set out a third time, our young hero, unable to support it any longer, begged as a favor they would be so obliging as to shoot him through the head. The favor being granted, a bandage was tied over his eyes, and he was made to kneel down. At that very instant, his Bulgarian Majesty, happening to pass by, inquired into the delinquent's crime, and being a prince of great penetration, he found, from what he heard of Candide, that he was a young meta-physician, entirely ignorant of the world. And, therefore, out of his great clemency, he condescended to pardon him, for which his name will be celebrated in every journal, and in every age. A skillful surgeon made a cure of Candide in three weeks by means of emollient unguents prescribed by Dioscorides. His sores were now skinned over, and he was able to march when the King of the Bulgarians gave battle to the King of the Abares.[2]

CHAPTER III

How Candide Escaped from the Bulgarians, and What Befell Him Afterwards

Never was anything so gallant, so well accoutered, so brilliant, and so finely disposed as the two armies. The trumpets, fifes, oboes, drums, and cannon, made such harmony as never was heard in hell itself. The entertainment began by a discharge of cannon, which, in the twinkling of an eye, laid flat about six thousand men on each side. The musket bullets swept away, out of the best of all possible worlds, nine or ten thousand scoundrels that infested its surface. The bayonet was next the sufficient reason for the deaths of several thousands. The whole might amount to thirty thousand souls. Candide trembled like a philosopher and concealed himself as well as he could during this heroic butchery.

At length, while the two kings were causing *Te Deum*[3] to be sung in each of their camps, Candide took a resolution to go and reason somewhere else upon causes and effects. After passing over heaps of dead or dying men, the first place he came to was a neighboring village, in the Abarian territories, which had been burned to the ground by the Bulgarians in accordance with international law. Here lay a number of old men covered with wounds, who beheld their wives dying with their throats cut, and hugging their children to their breasts all stained with blood. There several young virgins, whose bellies had been ripped open after they had satisfied the natural necessities of the Bulgarian heroes, breathed their last; while others, half burned in the flames, begged to be dispatched out of the world. The ground about them was covered with the brains, arms, and legs of dead men.

Candide made all the haste he could to another village, which belonged to the Bulgarians, and there he found that the heroic Abares had treated it in the same fashion. From thence continuing to walk over palpitating limbs or through ruined buildings, at length he arrived beyond the theater of war, with a little provision in his pouch, and Miss Cunegund's image in his heart.

---

[2]I.e., French. The Seven Years' War had begun in 1756.

[3]A Te Deum ("We praise thee, God") is a special liturgical hymn praising and thanking God for granting some special favor, like a military victory or the end of a war.—Eds.

Denis Diderot
SUPPLEMENT TO THE VOYAGE OF BOUGAINVILLE

Enlightenment thinkers often used examples from the non-European world in order to attack European values that seemed contrary to nature and reason. Denis Diderot reviewed Louis Antoine de Bougainville's *Voyage Around the World* (1771) and in the next year wrote *Supplement to the Voyage of Bougainville* (published posthumously in 1796). In this work, Diderot explored some ideas, particularly the sex habits of Tahitians, treated by the French explorer. In the process Diderot denounced European imperialism and the exploitation of non-Europeans, and questioned traditional Christian sexual standards. In *Supplement*, Diderot constructed a dialogue between a Tahitian (Orou), who possesses the wisdom of a French philosophe, and a chaplain, whose defense of Christian sexual mores reveals Diderot's critique of the Christian view of human nature. Diderot thus used a representative of an alien culture to attack those European customs and beliefs that the philosophes detested. In the opening passage, before Orou's dialogue, a Tahitian elder rebukes Bougainville and his companions for bringing the evils of European civilization to his island.

"We [Tahitians] are free—but see where you [Europeans] have driven into our earth the symbol of our future servitude. You are neither a god nor a devil—by what right, then, do you enslave people? Orou! You who understand the speech of these men, tell every one of us, as you have told me, what they have written on that strip of metal—'This land belongs to us.' This land belongs to you! And why? Because you set foot in it? If some day a Tahitian should land on your shores, and if he should engrave on one of your stones or on the bark of one of your trees: 'This land belongs to the people of Tahiti,' what would you think? You are stronger than we are! And what does that signify? When one of our lads carried off some of the miserable trinkets with which your ship is loaded, what an uproar you made, and what revenge you took!

And at that very moment you were plotting, in the depths of your hearts, to steal a whole country! You are not slaves; you would suffer death rather than be enslaved, yet you want to make slaves of us! Do you believe, then, that the Tahitian does not know how to die in defense of his liberty? This Tahitian, whom you want to treat as a chattel, as a dumb animal—this Tahitian is your brother. You are both children of Nature—what right do you have over him that he does not have over you?

"You came; did we attack you? Did we plunder your vessel? Did we seize you and expose you to the arrows of our enemies? Did we force you to work in the fields alongside our beasts of burden? We respected our own image in you. Leave us our own customs, which are wiser and more decent than yours. We have no wish to barter what you call our ignorance for your useless knowledge. We possess already all that is good or necessary for our existence. Do we merit your scorn because we have not been able to create superfluous wants for ourselves? When we are hungry, we have something

Denis Diderot, *Rameau's Nephew and Other Works,* translated by Jacques Barzun and Ralph H. Bowen, pp. 188–190, 194–195, 197–199, 213. 1st Edition, © 1964. Reprinted by permission of Pearson Education, Inc., Upper Saddle River, NJ.

to eat; when we are cold, we have clothing to put on. You have been in our huts—what is lacking there, in your opinion? You are welcome to drive yourselves as hard as you please in pursuit of what you call the comforts of life, but allow sensible people to stop when they see they have nothing to gain but imaginary benefits from the continuation of their painful labors. If you persuade us to go beyond the bounds of strict necessity, when shall we come to the end of our labor? When shall we have time for enjoyment? We have reduced our daily and yearly labors to the least possible amount, because to us nothing seemed more desirable than leisure. Go and bestir yourselves in your own country; there you may torment yourselves as much as you like; but leave us in peace, and do not fill our heads with a hankering after your false needs and imaginary virtues. Look at these men—see how healthy, straight and strong they are. See these women—how straight, healthy, fresh and lovely they are. Take this bow in your hands— it is my own—and call one, two, three, four of your comrades to help you try to bend it. I can bend it myself. I work the soil, I climb mountains, I make my way through the dense forest, and I can run four leagues [about 12 miles] on the plain in less than an hour. Your young comrades have been hard put to it to keep up with me, and yet I have passed my ninetieth year. . . .

"Woe to this island! Woe to all the Tahitians now living, and to all those yet to be born, woe from the day of your arrival! We used to know but one disease—the one to which all men, all animals and all plants are subject—old age. But you have brought us a new one [venereal disease]: you have infected our blood. We shall perhaps be compelled to exterminate with our own hands some of our young girls, some of our women, some of our children, those who have lain with your women, those who have lain with your men. Our fields will be spattered with the foul blood that has passed from your veins into ours. Or else our children, condemned to die, will nourish and perpetuate the evil disease that you have given their fathers and mothers, transmitting it forever to their descendants." . . .

> Before the arrival of Christian Europeans, love-making was natural and enjoyable. Euronpeans introduced an alien element, guilt.

"But a while ago, the young Tahitian girl blissfully abandoned herself to the embraces of a Tahitian youth and awaited impatiently the day when her mother, authorized to do so by her having reached the age of puberty, would remove her veil and uncover her breasts. She was proud of her ability to excite men's desires, to attract the amorous looks of strangers, of her own relatives, of her own brothers. In our presence, without shame, in the center of a throng of innocent Tahitians who danced and played the flute, she accepted the caresses of the young man whom her young heart and the secret promptings of her senses had marked out for her. The notion of crime and the fear of disease have come among us only with your coming. Now our enjoyments, formerly so sweet, are attended with guilt and terror. That man in black [a priest], who stands near to you and listens to me, has spoken to our young men, and I know not what he has said to our young girls, but our youths are hesitant and our girls blush. Creep away into the dark forest, if you wish, with the perverse companion of your pleasures, but allow the good, simple Tahitians to reproduce themselves without shame under the open sky and in broad daylight."

> In the following conversation between Orou and the chaplain, Christian sexual mores and the concept of God are questioned. Orou addresses the chaplain.

[OROU] "You are young and healthy and you have just had a good supper. He who sleeps alone, sleeps badly; at night a man needs a woman at his side. Here is my wife and here are my daughters. Choose whichever one pleases you most, but if you would like to do me a favor, you will give your preference to my youngest girl, who has not yet had any children."

The mother said: "Poor girl! I don't hold it against her. It's no fault of hers."

The chaplain replied that his religion, his holy orders, his moral standards and his sense of decency all prevented him from accepting Orou's invitation.

Orou answered: "I don't know what this thing is that you call 'religion,' but I can only have a low opinion of it because it forbids you to partake of an innocent pleasure to which Nature, the sovereign mistress of us all, invites everybody. It seems to prevent you from bringing one of your fellow creatures into the world, from doing a favor asked of you by a father, a mother and their children, from repaying the kindness of a host, and from enriching a nation by giving it an additional citizen. I don't know what it is that you call 'holy orders,' but your chief duty is to be a man and to show gratitude. . . . I hope that you will not persist in disappointing us. Look at the distress you have caused to appear on the faces of these four women—they are afraid you have noticed some defect in them that arouses your distaste. But even if that were so, would it not be possible for you to do a good deed and have the pleasure of honoring one of my daughters in the sight of her sisters and friends? Come, be generous!"

THE CHAPLAIN "You don't understand—it's not that. They are all four of them equally beautiful. But there is my religion! My holy orders! . . .

. . . [God] spoke to our ancestors and gave them laws; he prescribed to them the way in which he wishes to be honored; he ordained that certain actions are good and others he forbade them to do as being evil."

OROU "I see. And one of these evil actions which he has forbidden is that of a man who goes to bed with a woman or girl. But in that case, why did he make two sexes?"

THE CHAPLAIN "In order that they might come together—but only when certain conditions are satisfied and only after certain initial ceremonies have been performed. By virtue of these ceremonies one man belongs to one woman and only to her; one woman belongs to one man and only to him."

OROU "For their whole lives?"

THE CHAPLAIN "For their whole lives."

OROU "So that if it should happen that a woman should go to bed with some man who was not her husband, or some man should go to bed with a woman that was not his wife . . . but that could never happen because the workman [God] would know what was going on, and since he doesn't like that sort of thing, he wouldn't let it occur."

THE CHAPLAIN "No. He lets them do as they will, and they sin against the law of God (for that is the name by which we call the great workman) and against the law of the country; they commit a crime."

OROU "I should be sorry to give offense by anything I might say, but if you don't mind, I'll tell you what I think."

THE CHAPLAIN "Go ahead."

OROU "I find these strange precepts contrary to nature, and contrary to reason. . . . Furthermore, your laws seem to me to be contrary to the general order of things. For in truth is there anything so senseless as a precept that forbids us to heed the changing impulses that are inherent in our being, or commands that require a degree of constancy which is not possible, that violate the liberty of both male and female by chaining them perpetually to one another? Is there anything more unreasonable than this perfect fidelity that would restrict us, for the enjoyment of pleasures so capricious, to a single partner—than an oath of immutability taken by two individuals made of flesh and blood under a sky that is not the same for a moment, in a cavern that threatens to collapse upon them, at the foot of a cliff that is crumbling into dust, under a tree that is withering, on a bench of stone that is being worn away? Take my word for it, you have reduced human beings to a worse condition than that of the animals. I don't know what your great workman is, but I am very happy that he never spoke to our forefathers, and I hope that he never speaks to our children, for if he does, he may tell them the same foolishness, and they may be foolish enough to believe it." . . .

OROU "Are monks faithful to their vows of sterility?"

THE CHAPLAIN "No."

OROU "I was sure of it. Do you also have female monks?"

THE CHAPLAIN "Yes."

OROU "As well behaved as the male monks?"

THE CHAPLAIN "They are kept more strictly in seclusion, they dry up from unhappiness and die of boredom."

OROU "So nature is avenged for the injury done to her! Ugh! What a country! If everything is managed the way you say, you are more barbarous than we are."

Montesquieu
THE PERSIAN LETTERS

Like other philosophes, Charles Louis de Secondat, baron de la Brède et de Montesquieu (1689–1755), was an ardent reformer who used learning, logic, and wit to denounce the abuses of his day. His principal work, *The Spirit of the Laws* (1748), was a contribution to political liberty. To safeguard liberty from despotism, which he regarded as a pernicious form of government that institutionalizes cruelty and violence, Montesquieu advocated the principle of separation of powers—that is, the legislative, executive, and judiciary should not be in the hands of one person or body. Montesquieu's humanitarianism and tolerant spirit are also seen in an earlier work, *The Persian Letters* (1721), published anonymously in Holland. In the guise of letters written by imaginary Persian travelers in Europe, Montesquieu makes a statement: He denounces French absolutism, praises English parliamentary government, and attacks religious persecution, as in this comment on the Spanish Inquisition, excerpted below.

LETTER XXIX

Rica to Ibben, at Smyrna

. . . I have heard that in Spain and Portugal there are dervishes who do not understand a joke, and who have a man burned as if he were straw. Whoever falls into the hands of these men is fortunate only if he has always prayed to God with little bits of wood in hand, has worn two bits of cloth attached to two ribbons, and has sometimes been in a province called Galicia![1]

Otherwise, the poor devil is really in trouble. Even though he swears like a pagan that he is orthodox, they may not agree, and burn him for a heretic. It is useless for him to submit distinctions, for he will be in ashes before they even consider giving him a hearing.

Other judges presume the innocence of the accused; these always presume him guilty. In doubt they hold to the rule of inclining to severity, evidently because they consider mankind as evil. On the other hand, however, they

---

Montesquieu, *The Persian Letters* (Indianapolis: Bobbs-Merrill, 1964), pp. 53–54.

[1]The references are to a rosary, a scapular, and the pilgrimage shrine of St. James of Campostello in the Spanish province of Galicia.

hold such a high opinion of men that they judge them incapable of lying, for they accept testimony from deadly enemies, notorious women, and people living by some infamous profession. In passing sentence, the judges pay those condemned a little compliment, telling them that they are sorry to see them so poorly dressed in their brimstone shirts,[2] that the judges themselves are gentle men who abhor bloodletting, and are in despair at having to condemn them.

Then, to console themselves, they confiscate to their own profit all the possessions of these poor wretches.

Happy the land inhabited by the children of the prophets! There these sad spectacles are unknown.[3] The holy religion brought by the angels trusts truth alone for its defense, and does not need these violent means for its preservation.

PARIS, THE 4TH OF THE MOON OF CHALVAL, 1712

---

[2]Those condemned by the Inquisition appeared for sentencing dressed in shirts colored to suggest the flames of their presumed postmortem destination.

[3]The Persians are the most tolerant of all the [Muslims].

REVIEW QUESTIONS

1. What does *Candide* reveal about Voltaire's general outlook?
2. How did Diderot attempt to use the Tahitians to criticize the sexual morals of Europeans?
3. How did Diderot use the concept of the law of nature to undermine Christian sexual morality?
4. How did Montesquieu characterize Spanish and Portuguese inquisitors?

---

9 Madame du Châtelet: A Woman of Brilliance

Gabrielle Emilie Le Tonnelier de Breteuil du Châtelet (1706–1749), known simply as Madame Châtelet, was the daughter of a Parisian nobleman. She early showed signs of a superior intelligence, and her father provided tutors for the young Gabrielle Emilie. Since females were excluded from a university education, her husband, Marquis Florent-Claude Chastellet, later supported Emilie du Châtelet's love of learning by arranging for university professors of physics and mathematics to tutor her at home.

Madame du Châtelet
AN APPEAL FOR FEMALE EDUCATION

In her lifetime Madame Châtelet learned Latin, Italian, German, and English and read and translated works in these languages. She collaborated with Voltaire, who was both her intellectual companion and lover, in writing *The Elements of the Philosophy*, an attempt to explain Newton's theories to nonmathematicians. And she translated Newton's *Principia Mathematica* from the Latin into French.

In the following passage, drawn from the introduction of her translation of Bernard Mandeville's *The Fable of the Bees*, Madame Châtelet makes a fervent appeal for educating women.

. . . Thus, while it is true to say that a good translation requires application and labor, it is, nonetheless, at best, a very mediocre work.

However mediocre this kind of work, it may be thought that it is audacious for a woman to aspire to do it.

I feel the full weight of prejudice that excludes us [women] so universally from the sciences, this being one of the contradictions of this world, which has always astonished me, as there are great countries whose laws allow us to decide their destiny, but none where we are brought up to think.

Another observation that one can make about this prejudice, which is odd enough, is that acting is the only occupation requiring some study and a trained mind to which women are admitted, and it is at the same time the only one that regards its professionals as infamous.

Let us reflect briefly on why for so many centuries, not one good tragedy, one good poem, one esteemed history, one beautiful painting, one good book of physics, has come from the hands of women. Why do these creatures whose understanding appears in all things equal to that of men, seem, for all that, to be stopped by an invincible force on this side of a barrier, let someone give me some explanation, if there is one. I leave it to naturalists to find a physical explanation, but until that happens, women will be entitled to protest against their education. As for me, I confess that if I were king I would wish to make this scientific experiment. I would reform an abuse that cuts out, so to speak, half of humanity. I

would allow women to share in all the rights of humanity, and most of all those of the mind. Women seem to have been born to deceive, and their soul is scarcely allowed any other exercise. This new system of education that I propose would in all respects be beneficial to the human species. Women would be more valuable beings, men would thereby gain a new object of emulation, and our social interchanges which, in refining women's minds in the past, too often weakened and narrowed them, would now only serve to extend their knowledge. Some will probably recommend that I ask M. the abbé of St. Pierre to combine this project with his.[1] Mine will perhaps seem as difficult to put into practice, even though it may be more reasonable.

I am convinced that many women are either ignorant of their talents, because of the flaws in their education, or bury them out of prejudice and for lack of a bold spirit. What I have experienced myself confirms me in this opinion. Chance led me to become acquainted with men of letters, I gained their friendship, and I saw with extreme surprise that they valued this amity.[2] I began to believe that I was a thinking creature. But I only glimpsed this, and the world, the dissipation, for which alone I believed I had been born, carried away all my time and all my soul. I only believed in earnest in my capacity to think at an age when there was still time to become reasonable, but when it was too late to acquire talents.

Being aware of that has not discouraged me at all. I hold myself quite fortunate to have

---

Emilie du Châtelet, *Selected Philosophical and Scientific Writings,* ed. Judith P. Zinsser, trans. Isabelle Bour and Judith P. Zinsser (Chicago: The University of Chicago Press, 2009), pp. 48–49.

---

[1]Charles-Irénée Castel, Abbé de St. Pierre (1658–1743). wrote a number of well-known treatises on education, including one that advocated *colleges* for girls with a course of study similar to that for boys.
[2]*L'amitié*, the French word used here, means more than simple friendship and carries the connotation of affection and concern.

renounced in mid-course frivolous things that occupy most women all their lives, and I want to use what time remains to cultivate my soul. Feeling that nature has refused me the creative genius that discovers new truths, I have done

justice to myself, and I am content to render with clarity the truths others have discovered, and which the diversity of languages renders useless for most readers.

REVIEW QUESTION

Why did Madame du Châtelet advocate a new system of education?

10 On the Progress of Humanity

During the French Revolution, the Marquis de Condorcet attracted the enmity of the dominant Jacobin party and in 1793 was forced to go into hiding. Secluded in Paris, he wrote *Sketch for a Historical Picture of the Progress of the Human Mind*. Arrested in 1794, Condorcet died during his first night in prison from either exhaustion or self-inflicted poison.

Marquis de Condorcet
PROGRESS OF THE HUMAN MIND

Sharing the philosophes' confidence in human goodness and in reason, Condorcet was optimistic about humanity's future progress. Superstition, prejudice, intolerance, and tyranny—all barriers to progress in the past—would gradually be eliminated, and humanity would enter a golden age. The following excerpts are from Condorcet's *Sketch*.

. . . The aim of the work that I have undertaken, and its result will be to show by appeal to reason and fact that nature has set no term to the perfection of human faculties; that the perfectibility of man is truly indefinite; and that the progress of this perfectibility, from now onwards independent of any power that

Antonie-Nicolas de Condorcet, *Sketch for a Historical Picture of the Progress of the Human Mind*, trans. June Barraclough, pp. 4–5, 9–10, 128, 136, 140–142, 173–175, 179. Copyright © Weidenfeld & Nicolson, an imprint of The Orion Publishing Group. Used by permission of The Orion Publishing Group, London.

might wish to halt it, has no other limit than the duration of the globe upon which nature has cast us. This progress will doubtless vary in speed, but it will never be reversed as long as the earth occupies its present place in the system of the universe, and as long as the general laws of this system produce neither a general cataclysm nor such changes as will deprive the human race of its present faculties and its present resources. . . .

. . . It will be necessary to indicate by what stages what must appear to us today a fantastic hope ought in time to become possible, and even likely; to show why, in spite of the transitory successes of prejudice and the support that it receives from the corruption of governments or peoples, truth alone will obtain a lasting victory; we shall demonstrate how nature has joined together indissolubly the progress of knowledge and that of liberty, virtue and respect for the natural rights of man. . . .

After long periods of error, after being led astray by vague or incomplete theories, publicists have at last discovered the true rights of man and how they can all be deduced from the single truth, that *man is a sentient being, capable of reasoning and of acquiring moral ideas*. . . .

At last man could proclaim aloud his right, which for so long had been ignored, to submit all opinions to his own reason and to use in the search for truth the only instrument for its recognition that he has been given. Every man learnt with a sort of pride that nature had not forever condemned him to base his beliefs on the opinions of others; the superstitions of antiquity and the abasement of reason before the [deception] of supernatural religion [had] disappeared from society as from philosophy.

Thus an understanding of the natural rights of man, the belief that these rights are inalienable and [cannot be forfeited], a strongly expressed desire for liberty of thought and letters, of trade and industry, and for the alleviation of the people's suffering, for the [elimination] of all penal laws against religious dissenters and the abolition of torture and barbarous punishments, the desire for a milder system of criminal legislation and jurisprudence which should give complete security to the innocent, and for a simpler civil code, more in conformance with reason and nature, indifference in all matters of religion which now were relegated to the status of superstitions and political [deception], a hatred of hypocrisy and fanaticism, a contempt for prejudice, zeal for the propagation of enlightenment: all these principles, gradually filtering down from philosophical works to every class of society whose education went beyond the catechism and the alphabet, became the common

faith . . . [of enlightened people]. In some countries these principles formed a public opinion sufficiently widespread for even the mass of the people to show a willingness to be guided by it and to obey it. . . .

Force or persuasion on the part of governments, priestly intolerance, and even national prejudices, had all lost their deadly power to smother the voice of truth, and nothing could now protect the enemies of reason or the oppressors of freedom from a sentence to which the whole of Europe would soon subscribe. . . .

Our hopes for the future condition of the human race can be subsumed under three important heads: the abolition of inequality between nations, the progress of equality within each nation, and the true perfection of mankind. Will all nations one day attain that state of civilization which the most enlightened, the freest and the least burdened by prejudices, such as the French and the Anglo-Americans [by virtue of their revolutions], have attained already? Will the vast gulf that separates these peoples from the slavery of nations under the rule of monarchs, from the barbarism of African tribes, from the ignorance of savages, little by little disappear? . . .

Is the human race to better itself, either by discoveries in the sciences and the arts, and so in the means to individual welfare and general prosperity; or by progress in the principles of conduct or practical morality; or by a true perfection of the intellectual, moral, or physical faculties of man, an improvement which may result from a perfection either of the instruments used to heighten the intensity of these faculties and to direct their use or of the natural constitution of man?

In answering these three questions we shall find in the experience of the past, in the observation of the progress that the sciences and civilization have already made, in the analysis of the progress of the human mind and of the development of its faculties, the strongest reasons for believing that nature has set no limit to the realization of our hopes. . . .

The time will therefore come when the sun will shine only on free men who know no other master but their reason; when tyrants and slaves, priests and their stupid or hypocritical instruments will exist only in works of history and on the stage; and when we shall think of them only to pity their victims and their dupes; to maintain ourselves in a state of vigilance by thinking on their excesses; and to learn how to recognize and so to destroy, by force of reason, the first seeds of tyranny and superstition, should they ever dare to reappear amongst us.

REVIEW QUESTIONS

1. According to Condorcet, what economic, political, and cultural policies were taught by the philosophes?
2. What image of human nature underlies Condorcet's theory of human progress?